MARKETING ANALYTICS

Strategic Models and Metrics

Stephan Sorger

Technologies: The book includes references to specific analytics technology companies, their products/services, and websites to illustrate typical example resources for marketing analysts in industry. Company strategies, offerings, pricing, and website details can change over time and might not agree with the descriptions provided in this book.

Edition: First Edition, Version 1.2, June 2016. Incorporates minor corrections and edits.
Retains same page layout as original release (First Edition, Version 1.0).
See StephanSorger.com for a complete record of all changes.

For more information, please go to StephanSorger.com or Admiral Press at AdmiralPress.com.

ISBN-13: 978-1481900300
ISBN-10: 1481900307
Library of Congress Control Number: 2013900332

CONTENTS

PREFACE

Purpose

The purpose of this book is to give marketing students and professionals a practical, structured, and comprehensive guide to marketing analytics. This book covers a number of strategic models and metrics to help marketers quantify and monitor their marketing efforts, as well as predict their results. The insight gained from the models and metrics help marketers make better decisions and maximize the effect of their resources.

In the title, "Marketing Analytics: Strategic Models and Metrics," we refer to the models and metrics as "strategic" to differentiate this book from others focusing on tools for website analytics. This book is not limited to website analytics. This book shows how to apply models and metrics throughout the entire range of marketing efforts—from market sizing to sales—to demonstrate the strategic relevance of analytics in virtually every marketing endeavor.

In a world where marketing professionals are held accountable for results, the ability to quantify the outcome of one's efforts, and to show how they relate to organizational objectives, is a critical competitive advantage.

Marketing Analytics

For purposes of this book, we will define marketing analytics to include models and metrics that provide actionable insight. Here, "models" are decision tools, such as spreadsheets, that aid decision-making, and "metrics" are key performance indicators that provide insight into business operations. Metrics for business operations, as we shall soon see, can span from profitability-related measures to social media engagement.

Practical, Structured, and Comprehensive

This book gives marketers a guide into methods to derive actionable insight into their efforts by introducing a practical, structured, and comprehensive approach to marketing analytics, using a business-oriented structure. With the approach, marketers will gain a solid understanding of marketing analytics fundamentals and how to apply them.

Practical: The book focuses on practical applications to common marketing issues. The examples leverage existing tools such as Microsoft Excel-based spreadsheets so marketers can put the knowledge to use without having to implement special software. The book emphasizes established marketing principles in publicly available marketing books (rather than focusing on university papers) to further emphasize its applied, practical nature.

Structured: Traditional operations research books often structure their content around math-oriented concepts, such as "conjoint models" and "optimization models." Such a structure can make it difficult to interpret and apply the information. To make the book more relevant to its intended audience, the book structures its content according to familiar marketing functions, such as "competitive analysis" and "pricing."

Comprehensive: Unlike existing books limited to specific areas within marketing analytics (such as books limited to website analytics), this book introduces a spectrum of essential analytics tools required for a fundamental understanding of marketing analytics. Each chapter includes indispensable models and metrics applicable to typical marketing functions, such as competitive analysis.

Organization

As shown in Figure 0.1, the book's content is organized into six areas, from strategic affairs to tactical actions, with chapters mapped to those areas. Using this organizational approach, readers can quickly identify which models and metrics to use for different marketing situations.

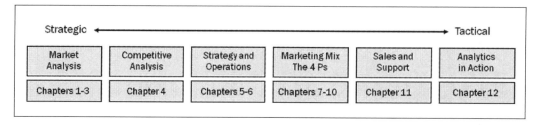

Figure 0.1: Book Organization

Intended Audiences

This book is intended for use with three types of readers:

Undergraduate students: The book is ideal for upper division undergraduate business or marketing students in dedicated marketing metrics and analytics courses. In addition, the book is relevant for courses that incorporate marketing analytics into their topics, such as courses in marketing research, competitive analysis, pricing, web-based marketing, and strategic marketing. Depending on the nature of the course, this book could either be used as a supplement to the main text or as a stand-alone resource.

Graduate students: The book is useful for graduate masters of business administration (MBA) students in dedicated marketing metrics and analytics courses, as well as courses incorporating marketing analytics topics.

Marketing professionals: Professionals involved in areas where marketing analytics can provide a competitive advantage. Example areas include: strategic marketing, corporate marketing, lead generation, product management, product marketing, brand management, social media, new product development, and others.

Learning Features

The book employs several features to enhance learning. Additional learning resources are available on the author's website, StephanSorger.com, as explained on the next page.

Chapter Outline: Each chapter starts with an overview of the contents.

Marketing Made Measurable: Brief case studies demonstrate how analytics can be applied in real-world situations.

Figures: The book includes almost 400 figures, including diagrams, tables, and illustrations.

Summaries: Each chapter ends with a summary to help digest the chapter's topics.

Terminology: Principal terms are listed at the end of each chapter.

Class Discussion: Suggested topics for classroom instruction are included.

Practice Problems: Exercises are given in each chapter. Excel-based case study problems, along with their solutions, are available on the author's website. See below.

Instructor Supplements

Academic faculty and interested professionals may obtain access to instructor supplements. The supplements are ideal for adopting the book in classroom environments. Supplements are made available at the author's website, StephanSorger.com, on the Marketing Analytics course webpage. The webpage shows a sample of the resources. To access the complete set of supplements, please provide a request for the access password via the Contact page on the author's website, StephanSorger.com. Supplements include:

Microsoft PowerPoint Presentations: PowerPoint slides for each chapter, including outlines, key points, and figures from the text, are available for download.

Test Bank: Questions to test concepts and terminology, in multiple choice format are available. Instructors are responsible for tailoring and testing the questions for their respective classes. Due to the sensitive nature of exam questions, faculty members are asked to contact the author directly via the Contact page on StephanSorger.com, in lieu of downloading.

Excel-based Cases with Solutions: Business cases for each chapter use Microsoft Excel-based spreadsheets to demonstrate the application of decision models. The cases involve a variety of industries to show the wide applicability of the models. Solutions for each case are provided.

Web Resources: Links to various Internet-based articles and useful marketing analytics resources are provided on the webpage.

Videos: The webpage includes links to videos that illustrate various topics discussed in the book. Students often find watching the videos enjoyable, relevant, and educational.

Instructor Feedback

We encourage faculty members and other professionals to provide feedback on models, metrics, and examples for future editions of this book. We welcome any suggestions to continue to make this book useful for instructors and professionals as the dynamic field of marketing analytics continues to evolve. Please contact the author through the Contact page on the author's website, StephanSorger.com.

Acknowledgements

The author wishes to acknowledge the many people that helped inspire this book. Their guidance aided in transforming the book from a vision into a reality.

The book started out as a series of lecture notes for the author's course in Marketing Analytics taught at the University of California, Berkeley Extension. The course started back in 2008, when marketing analytics did not enjoy the popularity it does today. Since then, interest in the topic has grown considerably—and so has the number of academic institutions offering analytics courses. One factor driving this swift growth is the demand for skilled marketing analysts in virtually every industry. In the professional world, many employers look for analytics expertise in new marketing employees.

Thanks go out to the many students enrolled in the course over the years. Those students offered considerable feedback. The feedback helped to drive the selection of models and metrics discussed in this book. Many of the examples in the book originated from examples originally developed for the class.

Beyond the world of academia, the author also owes thanks to the organizations with which he has been involved, such as Oracle, 3Com (now part of Hewlett-Packard), and NASA (National Aeronautics and Space Administration). The author leveraged many of the models and metrics discussed in this book to help solve the complex challenges faced by those organizations. Usage in those "real world" environments aided in shaping and validating the techniques.

The author wishes to thank the following people in particular:

- Jim Prost, Adjunct Professor of the University of San Francisco, for his continual support of the author's academic writing activities.
- Tom McGuire, University of California, Berkeley Extension Program Director, for his belief in the course back in 2008, before marketing analytics enjoyed the popularity it has today.
- Vishag Badrinarayanan, Associate Professor, Department of Marketing, McCoy College of Business Administration, Texas State University, for his inspiration and feedback.
- John Follett, Chief Analyst at Demand Metric, a company specializing in analytics-based tools for marketers and consultants, for his review of the early manuscript of this book.
- Jerry Rackley, Vice President of Marketing and Product Development, also with Demand Metric, for his insight into the usability of the models and metrics in a practical setting.

About the Author

Stephan Sorger, M.S., M.B.A., is an authority on marketing analytics, supported with both professional and academic work on the subject.

Professionally, Mr. Sorger applies quantitative methods for business strategy, competitive analysis, and marketing research as Vice President of Strategic Marketing at marketing consulting firm On Demand Advisors. Before On Demand Advisors, Mr. Sorger held leadership positions at Oracle, 3Com, NASA, and other leading organizations.

As an instructor, Mr. Sorger teaches marketing analytics courses to post-graduate students at the University of California, Berkeley Extension. He spearheaded the first dedicated marketing analytics course to be offered on the West Coast, and has been teaching the topic since 2008. He is also an Adjunct Faculty member at the University of San Francisco (USF) MBA program, teaching marketing analytics.

He is a contributing writer to the online column of Demand Metric, a company specializing in marketing analytics tools.

Other books from Mr. Sorger include the textbook "Marketing Planning: Where Strategy Meets Action." The book offers a practical, streamlined, and comprehensive approach to marketing planning. The textbook is published by Pearson - Prentice Hall, and has been adopted by several major universities.

For further information, please visit the author's website at StephanSorger.com.

Chapter 1.

INTRODUCTION

Chapter Outline

We cover the following marketing analytics topics in this chapter:

- ☑ **Introduction to Marketing Analytics**: Models and Metrics; Adoption; Advantages
- ☑ **Introduction to Models:** Definition; Forms; Variables; Terminology
- ☑ **Introduction to Metrics:** Definition; Purpose; Metrics Families; Dashboards

---

"If you cannot measure it, you cannot improve it."
– Lord Kelvin

William Thomson, the 19th century mathematical physicist and engineer later known as Lord Kelvin, understood the power of measurement. Lord Kelvin made important contributions to science and measurement. Some examples include his work in developing the electric telegraph, improving the mariner's compass, and helping to formulate the first and second laws of thermodynamics. He also realized that temperature had a lower limit, absolute zero. Today, scientists state absolute temperatures in the units of Kelvin in his honor. [1-1]

INTRODUCTION TO MARKETING ANALYTICS

For purposes of this book, we define marketing analytics to cover models and metrics that provide actionable insight. Note that this definition differs from the traditional version, which describes marketing analytics as data analysis for marketing purposes. In the author's view, the traditional view is too vague to be useful. In addition, the inclusion of the word "actionable" in the new definition emphasizes the practical, directly applicable nature of the book's approach.

Models and Metrics: An Introduction

Models: In this book, we define models as tools that aid us in making decisions based on marketing data and organizational objectives. Models simplify and represent the real world along a dimension of interest. Models allow us to focus our efforts.

We can use computer-based spreadsheets (such as those from Microsoft Excel) to implement decision models. We discuss several spreadsheet-based models in this book.

As an analogy for models, one could consider a GPS (global positioning system) navigational unit in an automotive dashboard, as shown in Figure 1.1. The system is a simplification of the real world (the maps do not show rocks and trees), it is representative (the maps are to scale), and it serves as a decision-making tool (drivers can decide which route to take, based on information in the maps).

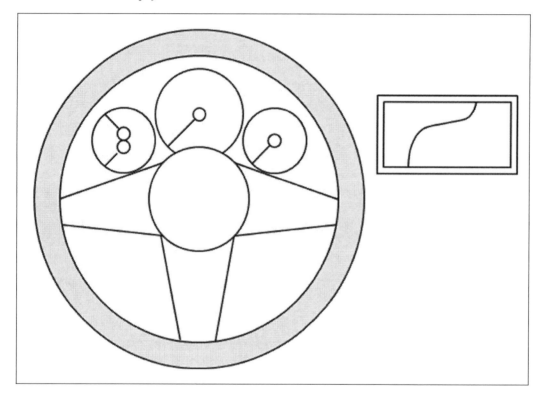

Figure 1.1: Automotive Dashboard, with Instruments (Left) and GPS Unit (Right)

Metrics: In this book, metrics are measurements representing performance levels of important variables within an organization, such as sales revenue. Marketers can apply metrics to monitor situations and diagnose problems. Some organizations refer to especially important metrics as key performance indicators (KPIs), because they indicate the performance of important attributes of the company, such as sales in different markets. Marketers can leverage the information gained by metrics as insight toward the performance of the system.

In this book, we review several relevant metrics for different aspects of marketing. Although many possible metrics are available, we urge marketers to exercise caution when selecting them. We want to ensure that the metrics we select provide strong indicators of results. As physicist Albert Einstein said: "Everything that can be counted does not necessarily count; everything that counts cannot necessarily be counted."

As an analogy for metrics, one could consider the instruments in a car (speedometer, odometer, fuel gauge, temperature, etc.) to display key metrics. The instruments display vital information to monitor the status of the vehicle. The driver can see the speedometer, and notice that she is driving above the posted speed limit (she had better slow down!). The driver can also see the odometer and the fuel gauge, and notice that her fuel consumption is above-average (probably from driving too fast). The driver can also use the metrics to diagnose problems (the quickly climbing temperature gauge could signal an overheating engine).

MARKETING MADE MEASURABLE

Metrics in the Military: In World War II, many airplanes returned from battle with significant damage. The damage was often concentrated in certain areas, such as tail sections riddled with bullet holes, as shown in Figure 1.2. Military personnel noticed the damage and came to the conclusion that those areas were vulnerable and thus should be reinforced.

Abraham Wald, a statistician skilled in analytics, came to the opposite conclusion. He reasoned that the planes that made it back in one piece (albeit with damage) were fine. Instead, we should be concerned with the planes that failed to return. Those planes must have been hit in areas that the plane simply could not survive. Therefore, the planes must be reinforced in the areas not seen as damaged in returning airplanes.

The problem, Wald stated, was that military personnel were using the wrong metrics because of the inherent selection bias in the data. [1-2]

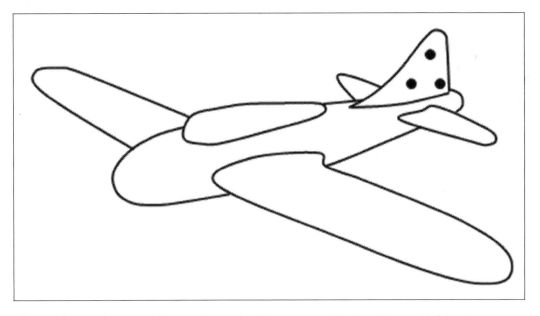

Figure 1.2: Metrics in the Military: Example of Airplane with Bullet Holes in Tail Section

Marketing Analytics Adoption

Several factors are driving increased adoption of marketing analytics.

Accountability: Organizations are searching for ways to improve productivity to reduce costs and improve profitability. To improve productivity, chief executive officers (CEOs) are following the old adage, "what gets measured gets done." In the military, some officers express this sentiment by saying, "people don't do what you expect; they do what you inspect." Therefore, they are holding marketers responsible for delivering measurable results from their marketing efforts.

Data-Driven Presentations: Similar to the accountability factor mentioned above, executives want to confirm that decisions that could affect organizational profitability (such as increased marketing spending) are backed by solid data during presentations.

Massive Data: Many organizations are awash in data. For example, some customer databases are over 1TB (one Terabyte) in size, thanks to initiatives to capture detailed customer information. Effective organizations seek to wield the power of all that data. We discuss several ways to leverage data in the coming chapters.

Online Data Availability: Marketers can now access tremendous amounts of data over computer networks. In fact, many organizations have moved significant amounts of data to the Cloud. Online availability improves the speed and convenience of accessing data. In a world where every second counts, this is a powerful advantage.

Reduced Resources: Many organizations now live by the mantra, "Doing more with less." In such organizations, every marketing dollar is scrutinized. Marketers must show the outcome of their efforts if they want to keep their marketing budgets intact.

Figure 1.3 summarizes the adoption factors.

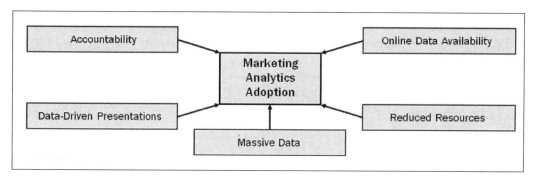

Figure 1.3: Factors Driving Marketing Analytics Adoption

Marketing Analytics Advantages

The field of marketing analytics provides powerful advantages to organizations.

Drive Revenue: In the past, some organizations considered marketing departments as a "cost center," because marketing departments failed to show the correlation between marketing spending and marketing results. Using marketing analytics, some marketing departments are transforming themselves into "revenue centers," emphasizing their role in driving revenue for the organization.

Save Money: The traditional approach to marketing has been to execute a campaign and guess at its outcome. Many organizations will no longer tolerate such an approach. Thanks to marketing analytics, organizations can predict the outcome of many campaigns.

Persuade Executives: Before the advent of marketing analytics, marketers sought to persuade decision makers to increase their marketing budget to fund campaigns such as those to build brand equity. The approach often failed, for at least two reasons. First, many decision makers are more focused on driving revenue or reducing costs than they are in branding campaigns. Second, the marketers were unable to prove how the extra budget would drive results. With marketing analytics, marketers can now predict (in many cases) the revenue impact of specific campaigns.

We have found marketing analytics particularly important in the case where executives do not come from a marketing or sales background, and sometimes do not appreciate (or even fully understand!) the role of marketing. In these cases, supplementing marketing proposals with models and metrics can be a powerful persuasion tool.

Encourage Experimentation: Without marketing analytics, it is difficult to experiment with different versions of advertisements and other vehicles due to the high cost of executing each version and comparing the results. Marketing analytics give us the power to test multiple scenarios using models. With the models, we can run simulations of different approaches and predict which one will work best—all without spending a dime of advertising budget.

Decrease Effect of Politics: In the past, marketers could be subject to the whims of organizational politics. If the CEO did not appreciate marketing (or worse, disliked it), the marketer's fate was sealed. Thanks to marketing analytics, marketers can use the power of models and metrics to show the correlation of their efforts with the areas in which the CEO feels most passionately about: revenue and cost.

In fact, marketing analytics can even help improve job security. According to executive search firm Spencer Stuart (spencerstuart.com), the average tenure for chief marketing officers (CMOs) can be only 25 months in volatile industries, such as automobiles and restaurants. Compare the tenure to that of chief executive officers (CEOs), at 111 months, and we can observe that the CMO's role is a perilous one. [1-3]

Figure 1.4 summarizes the advantages.

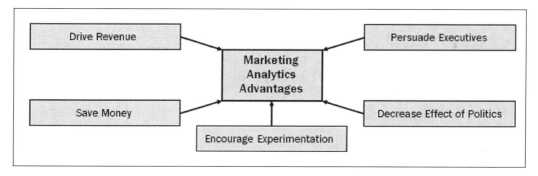

Figure 1.4: Marketing Analytics Advantages

MARKETING MADE MEASURABLE

Data Analysts: From Geek to Google: Organizations have changed their perception of data analysts. Once associated with pocket protectors, data analysts are now highly regarded for their analytics skills.

Internet search powerhouse Google is a driving force in this change. The company depends on quantitatively-motivated individuals in its quest to track, interpret, and manage data to drive profit.

Other companies, attracted by Google's billions in profit, are gaining respect for analytics as well. In fact, the United States Bureau of Labor Statistics estimates that the job category will grow by 45% by 2018, making it among the fastest growing careers available. [1-4]

INTRODUCTION TO MODELS

Earlier, we briefly introduced the concept of models. We now explore them in detail.

Models: Definition and Detail

Definition: Models are simplified representations of reality we use to solve problems and gather insight to make decisions. Models are "simplified" in that they intentionally leave out detail in non-essential areas, so we can focus on the areas that matter. In our earlier GPS example, the navigational maps are simplified in that they do not show rocks, trees, and other geological features. Models are "representational" in that they approximate reality for the attributes in which the marketer is most interested. In the GPS example, the maps are to scale and the distances are accurate because those characteristics are vital to our decision-making.

Purpose: The purpose of models is to understand the nature of marketing phenomenon and use that understanding to predict the outcome of our marketing actions. For example, we might wish to understand the relationship between advertising levels and resulting sales revenues. The purpose of this model would be to assess a particular campaign's advertising effectiveness.

Accuracy: Models are useful because they allow us to study important attributes of marketing situations. Nevertheless, all models are inherently limited in that they are simplified representations of reality, not reality itself. As we will see later in the book, models can be made more accurate by considering more data and more variables, but they can only approximate reality, not duplicate it.

Decisions: Models provide marketers with insight into decisions. For example, understanding how advertising affects sales revenue allows us to select an optimum level of advertising spending for a given amount of target revenue.

Model Styles: Verbal, Pictorial, and Mathematical

Models can be expressed in different styles. We can express them verbally, pictorially, or mathematically, depending on the type of phenomenon and the amount of information known about it.

Verbal Models: Verbal models are models expressed in words. Continuing the advertising example above, we could express our verbal model as, "sales revenue increases with advertising spending up to a point, and then falls." Marketers often use analogies and metaphors as a form of verbal models, such as the "marketing funnel." Verbal models are a good start to understanding marketing phenomenon, but are insufficient for complete understanding. We need to develop the model further (to pictorial and mathematical forms) to gain the most benefit from it.

Pictorial Models: Pictorial models show marketing scenarios in a diagram. Different diagrams can serve different purposes. A block diagram could show a process (such as a block diagram representing a typical marketing campaign flow). A graph could show the relationship between different variables. Figure 1.5 shows an example graph displaying the relationship between advertising and sales revenue, where it hits a peak at point A, and declines thereafter.

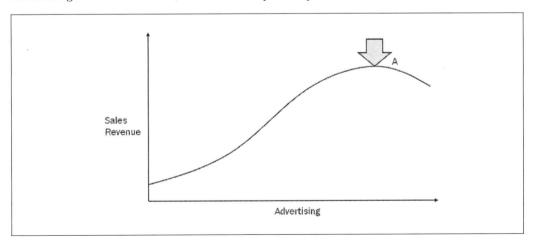

Figure 1.5: Sample Pictorial Model, Relationship of Advertising and Sales Revenue

Mathematical Models: Mathematical models specify a direct relationship between one set of variables (such as advertising spending levels) and another set of variables (such as sales revenue). Mathematical models are often set in the form of an equation, such as S = f(advertising), which means that sales revenue is a function of advertising. Mathematical models are the most useful form of models because we can use them directly in spreadsheets and other decision-making tools. Of course, the accuracy of mathematical models is limited by the accuracy of the input data. As the old adage states, "garbage in, garbage out."

Figure 1.6 summarizes the different styles of models.

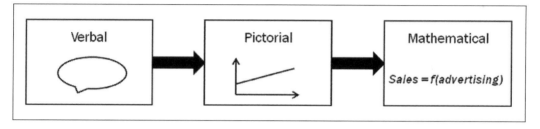

Figure 1.6: Model Styles: Verbal, Pictorial, and Mathematical

Model Forms: Descriptive, Predictive, and Normative Forms

We can categorize models by their forms. The forms range in terms of complexity and usefulness from the most basic (called descriptive) to a medium level (called predictive) to the most advanced level (called normative). Figure 1.7 shows the different forms.

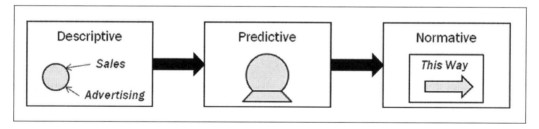

Figure 1.7: Model Forms: Descriptive, Predictive, and Normative

Descriptive Models: Descriptive models simply characterize (describe) marketing phenomena. They identify the components of the phenomena (such as variables) and specify the causal relationships between variables. Continuing our advertising model example, we can express the relationship in a simple linear equation. The equation is: "Sales Revenue = a + b * Advertising" where "a" is a constant and "b" is the degree to which advertising affects sales revenue. In the figure, the descriptive model is represented as the phenomenon with certain characteristics (sales and advertising) associated with it.

Descriptive models provide a structured basis for definition, analysis, and understanding of the problem at hand. However, descriptive models are limited to description only; they generally offer little if any predictive power or insight into the best course of action.

Predictive Models: Predictive models determine likely outcomes given certain inputs. In other words, they predict what will happen. A typical example would be a sales forecast, where an organization predicts its sales for the coming quarter or year. An even more common example is the "what if" spreadsheet—"What would happen to sales if we were to decrease prices?" In the figure, the predictive model is represented as a crystal ball, to forecast the future.

Predictive models go beyond purely descriptive models to make inferences about the underlying structure of variables governing a marketing phenomenon. For example, rather than simply relate advertising to sales revenue (as in the descriptive model), we can predict the effect of components of advertising, such as frequency (the number of times the target market sees the ad in a given time period) and reach (the number of people exposed to the ad), to advertising effectiveness.

Normative Models: Normative models provide guidance on the appropriate course of action given a certain set of circumstances. In that way, normative models go beyond simply describing the phenomenon (the role of a descriptive model) and predicting possible futures (the role of a predictive model). For example, we could determine the optimum price by considering sales forecasts at different prices. In the figure, the normative model is represented as a road sign, showing the way to success.

Instead of asking, "What if we were to change advertising levels?" as we would in a predictive model, we can use the normative model to ask, "What is the best level of advertising given our current market condition?" Not surprisingly, normative models are the most complex of the three forms and the most difficult to develop.

Models: Independent and Dependent Variables

Mathematical models use independent and dependent variables to describe marketing phenomena, such as the relationship between advertising levels and sales revenue. We can classify variables into independent and dependent variables, as shown in Figure 1.8.

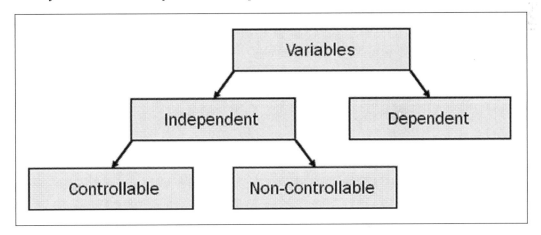

Figure 1.8: Independent and Dependent Variables

Variable: The definition of a variable is a quantity that can be changed, or varied. We can change the level of advertising, so that is a variable. Sales revenue can also change, so it too is a variable.

Independent Variable: The definition of an independent variable is a variable whose value can impact a dependent variable. Because the level of advertising can impact sales revenue (which we will soon learn is a dependent variable), the level of advertising is an independent variable. Independent variables are customarily assigned to the horizontal, or x, axis of graphs. Independent variables can be classified as controllable or non-controllable:

- **Controllable**: We consider independent variables controllable if we can exert some control over them. For example, marketers can control the amount of money they spend on advertising, so the advertising level would be considered a controllable independent variable.

- **Non-controllable**: We classify independent variables as non-controllable if we cannot exert control over them. For example, we might find that different customer age groups buy different amounts of our product, so age would be considered an independent variable. Because we cannot control our customer's age, it is considered a non-controllable independent variable.

Dependent Variables: The definition of a dependent variable is a variable that responds to changes in the independent variable. In our earlier example, sales revenue would be a dependent variable because it responds to changes in advertising levels. Dependent variables represent our marketing objective (what we seek to achieve).

Typical dependent variables for marketing groups in for-profit organizations include sales revenue, profitability, brand awareness, exposure levels, and any other characteristic that demonstrates the impact of our marketing efforts. For non-profit organizations, dependent variables could include donation proceeds or number of donors. Dependent variables are customarily assigned to the vertical, or y, axis of graphs.

Models: Terminology

Figure 1.9 shows how model terminology is used in one of the simplest models, a linear response model. The figure shows a linear response model with only two variables. The two variables are an independent variable and a dependent variable. The independent variable is customarily drawn on the horizontal axis, also called the x axis. The dependent variable is drawn on the vertical axis, also called the y axis. As the name suggests, linear models are represented as a line. The line has a slope, defined as the rise (vertical portion) over the run (horizontal portion).

For the example shown in the figure, we show that the linear model has the form "$y = a + b * x$":
- y is the dependent variable (which in this case is sales revenue)
- x is the independent variable (which in this case is advertising level)
- a is the y intercept (where the line crosses the y axis)
- b is the slope (steepness of the line)

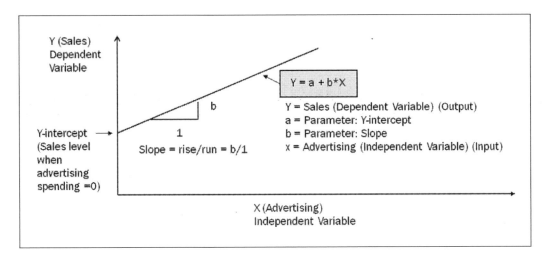

Figure 1.9: Linear Response Model

INTRODUCTION TO METRICS

Next, we turn our attention to metrics.

Metrics: Definition and Purpose

Definition: Metrics are measurements quantifying important attributes of marketing phenomena. We consider two examples. The metric "sales revenue by store" measures the amount of money each store generates, on average, from our products and services. The metric "sales revenue by product" measures the amount of money each of our products generates. Both would be useful to assess the effectiveness of our retail product marketing efforts. We can extend these examples to include hundreds, perhaps even thousands, of metrics we can potentially track.

Purpose: Metrics are used to monitor and diagnose marketing phenomenon. By monitoring important marketing attributes, we can quantitatively seek to improve the system. In the example of "sales revenue by store," we can use the metric to measure the effectiveness of different marketing activities. We can also use metrics to diagnose situations. For example, we might identify a problem store by assessing that its "sales revenue by store" metric is much lower than average, and take corrective action to remedy its low performance.

Metrics: Metrics Families and Dashboards

With so many metrics available, we need a way to logically group them so we can quickly monitor and diagnose marketing results. [1-5]

Metrics Families: Metrics families are groups of related metrics. Grouping related metrics makes it easier to assess marketing situations and take action if something is wrong. Many different types of metrics families are possible. For example, a typical metrics family could be sales metrics sorted by geography, business unit, products, and market segments. Many other metrics families are available, such as those for customer service and brand equity.

Metrics Dashboards: Metrics dashboards aggregate important metrics on a single display. The dashboard often displays the metrics using graphics, such as trend graphs, dial gauges, and pie charts, for easier interpretation of the data. The graphics frequently include color coding, such as green for good (indicating that the metric is within acceptable limits), yellow for caution (indicating that the metric is about to stray into dangerous territory), and red for problem areas (alerting the user that immediate action is required).

Dashboards are included in many marketing automation systems and sales force automation systems. **Marketing automation systems** are software tools that automate common marketing tasks, such as campaign management. Some well-known marketing automation systems include Eloqua (eloqua.com), Marketo (marketo.com), and Pardot (pardot.com). **Salesforce automation systems**, such as those of Netsuite (netsuite.com) and Salesforce.com, are software tools that automate and coordinate sales efforts, such as tracking sales progress.

Figure 1.10 shows a sample typical metrics dashboard. The dashboard shows metrics around a Google AdWords search engine marketing (SEM) campaign. On the left hand side, we see a speedometer style graph for total number of leads from Google AdWords, and a pie chart showing the contribution of five different campaigns to the total number of leads. In the middle, we see metrics of top performers, including top 10 keywords, top 10 ad headlines, and top 10 campaigns (the figure shows only the top four in each category). On the right hand side, we see how leads from Google AdWords campaigns are being pursued within the sales pipeline. For example, the chart shows that salespeople are using nine leads from Google AdWords to conduct prospecting (following up with people who showed interest in the ads).

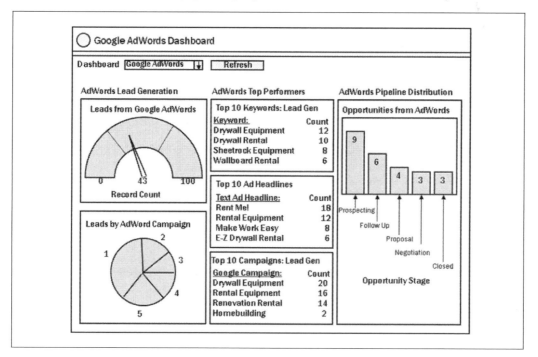

Figure 1.10: Typical Metrics Dashboard (Also Called Marketing Dashboard)

SUMMARY

We define marketing analytics as the use of models and metrics that offer actionable insight. We refer to the term "actionable" as providing concrete information with which we can take steps to make important marketing decisions, correct or improve results of marketing programs, or engage in other actions.

Models are tools that aid us in making decisions based on marketing data and organizational objectives. Models simplify and represent the real world, enabling us to focus our efforts on a specific problem. Many of the models discussed in this book can be implemented as computer spreadsheets, such as Microsoft Excel.

Metrics are measurements of marketing phenomena. We use metrics to monitor situations and diagnose problems. Marketers can apply the information gained by metrics as insight to the performance of specific marketing initiatives, such as campaigns.

Several factors are propelling the popularity of marketing analytics. The factors include increased accountability for results from marketing professionals, greater use of data in presentations, the huge size of most organizational databases (and the secrets they could reveal), online availability of marketing data, and reduced marketing resources.

Models come in different styles. At the lowest level are verbal models, which are simply verbal statements expressing a marketing phenomenon. The next level is pictorial models, which consist of pictures, diagrams, and graphs that express a relationship. The highest level is mathematical models, which represent relationships in equations.

Models also come in different forms, with progressively increasing power in gaining insight. The simplest form is descriptive models, which characterize marketing phenomena. Next are predictive models, which can determine likely outcomes given certain inputs. The most insightful forms are normative models, which can provide guidance on an appropriate course of action given a certain set of circumstances.

Models expressed in equation form include independent and dependent variables. Independent variables are defined as those whose values can affect dependent variables. Independent variables can be classified as controllable or uncontrollable, depending on the degree to which marketers can change them. Dependent variables are defined as those that respond to changes in the independent variables. For marketing problems, dependent variables represent our marketing objective (what we want to achieve), such as sales revenue and profitability.

Metrics are values measuring important attributes of marketing phenomena. Marketers apply metrics to monitor and diagnose marketing phenomenon. Marketers can view families of related metrics using tools such as metrics dashboards.

Terminology

Controllable Variables: Independent variables that the marketer can exert some control over, such as advertising levels

Descriptive Models: Models that characterize (describe) marketing phenomena

Metrics: Values measuring important attributes of marketing phenomena

Metrics Families: Groups of related metrics

Metrics Dashboards: Displays showing multiple metrics on one screen, or set of screen, for quick evaluation of conditions

Models: Tools that aid us in making decisions based on marketing data and organizational objectives

Normative Models: Models that provide guidance on the appropriate course of action given a certain set of circumstances

Predictive Models: Models that determine likely outcomes given certain inputs

Uncontrollable Variables: Independent variables that the marketer cannot exert control over, such as the age of the customer base

Class Discussion

1. How is the field of marketing analytics affecting your organization? What changes will occur as a result?

2. How do the tools and techniques of marketing analytics help persuade executives? What types of executives would find marketing analytics particularly persuasive?

3. What dependent variables does your organization track at the executive level? How do those variables change as one goes lower in the organization, such as the product or service level?

Practice Problems

1. Identify specific factors driving adoption of marketing analytics in your organization. Explain how the adoption is changing marketing operations.

2. State which dependent and independent variables your organization tracks at the marketing level. Which independent variables are controllable? Which are uncontrollable?

3. Identify examples of descriptive, predictive, and normative models used by your organization.

4. Which metrics families do you currently track in your organization? Which metrics do you plan to track in the future?

Chapter 2.
MARKET INSIGHT

Chapter Outline

We cover the following marketing analytics topics in this chapter:

☑ **Market Terminology**: Defining key terms
☑ **Market Data Sources:** Recommended sources for researching the market
☑ **Market Sizing**: Top-down and bottom-up approaches, and triangulation
☑ **PESTLE Market Analysis**: Identifying potential trends and underlying forces
☑ **Porter Five Forces Analysis**: Understanding the forces driving markets

"Before you build a better mousetrap, it helps to know if there are any mice out there."
– Mort Zuckerman

Mortimer "Mort" Zuckerman, Canadian-born American businessman, knows the value of understanding markets before investing in them. Thanks to his shrewd market knowledge, he amassed vast holdings in magazines, publishing, and real estate over his lifetime. In 2007, Forbes reported he was the 188th richest person, with a net worth of $2.4 billion. [2-1]

This chapter covers tools and techniques for market insight. It defines market terminology, recommends sources for market data, and addresses three approaches to market sizing. The three approaches are market research, top down market sizing, and bottom up market sizing. In addition, we study current forces and trends acting on markets to predict their characteristics in the future.

MARKET TERMINOLOGY

In this section, we review some common market definitions that we will need to understand for market sizing. [2-2]

Market: At its essence, a market is a group of customers who purchases products and services from sellers. That group can be made up of different segments with different needs. For example, we can break down the market for personal computers into multiple segments. The market segment called "business travelers" has a need for portable, lightweight computing power. Compare that group to the market segment called "gamers," who have a need for high-performance computing power.

We recommend that marketers define markets based on market need instead of product or service form. For example, personal computer manufacturers focused on selling "ultra-portable" machines into the "business traveler" segment. But they should have been defining their market in terms of the market need, which was portable, convenient computing power. Meanwhile, Apple focused on the need, not the form, and sold its iPad product to travelers. Many business travelers found the iPad preferable to an ultra-portable PC. As a result, Apple has cut into ultra-portable PC manufacturers' market share. [2-3]

Potential Market: Potential markets, also known as total markets, are defined as all customers in the population who have interest in acquiring the product or service. The term is more useful in theory than it is in practice, because it only considers interest. For example, customers who are interested in acquiring a Ferrari automobile, but do not have the means (money) to do so, are considered in the potential market. Therefore, the potential market size does not always reflect how many people will actually buy.

Available Market: Also known as Total Available Market (TAM), the available market is defined as the set of customers who are interested in a product and service, and have the means to purchase it.

Qualified Available Market: This term is defined as those customers in the available market who possess the required qualifications to purchase the product or service. For example, one must be 21 years of age to purchase liquor in many states.

Served Market(s): The served market(s) is the market segment or segments that the company has chosen to target. For example, the Sheraton Suites hotel chain (sheratonsuites.com) targets business travelers.

Figure 2.1 shows how the different market definitions nest into one another. For the remainder of this book, when we mention the general term "market" we are referring to qualified available markets, because the vast majority of markets place no legal restrictions on consumption.

Figure 2.1: Hierarchy of Market Definitions

When we study markets, we focus on the buying side—the people who purchase goods and services from companies. Alternatively, we can examine industries, which focus on the sellers of goods and services to those markets. Assuming the markets buy all of the output industries offer to sell (which in the long run they do, barring catastrophic recessions, obsolete technologies, and natural disasters), we can study the sales of industries to markets as a proxy for the amount of goods and services individuals purchase from those industries. [2-4]

To that end, we define industry-related terminology:

Industry: An industry is a group of sellers that produce products or services that customers find similar. For example, customers shopping for household appliances (known as "white goods" in the trade) would find the goods of major appliance manufacturers (General Electric, Westinghouse, Samsung, and so forth) to be similar, and therefore relevant for their search.

Category: A category is a subset of an industry. It is a group of competing firms selling to the same market segment. For example, high end appliance manufacturer Sub Zero (famous for its elegant, high-capacity refrigerators) is in the high-end kitchen appliances segment, which is within the household appliances industry. Sub Zero sells into a market which consists of affluent, discriminating homeowners and builders constructing luxury residences.

Figure 2.2 shows how categories exist within industries.

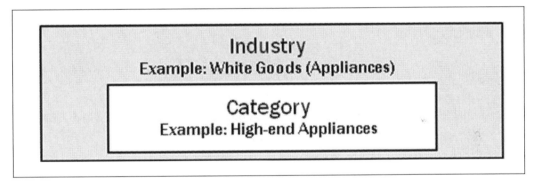

Figure 2.2: Hierarchy of Industry Definitions

MARKET DATA SOURCES

Marketers should begin their journey into market insight by researching the market. Researchers classify research into two types: primary and secondary. Primary data is data created directly by the researcher for a specific purpose. Secondary data is data created by others. We recommend searching for available secondary data before embarking on generating primary data. Figure 2.3 shows the approach.

To mirror our recommended approach, we begin this section with secondary data sources, and then move on to primary data.

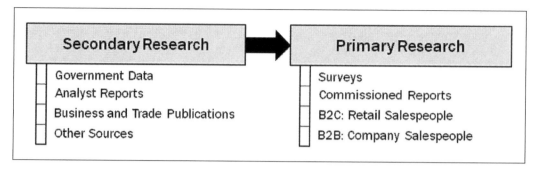

Figure 2.3: Market Data Sources: Secondary and Primary Research Data Sources

Secondary Research

One can often find abundant secondary data for virtually every market. In this section, we cover several relevant sources.

Government Data: The United States government publishes a wealth of data relevant for market insight. Government data sources have several advantages. The data is free, generally available online, and adheres to mandated processes and standards to maintain data accuracy and reliability. The disadvantages of government data are that the information is often several years old and covers broad markets, making it less useful for specific, smaller markets.

Here are some typical sources:

- **United States Census Bureau (census.gov)**: The U.S. Census Bureau conducts a census (complete count) of the U.S. population every 10 years, as dictated by the Constitution. In addition, it collects data in other ways, such as with its New American Community Survey 5-Year Estimates. The information includes detail on people and households, such as statistics on housing, median income, and population densities. Census bureau information also includes data on business and industry, such as statistics on different industries. [2-5]

- **United States Bureau of Labor and Statistics (bls.gov):** The U.S. Bureau of Labor publishes data on various labor-related topics, such as employment, productivity, and inflation statistics. [2-6]

- **United States Bureau of Economic Analysis (bea.gov):** The Bureau of Economic Analysis, part of the U.S. Department of Commerce, publishes statistics on U.S. economic accounts, such as nationwide gross domestic product (GDP), personal income, international trade, regional GDP (by state and metropolitan area), and industry data. [2-7]

- **Local Chambers of Commerce:** Most mid to large sized cities and metropolitan areas maintain a chamber of commerce. The chambers often hold significant data over the local area. For example, the Atlanta chamber of commerce (metroatlantachamber.com) has special sections on its website devoted to featured industries, such as bioscience, global commerce, supply chain, and technology. [2-8]

Government data sources (and many private sources) index industry data using the North American Industrial Classification System (NAICS) code (census.gov/naics). The intent of the NAICS code is similar to the United States Postal Service's ZIP code plan. The government enacted the zone improvement plan (ZIP) in 1963 to clearly define different geographical areas. Analogously, the NAICS code clearly defines different industries by assigning a unique code to virtually every industry.

NAICS uses a hierarchical system, starting with a two-digit code at the top designating 20 industry groups. Figure 2.4 shows the groups.

Code	Industry Title
11	Agriculture, Forestry, Fishing, and Hunting
21	Mining
22	Utilities
23	Construction
31 - 33	Manufacturing
42	Wholesale Trade
44 - 45	Retail Trade
48 - 49	Transportation and Warehousing
51	Information
52	Finance and Insurance
53	Real Estate and Rental and Leasing
54	Professional, Scientific, and Technical Services
55	Management of Companies and Enterprises
56	Administrative and Support and Waste Management and Remediation Services
61	Educational Services
62	Health Care and Social Assistance
71	Arts, Entertainment, and Recreation
72	Accommodation and Food Services
81	Other Services (except Public Administration)
92	Public Administration

Figure 2.4: NAICS Industry Groups

Additional digits are appended to the end of the NAICS code as industries become more specific, ultimately leading to a six digit code. For example, Figure 2.5 shows the NAICS hierarchy for insurance agencies and brokerages, such as those offering homeowner's insurance. [2-9]

Code	Industry Title
52	Finance and Insurance
524	Insurance carriers and related activities
5242	Agencies, brokerages, and other insurance related activities
52421	Insurance agencies and brokerages

Figure 2.5: NAICS Example Hierarchy for Insurance Agencies and Brokerages

Having obtained the NAICS code for the desired industry, marketers can access significant amounts of information made available by the U.S. government. Private organizations also use the NAICS code to classify their own materials, as we will see with industry analysts below.

The U.S. Census Bureau offers industry statistics reports, such as their Industry Samplers and Industry Snapshots, for many industries. Figure 2.6 shows an excerpt of an Industry Snapshot table for NAICS 52421, Insurance Agencies and Brokerages. The figure shows 2002 and 2007 data for total revenue, number of establishments, and total employment within the industry. [2-10]

Metrics	2002 Data	2007 Data	% Change
Total Revenue	$80.9 billion	$106.1 billion	31.2%
Number of Establishments	125,868	136,995	8.8%
Total Employment	627,346	695,275	10.8%

Figure 2.6: Industry Snapshot for NAICS 52421, Insurance Agencies and Brokerages: Sample Data

Analyst Reports: Market research and analysis firms routinely develop and publish reports on market sizing and trends. In fact, industry reports are one of their principal sources of revenue. Subscribers to the reports often spend thousands of dollars a year to see what insight the analysts can offer. Analysts are categorized into industry analysts and financial analysts. [2-11]

Industry analysts focus on events and trends in the markets they cover. They develop their reports principally for manufacturers and service providers, who use the reports to make changes in the development or marketing of their products and services, with the goal of increasing sales.

For example, research firm IBISWorld (ibisworld.com) acts as an industry analyst by estimating the sizes of many industries. Like many research firms, it categorizes the industries it studies using the U.S. Census Bureau's NAICS system. According to an IBISWorld July 2012 report, the market size for NAICS 52421 (Insurance Agencies and Brokerages) is estimated at $154 billion in 2012. This size agrees fairly well with the 2007 U.S. Census Bureau estimate of $106 billion, considering the market's strong growth rate.

Analyst companies focus on either business to consumer markets (B2C, such as the sale of food and beverage products to consumers) or business to business markets (B2B, such as the sale of machinery to companies). For example, B2C analyst Nielsen (nielsen.com) measures effectiveness of consumer packaged goods (CPG) advertising, and reports the results. B2B analyst Gartner (gartner.com) covers sales of enterprise software and other areas for the businesses that subscribe to their information services. [2-13]

Financial analysts also study markets, but primarily to identify potential financial investment opportunities. For example, financial analyst firm Barclays Capital (barcap.com) covers the personal computing market, and predicted back in July 2010 that Apple would sell 20 million iPads in 2011. [2-14]

Here are some examples of large industry and financial analyst firms:

- **Industry analysts, B2C**: Mintel (mintel.com), Nielsen (nielsen.com), and NPD Group (npd.com)

- **Industry analysts, B2B**: Forrester Research (forresterresearch.com), Gartner (gartner.com), IDC (idc.com)

- **Financial analysts**: Barclays Capital (barcap.com), (Dunn & Bradstreet (dnb.com)

Business and Trade Publications: Business and trade publications often cover events in major markets, and predict market sizes as well. Business publications work well for researching large consumer markets.

Examples of business publications include magazines (and their websites), such as Business Week and Fortune for general market coverage, newspapers (and their websites), such as the New York Times and the Wall Street Journal for late-breaking stories, and niche magazines, such as Fast Company and Wired, for high technology.

For business markets, trade publications can provide relevant market information. Specialty publishers publish trade publications for virtually every industry. For example, trade publication Adweek (adweek.com) covers the advertising industry, and is delivered in print and online formats. The publication covers major events and trends in the industry, and often predicts future market sizes, such as the potential advertising revenue to be expected through Apple iPad apps. [2-15]

Other Sources: Often, a thorough hunt for information using a popular search engine like Google will yield significant relevant information. For example, aggressive Internet searching can uncover a press release from an industry analyst with "teaser data" to coax companies into buying the full report. Often, the teaser data is sufficient. One caution: Be wary of information from blogs and other social media sources. While some of the information is authenticated and fact-checked, much of it is not. *Caveat emptor.*

Primary Research

Primary research is completed directly by the researcher. Often, it consists of surveys conducted with customers, prospects, distribution channel members, and other stakeholders related to the market. Marketers can also commission dedicated market research studies from specialty market research firms.

The advantages of primary research are that it is current (because marketers can conduct periodic surveys to ensure up-to-date information), accurate (because marketers can control the survey process to ensure high quality), and relevant (because marketers control the content of the questions). The disadvantages of primary research are that it is time consuming (diligent research can take weeks or perhaps even months), expensive, and difficult.

Nevertheless, some quick, low-cost, and easy primary sources exist. For business to consumer companies, marketers can get feedback from retail salespeople representing the company's brand. For example, a marketer working at apparel manufacturer Donna Karan can interview sales managers at retail outlets selling the brand, such as Macy's, to gain insight into the market, likely trends, and opportunities for revenue growth. For business to business companies, marketers can ask the company's sales team about their observations on the company's market, its trends, and likely growth.

MARKET SIZING

Understanding a market's size is critical for effective marketing. As we will see in this section, market size estimates are used for a variety of purposes, from deciding whether to enter a quickly growing market to deciding to exit a failing one.

Sometimes, we stumble across an industry analyst report or other data source that gives us exactly the data we need—the exact size of our market. Alas, this is rarely the case. Even if did "strike it rich" with this lucky find, we recommend that marketers apply several approaches to size the market, and then combine the results to arrive at the final estimate. We do not want to rely too heavily on any one approach.

In this section, we cover top-down and bottom-up approaches to sizing the market, then discuss how to triangulate the results. We start by addressing the stakeholders (the affected parties) of marketing sizing efforts.

Stakeholders for Market Sizing

As we discover in this section, many individuals and departments in an organization (and many outside of it!) are affected by market sizing estimates. Figure 2.7 provides an overview of the principal stakeholders. [2-16]

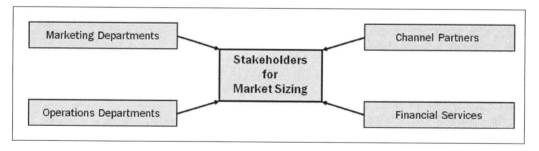

Figure 2.7: Stakeholders for Market Sizing

Marketing Departments: Market sizing will definitely affect individuals in the marketing department. For example, marketing executives (such as vice presidents of marketing) will need to conduct market sizing efforts when investigating new markets or calculating market share within existing markets.

Operations Departments: Market sizing will also affect manufacturing personnel (in companies which manufacture products) and service provider personnel (in companies delivering services). Manufacturers need company forecasts (which are based on market size) to determine how many units to make, what type of machinery to use, and what special manufacturing processes to apply. High volumes will require different types of machinery and processes than low volumes. Service providers need company forecasts to determine how many service personnel to hire and deploy, and to decide on the type and amount of support equipment required.

Distribution Channel Partners: Distribution channel partners are intermediary organizations that move products and services from the manufacturer (in the case of products) or service provider (in the case of services) to the customer.

For a product example, consumer product giant Unilever (unilever.com) sells its Skippy brand of peanut butter to customers using a variety of distribution channel partners, including wholesalers and retail stores, such as Safeway supermarkets.

In the case of services, high end audio specialist Magnolia (magnoliaav.com) sells its line of luxury home theater and audio equipment in dedicated areas of selected Best Buy consumer electronics stores.

Channel partners are affected by market sizing because the company sales forecasts (which are related to market size) will impact the amount of product they will be expected to sell.

Financial Services: Companies providing financial services, such as banks, venture capitalists (VCs), and angel investors, use market sizing as an important metric when deciding on how much money to invest or lend in companies. For example, many VC firms require that a firm demonstrate a $500 million to $1 billion market size before lending money to that firm. [2-17]

Applications for Market Sizing

Market sizing is useful for many different scenarios. Figure 2.8 provides an overview of the applications. [2-18]

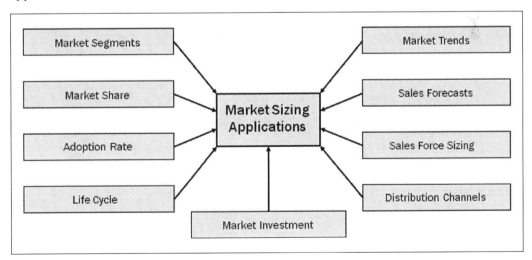

Figure 2.8: Typical Applications for Market Sizing

Market Investment: Organizations conduct market sizing efforts to determine if they should invest in a new market (also called a "Go/No Go" decision) and the amount of money to invest (also called a "Market Allocation" decision). Many marketers believe that organizations should also periodically conduct market sizing efforts for their existing markets, to ensure that their market is still a profitable one.

Market Segments: Companies can also benefit from market sizing efforts to determine the number of market segments available within a given market, as well as which ones to target. Larger markets generally offer more segments than smaller ones.

For example, according to industry analyst Gartner, the worldwide personal computer market size for 2011 was 364 million units. Because of the market's vast size, one can consider segments based on need (business travel, gaming, etc.), form factor (laptop, tablet, etc.), geography (North America, Europe, etc.), as well as other categories. Growing markets also generally offer more segments than stagnant ones, because new use cases are found as the market expands and customers become familiar with the product or service. [2-19]

Market Share: Market share is defined as the sales of a given type of product or service attributable to a given company, compared to the market as a whole. Therefore, to calculate market share, one must know the overall market size.

Adoption Rate: Adoption rate is the relative speed with which customers purchase and use a new product or service. Organizations can compare the adoption rate with the market growth rate to determine if they are exceeding it, or lagging behind it.

Life Cycle: The market adoption of virtually every product or service follows a life cycle similar to that of the human body. The life cycle continues over time in four stages. In the introductory stage, the company introduces the product or service into the market and sales grow slowly from zero. In the growth stage, adoption of the new product or service quickly increases. In the maturity stage, the product or service maintains a steady level of sales. In the decline stage, sales wither and eventually die. Periodic market sizing can aid in indicating the current stage of the life cycle.

Market Trends: Periodic market sizing efforts identify growing trends, be they positive or negative. Alert marketers can use the information to take advantage of the trend (in the case of a positive upswing) or take corrective action (in the case of a negative trend).

Sales Forecasts: Companies can also apply market sizing for assessing sales forecasts. Sales forecasts estimate the amount of sales the company expects to achieve in the coming period, usually one quarter or one year. If forecasts are an excessively high percentage of the total market, then the forecasts are not likely to be realized.

Sales Force Sizing: Business to business organizations need to decide how many salespeople to assign to a given market. Companies in large and quickly growing markets may need to add salespeople to keep up with increasing demand.

Distribution Channels: Distribution channel decisions benefit from market sizing. We can apply the information in various ways:

- **Number of Channels**: Large and growing markets need more retail stores than small and shrinking ones.

- **Type of Channels Needed**: Large and growing markets often require different types of retailers to cater to different market segments. Small and shrinking markets could require liquidation stores if the situation is dire enough.

- **Channel Location**: Large and growing markets need retail stores near growing areas to feed demand.

Market Sizing: Top-Down Approach

In this section, we cover top-down approaches. In the next section, we discuss bottom-up approaches. We close market sizing by discussing how to triangulate, or aggregate, the estimates from the different approaches for a final market size estimate.

Total Market Demand: In top down market sizing, we start with the size of a large, general market that includes the segment in which we are interested (plus many others). We multiply the size of the large, general market by successive factors to narrow the market down to our objective market (the market whose size we wish to estimate). This method is sometimes referred to as the chain ratio method. Figure 2.9 shows an overview of the top down approach using three factors; we can add more factors if necessary. [2-20]

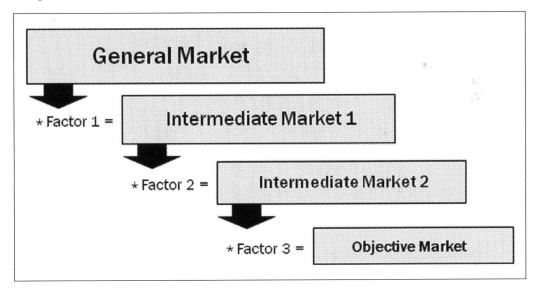

Figure 2.9: Overview of Top-Down Market Sizing Approach

The values for the large, general market are often called population numbers, because they represent an entire population of interest. Figure 2.10 shows some typical examples of population numbers. When using the top down market sizing approach, we start with these population numbers. [2-21, 2-22, 2-23]

General Market/ Population	Data and Source
Total population of the United States	308 million people in 2010 - U.S. Census Bureau
Total U.S. healthcare expenditures	$2.5 trillion in 2009 - Center for Medicare and Medicaid Services
Total number of motorcycles in U.S.	7.9 million motorcycles in 2009 - U.S. Bureau of Transportation Statistics

Figure 2.10: Top Down Market Sizing: Example General Market/Population Values

To demonstrate how top-down sizing works, we will describe how to calculate the market demand for a new type of eco-friendly biodegradable dental floss for the United States market. We show the steps to calculate the demand, based on the top-down approach:

- **Determine the population value** (in this case, the total number of people in the United States): According to the United States Census, the United States population was about 308 million people in 2010. [2-24]

- **Determine factor #1.** Factor #1 narrows the entire population of the United States to those who floss every day. According to the American Dental Association, about 12% of Americans floss daily. [2-25]

- **Determine factor #2.** Factor #2 represents the number of consumption occurrences per year. For daily flossing, this value will equal 365 uses per year.

- **Determine factor #3.** Factor #3 incorporates the amount of floss consumed per use. We shall estimate that each floss usage consumes one foot of floss.

- **Determine factor #4.** Factor #4 examines the price for one foot of floss. According to Walgreens.com, a standard 43.7 yard package of floss retails for $3.99. This works out to about $0.03 per foot. [2-26]

- **Determine factor #5.** Factor #5 takes into account the percentage of consumers who choose eco-friendly products. According to an article by consulting firm McKinsey (mckinsey.com), eco-friendly laundry detergents and household cleaners accounted for about 2 percent of all such cleaning products. [2-27]

We now multiply the population value by the various factors to get our market size for eco-friendly dental floss, calculated in dollars per year:

(Demand for eco-floss)   = (Total U.S. population)
                                          * (percentage of population that flosses)
                                          * (number of consumption occurrences per year)
                                          * (amount of floss consumed per use)
                                          * (price per foot)
                                          * (percentage of population who choose green products)

(Demand for eco-floss)   = (308 million)
                                          * (12%)
                                          * (365 uses/ year)
                                          * (1 foot/use)
                                          * ($0.03/ 1 foot)
                                          * (2%)
                                          = $8.1 million per year

By leaving out the percentage of customers choosing eco-friendly products (in our case, 2%), we arrive at the total demand for all dental floss as $404.7 million per year.

Figure 2.11 summarizes the example.

Step	Data
1. Determine relevant population value	Population of United States = 308 million people in 2010
2. Determine factor #1	% of Americans who floss daily = 12%
3. Determine factor #2	Number of uses per year (assume daily flossing) = 365
4. Determine factor #3	Amount of product (floss) consumed per use = 1 foot
5. Determine factor #4	Price for one usage of floss (1 foot) = $0.03
6. Determine factor #5	% of customers choosing eco-friendly products = 2%
7. Calculate demand by multiplying factors	= 308 million * 12% * 365 uses/year * 1 foot/use * ($0.03/use) * 2% = $8.1 million per year

Figure 2.11: Top Down Market Sizing: Eco-Friendly Dental Floss Market Size Estimation

For a comparison of our marketing sizing results, an Internet search reveals that Swiss yarn and fiber manufacturer Swicofil (swicofil.com) reported that the United States used over 2.5 million miles (4.4 billion yards) of dental floss in 1994. A standard 43.7 yard package retails for $3.99, which equates to about a $402 million market. According to the United States Census, the population of the United States in 1994 was about 260 million people. Using the values we estimated earlier, we would have predicted a total market size (not including "green" effects) of

260 million x 12% x 365 uses/year x 1 foot/use x $0.03/ use = $341 million, which differs from our previously calculated $404.7 million estimate by only about 16%. [2-28]

From the example, we see that the top-down method is fairly logical and straightforward to implement, and can result in reasonably close estimates if executed skillfully. But it has several disadvantages. First, one must take care in keeping the units of measurement consistent. In our case, we took care to always use feet, and not use some other dimension, such as yards, by mistake. Second, some of the estimates can be questionable, such as our choice of one foot of floss per use. Third, we must question the applicability of our estimates for our case. For example, spending patterns on eco-friendly laundry detergents might not match those of eco-friendly dental products. And fourth, it can be difficult to find data to support the factors.

Area Market Demand: We can modify the method reviewed above to determine the market demand in specific geographic areas, such as a cities and states. Figure 2.12 expresses an example of the concept, where we know the market size for the entire United States (the general geographic area), and wish to determine the market size for just the state of Ohio (the geographic area of interest).

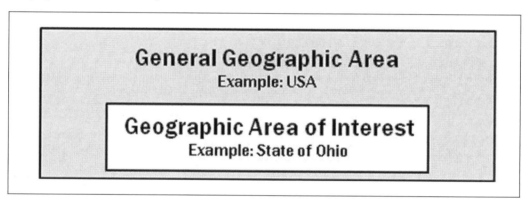

Figure 2.12: Area Market Demand

Two approaches are used, depending on the level of accuracy required. The two approaches are the single factor approach and the multiple-factor approach. In both cases, we seek to find out the percentage by which to multiply total demand to arrive at area market demand. [2-29]

In the **single factor approach**, we multiply the total market size by the percentage of the population the area of interest represents. To continue our flossing example, if we wanted to calculate the demand for bio-degradable floss in the state of Ohio, we could multiply the total demand by the ratio of the Ohio population over the U.S. population. According to the U.S. Census Bureau, the population of Ohio in 2010 was about 11.5 million. Thus, our factor is calculated as (11.5 million/ 308 million) = 3.7 percent. [2-30]

Critics might complain that multiplying by a population percentage is overly simplistic, and does not adequately represent the portion of consumption of the area. To increase the level of accuracy, we can employ the **multiple-factor approach**. In the approach, we use weighted levels of multiple factors to fine-tune our area estimates.

We can see how this approach would work by continuing our flossing market size example for the state of Ohio. We might assert that Ohio has an unusual level of retail sales compared to the rest of the nation, so we should include a factor that incorporates retail sales. According to the U.S. Census Bureau, the total level of retail sales in 2007 was about $138.8 million, compared to $3.92 billion in the United States as a whole. We can calculate our "retail sales" factor as ($138.8 million / $3.92 billion), or about 3.54%. [2-31]

We can assign weights to the various factors if we believe that some factors are more important. For example, we might believe that the level of retail sales plays a greater role in floss consumption than that of population. Therefore, we could assign a weight of 60% to retail sales and 40% to population. The adjusted weight would now be calculated as follows:

(Percentage of Floss Market in Ohio) = (Weight for Retail Sales) * (Retail Sales Ratio)
                                       + (Weight for Population) * (Population Ratio)

Inserting our values, we arrive at the following finding:

(Percentage of Floss Market in Ohio)   = (60%) * (3.54%)
                                          + (40%) * (3.7%)
                                          = 3.6%

Figure 2.13 summarizes the example.

Step	Data: Values	Data: Weights
1. Determine factor #1	Retail Sales Value USA: $3.92 billion Ohio: $138.8 million Percentage = 0.1388/ 3.92 billion = 3.54%	Retail Sales Weight Assign high weight due to perceived higher effect from retail sales Weight = 60%
2. Determine factor #2	Population Value USA: 308 million Ohio: 11.5 million Percentage = 11.5/ 308 million = 3.7%	Population Weight Assign lower weight due to perceived lower effect from population Weight = 40%
3. Calculate area market demand by multiplying factors by weights	% of Floss Market in Ohio = 60% * 3.54% + 40% * 3.7% = 3.6%	Note that sum of all weights must equal 1.0. In our case: 0.60 + 0.40 = 1.00 → OK

Figure 2.13: Top Down Market Sizing: Area Market Demand Example

The top-down approach must be used with caution, as it can over-estimate market size if one makes aggressive assumptions on factor values. For example, aggressively stating that 1% of all Americans will purchase a new $5,000 luxury watch (thus creating a $15.4 billion market) will not be realistic. For that reason, it is wise to temper top-down approaches with bottom-up ones, which we discuss in the next section.

Market Sizing: Bottom-Up Approach

In contrast to top-down approaches, bottom-up approaches start with individual elements and build them up to create the total market. Figure 2.14 shows the bottom-up approach.

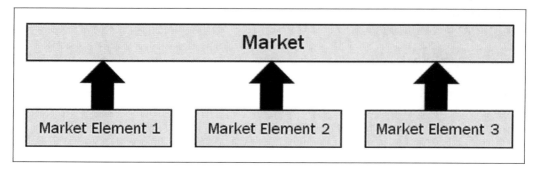

Figure 2.14: Overview of Bottom-Up Market Sizing Approach

The bottom-up approach is especially useful when dealing with the following situations:

- Niche markets
- Markets with a limited number of segments
- Markets with a limited number of distribution channels

Niche Markets: Some products or services are so specialized that only a very limited number of customers would buy them. For example, the Robbins Company (robbinstbm.com) manufactures tunnel boring machines (TBMs) to cut large holes in rock for highway or pipeline construction. Their largest unit, the 50 foot diameter Main Beam TBM, can cut a hole as tall as a small office building. Such a machine was featured in the 2007 motion picture "Oceans 13." [2-32]

The market for such a machine would be limited to major organizations planning to construct large motorways, pipelines, or other subterranean projects. Examples of such organizations include federal, state, and local governments (to build motorway tunnels, etc.), major utilities (to build underground water channels for hydroelectric power), and other similar large entities involved in developing large-scale infrastructure.

Calculating market size for niche markets is a relatively straightforward three step process, summarized in Figure 2.15. The example below demonstrates the process.

Step	Description
1. Identify Relevant Organizations	Determine which organizations would be interested in the product or service
2. Determine Quantity of Relevant Organizations	Determine the quantity of those organizations
3. Multiply Quantity by Price to Get Market Size	Multiply the quantity by the price of the product or service to get the market size

Figure 2.15: Bottom-Up Market Sizing: Approach for Niche Markets

MARKETING MADE MEASURABLE

Market Sizing for Niche Markets: General Electric Healthcare (gehealthcare.com) designs and manufactures PET/CT scanning machines (positron emission tomography – computed tomography). The complex machines produce three-dimensional images of functional body processes, essential for diagnosing disease. But they are very expensive at about $3 million each, so only the largest hospitals can afford them. [2-33, 2-34]

We will calculate the market size for PET/CT machines using the three steps we discussed:

1. **Identify Relevant Organizations**: For this step, we know that only large hospitals have the need and budget for such machines.

2. **Determine Quantity of Relevant Organizations**: According to the American Hospital Association (AHA), large hospitals (defined as those with over 500 beds) constitute five percent of all hospitals. Five percent of the 5,795 hospitals in the United States equates to about 290 hospitals.

3. **Multiply Quantity by Price to Get Market Size**: We multiply the quantity of potential customers (290 in this case) by the price ($3 million) to get the market size ($870 million).

Markets with a Limited Number of Segments: Many products or services are intended for a limited number of markets or market segments, but not so limited that they are classified as niche markets. For example, fork lift manufacturers sell to multiple markets (warehouses, industrial yards, marine boat lifts, etc.), but they can hardly be classified as mass market goods (such as soft drinks).

Calculating market size with a limited number of market segments is similar to that of niche markets.

- **Identify Groups of Buyers**: First, identify the groups of buyers for the product or service. If previous sales data exists, study it to determine what types of buyers purchased the product or service in the past. For new products or services, list all the relevant groups of buyers that could likely be interested in the product or service and conduct surveys in those groups to gauge their level of interest.

- **Identify Buying Rate**: Second, identify the buying rate of the different groups of buyers. For sales to consumers, surveys of buying intent can again be used.

- **Sum up Potentials:** Third, add up the potentials from each group of buyers identified in step one.

To identify buying rate for sales of products and services to businesses, it is helpful to categorize the buying rate as a function of one of three parameters:

- **Percentage of Total Revenue**: The first parameter is the amount of money the company spends on the product or service category, as represented as a percentage of the company's annual sales revenue. For example, some companies spend about 10% of their annual revenue on advertising agency services to promote the companies' offerings. As a result, advertising agencies gauge potential revenue in a company as a function of the company's annual sales.

- **Number of Employees:** The second parameter is the number of employees at the company. For example, insurance companies assess potential revenue as a function of the total number of employees, because each represents a potential new health insurance or other policy.

- **Number of Facilities**: The third parameter is the number of facilities, or locations. For example, building maintenance service companies gauge potential revenue as a function of the number of buildings, because each building will require regular maintenance.

We can apply the market research discussed earlier in the chapter to gather the information needed to address the three categories above.

Figure 2.16 shows an excerpt from the U.S. Census Bureau Industry Statistics Sampler for NAICS 541213, Tax Preparation Services for 2007. The figure shows Receipts (gross sales revenue) by state. We can apply the Receipts data for the Percentage of Total Revenue approach we discussed above.

The figure also shows the number of total employees by state, which we can apply for the Number of Employees approach. For example, if we decided to focus our efforts on sales of insurance policies to employees of tax preparation services, the data shown would provide us with the relevant market size (number of employees). [2-35]

Description	Receipts ($1000)	Employees	Establishments
United States	5,250,871	198,445	24,911
California	903,290	22,557	3,298
Texas	352,189	14,753	1,718
New York	322,989	11,001	1,364
Florida	309,453	12,557	1,615

Figure 2.16: Bottom-Up Market Sizing: NAICS 541213 Tax Preparation Services (Excerpt)

Figure 2.17 summarizes the three step procedure. The example below demonstrates the process.

Step	Description
1. Identify Groups of Buyers	Determine which groups of buyers would be interested in the product or service, based on historical data or surveys
2. Identify Buying Rate	Determine the buying rate of the product or service by those groups
3. Sum Up Potentials	Add up the potential from each group of buyers

Figure 2.17: Bottom-Up Market Sizing: Approach for Markets with Limited Numbers of Segments

---

MARKETING MADE MEASURABLE

Market Sizing for Limited Number of Markets: Acme Advertising is a fictitious advertising agency in the state of Arizona. It sells advertising services to three markets: Arizona accounting services companies, Arizona engineering services companies, and Arizona legal services companies. Acme chooses to focus on Arizona companies only, and in those three markets only. It therefore has developed great expertise in those markets. We will calculate Acme's potential market size: [2-36]

1. **Identify Groups of Buyers**: We can access the U.S. Census Bureau website to determine the total revenue in Arizona for Acme's three markets:
- Accounting services companies (NAICS code 541211): $400 million
- Engineering services companies (NAICS 541330): $1.1 billion
- Legal services companies (NAICS 541110): $1.4 billion

2. **Identify Buying Rate**: Acme's market research (and experience to date) shows that accounting services companies spend about 2% of their annual sales on advertising services. Similarly, engineering services companies spend about 1% and legal services companies spend about 3%.

3. **Sum Up Potentials**: To obtain the amount expected to be spent by Arizona accounting services for advertising, multiply the total revenue ($400 million) by the percentage of revenue spent by that market (in this case, 2%) to get $8 million. Similarly, we calculate the potential sales to the engineering and legal services markets to be $11 million and $42 million, respectively. We add the figures to arrive at a total of $61 million.

Markets with a Limited Number of Distribution Channels: Some markets are characterized as having a limited number of distribution channels. Distribution channels are intermediary organizations that distribute goods between manufacturers and customers. Examples of distribution channel members include wholesalers, retailers, auto dealerships, and retail stores.

Marketers often encounter situations where companies distribute their products and services through a limited number of distribution channels. In such situations, one can calculate potential annual sales by multiplying the number of goods each distribution channel member expects to move in one year by the total number of channel members.

Figure 2.18 shows a typical situation. In this case, six distribution channels supply the needs of all the individual customers interested in the company's product or service. The limited number of distribution channels governs the amount of sales possible. Thus, one can calculate the aggregate market size by determining the number of sales through each distribution channel.

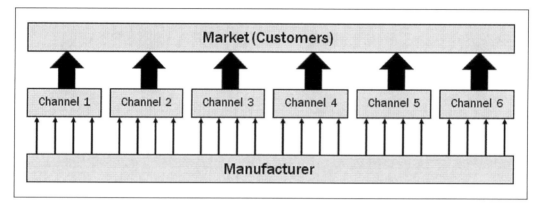

Figure 2.18: Bottom-Up Market Sizing: Limited Number of Distribution Channels

For example, according to Ferrari's dealer locator on its website (ferrari.com), it offers only 39 dealerships in the United States, a country of over 308 million people. If each Ferrari dealership sold 100 of its super-premium vehicles to customers every year, total sales would be limited to only 3,900.

The U.S. Department of Energy's Energy Efficiency and Renewable Energy agency reports that the average number of light vehicles sold per dealership is 777. Therefore, the 100 vehicles each Ferrari dealership sells is well below the industry average. Thus, Ferrari's dealership distribution channel model limits the market that the company can serve. The limited number of distribution channels in this case is not a problem because Ferrari, like many luxury auto brands, limits the number of cars it sells to a fairly low number to stimulate demand. [2-37, 2-38]

Market Sizing Triangulation

In this chapter, we have discussed three different ways to estimate market sizes:

- **Data Sources**: We reviewed how to access secondary data sources to leverage market sizing data already calculated by some other person or organization. For example, trade publications and analyst reports often size popular markets, such as the cell phone device market. We might also decide to conduct primary data research to establish the size. We will denote the market size we estimate using this method as "Market Size (Data Source)."

- **Top Down**: We also reviewed the method to calculate market size starting with a large, general market, and then narrowing it down to the market of interest using the top-down method. We call the resulting market size "Market Size (Top Down)."

- **Bottom Up**: We discussed how to determine the market size by building up the market from the bottom up, adding up portions of the market into one overall market. We indicate the market size using this method as "Market Size (Bottom Up)."

We recommend using multiple techniques to size the market whenever feasible. If we engage all three methods, we will have three market size estimates: We can combine multiple sizes into one number using a weighted average.

We will use corresponding weights for the different market size estimates. We designate the weight for the market size acquired through the data source as "Weight (Data Source)," for the market size calculated through top down means as "Weight (Top Down)," and for the market size resulting from the bottom up approach as "Weight (Bottom Up)."

The combined weights must equal 100%. We form a weighted average of the three sizes using the following equation:

Market Size (Combined) = Weight (Data Source) * Market Size (Data Source)
+ Weight (Top Down) * Market Size (Top Down)
+ Weight (Bottom Up) * Market Size (Bottom Up)

For example, we might obtain a market size using a particularly trustworthy data source, and so want to weight that market size higher. In this case, we could weight the Market Size (Data Source) weight as, say, 40% and weight the top down and bottom up averages at 30% each. If the Market Size (Data Source) was $100 million, the Market Size (Top Down) was $110 million, and the Market Size (Bottom Up) was $105 million, then we would calculate the combined estimate using the following equation:

Market Size (Combined) = 40% * $100 million
+ 30% * $110 million
+ 30% * $105 million
= $104.5 million

If each market size estimate represents the same level of robustness, then we could simply use a straight arithmetic average to reflect that fact. In this case, we would set all three weights at 33.3%.

PESTLE MARKET ANALYSIS

Sizing a market is a good start, but to truly gain insight into the market one must study the forces driving it. To that end, this chapter presents two market force analysis tools. The first tool, PESTLE market analysis, studies the political, economic, social, technological, legislative, and environmental trends in markets, based on the forces acting on those markets. The second tool is Porter's Five Forces Analysis. The Porter's analysis examines five key forces in markets to predict how companies serving the market will behave in the future. We will use an ongoing example of the laptop computer market to demonstrate the tools. We start with the PESTLE market analysis.

In the PESTLE market analysis, we study the trends caused by market forces to predict the future states of markets. As Figure 2.19 shows, we can essentially "fast forward into the future" using the technique.

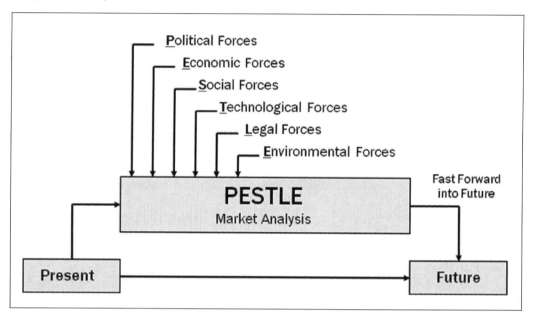

Figure 2.19: PESTLE Market Analysis

PESTLE Overview: Each letter of the acronym PESTLE represents a category of trends whose underlying forces affect the future state of the market--political, economic, social, technological, legal, and environmental. Each category can have a profound effect on markets. [2-39]

For example, the advent of the modern microprocessor in 1971 had a profound impact on the development of the modern laptop computer. Some might even argue that mobile devices like laptops and pocket-sized cell phones would have been impossible without the microprocessor. In this case, the invention of the microprocessor was a technological force.

We will cover different types of trends and their underlying forces, give examples of each, and show how they affect markets.

Political Trends: National and local politics can profoundly affect markets. Political forces drive virtually every organization, as its constituents struggle for control and power. Examples at the national level include taxation policy, trade restrictions and tariffs, party-dependent decision models (differences in behavior between republican and democratic representatives), and influencing and lobbying efforts.

MARKETING MADE MEASURABLE

Political Trends in the Laptop Market: The Indian government responded to lobbying by information technology (IT) firms in 2004 by eliminating import duties on a range of products. The government cut customs duty on mobile phones from 10 per cent to five per cent. Duty on computer equipment was reduced from 16 percent to eight per cent. And the government eliminated an odd rule that subjected laptop computers (aka notebook computers) to customs duty if they were in Indians' baggage. Laptop sales have increased since the duties were reduced. [2-40]

Economic Trends: As the poor economic conditions of 2007-2012 demonstrated, the state of the economy can have a lasting impact on virtually every market. Economic forces are categorized as macroeconomic factors and microeconomic factors.

- **Macroeconomic Factors**: Macroeconomics studies the behavior of the aggregate economy. Example factors involved in macroeconomics include inflation rates, unemployment levels, exchange rates, trade balances, and other nationwide and international parameters.

- **Microeconomic Factors**: Microeconomics studies the market behavior of individual consumers and firms. Example microeconomic factors include supply and demand of important resources, marketplace competition, characteristics of labor markets and wages, and other areas.

MARKETING MADE MEASURABLE

Economic Trends in the Laptop Market: Unfavorable economic conditions in 2007 – 2012 caused declines in virtually every sector of business spending, including IT purchases. Industry analyst Forrester Research predicted a 3 percent decline in global IT purchases in its January 2009 report, stating that "the global IT market will be a gloomy one in 2009..." This forecast indeed proved to be the case. [2-41]

Social Trends: Social forces acknowledge that cultural aspects of society can shape markets. Sources of social forces include people's values, beliefs, traditions, and taboos.

MARKETING MADE MEASURABLE

Social Trends in the Laptop Market: Two social forces have combined to drive sales of so-called ultra-portable laptop computers. The first is the desirability of ultra-portables by business executives. Ultra-portable laptops are thinner and lighter than traditional laptops—and more stylish to boot. With aluminum skins and svelte styling, the premium-priced machines are considered "objects of executive desire," according to a Financial Times article. The second force is the increase in business travel. The travel-friendly nature of ultra-portables make them a "must-have" on business trips. [2-42]

Technological Trends: Technological forces, such as the effect of the invention of the microprocessor on the computer market, are one of the greatest drivers of future products. This is especially true in high technology markets. Examples of technological forces include the low-cost widespread availability of information, low-cost communications channels (such as email and text), as well as the many advances in materials, electronics, manufacturing processes, and other areas in the past century.

MARKETING MADE MEASURABLE

Technological Trends in the Laptop Market: The laptop market has benefited from great technological advances, such as increases in processor speed and battery life.

The latest technological threat is particularly severe—is a laptop still relevant in an age of tablets and smartphones? After all, even a five pound ultra-portable laptop feels clumsy when compared with a sleek Apple iPad tablet.

As a result, tablet computers have been encroaching into laptop sales. Computer makers are fighting back with their new thin and light ultrabook models. Examples include the Apple MacBook Air at 2.85 pounds, the ASUS Zenbook at 2.86 pounds, and the HP Folio at 3.3 pounds. Industry analyst HIS predicts the sales of ultrabooks to rise to 28% in 2013 and 38% in 2014. [2-43]

Legal Trends: Legal forces, such as those caused by new legislation and regulations, can have a dramatic impact on markets.

Legislation is defined as directives proposed by legislative bodies (such as the Congress of the United States), whereas regulations are defined as specific requirements within legislation. For example, Congress might pass legislation concerning automotive safety, and have it enforced using specific regulations.

Examples of legal forces on for-profit organizations include anti-trust legislation and corporate taxation, incentive grants, and allowances. Examples of legal forces on non-profit organizations include limits on contributions from donors, as well as reporting requirements.

MARKETING MADE MEASURABLE

Legal Trends in the Laptop Market: About the only force fiercer than technological change in the laptop market is the legal force to enforce the patents that support those technologies. Companies understand they live or die by the competitive advantage they hold in their intellectual property assets, which includes their quiver of patents. Computer manufacturers are becomingly increasingly threatened by so-called "patent trolls," companies whose only "product" appears to be the production of new patents. And the courts have been clogged with massive litigation over ownership of ideas. In fact, PC World magazine estimated that patent trolls cost businesses $80 billion per year. [2-44]

Environmental Trends: Environmental forces arise from society's concern for the physical environment in which we live. This concern often manifests itself as specific regulations within certain industries, such as limits on sulfur emissions on coal production in the energy industry.

Examples of environmental forces include environmentally-oriented legislation and regulations. Examples also include societal forces intending to protect the environment, such as public reaction to changes in the global environment (such as global warming) and preservation of the earth's inhabitants (such as protection of endangered species).

MARKETING MADE MEASURABLE

Environmental Trends in the Laptop Market: The rapid obsolescence of laptop computers results in massive amounts of e-waste. In fact, Wired Magazine reports that more than 4.6 million tons of e-waste entered U.S. landfills in 2000, with that amount projected to grow at least fourfold. An estimated 50 to 80 percent of e-waste collected in the United States is exported to countries such as China, India, or Pakistan, where workers harvest the old machines for precious metals. But the machines contain toxic chemicals that pose serious health concerns.

To slow the spread of toxic waste, the European Union adopted the Restriction of Hazardous Substances directive (RoHS) in 2003, which restricts the use of certain hazardous materials. RoHS is associated with the Waste Electrical and Electronic Equipment (WEEE) directive, which sets collection, recycling, and recovery targets for electrical goods. [2-45]

PORTER FIVE FORCES ANALYSIS

Harvard professor Michael Porter developed the Five Forces analysis framework. The Five Forces analysis framework examines the forces acting on markets to anticipate changes likely to occur as a result of the forces. In this way, the Porter Five Forces framework is similar to the PESTLE market analysis. The five forces include the threat of new entrants, intensity of rivalry from existing competitors, pressure from substitute products, bargaining power of buyers, and the bargaining power of suppliers. [2-46]

Just as with the PESTLE market analysis, we can apply the five forces to predict the future states of markets. As Figure 2.20 shows, we can essentially "fast forward into the future" using the technique.

To demonstrate the Porter Five Forces framework, we will show the impact of the five forces on a company delivering dog walking services. The dog walking company turns to the Porter framework to predict how market forces will shape its market over time. We start by examining the threat of new entrants.

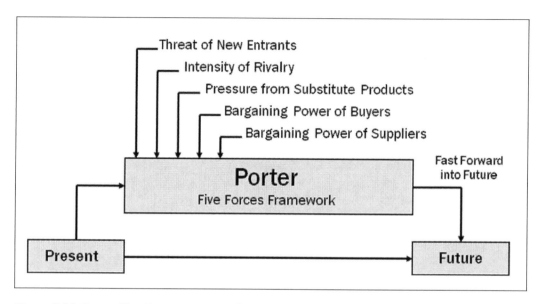

Figure 2.20: Porter Five Forces Framework

Threat of New Entrants: New entrants into markets can threaten the profitability of existing companies due to three factors. The factors are the delivery of new capacity into the market, the new entrants' desire to grow market share, and the availability of resources for the new entrant. For example, the dog walking service could be threatened by a new entrant moving into the same local area. We can examine the impact using the three factors:

- **Delivery of new capacity into a market**: The new entrant gives pet owners an additional choice in dog walking services (i.e., new capacity).

- **New entrants' desire to grow market share**: The new entrant might offer lower prices to establish its sales (and grow market share).

- **Availability of resources for the new entrant**: The new entrant might have many dog walkers at its disposal, and could thus take on many clients at once (i.e., high availability of resources).

To help reduce the threat of new entrants, existing companies can erect barriers to entry. The barriers to entry make it more difficult for a new entrant to succeed in the market. Porter cites several possible barriers to entry. We show how each would be used in our dog walking service example.

- **Economies of scale**: Economies of scale are the reduction in operating costs due to increasing the scale of operations. For example, our dog walking service could decrease its operating costs by establishing large-scale operations and spreading the cost of promotion programs over many prospects.

- **Product Differentiation**: In product differentiation, companies introduce new features to emphasize the difference in products and services from those of other providers. Our dog walking service could differentiate its service by offering new features, such as kennel services to accommodate pets when their owners were out of town.

- **Capital Requirements**: Capital requirements refer to the money required to enter a new market. If our dog walking service were to introduce the new kennel service proposed above, the capital costs for purchasing the required facilities could be substantial. Any new entrant into the market would be expected to match existing services (or sacrifice market share), thus discouraging new entrants.

- **Switching Costs**: Switching costs are the costs to switch from one supplier to another. In our dog walking service, we can introduce contracts that lock in customers for a period of time.

- **Access to Distribution Channels:** Access to distribution channels refers to the availability of intermediary organizations, such as retail stores, that offer the product or service. In our dog walking service example, we might foster exclusive relationships with all major pet stores. Such an arrangement would make it difficult for new entrants to gain access to distribution.

- **Cost Disadvantages Independent of Scale**: The notion of cost disadvantages refers to the reduced costs available to existing suppliers that would be difficult for new entrants to match. For example, our dog walking service might have a proprietary scheduling tool that efficiently assigns dog walkers to time slots. In addition, the dog walking service can target areas with a high density of potential customers, such as pet-friendly apartment complexes and high-rise buildings. High densities of customers cost less to serve than widespread geographies. The dog walking service can also leverage the lessons it has learned from its many years in the area, which a new entrant cannot match.

- **Government Policy**: Existing companies can leverage government policy to dissuade new entrants. For example, our dog walking service could petition city government, insisting that all new dog walking services be required to maintain a special business permit (with a grandfathering provision for existing services).

Intensity of Rivalry from Existing Competitors: As an industry matures, competitors within it jockey for position. Successful companies strive to grow their business. Growth efforts can take the form of price competition, new product development, new services, savvy promotion, and other tactics.

This rivalry is especially pronounced with the top two to three companies in the industry. Few markets will tolerate more than two or three market leaders, as can be observed in many markets: soft drinks (Coca-Cola and Pepsi), package delivery (UPS and Federal Express), home improvement (Home Depot and Lowes), microprocessors (Intel and AMD), and many others.

Brand consultancy firm Interbrand (interbrand.com) found an S-curve relationship between brand value and brand strength. Brand value is the estimated monetary value of the brand. Brand strength considers the brand's potential for market leadership and other factors. As the brand's strength increases from zero (such as that for a new brand), the corresponding brand value slowly increases. As the brand ascends into the top one or two brands in a market, its brand value sharply increases, and then plateaus. Many rivals find themselves at this plateau stage. Figure 2.21 shows the relationship. [2-47]

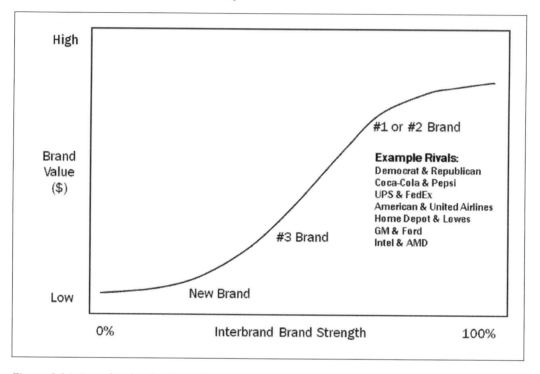

Figure 2.21: Brand Value for Rival Firms

Several factors can intensify rivalry:

- **Nearly Equal Competitors**: The condition of equally balanced competitors is a highly unstable one. Competitors will often resort to cut-throat tactics to topple the other. In our dog walking example, the competition between two nearly equal competitors in the same neighborhood would likely lead to price wars and other potentially destructive behavior.

- **Slow Industry Growth**: When the total size of the market does not grow, companies must acquire customers from competitors in order to grow. For example, cellular phone companies promote their services to customers of competitors in order to steal them away. In our dog walking example, we might employ a special promotion to target customers of competitors to grow our business.

- **High Fixed Costs**: When high fixed costs are involved, competitors will increase rivalry as they attempt to leverage those costs over higher volumes to reduce their cost per unit. In our dog walking example, we might be forced to reduce prices sharply to keep our expensive kennel facility filled with as many dogs as possible, to spread out the cost. The price reduction could spark a price war from our competitor.

- **Lack of Differentiation**: When customers perceive products or services as commodities, they will choose alternatives by price alone. Our dog walking service must therefore introduce features that differentiate it from its competitor. For example, it could provide dog grooming services as part of its portfolio of services.

- **Capacity Augmented in Large Increments**: Some industries demand that capacity be added in large increments, which can be disruptive to the balance between competitors. In our dog walking example, it might expand into a new city, causing an imbalance with its competitor, which only serves the local area.

- **Diverse Competitors**: Competitors with differing strategies and ways of doing business can intensify rivalry, because each has difficulty in understanding the other. Our dog walking service might run into a competitor coming from a foreign land. The competitor might run its business in a very different way from traditional domestic small businesses. The diversity could result in frustration and confusion for both companies.

- **High Strategic Stakes**: Under certain situations, rivals might believe the consequences for success are significant. In an expanding market, companies strive to grow market share to secure leadership once the market matures. In a declining market, companies also strive to maintain the last few remaining customers (or face possible bankruptcy). In our dog walking service, we might aggressively compete with our rival to gain market share in a new skyscraper with many dog owners.

- **High Exit Barriers**: Barriers that make it difficult for companies to abandon markets tend to intensify rivalry. For example, companies might have specialized assets that might be difficult to leverage elsewhere, or could have long-term contracts for labor or building rentals. Our dog walking service might have built a special kennel facility that would be difficult to use for another purpose.

Pressure from Substitute Products: In addition to traditional competitors, companies face competition from products and services that can fulfill the same role. Savvy companies identify substitute products early and seek to differentiate from them. In our dog walking service, we can identify several substitute products and services which could compete with our service (in addition to other professional dog walking services like ours).

Substitute "products" could include other pet-related services (such as dog grooming companies that provide dog walking services), neighbors walking dogs while the owner is away, and pet doors that allow pets to enter and exit buildings by themselves. Of course, substitute products are limited only by the imagination. Design company SchultzeWORKS has created a dog-walking robot called Luna. [2-48]

Bargaining Power of Buyers: Demanding buyers can drive prices (and profits) down by bargaining for higher quality, more services, and lower prices. Several situations can make groups of buyers particularly powerful:

- **Large Accounts**: Some groups of buyers represent a large portion of a company's overall business. These groups wield a great deal of power. In our dog-walking service example, a large skyscraper with many pet owners might demand price concessions from our service.

They would likely win the concessions if their business represents a large portion of our total business, because we cannot afford to lose them.

- **Large Purchases**: Buyers are likely to bargain for purchases that represent a large portion of their income, such as house and automobile purchases. Because our dog walking service accounts for only a small portion of income, we are not likely to be affected by this element.

- **Undifferentiated Products**: Buyers faced with seemingly identical products and services (such as selecting different cellular telephone providers) are more likely to bargain. With our dog walking service, we must emphasize our differences compared to other similar services so buyers can appreciate the superiority of our services.

- **Few Switching Costs**: Switching costs, such as long-term contracts, tend to lock the buyer to particular suppliers. We can use contracts in our dog walking service to decrease customer defection to competitors.

- **Backward Integration**: Buyers are more likely to bargain if they have opportunities to bypass suppliers with alternative methods. In our dog walking service example, dog owners might choose to walk their dog themselves, for fitness or other reasons, thus no longer needing our services.

- **Low Impact from Supplier Quality**: Buyers are likely to bargain if they believe the quality of the products and services they receive has little impact to their lives. In the case of business markets, we can extend this statement to say that the quality of the goods or services sold by the supplier (which we use as ingredients for our product) has little impact on our product. In our dog walking service, we must emphasize how important it is to pet health to give the dog regular walks, and how important the pet is to the owner's life.

- **Buyer has Full Information**: Buyers with complete knowledge to competitors' offerings and prices are more likely to bargain. In fact, many businesses fear price-checking software, such as Amazon's Price Check App for the Apple iPhone, because it allows rapid and convenient price checking of similar products and services. We would be concerned if other dog walking services began posting their prices online. [2-49]

Bargaining Power of Suppliers: Some market conditions permit suppliers to dictate terms to buyers. Predictably, they are similar to the conditions where buyers bargain with suppliers:

- **Concentrated Industry**: Suppliers in concentrated industries, dominated by only a few firms, are less likely to concede to demands to reduce prices. For example, our dog walking service might be one of several large dog walking services in the city, which has established a "going rate" for dog walking services that is not open to negotiation with pet owners.

- **Few/No Substitute Products**: Suppliers not facing strong substitute products are in a better position to demand higher prices. If pet owners perceive few alternatives to our dog walking service, we feel less pressure to reduce prices.

- **Buyer Not an Important Customer**: Buyers that do not represent an important class of customers to the supplier are in a weaker position to demand lower prices. For example, if our dog business deals mostly with large accounts from skyscrapers (with many dog owners), individual pet owners will have less pull.

- **Suppliers' Products Important to Buyer**: Buyers who perceive that the suppliers' product or service is essential to them are less likely to demand lower prices. For example, pet owners are often enthusiastic over their dogs, and will pay higher prices if they feel the dog walking service to be of high quality.

- **High Switching Costs**: Buyers with high switching costs are less likely to bargain. For example, buyers might have long-term contracts with suppliers, which can be costly to terminate. Our dog walking service can use long term contracts to increase switching costs for pet owners. However, we recommend against taking advantage of buyers once locked into long-term contracts. For example, the popularity of pre-paid cell phone service plans is growing, due to the public's reluctance to enter multi-year contracts.

We demonstrate the application of the Porter Five Forces framework in the following example.

MARKETING MADE MEASURABLE

Groupon or Group-Off? Application of Porter Five Forces Framework: We can apply the Five Forces model to the situation that group coupon ("groupon") company Groupon faced shortly after its initial public offering (IPO) in November 2011.

- **Threat of New Entrants**: The group coupon discounter category has few barriers to entry, which tends to attract new entrants. If the space proves to be profitable, one can expect many new companies to enter, which would tend to reduce profitability for Groupon.
- **Intensity of Rivalry**: Existing competitors include LivingSocial (backed by Amazon.com) and Google, to name just two. The competitors are well-funded and some (such as Google) have proven to fiercely defend their territory. Therefore, one can expect the intensity of rivalry to escalate if the market proves to be a profitable one.
- **Pressure from Substitute Products**: Coupon seekers can select from many sources of coupons, from online coupons to traditional newspaper coupons. Searching for the word "coupon" in Google produces over 560 million results. Therefore, pressure from substitute products is very high.
- **Bargaining Power of Buyers**: Groupon's products are largely undifferentiated, and "buyers" (people searching for coupons) have essentially no switching costs. Therefore, buyers have substantial bargaining power.
- **Bargaining Power of Suppliers**: Groupon is in a so-called "fragmented" (non-concentrated) industry, with many substitute products. In addition, the coupons are not essential to many buyers, because buyers can find other ways to save money. Therefore, suppliers like Groupon have little bargaining power.

The Five Forces model shows the group coupon provider market to not be a very attractive one. It should not be surprising, then, that share prices for Groupon fell over 14% within the first few days after opening. [2-50]

SUMMARY

A market is defined as a group of customers who purchase products and services from sellers. That group can be made up of different segments with different needs. We can determine the monetary value of sales of our products and services to the market. That value is the market size. In this book, when we refer to the "market" we intend to mean the qualified available market, which is the group of people with interest in the product/service, the means to pay for it, and the qualifications (such as legal age) to purchase it.

When searching for market data, we recommend first considering secondary data, which consists of data created by others. Once secondary sources are exhausted, marketers should move on to primary sources, which consist of data created directly by the researcher for a specific purpose. A quick Internet search will often return a wealth of information about a market. We can supplement that information with industry and financial analyst reports, as well as other sources.

Government sources represent a rich source of data. The U.S. government categorizes market information using its North American Industrial Classification System (NAICS). The NAICS coding system assigns unique numbers to virtually every industry. Establishing the NAICS code makes it easier to find information from government sources, as well as private ones.

Multiple parties hold interest in market sizing results. The parties include marketing departments (to calculate market share and other metrics), operations departments (to establish operations requirements, such as production schedules), distribution channel partners (to assign levels of resources required for different channels), and financial analysts (for companies to obtain financing).

Marketers can use market sizing data for multiple applications. The applications include understanding different market segments, calculating market share, estimating adoption rate, establishing the product or service's position in its life cycle, determining the level of market investment, identifying market trends, predicting sales forecasts, sizing the sales force, and working with distribution channels.

We can determine the size of markets using top-down and bottom-up approaches. In top-down market sizing, we start with the size of a large, general market that includes the segment in which we are interested (plus many others). We multiply the size of the large, general market by successive factors to narrow the market down to our objective market (the market whose size we wish to estimate). This method is sometimes referred to as the chain ratio method. We can focus on one particular area using the area market demand approach.

In the bottom-up market sizing method, we start with individual sub-segments of the market and build them up to create the total market. Bottom-up methods are particularly useful for three situations. The first is niche markets, where the entire market consists of only a handful of customers. The second situation is the case of markets with a limited number of segments, where we can calculate the demand for each market, and then sum the demand. In the third situation, we face a market with a limited number of distribution channels, where we add the sales through each channel to determine the total market.

Having estimated the size of the market, we now wish to predict its status in the future, to ensure our investments in that market are warranted. We discuss two tools to predict future states of the market based on current market forces.

The first tool is the PESTLE Market Analysis. Each letter of the acronym PESTLE stands for a category of forces that affect the future state of the market--political, economic, social, technological, legal, and environmental. Each category can have a profound effect on markets.

The second tool to predict the future state of markets is the Porter Five Forces Framework. The framework examines the forces acting on markets to anticipate changes likely to occur as a result of the forces. The five forces include the threat of new entrants, intensity of rivalry from existing competitors, pressure from substitute products, bargaining power of buyers, and the bargaining power of suppliers.

Terminology

Available Market: (also known as the Total Available Market, or TAM) Set of customers who are interested in a product or service, and have the means to purchase it.

Bottom Up Market Sizing: Method of market sizing which starts with individual sub-segments of a market and builds them up to create the total market.

Market: Group of customers who purchase products and services from sellers.

Market Sizing Triangulation: Combining multiple market sizing results using weighted average techniques.

NAICS Code: North American Industrial Classification System, which assigns a unique identifier to virtually every industry.

PESTLE Market Analysis: Predicting future states of markets by studying trends resulting from political, economic, social, technological, legal, and environmental forces.

Porter Five Forces Framework: Predicting future states of markets by studying the forces that act upon them, including the threat of new entrants, intensity of rivalry from existing competitors, pressure from substitute products, bargaining power of buyers, and the bargaining power of suppliers.

Potential Market: (also known as Total Market) All customers in the population who have interest in acquiring the product or service.

Primary Data: Data created directly by the researcher for a specific purpose.

Qualified Available Market: Customers in the available market who possess the qualifications to purchase the product or service (such as legal age).

Secondary Data: Data created by others.

Served Market: Segment(s) the company has chosen to target.

SIC Code: Standard Industrial Classification code, replaced by NAICS code.

Top Down Market Sizing: Method of market sizing which starts with the size of a large, general market, and then multiplies it by successive factors to narrow the market down to the objective market.

Class Discussion

1. How would the sizes of the potential market, available market, qualified available market, and served market vary for your organization?

2. What are some limitations of the NAICS categorization scheme?

3. Under what circumstances do you believe the top-down market sizing approach would be more accurate? What about the bottom-up approach?

Practice Problems

1. Identify at least three secondary data sources to obtain information about the market(s) on which your organization focuses.

2. Determine the NAICS code for the industry of your organization and your primary markets.

3. Identify at least three stakeholders in your organization interested in market sizing results.

4. Calculate the size of one of your organization's primary markets using the top-down market sizing approach.

5. Calculate the size of one of your organization's primary markets using the bottom-up market sizing approach.

6. Compare the results for market size between the top-down and bottom-up approach. Are they different?

7. Conduct a PESTLE market analysis for your organization's market. Of the six categories of trends, which has the largest potential to make significant change?

8. Identify the forces acting on your organization's market using the Porter five forces framework. How will they change the market over time?

Chapter 3.

MARKET SEGMENTATION

Chapter Outline

We cover the following marketing analytics topics in this chapter:

☑ **Segmentation:** Dividing large, general markets into smaller, specific segments
☑ **Targeting:** Selecting market segments on which to focus
☑ **Positioning:** Establishing a distinct position in the buyer's mind

"Please all and you will please none."
– Aesop

Ancient Greek story teller Aesop understood the power of market segmentation even back in 600 BC. Aesop's fables, such as *The Tortoise and the Hare*, taught important lessons through the vehicle of story. The method conveyed the concepts in a way that connected with the audience. In the same way, market segmentation and positioning seek to connect the company with its audience--the market. Companies connect to different segments of the market by understanding each segment's unique attributes. [3-1]

This chapter covers several popular techniques to conduct market segmentation, targeting, and positioning (STP). Many marketers refer to the set of techniques as STP, as shown in Figure 3.1. In this section, we define each term and discuss their advantages to marketing.

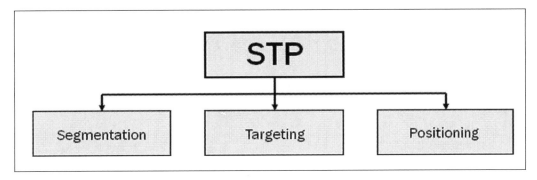

Figure 3.1: STP: Segmentation, Targeting, and Positioning

Market Segmentation: Market segmentation is the process of subdividing general markets into distinct segments with different needs, and which respond differently to marketing efforts. Through market segmentation, we can increase customer satisfaction by providing buyers with products or services that meet their unique needs. In today's competitive environment, market segmentation is seen as more effective than mass marketing, which offers "one-size-fits-all" offerings to everyone.

MARKETING MADE MEASURABLE

Tide: From Mass Market to Multiple Segments: Procter and Gamble's (P&G) Tide laundry detergent started in the 1940s with only one version, sold to the mass market. Over time, Procter and Gamble discovered that different groups of people had different needs in their laundry detergent.

One group favored convenience, so P&G launched mini-packets of Tide detergent. A second group preferred detergent gentle to the skin, so P&G created Tide Free. A third group traveled extensively and wanted a travel-ready product to clean stains while on the go; P&G responded with its Tide To Go Instant Stain Remover.

By early 2012, P&G offered no fewer than 41 variants to accommodate its various market segments. [3-2]

Targeting: Targeting is the selection of market segments to which a company plans to sell products or services. Few companies have the resources to service every possible segment, so they must choose the segments on which to focus.

For example, Procter and Gamble chose not to target the price-conscious market segment with its premium Tide product. Instead, it offers other products that fulfill the needs of that segment, such as its Bonux laundry detergent, launched in Egypt in 2006. [3-3]

Positioning: Positioning seeks to make consumers perceive that a brand occupies a distinct position relative to competing brands.

For example, Procter & Gamble sought to position Tide in the 1940s and 1950s as superior to traditional soaps through ads with slogans such as "cleaner than soap" and "oceans of suds." In fact, the performance of Tide, one of the earliest synthetic soaps, was considered superior to other soaps, and the positioning holds to this day. [3-4]

Market segmentation, targeting, and positioning offers several advantages over mass marketing, as explained below and summarized in Figure 3.2.

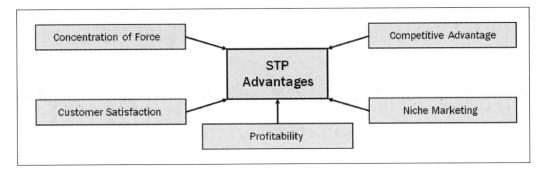

Figure 3.2: Advantages of Segmentation, Targeting, and Positioning

We now discuss the advantages.

Efficiency through concentration of force: With segmentation and targeting, we can apply a "concentration of force." In "concentration of force," we focus the core competencies of the organization on relevant market segments, rather than diffusing our energies over a broad market. The term "concentration of force" comes to us from military strategy, which seeks victory by focusing resources on specific targets. For example, smaller second-run movie theaters focus on price-conscious customers. They do not diffuse their energy by attempting to cater to people demanding newly-released movies.

Increased customer satisfaction: As the Tide example showed, even markets for "commodity" products such as laundry detergent can have segments. For example, travelers wanting to bring Tide on a trip prefer small sizes for portability, but value-conscious people prefer larger sizes for cheaper per-ounce prices. Attempting to satisfy both segments with one "in-between" size would likely satisfy neither.

Profitability: Segmentation acknowledges that different groups have different needs and value perceptions of the same (or similar) product or service. We can grow profits by determining the maximum amounts the different groups of buyers will pay. For example, price conscious shoppers might only purchase Tide in bulk packages because of the greater economy. But travel-minded individuals will pay more per ounce of detergent for smaller sizes, due to the convenience it affords them.

Competitive advantage: Segmentation, targeting, and positioning techniques provide tools to succeed in the market despite formidable competitors. For example, rental car agencies Hertz (hertz.com) and Enterprise (enterprise.com) battle in the competitive rental car market. But both succeed financially because they target different segments. Hertz targets business travelers by locating virtually all of its facilities at major airports. By contrast, Enterprise locates many of its facilities away from airports to target long-term renters such as those needing a car while theirs is under repair.

Niche marketing: Companies can identify specific segments in the market that desire a product or service not currently provided by existing suppliers. For example, Panasonic targets customers with rigorous physical demands, such as law enforcement and military personnel, with its special Panasonic Toughbook ruggedized personal computers.

SEGMENTATION

We study segmentation so we can more effectively market to our customers. We recognize that different groups of customers have different needs, so we tailor our marketing efforts to those unique needs.

Segmentation-based Marketing

Segmentation links customer needs to marketing actions. Examples of customer needs include quality, durability, cost savings, time savings, style, and many others. Marketing actions are tactics marketers can execute to address those needs. Examples of tactics include changes to the features of products and services, their prices, the places where they are distributed, and how they are promoted. Marketers refer to the group of tactics as the marketing mix. Marketers often refer to the four types of tactics as the four Ps—product, price, place, and promotion. [3-5]

Different segments demand different marketing tactics due to their varying needs, as explained below and summarized in Figure 3.3.

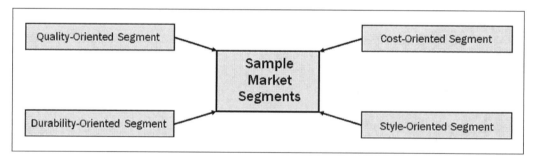

Figure 3.3: Sample Market Segments with Different Needs

We now discuss the different segments.

Quality-Oriented Segment: Rolex (rolex.com) targets quality-oriented people with their fine Swiss watches:
- **Product:** Finely machined stainless steel and precious metals
- **Price:** High prices, to signal high quality
- **Place (Distribution):** Sold only through carefully selected retail stores
- **Promotion:** Advertisements emphasize quality, often set in luxurious surroundings

Durability-Oriented Segment: Durability-oriented people appreciate Briggs and Riley Travelware (briggs-riley.com) luggage:
- **Product:** Extra-tough hardware and materials
- **Price:** Mid level, to signal durability and practicality
- **Place (Distribution):** Retail stores targeted to frequent business travelers, who value durability
- **Promotion:** Marketed as "serious" luggage, not as a mass merchandise good

Cost-Oriented Segment: Geico insurance (geico.com) targets cost-conscious people:
- **Service:** Similar coverage to other, higher-priced insurance carriers
- **Price:** Lower than competitors for some types of insurance
- **Place (Distribution):** Internet-based sales, not agents, to reduce costs
- **Promotion:** Pervasive multi-channel advertising campaigns declaring 15% savings on automobile insurance

Style-Oriented Segment: Apple (apple.com) tailors its products and services to style-conscious people:
- **Product:** Strong sense of style, with rounded corners, sleek styling, and high quality materials
- **Price:** High pricing to signal high style and quality
- **Place (Distribution):** Sold through Apple's stylish retail stores
- **Promotion:** Apple billboards, web pages, and advertisements all evoke a strong sense of style

Segment Selection Guidelines

We use several criteria when determining how to select segments, as summarized in Figure 3.4. Marketers should seek to satisfy all criteria when selecting segments.

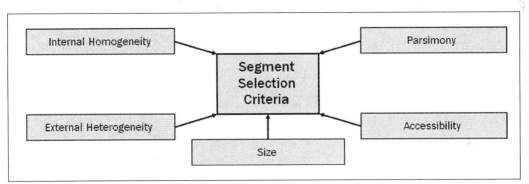

Figure 3.4: Segment Selection Criteria

We now discuss the guidelines.

- **Internal Homogeneity:** Internal homogeneity means that individuals in the segment respond similarly to marketing efforts. For example, if we selected price sensitivity as a segmentation variable, we would expect everyone in the "thrifty" group to be budget-oriented.

- **External Heterogeneity**: External heterogeneity means that individuals in one segment behave differently from those in another segment. Again, if we selected price sensitivity as a segmentation variable, we would expect the spending habits of the "thrifty" group to be different from those in the "big spenders" group.

- **Parsimony**: Marketers should strive to segment the market in as few groups as possible, while still maintaining an adequate number of groups for marketing effectiveness. We recommend segmenting most markets using ten groups at most whenever possible. While we acknowledge there are rare cases where more groups are required, marketers must balance the utility of having many groups with the time and expense of managing and marketing to all those separate groups.

- **Accessibility**: Knowing the segments does us little good if we cannot access them with our marketing efforts. We can access a segment such as "Sports Cars Enthusiasts" through many means, such as sports car magazines, websites, etc. But it would be difficult to access a segment such as "People Who like the Color Blue" because we have no direct means of reaching such a segment.

- **Size**: Segments must contain sufficient potential profitability to make them worthwhile to pursue. This does not mean the segment must have thousands of individuals. Many niche segments consist of only a few individuals, but the high price points of the products and services needed make pursuing those niches worthwhile.

Overview of Segmentation Approaches

The basic approach of segmentation is to divide a large, general market into smaller, specific segments. In segmentation, we make the fundamental assumption that large, general markets are made up of many different kinds of people with different wants and needs.

In this section, we cover segmentation variables (variables used to segment the market), different classifications of segmentation techniques, and several popular segmentation approaches.

Segmentation Variables: In segmentation, we use segmentation variables to segment the market and identify in which group particular individuals belong. We denote two types of segmentation variables to help us with this task: response variables and identifier variables.

- **Response Variables**: We use response variables to describe how individuals respond to an offer. We can classify response variables into several major categories. We will use a running example of the airline industry to demonstrate the different categories: [3-6]

  o **Functional:** Functional response variables consider the function of company products and services. Specific variables in this category include performance, reliability, durability, quality, and so forth. For example, Forbes magazine (Forbes.com) studied the on-time arrival performance of several major airlines, and declared Japan Airlines the winner, with a 91% on-time record. [3-7]

  o **Service and Convenience:** Service and convenience response variables study how company products and services deliver service and convenience to their customers. Specific variables in this category include time savings, ease of use, ease of purchase, convenience and location of a retail store, and so forth. For example, USA Today (usatoday.com) reported on the results of a J.D. Power and Associates Airline Satisfaction Study. It found that Alaska Airlines received the highest score for customer service in the "traditional network" category. [3-8]

○ **Financial**: Financial response variables focus on the monetary performance delivered by products and services. Specific variables in this category include cost savings, potential revenue gain, sensitivity to price-related promotions, liability avoidance, and so forth. For example, the Wall Street Journal (wsj.com) reported on the results of a J.D. Power and Associates poll. It found that the lowest fare airline carriers with good customer service scores included JetBlue Airways, Southwest Airlines, WestJet Airlines, AirTran Airways, and Frontier Airlines. [3-9]

○ **Usage**: Usage response variables consider how customers will use the product or service. Specific variables in this category include usage scenario or occasion, usage rate, usage frequency, application of the product or service, usage patterns, and so forth. For example, USA Today (usatoday.com) reported on the results of an Air Transport Association study. It indicated that the Thanksgiving holiday period represents the highest usage period for airline travel in the United States. [3-10]

○ **Psychological**: Psychological response variables study how products and services affect psychological aspects. Specific variables in this category include trust, esteem, status, and so forth. For example, the New York Times (nytimes.com) reported on tips for flying with very important person (VIP) status on major airlines. It discussed topics such as how to get low-cost upgrades to business class, gaining access to exclusive airline lounges, and obtaining priority security screening and boarding privileges. [3-11]

Figure 3.5 summarizes the categories.

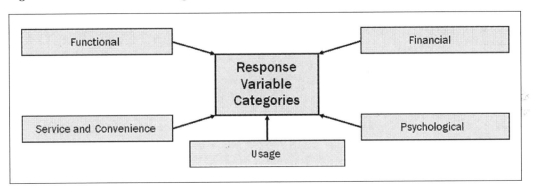

Figure 3.5: Segmentation Response Variable Categories

- **Identifier Variables**: We use identifier variables to categorize and describe the individuals in segments. For example, Forbes magazine (forbes.com) found that the segment of the population who purchases Porsche 911 sports cars is predominantly male (87%), financially successful (median income $390,000), and enjoys a lifestyle in which they can reward themselves for achieving major milestones. [3-12]

We can conduct market research to determine the correct identifier variables to describe different groups. Most times, however, we can use established identifier variable categories. Marketers find the established categories useful and convenient because they have a long history of using them for traditional media marketing, such as in print-based and television-based campaigns.

For consumer markets, we can use identifier variable categories such as the following: [3-13]

- o **Consumer Demographics:** Age, gender, family size, income, occupation, etc.
- o **Consumer Geographics:** Country, region, county, city, density, climate, etc.
- o **Consumer Psychographics:** Personality, lifestyle, values, interests, attitudes, etc.

For business markets, we can use identifier variable categories such as the following: [3-14]

- o **Business Demographics**: Industries, company size, etc.
- o **Business Geographics**: Company location, proximity to customers, etc.
- o **Business Situational Factors**: Specific applications, order size, etc.

Figure 3.6 summarizes identifier variables for consumer and business markets.

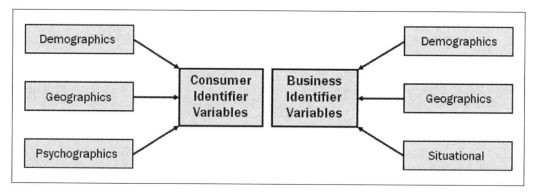

Figure 3.6: Segmentation Identifier Variables: Consumer and Business Markets

We will use response and identifier variables in the segmentation techniques in this chapter. For example, in the regression analysis techniques we cover later in this chapter, we portray response variables as the dependent variables and the identifier variables as the independent variables.

We characterize response variables as the dependent variables because they represent the behavior in which we are interested. We describe identifier variables as the independent variables because they represent variables which help explain behavior. Figure 3.7 shows the concept. [3-15]

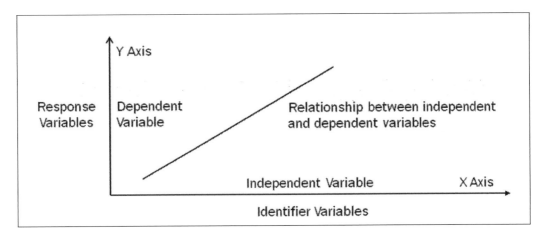

Figure 3.7: Relationships between Identifier and Response Variables

A Priori and Post Hoc Segmentation Techniques: **A priori** (Latin for "from before") and **post hoc** (Latin for "after this") describe the time at which the segments are declared (before or after primary market research and analysis).

Both methods accomplish the same result in that they both enable us to segment the market, but take different routes to get there. Figure 3.8 summarizes the difference. [3-16]

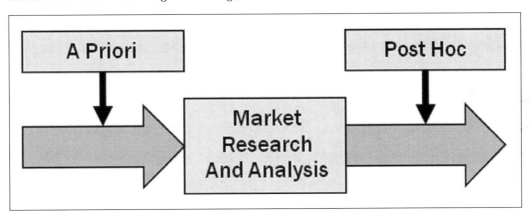

Figure 3.8: A Priori and Post Hoc Segmentation Techniques

In **a priori segmentation**, marketers divide the market into segments before primary market research and analysis are conducted. Generally, marketers apply a priori segmentation techniques when they have existing knowledge from earlier experience about the basis for assigning customers to segments.

In this approach, marketers specify the segmentation variables to use, as well as the number of segments, in the hope that resulting segments behave differently in response to marketing mix variables (product, price, place, and promotion).

A priori segmentation projects typically involve several stages. We will discuss a typical process, as applied to a segmentation project conducted by a luxury hotel chain to identify market segments that frequent luxury hotels. [3-17]

Figure 3.9 shows the step by step approach.

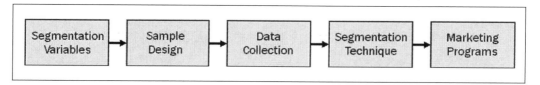

Figure 3.9: A Priori Market Segmentation Process

We discuss each step in turn.

- **Segmentation Variables**: We select segment identifier and response variables to study. To select response variables, we consider which types of responses we wish to know, such as the following examples:

   - **Usage scenarios**: Under what occasions do travelers select luxury hotels?
   - **Usage rates**: How many times per year do travelers stay at luxury hotels?
   - **Usage duration**: How long do travelers stay?
   - **Expected services**: What do travelers expect to find at luxury hotels?
   - **Differentiating services**: What sets one luxury hotel apart from another?

   Similarly, we consider the types of identifier variables we could find useful, such as the following examples:

   - **Demographics**: Age, income, education level, occupation, etc.
   - **Geographics**: Home location of traveler
   - **Psychographics**: Luxury traveler lifestyles, hobbies, interests, etc.

   To gather this preliminary information, we could study several sources:

   - **Company records**: Study hotel records to assess what we already know
   - **Informal interviews**: Ask frequent hotel guests what they want in a luxury hotel
   - **Secondary research**: Determine what industry analysts are saying
   - **Competitor trends**: Find out how competitors are changing their hotels

- **Sample Design**: Here, we design a survey sample to study. The survey sample is the set of individuals to whom marketers will be sending the survey. For sizable surveys, we might employ a random sample, where every individual in the target market has an equal chance of being included in the survey. For smaller, more focused surveys, we might select a non-random sample to favor individuals that will be more relevant to the topic at hand. For example, we might choose to only contact social media-savvy individuals on a survey for a new social media service.

In our luxury hotel example, we will send out a survey to readers of luxury travel magazines such as Departures (departures.com), Four Seasons (magazine.fourseasons.com), and Conde Nast Traveler (cntraveler.com). We will also hold in-depth personal interviews with frequent luxury travelers in exchange for something of value, such as a one week stay at one of our properties.

- **Data Collection**: In this step, we gather the data. This step is increasingly done with online survey tools, such as Survey Monkey (surveymonkey.com) and Zoomerang (zoomerang.com). Online tools offer speed, reliability, and convenience.

In our luxury hotel example, we would collect data using the identifier and response variables we selected earlier. For example, we could ask about a person's age and income, and what they look for in a luxury hotel.

- **Segmentation Technique**: We form segments using a priori segmentation techniques, such as cross-tabulation and regression segmentation, discussed later in this chapter.

In our luxury hotel example, we would apply the identifier variables we selected earlier, and determine if we can find relationships with the response variables by using our segmentation techniques.

- **Marketing Programs**: We estimate the size and potential profitability of the resulting segments to determine which ones we want to pursue (known as our target markets). For our target markets, we establish marketing programs that leverage the data we learned from the segmentation process. For example, we will highlight product or service attributes known to be of prime importance to segments.

In our luxury hotel example, we might find that the market segment that stayed often at luxury hotels are often executives at international organizations who appreciate perks and VIP treatment while on the road, as the example below illustrates.

MARKETING MADE MEASURABLE

Starwood Hotels Targeting the Elite Traveler Segment: According to a Business Week report on luxury travelers, so-called Elite Travelers represent the most sought-after type of traveler by hotels and airlines. "Our top 2 percent of travelers are responsible for 30 percent of our profit," said Starwood hotel chain Chief Executive Officer Frits van Paasschen. Starwood coined the name "mega-traveler" to denote this market segment. Mega-travelers yield as much revenue for the hotel as 50 regular guests.

Although Starwood offers the typical gold and platinum loyalty programs for certain travelers, it reserves its personal Ambassador program to the elite few who stay more than 100 nights per year. Starwood charges the Ambassador to do whatever it takes to make these mega-travelers happy. David Neuman, mega-traveler due to his role as president of olive oil company Lucini Italia, refers to his Ambassador as "my angel" due to the extra level of service she orchestrates on Starwood's behalf. [3-18]

The post hoc process is similar, but we do not select the variables before conducting the research.

In **post hoc segmentation**, marketers hold little knowledge about the type of segments in a particular market, or even the quantity. The post hoc approach determines the segments after research and analysis are conducted. For example, a new product or service could require post hoc segmentation techniques, because of lack of earlier experience. Complex markets often benefit from a post hoc segmentation approach, because the segments are not always clearly evident.

In our luxury hotel example above, we applied a priori techniques because the luxury hotel market is well established. But if we did not know much about it, we would have applied post hoc techniques. For example, space-liner operator Virgin Galactic (virgingalactic.com) offers space enthusiasts with $200,000 to spend chances to ride into outer space. Because we know little about civilian space travel, such as which segmentation variables are relevant, we would want to apply post hoc segmentation techniques in that market. [3-19]

Post hoc segmentation models use response variables to segment groups based on how customers behave, and then test that the resulting segments differ enough in terms of their customer profiles to enable identification.

For example, when segmenting potential civilian space travelers for Virgin Galactic, we could identify different segments based on expected usage. But we could experience difficulty assigning typical demographic profiles to them. A space traveler prospect could have either a high income ("to complete the list of places the high-roller has visited") or low income ("to enjoy a once-in-a-lifetime experience").

In practice, we recommend marketers apply both a priori and post hoc segmentation techniques whenever feasible.

Factor Analysis: Post hoc segmentation techniques often use a technique called factor analysis. Factor analysis reduces the original set of variables into a manageable number before attempting to cluster the individual customers into groups.

Two major types of factor analyses are popular with marketing segmentation efforts. R-factor analysis reduces the number of variables by finding similarities in responses among variables, indicating which variables are redundant and therefore can be eliminated. Q-factor analysis discovers groupings of people who respond similarly during marketing research studies.

Descriptive and Predictive Segmentation Techniques: Marketers use either descriptive or predictive segmentation techniques, depending on the objective of the segmentation efforts. Figure 3.10 summarizes the differences between the two. Marketers can use descriptive and predictive techniques on both a priori and post hoc approaches. [3-20]

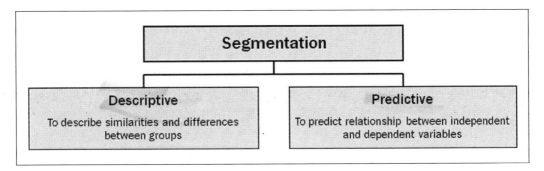

Figure 3.10: Descriptive and Predictive Segmentation Techniques

Marketers apply descriptive segmentation techniques if the objective is to describe the similarities and differences between customer groups. We study similarities and differences among customers to market more effectively to them. One common descriptive segmentation approach is cross-tabulation analysis, which we cover later in this chapter.

Conversely, marketers apply predictive segmentation techniques if the objective is to predict how changes in independent variables affect the values of dependent variables. For example, we might wish to find out how advertising spending (an independent, controllable variable) affects sales revenue (a dependent variable). We achieve the objective by studying the relationship between the two. One common predictive segmentation approach is regression analysis, which we cover later in this chapter.

Figure 3.11 shows a simplified representation of several popular marketing segmentation methods. The figure classifies the methods by the point in time in which the market is divided into segments (before conducting market research, or a priori, versus after conducting market research, or post hoc) and the objective of the segmentation (descriptive or predictive).

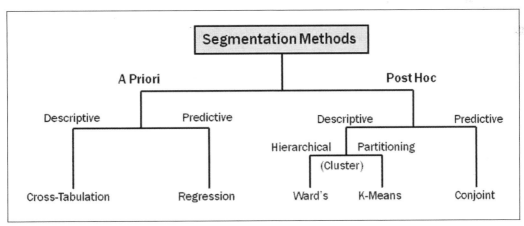

Figure 3.11: Classification of several popular market segmentation methods

Sample Marketing Segmentation Techniques

We now cover several popular marketing segmentation techniques, beginning with cross-tabulation, used by marketers worldwide for decades.

Cross-tabulation Segmentation: Cross-tabulation is considered an a priori, descriptive segmentation technique (although it does have some predictive qualities). The technique is often called "cross-tab" for short. It is very popular due to its ease of application.

Cross-tabulation is a procedure that cross-tabulates two variables, expressing their relationship in a table. The process thus "describes" our market segments, allowing us to understand them more fully so we can market to them more effectively. [3-21]

We will demonstrate cross-tabulation segmentation using an example. Acme Restaurant (fictitious name) wants to discover the segments existing in the market (their local area). Acme is especially interested in how the segments vary with respect to the number of times they dine out per month. Acme plans to focus its marketing budget on diners who like to dine out often, and not waste money on diners who rarely go out to eat.

Figure 3.12 shows the step by step process to conduct cross-tabulation segmentation for the Acme example.

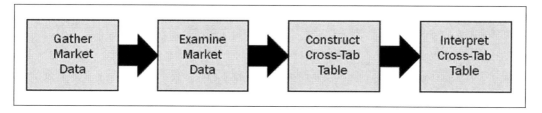

Figure 3.12: Cross-Tabulation Segmentation Process

We now discuss each step in turn.

- **Gather Market Data**: Acme surveys the local community during a local town fair, asking individuals how frequently they dined out per month over the past year. They also ask questions for identifying demographic variables, such as annual income, age, and occupation. Figure 3.13 shows a small excerpt of the resulting data. Actual surveys can have hundreds, or even thousands, of respondents.

Respondent	Frequency	Annual Income	Age	Occupation
Respondent 1	4 times/ month	$150,000/year	35	Physician
Respondent 2	1 time/ month	$60,000/year	32	Auto repair
Respondent 3	Under 1/month	$25,000/year	34	Security guard

Figure 3.13: Cross-Tabulation Market Segmentation: Market Data Table (Excerpt)

- **Examine Market Data**: A quick look at the data in Figure 3.13 reveals some market insight. Dining frequency definitely varies with annual income. Greater annual income is associated with greater dining frequency. The frequency does not appear to vary with age. Age remained consistent despite a wide range in dining frequency. The Occupation variable appears to be redundant, because the stated annual incomes correlate with the typical incomes expected from those occupations. For large data sets, it can help to sort the data by the variable of interest (in this case, Dining Frequency) to more readily perceive the underlying patterns.

- **Construct Cross Tabulation Table**: Based on our quick analysis in the previous step, we decide to focus on dining frequency and income. We can construct a cross-tab table as shown in Figure 3.14 using a dedicated cross-tabulation tool. Commercial statistics software packages provide cross-tabulation tools. Examples of such packages include SPSS (Statistical Package for the Social Sciences, sold by IBM) and MarketSight (marketsight.com).

  Alternatively, we can simply count the number of respondents dining out four times per month that make $10,000 - $49,000 per year, $50,000 - $99,999 per year, and over $100,000 per year, and divide by the total to get the percentages. As typical of a priori segmentation, we apply existing knowledge to decide on the income brackets to use.

Frequency	$10,000 - $49,999 Annual Income	$50,000 - $99,999 Annual Income	$100,000 – over Annual Income	Total
4 times/ month	10%	30%	60%	100%
1 time/ month	20%	60%	20%	100%
Under 1/ month	60%	30%	10%	100%

Figure 3.14: Cross-Tabulation Market Segmentation: Cross Tabulation Table

- **Interpret Cross Tabulation Table**: The cross-tabulation chart shows three distinct segments, as shown in Figure 3.15. The first segment (which we shall call Dining Misers) consists of relatively low income individuals who dine out rarely (less than once per month). Acme is not likely to target this segment, due to its low revenue potential. The second group (which we shall denote as Dining Medians) consists of mid-income individuals dining out about once per month. The third group (which we shall call Dining Mavens) appears to be our most attractive segment: individuals who dine out about once per week, with relatively high income.

  With this knowledge, we would seek to increase the number of diners eating at Acme by executing a campaign targeting high income individuals.

Frequency	$10,000 - $49,999 Annual Income	$50,000 - $99,999 Annual Income	$100,000 – over Annual Income	Total
4 times/ month	10%	30%	60% ←Mavens	100%
1 time/ month	20%	60% ←Medians	20%	100%
Under 1/ month	60% ←Misers	30%	10%	100%

Figure 3.15: Cross-Tabulation Market Segmentation: Market Segments

Regression-based Segmentation: Regression-based segmentation is an a priori, predictive segmentation technique. In regression, we seek to determine the relationship between independent variables and dependent variables. The discussion here assumes linear regression. Many commercially available software packages, including Microsoft Excel, include tools for linear regression. [3-22]

The goal of regression-based segmentation is to group different customers together based on the similarity they have in their relationships between the independent and dependent variables. For example, we might find that customers within a certain age bracket have similar usage rates, which would indicate an actionable market segment.

The relationship between the independent and dependent variables is expressed can be expressed in a regression equation. A typical example of a regression equation using demographic variables is shown below. The equation predicts the spending level of individuals for a particular product or service, given their age and personal income.

Spending = a + b*(Income)

In the equation, "a" is the y-intercept and "b" is the coefficient for the variable Income.

By calculating the coefficients "a" and "b," we can determine how income affects spending, and assess if we can categorize certain groupings of people at certain income levels as segments. In this case, we estimate spending based on the single variable Income. Regression on one variable is called **simple regression**. We refer to regression involving more than one variable as **multiple regression.**

One major advantage of linear regression-based techniques is that they can be executed using common spreadsheet programs, such as Microsoft Excel. To demonstrate the process, we will work through an example of determining potential segments for automotive spending by consumers.

Figure 3.16 shows a simplified version of the process we will use for our example.

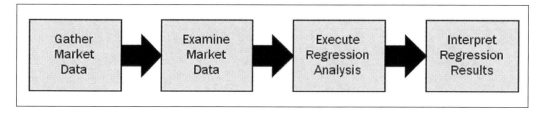

Figure 3.16: Regression-based Segmentation Process

Here is the step by step process, using Microsoft Excel and fictitious data:

- **Gather Market Data**: We can obtain the data for our technique using standard market research tools, such as online questionnaires with online tools such as Survey Monkey.

  For our example, we conduct an online survey, asking a random group of individuals about how much they intend to spend on their next automobile. We also ask questions to gather demographic information, such as age and personal income. Figure 3.17 shows an excerpt of the table showing spending levels and personal income for several respondents (the respondent data names have been deleted for anonymity).

A: Respondent	B: Spending	C: Income
Respondent 1	$70,000	$190,000
Respondent 2	$6,000	$20,000
Respondent 3	$23,000	$50,000
Respondent 4	$60,000	$150,000
Respondent 5	$9,000	$30,000
Respondent 6	$25,000	$54,000
Respondent 7	$8,000	$25,000
Respondent 8	$25,000	$55,000
Respondent 9	$70,000	$200,000
Respondent 10	$7,000	$22,000
Respondent 11	$62,000	$170.000
Respondent 12	$22,000	$45,000

Figure 3.17: Regression-based Segmentation: Typical Market Survey Data Table (Excerpt)

- **Examine Market Data**: We prepare the market data for review by sorting it by the dependent variable. Here, the dependent variable is "Spending" (because it is our primary interest), so we sort by it. Figure 3.18 shows the sorted results.

A: Respondent	B: Spending	C: Income
Respondent 2	$6,000	$20,000
Respondent 10	$7,000	$22,000
Respondent 7	$8,000	$25,000
Respondent 5	$9,000	$30,000
Respondent 12	$22,000	$45,000
Respondent 3	$23,000	$50,000
Respondent 6	$25,000	$54,000
Respondent 8	$25,000	$55,000
Respondent 4	$60,000	$150,000
Respondent 11	$62,000	$170,000
Respondent 1	$70,000	$190,000
Respondent 9	$70,000	$200,000

Figure 3.18: Regression-based Segmentation: Survey Data Sorted by Spending

We examine the data and note that spending clearly varies with income. If we were to plot out the data, we would not see a uniform line for the entire data set, but rather a jagged line with three distinct line segments with different slopes. We can interpret the line segments as market segments. If we apply a strict a priori approach, we would segment the data using the independent variable (Income) and use our existing knowledge of the market to define segments based on our three pre-assigned bands of income, which in this case would be $0-$30,000, $31,000-$99,999, and $100,000-above. We can apply regression analysis to predict behavior within those three segments. In this simple case, we could also segment the data using the dependent variable (Spending) by noticing the obvious gaps in the Spending data between $9,000 and $20,000, and again between $25,000 and $60,000, indicating three segments. Later in this chapter, we discuss segmentation techniques (such as K-Means) that identify these segments in a more automated manner.

Figure 3.19 thus shows three segments, with associated ranges of Income and Spending: Segment 1 ("low budget"), Segment 2 ("mid budget"), and Segment 3 ("high budget").

Segment	B: Spending	C: Income
Segment 1		
Respondent 2	$6,000	$20,000
Respondent 10	$7,000	$22,000
Respondent 7	$8,000	$25,000
Respondent 5	$9,000	$30,000
Segment 2		
Respondent 12	$22,000	$45,000
Respondent 3	$23,000	$50,000
Respondent 6	$25,000	$54,000
Respondent 8	$25,000	$55,000
Segment 3		
Respondent 4	$60,000	$150,000
Respondent 11	$62,000	$170,000
Respondent 1	$70,000	$190,000
Respondent 9	$70,000	$200,000

Figure 3.19: Regression-based Segmentation: Sorting by Spending

- **Execute Regression Analysis**: Next, we execute regression analysis to determine the relationship between income and spending for each segment. Figure 3.20 shows the four-step process to execute regression analysis in Microsoft Excel.

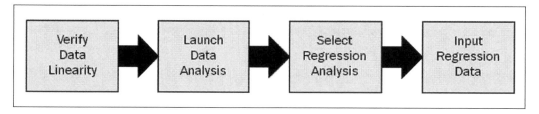

Figure 3.20: Regression Execution Process in Microsoft Excel

We start by verifying the linearity of our data. Linear regression demands that the data show linearity. We can quickly check for linearity by plotting out the data. Figure 3.21 shows an example scatter plot of spending versus income for Segment 1, with a dashed line superimposed over the data to estimate the resulting relationship.

By examining the plot, we can quickly confirm the linearity of the data, as evidenced by the nearness of the data points to the dashed line we inserted into the figure. Had the points formed a U-shape or other nonlinear pattern, we would need to apply nonlinear regression techniques.

Microsoft Excel uses an algorithm called **least squares estimation** for regression analysis. In the algorithm, Excel selects the line to fit through the data by minimizing the squared values of the differences between the data points and the line. [3-23]

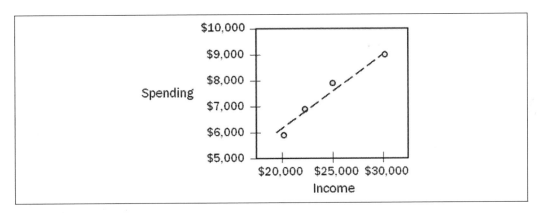

Figure 3.21: Linearity Verification

Having verified linearity, we launch the data analysis set of functions in Microsoft Excel. To launch Data Analysis, select the Data menu tab, and then select Data Analysis in the area below the tab. Some versions of Excel may require that the user install the Analysis ToolPak Add-In to obtain the Data Analysis set of functions. Figure 3.22 shows a simplified diagram of the process.

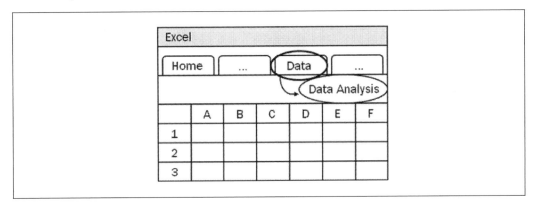

Figure 3.22: Launching Data Analysis in Microsoft Excel

Clicking on Data Analysis will reveal the Data Analysis dialog box. Scroll down the various data analysis tools, select Regression, and then click OK. Figure 3.23 shows a simplified diagram of the dialog box.

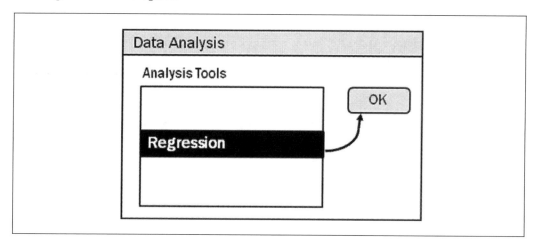

Figure 3.23: Selecting Regression in the Data Analysis Dialog Box

Selecting the Regression function will reveal the Regression dialog box, as shown in Figure 3.24. Highlight the Spending data in the spreadsheet to input data into the Input Y Range box. We highlight Spending because it represents the dependent variable. Highlight the Income column to input data into the Input X Range box. Include the labels at the top of the columns (Spending and Income) when selecting the data.

Check the "Labels" box to let Excel know the labels are included in the selection. Do not check the "Constant is Zero" box because we do not know if the regression constant will be zero. Check the "Confidence Level" box and enter "95%" in the percentage box, to indicate we are using a standard 95% confidence level. Click OK.

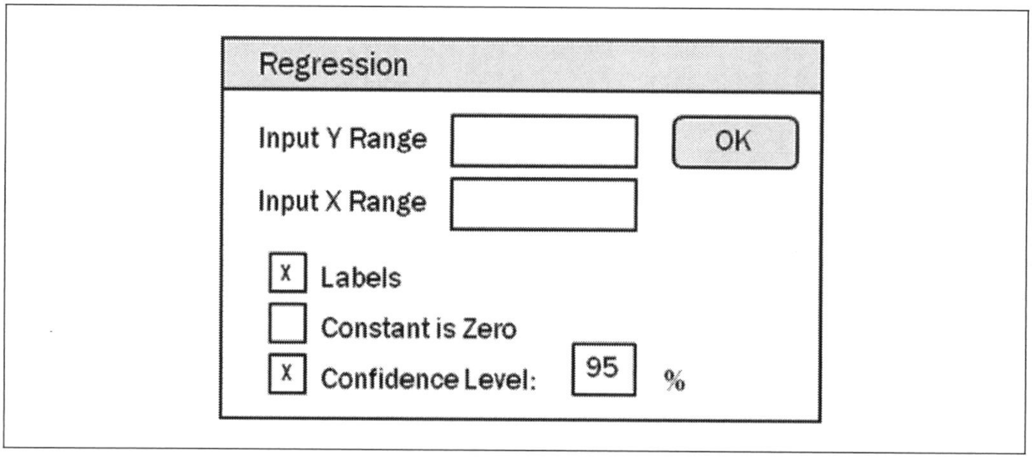

Figure 3.24: Entering Data into the Regression Dialog Box

- **Interpret Regression Results**: Excel will open a new tab titled SUMMARY OUTPUT, with the results of the regression analysis. Excel displays the results in three tables: Regression Statistics, ANOVA, and Coefficients.

  The primary statistic of interest in the first table is the R-Squared value. The R-Squared value is also called the coefficient of determination, and varies from 0 to 1. R-Squared represents the degree to which the independent values explain the estimated function (in this case, a line through the data). If they explain the relationship perfectly (i.e., all the data points lie directly on the line), then R-Squared is equal to 1.

  If no relationship exists, then R-Squared is equal to zero. When plotting the data, we can infer that R-Squared will be equal to zero if the scatter plot looks like a cloud of random points, without any real pattern. In our automotive example, the regression analysis resulted in an R-Squared of 0.96, so we can infer that the regression model explains spending behavior well.

  In well-defined situations, such as scientific applications using precise instrumentation, R-Squared values are very high, often 0.9 or greater. In less manageable situations, such as social science studies, R-Squared values can be small, such as 0.3. In most marketing research applications, values of R-Squared fall in between the two extremes, generally near 0.6. Figure 3.25 summarizes the values. [3-24]

Scenario	R-Squared
No Relationship	0.0
Social Science Studies	0.3
Marketing Research	0.6
Scientific Applications	0.9
Perfect Relationship	1.0

Figure 3.25: Typical Values for R-Squared, the Coefficient of Determination

  If the value of R-Squared is lower than the values mentioned above, the cause could be that the existing variables are insufficient to explain the phenomenon, and that more variables are needed. We can test if a variable is relevant by examining if the value of R-Squared improves when we add the variable.

  For example, had our automotive regression example resulted in a low R-Squared value, we could test other variables, such as gender, to gauge any improvement in R-Squared. We must balance the boost given in R-Squared through adding variables with the goal of parsimony. In parsimony, we seek to explain behavior using as few variables as possible.

  The second table, **ANOVA (analysis of variance)**, tests for the significance of the model as a whole. ANOVA computes an F-statistic for testing the two hypotheses H(0) and H(1). H(0), the **null hypothesis**, states that the dependent variable has no relationship with the independent variable. H(1), the **alternative hypothesis**, states the opposite—that a relationship exists.

To test if we can reject the null hypothesis, Excel provides us with a **Significance F** value in the ANOVA table. If Significance F is very small (generally, under 5%), we reject the null hypothesis. In the case of our automotive spending example, Excel indicates a Significance F value of 0.02 (2%), which is acceptable to reject the null hypothesis and thus declare that the overall model does indeed represent the relationship.

The third table shows the regression equation coefficients. Figure 3.26 shows an excerpt of the coefficient table for segment #1, which we called "low budget."

Parameter	Coefficient	Standard Error	t-Stat	P-value
Intercept	449.339	1036.95	0.433329	0.707034
Income Coefficient	0.290749	0.042254	6.880976	0.020474

Figure 3.26: Coefficient Table for Automotive Spending Regression Study, Segment 1

The first column of the coefficient table shows the names of the parameters (the y-intercept and the coefficient for the income variable). The second column shows the value of the coefficient. We insert the values for the y-intercept and the income coefficient into the regression equation as follows:

Spending = a + b*(Income)

Substituting the information from the table:

Spending = (449.339) + (0.290749) * Income

The third, fourth, and fifth columns of the table indicate the relevant Standard Error, t-Stat, and P-value metrics, respectively, for the regression coefficients.

The **Standard error** is an estimate of the standard deviation of the coefficient. The **t-Stat** is the coefficient divided by the Standard Error. We can think of the Standard Error as a measure of the precision with which the regression coefficient is measured. Statistically significant coefficients are large compared to zero. To determine if the value is large enough, Excel compares the t-statistic with values in the Student's t distribution to calculate the P-value.

The **P-value** is the probability of encountering an equal t value in a collection of random data in which the variable had no effect (i.e., the null hypothesis). Marketing researchers generally regard 5% or less as the generally accepted point at which to reject the null hypothesis. With a P-value of 5%, we have only a 5% chance that the results would come from a random distribution. Alternatively, we can state with 95% probability that the variable does indeed affect the model. In the case of our automotive example, our P-value of only 2% (0.02...) for the Income coefficient satisfies the 5% cutoff, so we can state that the Income variable makes a significant contribution to the model. [3-25]

Figure 3.27 summarizes the descriptions of the regression statistics.

Statistic	Description
Standard Error	Estimate of standard deviation of the coefficient
t-Stat	Coefficient divided by the Standard Error
P-value	Probability of encountering equal t value in random data (P-value should be 5% or lower)

Figure 3.27: Regression Statistic Descriptions

We repeat the process for the other two segments (Segment 2 and Segment 3) and get the regression coefficients shown in Figure 3.28. From the data, we observe that spending behavior increases with personal income in all three segments, but at different rates. Segmenting the market into the three segments allows us to pinpoint estimated spending levels more accurately than if we had aggregated all buyers into one mass market.

Parameter	Segment 1	Segment 2	Segment 3
Intercept	449.339	7,298.387	25,186.44
Income Coefficient	0.290749	0.322581	0.227119

Figure 3.28: Regression Coefficients, Automotive Segments

Using the regression results we just calculated, we can estimate the anticipated spend level for three example buyers. The first buyer is in Segment 1, and has an income of $24,000. The second buyer is in Segment 2, and makes $52,000. The third buyer is in Segment 3, and generates $180,000 in income. We can estimate the spending level for each buyer using the regression equations we developed:

Spending = (Intercept) + (Income Coefficient) * (Income)

Spending (Buyer 1) = (449.339) + (0.290749) * ($24,000) = $7,427

Spending (Buyer 2) = (7,298.387) + (0.322581) * ($52,000) = $24,073

Spending (Buyer 3) = (25,186.44) + (0.227119) * ($180,000) = $66,068

We now move on to discussing other market segmentation techniques.

Cluster Analysis Techniques: Cluster analysis techniques, such as Ward's and K-Means, are classified as post hoc and descriptive, and are fairly popular for market segmentation.

Different types of cluster analysis techniques exist, but all have two aspects in common. First, they all use a numerically-based index to indicate the degree of similarity of two individuals. Second, all use the index to group individuals into homogeneous segments using a defined clustering process. [3-26]

As shown in Figure 3.29, we can choose from two types of clustering methods. The first type is called **hierarchical clustering**. Hierarchical clustering groups differing clusters in a hierarchy, from a top level to lower levels (called **divisive hierarchical clustering**) and from the bottom up (called **agglomerative hierarchical clustering**). The result of hierarchical methods is a hierarchical structure similar to a family tree, called a **dendogram** (sometimes also called a **tree diagram**). In dendograms, roots branch off into two branches, which in turn branch off into further branches, and so on.

The second type of clustering process is called **partitioning clustering.** Partitioning clustering constructs clusters by maximizing specific criteria.

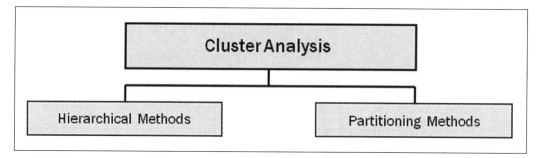

Figure 3.29: Cluster Analysis Techniques

Ward's method is a popular example of agglomerative hierarchical clustering. In Ward's, we start with individual elements and merge them together (combine them) into clusters. During the merging process, our goal is to lose as little information as possible. For example, if we group two individuals into a cluster, the cluster will not be as precise as each individual on their own. The information lost during clustering is sometimes referred to as the **merging cost**. To reduce the potential information lost during merging two elements into one, Ward's method minimizes the error sum of squares. The error sum of squares (ESS) is a popular algorithm that subtracts one value from another (to find the distance between them), then squares the result (to ensure positive values for distance).

For example, we might survey 100 people, asking them about the degree to which they recognize our brand and three competing brands. We ask them to rate the recognition of each on a scale of one to ten. We could then use Ward's method to group the data into clusters. Techniques based on measuring distances, such as Ward's, are well-suited for scaled data, such as the one to ten scale mentioned. We would market to the different clusters differently, because one cluster might have low brand knowledge and require education on the brand, whereas a cluster with strong brand awareness would find such education redundant and tedious. In our case of brand recognition, we do not know how many clusters to expect, which is why a post hoc technique like Ward's is appropriate.

K-Means is a popular example of partitioning clustering. In K-Means, we specify K, the number of final clusters to expect. Next, we run the K-Means algorithm. The algorithm consists of three steps, which continue to iterate until a stable solution is reached. A stable solution is reached when individuals converge into specific groups, and cease to change groups. The first step is to determine the centroid coordinates. The centroid coordinates define the location of the "center" of the system, as calculated using a weighted mean, similar to finding a center of mass in physics. Second, we determine the distance of each individual object to the centroid coordinates. Third, we form groups based on the shortest distance from the individual object to the centroid. For example, for two groups which differed in gender, the algorithm could place "females" in one group and "males" in the other. Here, the "distance" between a "female member" to the "female" group is shorter than the distance to the "male" group. Therefore, the algorithm would assign the "female member" to the "female" group.

The mathematics behind cluster analysis techniques can be difficult and time consuming to render through Microsoft Excel. Therefore, we recommend using the cluster analysis functions built into commercial statistical software packages, such as SAS (Statistical Analysis Software, available at sas.com) and SPSS (Statistical Package for the Social Sciences, available at ibm.com).

Conjoint Analysis-based Segmentation: Conjoint-based segmentation is a post hoc, predictive technique. The conjoint analysis process reduces preferences for certain goods and services into the worth that particular attributes hold for individuals, called **part worths**. We then use the part worths to segment the market. Conjoint-based segmentation holds the formidable advantage that the resulting segments represent demonstrated preferences held by different groups in the market. [3-27]

Figure 3.30 shows the conjoint analysis process for segmentation. We start by defining the attributes. Attributes are characteristics of the company's product or service that customers find relevant. We combine the attributes to form bundles. Bundles are different variations of the product or service for customers to evaluate. In the data collection step, we gather customer feedback on the bundles. Using the conjoint analysis process, we calculate the part-worth values that customers hold for the attributes. We can then apply that knowledge to execute marketing programs, such as campaigns.

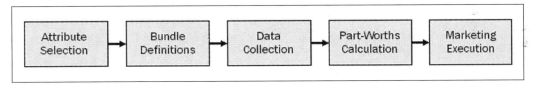

Figure 3.30: Conjoint Analysis-based Segmentation: Process

For example, we can conduct a conjoint analysis to segment the market of people wanting laptop computers. We start by defining attributes. In our example we declare the attributes as screen size (13 inch, 14 inch, and 15 inch), processor speed (2.0 GHz and 2.5 GHz) and battery life (3 hours, 4 hours, and 6 hours). We then combine the attributes in different ways to form different laptop bundles (Laptop A, B, and C) as shown in Figure 3.31.

Laptop Bundles	Screen Size	Processor Speed	Battery Life
Laptop A	13 inch	2.0GHz	6 hours
Laptop B	14 inch	2.0GHz	4 hours
Laptop C	15 inch	2.5GHz	3 hours

Figure 3.31: Conjoint Analysis-based Segmentation: Attribute Selection and Bundles

The different bundles represent different **trade-offs** between screen size, processor speed, and battery life. Laptop A features a small screen for portability, relatively slow processor speed, and fairly long battery life. Laptop B trades off a larger screen for less battery life. Laptop C trades off a yet larger screen and faster processor speed for even shorter battery life. The notion of trade-offs is important here—buyers are forced to choose among screen size, processor speed, and battery life. Using conjoint analysis, we can learn the values people place on each attribute based on the bundle they prefer.

In the data collection stage, we can conduct a survey asking each respondent to rate each laptop bundle on a scale of one to ten. In the part-worths calculation, we analyze the data to determine the market's assessment of each of the attributes, including screen size, processor speed, and battery life.

We then employ our part-worth knowledge to develop and execute marketing programs. For example, we could determine that a certain market segment places a high value on battery life, so we could execute battery life-based campaigns to that segment.

In conjoint analysis-based segmentation, we group potential customers according to how the value they place on specific attributes of products and services. The direct correlation between product/service attributes and market preferences make conjoint analysis a highly useful technique. We cover conjoint analysis in further detail in the Product and Service Analytics chapter later in this book.

Other Segmentation Techniques: Many other market segmentation techniques exist to suit different conditions that marketers might experience. Again, due to the advanced nature of the mathematics behind the models, we recommended the use of commercial statistical software packages, such as SAS or SPSS, to execute the techniques. A handful of techniques includes the following. [3-28]

- **AID (Automatic Interaction Detection):** AID is a post hoc, predictive segmentation technique. It is similar to Ward's Method in that it also produces dendograms. The technique divides elements in a "top down" fashion, instead of merging them "bottom up" like Ward's. An advantage of the AID technique lies in its ability to discover underlying interactions among variables, with the goal of identifying which independent variables have the most effect on dependent variables. One weakness of the AID technique is that it requires a large sample size. The large sample size is required because the sample is split in two at each stage of the dendogram "tree." Researchers tend to use the AID technique less frequently than the more versatile CHAID method.

- **CHAID (Chi Square Automatic Interaction Detection):** CHAID is an extension of the AID technique. It is similar to AID in that it also produces top-down tree diagrams. It is different from AID in that CHAID applies a statistical technique known as chi-square to select predictor variables. CHAID allows dependent and independent variables to be in category form with no intrinsic ordering, such as male/female, blonde/redhead/brunette, and so forth. In addition to this advantage, CHAID also allows the dendogram tree to branch into three or more branches (three levels of each variable) instead of just two branches.

- **CART (Classification and Regression Trees):** CART combines elements of AID, CHAID, and regression analysis. Like AID and CHAID, it produces top-down tree diagrams. It extends AID and CHAID by using regression analysis to further split each division into subdivisions.

- **Logit segmentation**: Also called **multinomial logit (MNL)** and **choice-based segmentation**, this technique segments markets based on individuals' likelihoods to choose to purchase a good or service. For example, one could segment customers in a customer database in terms of their probability of making future purchases from the company. Direct marketing campaigns can benefit from this technique by segmenting by likelihood of purchase.

- **Overlapping Segments**: Also called **fuzzy segmentation** or **probabilistic segmentation**, this group of techniques uses assignment weights to spread an individual across multiple segments. By comparison, the techniques we discussed earlier result in non-overlapping segmentation. Overlapping segments can be more intuitively appealing, because it can be difficult to place individuals into one and only one category. However, the mathematics associated with probabilistic segmentation can complicate execution.

Figure 3.32 summarizes the techniques.

Segmentation Technique	Description
AID	Automatic Interaction Detection Post hoc, predictive segmentation technique producing dendograms
CHAID	Chi Square Automatic Interaction Detection Extension of AID technique, using Chi-Square statistical technique
CART	Classification and Regression Tree Extension of AID and CHAID using regression analysis
Logit/ MNL	Multinomial Logit Segments markets based on individuals' choices
Overlapping Segments	Fuzzy Segmentation or Probabilistic Segmentation Uses weights to spread individuals over several segments

Figure 3.32: Other Segmentation Techniques

TARGETING

Having identified segments in the market, we now turn our attention to targeting those segments. We proceed in three steps. The first step is to establish criteria with which to select target segments. The second step is to consider the role of segment selection in the company's strategy for markets and products/services. The third step is to determine how to market effectively to those target segments.

Selection of Segment Targeting Criteria

To maximize potential revenue and minimize cost (and thus increase profitability), we select segments to target by maximizing three criteria: potential, alignment, and marketability. [3-29]

Potential: To maximize profitability, we target segments which have significant financial potential. Therefore, we seek segments which are large and growing, because they can deliver more revenue than those which are small and shrinking.

MARKETING MADE MEASURABLE

Apple: Digital Entertainment Potential: Forbes reported that digital entertainment such as video on demand, streaming and films purchased through online services like Apple's iTunes was a large and growing market, up 51% in 2012, to $3.4 billion. Meanwhile, sales of the once mighty JVC video home system (VHS) machines, which peaked at 23 million units in 2000, plummeted 39.8% per year to 1.36 million units in 2005, and were basically dead by 2012. [3-30, 3-31]

Alignment: The products and services associated with the selected segment should align with the company's mission, resources, and capabilities to minimize the cost of entering the segment. Entering new segments, even if they are large and growing, is risky for companies if they do not align with the organization's competencies.

MARKETING MADE MEASURABLE

HP: Tablet Computer Alignment: Hewlett-Packard (HP) entered the growing tablet computer segment but quickly found that its capabilities were no match for market leader Apple. Users found the HP TouchPad tablet's WebOS operating system not as intuitive as Apple iOS system, among other problems. By August of 2011, HP had sold only 25,000 TouchPads after ordering 270,000 units to sell in Best Buy retail stores. HP acknowledged defeat, discontinuing the device and liquidating its inventory by slashing the price from $499 to only $99. [3-32]

Marketability: In addition to potential and alignment, the selected segments must have certain characteristics to facilitate our marketing efforts. The segments must be accessible, distinct, and have the potential of responding favorably to our offering's value proposition. Here "accessible" means the ability to reach customers with messages. By "distinct," we mean that different segments respond differently to marketing efforts.

MARKETING MADE MEASURABLE

L'Oreal: Cosmetics Marketability: Cosmetics and beauty product giant L'Oreal maintains a stable of brands to target different segments. It markets its Garnier and Maybelline brands to mass consumer markets through consumer channels (print media, television, web, and so on), its luxury brands, such as Lancome, to luxury outlets, and its professional brands, such as Redken, to hair salons and other beauty professionals. [3-33]

Figure 3.33 summarizes segment targeting criteria.

Criterion	Description	Example
Potential	Segments with significant financial potential	Digital entertainment market (e.g., Apple iTunes) large and growing
Alignment	Segments aligned with company's mission and competencies	HP losing ground to Apple in tablet PCs due to lack of competencies
Marketability	Segments accessible, distinct, and responsive to value proposition	L'Oreal maintains multiple cosmetics brands to increase marketability

Figure 3.33: Segment Targeting Criteria

Target Segment Selection to Support Market Strategy

The selection of target segments plays a major role in an organization's market and product/service strategy. Organizations can apply one of five approaches to targeting, depending on their corporate objectives. [3-34]

Single-Segment Concentration: Some companies choose to concentrate their efforts on one specific market segment with one specific product or service. The advantage of this approach is the focus organizations can render on their market and product/service. The disadvantage of this approach is that the company is strongly exposed to market changes in demand.

MARKETING MADE MEASURABLE

Bare Escentuals: Unique Focus for a Unique Segment: Cosmetics maker Bare Escentuals (bareescentuals.com) originally sold only their bareMinerals line of mineral-based cosmetics to women who preferred natural makeup. To keep the focus a single segment concentration demands, Bare Escentuals only sold their products through limited channels, including television shopping channel QVC (Quality Value Convenience). It avoided the typical mass distribution channel of multiple department stores, as used by most other cosmetics brands.

Today, it still markets its products using selective distribution channels, offering them only in Bare Escentuals retail stores, Sephora specialty cosmetics stores, and QVC. Cosmetics still contributes 95.8% of their net sales, with other products (skin care brands) contributing only 4.2%. [3-35]

Selective Specialization: Some organizations market to several different segments, offering different products or services to each. In this approach, each segment is essentially independent from the rest, and sometimes no synergies exist.

This approach can be a deliberate choice or an incidental one. In the deliberate case, the company finds unique pockets of opportunity and moves to exploit them. The incidental case is often the result of mergers and acquisitions, where some of the assets acquired (which are often business units in a new industry for the company) might not align closely with other organizational divisions. If the newly acquired business unit is highly profitable, it can sometimes make sense to maintain it, despite its misalignment with the rest of the organization.

The advantage of this approach is the potential profitability additional segments and products can bring. The disadvantage is the lack of synergy among the segments, making long-term strategy difficult.

MARKETING MADE MEASURABLE

Selectica: Selecting Multiple Segments: Software technology company Selectica (selectica.com) sells two different product lines to two distinct markets, with no significant overlap.

The first product line is sales configuration software, which companies use to tailor products and services to user preferences. The company markets the configuration software to sales and marketing departments. The other product line is contract management software, which companies use to develop and execute corporate contracts. The company markets the contract software to corporate counsel departments. The two product lines are managed as two independent business units. [3-36]

Product/Service Specialization: Many organizations specialize in particular products or services, and market those products or services to multiple segments. Companies using this type of specialization can gain impressive knowledge and expertise in delivering their products or services. The advantage of this specialization is the expertise the firm acquires. The disadvantage is the exposure the company faces if the product or service falls out of favor.

MARKETING MADE MEASURABLE

Starwood Hotels: Starring Top Hotel Brands: For example, the Starwood Hotels and Resorts group (starwoodhotels.com) specializes in providing hotel lodging services to travelers. It features several major brands, such as Westin, W hotels, and Sheraton. This specialization gives them a competitive advantage in hotel operation.

Of course, when general hotel occupancy declined after the 9/11 terrorist attacks, Starwood was affected throughout its line of hotels just like all other hotel chains. [3-37]

Market Specialization: Here, organizations choose to specialize in a specific market segment, often selling a wide variety of products and services to that segment. The advantage of this approach is the expertise this specialization provides for this segment. The disadvantage is the exposure the company faces if the market segment suffers a downturn.

> ## *MARKETING MADE MEASURABLE*
>
> **American Hospital Supply: One-Stop Medical Shop** American Hospital Supply (americanhospitalsupply.com) markets medical equipment and other medical supplies to hospitals and other healthcare facilities. Hospitals benefit from the vast selection of the company, which offers medical and surgical supplies, health care equipment and furniture, clinical diagnostic equipment, and many other products. [3-38]

Full Market Coverage: In this approach, organizations serve multiple segments with multiple products or services. The approach works best for very large organizations, due to the significant resources required. The advantage of this approach is the potential revenue it can provide, due to the wide span of operations. The disadvantage is the difficulty of managing multiple products and markets simultaneously. In military strategy, the approach would be similar to fighting a multi-front war.

> ## *MARKETING MADE MEASURABLE*
>
> **Oracle: Multiple Products and Markets**: Enterprise software vendor Oracle (oracle.com) offers more than 100 different products and services, in multiple categories. It markets them to more than 20 industries, such as automotive, chemical, consumer goods, and others. The revenue from this approach is significant, earning over $10 billion in 2011. But the scope of the operations is significant as well, requiring an army of more than 108,000 people. [3-39]

We recommend selecting the segment specialization approach for a particular organization by applying the principles of potential, alignment, and marketability discussed earlier. Figure 3.34 summarizes the strategic roles of target segments.

Segment Strategy	Description	Example
Single-Segment Concentration	Concentrate efforts on one specific market segment	Bare Escentuals originally concentrated its efforts on mineral-based cosmetics
Selective Specialization	Marketing multiple independent products to multiple segments	Selectica marketing two different products to two different markets
Product/ Service Specialization	Focusing on specific product or service	Starwood hotel chain focuses on providing lodging services to travelers
Market Specialization	Market variety of goods and services to one market	American Hospital Supply sells variety of equipment and supplies to hospitals
Full Market Coverage	Offer multiple categories of products to multiple markets	Oracle markets 100 different products to over 20 industries

Figure 3.34: Target Market Selection to Support Market Strategy

Marketing to Target Segments

Now that we have identified potential segments in the market, and selected the segments to target, we turn our attention to implementing the results of our market segmentation efforts to market to those segments.

In this section, we discuss several different methods to market to target segments, depending on the organization's objectives.

Full Marketing Mix Campaigns: Many organizations market their products and services using the complete marketing mix. As we discussed, the marketing mix is also known as the four Ps: product/service, price, place (distribution channels), and promotion. We can market to our target segment(s) using each of the four Ps. We demonstrate the approach through a running example of Chanel No. 5 perfume.

- **Product/Service**: We emphasize different features or attributes of our product or service to different segments. For example, Chanel (chanel.com) offers its famous Chanel No. 5 perfume in luxurious packaging and elegant, delicate glass containers to support its position as a premium fragrance, selling to a discerning market segment. [3-40]

- **Price**: Many markets include a premium segment willing to pay a high price for high quality goods and services, a price-sensitive segment more concerned with price than with quality, and a mass market falling in between. Thus, marketing to the premium segment should emphasize quality over price. For example, Chanel originally marketed its Chanel No. 5 fragrance as "the most expensive perfume in the world."

- **Place**: The selection of distribution channels should support the target market. The values of AM/PM convenience stores do not support those of Chanel No. 5 perfume, so we should not sell the fragrance there.

- **Promotion**: Advertising and other promotion tools must use the language and marketing channels (print media, web, and so on) desired by the target segment. Chanel promotes its Chanel No. 5 in print media read by the premium segment, such as Vogue and Bazaar. Chanel also runs dramatic "mini-movies" on television and web channels, designed to evoke the essence of its famous perfume.

Direct Marketing Campaigns: Companies using direct marketing techniques leverage customer databases to sell directly to their customers. In the past, direct marketing would consist of print catalogs being sent to a specific list of people. Today, print catalogs have been largely replaced by online sites, but the approach is the same. Companies track what customers buy and segment their customer list based on their behavior.

MARKETING MADE MEASURABLE

Amazon.com: 5-Star Campaigns: Online eCommerce giant Amazon.com (amazon.com) tracks customer purchase history and browsing history.

It segments its vast customer database to find others who behave similarly. It uses the knowledge thus gained to give recommendations, such as "others who have purchased X have also purchased Y."

In this way, Amazon.com gains additional revenue by "up-selling" customers through their segmentation techniques. [3-41]

Website Marketing Campaigns: Many companies apply self-selection techniques when developing website navigation. In **self-selection**, customers select their own segment based on questions introduced on the website's home page or other area. Customers then navigate to the relevant section of the website dealing with their particular segment.

MARKETING MADE MEASURABLE

Cisco: Multi-Segment Website Marketing: Networking giant Cisco (cisco.com) markets to three major segments—mid to large sized businesses, small businesses, and consumers. To allow customers to perform self-selection, the cisco.com website features a How to Buy section, which shows different areas for business and for home.

Clicking on the Small Business icon reveals a page devoted to the messaging and the types of products small businesses purchase. Clicking on the Reseller link shows a list of industry-related resellers, which is the preferred method of purchasing by large businesses. Clicking on the For Home Products Store link reveals an eCommerce page with an Amazon-like layout, perfect for targeting the consumer segment. [3-42]

Alternatively, companies can leverage the interactive nature of the Internet to allow **self-configuration** of product and service choices. Here, the company permits customers to tailor products to suit their unique needs.

Configuration tools provide menus of attributes, components, and prices for customers to make informed choices. The tools also check for compatibility of choices.

Self-configuration works well for industries with base models that are customized to meet a need, such as automobiles and computers. Self-configuration is fast, because customers often know exactly what they want. It is cost-efficient, because customers are not required to pay for features they do not want. It is also precise, in that customers get the exact configuration they desire, and do not have to compromise.

MARKETING MADE MEASURABLE

Dell: Configure Your System Your Way: Computer manufacturer Dell (dell.com) maintains self-configuration capabilities on its website. When ordering a new personal computer, customers can select from a myriad of choices, such as processor speed, hard drive sizes, graphics processing capabilities, and so on.

The configuration tool checks for compatibility of the components selected by the user. For example, if a user ordering a new laptop selects a high-resolution screen, the configuration tool will warn the user that the high-resolution screen requires the addition of a high performance graphics processor. [3-43]

Retail Marketing: Retail stores can carry hundreds, if not thousands of different goods for sale. Stores index the goods using stock keeping units (SKUs). Retailers address segmentation by displaying their broad assortment of SKUs on accessible shelves and displays. By displaying the goods in this way, customers can perform self-selection, and choose the product that best fulfills their needs.

MARKETING MADE MEASURABLE

Home Depot: More Selection for More Doing: Home improvement warehouse store The Home Depot (homedepot.com) stocks thousands of different goods for the do it yourselfer. They stock multiple brands of popular categories to allow customers to choose the brand that best suits their needs and budget. For example, the paint aisle contains dozens of different brands at different quality levels and price points, from inexpensive basic paint to premium Ralph Lauren paint retailing for over $40 a gallon. [3-44]

Figure 3.35 summarizes marketing to target segments.

Marketing Approach	Description	Example
Full Marketing Mix Campaigns	Product, price, place, and promotion tactics must all align with segment characteristics and expectations	Chanel executes product, price, place, and promotion tactics to support the luxury image of its brand
Direct Marketing Campaigns	Sell products and services directly to customers using direct marketing	Amazon.com tracks customer purchases to recommend related products and gain incremental revenue
Website Marketing Campaigns	Enable customers to select and configure purchases when shopping online	Cisco dedicates different areas of its website to serve different markets
Retail Marketing	Carry wide selection to serve multiple segments	Home Depot stocks thousands of SKUs to cater to different customer segments

Figure 3.35: Marketing to Target Segments

POSITIONING

In their bestselling book, "Positioning: The Battle for Your Mind," authors Al Ries and Jack Trout define **positioning** as placing the product or service in the mind of the prospect. Before the Ries and Trout book, advertising agencies had based their media campaigns on the benefits they conceived the product had, instead of basing them on what prospects thought about the product or service. [3-45]

Figure 3.36 illustrates the concept of positioning brands in relevant areas of the prospect's mind. For example, when an individual thinks of "overnight shipping," he might think of popular shipping firm FedEx (fedex.com). Similarly, he could associate the Kimberly Clark brand Kleenex with "facial tissue" and Johnson & Johnson brand Band-Aid with "adhesive bandages." Companies spend significant resources to achieve this positioning.

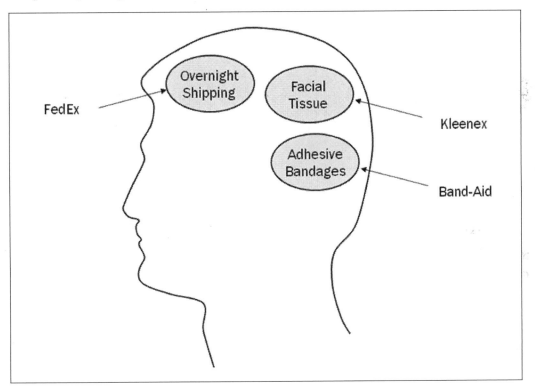

Figure 3.36: Positioning Brands in the Mind of the Prospect

Positioning Companies in Markets

To position companies in markets, one must differentiate the company and ensure prospective customers acknowledge that difference. It is not enough to be different, although differentiation is a prerequisite for positioning. As the example below shows, many ways exist to position one's product or service.

For example, the rental car market can maintain several major brands because each brand has established a unique position along a distinct differentiation vector. [3-46]

- **Positioning to Airport Business Travelers**: Hertz (hertz.com) offers its rental cars in virtually every airport in the world.

- **Positioning to Auto Repairs**: Enterprise (enterprise.com) locates its rental facilities in cities to cater to people whose car is under repair, and need a rental while it is being fixed.

- **Positioning to Relocated Employees:** Thrifty (thrifty.com) features a multi-month rental program to cater to employees on temporary assignment.

- **Positioning to Price-Conscious:** Budget (budget.com) rents its cars for a bit less than major chains Hertz and Avis, ideal for price-conscious travelers.

- **Positioning to Exotic Car Aficionados**: Xotic Dream Cars (xoticdreamcars.com) rents Ferrari and Lamborghini exotic cars in Miami, Orlando, and New York to satisfy exotic tastes.

MARKETING MADE MEASURABLE

Staples: Repositioning Was Easy: Sometimes, companies must reposition themselves to respond to market changes. For example, office retailer Staples (staples.com) founded the office store superstore model, emphasizing its convenience and selection with its tagline, "Yeah, We've Got That."

But soon other office superstores, such as Office Max and Office Depot, entered the market, which eliminated Staple's differentiating area. To prevent sales erosion, Staples conducted market research with the help of the brand consultancy Prophet and learned customers were frustrated by the difficulty of finding office supplies. As a result, it repositioned itself from a store around convenience and selection to a store around easy shopping with its new tagline, "That Was Easy." [3-47]

Positioning using Perceptual Maps

Perceptual mapping graphically represents customers' perceptions of important attributes of areas of interest for marketers, such as product or service categories and brands. The maps show us the "position" of products and services in the customer's mind. [3-48]

Figure 3.37 shows a simple example of a two-dimensional perceptual map for household blenders. Two-dimensional perceptual maps use the x and y axes to denote the two primary purchasing criteria consumers consider when buying a product or service. In the case of blenders, the figure shows that consumers evaluate blenders (within a given price range) by considering feature availability and blending power.

Brands shown far to the right (along the x axis) on the graph are perceived as having more features than those on the left. Brands shown near the top of the graph (along the y axis) are perceived as having more power than those at the bottom. The closer brands are together, the closer consumers perceive those brands to be.

The map also shows us that competitors are clustered in one quadrant, with few competitors in the other quadrants. The map thus gives us valuable insight into the market (i.e., how customers perceive products and services) and competitors (i.e., how consumers perceive different companies).

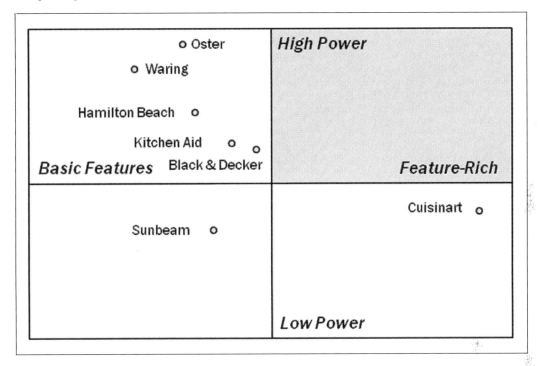

Figure 3.37: Sample Perceptual Map for Household Blenders

Perceptual mapping is highly versatile and can fulfill several objectives. [3-49]

- **Cluster Identification**: Perceptual mapping can be used to identify clusters (segments) of potential customers with similar needs and/or attitudes toward products or services. For example, we can identify clusters of individuals and determine which attributes they have in common.

- **Competition**: Perceptual mapping can also be used to assess the perception of different competitors within product or service categories. For example, close distances between competitors on perceptual maps indicate that customers view the competitors as similar.

- **New Opportunity**: Blank areas in perceptual maps signify the absence of significant competitors in that area. The blank area could signify a new market opportunity. Of course, management must decide if it is worthwhile to pursue that opportunity.

- **Communications Vehicle**: Perceptual mapping can be used as a communications vehicle. For example, the maps can be shown to company executives to visually show how "close" a competitor is to their company.

- **Customer Perceptions**: Perceptual mapping, if done at regular intervals, can alert company management of changes in customer perceptions over time. Management can thus alter course before sales are reduced. The Staples example presented earlier demonstrates this objective.

Figure 3.38 summarizes the applications for perceptual mapping.

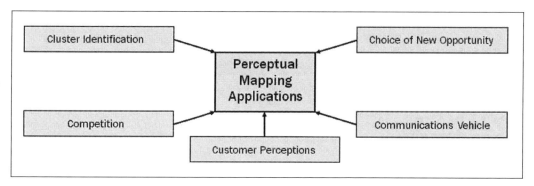

Figure 3.38: Perceptual Mapping Applications

Mapping Methods

In this section, we review several mapping methods. In general, all of the methods described here will require the use of commercial software packages such as SPSS and SAS. Some require specialized packages, such as MDPREF (Multi Dimensional PREFerence scaling, from newmdsx.com), KYST (named after its creators, Kruskal, Young, Shepard, and Torgerson), and MDSCAL (Multi Dimensional SCALing) . In the next section, we cover a simplified approach. The simplified approach produces a two-dimensional perceptual map using Microsoft Excel. [3-50, 3-51]

Mapping methods are classified into three types: perceptual maps, preference maps, and joint-space maps. We will briefly discuss each type, along with examples of each. [3-52]

Perceptual Maps: Perceptual maps, as we discussed, display customer perceptions. The category is separated into attribute-based methods and similarity-based methods.

- **Attribute-based Perceptual Maps**: Attribute-based perceptual maps are quite popular. In fact, when marketers mention "perceptual maps," they generally mean attribute-based perceptual maps. Attribute-based perceptual maps display data from customer evaluations of products and services using attributes they find relevant. Attributes are tangible descriptors customers use when considering the purchase of a product or service. Examples include reliability, durability, style, luxury, comfort, sportiness, and other directly observable characteristics. We cover attribute-based maps further in the simplified approach later in this chapter.

- **Similarity-based Perceptual Maps:** Similarity-based perceptual maps show how similar customers perceive one brand to be to another. Brands adjacent to each other in similarity-based perceptual maps are perceived to be similar, whereas wide gaps denote dissimilarity. Similarity-based methods are used in categories where customers apply intangible characteristics, such as "image" or "class" to compare alternatives. For example, similarity-based methods could be appropriate in such areas as perfume, fine cuisine, and fashion, where assessment of intangibles plays an important role in brand selection.

Preference Maps: Perceptual maps show how customers perceive existing competing goods and services, but they do not include information about what customers prefer. Preference maps fill that gap by including "preference vectors" showing the "ideal choice." The category is separated into ideal-point models and vector models.

- **Ideal-Point Preference Maps:** Ideal-point preference maps acknowledge a "most-preferred" version of certain attributes where customers can exercise significant personal judgment during evaluation. For example, tomato sauce can vary from bland to excessively spicy. Between those two extremes, customers will desire a "most preferred" amount of spiciness. Ideal-point maps are often in the shape of an upside-down U, recognizing an optimum point between two extremes. Predictably, these types of maps are often used in food and beverage studies.

- **Vector Model Preference Maps:** Vector model preference maps are the opposite of ideal-point maps. Vector model preference models suit "universal attributes" that most everyone will agree are desirable or undesirable, such as performance, reliability, and convenience. Rather than model an attribute in an upside-down U (with an "ideal point" at the top), vector model attributes are modeled as a straight line (a vector). For example, "reliability" can be modeled as a straight line, where customers uniformly rate reliable products higher than unreliable products.

Joint-Space Maps: Joint space maps seek to combine the best of both worlds. They combine the perceptual data from perceptual maps with the preference data from preference maps for greater insight into the market. The category consists of simple joint-space methods and external analysis methods.

- **Joint-Space Methods**: Joint-space methods combine perceptions and preferences in the same map. For example, in an attribute-based study, we could start by asking customers to evaluate existing brands over several different evaluation criteria. This process would result in perception data. We could then ask the same customers for their preference, which could be entirely different from the brands they evaluated. In practice, attribute-based joint space maps look like traditional attribute-based perceptual maps, but with the addition of a preference vector.

- **External Analysis Methods**: External analysis methods leverage the analytical power of tools such as PREFMAP3. Like regular joint space maps, external analysis maps start by mapping perceptual data. But instead of just adding a preference vector, PREFMAP3 adds groupings of ideal customer points on the perceptual map, rendered as circles. The position of the circles on the perceptual map indicates the degree of importance of different attributes on customers' preferences. The size of the circles indicates the proportion of the population desiring particular types of products and services. The size of the circles can be interpreted as potential market share for products and services of that type.

Figure 3.39 summarizes the different types of mapping methods.

Mapping Method Category	Methods
Perceptual Maps	Attribute-based: Good for tangible descriptors, such as weight Similarity-based: Good for intangible descriptors, such as image
Preference Maps	Ideal Point: Adds "most-preferred" point for judgment attributes Vector Model: Adds "preference vector" for universal attributes
Joint Space Maps	Joint Space: Combines perceptions and preferences on one map External Analysis: Leverages analytical power of software programs

Figure 3.39: Mapping Methods

Perceptual Map Development

In this section, we describe a simplified approach to developing perceptual maps. The approach covers the creation of two-dimensional attribute-based perceptual maps, the most popular type of perceptual maps. Marketers can execute the approach using the standard functions available in Microsoft Excel.

As Figure 3.40 shows, we follow a five-step process, from determining the selection criteria to interpreting the resulting perceptual map.

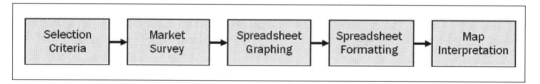

Figure 3.40: Perceptual Map Development: Process

To demonstrate the approach, we will show how to build a simplified perceptual map for consumer blenders. According to Consumer Reports magazine (consumerreports.org), some leading brands and models for popular consumer blenders at about $60 are as follows:

- Black & Decker BL 1900
- Cuisinart BFP-703CH
- Hamilton Beach 56221
- KitchenAid KSB560
- Oster 4093 Beehive
- Sunbeam 3350W
- Waring WPB80BC

Selection Criteria: We start by researching the market segment to determine the selection criteria. We recommend conducting secondary research first to become familiar with the terminology and typical purchasing behavior. For example, marketers should study the criteria third party review sources, such as Consumer Reports and J.D. Powers, consider when evaluating products and services.

Once marketers have exhausted secondary information sources, they can move on to conduct primary research. For example, we can conduct consumer interviews, asking them what evaluation criteria they consider when deciding on the purchase of goods and services.

Figure 3.41 shows typical examples of purchasing selection criteria.

Selection Criterion	Rating of 1 on 1 to 10 Scale	Rating of 10 on 1 to 10 Scale
Style	Traditional style	Fashionable style
Ruggedness	Delicate; Fine	Rugged; Durable
Size	Compact size	Full size
Economic Orientation	Economy-oriented	Luxury-oriented
Comfort Orientation	Comfort oriented	Sportiness oriented

Figure 3.41: Perceptual Map Development: Selection Criteria

In our blender example, customers used two decision criteria—features and power—when shopping for blenders. "Features" referred to the number of speed settings and other adjustments available on the machine. For example, features in our set ranged from simple, as in the Off-Low-High switch in the Waring, to elaborate, as in the Cuisinart.

"Power" referred to the effective chopping power of the blender, ranging from the relatively weak Sunbeam to the ferocious Oster.

Market Survey: Next, we survey individuals in the market segment for their perceived rating for each choice within the category. We ask them to rate each choice against the two selection criteria discovered earlier. We recommend using a 1 – 10 rating scale.

In our case, we designate a "5" for expected features, such as three or four speeds, with lower scores for more Spartan features and higher scores for extensive features. Similarly, ratings for effective ranged from "1," designating relatively weak performance, to "5," indicating expected power, to "10," designating very strong chopping power.

After surveying the individuals, we averaged the results. They are shown in Figure 3.42.

Blender	Features: 1 to 10 Scale	Effective Power: 1 to 10 Scale
Black & Decker BL 1900	4.6	6.1
Cuisinart BFP-703CH	9.2	4.2
Hamilton Beach 56221	3.4	7.2
KitchenAid KSB560	4.1	6.2
Oster 4093 Beehive	3.1	9.4
Sunbeam 3350W	3.8	3.6
Waring WPB80BC	2.1	8.6

Figure 3.42: Perceptual Map Development: Market Survey on Perceptions

Spreadsheet Graphing: We graph the results using Microsoft Excel's XY Scatter Plot function. Figure 3.43 shows the raw result after graphing, before applying any formatting changes.

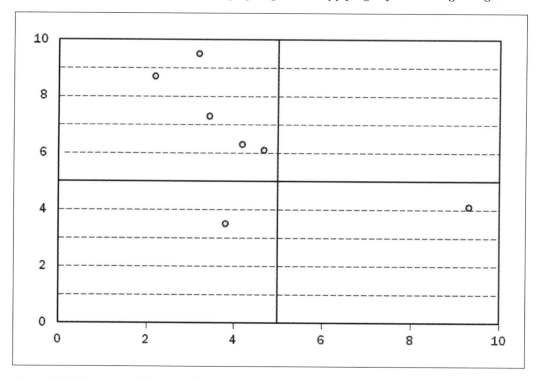

Figure 3.43: Perceptual Map Development: Spreadsheet Graphing

Spreadsheet Formatting: As an optional next step, we can change the standard formatting to make the chart more presentable. Microsoft Excel offers a multitude of formatting options. We present a straightforward approach in this section.

We start by removing any legends from the graph. Next, remove the horizontal grid lines and axis values. Add labels for each brand by selecting the Text Box function from the Insert tab. Alternatively, Excel can insert labels automatically, but the result is generally not acceptable for executive-level reports. Add labels to the axes in the same way.

Next, we will add some formatting to separate the graph into four quadrants. Click on any area outside the graph to bring up the standard menu (instead of the Chart Tools menu, which is the default after creating a graph), and click on the Insert tab. Click on the Shapes icon in the Illustrations area. Select the Rectangle shape and draw a rectangle to cover the entire plot. Use the No Fill option. Repeat the process, drawing four more rectangles to form the four quadrants.

Figure 3.44 shows the finished result after formatting. Note that we shaded the upper right quadrant using the Format Shape option on the upper right rectangle. By forming the quadrants using rectangles (instead of using lines), we can emphasize quadrants by shading, which can be handy, as we shall soon see.

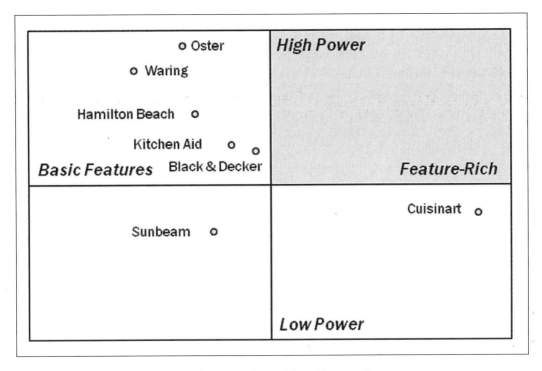

Figure 3.44: Perceptual Map Development: Spreadsheet Formatting

Perceptual Map Interpretation: From the map, we see several brands competing in the "Basic Features & High Power" quadrant. We see only one brand each in the "Basic Features & Low Power" and "Feature Rich & Low Power" quadrant. Surprisingly, we do not see any brands at all in the "Feature Rich & High Power" quadrant (shaded in the figure).

Marketing Strategy: The perceptual map suggests that we investigate the "Feature Rich & High Power" quadrant to determine market demand for a potential product. If indeed strong demand exists, it could be profitable for us to launch such a product, because we face no competition from established brands there.

SUMMARY

Market segmentation is the process of subdividing general markets into distinct segments with different needs, and which respond differently to marketing efforts. Targeting is the selection of market segments to which a company wishes to sell products or services. Positioning is the approach that seeks to make a brand occupy a distinct position (relative to competing brands), as perceived by the consumer.

Together, segmentation, targeting, and positioning (called STP for short) can achieve several significant advantages, such as efficiency through concentration of force, increased customer satisfaction, higher profitability, competitive advantage, and ability to execute niche marketing.

When segmenting markets, we seek to satisfy five goals simultaneously. These goals are internal homogeneity (all individuals in a group respond similarly to marketing efforts), external heterogeneity (individuals in different segments behave differently), parsimony (we use as few segments as possible), accessibility (ability to reach segment individuals), and size (we favor large and growing markets).

We segment markets using response variables and identifier variables. Response variables describe how individuals respond to marketing offers. Identifier variables categorize and describe individuals in segments.

We can categorize segmentation techniques in several different ways. We can categorize by the time at which we execute the segmentation, either a priori (before market research and analysis) or post hoc (after research and analysis). We can also categorize by the objective of the segmentation, either descriptive (to describe similarities and differences between groups) or predictive (to predict relationships between independent and dependent variables).

In the chapter, we covered the execution of several straightforward segmentation techniques, such as cross-tabulation and regression-based methods. Advanced techniques are also available, such as cluster analysis, conjoint-based regression, AID, CHAID, and other methods. Advanced methods work best when executed using sophisticated software programs suited for the purpose, such as SAS and SPSS.

Once the segments are identified, we must select the segments on which to focus, called targeting. When targeting segments, we seek to select segments with high potential revenue, those with strong alignment with the company's mission and competitive advantage, and those we can access effectively using marketing programs.

We must position our products and services to the targeted segments to differentiate the company and ensure prospective customers acknowledge the difference. We can apply tools such as perceptual maps to determine how customers currently perceive products and services in the market segment, and interpret potential areas of opportunity for new products and services into the segment.

Terminology

A Priori Segmentation: Segmentation technique category where marketers divide the market into segments before primary market research and analysis are conducted

Accessibility: Ability to reach individuals in market segments with marketing efforts

Agglomerative Hierarchical Clustering): Type of cluster-based segmentation technique which clusters group in a hierarchy by combining groups from bottom to top

AID: Automatic Interaction Detection; Post hoc, predictive segmentation technique

ANOVA: Analysis of Variance; In regression analysis, tests for the significance of the model as a whole

Attribute-based Perceptual Maps: In positioning, perceptual maps suited to tangible descriptors

CART: Classification and Regression Trees; Segmentation technique that combines elements of AID, CHAID, and regression analysis

CHAID: Chi Square Automatic Interaction Detection; Extension of AID segmentation technique

Conjoint Analysis-based Segmentation: Post hoc, predictive technique that reduces preferences for certain goods and services into part worths

Cross-Tabulation: Segmentation procedure to cross-tabulate variables, expressing their relationship in a table

Dendogram: Also called tree diagram; Segmentation technique producing tree-like diagram where root branches off into two or more branches

Descriptive Segmentation: Segmentation with the objective of describing the similarities and differences between customer groups.

Divisive Hierarchical Clustering: Type of cluster-based segmentation technique which clusters groups in a hierarchy, from a top level to lower levels

External Analysis: In positioning, technique which leverages analytical power of software programs

External Heterogeneity: Segmentation goal, where individuals in one segment behave differently from those in another group

Factor Analysis: In segmentation, reducing the original set of variables into a manageable number before attempting to cluster the individual customers into groups

Full Market Coverage: Targeting technique that offers multiple categories of products to multiple markets

Fuzzy Segmentation: Segmentation techniques giving ability to assign individuals to multiple market segments

Hierarchical Clustering: Type of cluster-based segmentation technique which groups differing clusters in a hierarchy, from a top level to lower levels

Ideal Point Preference Maps: In positioning, preference maps that add "most-preferred" point for judgment-oriented attributes

Identifier Variables: Segmentation variables to categorize and describe the individuals in segments.

Internal Homogeneity: Segmentation goal, where every individual in a segment behaves the same way relative to the variable

Joint-Space Maps: In positioning, graphical instruments that combine customer perceptions and preferences on one map

K-Means: A popular example of partitioning clustering

Logit segmentation: Also called multinomial logit (MNL) and choice-based segmentation; Segmenting a market based on individuals' likelihoods to choose to purchase a good or service

Market Specialization: Targeting technique that markets a variety of goods and services to one market

MNL Segmentation: Multinomial Logit segmentation; Also called Logit Segmentation; Segmenting markets by individual choice

P-value: Probability of encountering an equal t value in a collection of random data in which the variable had no effect (the null hypothesis)

Partitioning Clustering: Type of cluster-based segmentation technique which constructs clusters by maximizing specific criteria

Parsimony: Segmentation goal, where marketer describes markets in as few groups as possible, while still being effective

Perceptual Mapping: Graphical positioning technique which represents customers' perceptions of important attributes of areas of interest for marketers

Predictive Segmentation: Segmentation with the objective of predicting the relationship between independent and dependent variables

Preference Maps: In positioning, graphical tools showing customer preference

Positioning: Establishing a distinct position in the buyer's mind relative to competitors

Post Hoc Segmentation: Segmentation technique category where marketers divide the market into segments after primary market research and analysis are conducted

Product/ Service Specialization: Targeting technique that focuses company efforts on one specific product or service

R-Squared: Also called the coefficient of determination; Represents the degree to which the function estimated through regression represents the original data

Regression-based Segmentation: Segmentation technique to determine the mathematical relationship between independent variables and dependent variables

Response Variables: Segmentation variables to describe how individuals respond to an offer

Segmentation: Dividing larger, general markets into smaller, specific segments

Selective Specialization: Targeting technique that targets company efforts over multiple independent products to multiple segments

Similarity-based Perceptual Maps: In positioning, perceptual maps suitable for intangible descriptors

Single-Segment Concentration: Targeting technique that concentrates company efforts on one specific market segment

Targeting: Selecting market segments on which to focus

Vector Model Preference Maps: In positioning, preference maps that add "preference vector" for universal attributes

Ward's: A popular example of agglomerative hierarchical clustering

Class Discussion

1. What segments does your organization target? How are they similar? How are they different?
2. What changes do you plan to make to your organization's marketing efforts based on the information presented in this chapter?
3. What are some inherent limitations of segmentation?
4. What are some problems with targeting multiple markets simultaneously?
5. How are your organization's products and services positioned relative to those of your competitors?
6. How would you approach a repositioning project to make your company's brand more relevant to your customers?

Practice Problems

1. Identify several response variables that measure the behavior of your customers.
2. Identify several identifier variables you can use to describe and characterize the segments interested in your products and services.
3. Conduct a segmentation project employing cross-tabulation analysis on a segment of your customers. What insights did you learn?
4. Conduct a segmentation project using regression-based techniques. What are the strengths and weaknesses over the cross-tabulation technique?
5. Determine the type of segment specialization used currently by your organization. Identify the anticipated changes in revenue if the specialization were to be changed.
6. Prepare a perceptual map for one of your organization's products or services using the techniques described in this chapter.

Chapter 4.
COMPETITIVE ANALYSIS

Chapter Outline

We cover the following marketing analytics topics in this chapter:

- ☑ **Competitive Information:** Gathering actionable competitive information
- ☑ **Competitive Analysis:** Applying models to analyze competitive situations
- ☑ **Competitive Actions:** Deciding on defensive or offensive actions

---

"The wise learn many things from their enemies."
– Aristophanes

Ancient Greek comic playwright Aristophanes understood the power of competitive analysis even back in 400 BC. Aristophanes competed at the great dramatic festivals of Athens. Judges assessed his works along with other comic dramatists.

He won second prize with his first play "The Banqueters." He won first prize with his next play, "The Babylonians." His skill was so great that today he is known as the "Father of (Old) Comedy." Clearly, he learned much from his enemies. [4-1]

For the purposes of this book, we will define **competitive analysis** as the gathering and interpretation of competitive information, with the objective of establishing marketing strategies and tactics to make use of that information.

We advocate the ethical collection and usage of information. We specifically do not endorse unethical practices, such as industrial espionage, like the example described in the following brief case study.

MARKETING MADE MEASURABLE

Oracle: Dumpster Diving for Data? The quest for competitive information can turn nasty. Rivalry between competing firms, such as technology firms Oracle and Microsoft, can lead companies (and their CEOs) to do extraordinary actions.

In 2000, at the height of the rivalry, Oracle CEO Larry Ellison was accused of digging through the garbage of Microsoft CEO Bill Gates. Presumably, he was searching for any scrap of information which could give him a competitive advantage.

Only a year later, a similar incident occurred, this time between consumer packaged goods giant Procter & Gamble and its rival, Unilever. In that case, Procter & Gamble admitted that employees had hired investigators to dig through the garbage of Unilever, again with the intention of finding tasty tidbits of knowledge. [4-2]

Competitive analysis can yield many benefits. Its power and versatility make it essential for virtually every organization. Figure 4.1 shows some of the benefits.

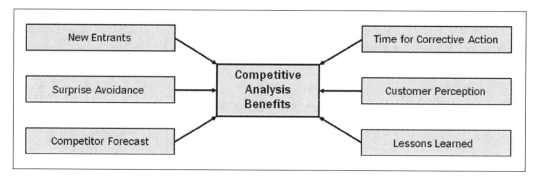

Figure 4.1: Competitive Analysis Benefits

Organizations find several benefits with competitive analysis:

New Entrants: Vigilant monitoring can detect new companies entering the market. Competitive analysis can assess the potential threat these new entrants will cause.

Surprise Avoidance: Executives rarely appreciate surprises, especially nasty ones. Ongoing competitive information gathering and analysis keeps organizations aware of the latest developments.

Competitor Strategy Forecast: We can anticipate the strategy of competitors by examining their strengths and weaknesses, and how they have behaved in the past to various situations.

Time for Corrective Actions: By monitoring the competitive landscape, organizations maintain an early warning system that gives them time to take corrective actions before it is too late.

Customer Perception: With effective competitive analysis, companies maintain awareness of customer perception of companies and markets. Without such analysis, companies can focus on their rivals, not even realizing that customers see the market more broadly.

Lessons Learned: Attentive marketers can learn from the lessons learned by other companies in the market. We can learn from both successes and failures, as we see in the Marketing Made Measurable brief case study on Snapple below.

MARKETING MADE MEASURABLE

Snapple: Best Stuff on Earth or Worst Merger on Earth? Competitive analysis includes both short term and long term applications. We can see both in the unfortunate merger between the quirky Snapple Beverage Corporation and the conservative food giant Quaker Oats in the 1990s. In the short term, food and beverage companies conducting effective competitive analysis were aware of the merger. They keenly followed the ensuing drama, as Quaker purchased Snapple for $1.7 billion in 1994.

The merger, originally thought to provide Quaker with an unbeatable competitive advantage, proved to be anything but. After several years of disappointing sales, Quaker sold Snapple to Triarc for a paltry $300 million. In the long term, competitors in other industries were reminded of the importance of alignment of cultures and brand understanding during mergers and acquisitions. [4-3]

Figure 4.2 shows the competitive analysis process outlined in this book. We start by researching information about the competitive landscape. This chapter presents several recommended sources to gather the information. In addition to traditional sources, such as industry and financial analyst reports, we discuss website traffic analysis and social media monitoring tools.

Next, we conduct a competitive analysis using the information. We start the analysis process by narrowing down the list of potential competitors (of which there could be hundreds) to the principal competitors on which to focus (generally fewer than ten). We analyze the competitors using several different kinds of models.

Based on the assessment of the models, we conclude by evaluating potential defensive and offensive competitive actions. We refer to defensive competitive actions as those meant to defend the organization against anticipated competitive attacks. Alternatively, companies can take offensive actions, where they seek to exploit market opportunities.

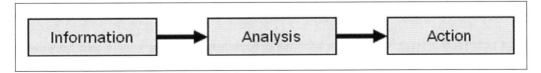

Figure 4.2: Competitive Analysis Process

COMPETITIVE INFORMATION

Figure 4.3 provides an overview of several different competitive information sources. In this section, we will discuss the sources.

As time and resources permit, marketers can choose to include additional sources, such as personal interviews and other primary research. We advise using as many sources of information as possible. The use of multiple sources reduces reliance on any one source, allows cross-checking of facts, and provides different viewpoints. [4-4]

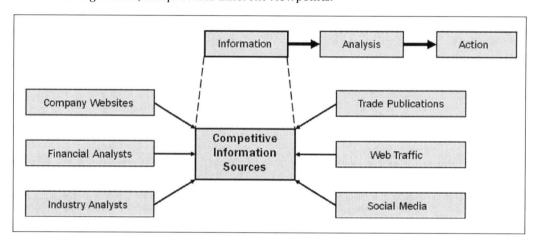

Figure 4.3: Competitive Information Sources Overview

Company Websites

Company websites offer a rich source of competitive information. Inquisitive marketers can find financial statements, product/service descriptions, management profiles, and many other useful facts.

For public companies, the United States Securities and Exchange Commission (SEC) requires that companies post their financial information publicly, and many companies maintain a financial section on their website to comply with the request. The financial section will include financial statements, which give detailed revenue and profit information. For private companies, one can often obtain basic financial information through financial analyst firms, mentioned later in this section.

Websites also list out company-specific details, such as the management team and partners. Websites give detailed product and service collateral (company-created information), such as data sheets, brochures, and videos. When evaluating the information, marketers must consider the inherent bias in company-supplied information, and filter the data accordingly.

Websites also provide profiles of the senior management team. The profiles indicate the senior managers' responsibilities, their background, their education, and highlights of their achievements to date. We find profiles useful in competitive analysis because we can predict the future behavior of individuals based on their past actions.

Financial Analysts

We often need to know the financial health of our competitors. As we mentioned earlier, public firms trade their stock on public stock exchanges, so the Securities and Exchange Commission requires that those companies disclose key financial data. Therefore, public firms include financial sections on their website.

But finding data on private firms (those whose fund through private equity) can prove more difficult. Here we have two choices—enroll in the services of a large full-service financial analyst, such as the American International Group (AIG; aig.com), or access the database of a smaller financial research company.

Financial research companies maintain databases with basic financial information of many private companies. The basic information typically includes annual sales revenue and recent rounds of funding (if applicable). Much of the data from these sources is available for free online. Examples of such research companies include Hoovers (hoovers.com), InsideView (insideview.com), Jigsaw (jigsaw.com), and Manta (manta.com). [4-5, 4-6, 4-7, 4-8, 4-9]

Industry Analysts

Industry analyst firms provide in-depth research on many prominent industries. Such analysis often includes overviews of the market and competitors. Many industry analysts and market research firms offer annual subscriptions to their content, which can be expensive, costing thousands of dollars per year. Alternatively, marketers can purchase individual research reports for less cost than an annual subscription, but such an approach can prove more expensive in the long run. Because industry analysts do not analyze every market every year, information might be several years old and thus less pertinent.

Examples of industry analysts include the NPD group (npd.com) for consumer markets and Forrester Research (forrester.com) for business markets.

Trade Publications

Virtually every industry features a number of publications and associated websites devoted to knowledge over the industry (also called the "trade"). These trade-related sources offer fast, easy, and often free access to a wealth of industry-related content.

For example, the apparel industry features websites rich in content such as Women's Wear Daily (wwd.com), Textile World (textileworld.com), and Footwear News (footwearnews.com). The sites routinely discuss major trends and events occurring in their industries, as well as the overall performance of the industry. The sites do not go into great detail on individual firms.

Web Traffic Analysis

In today's online world, information on web traffic to competitors' sites can prove useful to assess web popularity and strategy. Marketers can access web traffic analysis tools which offer information applicable to competitor site analytics and search analytics. Site analytics information includes various data points, such as traffic volume, about selected sites. Search analytics information shows which keywords users are entering to send traffic to websites.

In this section, we cover several online competitive analysis tools to assist with web traffic analysis and other website-related competitive information gathering. We will demonstrate the use of the online tools through a running example.

In the example, we represent wrinkle cream manufacturer Dermagist (dermagist.com). We will engage in online competitive analysis to determine how our website characteristics compare with those of our competitors, Life Cell Skin (lifecellskin.com) and Athena 7 Minute Lift (7minutelift.com).

We start with online competitive analysis tool **Alexa** (alexa.com). As shown in Figure 4.4, to use the tool, we go to Alexa.com and enter our search term. We can research our own website characteristics by entering "dermagist.com" in the search box, and then clicking the "search" button. Alexa.com changes over time, so exact details might vary from those discussed here.

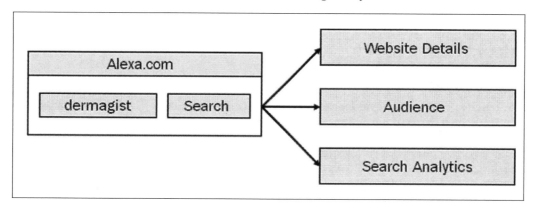

Figure 4.4: Online Competitive Analysis Tools: Alexa

Alexa returns several different types of information, some examples of which are shown in the figure. We start by clicking on the "Details" button to find website details. Some details include our Alexa Traffic Rank (how we compare with other websites), and the number of sites linking in. By selecting the "Audience" tab on Alexa, we can see age, education, gender, and other demographic data on site visitors.

By selecting the "Search Analytics" tab, we can see graphs of the dermagist.com website traffic over time. The tool also shows keyword popularity for different search terms. We can repeat the procedure to obtain similar information for our competitors, lifecellskin.com and 7minutelift.com. We then compare the results to determine how we fare. [4-10]

The advantages of Alexa are its cost (it is free), its ease of use, and the relevance of its data to assess traffic volume trends. The disadvantage of Alexa is that it obtains its data from people who have installed the Alexa toolbar. Therefore, the data represent Internet data analysts (who often have the toolbar installed) more accurately than standard consumers. Remember this fact when interpreting the data.

Online competitive analysis tool **Compete** (compete.com) allows users to simultaneously compare the web traffic of up to five domain names over time. As shown in Figure 4.5, the tool provides graphs showing the number of unique visitors over time, monthly metrics for each domain name (such as number of referring sites), and top search terms for each of the domain names entered. Compete.com changes over time, so features might differ from this description.

For our example, we would enter all three domain names—dermagist.com, lifecellskin.com, and 7minutelift.com—into the tool, click on the "search" button, and observe the results.

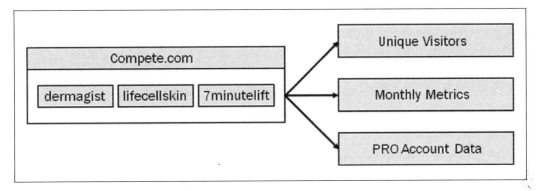

Figure 4.5: Online Competitive Analysis Tools: Compete

Compete gets its traffic estimates from a panel of over 2 million U.S. Internet users. Users opting to pay extra for the PRO account get additional data, such as audience profiles and the number of pages viewed per visit. [4-11]

The advantages of Compete are that it provides much of the functionality without an upgrade to the PRO account, that it is easy to use, and that it allows users to quickly compare important information among several sites simultaneously. The disadvantage of Compete is that it reflects the United States more than other countries because the data comes from a U.S.-based panel.

Google offers two helpful tools to assess the competitive landscape, as well as overall trends, over time. The first tool is **Google Alerts**, shown in Figure 4.6. To use Google Alerts, we enter the topic of interest and the type of data desired (news, blogs, video, discussions, product reviews, etc.). We select how often we wish to receive alerts, provide our email address, and click on the "Create Alert" button. Google will deliver alerts relevant to the topic entered.

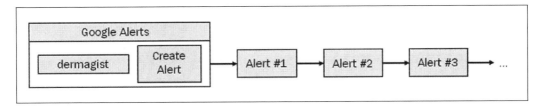

Figure 4.6: Online Competitive Analysis Tools: Google Alerts

In our case, we enter "dermagist" into Google Alerts, and the tool will alert us with regular messages whenever the term "dermagist" comes up. We can also request to get alerts for the terms "Life Cell Skin" and "7 Minute Lift" occur. We advise users to select the type and frequency of alerts carefully to avoid receiving a deluge of information.

Google also offers **Google Trends** (google.com/trends), shown in Figure 4.7. To use the tool, we enter the category represented by the company and its competitors. In our case, we enter the category term "wrinkle cream" After clicking the "Explore" button, Google Trends returns three types of information.

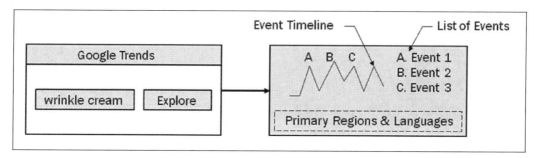

Figure 4.7: Online Competitive Analysis Tools: Google Trends

The first type of information is an event timeline. The event timeline shows the search frequency of the entered term (in this case, "wrinkle cream"). The event timeline indicates times of intense searching, such as shortly after a product introduction from a competitor.

The second type of information is a list of events. Each event in the list is indexed with alphabetical letters and includes a headline, a link to further information, and a corresponding letter on the event timeline, as shown in the figure.

The third type of information is a section on primary regions and languages. This section shows the popularity of searches by regions (such as comparing the popularity of the search term in the United States and Canada), by cities (such as comparing the search frequency in Tampa and Chicago), and by languages (such as comparing the number of occurrences in English and in French).

In our case, we would enter "wrinkle cream" into the tool and examine the results. The results could show us that search results spiked after one of our competitors released a new version of their product, or it could show the effect of a trend. For example, if a medical-oriented television program promoted the benefits of wrinkle cream to avoid sun damage, we could see increased interest in wrinkle cream as a whole.

Social Media Analysis

Many organizations actively engage with their customers via social media channels, such as Facebook (facebook.com), LinkedIn (linkedin.com), and Twitter (twitter.com). Each channel includes some limited analysis tools, such as displaying the number of followers.

For example, Twitter shows the number of followers and the number of people being followed. Third-party tools, such as TweetDeck (tweetdeck.com) are available to provide more in-depth analysis. Social media aggregator tools, such as Samepoint (samepoint.com) and Socialmention

(socialmention.com), can speed the social media analysis process by incorporating multiple social media channels in one tool. [4-12, 4-13, 4-14]

Social media aggregation tools typically show mentions per channel (Facebook, LinkedIn, and so forth), the top hashtags (user-defined categories), keywords, and users. Large businesses, with demanding social media analysis needs and substantial budgets, should consider enterprise-class tools, such as Radian 6 (radian6.com). Radian 6 enables deep analysis into social media data but can be expensive, starting at about $600 per month per user. [4-15]

Figure 4.8 summarizes recommended competitive information sources, along with their advantages, disadvantages, and typical data available.

Information Source	Advantages	Disadvantages	Typical Data
Company Websites	Fast, Easy, Free	Biased	Financial information Management team Product/service data Press releases
Financial Analyst	Detailed financial data	Can be expensive	Revenue Profit Financial analysis
Industry Analyst	Credible	Expensive; Can be dated	Industry analysis reports Comparisons of firms
Trade Publications	Fast, Easy, Free	Limited detail on individual companies	Industry performance Industry events Industry trends
Web Traffic Analysis	Fast	Some services require fees	Web traffic over time Top keywords
Social Media Analysis	Fast, Easy, Free	Requires much filtering	Mentions/ channel Top hashtags Top keywords Top users

Figure 4.8: Recommended Competitive Information Sources

COMPETITIVE ANALYSIS

In this section, we apply several models to analyze the competitive information we just gathered. We start by identifying our principal competitors.

Competitor Identification

Thanks to the information we gathered on the industry in the previous section, we should now have a good oversight of our competitive landscape. Our preparations put us in a good position to identify the competitors on which to focus our efforts. We start by listing all competitors, both direct and indirect, and then narrow down the list to the principal competitors on which to focus.

Direct and Indirect Competitors: Our first step is to list all organizations offering products and services that customers perceive as fulfilling the same need as our own company's offerings. We can divide the list into direct and indirect competitors. [4-16]

- **Direct Competitors:** Direct competitors are those offering similar products and services to the same market. Prices and availability will often be similar. Sometimes, customers find it difficult to tell the difference among the similar offerings.

- **Indirect Competitors**: Indirect competitors are those fulfilling the same function, but with a product or service that appears different from the original. Prices and availability often vary widely.

For example, suppose we made gasoline-powered push lawn mowers for consumer lawn care, and we wished to identify our competitors. For direct competitors, examples include traditional lawn mower brands such as Toro, Snapper, and Honda.

For indirect competitors, examples include products and services that could also accomplish the task of mowing grass, such as manual push mowers and electric-powered mowers. As a green alternative to gas-powered mowing, Google rents a team of 200 goats to eat the grass around its Mountain View, California campus. [4-17]

While it is admirable to be thorough, it is unlikely that rented goats will prove to be a worthy alternative to traditional mowers for most homeowners in the near future. What we need to do is to narrow down the list to more reasonable alternatives.

Principal Competitors: Organizations do not have the resources to address every conceivable competitor. Therefore, we must narrow down the list to **principal competitors**, those that pose the most likely threat to the organization. We can use several factors to converge from all competitors to principal competitors. [4-18]

- **Time Horizon**: We can reduce the list of competitors by eliminating the ones not likely to pose a threat in the planning horizon of the company, generally one year. A one year time horizon is likely to emphasize direct competitors, with only the most robust indirect competitors making the cut.

  In our lawn mowing example, we would thus include traditional gasoline-powered lawnmower manufacturers (direct competitors) on our list of principal competitors. We include them because consumers are likely to continue to appreciate their convenience and power for the foreseeable future, and certainly for at least one year.

  We might also consider electric mowers as an indirect competitor. Some consumers might find them an attractive alternative given their quiet operation and lack of exhaust. Electric mowers will likely be more of a niche product, however, due to their low power (for battery-powered units) and limited range (for cord-powered units). And few consumers could afford hiring a goat herd and shepherd to mow their lawn, so we will eliminate that option.

- **Product/Service Life Cycle**: We can also reduce our list to those competitors in the same stage of the product/service life cycle as our own. The product/service life cycle, like the human life cycle, starts with introduction, then growth, followed by maturity and decline. Using this approach, we will include direct competitors in our principal competitor list. We will include indirect competitors only if they are in a similar life cycle stage with ours.

    In our lawn mowing example, we will include other gasoline-powered lawn mowers, because they are in the maturity stage of their product life cycle. We are less likely to consider alternatives in other stages of the life cycle.

    For example, Lawnbotts (lawnbotts.com) manufactures robotic lawn mowers, such as its LB3510 unit, for consumer use. We would not likely include them as principal competitors because they are a new invention, and thus are in the introductory stage of their life cycle. Like many new products, the market must still decide if the new product's advantage (automatic operation) outweigh its significant disadvantages. Disadvantages include the possible safety hazards to pets and children, the difficulty of repairing and servicing the units, and the high price (the LB3510 costs a staggering $4000). [4-19]

- **Rate of Technological Change**: The third step to reducing our list of competitors is by considering the rate of technological change. The faster technology changes, the more relevant indirect competitors become. In the fast changing computer market, for example, hard disk drive manufacturers, such as Seagate and Hitachi, fight furiously to grow market share. Meanwhile, solid state drives, an indirect competitor to traditional spinning drives, are slowly growing their market share.

    In our lawn mowing example, few major changes have been made to the basic design for several decades. In fact, one can still recognize the basic design from early lawn mowers made by Toro (thetorocompany.com) back in 1920. Because the rate of technological change in lawn mowers is so slow, we will focus our efforts on direct competitors. [4-20]

Figure 4.9 summarizes the three criteria for identifying principal competitors.

Criterion	Description	Example
Time Horizon	Considering the time at which the competitor will pose a substantial threat	**Electric Lawn Mowers:** Not a principal competitor because range and power problems not likely to be solved in next year
Product/ Service Life Cycle	Considering stage of life cycle of competitor's product or service	**Lawnbotts:** Robot lawn mower not a principal competitor because product is still in infancy
Rate of Technological Change	Considering indirect competitors more seriously in cases of rapid technological change	**Toro:** Basic lawn mower design little changed since version introduced by Toro back in 1920

Figure 4.9: Criteria for Identifying Principal Competitors

Identifying the relevant set of principal competitors might seem obvious. Nevertheless, many companies focus their efforts on the wrong competitors, as the following example shows.

MARKETING MADE MEASURABLE

American Airlines: Fighting the Wrong Competitor? Airline giant American Airlines perceived its competitor to be United Airlines (and vice versa). As a result, the two engaged in a bitter rivalry for many years.

But both were fighting the wrong competitor. Customers perceived the market more broadly. Customers fled the big carriers when smaller airlines such as Southwest Airlines and JetBlue started up, attracted by their lower fares and friendlier service. [4-21]

Now that we have identified our principal competitors, we will apply the models shown in Figure 4.10 to analyze the information we have gathered thus far.

We will discuss each model and its relevance to competitive analysis. Depending on the complexity of the market, we can engage all of them, or only one for straightforward situations. Of the four models discussed, three have already been introduced earlier in the book. We discuss the application of each, continuing our household blender example from Chapter 3.

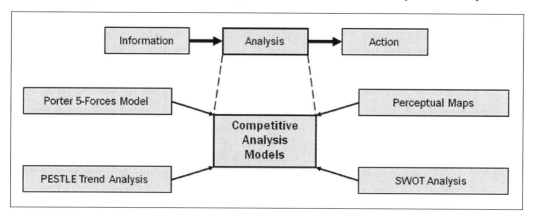

Figure 4.10: Competitive Analysis Models

PESTLE Market Analysis

As we saw in Chapter 2, the PESTLE market analysis model examines the political, economic, social, technological, legislative, and environmental trends affecting markets. For market insight, we examine the trends so we can predict how the market could change over time.

For competitive analysis, we examine the trends so we can assess how those trends might favor particular firms. We discuss examples of each area in PESTLE as they pertain to the household blender market.

Political: We start by examining political trends affecting the household blender market.

MARKETING MADE MEASURABLE

Deer: Political Impact of Tariff Reduction: Chinese consumer manufacturer Deer (deerinc.com) produces blenders, juicers, and other electronic countertop appliances for other manufacturers, such as Black and Decker, West Bend, and Toastmaster.

To boost the sales of blenders and other consumer products made in its country, China turned to the World Trade Organization (WTO) to block tariffs on 22 types of Chinese products, from steel wheel hubs to consumer products.

China stated that existing duties levied on Chinese products by the U.S. Commerce Department could be viewed as trade protectionism. The USA complains that China subsidizes many of the products it exports, giving it an unfair advantage. Sales of US blenders could suffer if the tariff reduction were passed. [4-22, 4-23]

Economic: Next, we consider economic trends relating to consumer durables, such as household blenders.

MARKETING MADE MEASURABLE

India: Economic Slowdown: According to the Economist (economist.com), the growth slowdown in India has caused sales of consumer durables, such as blenders and other small appliances, to fall.

In fact, sales of consumer durables decreased by 10 – 15% in the year leading to March 2012. Prolonged economic slowdowns can ruin smaller competitors, which do not have the cash reserves to weather economic storms. [4-24]

Social: Social trends, such as social media, can affect the household blender market as well, as we see in our next example.

MARKETING MADE MEASURABLE

BlendTec: Social Media Campaigns: Premium blender manufacturer BlendTec (blendtec.com) took advantage of the trend in social media to help sell its products in its "Will it Blend?" campaign.

The "Will it Blend?" campaign featured a collection of bizarre short videos highlighting the power of the BlendTec blender. In the videos, the blender demolished everything from garden rakes to iPhones.

Campaigns taking advantage of social trends, such as the "Will it Blend?" program, can increase a company's standing against the competition. [4-25]

Technology: Technological trends affect virtually every market, including that for household blenders.

MARKETING MADE MEASURABLE

Waring and Cuisinart: Advances in Blender Technology: In the 1960s, blender originator Waring introduced a blender with solid state control, permitting multiple speeds.

Thanks to modern electronics, Cuisinart can now offer its SmartPower Electronic Blender, with no fewer than 18 speeds. Technical advances in products can make them more competitive in the market. [4-26]

Legal: In today's strict legal environment, even household blenders suffer under legislation prohibiting their use.

MARKETING MADE MEASURABLE

Kansas: Illegal Use of Blenders: The state of Kansas makes it a crime to use blenders in some circumstances.

According to Kansas Statute Chapter 21, Part II, Article 36a (Crimes Involving Controlled Substances), "Blenders, bowls, containers, spoons and mixing devices used or intended for use in compounding controlled substances" are considered "drug paraphernalia" and are therefore illegal to possess, market, or distribute.

In most cases, legislation prohibiting the use of products and services depresses sales, although exceptions exist. For example, cell phone legislation requiring "hands free" operation in automobiles led to a boom in the sale of Bluetooth-enabled headsets. [4-27]

Environment: Concern for environmental responsibility extends to household blenders.

MARKETING MADE MEASURABLE

EPA: Environmentally Friendly Disposal of Blenders and Other Small Appliances: The disposal of consumer electronics and small appliances, such as blenders, is a concern to many governments.

In 2005, the Environmental Protection Agency (EPA) estimated that the "e-waste" from computers alone amounted to 1.9 to 2.2 million tons of waste annually. Accordingly, the EPA recommends the practice of properly recycling such goods, or as it calls the practice, "eCycling."

Some companies choose to increase their competitiveness by embracing such environmental concerns. For example, Apple boasts of the easy recyclability of its Macbook line of personal computers. [4-28]

Figure 4.11 summarizes the PESTLE market analysis for household blenders.

Area	Description	Example
Political	Governmental effect on market, especially as it pertains to competition	**Deer:** Proposed tariff reductions in Chinese small appliances could increase threat level of Chinese small appliances
Economic	Effect of economic conditions on competition	**India:** Economic slowdown results in reduced purchases of small appliances.
Social	Social trends and their impact on products and services, such as blenders	**BlendTec:** Took advantage of social media trend in "Will It Blend?" campaign.
Technological	Technological advances can improve competitiveness of companies	**Waring and Cuisinart:** Introduced electronic controls on its blenders.
Legal	Legislation prohibiting the use of certain products and services, such as blenders	**Kansas:** Enforces statute prohibiting use of blenders in some conditions.
Environmental	Addressing environmental concerns, such as the disposal of small appliances	**EPA:** Promoting use of "eCycling" to reduce e-waste from consumer durables

Figure 4.11: PESTLE Market Analysis for Household Blenders

Porter Five Forces Analysis

As we saw in chapter 2, the Porter Five Forces framework examines five forces acting on markets to anticipate changes likely to occur as a result. The five forces include the threat of new entrants, intensity of rivalry from existing competitors, pressure from substitute products, bargaining power of buyers, and the bargaining power of suppliers. For competitive analysis, we can use the model to predict specific organizations that stand to profit from the five forces.

Threat of New Entrants: The market for household blenders had traditionally been dominated by established U.S. manufacturing companies such as Oster and Waring.

New entrants pose a threat to the blender market. Earlier, we discussed the entrance of Chinese manufacturer Deer into the blender market. Other foreign firms may soon follow. In fact, a search on international trade site Alibaba (alibaba.com) reveals no fewer than 9,637 blender products from China, 65 from Taiwan, 11 from Thailand, 32 from the United Arab Emirates, and 10 from Vietnam. [4-29]

Intensity of Rivalry: Many people find the brand names "Oster" and "Waring" synonymous with blenders, with a moderate rivalry between the brands. Because of the limited promotion efforts each company takes in response to the others, it is difficult to justify classifying this as an "intense" rivalry.

Consumers perceive the two brands as rivals. For example, "foodie" website Chowhound (chowhound.com) initiated a fierce discussion in the comments section of an article comparing the iconic Oster Beehive blender with the Waring Professional model. Some users swore to the great power of the Oster, despite reports of loud operation; others preferred the Waring for its superior ice-crushing ability. [4-30]

Pressure from Substitute Products: Consumers can select from several substitute products for traditional blenders.

For manual tools, they can use hand mixers and whisks. Manual tools have the advantage of gentle application, such as delicately frothing egg whites. Manual tools have the disadvantage of the limitations caused by low power. After all, manually crushing large amounts of ice can be laborious and time-consuming.

For electric tools, chefs can select immersion blenders. Immersion blenders are handheld blenders with blades at the end of the device. Immersion blenders can provide a delicate touch to certain tasks. For example, immersion blenders work well for pureeing soups. However, their limited power makes them unsuitable for difficult jobs, such as crushing ice. Chefs and bartenders can select food processors instead of blenders, but many chefs do not find them to be good substitutes. The chefs find that food processors work well for chopping, but not as well for liquid mixing. [4-31]

Therefore, we find only a moderate amount of pressure from substitute products. While substitutes exist, serious chefs and bartenders desire traditional blenders for many tasks such as liquid mixing and ice crushing.

Bargaining Power of Buyers: The recession of the late 2000s caused significant changes in spending for many industries, including blenders and other small appliances. Before the recession, some consumers chose high-end appliances for their luxury features and status. That ended when consumers had to cut costs during the prolonged recession.

Evidence of this trend surfaced during a December 2008 study by the Riedel Marketing Group (4rmg.com). The group found that Americans are making long-term spending changes due to the recession. According to the research results, 55% of those surveyed indicated they would not return to pre-recession spending habits. A repeat of the study in June 2009 found that the percentage had increased from 55% to 73%. [4-32]

Therefore, we would anticipate significant bargaining power of buyers, due to increased consumer demand for low prices.

Bargaining Power of Suppliers: As we mentioned earlier, home appliance manufacturers worldwide compete to supply goods for the blender market. The glut of manufacturers makes the bargaining power of suppliers low.

Figure 4.12 summarizes the Porter Five Forces analysis for household blenders.

Area	Description	Household Blender Market
Threat of New Entrants	Lower profits due to new competitors coming into market	**Household Blenders:** Thousands of new blender manufacturers entering market
Intensity of Rivalry	Lower prices and new product development spurred by rivalry between two firms	**Household Blenders:** Moderate levels of rivalry, with more emphasis on price than on product development
Pressure from Substitute Products	Buyers can choose alternative products or services, making product less important	**Household Blenders:** Alternatives available, but no perfect substitutes
Bargaining Power of Buyers	Buyers can dictate pricing and terms due to their importance	**Household Blenders:** Strong bargaining power by buyers due to reduced consumer spending
Bargaining Power of Suppliers	Suppliers can dictate pricing and terms due to their importance	**Household Blenders:** Little bargaining power, due to glut of manufacturers

Figure 4.12: Porter Five Forces Analysis for Household Blenders

We repeat the Porter Five Forces model process, this time with daily deal company LivingSocial.

MARKETING MADE MEASURABLE

LivingSocial: From Daily Deal to Local Commerce: The daily deal industry, made popular by market leader Groupon (groupon.com), clearly demonstrates the Porter Five Forces model.

In terms of new entrants, the potential profitability of the industry has attracted over 700 new copycat businesses.

In terms of intensity of rivalry, the number two player in the market, LivingSocial (livingsocial.com), is fiercely battling Groupon for market share.

In terms of pressure from substitute products, many substitutes exist, from special deals offered by online merchants to traditional newspaper coupons.

In terms of bargaining power of buyers and suppliers, buyers (people searching for deals) clearly have the upper hand because they have no switching costs.

Competitor LivingSocial deals with the five forces by changing the game. Instead of focusing strictly on the daily deal industry, it is expanding its business model to what it calls the "local commerce space." The new model allows the company to expand from small businesses (the target for Groupon) into larger ones, such as upscale supermarket chain Whole Foods (wholefoods.com). [4-33]

Perceptual Maps

As we saw in chapter 3, perceptual maps assess the perceived similarities and differences of competitors, based on market research. The beauty of perceptual maps is that they represent consumer perception, and not just the organization's view of itself, and thus are highly relevant to competitive analysis.

Figure 4.13 repeats the perceptual map we developed in Chapter 3 for household blenders. By studying the map, we notice the large distance between the location of the Cuisinart rating and those of its competitors. Based on the large distance, we can assert that consumers perceive Cuisinart differently from other blender manufacturers.

Of the seven major brands tested, five were clustered in the "Basic Features and High Power" quadrant of the perceptual map. Therefore, consumers perceived the five brands as similar.

Of the other two brands, Sunbeam was in the "Basic Features and Low Power" quadrant, and Cuisinart was in the "Feature Rich and Low Power" quadrant. The positioning of Sunbeam is odd, as we are not sure who would be interested in such a combination. In the case of Cuisinart, consumers appear to be perceiving the machine as one targeting connoisseurs who value the extra features and do not need the extra power.

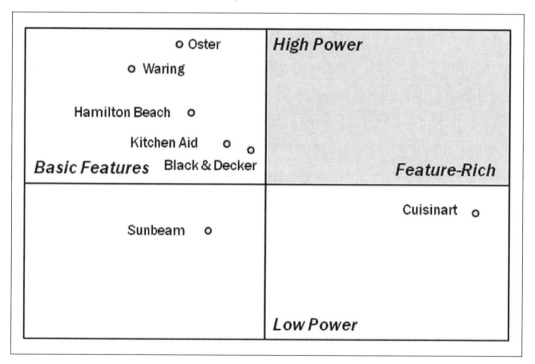

Figure 4.13: Perceptual Map for Competitive Analysis of Household Blender Market

SWOT Analysis

We can analyze the strengths, weaknesses, opportunities, and threats (SWOT) of competitors to understand them. Strengths and weaknesses evaluate the internal environment of the competitor. Opportunities and threats address the external environment. [4-34]

We start by examining strengths and weaknesses. For strengths and weaknesses, we focus on the areas of leadership, finance, strategy, market segments, positioning, operations, product, price, place, promotion, and support.

We can continue our example of the household blender market by studying the apparent strengths and weaknesses for consumer appliance company Jarden (jarden.com). Jarden heads the Oster and Sunbeam brands, as well as other well-known consumer brands such as Mr. Coffee (coffee makers) and VillaWare (European kitchen appliances). [4-35]

Leadership: In leadership, we study the competency and experience of the individuals in charge of managing the organization. We want leaders to have knowledge in their respective spaces, and have a track record of making sound, ethical, and timely strategic decisions.

In the case of Jarden, the company benefits from a CEO with significant experience within the firm. The CEO, James Lillie, joined Jarden in 2003 as chief operating officer (COO) and served eight years before being promoted to CEO in 2011. Therefore, we assess that leadership is strong at the Jarden organization. [4-36]

Finance: According to its 2011 Annual Report, Jarden grew both Net Sales and Operating Earnings from 2007 – 2011, despite the economic uncertainty that plagued that time period. Net Sales expanded from $4.66 billion in 2007 to $6.68 billion in 2011. Operating Earnings grew from $232 million in 2007 to $523 million in 2011. [4-37]

Conducting further financial research on Jarden, we find that the company suffers from the highest debt to EBITDA (earnings before interest, taxes, depreciation, and amortization) in the house-wares and specialties industry. The debt to EBITDA ratio measures how many years it would take the company to pay back all its debt using its earnings. In the EBITDA ratio, lower numbers represent faster paybacks, and are therefore better. Jarden ranks highest with a debt to EBITDA ratio of 4.5. [4-38]

We balance our praise for its revenue and earnings growth with our concern over its high debt load and assess Jarden with a rating of "medium" for financial strength.

Strategy: We refer to strategy as the soundness of the company's general approach to achieving the objectives of the organization. We assess strategy on the basis of its alignment with organizational mission, its effectiveness against competitors, and of course the resulting revenue and profit.

According to a Jarden press release, its primary organizational objective is long-term growth. Its strategy to achieving long-term growth is merger and acquisition (M & A) of other consumer brands, as well as geographic expansion. The annual report states that net sales have grown from $368 million in 2002 to $6.68 billion in 2011, for a compound annual growth rate (CAGR) of 38%. With such a strong growth result, we rate Jarden strong in its strategy. [4-39, 4-40]

Market Segments: For market segments, we study the degree to which the company has clarity in its knowledge about its target market segments. We look for alignment of the product/service line with the needs of the segment. We also consider the company's ability to deliver to that segment.

In the case of Jarden, the market segmentation strategy appears strong, with a clear commitment to the household small appliance market. The company has a strong product lineup for the segment, with ample development and distribution resources to deliver to the segment. We therefore rate market segments as strong.

Positioning: As we discussed in chapter 3, positioning is the placement of brand names of products or services in prospects' minds. We want to associate the brand with relevant categories (such as "kitchen appliances") and desirable attributes (such as "reliable" and "stylish").

Jarden provides an excellent example of positioning with its relatively new VillaWare brand. Jarden went to industrial design firm Frog Design (frogdesign.com) to reinvigorate the VillaWare brand. Frog conducted research in the European appliance market to understand what it wanted before designing the products. Then it applied a unique design language to differentiate VillaWare's products from others. The designs applied unique shapes, surfaces, and materials to set the products apart. Because of Jarden's commitment to positioning, we rate it as strong. [4-41]

Operations: We define operations here broadly to include manufacturing for product-oriented organizations, service delivery for service-oriented organizations, and support processes, which include a variety of activities required to run a business. We judge manufacturing performance on cost, speed, quality, and other related factors. We judge service-oriented operations on cost of delivery, reliability, customer satisfaction, and so on.

Jarden places significant effort into its manufacturing operations to achieve strong results. According to its 2011 Annual Report, it operates over 60 manufacturing plants all over the globe. The growth to 60 plants demonstrates a strong commitment to manufacturing, considering Jarden operated only six manufacturing facilities in 2001. The Annual Report also discusses their work in optimizing its plants for higher efficiency. We therefore judge Jarden's manufacturing operations as strong. [4-42]

Product: We consider consumer assessment of the company's products and services when evaluating the "Product" strength/weakness rating. Consumers increasingly demand innovative, reliable, and cost-effective products and services. Because so many people associate companies with their products and services, consumer assessment of their offerings forms an essential part of the SWOT analysis.

In the case of Jarden, the product reviews are mixed. According to the 2011 Annual Report, the Jarden Corporation won a number of awards for its products. Examples of awards include the Powder Magazine Skier's Choice 2012 award and the Backpacker magazine Editor's Choice

2011 award (although we doubt these awards were for its blenders). For a fair and balanced treatment, we also accessed the Consumer Reports website (consumerreports.org) for its independent assessment of their household blenders. [4-43]

The Consumer Reports website indicates an average user rating of three stars out of five (based on 17 ratings) for the Oster blender line. Fans of the Oster cited its ease of cleaning, its pleasing pitcher, and admirable power output. Detractors of the Oster complained of its loud noise and poor mixing ability. By comparison, the Consumer Reports website indicated an average user rating of only two stars out of five (based on five ratings) for one of Jarden's principal competitors, the Waring blender line. Because of the lackluster reviews, we judge Jarden's product prowess as a medium. [4-44, 4-45]

Price: We assess price performance in SWOT analyses as the company's ability to command price premiums for their products and services. For example, a PC World study in 2009 compared the price of an Apple MacBook computer with a similarly configured Dell machine. The Apple unit commanded a price premium of $359. Such price premiums are a result of successful product innovation and branding, and contribute significantly to company profitability. [4-46]

To assess price premium for our blender example, we consulted Consumer Reports' research in pricing for popular blenders. As part of its research, Consumer Reports generated a price list of different blenders, from high to low, to reflect the type of blenders that consumers considered purchasing. At the bottom of the list were low-priced blenders from Hamilton Beach and Black and Decker. In the middle of the list were several Oster units, as well as competing major brands (such as Cuisinart and Waring) and niche brands (such as Nesco and Ninja Master). At the top of the price list Consumer Reports only included units from Waring and Cuisinart, as well as niche brands (such as Ninja Professional and Omega). Therefore, we list the price performance as "medium" compared to the price premium enjoyed by the higher-level Cuisinart and Waring units. [4-47]

Place: Place refers to the distribution of goods and services. As we shall see in Chapter 9, different types of companies use different distribution channel structures. Some companies use direct channels with no intermediaries, such as Internet-based sales directly to consumers. Conversely, mass merchandise goods such as household blenders use multiple intermediaries, including wholesalers, distributors, and retailers.

Jarden operates an impressive network of distribution channels. According to its 2011 Annual Report, it maintains 59 distribution and warehousing facilities across 28 countries. Jarden sells its products through a number of retail channels. For example, consumers can purchase its Oster brand of household blenders in department stores, such as Macy's and Kohl's, in consumer electronic stores, such as Best Buy, home improvement stores such as Lowes, discount stores such as Walmart, and etail stores, such as Amazon.com. [4-48]

Promotion: For SWOT purposes, we regard promotion strength in terms of the company's ability to communicate the benefits of its products and services to its consumers.

In the case of Jarden household blender products, Internet research revealed few efforts by the company to promote its products. The company appears to rely on word of mouth and retail store placement to promote its products. Compare those efforts to the effective social media campaign by BlendTec discussed earlier, and we can see that the company could do more to promote its products effectively. Therefore, we rate promotion strength as "medium."

Support: Companies understand that customer support forms a significant amount of consumer perception of a brand. Accordingly, many companies place a great deal of emphasis on their customer support function. To rate well in the support category, replacement parts should be readily available, repair locations should be available, and the company should be responsive to customer support requests.

In the case of Jarden household blender products, an Internet search revealed ready availability of replacement parts. Few repair facilities were found, however. The low number of facilities is not surprising given the general low cost of consumer blenders compared with the high cost of repair labor. To gain an understanding of consumer perception of Oster appliance support, we searched for positive and negative reviews for Oster blender customer support.

Reviews on Amazon.com praised Oster's customer service. One reviewer wrote that his Oster blender leaked, and when he reported to Oster customer service, they sent him a brand new blender. Oster's competitor Waring did not fare as well. Blender review website bestblenderreviews.com reported poor customer service from the Waring customer service organization. We therefore rate Oster as strong in support. [4-49, 4-50]

We move now to evaluating opportunities and threats for the organization. In the descriptions below, we refer to "short-term" as generally one quarter or less. Conversely, "long-term" comprises more than one quarter and can span several years.

Opportunities: We define a marketing opportunity as an unfulfilled market need or needed improvement in existing products or services. In order for the opportunity to be relevant, the company should possess the requisite knowledge and skill to fulfill the need or improve the product or service, or plan to develop those capabilities. Here are some examples of market opportunities for blender manufacturers:

- **Short-Term Opportunity**: Take advantage of social media trend with new social-based campaigns.
- **Short-Term Opportunity**: Cross-promote blenders in advertisements for spirits often mixed using blenders, such as tequila for margaritas.
- **Long-Term Opportunity**: Consider diversification into adjacent sectors, such as other small appliances, to reduce dependence on blender sales.
- **Long-Term Opportunity:** Consider regional manufacturing and distribution system to reduce dependence on fuel costs.

Threats: We define a marketing threat as a short-term or long-term event that can cause revenue or profitability to suffer. Here are some examples of short-term and long-term threats in the blender market:

- **Short-Term Threat**: A competitor could introduce a new blender with superior features, a lower price, a new distribution channel, or a well-funded promotion campaign.
- **Short-term Threat**: Most state governments could pass legislation prohibiting the use of blenders under certain conditions, as we saw in the Kansas example earlier.
- **Long-Term Threat**: Gasoline costs could rise over the long run, increasing transportation costs and reducing profits.
- **Long-Term Threat**: A prolonged recession could stifle consumer demand for non-essential items such as household blenders.

Figures 4.14 and 4.15 summarize the SWOT analysis for Jarden. We recommend adopting different evaluation criteria as required to suit the analysis. In the next chapter, we will investigate the Quantitative Strategic Planning Matrix (QSPM), a decision model similar to the SWOT approach, but which applies weights to emphasize certain aspects of the business.

Criterion	Category	Assessment
Strengths and Weaknesses	Leadership Finance Strategy Market Segments Positioning Operations Product Price Place Promotion Support	Strength: Seasoned CEO Medium: Robust growth, but high debt Strength: Skill in growth through M & A Strength: Good alignment Strength: Strong understanding Strength: Growth in manufacturing Medium: Mixed product reviews Medium: Some price premium Strength: Worldwide distribution Medium: No social media Strength: Responsive support

Figure 4.14: SWOT Analysis Summary for Jarden Corporation: Strengths and Weaknesses

Criterion	Category	Assessment
Opportunities and Threats	Opportunities	Short Term Opportunities: -Develop social media campaigns -Cross-promote with spirits Long Term Opportunities -Diversification into adjacent areas -Regional operations
	Threats	Short Term Threats: -New competitor -New legislation Long Term Threats: -Prolonged recession -Increased fuel costs

Figure 4.15: SWOT Analysis Summary for Jarden Corporation: Opportunities and Threats

In SWOT analyses for highly competitive markets, we may wish to identify the **core competencies** enjoyed by each of the principal competitors. We consider a competency to be elevated to a core competency when it becomes central to the company's strategy, competitiveness, and profitability. To aid in the identification of competitors' core competencies, we introduce a framework that evaluates core competencies from an organizational function perspective.

In the organizational function approach, marketers can systematically consider the functions within their competitors' organizations, and specifically identify the area of core competency. Any of the functions are candidates for the core competencies of the organization.

Figure 4.16 displays the functions found in typical organizations. In the figure, we interpret the "operations" function as relevant for both product-related and service-related organizations. For product related organizations, the operations function signifies manufacturing and supply chain operations. For service related organizations, the operations function designates the management of service execution processes and facilities. We review each function.

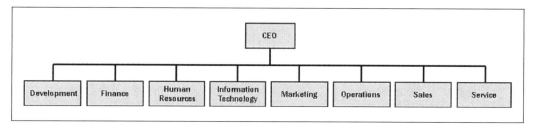

Figure 4.16: Core Competency Identification: Typical Organizational Functions

Development: Typical core competencies associated with development include the ability to innovate new products and services, technological expertise, the company's speed of development, and the company's accuracy of development. For example, social gaming developer Zynga (zynga.com) created a fast development organization to create new versions daily, to keep its demanding market satisfied.

Finance: Finance department core competencies include ongoing tasks, such as managing cash flow, assets, and debt, as well as occasional tasks, such as merger and acquisition support. For example, search giant Google (google.com) leverages its considerable company assets, such as its enormous cash reserves, to support its ongoing strategy through mergers and acquisitions.

Human Resources: Human resource departments strive to fulfill the organization's needs for hiring, developing, and supporting employees. For example, technology and finance company General Electric (ge.com) has built a reputation for recruiting and developing outstanding managerial talent.

Information Technology: Information technology (IT) department core competencies include the ability to apply information assets within the organization toward more intelligent solutions to business problems. For example, financial services provider Allstate (allstate.com) leverages information technology tools for risk management of its insurance policies.

Marketing: Core competencies within the marketing function include the ability to understand what customers need, and then provide products and services that meet that need. For example, consumer electronic company Apple (apple.com) specializes in delighting its customers with elegant product designs and sophisticated promotions.

Operations: Core competencies for the operations function in manufacturing-related organizations include areas such as quality, speed, consistency, and customization capabilities. For service-oriented organizations, these same areas are also vital. For example, fast food franchise McDonald's (mcdonalds.com) painstakingly develops and enforces operational guidelines to ensure consistency of its products throughout its worldwide network.

Sales: Sales department core competencies include the ability to understand buyers' wants and connect them with the appropriate product or service. Competencies also include sales operations skills, such as customer order processing, retail management and merchandising. For example, industrial supply distributor Grainger (grainger.com) provides consulting to assist its business customers in the selection of Grainger's 900,000 products.

Service: Customer service core competencies include the ability to add value to the purchase experience before, during, and after the sale. Leading companies leverage customer service to deliver a positive customer experience that sets their organizations apart. For example, department store retailer Nordstrom (nordstrom.com) delivers on its stellar reputation for helpful and friendly customer service.

Figure 4.17 shows a table summarizing core competencies based on organizational functions.

Function	Description	Example
Development	Innovating new products and services	**Zynga:** Engages demanding online audience by creating new software version every day
Finance	Manages financial assets toward security and growth of the organization	**Google:** Leverages its considerable company assets to grow the company
Human Resources	Recruiting and developing top talent	**General Electric:** Grooms impressive management talent
Information Technology	Applying technology to business problems	**Allstate Financial:** Leverages IT for risk management of life insurance
Marketing	Satisfying customer needs	**Apple:** Meets and exceeds customer needs
Operations	Converts labor and materials into goods and services	**McDonald's:** Develops and enforces operations guidelines to ensure consistent taste
Sales	Aids the buyer in finding the correct product or service to purchase	**Grainger:** Provides consulting to business users on the application of its 900,000 products
Service	Adding value to the purchase experience before, during, and after the sale	**Nordstrom:** Delivers on its reputation for helpful and friendly customer service

Figure 4.17: Core Competency Identification by Organizational Function

Returning to the SWOT analysis for the Jarden Corporation in the household blender example, we note that its 2011 Annual Report cites its core competency as the "ability to successfully integrate acquisitions into our operating platform and culture." This statement suggests core competencies in the finance department (skills in mergers and acquisitions) and operations (skills in operating multiple lines of business). [4-51]

MARKETING MADE MEASURABLE

Zynga: Mafia Wars 2 Sleeping with the Fishes? Zynga (zynga.com) developed its core competency around development speed to address the fickle nature of the $14.2 billion social gaming market. While the market size is huge, most players' tolerance for boredom is not. Social gamers demand continual excitement in their online gaming experience. Therefore, Zynga has developed its core competency around speed. It develops and releases new versions of its games daily.

But even this is not enough—users want more. Zynga's Mafia Wars 2 game (a sequel to the popular Mafia Wars game) has disappointed fans. The fans demand excitement and change, but the game does not deliver. As one gamer said, "once you hit level 50, there was nothing to do. It was literally like hitting a ceiling." [4-52]

COMPETITIVE ACTIONS

Now that we have gathered competitive information and analyzed it, we will use the results to determine defensive and offensive competitive actions. Figure 4.18 provides an overview.

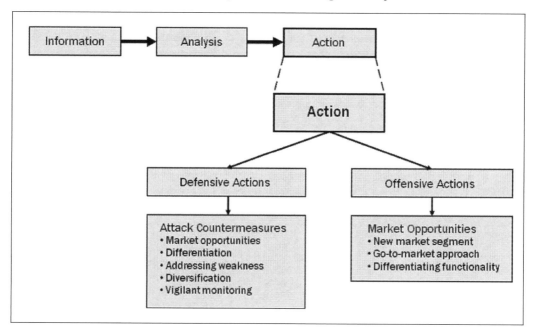

Figure 4.18: Competitive Actions

We define defensive competitive actions as those to prepare the organization for an anticipated competitive attack. Conversely, offensive competitive actions are classified as pursuing actions to take advantage of market opportunities.

Defensive Actions: Defending Against Competitor Attacks

Once intelligence has been obtained about the competitive strengths and weaknesses, one is in a better position to predict the type of attack that competitors will levy against the organizations in the industry.

Figure 4.19 shows common types of attacks between companies. The figure portrays Company 1 as the attacker and Company 2 as the defender. We will address each type of attack in turn, and discuss countermeasures against the attacks. [4-53]

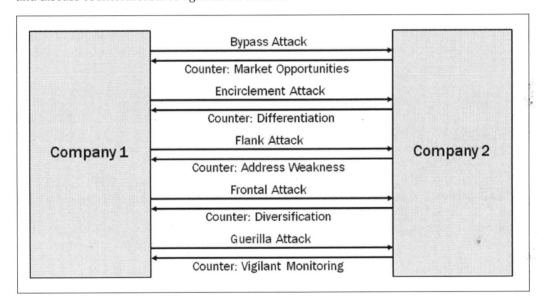

Figure 4.19: General Attack and Counter-Attack Strategies

Bypass Attack: In a bypass attack, the attacker bypasses the defender entirely and expands into new areas. The new area can be a new product. For example, Apple bypassed its arch rival Microsoft to launch Apple's iconic iPod MP3 player in 2001. The new area can also be new geographies. For example, Starbucks aggressively expanded into China to stop potential competitors from investing there. [4-54, 4-55]

To counter the threat of bypass attacks, companies must identify and pursue market opportunities on an ongoing basis. By pursuing market opportunities, companies can head off competitor actions to do the same thing. We cover market opportunities in the next section of this chapter.

MARKETING MADE MEASURABLE

Nintendo: Bypassing its Rival: Nintendo (nintendo.com) employed a bypass attack when it introduced its Wii video game console. Before the Wii, competition had been centered on advanced graphics capabilities. The competitors, Microsoft X-Box and Sony Playstation, had impressive graphics. Rather than competing head-on by developing yet more advanced graphics, Nintendo leapfrogged Sony by introducing its Wii console with new motion-sensing technology. The interactive play environment proved extremely popular, and attracted a whole new category of casual gamers. [4-56]

Encirclement Attack: Also called a Blitz attack, this strategy focuses on overwhelming the enemy (the competitor) with vastly superior resources.

To counter an encirclement attack, the defender must show how its products and services are different from those of the attacker. For example, credit unions were largely unharmed during Bank of America's encirclement attack described in the brief case study below because consumers saw them as fundamentally different from traditional banks.

MARKETING MADE MEASURABLE

Bank of America: Blitzing other Banks: Bank of America (bankofamerica.com) employed an encirclement attack to maintain its market leader position in the California banking market by emphasizing its impressive resources—over 17,000 ATMs (automated teller machines). Customers understood that the vast number of ATMs meant that they could access their accounts from virtually anywhere in the state and beyond. The approach also gave Bank of America the opportunity to further leverage its ATM investment by charging ATM access fees for non-customers. [4-57]

Flank Attack: In a flank attack, one combatant attacks the sides of another. In the case of business, targeting the "sides" refers to attacking a perceived weakness of another.

To counter a flank attack, companies must fix any areas of the business that could be perceived as weak by competitors. Alternatively, companies can show how they bring new capabilities to the market that the attacker cannot offer.

MARKETING MADE MEASURABLE

Cisco: Attacking HP's Flanks with Blades: Cisco Systems (cisco.com) is an acknowledged leader in computer networking hardware, such as routers and switches. As part of Cisco's growth strategy, it planned to enter the data center server market with a new blade server chassis code-named California. Blade servers, which perform web hosting and other critical activities, represent a multi-billion dollar market. Blade servers are a traditional product line at Cisco's competitor, Hewlett Packard (HP). To avoid losing market share to Cisco in its blade server line, HP could execute a flank attack against Cisco by exploiting Cisco's relative inexperience with servers. [4-58]

Frontal Attack: In a frontal attack, one company attacks the strength of another. Frontal attacks incur great risk and require tremendous resources and dedication to win.

The defender has multiple countermeasures at their disposal. The most common approach is to invade the attacker's territory. For example, United Parcel Service (UPS; at ups.com) attacked Federal Express's (FedEx, at fedex.com) airborne package delivery operations by promoting its Next-Day air service. FedEx counterattacked by investing in its ground delivery system, a traditional strength of UPS. [4-59]

The second counterattack approach is diversification, where the defender prepares for future frontal attacks by diversifying or broadening its market into new areas and establishing multiple centers for offense and defense. For example, BP (British Petroleum) employed a diversification strategy when it switched its focus from being a petroleum company to an energy company. It did so by adding alternative energy sources. As part of its broadening to include alternative energies, BP announced a new $500 million energy research program for farm-based Bioenergy production. [4-60]

The third countermeasure is contraction, where the defending company eliminates operating units which do not contribute to its core operations, making it easier to focus its resources on the processes that matter most. For example, Sara Lee (saralee.com) spun off its Hanes hosiery line, as well as other popular products, to fortify its famous food brands. [4-61]

MARKETING MADE MEASURABLE

Microsoft: Bing Searches for a Lead: Microsoft (microsoft.com) engaged in a frontal attack against Google by developing its new Bing search engine to rival Google's search engine.

Bing was launched in June 2009 with a marketing blitz that reportedly cost Microsoft $80 million. Bing gathered 8.4% of the search share in its first week of operation, but lost momentum once the novelty factor wore off.

Thanks to additional spending by Microsoft, Bing's market share increased to 15% by 2012, still dwarfed by its rival Google at over 66%. [4-62, 4-63]

Guerrilla Attack: Guerrilla attacks are random attacks, often against multiple competitors at different times. For example, posting negative blog entries against major firms could be considered a guerrilla attack. This type of attack is frequently employed by smaller firms, which do not have the resources to wage encirclement and frontal attacks.

To counter guerrilla attacks from competitors, companies must maintain vigilant monitoring of competitive actions. Stay up on posts in forums. Use social media aggregator tools to check for guerrilla attacks.

Figure 4.20 summarizes the different types of competitive attacks. It also shows which core competencies lend themselves to each type of attack.

For example, encirclement and frontal attacks require tremendous amounts of resources. Therefore, marketers should be wary when they notice competitors build up their cash reserves. It may very well be a war chest.

Bypass and flank attacks require development and marketing skills, because those skills are needed to enter the company into new areas. Other areas, such as finance and sales, could also be involved to facilitate rapid expansion into the new areas.

Guerrilla attacks are the hardest to predict due to their random nature. The best indicator for these attacks is to monitor the hiring of new executives. When competitors hire executives with a track record of executing guerrilla attacks, a new wave of such attacks is not far behind.

Attack Type	Description	Indicators: Core Competencies
Bypass Attack	Bypass defender and expand into new areas	Development Finance Marketing Sales
Encirclement Attack	Use of overwhelming force to beat competitors	Finance Operations
Flank Attack	Attack "sides" (weak areas) of competitors	Development Marketing
Frontal Attack	Attacks strengths of competitors	Finance Sales
Guerrilla Attack	Random attacks against competitors	HR

Figure 4.20: Core Competencies Indicating Different Types of Competitive Attacks

Offensive Actions: Pursuing Market Opportunities

Growth-minded companies must pursue offensive actions to drive revenue, in addition to warding off attacks using defensive actions.

Here, offensive actions consist of pursuing market opportunities. We consider market opportunities in three categories: new market segments, new go to market approaches, and differentiating functionality. [4-64]

New Market Segments: This strategy consists of identifying and pursuing market segments not currently being pursued by the company or its competitors. To identify such market segments, use the segmentation models and perceptual maps discussed in Chapter 3. To pursue the segments, companies must assess if they have the core competencies required to succeed in the new endeavor.

MARKETING MADE MEASURABLE

Skoda and the Czech Republic: Turning to New Markets: The Czech Republic exports its products, including Skoda automobiles, primarily to the European Union (EU). In 2011, exports to the 27-nation EU made up 83.8% of all shipments. The dependency on the EU worries Czech deputy trade minister Martin Tiapa, who believes slowdowns in the EU market will harm the Czech economy.

Therefore, he and other government officials have embarked on a strategy to discover new markets for Czech goods. According to Tiapa, "We're looking for opportunities in Asia, India, China, Russia, and also the Latin America." As a result of the new strategy, its sales to China increased 15.4%, and sales to Russia rose 22.7%. [4-65]

Go To Market Approaches: Here, the term "go to market" designates the method in which companies deliver their products and services. One problem with mass marketing (marketing goods and services to large markets) is that consumers perceive many products and services from different companies to be virtually identical. They perceive few, if any, differences to convince them to select one brand over the other. Indeed, we saw in Chapter 3's consumer blender perceptual map that respondents perceived many blenders as similar, clustering most models into the same quadrant.

We can choose from several different types of go to market approaches.

- **Bundling**: We can include a product or service as part of a package. For example, General Motors (gm.com) automobile dealers can add the GM Protection Plan extended warranty as part of the sale of its vehicles to form a bundle, offering piece of mind for new car buyers.

- **Distribution channels**: We can offer a product or service in different types of distribution channels, such as retail stores, online, or through a channel partner, such as a specialist in a particular industry. For example, Nike sells its athletic shoes through outlet stores (for cost-sensitive buyers), through department stores (for convenience-oriented buyers), and specialty stores (for performance-oriented buyers).

- **Interval ownership**: Instead of making consumers pay for the entire purchase up front, we can offer partial or interval ownership such as timeshare condominiums. For example, airline service provider NetJets (netjets.com) offers fractional ownership of business jets.

- **Leasing**: We can make it easier for consumers to trade up to nicer cars through leasing, and provide options to purchase the car outright at the end if they want to keep it. For example, Ford Credit (credit.ford.com) offers leasing plans on new Ford vehicles.

- **Prepaid Plans**: We can offer consumers the choice to pay up front for services instead of billing them at the end of the month. For example, cell phone service provider Virgin Mobile (virginmobile.com) specializes in prepaid plans.

- **Rental**: We can offer consumers the choice of renting products instead of purchasing them. For example, fashion-conscious consumers can rent haute couture clothing through Rent the Runway (renttherunway.com).

Figure 4.21 summarizes the different types of go to market approaches. Companies can apply different go to market approaches for different markets, as shown in the example below.

Go To Market Approach	Description	Examples
Bundling	Including product or service as part of a package	**GM**: Offers GM Protection Plan, which dealers can bundle with new car sales
Distribution Channels	Offer product or service through multiple distribution channels	**Nike**: Sells its shoes in outlet malls, department stores, and specialty stores
Interval Ownership	Own portion of product or service	**NetJets**: Offers fractional ownership in business jets
Leasing	Payment terms over time	**Ford Credit**: Offers leasing plans on new Ford vehicles
Prepaid Plans	Pay for services before using them	**Virgin Mobile**: Specializes in prepaid cell phone service plans
Rental	Pay for products and services only when used	**Rent the Runway**: Rents haute couture clothing for special occasions

Figure 4.21: Go To Market Approaches

MARKETING MADE MEASURABLE

Lenovo: Different Go To Market Approaches for Different Markets: Computer maker Lenovo (lenovo.com) goes to market with different distribution channels to target different market segments.

For performance-minded customers, Lenovo includes configuration ability on its website. The configuration ability allows those customers to build their machines to their exact specifications, similar to the capabilities of dell.com.

For cost-conscious shoppers, Lenovo sells popular configurations of their machines on general ecommerce sites, such as Amazon.com. The prices on those sites tend to be a bit lower than those on lenovo.com.

For convenience-oriented consumers, Lenovo sells their lower-end models at consumer retail stores, such as Best Buy. Thus, consumers can simply walk into the store, check out the machine, and walk out with a brand new computer. [4-66]

Differentiating Functionality: To drive growth and make their products and services more distinctive, companies can develop differentiating functionality. Done correctly, customers might prefer the company's brand over others because of a new "must-have" feature. But more often than not, this pursuit of new features results in the unfortunate condition of "feature bloat." In feature bloat, products become so laden with extra features (often of dubious utility) that they become a burden to use. Companies must engage market research studies when developing new functionality to ensure that the market finds planned new features relevant.

Differentiating functionality is not the sole province of products. Services can benefit as well, as the next example shows.

MARKETING MADE MEASURABLE

Westin: Exploring the Westin Difference: Hotel chain Westin (westin.com) introduced several new features into its services to differentiate its hotels from the others. In fact, the company's website includes a section called, "The Westin Difference," where it discusses what makes its hotel services unique. For example, the chain describes its "mood enhancing" lobbies, scented with "vivid Jane Packer botanicals, the scent of White Tea...[and the] atmospheric lighting."

The Westin Difference also includes its Westin Heavenly Beds, with "layers of down, 250-count sheets, five plush pillows and our exclusive pillow-top mattress." The chain even describes its differentiating restaurant menu on its site, with its "SuperFoodsRx" offerings, "designed by experts in food synergy to keep you on top of your game." [4-67]

SUMMARY

Competitive analysis is defined as the gathering and interpretation of competitive information, with the objective of establishing marketing strategies and tactics to make use of that information.

Competitive analysis affords organizations many benefits, such as the ability to identify new entrants into the market, the ability to forecast competitor actions, and time for corrective action.

We reviewed a three step approach to competitive analysis in the chapter. The three steps are gathering information, analyzing it, and then acting on the results.

We can gather information using several different sources, such as the websites of competitors, financial and industry analyst reports, business and trade publications, web traffic sources, and social media. Online competitive analysis tools such as Alexa and Compete can be effective in finding website characteristics of competitors.

Having gathered relevant competitive information, our next step is to analyze it. We start by narrowing down the list of competitors to the most relevant ones, called principal competitors. We narrow down the list by considering the time horizon when they will pose a threat, by assessing their stage in their product/service life cycle, and by evaluating the rate of technological change on the category of interest.

Next, we apply several models to analyze the data. The first is the PESTLE market analysis to discover the impact of political, economic, social, technological, legal, and environmental trends on the market. The second model is Porter's Five Forces analysis, which studies the impact of the threat of new entrants, the intensity of rivalry, pressure from substitute products, the bargaining power of buyers, and the bargaining power of suppliers, on the market. The third is the study of perceptual maps to gauge consumer perception toward the different competitors. The fourth model is a SWOT analysis to assess the strengths, weaknesses, opportunities, and threats of each competitor.

Once we have analyzed the data, we apply the results to determine defensive and offensive competitive actions. Defensive competitive actions are classified as those to prepare the organization for an anticipated competitive attack. Offensive competitive actions are classified as pursuing actions to take advantage of market opportunities.

Competitive attacks come in different types, such as bypass attacks, encirclement attacks, flank attacks, frontal attacks, and guerilla attacks. For each attack, we can identify a counterattack plan to defend against the attacker.

Market opportunities come in three types—new market segments (such as geographic expansion), new go to market approaches (such as renting products to consumers instead of selling them outright), and differentiating functionality to set the brand apart from others.

Terminology

Bypass Attack: Competitive attack where the attacker bypasses the defender entirely and expands into new areas

Competitive Analysis: Gathering and interpreting competitive information with the objective of establishing marketing strategies and tactics to make use of that information

Direct Competitors: Companies offering similar products and services to the same market

Encirclement Attack: Also called a Blitz attack, this type of competitive attack focuses on overwhelming the enemy (the competitor) with vastly superior resources

Flank Attack: Competitive attack where the attacker targets perceived weaknesses of another company

Frontal Attack: Competitive attack where the attacker targets the perceived strengths of another company

Guerrilla Attack: Competitive attack where the attacker strikes competing companies randomly

Indirect Competitors: Competitors with a product or service different than the company's offering, but fulfilling the same function

Principal Competitors: Organizations posing the most serious threat to the company

SWOT Analysis: Studying the strengths and weaknesses of an organization to assess the internal environment, and the opportunities and threats to gauge its external environment

Class Discussion

1. How is the Internet changing the competitive information gathering process?
2. What advantages would superior competitive analysis provide your existing organization?
3. What are your favorite sources of competitive information?
4. Which companies are your organization's principal competitors?
5. What core competencies do your organization's principal competitors enjoy?
6. What type of competitive attacks (if any) has your organization endured? How did it react?

Practice Problems

1. Conduct a competitive information gathering project for your organization. Apply the latest online competitive analysis tools in the search, such as Alexa, Compete, and social media intelligence gathering applications.
2. Prepare a PESTLE market analysis, Porter Five Forces Analysis, and Perceptual Map for your organization, if you have not already done so for Chapter 2 and 3.
3. Perform a SWOT analysis for your own organization and at least two of your principal competitors.
4. Identify the core competencies of your own organization and at least two of your principal competitors.
5. Predict the types of attacks you can expect from your principal competitors, given the types of core competencies they possess.

Chapter 5.
BUSINESS STRATEGY

Chapter Outline
We cover the following marketing analytics topics in this chapter:

- ☑ **Strategic Scenarios:** Identifying strategic options from which to select
- ☑ **Strategic Decision Models:** Selecting the most effective strategic option
- ☑ **Strategic Metrics:** Evaluating performance based on key performance indicators

"However beautiful the strategy, you should occasionally look at the results."
– Sir Winston Churchill

Sir Winston Churchill, English statesman and prime minister, focused on military strategy during World War I. The strategic advantage of defenders in the trench warfare used in that war thwarted England's efforts to gain ground on the Western Front, the war's primary battleground. Because a direct attack on the Western Front would not be effective, he weakened the enemy by attacking on multiple distant fronts, where the enemy was more vulnerable. He combined the approach with a focus of fusing alliances with the Axis powers to gain the additional resources required by this strategy. [5-1]

This chapter introduces an analytics-based approach to organizational strategy decisions. Figure 5.1 shows an overview of the process.

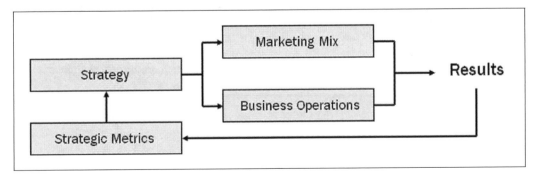

Figure 5.1: Analytics Approach to Strategy

We start by identifying the strategy to use, based on the strategic scenario facing the company. For example, the company might be facing a strategic scenario of deciding how to enter a new market (or even whether to enter it at all!). We then select a strategy to implement, based on the strategic scenario and other factors. In this chapter, we show how to use decision models to perform this selection.

We implement the strategy using the marketing mix and business operations. The marketing mix is often referred to as the 4Ps and is the set of product, price, place (distribution), and promotion approaches to execute the strategy. We cover analytics for the marketing mix in chapters seven through ten.

To support us in executing the marketing mix, we apply certain business operations, such as forecasting. We cover analytics for business operations in the next chapter.

We measure the results of our strategy using strategic metrics. We use the term "strategic metrics" here to emphasize their "big picture" nature. Based on the metrics, we adjust our marketing mix elements, business operations, and even strategy as necessary to ensure we are meeting organizational objectives. We apply the feedback from our strategic metrics to monitor the effectiveness of our strategy, and make changes if necessary.

In this chapter, we begin by reviewing three typical strategic scenarios facing many organizations. We discuss the different options available to us in those scenarios. We then review different decision models to decide on an option, based on our selection criteria. We cover strategic metrics to measure our results.

In the past, the decisions to embark on a new strategy have often been made on "gut instinct" or experience. While the gut instinct approach is fast, it frequently does not work.

MARKETING MADE MEASURABLE

Gap: Gut Instinct Could Make You Lose Your Shirt: Clothing retailer Gap (gap.com) founder Donald Fisher recalls how in the 1990s, he would simply stand in front of potential new store locations in New York City and let his gut decide if he should lease them. But that was then.

Now, "gut instinct is no longer sufficient," according to Jeffrey Roseman, principal at commercial real estate firm Newmark Knight Frank (newmarkkf.com). Since the 1990s, national and global chain stores have swarmed New York, raising rents to $1,500 per square foot. As a result, companies like the Gap now select sites only after considering reams of data, with analysis of maps detailing subway access and foot traffic, as well as profiles of incomes of nearby residents and sales figures for nearby stores.

And they certainly would not let company founders pick the location—that decision is left up to real estate consultants and executives, to prevent any emotional bias. [5-2]

STRATEGIC SCENARIOS

Organizations find themselves in situations where they must decide on specific strategies to achieve organizational objectives. We label these situations strategic scenarios. Figure 5.2 shows three sample strategic scenarios.

Figure 5.2: Sample Strategic Scenarios

The figure recognizes that most organizations must first decide if they want to enter particular markets (or if they wish to exit one of their existing markets). Once in the market, organizations must decide which approach they wish to take to succeed in the market. Do they want to lead through differentiation, through cost leadership, or through focus on a niche? Having decided on their general approach, they must then decide how they wish to grow revenue in those markets. Of course, many other strategic scenarios exist; the approach discussed in this chapter will work for those as well.

Market Entry

Figure 5.3 summarizes the market entry strategic scenario. In the market entry scenario, organizations must decide whether or not to enter a new market. Conversely, they can decide to exit an existing market they no longer find attractive.

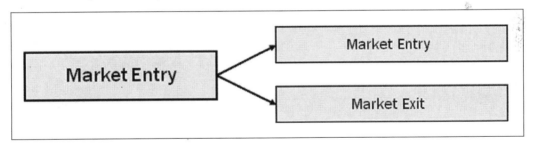

Figure 5.3: Market Entry Strategic Scenario

Market Entry Strategies: Companies enter new markets when they determine they can leverage their competitive advantages to take advantage of strong market demand.

Companies can enter markets by growing their internal processes and product/service line to accommodate the new market. This is often referred to as **organic growth**.

Alternatively, companies can enter new markets by acquiring companies already in that market. This is referred to as an **acquisition-driven growth** approach.

For example, social media company Diaspora (diaspora.com) entered the social networking market after predicting strong demand, much like its competitor Facebook.

Market Exit Strategies: Conversely, companies exit flat or shrinking markets that hold little customer demand, or those suffering from intense competition. Those conditions can cause profit margins to shrink, making a continued investment in the market unappealing.

For example, European radiation therapy company Siemens (Siemens.com) exited the radiation therapy market as it struggled with arch rival Varian Medical Systems. Varian stock jumped on the news. [5-3]

In a market entry strategic option, companies must determine the size, growth, and likely trend of their intended market. Use the methods shown in Chapter 2 to gain the market insight required to make a rational market entry choice.

In a market exit strategic option, companies must analyze their competition (as well as confirm their predictions of shrinking markets). Use the methods shown in Chapter 3 to gain the competitive understanding required to make a rational market exit decision.

Figure 5.4 summarizes the different strategic options for market entry strategy.

Strategy	Description	Example
Enter/ exit market based on demand	Market sizing models (see Chapter 2)	**Diaspora:** Entered lucrative social networking market
Enter/exit market based on competition	Competitive analysis models (see Chapter 3)	**Siemens:** Exited radiation therapy market

Figure 5.4: Strategic Options for Market Entry and Exit Decisions

---

MARKETING MADE MEASURABLE

Pfizer: Entering Insulin Market by Tapping Beer Skills: Major pharmaceutical manufacturer Pfizer (pfizer.com) entered into an agreement with drug development company Biocon (biocon.com) to supply Pfizer with four generic insulin products.

Pfizer will use the insulin to re-enter the $14 billion global insulin market after leaving it four years earlier. The deal will contribute to the global demand for insulin, forecast to expand 20% per year through 2015.

Kiran Mazumdar Shaw founded Biocon in 1978 for about $1,200. It is now Asia's biggest supplier of insulin, with a market value of about $1.35 billion. Ms. Shaw originally studied how to brew beer, where she learned the intricacies of enzymes. Now it appears that Pfizer will be tapping that knowledge to re-enter the insulin market. [5-4]

Market Approach

Figure 5.5 summarizes the generic strategy strategic scenario. After deciding to enter a market, organizations must decide on the generic approach they plan to pursue within that market.

When considering the generic approach to the market, we find it useful to adopt the generic strategy model introduced by Harvard Professor Michael Porter in his book "Competitive Advantage: Creating and Sustaining Superior Performance." In the book, Professor Porter discusses three generic strategies to suit different markets and organizational objectives: cost leadership, differentiation, and focus. [5-5]

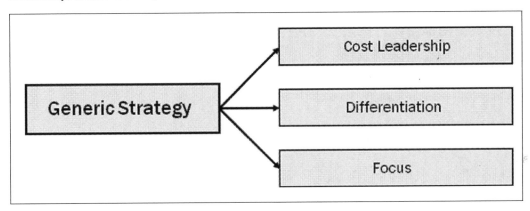

Figure 5.5: Generic Strategy Strategic Scenario

Cost Leadership: With cost leadership, the organization applies their core competencies in low-cost production (in the case of products) or low-cost service delivery (in the case of services) to maximize volume and thereby increase revenue. For example, computer product manufacturer PNY (pny.com) manufactures and sells inexpensive memory products.

In a cost leadership strategy, we evaluate the potential core competencies available to the organization that give it a competitive edge in saving costs. Porter cites advantages through economies of scale and the experience curve. Economies of scale reduce costs on a per-unit basis through the use of specialized equipment or operations designed for high volume. The experience curve describes how companies can apply their lessons-learned to reduce costs.

For example, airline carrier Southwest Airlines (southwest.com) keeps costs low by consolidating operations on only one type of aircraft, the Boeing 737. The approach reduces spare parts inventory and maintenance costs.

Differentiation: With differentiation, the organization emphasizes unique areas that make its offerings stand out from those of competitors in ways that customers value. The uniqueness translates into higher prices demanded for its products and services.

For example, consumers perceive the New York Times newspaper (newyorktimes.com) as different from other newspapers. The paper's in-depth coverage and lively writing style contribute to the perception of differentiation. As a result of the differentiation, consumers are willing to pay to access online content in a market where many newspapers allow free access.

In a differentiation strategy, organizations must seek to understand what customers value highly enough that they are willing to pay a premium for it. They must also create product development and service delivery processes so they can deliver them profitably to the market.

Focus: The focus generic strategy targets niche markets using the cost or differentiation approaches. To address cost, companies can reduce cost through specialized infrastructure. To address differentiation, companies can emphasize their unique offerings. For example, sunglass retailer Sunglass Hut (sunglasshut.com) specializes in the retail sales of sunglasses.

In a focus strategy, companies must decide in which niche they wish to specialize. Few companies find this to be a problem, because they are already active in their particular niche. In fact, the decision is likely to be closer to one of fully committing to their existing niche.

The company must then develop the required specialized equipment or processes to deliver their products and services profitably. In addition, they must promote their focus in a way that will be appreciated by their niche market.

For example, people seeking vision improvement would likely be influenced by a physician's promotion stating that she specialized only in LASIK-based vision treatments.

Figure 5.6 summarizes different strategic options for market approach decisions.

Strategy	Description	Example
Increase profitability through cost leadership	Porter generic strategy: Cost Leadership	**Southwest:** Leverages low-cost operations to keep profits high
Increase profitability through differentiation	Porter generic strategy: Differentiation	**New York Times:** Commanding premium pricing thanks to its unique writing style
Increase profitability through focus	Porter generic strategy: Focus	**Sunglass Hut:** Emphasizes specialty in sunglasses only

Figure 5.6: Strategic Options for Market Approach Decisions.

MARKETING MADE MEASURABLE

Sunglass Hut: Focus on the Eyewear Market: Specialty retailer Sunglass Hut (sunglasshut.com) concentrates exclusively on shades. Their salespeople specialize in matching the look of the sunglasses with the characteristics of the wearer. Sunglasses at the store vary from Bausch & Lomb's Killer Loops (for surfer dudes and dudettes) to Revo's modified cat's-eye style graphite sunglasses (for conservative, older gentlemen), to the Ray-Ban Clubmaster (for well-off ladies in their late 20s), to the 1960s retro-look wire rim models (for hipsters in their late teens or early 20s).

"Sunglasses are mysterious. They're sexy. It's a fun product," said Steve Lemack, Sunglass Hut regional director. [5-6]

Growth

Figure 5.7 summarizes the growth strategic scenario. Once companies have entered a market and decided on the generic approach to it, they will seek to grow the amount of revenue they gain from that market. To address the growth strategic scenario, we turn to the growth strategies laid out in H. Igor Ansoff's Harvard Business Review's paper, "Strategies for Diversification." His paper outlined four approaches to growth: market penetration, market development, product/service development, and diversification. [5-7]

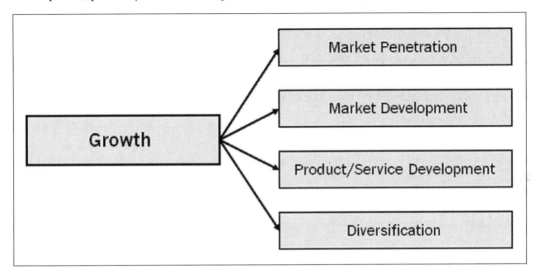

Figure 5.7: Growth Strategic Scenario

Market Penetration: In this method, organizations grow by increasing sales of existing products and services to existing customers.

For example, online travel agent Expedia (expedia.com) encourages travelers to book airline and hotel reservations together, thereby increasing referral revenue for Expedia.

To execute a market penetration strategy, three different approaches are available to marketers:

- **Targeting Competitors:** In the first market penetration approach, companies go after competitor's customers, enticing them to switch. For example, cellular phone provider T-Mobile touts its unlimited data plans to customers using AT&T cell phone plans, which offers only limited data plans.

- **Targeting Usage**: In the second approach, companies encourage customers to increase their purchase frequency. For example, T-Mobile advertises low-cost upgrades to new 4G phones to its existing customers, even though their 3G phones are still operational, and could function for several more years.

- **Targeting Revenue Per Order**: In the third approach, companies increase the size per order, often encouraging customers to purchase additional products and services through bundling. For example, T-Mobile advertises its Android Device Packages, which include a voice plan, a text plan, and an Android device for one monthly fee.

Market Development: This strategy targets growth by increasing sales of existing products and services to new markets. The new markets could be new types of customers (such as older or younger buyers) or new geographies. For example, donut franchise Dunkin' Donuts (dunkindonuts.com) expanded geographically to meet its growth objectives.

In a market development strategy, companies must assess potential new markets, and determine which make sense to pursue. Companies must decide if they can extend their brand to satisfy the demands of a new class of buyers. Alternatively, companies must decide if they have the resources to support geographic expansion, which can be expensive.

Product/Service Development: In this strategy, we target growth by marketing new products and services to existing customers.

For example, cosmetics and beauty company L'Oreal (loreal.com) markets many different types of products to its customers to maximize revenue. Some of its products include cosmetics, hair care, skin care, hair color, hair styling, and men's grooming products.

To execute a product/service development strategy, companies must decide if their brand can be extended to support the proposed new product or service. In our L'Oreal example above, the company would not shock most customers by introducing a new type of hair coloring product. But their brand would not support a radically different type of product, such as the L'Oreal Riding Lawn Mower.

Diversification: This strategy targets growth by marketing new products and services to new markets. Of the four growth strategies, diversification entails the most risk. To execute the strategy, companies must not only be successful with new products and services, they must do so in markets new to the company. Few companies have the resources to successfully execute this type of strategy.

For example, for many years, manufacturer General Electric (ge.com) pursued a diversification strategy, marketing everything from blenders for consumers, to jet turbines for aircraft builders. Even with the prowess of GE's management team, they were forced to divest several businesses to remain competitive in the remaining ones.

Execution of a diversification strategy is a combination of market development and product/service development. Companies must conduct market research to establish what types of products and services the proposed new market will accept. They must develop the processes necessary to develop the new products and services, and the infrastructure to deliver the new offerings to the new market. This is a not a market strategy for the timid or uncommitted.

Figure 5.8 summarizes different strategic options for growth decisions.

Strategy	Description	Example
Growth through market penetration	Ansoff growth strategy: Market Penetration	**Expedia:** Encourages shoppers to book airline and hotel together
Growth through market development	Ansoff growth strategy: Market Development	**Dunkin' Donuts:** Expanding geographically
Growth through product/ service development	Ansoff growth strategy: Product/ Service Development	**L'Oreal:** Markets multiple types of hair color products to customers
Growth through diversification	Ansoff growth strategy: Diversification	**GE:** Markets multiple products to multiple markets

Figure 5.8: Strategic Options for Growth Decisions

MARKETING MADE MEASURABLE

Dunkin' Donuts: International Expansion: Restaurant franchise chain Dunkin' Donuts (dunkindonuts.com) is expanding aggressively into new markets to fuel growth. In early 2012, the franchise opened its 80th store in China, increasing the total number of stores to 10,000 worldwide.

Low average revenue per outlet (ARO, the amount of money made per store) in Chinese stores concerns the chain. The low ARO threatens to slow expansion in the Chinese market. Dunkin' Donuts seeks to bring ARO up to domestic levels by catering to country-specific lifestyles. In China, it plans to shift its focus to afternoon snacks, such as savory bagels, because breakfast is not a big business there.

According to CEO Nigel Travis, the company also intends to expand in the U.S., with plans to double domestic units from over 7,000 to 15,000 in the next 20 years. [5-8]

STRATEGIC DECISION MODELS

Now that we have outlined the various strategic options available to organizations, given different strategic scenarios, we must decide which options to pursue. To accomplish this task, we turn to decision models. [5-9]

In this section, we review several different types of decision models useful for selecting among strategic option alternatives. We acknowledge that virtually any decision model discussed in this book could be applied to strategic option selection. However, we have found that the models discussed in this section are particularly relevant for decisions at the strategic level.

Specifically, we have found that most decisions on strategic alternatives fall into one of three types—those with multiple consideration criteria, those with high risk and uncertainty, and those with a mix of hard and soft data.

Figure 5.9 presents an overview of the different types of strategic decision situations.

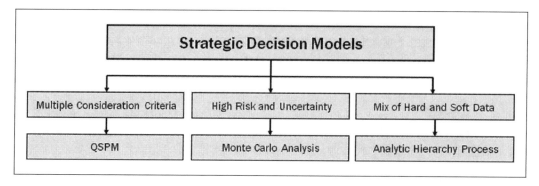

Figure 5.9: Strategic Decision Situations

We discuss each type of model, and then show how to apply them.

Multiple Consideration Criteria: Major decisions in large organizations can affect many departments, operations, products/services, and other areas.

For example, the decision to launch a new customer loyalty program to boost retention can have many organizational consequences. The decision will impact multiple departments:

- **Customer Service:** New customer tiers (levels) will need to be created, such as Silver, Gold, and Platinum. We can also address this with the analytic hierarchy process, discussed later.
- **Operations:** The company will need to deliver VIP services to top tier customers
- **Finance:** The company will need to finance the new program
- **Sales:** Different salespeople will need to be assigned to different customer tiers
- **Human Resources:** The company will need to staff the new program
- **Information Technology:** The company will need IT support for the new program

The company must also consider if it wishes to weight some factors higher than the others, to acknowledge their importance to the success of the new program. For example, the company could determine that the customer service organization will play a greater role in the new loyalty program than the IT organization.

When dealing with complex decisions with multiple weighted criteria, marketers should consider the Quantitative Strategic Planning Matrix (QSPM). We will demonstrate the application of QSPM using the Market Entry strategic scenario, because of the many factors involved in the decision to enter or exit markets.

High Risk and Uncertainty: Some decisions involve situations characterized by unusual levels of risk and uncertainty.

For example, organizational growth into new geographical areas or entirely new product/ service lines can entail significant risk and uncertainty. Because the organization has no experience with the new areas, it cannot predict the outcome with certainty.

In decision making environments involving risk and uncertainty, Monte Carlo Analysis works well. We will demonstrate the application of Monte Carlo Analysis using the Growth strategic scenario, because of the risks inherent with growth through new markets and products/services.

Mix of Hard and Soft Data: Some areas of strategy inherently combine "hard" quantitative data with "soft" subjective data.

For example, brand management includes hard numbers such as brand awareness measurement values. Brand management also includes soft subjective data such as general feelings and goals for the brand, which can be difficult to quantify.

In such a mixed environment, the decision making model of choice is the Analytical Hierarchy Process (AHP). We will demonstrate the application of the AHP using the Market Approach strategic scenario. The Market Approach scenario involves a mix of hard data (such as potential profitability) and soft data (such as alignment of organizational resources with the market).

Figure 5.10 summarizes the strategic alternative selection models and the type of strategic option selections for which they are well suited.

Model	Description	Strategic Option Applications
Quantitative Strategic Planning Matrix (QSPM)	Systematic approach for evaluating alternative strategies	Entry/ Exit
Monte Carlo Simulation	Incorporates uncertainty in forecasting future results	Growth
Analytical Hierarchy Process (AHP)	Multi-criteria decision analysis framework, combining quantitative "hard" numbers with subjective "soft" criteria	Market Approach

Figure 5.10: Decision Models to Select Among Strategic Options

We now discuss the strategic decision models, covering their applications, advantages, disadvantages, techniques to implement, and recommendations for executing within organizations.

Quantitative Strategic Planning Matrix (QSPM)

The **Quantitative Strategic Planning Matrix (QSPM)** decision model works well for situations involving many evaluation criteria. The model can assign different weights to different criteria to reflect the priorities of the decision.

For example, we might wish to evaluate three possible strategic options to entering a new market. Entering a new market is a big decision for a company, and the company would want to evaluate the impact of each option on the critical success factors of the company before moving forward. [5-10]

Applications: The Quantitative Strategic Planning Matrix decision model is recommended for strategic decisions characterized by large numbers of evaluation criteria. Several applications are particularly suited for the QSPM model.

- **Market Entry and Exit Decisions:** As indicated earlier, market entry and exit decisions can involve large investments and multiple evaluation criteria.

- **Customer-Related Decisions**: Decisions regarding customer-related strategic options, such as launching a new customer loyalty program, can also benefit from the attributes of the QSPM model. The critical nature of customers on profitability means that such decisions should consider all relevant criteria. We cannot afford to make a mistake with customers.

- **Major Organizational Changes**: Acquisitions of new companies, divestitures of failing companies, or major re-organizations can also benefit from QSPM. Such decisions are large in scope, and require consideration of many criteria.

Advantages: The QSPM decision model is suited for large organizations with many stakeholders and issues, because it incorporates many evaluation criteria. Through its many weighting factors and criteria, it can accurately reflect the diverse values of the organization. The model also provides a useful framework to prioritize strategic decisions by weighting evaluation criteria. QSPM integrates internal factors (such as department resource demands required with new strategies) with external factors (such as competition) into a single model.

Disadvantages: The QSPM decision model requires judgment in assigning criteria weights, which can make the model subjective. At times, the model's result, called the total attractiveness score, can be similar among the decision candidates, making the final decision unclear. The results of the QSPM model should be used to guide decisions, not dictate them—our recommendation for all decision models in general.

Technique: The Quantitative Strategic Planning Matrix sums weighted scores of multiple evaluation criteria to arrive at what it calls its Total Attractiveness Score.

We demonstrate the process with an example. For the example, we are considering whether to enter a new market by acquiring a competitor, or by growing organically (developing the capabilities for the new market internally). Figure 5.11 shows an overview of the technique.

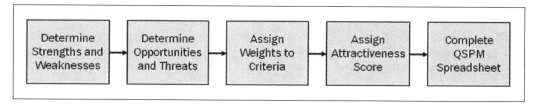

Figure 5.11: Quantitative Strategic Planning Matrix Technique

We follow the process through each step in turn, applying the familiar SWOT format (strengths, weaknesses, opportunities, and strengths) we covered in the previous chapter.

- **Determine Strengths and Weaknesses**: We start by determining the strengths and weaknesses of the different options.

  For example, the market might place a value on a wide product line (i.e., a large assortment of products available for sale). This could favor the acquisition route, if the company we plan to acquire already has a wide product line.

  An example of a weakness would be market perception of low product differentiation. This could favor the organic growth route, because we could design our new product from scratch to be highly differentiated from existing models.

- **Determine Opportunities and Threats**: Next, we examine areas of the market benefiting from our strengths, which we classify as opportunities. We also examine areas where we must manage risk, which we categorize as threats.

  For example, we could face increasing demand (an opportunity). This would favor the acquisition route, because we can develop the capabilities required to address the demand faster through acquisition than we can by growing them organically.

  An example of a threat would be increasing costs of key materials. This could favor organic growth, if our company had access to lower cost materials than the acquisition candidate.

- **Assign Weights to Criteria**: **Weights** indicate the relative importance of individual criteria. For example, we might assert that "increasing demand" is of greater importance than "industry consolidation," so we assign it a higher numeric weight. For consistency, weights must total 100% for the strengths and weaknesses section, as well as the opportunities and threats section, for both strategic alternatives. We research the market to discover the weights.

- **Assign Attractiveness Scores:** The **attractiveness score** for each criterion reflects the company's evaluation of the strategic alternative against that criterion. A one to four scale is commonly used. In the scale, enter "1" for not attractive, "2" for somewhat attractive, "3" for reasonably attractive, and "4" for highly attractive. Enter "0" if the criterion is not relevant to a particular strategic alternative. Consider removing criteria that result in many "0" scores, because they are not relevant to the decision.

- **Complete QSPM Spreadsheet:** Prepare the QSPM tool using common spreadsheet tools, such as Microsoft Excel. Assign separate columns for criteria, weights, attractiveness scores, and total attractiveness. The **total attractiveness score** is calculated by multiplying the weight of each criterion with its associated attractiveness score.

Figure 5.12 shows a simplified QSPM table to evaluate the organic growth option to market entry. Figure 5.13 shows the same table for the acquisition approach. The evaluation criteria are the same. We only show two criteria for each SWOT area, but one can easily expand the model to incorporate many criteria.

Criteria	Weight	Attractiveness Score	Total Attractiveness
Strengths			
Wide product line	15%	2	0.30
High product quality	30%	4	1.20
Weaknesses			
Low differentiation	35%	3	1.05
Operating expenses	20%	3	0.60
Weights Total	*100%*		
Opportunities			
Increasing demand	30%	4	1.20
Industry consolidation	15%	2	0.30
Threats			
Increasing costs	25%	3	0.75
New legislation	30%	2	0.60
Weights Total	*100%*		
Total Sum of Attractiveness Score			*6.00*

Figure 5.12: Quantitative Strategic Planning Matrix: Organic Growth Option

Key Factors	Weight	Attractiveness Score	Total Attractiveness
Strengths			
Wide product line	15%	3	0.45
High product quality	30%	3	0.90
Weaknesses			
Low differentiation	35%	3	1.05
Operating expenses	20%	2	0.40
Weights Total	*100%*		
Opportunities			
Increasing demand	30%	4	1.20
Industry consolidation	15%	3	0.45
Threats			
Increasing costs	25%	2	0.50
New legislation	30%	2	0.60
Weights Total	*100%*		
Total Sum of Attractiveness Score			*5.55*

Figure 5.13: Quantitative Strategic Planning Matrix: Acquisition Option

Looking at the tables, we see that the total sum of attractiveness score is greater for the organic growth option than for the acquisition option. Therefore, based on the evaluation criteria, weights, and assessments of the model, the organic growth option is the superior choice.

Execution: The QSPM method is well suited for implementation using common spreadsheet programs, such as Microsoft Excel.

Monte Carlo Simulation

In today's dynamic environment, marketers cannot count on certainty. But markets must still make decisions. Monte Carlo simulation, named after the casinos at Monte Carlo in Monaco, incorporates random elements to address uncertain and risky situations. With Monte Carlo simulation, marketers can test whether a proposed strategy will work, even if actual revenue turns out to be lower than forecasted revenue and actual costs become higher than projected costs. [5-11]

Applications: Monte Carlo simulation is recommended for strategic decisions characterized by risk and uncertainty. Several applications are particularly suited for Monte Carlo simulation.

- **Growth Decisions**: Growth through the introduction of new products/services and new markets can contain uncertain elements.

- **Market Entry/Exit**: Entry into new markets can bring uncertainty, especially if the company has little familiarity with them.

- **Product/Service Development**: Adoption of new products and services can introduce uncertainty and risk.

Advantages: Monte Carlo simulation possesses several advantages. The technique allows marketers to incorporate uncertainty in a controlled way. By introducing uncertainty in a controlled fashion, marketers can study the distribution of recorded outputs of the simulation model. By studying the outputs, marketers can identify likely scenarios. The simulation model itself is easy to change, making it possible to study different types of uncertainties.

Disadvantages: Monte Carlo simulation also has several disadvantages. The output of the simulation gives estimated answers, not exact ones. This is not surprising, given the stochastic nature of the model. In addition, the random aspect of the model results in more complexity than non-probabilistic models. Monte Carlo simulation requires certain types of functionality not found in standard spreadsheet tools, such as Microsoft Excel. Luckily, marketers can supplement Excel with relevant add-ins, such as @Risk or Crystal Ball, as we will learn in the Execution section below.

Technique: We will demonstrate the technique with an example. For the example, we are considering growth through product development. We plan to introduce a new product, the Acme X1000. To evaluate the feasibility of the decision, we estimate the first year profit for the X1000.

Profit is dependent on several factors: the number of units we sell (Unit Sales), the amount of money we charge for each unit (Unit Price), our cost to build each unit (Unit Cost), and certain costs, such as rent and depreciation, which stay constant regardless of how many units we make (Fixed Costs). Profit is thus calculated using the following formula:

$$\text{Profit} = (\text{Unit Sales}) * (\text{Unit Price} - \text{Unit Cost}) - (\text{Fixed Costs})$$

We will apply the Monte Carlo Analysis technique to determine the probabilities of success and failure for our new product. Figure 5.14 shows an overview of the technique.

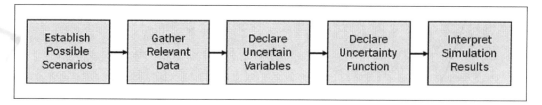

Figure 5.14: Monte Carlo Analysis Technique

We follow the process through each step in turn, starting by establishing possible scenarios.

- **Establish Possible Scenarios**: We start by establishing the possible scenarios we could face. Based on its market research, Acme forecasts equal likelihood for three scenarios:

    ○ **Weak Market**: The first scenario considers an economic recession.
    ○ **Typical Market**: The second scenario represents average conditions.
    ○ **Strong Market**: The third scenario proposes an economic boom.

- **Gather Relevant Data**: Next, we obtain data for the three scenarios around the variables identified above (Unit Sales, Unit Price, Unit Cost, Fixed Costs). Figure 5.15 shows data for our example (revised to include unit cost).

    In our case, Unit Cost is not a function of the strength of the market. But it is still uncertain because it changes due to the variability of manufacturing processes. According to Acme's manufacturing estimates, unit cost is expected to vary anywhere between $9.00 per unit and $11.00 per unit.

Variable	Weak Market	Typical Market	Strong Market
Unit Sales	40,000	50,000	60,000
Unit Price	$22.00/ unit	$20.00/ unit	$18.00/ unit
Unit Cost	$9.00 - $11.00/unit	$9.00 - $11.00/unit	$9.00 - $11.00/unit
Fixed Costs	$100,000	$100,000	$100,000

Figure 5.15: Monte Carlo Simulation: Data Table

- **Declare Uncertain Variables**: In Monte Carlo analysis, some variables are certain and some are uncertain. In our example, fixed costs will not vary, so they are certain. The Monte Carlo analysis software will ask the user to input the uncertain variables and the scenarios. For the scenarios, we tell the software of the three possibilities—weak, typical, and strong. We also input the uncertain variables—unit sales, unit price and unit cost.

    Unit price is an uncertain variable. Acme expects to sell more units during strong markets than weak ones, due to market demand. As a result, Unit Price is uncertain, because strong markets (and their resulting profits) can attract competitors, which can reduce prices. If that happens, Acme will need to reduce its Unit Price to remain competitive.

The variable Unit Cost is also uncertain. Unit cost does not vary with the strength of the market. The variability of Unit Cost is simply a reflection of uncertainties in manufacturing processes.

- **Declare Uncertainty Function**: For our example, the uncertainty function is the formula we showed earlier for profit.

- **Interpret Simulation Results**: Having entered the required information, we execute the Monte Carlo simulation. In the simulation, the software cycles through hundreds (perhaps thousands) of trials. The software incorporates probability through the use of a random number generator producing different numbers for each trial.

  Figure 5.16 shows a typical plot of the results. The plot shows potential profits and losses at different relative probabilities. For example, point A represents a situation where the new product would incur a significant loss, albeit at a relatively low likelihood of occurring. Point B shows a break-even situation. Point C designates the most likely condition (the one with the highest relative probability). At that point, we are making a healthy profit. And point D shows vigorous profit, albeit at a low probability.

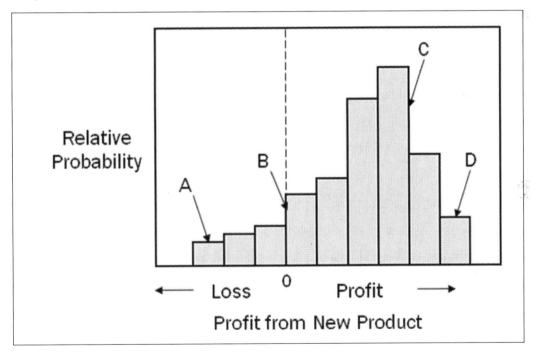

Figure 5.16: Sample Monte Carlo Analysis Output Plot

Execution: Several companies market software for Monte Carlo simulation. Examples include Palisade Corporation with its popular @RISK program (palisade.com/risk), Oracle Corporation with Crystal Ball (oracle.com), Structured Data with RiskAmp Professional (riskamp.com), and Frontline Systems (maker of the Solver function for Excel) with Risk Solver Pro (solver.com).

The more advanced software packages include specialized tools to gain additional insight. For example, Risk Solver Pro allows users to conduct sensitivity analyses on the results. Through sensitivity analysis, we can investigate ways in which we can reduce our probability of a loss, or reduce the variability of profit in general.

Analytic Hierarchy Process

The Analytical Hierarchy Process (AHP) is a multi-criteria decision analysis framework for complex decisions. Thomas Saaty introduced the Analytic Hierarchy Process in the 1970s. [5-12]

The technique provides a framework for structuring the problem, for applying evaluation criteria, for relating those elements to overall goals, and for evaluating alternative solutions. It incorporates psychological aspects within the model, allowing the model to accommodate subjective judgments. [5-13]

Applications: The analytic hierarchy process works well for decisions that involve personal judgment and subjective evaluation. Because it accommodates both quantitative and subjective data in one model, it works well for a variety of typical marketing situations.

- **Brand Decisions**: Deciding whether to extend an existing brand could involve both quantitative data (for example, incorporating measures of brand awareness) and subjective data (for example, assessing if the brand "fits" a proposed new service).

- **Generic Strategy Decisions**: Deciding whether to apply cost leadership, differentiation, or focus strategies to a market can include both hard and soft data.

- **Customer-Related Decisions**: Deciding on new customer-related initiatives, such as introducing tiered customer support. For example, we might wish to introduce Silver, Gold, and Platinum customer support levels, based on the amount of money spent on our services by customers. Such customer-related decisions can include quantitative data (such as cost savings from reduced support for lower tiers) and subjective data (such as considering the psychological effects such an initiative would create).

Advantages: Because the technique is based on both mathematics and psychology, it can incorporate both quantitative and subjective evaluation criteria.

Disadvantages: The process uses sophisticated linear algebra techniques difficult to replicate with standard spreadsheet tools such as Microsoft Excel. However, several companies offer software packages including AHP. See the Execution section below.

Technique: The Analytic Hierarchy Process interprets the selection of an alternative in a hierarchical fashion (as the name would suggest). The decision goal stands at the top of the hierarchy, because it is the most important outcome of the exercise. The decision goal is supported by the selection criteria, which in turn are supported by the decision alternatives.

AHP uses complex Eigenvectors and other linear algebra tools in its algorithm to calculate the decision goal best meeting the selection criteria for the alternatives given.

Figure 5.17 presents an overview of the technique.

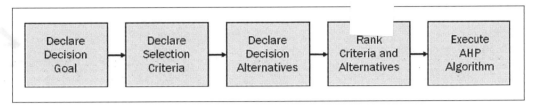

Figure 5.17: Analytic Hierarchy Process Technique

In the discussion that follows, we will demonstrate the technique by deciding on a generic strategy (cost leadership, differentiation, or focus) for a new market.

- **Declare Decision Goal**: We start by declaring our decision goal. In our case, we wish to decide on a generic strategy to apply to a new market.

- **Declare Selection Criteria**: Next, we select the criteria with which to select an alternative. To demonstrate the technique, we will select both quantitative and psychological criteria. For our quantitative criterion, we will choose the potential profitability of each alternative. For our psychological criterion, we will choose the alignment of the resources required by each alternative with those currently existing in the organization. We can express profitability in quantitative terms, but alignment requires more of a subjective measurement (hence the value of AHP).

- **Declare Decision Alternatives**: We can select from three generic strategies—cost leadership, differentiation, and focus.

- **Rank Criteria and Alternatives**: Next, we rank the criteria. For example, we could state that profitability is twice as important as alignment. We also must assign either a value (for quantitative criteria) or a rating (for psychological criteria) for each alternative and criterion. For example, we would enter the expected profitability for each alternative into the model as a numeric value. For alignment, we would rate the degree to which each alternative aligns with the company resources using an ordinal scale; say, a scale from 1 to 10.

- **Execute AHP Algorithm**: The AHP algorithm applies complex linear algebra techniques, such as the use of Eigenvectors, to determine the alternative that maximizes the user's stated criteria.

Execution: Because of the complexity in executing the AHP algorithm, we recommend using statistical software packages to execute AHP. The packages can range from large commercial packages such as SPSS (spss.com) and SAS (sas.com) to AHP templates for Microsoft Excel available from companies such as Business Performance Management Singapore (bpmsg.com).

With skillful execution, the analytical hierarchy process can be applied to a wide range of problems. For example, Northfield Information Services (northinfo.com) uses AHP for financial asset allocation, such as selecting mixes of mutual funds for people of different risk tolerances.

STRATEGIC METRICS

To monitor our marketing efforts at the strategic level, we present a number of strategic metrics in this section. The metrics help assess the market and take corrective actions as necessary. We can change tactics within the marketing mix or supporting business processes to adapt our marketing approach to changing market conditions.

In this section, we cover two sets of strategic metrics. The first set uses monetary metrics to directly measure the effectiveness of the strategic scenarios we covered earlier. The strategic scenarios include market entry/exit, market approach, and market growth.

The second set uses non-monetary metrics to measure the effectiveness of areas that support the organization at a strategic level. Such areas include brand development, customer development, and product/service development.

While we acknowledge other strategic-level metrics exist, we have found the set discussed here useful in measuring marketing performance at the strategic level. We will investigate lower level metrics for each of the marketing mix elements in chapters seven through ten.

Figures 5.18 and 5.19 provide an overview of strategic metrics for primary strategic scenarios and supporting strategic functions.

Strategic Scenario	Relevant Strategic Metrics
Market Entry/ Exit	Market size Market growth rate
Market Approach	Revenue Profit
Market Growth	Year on year growth CAGR

Figure 5.18: Strategic Metrics for Strategic Scenarios

Supporting Function	Relevant Strategic Metrics
Brand Development	Brand Awareness Brand Equity Index
Customer Development	Customer Lifetime Value Customer Profit
Product/ Service Development	Development process metrics Development innovation metrics

Figure 5.19: Strategic Metrics for Supporting Strategic Functions

Market Entry/Exit

In this section, we present two metrics relevant to the market entry/exit strategic scenario. The two metrics are market size and market growth rate.

Market Size: Marketers should routinely track overall market size over time to ensure that the size is adequate for potential profitability. For example, according to technology analyst firm TechCrunch (techcrunch.com), the global smartphone app download market could reach $15 billion by 2013. Such large markets attract investors. [5-14]

In fact, investors in new ventures, such as venture capitalists, generally look for market sizes of $1 billion (or more), according to venture capital sources. [5-15]

Venture capitalists target large market sizes for several reasons. First, market sizes near the $1 billion mark increase the chances for new companies to grow to large sizes, helping to support long-term success. By comparison, smaller companies in modest markets risk financial peril because they lack the brand awareness and economies of scale enjoyed by larger companies. In addition, larger markets offer more segments, increasing the likelihood of finding a segment that uniquely suits the company's competitive advantage.

For techniques to determine market sizes, please refer to Chapter 2.

Market Growth Rate: Just as marketers should monitor total market size over time, they should also monitor market growth rates. Marketers must maintain vigilance on market growth rates to ensure they do not find themselves in declining markets.

For example, Wang Laboratories in the 1980s failed to notice that the market for dedicated word processors was shrinking as general purpose personal computers were becoming popular. By the time they noticed, the market had already declined significantly, forcing them to reduce prices to remain competitive. Wang was unable to broaden its role in the workplace beyond word processing, and the company eventually declared bankruptcy in 1992. [5-16]

Figure 5.20 summarizes strategic metrics for market entry and exit.

Metric	Description	Example
Market Size	Calculation of potential revenue available in market	**Smartphone Apps:** Market size for apps to reach $15 billion by 2013
Market Growth Rate	Periodic evaluation of market to ensure continued growth	**Wang Laboratories:** Wang failed to notice shrinking market for word processors

Figure 5.20: Strategic Metrics: Market Entry and Exit

Market Approach

We select our approach to the market (cost leadership, differentiation, or focus) by choosing the one that will result in the highest revenue and profit. Accordingly, we show how to measure those two metrics in this section.

Revenue: Instead of calculating revenues manually, we can save time and increase accuracy by evaluating revenues using a marketing automation system. Marketing automation systems, such as those produced by Eloqua (eloqua.com), Marketo (marketo.com), and Pardot (pardot.com) feature user dashboards displaying revenue and other metrics.

For example, Marketo tracks many revenue-based metrics with its marketing dashboard. The dashboard allows users to create custom reports, plots, and charts, to suit individual needs. [5-17]

Marketing dashboards display revenue-based metrics in many different forms, allowing marketers to spot problem areas and areas of opportunity. Popular revenue-based reports include those such as the following:

- **Total Revenue**: Tracks total revenue to see how the company fares against its competitors.

- **Revenue by Business Unit**: Tracks revenue by unit to identify relative success of each.

- **Revenue by Product or Service**: Tracks revenue to discover most popular offerings.

- **Revenue by Geographic Region**: Tracks revenue by region to identify areas of high sales.

- **Revenue by Segment**: Tracks revenue by segment to determine the popularity of our products and services with our targeted segments.

Profit: In addition to revenue-based metrics, marketing automation systems also display profit-based metrics.

Typical profit-based reports include those such as the following:

- **Profits per Business Unit, Product/ Service, Region, Segment, etc.**: We can track profits in different ways to identify different trends and opportunities.

- **Profits from New Products and Services**: We can also track profits from products and services introduced in the past year to determine how quickly the new offerings are achieving profitability.

- **Profits from New Segments**: When launching products and services into new customer segments, it pays to monitor profitability in those segments. We want to ensure that the cost to service the new segments does not exceed the revenue created by those segments.

Profit is also related to contribution margin. **Contribution margin** is defined as follows: [5-18]

Contribution Margin = (Selling Price per Unit – Variable Cost per Unit) / (Selling Price per Unit)

In the formula, the variable cost per unit is the labor and materials to manufacture one additional product. The variable costs do not include fixed costs, such as rent and depreciation, which remain fixed regardless of production volume.

We can also calculate the profitability of our marketing efforts by calculating the **return on marketing investment (ROMI).** In the calculation, we apply the contribution margin. [5-19]

ROMI = [(Revenue from Marketing) * (Contribution Margin) – (Marketing Spending)]
(Marketing Spending)

In the equation, the term "Revenue from Marketing" refers to incremental revenue generated in a particular period of time as a result of marketing efforts. "Marketing Spending" refers to the amount of money spent on marketing in that period.

For example, if we spent $10,000 to market a product that generated $50,000 in <u>incremental</u> revenue and achieved a 50% contribution margin, we would calculate the following ROMI:

ROMI = [($50,000) * (0.50) - $10,000] / ($10,000) = <u>150%</u>

Figure 5.21 summarizes strategic metrics for the market approach strategic scenario.

Metric	Description	Example
Revenue	Sales of goods and services into market	**Revenue Reports:** Total revenue; Revenue by business unit; Revenue by product or service; Revenue by geographic region; Revenue by segment
Profit	Revenue of goods and services, less costs of doing business	**Profit Reports:** Profits per business unit, product/ service, region, segment, etc.; Profits from new product/service; Profits from new segments

Figure 5.21: Strategic Metrics: Market Approach

Market Growth

In this section, we present two metrics relevant to measuring growth. The two metrics are year on year growth and compound annual growth rate (CAGR).

Year on Year Growth: As marketers, we are always interested in growing the revenues of our organization. To express the growth in revenue from one year to another, we use the term **Year on Year Growth**, sometimes also called **Year over Year Growth**. For longer time periods, we use the term Compound Annual Growth Rate (CAGR); we review CAGR later in this section. We use the following formula to calculate the year on year revenue growth rate: [5-20]

Year on Year Growth = [Revenue (t) – Revenue (t-1)]
[Revenue (t-1)]

In the equation, Revenue (t) refers to the revenue at the end of the year. Revenue (t-1) refers to the revenue generated at the beginning of the year. Actually, we could replace the variable "Revenue" here with other variables, such as "Profit", to determine the year on year growth of those variables.

For example, Apple's 2011 Annual Report states that the company earned $108.2 billion in net sales in 2011, $65.2 billion in 2010, $42.9 in 2009, $37.5 in 2008, and $24.6 in 2007. We can calculate its year on year growth from 2010 to 2011 as ($108.2 - $65.2) / ($65.2) = 66%. [5-21]

Compound Annual Growth Rate: CAGR: To measure growth over multiple years, we use the term **compound annual growth rate**. Experienced marketers refer to the term in its abbreviated form (**CAGR**), pronouncing it "cager." As the name implies, compound annual growth rate reflects the compounding of interest rates over a period of time, such as those of a bank account. We use the following formula to calculate CAGR: [5-22]

$$CAGR = [(Ending\ Value\ /\ Starting\ Value)\ ^\wedge\ (1\ /\ Number\ of\ Periods)] - 1$$

In the equation, Ending Value is the value at the end of the period of consideration, and starting value is the value at the beginning. The symbol "^" is the exponent symbol, indicating that the expression (Ending Value / Starting Value) is taken to the power (1 / Number of Periods).

For example, if we start with revenues of $100,000 and grow them to $150,000 over a period of three years, we would calculate the CAGR as follows:

$$CAGR = [(\ \$150,000\ /\ \$100,000\ )\ ^\wedge\ (\ 1\ /\ 3\ )] - 1 = 14.5\%$$

In Microsoft Excel, we can use the XIRR function to calculate CAGR.

Figure 5.22 summarizes strategic metrics for market growth.

Metric	Description	Example
Year on Year Growth	Increase (or decrease) in revenue, profit, or some other measure from one year to the next	**Apple:** Year on Year Growth from 2010 to 2011 of 66%
Compound Annual Growth Rate (CAGR)	Increase (or decrease) in revenue, profit, or some other measure over a period of years, expressed as a compounded growth rate	**Microsoft Excel:** XIRR function to calculate CAGR in Excel

Figure 5.22: Strategic Metrics: Market Growth

Brand Development

We now move to the second set of strategic metrics. The second set uses non-monetary metrics to measure the effectiveness of areas that support the organization at a strategic level. We start with brand development, and then move to customer development and product/service development.

The development of an organization's brands forms a vital role in a company's strategic approach. To measure our effectiveness in brand development, we cover two strategic metrics: brand awareness and brand equity index.

Brand Awareness: Brand awareness can be measured using several dimensions: [5-23]

- **Brand Recognition**: Brand recognition is the ability to confirm prior exposure to a brand, such as recognizing a brand of breakfast cereal in a supermarket aisle after seeing an ad for it on television. For example, many consumers recognize Kellogg's brands of breakfast cereal, due to their intensive advertising efforts.

- **Brand Recall**: Brand recall is the ability to retrieve the brand out of memory, such as remembering the name of a good plumber when a pipe breaks. Brand recall is especially important for services, because of their intangible nature. For example, many consumers can recall the Roto-Rooter brand of plumbing services, due to their advertising and distinctive name.

- **Brand Depth**: The depth of brand awareness is the ease with which a brand comes to mind. For example, consumers have high brand awareness of brands such as GE, Maytag, and Whirlpool when shopping for washing machines. Such brands have high depth.

- **Brand Breadth**: The breadth of brand awareness refers to the range of usage scenarios in which the brand comes to mind. For example, many people recognize the Greyhound brand of bus transportation services, but few professionals would consider the service for a cross-country trip, preferring instead to travel by jet.

We can test brand awareness using tracking studies. Tracking studies monitor a brand's performance over time. Tracking studies consider brand awareness, brand preference, product/service usage, and brand attitudes. Research companies such as Millward Brown (millwardbrown.com) specialize in such studies.

Brand Equity Index: The **brand equity index** (BEI) measures the relative strength of brands. The index uses the following equation: [5-24]

$$\text{Brand Equity Index} = \text{Effective Market Share} * \text{Relative Price} * \text{Durability}$$

In the equation, Effective Market Share is a weighted average of the brand's market share in all segments, weighted by each segment's proportion of sales. We study the effective market share of brands because strong brands command higher market shares.

Relative Price is the ratio of the price for products and services sold under the brand's name, as compared to similar goods and services in the market. We track relative prices because strong brands can justify premium prices.

Durability is a measure of brand loyalty, and represents the percentage of a brand's customers who continue to purchase goods and services under that brand in the following year. We follow brand durability because strong brands last.

Figure 5.23 summarizes strategic metrics for brand development.

Metric	Description	Example
Brand Recognition	Ability to confirm prior exposure to brand	**Kellogg's:** Recognize names and boxes due to intense advertising
Brand Recall	Ability to retrieve brand from memory	**Roto-Rooter:** First name people remember when sink overflows
Brand Depth	Ease with which brand comes to mind	**GE:** Associated with appliances
Brand Breadth	Range of usage scenarios for brand	**Greyhound:** Limited use by professionals
Brand Equity Index	Measures relative strength of brands	**BEI:** Considers effective market share, relative price, & durability

Figure 5.23: Strategic Metrics: Brand Development

Customer Development

Customers form the lifeblood of any successful organization—without them, organizations would wither and die. To measure our effectiveness in customer development, we cover two strategic metrics: customer lifetime value and customer profit.

Customer Lifetime Value: Customer lifetime value (CLV) is defined as the total amount earned throughout the course of a customer relationship. Because the relationship could span many years, the metric incorporates the net present value of the projected cash flows from the customer relationship. Net present value is a mechanism to account for the time value of money over several years, calculating the equivalent total amount it would be worth today. [5-25]

The following equation defines customer lifetime value:

$$\text{Customer Lifetime Value} = \frac{\text{Margin} * (\text{Retention Rate})}{(1 + \text{Discount Rate} - \text{Retention Rate})}$$

In the equation, margin represents the revenue generated by the customer, less the costs to service the customer and market to them. For example, if media provider Netflix (netflix.com) earns $10 per month per customer through subscriptions, spends $3 per month per customer to deliver content to customers, and spends $1 per month per customer to promote its services, then the margin would be calculated as $10 - $3 - $1 = $6 per month, or $72 per year.

Discount rate represents the cost of capital for the organization. It is the amount an investment of equivalent risk would earn. The discount rate is generally expressed as an annual percentage interest rate.

Retention rate is the percentage of customers who remain loyal during the time period measured, generally one year.

For example, if Netflix had a $72 per year margin, a 99.5% retention rate, and a 5% discount rate, we would calculate the CLV as follows:

$$\text{Customer Lifetime Value} = (\$72) * (0.995) / (1 + 0.05 - 0.995) = \$1302.55$$

Customer Profit: Customer profit is defined as the difference between revenues earned from a customer, and the costs to service that customer, during the time period under study. [5-26]

The following equation expresses customer profit:

$$\text{Customer Profit} = \text{Customer Revenues} - \text{Customer Costs}$$

Unlike Customer Lifetime Value, which aggregates customer information to get an average value, Customer Profit recognizes that every customer is different. Some earn high revenues and demand little in the way of customer service. Such customers represent significant profit. Other customers earn relatively low revenues and have constant demands on customer service. Such customers do little for profit, and can in fact lose money for the company.

Using the notion of customer profitability, many companies have structured their customers into a profit hierarchy:

- **Tier 1 Customers**: High Revenue/ Low Cost. Tier 1 customers represent the most profitable type of customer. Such customers should be rewarded. For example, airline carrier American Airlines (aa.com) rewards its Executive Platinum AAdvantage loyalty club members (its highest level) with free flights, preferential boarding, and many other perks.

- **Tier 2 Customers**: Medium Revenue/ Medium Cost. Tier 2 customers represent the majority of customers, with average profitability. Such customers should be targeted for growth. For example, American Airlines maintains several AAdvantage loyalty club levels— from Gold, to Platinum, to Executive Platinum. The airline encourages moving up in the hierarchy by promising additional benefits with every new level.

- **Tier 3 Customers**: Low Revenue/ High Cost. Tier 3 customers can represent losses for companies. Such customers should be targeted for lower-cost service delivery. For example, customers not in American AAdvantage's Gold, Platinum, or Executive Platinum levels are limited to low-cost Internet booking services, and pay extra for basic amenities, such as early boarding privileges. If possible, companies should identify common characteristics of this type of customer so they can avoid acquiring them in the future.

Figure 5.24 summarizes strategic metrics for customer development.

Metric	Description	Example
Customer Lifetime Value (CLV)	Total customer spending over course of relationship	**Netflix:** Long-term retention rate important to customer lifetime value
Customer Profit	Customer revenues – Customer costs	**American Airlines:** AAdvantage customer loyalty program: Tier 1: Executive Platinum Tier 2: Gold, Platinum Tier 3: No loyalty status

Figure 5.24: Strategic Metrics: Customer Development

Product/Service Development

We conclude our discussion of strategic metrics with those for product and service development. We study development because products and services form an essential role in organizations. For example, many consumers associate the innovativeness of Apple's products (such as the Apple iPhone) and services (such as Apple's iCloud web services offering) as a core component of Apple as an organization.

To measure our effectiveness in product/service development, we cover two categories of product/service development metrics: development process metrics and development innovation metrics, as shown in Figure 5.25.

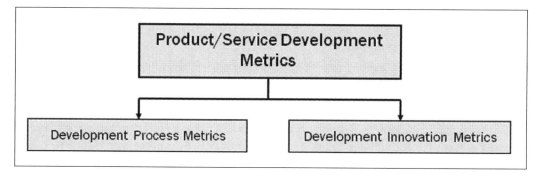

Figure 5.25: Product/Service Development Metrics Categories: Process and Innovation

Development Process Metrics Category: Many companies wish to improve their competitive advantage in product or service development. Such companies must maintain metrics measuring their development process capabilities. We present four different dimensions of metrics to measure the capabilities of the development process: customization capabilities, low cost capabilities, quality-oriented capabilities, and responsiveness capabilities.

Figure 5.26 shows an overview of the different groups of development process metrics.

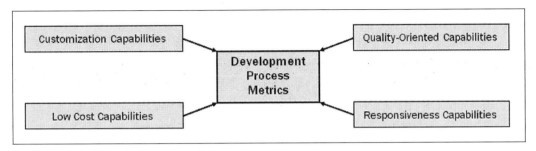

Figure 5.26: Product/Service Development Metrics: Development Process Metrics

We start by discussing **customization capabilities**, and then move on to the other development process capabilities. Companies seeking to differentiate themselves with their customization capabilities will need to measure their ability to do so. We discuss four typical types of customization capabilities, along with associated metrics.

In the first type of customization capability, organizations can incorporate **modular designs**. Modular designs employ configurable elements in the design which they can change to reflect unique customer demand. As a metric, we can track the degree of modularity in designs, such as the number of variations available per design.

For example, furniture retailer IKEA (ikea.com) specializes in modular furniture design. Its modular bookcase units allow homeowners to create wall storage to suit virtually any need. To further demonstrate its design skills, IKEA teamed up with pre-fabricated home builder ideabox (ideabox.us/models/aktiv) to create "aktiv." Aktiv is a 745 square feet pre-fabricated house based on modular design, with interior components from IKEA. The compact structure features an eco-friendly design, with fiber cement siding, energy-efficient appliances, and paint free of volatile organic compounds (VOC). Interested parties can purchase the house for about $86,500. [5-27]

In the second type of customization ability, organizations can develop **configuration systems**, which provide the ability for customers to select different configurations (specific arrangements of components) for their products, and check if the selections are compatible. As a metric, we can track the number of possible configuration options we can accommodate.

For example, Dell gives customers the ability to build their own computer configurations, and the online configuration system ensures system compatibility, such as ensuring that the amount of memory selected is adequate for the computer's processor.

In the third type of customization ability, organizations can develop **flexible manufacturing** systems. The systems allow the organizations to adapt to unique customer needs. As a metric, we can track build times for custom orders.

For example, Carvin Guitars (carvinguitars.com) maintains a custom shop, allowing customers to select fingerboards, finishes, pickups, and other features. [5-28]

In the fourth type of customization ability, organizations can develop **just in time** (JIT) inventory abilities. For products with many possible modules, companies must maintain vigilance on keeping inventory of the modules low, but prevent stocking out. Just in time (JIT) inventory systems address this need. We can measure JIT capability by tracking inventory cost and number of stock-outs.

For example, aircraft manufacturer Boeing (boeing.com) uses just in time inventory in its production of the F/A-18 military aircraft. [5-29]

Figure 5.27 summarizes strategic metrics for customization development process capabilities.

Capability	Description	Metric	Example
Modular Designs	Ability to change product attributes easily through modular design	Number of modular elements per design	**IKEA:** Modular bookcase units
Configuration Systems	Ability for customers to select different product configurations	Number of configuration options	**Dell:** Configure PC to suit consumer
Flexible Manufacturing	Ability to adapt to unique customer needs	Build times for custom orders	**Carvin Guitars:** Tailor instrument for customer
Just In Time Inventory	Ability to maintain minimum amount of inventory	Inventory cost; Number of stock-outs	**Boeing:** F/A-18 military aircraft uses JIT inventory

Figure 5.27: Development Process Metrics: Customization Capabilities

Next, we cover **low-cost capabilities** that allow us to develop low-cost products.

Companies seeking to develop low-cost products must maintain efficient development capabilities, production processes, and supply chain operations. Here, we present four metrics toward the goal of establishing low cost development capabilities.

In the first type of low cost development capability, organizations can apply **design for manufacturability** (DFM) techniques. DFM targets changes in the design of products to reduce the time and cost of manufacturing. For metrics, we can track cost savings due to DFM efforts, or related metrics, such as reduction in parts count. For example, Boeing applied DFM to the F/A-18 military aircraft, resulting in 40% fewer parts. [5-30]

The second type of low cost development capability is called **design for assembly** (DFA). Similar to DFM, DFA seeks to reduce costs through design changes. DFA targets reducing the amount of skilled labor and time required for assembly. For metrics, we can track reductions in assembly labor time and costs. For example, Boeing applied DFA techniques as part of their "lean manufacturing" initiative to reduce costs.

In the third type of low cost development capability, organizations can increase their **supply chain efficiency.** A company's supply chain consists of the movement of materials as they flow from their source to the end customer. Supply chain costs can be reduced through more efficient inventory control and trimming logistics costs, such as those for shipping. For metrics, we can track the costs of logistics and other elements of the supply chain.

For example, Motorola reorganized and consolidated its supply chain operations at its business units to reduce costs and improve customer service. [5-31]

The fourth type of low cost development capability is effective **purchasing capabilities**. We can reduce costs of incoming raw materials through the purchasing department by demanding lower prices and higher quality. We can measure purchasing capabilities by tracking amounts paid for parts and return rates of bad parts.

For example, piano manufacturer Steinway & Sons (steinway.com) purchases carefully selected woods for their soundboards and actions to ensure high quality, consistent sound. [5-32]

Figure 5.28 summarizes strategic metrics for low cost development capabilities.

Capability	Description	Metric	Example
Design for Manufacturing	Redesign products to reduce costs	Cost and parts savings due to DFM efforts	**Boeing:** Redesigned F/A-18 with 40% fewer parts
Design for Assembly	Reduce amount of skilled labor required for assembly	Cost and time savings due to DFA efforts	**Boeing:** Adopt lean manufacturing initiative
Supply Chain	Increase supply chain efficiencies	Cost of logistics and other supply chain elements	**Motorola:** Reorganized and consolidated supply chain operations
Purchasing Capabilities	Reduce costs and increase quality of incoming materials	Cost and defect rates of purchased materials	**Steinway:** Carefully selected wood for pianos

Figure 5.28: Development Process Metrics: Low Cost Development Capabilities

We now cover **quality-oriented capabilities** that promote the development of high quality products and services in organizations.

Companies with a goal of establishing development capabilities to emphasize quality (and other factors) must maintain relevant development capabilities and production processes. Here, we present four metrics toward the goal of establishing quality-oriented development capabilities.

In the first type of quality-oriented capability, organizations can benefit from **certifications and training** for their employees. We can measure training by tracking the number of relevant training programs completed per employee per year.

For example, health care provider Oneida Healthcare (oneidahealthcare.com) provides ongoing training for its surgical staff to ensure exceptional quality of care. [5-33]

The second type of quality-oriented capability is **employee involvement**. Commitment to quality must extend down to rank and file employees to be effective. We can measure employee involvement by tracking the number of times employees intervene in processes to improve quality, or the number of suggestions given by employees to improve quality.

For example, automotive manufacturer Toyota (toyota.com) encourages assembly workers to enforce high quality by stopping production lines if they spot problems.

In the third type of quality-oriented capability, organizations can implement effective **quality assurance** (QA) programs. Effective quality assurance programs ensure quality throughout the entire manufacturing or operations processes. We can measure quality assurance for products by tracking reject rates, and for services by tracking the numbers of recommendations (or complaints) generated by customers.

For example, hotel chain Four Seasons fastidiously measures customer feedback to encourage top service quality for guests.

The fourth type of quality-oriented capability is effective **personnel recruiting**. Just as low-quality materials result in low-quality finished goods, sloppy or uncommitted employees can cause quality problems. We can measure quality in our employees by tracking the percentage that earn high marks on evaluations and move up to leadership roles.

For example, diversified manufacturing company General Electric (ge.com) maintains its Experienced Leadership recruitment program to hire the best and brightest for its organization's future leaders. It monitors the personal attributes essential for quality-oriented employees. [5-34]

Figure 5.29 summarizes strategic metrics for quality-oriented development capabilities.

Capability	Description	Metric	Example
Certifications and Training	Provide certifications and training for staff to ensure high quality	Hours of training per year per employee	**Oneida Healthcare:** Ongoing training for surgical staff
Employee Involvement	Commitment to quality by everyone in organization	Hours of input by employees, or number of suggestions	**Toyota:** Encourage workers to enforce high quality
Quality Assurance	Ensure quality throughout entire manufacturing or operations process	Number of recommendations or complaints by customers	**Four Seasons:** Measures customer feedback to ensure top service quality
Personnel Recruiting	Hire high-quality individuals	Scores on personnel evaluations	**GE:** Monitors personal attributes essential for quality

Figure 5.29: Development Process Metrics: Quality-Oriented Development Capabilities

We now close the development process metrics section by discussing **responsiveness capabilities**. Companies wishing to develop core competencies around responsiveness to customer wishes must emphasize speed and attentiveness, while still maintaining quality. Here, we present four metrics toward the goal of establishing quality-oriented development capabilities.

In the first type of responsiveness capability, companies in dynamic markets can benefit by creating competencies around **speed of development**. Speed is especially important for some consumer markets, such as electronics, computer games, and fashion. We can measure speed capabilities by tracking development times.

For example, consider the Royal Wedding in Great Britain in 2011. After Kate Middleton wore her splendid Alexander McQueen dress during her wedding to Prince William, responsive clothing manufacturers quickly created copies, developing in 15 days what it took Sarah Burton of Alexander McQueen months to make. [5-35]

The second type of responsiveness capability is **attentiveness to needs**. In services, responsiveness translates to the ability to sense customer needs and deliver on them. We can measure attentiveness to needs by tracking customer recommendations and complaints.

For example, car rental agency Hertz (hertz.com) prides itself on its responsiveness to customer requests, especially those in its prestigious Gold program.

In the third type of responsiveness capability, companies can more quickly respond to unique customer needs through **specialized training and equipment**. We can measure the effectiveness of specialized training and equipment by tracking ratings and comments from discriminating customers. We can leverage social media feedback through sites such as socialmention.com.

For example, the French Culinary Institute (frenchculinary.com) provides specialized training and certifications for sommeliers aiming to work in leading restaurants. The specialized training prepares them to be responsive to the wishes of demanding patrons. [5-36]

The fourth type of responsiveness capability is the ability to gather and quickly act on **market feedback** to meet changing customer needs. We can measure our market feedback capabilities by tracking the speed with which we act on customer feedback.

For example, small businesses often follow their ratings on ratings website Yelp (yelp.com) so they can improve customer responsiveness. When customers post negative reviews in online sites, savvy businesses quickly make changes to avoid long-term consequences.

Figure 5.30 summarizes strategic metrics for development capabilities around responsiveness.

Capability	Description	Metric	Example
Speed of Development	Ability to quickly design goods and services	Development time	**Royal Wedding 2011:** Fast copies of Kate's wedding gown
Attentiveness to Needs	Ability to sense and deliver on customer desires	Number of customer recommendations and complaints	**Hertz:** Gold program for attentiveness to needs
Specialized Training and Equipment	Ensure quality throughout entire manufacturing or operations process	Ratings from discriminating customers	**French Culinary Institute:** Specialized training for sommeliers
Market Feedback	Gather and quickly act on market feedback	Comparison of actual and predicted behavior	**Yelp:** Small businesses follow ratings

Figure 5.30: Development Process Metrics: Responsiveness Development Capabilities

MARKETING MADE MEASURABLE

Red Robin: The Business of Burgers: Restaurant chain Red Robin (redrobin.com) developed an internal social network to aid in the development of its new Tavern Double hamburger line. The social network connects its managers together so the company can teach its managers the new recipes as well as the fastest ways to make them. In the past, Red Robin took six months to mail out spiral-bound books with the recipes, gather feedback from store visits, and make changes based on the feedback. The new network compresses the process to just a few days. [5-37]

Development Innovation Metrics: Companies planning to leverage core competencies around innovation must track metrics to determine how they are performing against that goal. To that end, we can measure the percentage of development projects that focus on significant innovations, as opposed to those of more modest goals. Companies typically work with five different types of development projects, as summarized in Figure 5.31.

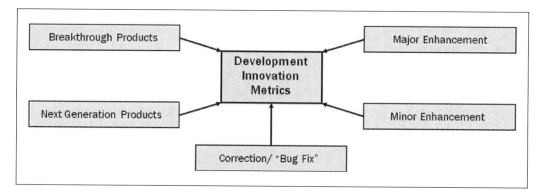

Figure 5.31: Product/Service Development Metrics: Development Innovation Metrics

We now discuss each of the different types of projects.

- **Breakthrough Products/Services**: Breakthrough projects are those that move the company in a new direction and have the potential of changing the entire industry. For example, many analysts consider the original Apple iPhone a breakthrough product.

- **Next Generation Products/Services**: Next generation products demonstrate significant advancement over existing products, but not to the extent of breakthrough products. For example, the Apple iPhone 4 was a significant advancement over the iPhone 3, with new materials, higher performance, and improved software.

- **Major Enhancement**: Projects targeting major enhancements to existing products result in big improvements, but do not represent a new generation. For example, the Apple iPhone 4S, with its introduction of the Siri personal assistant feature, would qualify as a major enhancement. It is not as significant as the leap from iPhone 3 to the iPhone 4.

- **Minor Enhancement**: Companies perform minor enhancement projects to extend products to a new class of users. For example, the Apple iPhone 3 was enhanced from 8GB of memory to 16GB of memory to satisfy the needs of some users who wished for more space for photos, songs, and videos on their phones.

- **Correction/ "Bug Fix"**: From time to time, even the savviest company makes mistakes and needs to correct them. For example, critics faulted the Apple iPhone 4's poor antenna design. Apple addressed the fault in the short term by giving away special cases that remedied the problem. Apple re-designed the antenna for the Apple iPhone 4S.

To measure a company's focus on innovation, we recommend tracking the percentage of each type of project using the metrics tracking tool shown in Figure 5.32. The percentages of all projects must equal 100%.

The tool includes sample data to demonstrate its use. As we review the data, we can see significant advancement in the company's focus on innovation from quarter 1 to quarter 2. In quarter 1, most of its projects revolve around minor enhancement and corrections. In quarter 2, it has succeeded in steering more of its resources to breakthrough, next generation, and major enhancement projects.

Innovation Categories	Quarter 1	Quarter 2	Quarter 3	Quarter 4
Breakthrough	5%	10%		
Next Generation	10%	20%		
Major Enhancement	15%	30%		
Minor Enhancement	40%	30%		
Correction/ "Bug Fix"	30%	10%		
Total	100%	100%	100%	100%

Figure 5.32: Development Innovation Metrics: Tracking Over Time

---

MARKETING MADE MEASURABLE

Apple: The Core of Innovation: A recent Forbes article hints at how Apple became such an "innovation pipeline." The article shared the story of the early relationship of Apple co-founder Steve Jobs and Intel co-founder Bob Noyce.

Mr. Noyce explained to the then-young Mr. Jobs how exponentially greater numbers of transistors would get packed into ever-smaller devices. The exponential effect would explode the capabilities of computing platforms in the future, thanks to Moore's law (named after Intel co-founder Gordon Moore).

As the story goes, that relationship started Mr. Jobs thinking about possible wild product ideas for the future. The lust for the unknown fueled Apple's drive for innovation, which still continues today. [5-38]

SUMMARY

This chapter introduced an analytics-based approach to organizational strategy decisions. In the approach, we start by selecting our strategy from several options using decision models. Next, we implement the strategy using the marketing mix and business operations. We measure the results of our strategy using strategic, "big picture" metrics.

We described three typical strategic scenarios facing many companies. The first is market entry, where we must decide if we wish to enter a new market (or exit one that no longer holds our appeal). The second is market approach, where we must decide which generic strategy we wish to pursue within that market. We have the choice of cost leadership, differentiation, or focus. The third is growth, where we must decide which growth path to take. We can sell existing products to existing markets (market penetration), sell existing products to new markets (market development), new products to existing markets (new product development), or new products to new markets (diversification).

We select different strategic decision models to suit different situations. For complex situations involving multiple consideration criteria, the quantitative strategic planning matrix (QSPM) works well. In the QSPM, we can factor in many different criteria, and weight them to show the relative importance. For situations involving an unusual level of risk and uncertainty, we turn to Monte Carlo analysis, which uses probability to introduce an element of chance in the analysis. For situations involving a mix of hard and soft data, we select the analytical hierarchy process (AHP).

To monitor and assess the effectiveness of our selected strategy, we measure our results using strategic metrics. We covered two sets of strategic metrics, one for strategic scenarios, and one for supporting functions. For strategic scenarios, we looked at metrics for market entry/exit, market approach, and market growth. For market entry/exit, we measure market size and market growth rate. For market approach, we measure revenue and profit indicators. For market growth, we examine year on year growth figures and compound annual growth rate (CAGR).

Supporting functions included brand development, customer development, and product/service development. For brand development, we track brand awareness and the brand equity index. For customer development, we measure customer lifetime value and customer profit. For product/service development, we measure metrics around our development process and our innovation capabilities.

Terminology

Acquisition-driven Growth: Growth achieved by acquiring companies in relevant markets

Analytical Hierarchy Process (AHP): Decision-assistance tool incorporating a mix of hard and soft data

Brand Breadth: Range of usage scenarios for brand

Brand Depth: Ease in which brand comes to mind

Brand Equity Index: Measurement of relative strength of brands

Brand Recall: Ability to retrieve brand from memory

Brand Recognition: Ability to confirm prior exposure to the brand

Breakthrough Products/ Services: Offerings that move company in new direction, and potentially change entire industry

Compound Annual Growth Rate: Measurement of growth over multiple years

Correction/ Bug Fix (to Products): Changes to existing products simply to address a problem or concern with product

Cost Leadership (Generic Strategy): Strategy emphasizing low-cost production

Customer Lifetime Value (CLV): Total amount earned from customer throughout their relationship with the company

Customer Profit: Difference between revenues earned by customers and costs to serve them

Differentiation (Generic Strategy): Strategy emphasizing unique benefits to customers

Diversification (Growth Strategy): Growth through selling new products and services to new markets

Focus (Generic Strategy): Strategy emphasizing niche, implemented using cost or differentiation approaches

Major Enhancements (to Products): Changes to existing products that are considerable, but do not constitute a significant enough advancement to be considered next generation

Market Development (Growth Strategy): Growth through selling existing products and services to new markets

Market Entry: Investing in new markets

Market Exit: Divesting holdings in existing markets

Market Penetration (Growth Strategy): Growth through selling existing products and services to existing markets

Minor Enhancements (to Products): Changes to existing products to target them to new classes of users

Monte Carlo Analysis: Decision-assistance tool incorporating elements of probability, for situations characterized by unusual levels of risk and uncertainty

Next Generation Products: Offerings demonstrating significant advancements over existing products

Organic Growth: Growth through internal organization processes using existing assets

Product/Service Development (Growth Strategy): Growth through selling new products and services to existing markets

Quantitative Strategic Planning Matrix (QSPM): Decision-assistance tool using multiple consideration criteria and weighting

Return on Marketing Investment (ROMI): Profitability of marketing efforts

Strategic Metrics: Metrics measuring high-level outcomes of marketing efforts

Year on Year Growth: Measurement of growth over one year

Class Discussion

1. What new markets could your organization potentially enter, given its current capabilities?
2. Which market approach (cost leadership, differentiation, or focus) does your organization currently use?
3. Which growth approach (market penetration, market development, product/service development, or diversification) does your organization currently use?
4. What criteria would your organization consider when deciding whether to enter a new market?
5. At what level does your organization measure revenue and profitability? At the product/service level, at the business group level, at the organizational level, or all of the above?
6. What brand performance metrics does your organization currently track?
7. What product/service development process metrics does your organization track?
8. What product/service development innovation metrics does your organization track?

Practice Problems

1. Prepare a Quantitative Strategic Planning Matrix (QSPM) model for entry into a new market. Ask your manager or professor about the type of evaluation criteria to use.
2. Perform a Monte Carlo analysis for a planned growth in an existing market. Create scenarios for a weak market, a typical market, and a strong market.
3. Obtain the values for revenue and profit for your organization at the product/service level and at the organizational level for the past five years.
4. Calculate the compound annual growth rate (CAGR) for revenue for the past five years.
5. Prepare a table showing the current mix of different innovation projects at your organization (breakthrough products/services, next generation products/services, major enhancements, minor enhancements, and corrections).

Chapter 6.
BUSINESS OPERATIONS

Chapter Outline

We cover the following marketing analytics topics in this chapter:

☑ **Forecasting**: Estimating future conditions
☑ **Predictive Analytics:** Predicting future events based on existing data
☑ **Data Mining**: Extracting patterns from data
☑ **Balanced Scorecard:** Establishing and tracking strategy and operations metrics
☑ **Critical Success Factors:** Defining and measuring business objectives

It's hard to make predictions, especially about the future.
- Yogi Berra

History attributes this famous quote to a variety of people, including Albert Einstein, Niels Bohr, Mark Twain, and others, but Yogi Berra usually gets the credit. After all, as a baseball manager, Berra's job relied on his ability to predict the future, in that he applied player statistics to anticipate the tactics the other team would use.

The game of baseball has a long tradition of applying statistics as part of its business "operations." Billy Beane, the former general manager of the Oakland Athletics, became famous for his analytical approach to applying statistics for baseball "operations" in Michael Lewis's book, "Moneyball." [6-1]

We define business operations as the set of processes, tools, and techniques that enable us to execute our selected strategy through the tactics of the marketing mix. As Figure 6.1 shows, business operations support the tactics we will use to carry out the strategy we selected.

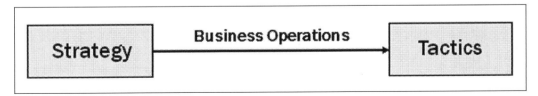

Figure 6.1: Role of Business Operations to Support Strategy and Tactics

Forecasting techniques support the implementation of our strategy through the marketing mix (product, price, place, and promotion), sales, and support functions, as shown in Figure 6.2.

- **Product**: Companies apply forecasting to tell them how many units to manufacture.

- **Price**: Organizations exercise forecasting to predict the break-even point for a given price.

- **Place (Distribution):** In order to specify the type of distribution channel to use, we need to anticipate the volume of goods we expect to sell, and for that we need forecasting.

- **Promotion**: Companies apply forecasting for promotion, so they can select relevant media. For example, we would select direct marketing media for low volume products and mass marketing media for high volume products.

- **Sales**: Organizations forecast future sales so they can track actual sales with expected sales.

- **Support**: Companies need forecasting information so they can staff support centers with sufficient personnel to manage the expected number of customers.

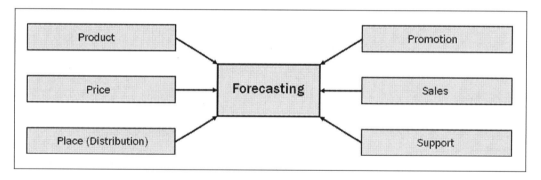

Figure 6.2: Applications for Forecasting

We cover the following business operations in this chapter:

- **Forecasting**: Tools and techniques to estimate future conditions

- **Predictive Analytics**: Tools and techniques to predict future events, based on existing data

- **Data Mining**: Tools and techniques to extract and identify patterns in data

- **Balanced Scorecard**: Approach to establishing and tracking strategy and operations metrics

- **Critical Success Factors**: Establishing competencies to ensure business success

MARKETING MADE MEASURABLE

Fiserv: Pricing Prediction of Housing Market: Financial services technology company Fiserv (fiserv.com) applies analytical techniques to forecast housing prices. Fiserv analyzes data from the Fiserv Case Shiller home price index and the Federal Housing Finance Agency to arrive at its estimates.

According to Fiserv's website, the Fiserv Case Shiller home price index measures the average change in home prices in various geographic markets. The U.S. government created the Federal Housing Finance Agency (FHFA, at fhfa.gov) in 2008 as part of the Housing and Economic Recovery Act of 2008. The FHFA monitors the country's secondary mortgage markets: Fannie Mae, Freddie Mac, and the Federal Home Loan Banks.

Fiserv tracks data from 384 housing markets to predict future home prices. Using the data, Fiserv predicted in 2012 that nationwide home prices would dip another 1% between March 2012 and March 2013, before rebounding in late spring 2013. [6-2]

FORECASTING

Sales forecasts predict the volume of products and services expected to be sold by a given organization for a given time period, generally one year. Sales forecasts are different from market sizing. Sales forecasts estimate sales for a given organization, whereas market sizing estimates sales for all organizations serving the needs of a market.

In this section, we will cover several different forecasting methods. As Figure 6.3 shows, we categorize them into four types.

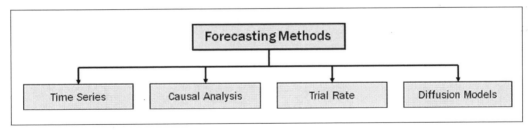

Figure 6.3: Forecasting Methods

- **Time Series:** The first type is **time series**, which studies sales history to date to extrapolate future sales.

- **Causal Analysis:** The second type is **causal analysis**, which examines underlying causes to calculate future conditions, given certain inputs.

- **Trial Rate:** The third is **trial rate**, which uses market surveys of initial trials of new products and services to predict future market share.

- **Diffusion Models:** The fourth type is **diffusion models**, which predict adoption rates of new products and services by comparing their characteristics to previous products and services.

We will cover each type of forecasting method in this chapter. We start by discussing the situations under which to apply each method.

Forecasting Method Selection

Different kinds of market and company situations call for different forecasting methods. We consider several criteria when deciding which forecasting method to use. As Figure 6.4 shows, we must consider accuracy, data availability, the time horizon, the life cycle stage, and resource availability when selecting our method. We will discuss each factor.

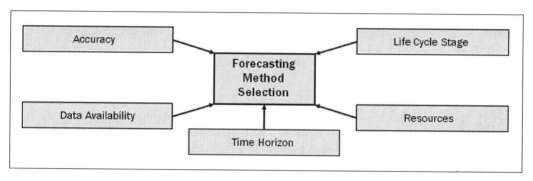

Figure 6.4: Forecasting Method Selection Factors

Degree of Accuracy: The first criterion to apply when deciding on which forecasting method to use is the degree of accuracy required. For example, the causal analysis approach lends a fairly high degree of accuracy to its estimates, because it examines the underlying causes driving sales trends (but requires significant time and money to execute).

Availability of Data: The second criterion is the availability of data. Causal analysis methods require significant amounts of historical data because the methods consider the impact of multiple factors. Diffusion models do not require a sales history to predict future sales.

Time Horizon: The third criterion is the time horizon for the sales forecast. For example, the validity of forecasts based on time series models erodes when extended time periods, such as multiple years. Causal analysis methods work better for long time horizons because the root causes it leverages are less likely to change over time. Nevertheless, all forecasting methods lose accuracy over long time periods.

Life Cycle Stage: The fourth criterion is the position of the products or services in their life cycle. For example, diffusion models can work well for the introduction and early growth life cycle stages because they forecast adoption rates based on the adoption rates of past products and services with similar characteristics. By contrast, time series methods are best suited for the maturity stages in the product/ service life cycle, when sales trends are more stable.

Resources: The fifth criterion is the availability of time and money resources. For example, trial rate methods to predict market share for new products and services can lend higher accuracy than diffusion model methods. However, trial rate methods cost more (due to the cost of market surveys) and take longer (due to the time to conduct the surveys and analyze the results). Similarly, causal analysis methods can hold greater accuracy than time series methods, but require a much greater time to gather, analyze, and interpret the data.

Figure 6.5 summarizes recommended usage for the different types of forecasting methods.

Forecasting Method	Description	Usage
Time Series	Leverage known sales history to extrapolate future sales	Best for rapid predictions of short-term future sales, where accuracy is not an issue
Causal Analysis	Examines underlying causes to predict future conditions	Best for in-depth analyses of sales, where time and cost are not issues. Require much data.
Trial Rate	Uses market surveys of initial trials to predict future market share	Best for introduction phase of product/ service life cycle, where cost is not an issue
Diffusion Models	Uses proxy to predict new product/ service adoption rate	Best for introduction phase of product/ service life cycle, when no sales data is available

Figure 6.5: Forecasting Method Usage Recommendations

Time Series Forecasting Method

We start our treatment of forecasting methods with one of the most popular approaches, **time series forecasting**. At its essence, the time series approach determines the underlying trend over time, and continues that trend to predict future conditions. Marketers frequently use the time series approach to predict sales volumes expected for their organization for the coming year (or quarter), based on sales data for the past few years.

Advantages: The time series approach has several advantages. As we will see in the example that follows, the process is quick and easy. The only data required is a record of sales volume over time, which is some of the easiest data to gather. It is also intuitive, because many people inherently understand that sales levels are likely to follow whatever trend they have been tracking over the past.

The technique is useful as a "sanity check" to confirm the accuracy of more sophisticated forecasting methods. If the results of other methods differ too strongly from that of the simple time series method, one must find out why. In fact, we recommend always conducting a time series-based forecast as part of the forecasting process, if only to provide checks and balances.

Some proponents say its biggest advantage lies in its ability to capture all of the underlying market drivers and forces. Whatever happened in the past, we know with certainty how sales behaved, because we are using the actual sales data.

Similarity to Technical Analysis for Stocks: In a way, the time series approach holds similarities to "technical analysts" in stock market investing. Technical analysts follow the movement of prices of stocks. They analyze the movement of stock prices over time to understand the trends, and then use that knowledge to predict the stock's next moves.

Figure 6.6 shows a typical graph used by a technical analyst stock trader, with stock price on the vertical axis and time on the horizontal axis. The vertical bars show the stock price movement during one day. The upper and lower limit lines show the band within which the stock moves in the short term. The slopes of the limit lines show the trend during that time period.

Figure 6.6: Technical Analysts Stock Market Investing as Analogy for Time Series Forecasting

Disadvantages: The time series approach holds several disadvantages. Dynamic market forces can cause trends to change. Therefore, we cannot state with certainty that trends affecting the sales volume will continue forever. Economic recessions, competitor actions, and even fickle customers can cause once-mighty sales figures to plunge, often quickly. The time series approach would not predict the plunges, because the approach assumes that trends continue unabated. Of course, the longer we extrapolate the trend, the more we increase the chance of error over time.

One less drastic disadvantage is the presence of **noise** in the raw sales data. Noise consists of short-term fluctuations in data that do not have material importance to the data. Noise can distract analysts from important underlying trends. This disadvantage is easily overcome by filtering the data. Analysts refer to the term **smoothing** to mean filtering the data to reduce the impact of noise. Common spreadsheet tools such as Microsoft Excel provide two powerful, easy methods to smooth the data.

The first smoothing process commonly available in spreadsheet tools is called **moving averages**. The process averages out the data over a number of periods. The process moves along the entire data set selected, hence the term "moving averages." Most marketers use three periods as a balance between sufficient filtering (which favors many periods) and the avoidance of losing important short-term data (which favors fewer periods). Analysts refer to the term **3PMA** to designate **3-Period Moving Average**.

The second smoothing process is called exponential smoothing. **Exponential smoothing** works similarly to moving averages in that it also filters out noise. Exponential smoothing works differently in that it applies an exponential equation instead of a simple averaging function. The equation weights recent data over older data. The emphasis on recent data is considered an advantage of the process, because recent data are more likely to be relevant to future conditions than data from the past.

Example: We demonstrate the time series forecasting approach with a simple example. We are given the sales history for the past seven periods, and are asked to forecast sales for the eighth period. Figure 6.7 shows the sales history data. The figure includes a blank space for Period 8, awaiting the results of our forecasting efforts.

Period 1	Period 2	Period 3	Period 4	Period 5	Period 6	Period 7	Period 8
110	110	120	130	120	130	140	

Figure 6.7: Sales History for Time Series Forecast Example

To come up with the sales value for the eighth period, we will use linear regression to draw a straight trend line through the sales data to date, and then extend the line to determine the sales in Period 8. Here is the equation for the straight line we wish to draw:

$$Sales = (Intercept) + (Slope) * (Time, in Periods)$$

We start the time series forecasting process by entering the sales history data into a spreadsheet tool such as Microsoft Excel. Use one column for the period information (such as Period 1, Period 2, Period 3, etc.) and the adjacent column for the corresponding data (such as 110, 110, 120, etc.). We use the data to plot out the sales history. We recommend plotting out the sales history to visually assess the information. Figure 6.8 shows the plot.

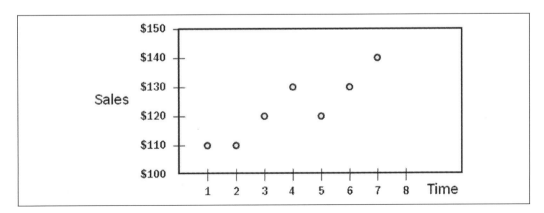

Figure 6.8: Sales History Plot, Showing Sales Results to Date

To execute the time series forecast, we will use the regression analysis function built into Microsoft Excel. We follow the same procedure as we did for regression analysis in chapter 3. In this case, we enter the sales data range (110, 100, 120, etc.) in the Excel regression dialog box asking for the Input Y Range. Select the periods (1, 2, 3, etc.) for the Input X range.

Excel will return a Summary Output table, showing regression statistics, ANOVA (analysis of variance) information and data on the regression coefficients. Figure 6.9 shows excerpts from the table we will use to calculate our sales forecast.

Output	Description	Value in Our Sales Example
R-Square	Goodness of fit of model (line) to data	0.81
Intercept	Point where line crosses Y (Sales) axis	104.3
Slope	Coefficient for time variable	4.64

Figure 6.9 Microsoft Excel Summary Output Table Excerpts

From the table, we see that our R-Square value is 0.81, which is quite good. We also learn that the Intercept is 104.3 and the slope of the resulting linear equation is 4.64. We insert the values into our equation to arrive at the result for period eight:

$$\text{Sales} = (\text{Intercept}) + (\text{Slope}) * (\text{Time, in Periods})$$
$$\text{Sales} = (104.3) + (4.64) * (8) = 141.4$$

Figure 6.10 shows the result. The figure shows the straight line Excel calculated, with a Y-Intercept of 104.3 and a slope of 4.64. It also shows the expected sales at period 8 of 141.4.

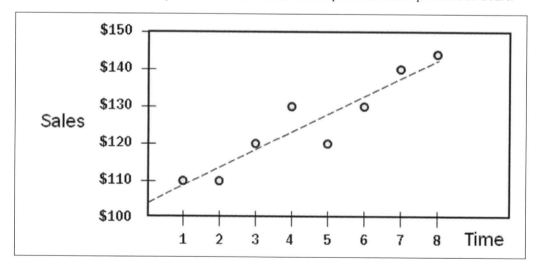

Figure 6.10: Sales History Plot, Showing Trend Line and Expected Sales in Period 8

To demonstrate the effect of smoothing data, we apply 3PMA (three-period moving averages) to the sales history to smooth our sales data. Figure 6.11 shows the result.

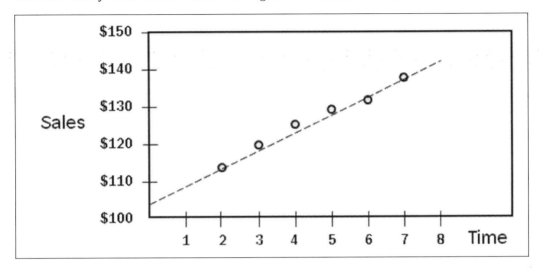

Figure 6.11: Sales History Plot, Smoothed using 3-Period Moving Averages (3PMA) Function

The smoothing process reduces the degree of short-term fluctuations, while keeping the trend intact. To calculate the values of the smoothed plot, we average the three values nearest each period. For example, to calculate the value of the smoothed plot for Period 2, we add the values for sales in periods one, two, and three (110, 110, and 120, respectively) and divide by 3 to arrive at 113. We plot the value of 113 for Period 2. We repeat the process for the remaining periods.

Microsoft Excel includes functions for moving averages and exponential smoothing in the Analysis ToolPak add-in.

Causal Analysis Forecasting Method

Earlier, we discussed how one could relate time series forecasting to technical analysis stock investing. Technical analysts concern themselves primarily with how stock prices fluctuate over time. In technical analysis, causal factors play a secondary role.

By contrast, so-called value investors carefully study crucial aspects of companies and their ability to affect the stock price. Crucial aspects include factors such as company strategy, competitive advantages, leadership capabilities of the executives, and so forth.
Value investors purchase stocks with relatively low price to earnings ratios, but strong crucial aspects, then hold the stock, waiting for its price to increase to its "intrinsic value."

Value investor champion Warren Buffett scrutinizes many aspects of companies in which he plans to invest. He believes in carefully researching companies, searching for underlying factors that could propel a company to greatness. [6-3]

With its focus on underlying factors, causal analysis shares the philosophy of value investing. Causal analysis seeks to find the underlying factors that explain behavior. Similarly, value investing seeks to find the intrinsic characteristics of companies that can cause significant stock price growth.

For example, Figure 6.12 shows the stock price of Apple (apple.com) between 2006 and 2012. We have included significant events on the chart, such as the launch of the first iPhone and iPad, as well as the death of Apple co-founder Steve Jobs. In causal analysis, we would be interested in the relationship between the string of product successes, such as the iPhone and iPad family, and the rising price of Apple stock. [6-4]

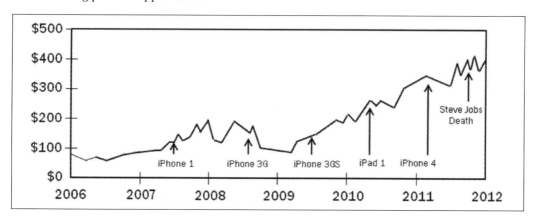

Figure 6.12: Apple Stock Price Chart, Including Significant Events

Advantages: Causal analysis features important advantages. If we can show which variables drive sales growth, we have unlocked a powerful advantage. We will know much more about how to drive sales. For example, if we can show a strong relationship between sales levels and advertising levels, we can manipulate advertising to boost sales. Causal analysis can hold greater accuracy than time series forecasting in the long run. The underlying factors driving causal analysis can last long after the trends affecting time series forecasting have dissipated.

Disadvantages: Causal analysis also holds disadvantages. As we might expect, causal analysis takes more work to execute. We need to study multiple variables and determine their effect on sales. Causal analysis also requires more data. We need data for each underlying factor we study, for as far back in time as we can get it. Often, the data is not available for some variables, forcing us to base the analysis on the variables for which data are available.

A variety of different factors can drive sales. Many factors will fall into the categories listed below, as summarized in Figure 6.13.

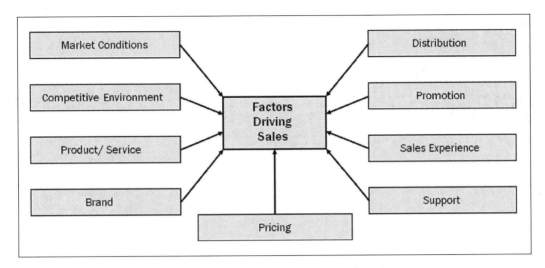

Figure 6.13: Causal Analysis Forecasting: Overview of Several Factors Driving Sales

- **Market Condition Factors**: Political, economic, and social changes within markets can affect individuals, which in turn can affect sales. For example, individuals make fewer larger purchases during recessionary periods, especially if general unemployment levels are high.

- **Competitive Environment Factors**: Competitive factors, such as significant price reductions by competitors, can affect sales levels. For example, an airline can initiate "fare wars" by introducing a deeply discounted fare on a popular route.

- **Product/ Service Factors**: Factors involving the products and services delivered by organizations can certainly affect sales. For example, Apple dramatically increased its overall sales when it introduced its revolutionary new iPhone.

- **Brand Factors**: Brand factors, such as brand awareness, can influence sales through the perception that others have on the brand. For example, automaker Audi (audi.com) spends a great deal of money associating its brand with luxury to support premium pricing.

- **Pricing Factors**: Pricing can have a dramatic effect on sales. For example, retailing giant Walmart (walmart.com) has established itself as the world's largest retailer through its emphasis on everyday low prices.

- **Distribution Factors**: The movement of goods and services through distribution channels can impact sales. For products, opening a new outlet store can boost sales in that area. For services, introducing a new channel to purchase services can increase sales, such as the expansion of H&R Block tax preparation services (hrblock.com) into a new geographic area.

- **Promotion Factors**: Advertising levels, advertising quality, social media usage, and many other promotion factors drive sales levels. For example, insurance service provider Geico (geico.com) advertises its services through a number of different promotion channels to increase insurance sales.

- **Sales Experience Factors**: The quality of the sales experience can affect sales. For example, many companies engage in sales training to increase their sales effectiveness.

- **Support Factors**: Stories of poor support told by disgruntled customers can decrease sales. For example, some consumers complain about rude customer service to many people, eroding the confidence those people associate with the brand.

MARKETING MADE MEASURABLE

Best Buy: Do Restocking Fees Cause Poor Sales? Consumer electronics retailer Best Buy (bestbuy.com) formerly charged restocking fees of 15% for many devices. Some analysts believe that the restocking fee gave Best Buy a poor reputation for customer support. Customers complained that the restocking fee made giving gifts risky. If the recipient wanted something else, the giver would be docked the restocking fee. So customers bought elsewhere, to avoid the fees.

Best Buy sales dropped in late 2010 as customers fled to Walmart, Target, Amazon.com, and other stores not charging restocking fees. As a result, Best Buy discontinued its policy of charging restocking fees. [6-5]

Figure 6.14 summarizes the different types of factors that can affect sales.

Category	Typical Variables	Examples
Market factors	Personal income; Unemployment levels; Gross domestic product; Inflation rates; Interest rates	Retail sales for virtually all types of goods and services decline during recessionary periods
Competitive factors	Competitive products; Competitive pricing; Competitive distribution	Airlines can trigger "fare wars" with deeply discounted fares
Product/ service factors	Product features; New products/services; Product history	Revolutionary new products and services can increase sales
Brand factors	Brand awareness; Brand perceptions	Audi emphasizes luxury attributes in its brand to increase sales
Pricing factors	Demand curves for pricing; Discount effects; Rebates	Walmart maintains high profitability through cost control
Distribution factors	Number of channels and stores; Locations of stores; Sizes of stores; Availability in stores	H&R Block expanding into new geographical areas to boost sales
Promotion factors	Advertising levels; Advertising quality; Advertising channels; Social media; Consumer promotions; Trade promotions	Geico advertises through integrated marketing communications program
Sales factors	Size of sales staff; Skill of sales staff; Compensation of sales staff	Companies train sales staff for greater sales effectiveness
Support factors	Number of customer complaints; Number of recommendations for brand; Quality of installation	Reports of rude customer service can reduce sales

Figure 6.14: Causal Analysis Forecasting: Categories of Factors Driving Sales

Example: We demonstrate the causal analysis forecasting approach with ▓▓▓▓ le example. Suppose we have identified two variables that affect sales strongly: mar▓▓▓▓ ▓eness and the number of retail locations. We compile a data set showing how sales rev▓▓▓▓ ary with different levels of market awareness and number of stores. Figure 6.15 shows the data set.

Period	Sales Level	Market Awareness	Number of Locations
Q1 2012	$1.0 million	80%	5
Q2 2012	$1.1 million	80%	5
Q3 2012	$1.3 million	85%	6
Q4 2012	$1.2 million	85%	6
Q1 2013	$1.3 million	85%	7
Q2 2013	$1.5 million	90%	8
Q3 2013	$1.5 million	90%	8
Q4 2013	$1.4 million	90%	8

Figure 6.15: Causal Analysis Forecasting: Example Data Set

We will use regression analysis to determine the relationship between the two causal variables (market awareness and number of locations) and sales level. The equation below defines the relationship. The coefficients act as "slopes," in that they define the level of contribution for the two causal variables. We seek to find the values for the intercept and the two coefficients.

Sales = (Intercept)   + (Coefficient 1) * (Market Awareness)
                          + (Coefficient 2) * (Number of Locations)

To find the intercept and coefficient values, we apply the regression analysis function in Microsoft Excel, as described in Chapter 3. We assign Sales Level as our dependent variable. We assign both Market Awareness and Number of Locations as the independent variables.

For our example, we select the column of data showing Sales Level for the "Input Y Range" Excel Regression input box. We select two columns of data—Market Awareness and Number of Locations—for the "Input X Range" input box.

After clicking OK, Excel returns a Summary Output table in a new sheet, showing regression statistics, ANOVA figures, and data on the regression coefficients. Figure 6.16 shows excerpts from the table we will use to calculate our sales forecast.

Output	Description	Value in Our Sales Example
R-Square	Goodness of fit of model to data	0.93
Intercept	Point where line crosses Y axis	-1.44
Coefficient 1	Coefficient for Market Awareness variable	2.86
Coefficient 2	Coefficient for Number of Locations variable	0.043

Figure 6.16 Microsoft Excel Summary Output Table Excerpts

The regression statistics show that we have an R-Square value of 0.93, which is very good. The output table shows an intercept value of -1.44, and coefficients of 2.86 and 0.043 for Market Awareness and Number of Locations, respectively. We insert the values to complete our equation:

Sales =   (Intercept) + (Coefficient 1) * (Market Awareness)
                 + (Coefficient 2) * (Number of Locations)

                 = (-1.44) + (2.86) * (Market Awareness)
                 + (0.043) * (Number of Locations)

For example, we could estimate our sales if we maintained a market awareness of 90% and expanded to 10 retail locations. We insert the values into our equation to arrive at the following result:

Sales   = (-1.44) + (2.86) * (90%)
                 + (0.043) * (10)

                 = $1.56 Million

We now move on to the next forecasting method, using trial rates to forecast demand.

Trial Rate Forecasting Method

The **trial rate forecasting method** calculates future sales based on the trial rate and repeat rate, as shown in Figure 6.17. Because the products and services are new, we cannot use past sales figures as we did in the time series and causal forecasting methods. Instead, we survey the market to determine the trial rate. We study initial sales or historical sales of similar products and services to determine the repeat rate. [6-6]

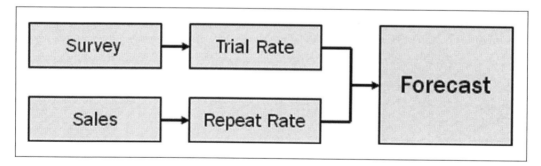

Figure 6.17: Trial Rate Forecasting Method: Overview

Terminology: To discuss the trial rate forecasting method, we need to define the terminology of trial rate, repeat rate, penetration, and projection of sales.

The **trial rate** is defined as the percentage of people who buy or use a new product or service for the first time, in a given population over a given time period. We call the current time period "t" and previous time periods "t - n" where n is the number of periods in the past. For example, the time period previous to the current one would be expressed as "t - 1." Two periods back would be expressed as "t - 2." We can express the trial rate concept in equation form:

Trial Rate = (Number of First-Time Purchasers or Users in Period t)
(Population)

Similarly, we can calculate the number of first-time purchasers or users in one period if we know the trial rate and population. We use the following formula:

Number of First-Time Purchasers or Users in Period t = (Trial Rate) * (Population)

The **repeat rate** is defined as the percentage of people who re-purchase or re-use a new product or service, compared to the number of people who purchased or used the new product or service at least once. We express the concept in the following equation:

Repeat Rate =   (Number of Repeat Purchasers or Users in Period t)   .
(Number of First-Time Purchasers or Users in Period t-1)

As marketers, we desire to know the market penetration for our product or service. The **penetration** of a new product or service is defined as the total number of people who have purchased the product or service at a given time.

Penetration at a given time is defined as the number of existing customers multiplied by the repeat rate (i.e., the number of people who continue using the product or service), added to the number of new purchasers we expect in the next period. We can express the calculations using the following equation:

Penetration in Period t = (Penetration in Period (t – 1))
* (Repeat Rate in Period t)
+ (Number of First-Time Purchasers or Users in Period t)

The **projection of sales** is defined as the penetration multiplied by the average frequency of purchase, in turn multiplied by the average units per purchase. We express projection of sales by the following equation:

Projection of Sales in Period t =   (Penetration in Period t)
* (Average Frequency of Purchase)
* (Average Units per Purchase)

Example: We will demonstrate the process using an example. Consider the fictional Acme Dog Walking service, as shown in Figure 6.18.

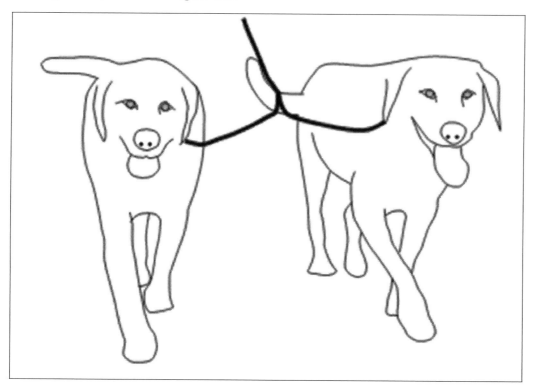

Figure 6.18: Trial Rate Forecasting Method: Acme Dog Walking Example

The service operates in a town with a population of 5,000. Acme realizes that dog owners are often too busy to groom their own dogs. Therefore, Acme introduces a new dog grooming service to supplement its existing dog walking service. Acme often has the dogs for several hours for their walks while the dog owners are at work or shopping, more than enough time to groom the dogs as well as walk them.

After a one month test period, Acme finds that 100 people have purchased their new grooming service. Using the data, we can calculate **the trial rate**:

Trial Rate =   (Number of First-Time Purchasers or Users in Period t) / (Population)

Trial Rate =   (100 first-time purchasers) / (5,000 inhabitants) = 2.0%

Acme holds a 90% **repeat rate** for its dog walking services, meaning that 90% of customers will continue to have their dogs walked by Acme in the following month. Acme believes the same repeat rate will work in their new grooming services. Acme expects to gain about 80 new purchasers of the grooming service in the next month (in addition to the 100 people who tried the service in the previous month). We can use the data to calculate the **penetration** expected in the next month:

Penetration in Period t = (Penetration in Period (t – 1))
                 * (Repeat Rate in Period t)
                 + (Number of First-Time Purchasers or Users in Period t)

Penetration in Period t = (100 customers in previous period)
                 * (90% repeat rate)
                 + (80 customers in current period)
                 = 170 customers

During the trial period, Acme determines that the average customer owns 1.5 dogs and gets their dogs groomed once per month. Therefore, for period t, where we have a penetration level of 170 customers, we can calculate expected sales as follows:

Projection of Sales in Period t =(Penetration in Period t)
                 * (Average Frequency of Purchase)
                 * (Average Units per Purchase)

Projection of Sales in Period t =(170 customers)
                 * (1 per month)
                 * (1.5 units per purchase)
                 = 255 units expected to be purchased

If we charge $50.00 for our grooming service, we can calculate the sales volume:

Sales Amount   = (Units Sold) * (Price/ Unit)
                 = 255 units * $50/ unit = $12,750

We can estimate expected total volume by calculating predicted trial volume and repeat volume.

Market Surveys: We can conduct market surveys to estimate **trial volume**. Trial volume is the total number of units we can expect to sell to the population over a given time period. Market surveys typically contain three principal sections, as shown in Figure 6.19.

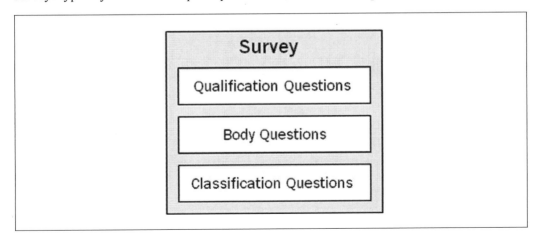

Figure 6.19: Trial Rate Forecasting Method: Market Survey Structure

The first section of the survey determines the **qualification** of respondents for the survey. In our Acme dog walking example, we could ask if the respondent has a dog that needs to be walked. If the respondent does not, then he or she is not qualified, and should not proceed with the remainder of the survey.

The second section of the survey is called the **body** of the survey, and contains the main information we wish to know, including the respondent's intention to buy.

The third section of the survey includes **classification** questions, such as demographic information, to classify the respondents into segments.

As we discussed, the body of the survey includes "intention to buy" questions, asking respondents if they intend to purchase the new product or service. Figure 6.20 shows typical answer choices for intention to buy questions.

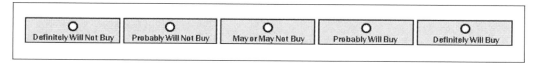

Figure 6.20: Trial Rate Forecasting Method: "Intention to Buy" Scale

Marketing research tells us that 80% of respondents who indicate "Definitely Will Buy" actually purchase the good or service in question. Only about 30% of those indicating "Probably Will Buy" do end up purchasing. [6-7]

Trial Volume: With the information from the survey, we can calculate **trial volume** by multiplying the trial population by the expected number of units per purchase:

Trial Volume = (Population) * (Units per Purchase)

In many cases, awareness and availability of new products and services might be low. For example, companies just starting out have not built up high levels of brand awareness. Also, new companies might not have access to (or afford) widespread distribution channels. In those cases, we can add factors for awareness and availability:

Trial Volume = (Population) * (Awareness) * (Availability) * (Units per Purchase)

We can shorten the expression "(Population) * (Awareness) * (Availability)" to simply **Trial Population** to designate the population we plan to target. The equation for trial volume can now be rewritten as follows:

Trial Volume = (Trial Population) * (Units per Purchase)

To incorporate the "intention to buy" findings we covered earlier, we modify the equation:

Trial Volume =   (Trial Population)
              * [(80% * Definitely Buy) + (30% * Probably Buy)]
              * (Units per Purchase)

Example: We demonstrate the process by continuing our Acme Dog Walking service example. To gather information about trial volume, Acme conducts a market survey. Acme sends out surveys to a random sample of people in the town of population 5,000.

The simple survey contains three sections. The first section includes a single qualification question. If the person receiving the survey does not own a dog and is not interested in dog grooming services, he or she is asked to not continue the survey.

The second section includes questions on usage, intention to buy, awareness, and availability.

- **Usage:** Usage questions gather information such as the number of dogs they own and their frequency of grooming.

- **Intention to Buy**: "Intention to buy" questions obtain information about the respondent's likelihood of purchasing dog grooming services from Acme.

- **Awareness**: Awareness questions ask about the respondent's awareness of the Acme brand, as compared to its competitors.

- **Availability:** Availability questions inquire into the pet stores the respondents visit, because Acme will be making its dog-related services available through national pet store chain Pet Store 1.

The third section includes classification questions. The intent of this section is to form segments to target. For example, if we learn that females between the ages of 35 to 49 years old, making $50,000 to $99,000 per year score high on the Intention to Buy scale, we will target that segment.

Figures 6.21 through 6.23 demonstrate the qualification, body, and classification sections of our Acme Dog Walking survey example.

Acme Dog Grooming Services Survey: Qualification
Do you own a dog?
___ Yes: Please proceed with the survey
___ No: Please stop the survey; Thank you for your interest

Figure 6.21: Market Survey Example: Qualification Section

```
Acme Dog Grooming Services Survey: Body
How many dogs do you own?
___ 1   ___ 2   ___ 3   ___ 4 or more

How often do you have your dogs groomed?
___ Every 4 weeks   ___ Every 8 weeks   ___ Every 12 weeks or more

How likely would you be to purchase dog grooming services from Acme?
___ Definitely will buy
___ Probably will buy
___ May or may not buy
___ Probably will not buy
___ Definitely will not buy

Of which dog grooming services are you aware?
___ Acme   ___ Groomer 2   ___ Groomer 3

Which pet store do you visit the most?
___ Store 1   ___ Store 2   ___ Store 3
```

Figure 6.22: Market Survey Example: Body Section

```
Acme Dog Grooming Services Survey: Classification
What is your gender?
___ Female   ___ Male

What is your age?
___ 0 – 17 years   ___ 18 – 34 years   ___ 35 – 49 years   ___ 50 and over

What is your annual household income?
___ 0 - $49,000   ___ $50,000 - $99,000   ___ $100,000 and over
```

Figure 6.23: Market Survey Example: Classification Section

Acme administers the survey to its target market. Figure 6.24 shows the results.

Question	Results
Number of dogs owned	1.5, on average
Frequency of dog grooming	Every 8 weeks, on average (or 0.5 purchases per month)
Likelihood to buy	Definitely will buy: 10% Probably will buy: 20%
Awareness of Acme	20%
Availability of Pet Store 1	30%

Figure 6.24: Market Survey Example: Results

Based on our survey results, we can calculate the trial volume:

Trial Volume =   (Population) * (Awareness) * (Availability)
                    * [(80% * Definitely Buy) + (30% * Probably Buy)]
                    * (Units per Purchase)

Trial Volume =   (5,000) * (20% Awareness) * (30% Availability)
                    * [(80% * 10% Definitely Buy) + (30% * 20% Probably Buy)]
                    * (1.5 units/ purchase)
                    = 63 units

As we discussed earlier, the total expected volume consists of predicted trial volume and repeat volume. Now that we have calculated the trial volume, we move on to repeat volume.

Repeat Volume: Repeat volume consists of people who try the product or service, and then like it so much they purchase it again. Companies actively encourage repeat volume through rewarding loyalty. For example, airlines offer frequent flier programs to reward continued repeat usage of their service. We can calculate repeat volume using the following formula: [6-8]

Repeat Buyers = (Trial Population) * (Repeat Rate)

To calculate the sales volume repeat buyers generate, we use the following formula:

Repeat Volume = (Repeat Buyers)
                    * (Repeat Unit Volume per Customer)
                    * (Repeat Occasions)

Substituting the equation for repeat buyers, we get the following formula:

Repeat Volume =[(Trial Population) * (Repeat Rate)]
                    * (Repeat Unit Volume per Customer)
                    * (Repeat Occasions)

Continuing our Acme dog grooming example, we formerly calculated the trial population:

Trial Population = (Population) * (Awareness) * (Availability)
                    = (5,000) * (20% Awareness) * (30% Availability)
                    = 300 people

We enter the remaining data into our equation to arrive at repeat volume:

Repeat Volume =(300 people) * (90% Repeat Rate)
                    * (1.5 units per purchase) * (0.5 purchase per month)
                    = 202.5 units per month * 12 months per year = 2,430 units/ year

Total volume consists of predicted trial volume and repeat volume, as shown in the formula below:

$$\text{Total Volume} = (\text{Trial Volume}) + (\text{Repeat Volume})$$

In our Acme dog grooming example, we assume that all trials will take place during the first year of introduction. Therefore, we calculate the expected total volume for the first year as follows:

$$
\begin{aligned}
\text{Total Volume} &= (\text{Trial Volume}) + (\text{Repeat Volume}) \\
&= (63 \text{ units}) + (2{,}430 \text{ units}) \\
&= 2{,}493 \text{ units in first year}
\end{aligned}
$$

We move now to estimating demand for discontinuous innovations using diffusion models.

Diffusion Models Forecasting Method

Sometimes, we must forecast demand for fundamental new innovations. For example, cable television programming services were revolutionary when they were introduced in the 1940s. In such cases, traditional forecasting methods such as time series, causal analysis, and trial rates will not work. The methods will not work because the sales history and the other data on which the methods rely are not available.

For fundamental new innovations, we turn to diffusion models. Diffusion models seek to explain at what rate new products and services spread through cultures. We want to know at what time people adopt new products and services. Different categories of people adopt new innovations at different rates. Everett Rogers framed innovation as a life cycle involving five distinct adopter categories. Figure 6.25 shows the categories. [6-9]

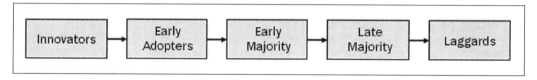

Figure 6.25: Diffusion Models: Adopter Categories

- **Innovators**: Innovators are the first people to adopt an innovation. They tend to have a high tolerance of risk, allowing them to adopt innovations which may ultimately fail.

- **Early Adopters**: Early adopters also adopt new innovations readily, but not as fast as innovators. Early adopters tend to hold a high degree of opinion leadership, fueled by their passion for new innovations.

- **Early Majority**: Early majority individuals adopt new innovations significantly more slowly than innovators and early adopters. They represent the beginning of the mass market adoption of the innovation.

- **Late Majority**: Late majority individuals hold a high degree of skepticism on new innovations. They adopt only after the majority of society has already decided to do so.
- **Laggards**: Laggards are the last segment of individuals to adopt a new innovation. They actively dislike change, and prefer instead to stick with established, traditional methods.

The research of Rogers indicated that the spread of new innovations depends on personal characteristics of two types of individuals: innovators and imitators, as shown in Figure 6.26.

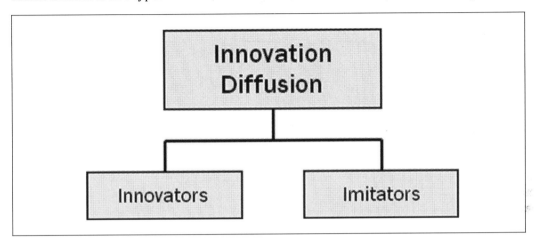

Figure 6.26: Diffusion Models: Innovators and Imitators

- **Innovators:** Innovators (individuals driven by innovation) seek new ideas and technologies, with little concern if others have adopted the new innovation.

- **Imitators:** Imitators, on the other hand, adopt new innovations primarily through the influence of other individuals. Imitators wait until others have tried the innovation first before trying it themselves. Imitators significantly outnumber innovators in society.

Characteristics of new innovations will affect the degree to which innovators and imitators drive adoption.

Diffusion Driven by Imitators: Imitators will play a larger role for innovations involving **network effects** and infrastructure investments. The network effect refers to innovations requiring networks to function properly. The usefulness of such innovations increases as more people adopt them, encouraging ever-increasing numbers of adopters.

For example, the adoption rate of cellular telephones started out slowly, because consumers would only find the phones useful if many other people had them. Once a certain number of people used them, adoption grew rapidly. The situation is similar to that in a nuclear reactor, where a minimum amount (called the critical mass) of nuclear material must be present before reaction can begin. Similarly, the high infrastructure investments required for high definition television (HDTV) meant initial slow growth for HDTV.

Adoption driven by imitators takes the form shown in Figure 6.27. The figure shows an **S-Curve**, where adoption of products and services starts out very slowly (because imitators do not adopt until others do). But once adoption starts in earnest, growth proceeds rapidly. As adoption continues, growth slows down and adoption asymptotically approaches 100% of the innovation's target market. The vast majority of adoptions follows this type of adoption profile.

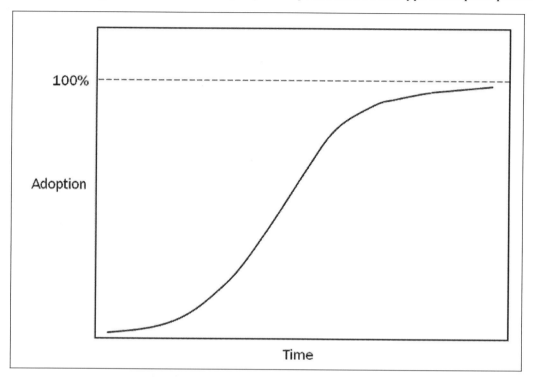

Figure 6.27: Diffusion Models: Imitator-Driven Adoption

Diffusion Driven by Innovators: Research shows that innovators play a greater role in some situations and cultures. Much of the role is based on supporting the innovators' tolerance for risk, so they are in a better position to take the risks new innovations bring. In general, the following situations and cultures tend to favor innovators over imitators: [6-10, 6-11]

- **Individualism**: According to a paper by Sundqvist, Frank, and Puumalainen, countries that value individualism, such as Anglo-Saxon cultures, tend to favor innovators compared to countries formerly based on communism, which favor collectivism.

- **Risk Taking**: Countries and cultures tolerating (or even embracing!) risk-taking show more of an impact from innovators than those emphasizing uncertainty avoidance.

- **High Per-Capita Income**: Countries and cultures with high per-capita incomes tend to show more of an impact from innovators than those with low per-capita incomes. We speculate that high per-capita countries and cultures are better prepared to absorb the risks inherent in innovation.

Adoption driven by innovation is shown in Figure 6.28. The figure shows a logarithmic curve. The curve shows adoption starting out rapidly, then decreasing its growth rate as the market saturates with the new innovation.

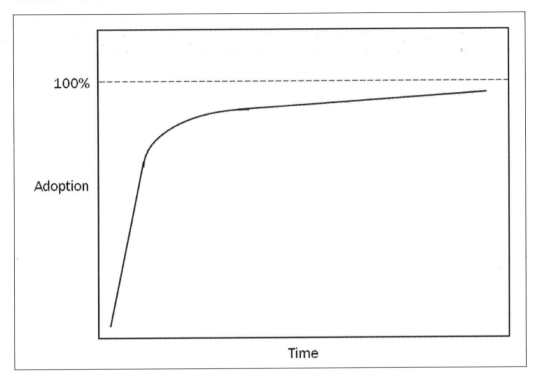

Figure 6.28: Diffusion Models: Innovator-Driven Adoption

Bass Diffusion Model: Professor Frank Bass published his model of diffusion in the 1960s. The Bass model, as it has become known, is widely used to predict adoption of new innovations. Bass studied the phenomenon of adoption and developed the Bass model principle: [6-12]

$$f(t)/[1 - F(t)] = p + q/M\ [A(t)]$$

The equation includes the following variables:

- $f(t)$: Portion of the potential market that adopts a new innovation at a certain time (t)

- $F(t)$: Portion of the potential market that has adopted the innovation at a certain time (t)

- $A(t)$: Cumulative adopters of the new innovation at a certain time (t)

- M: Potential market (the ultimate number of people likely to adopt the new innovation)

- p: Coefficient of innovation (the degree to which Innovators drive adoption)

- q: Coefficient of imitation (the degree to which Imitators drive adoption)

The equation asserts that the portion of the potential market that adopts at a certain time (t) is equal to a linear function of previous adopters. In practice, Bass model equations often use exponential functions, rather than the form discussed above, for ease in computation. Note that the equation is driven by two primary elements.

- **p: Coefficient of innovation**: Adoption by innovators is independent of the number of people who have adopted the innovation so far (i.e., the "p" component of the equation is independent of A(t), the cumulative adopters).

- **q: Coefficient of imitation**: Adoption by imitators is dependent on cumulative adopters. As more people adopt a new innovation, the more imitators will adopt it as well.

This observation confirms our previous finding that innovators and imitators behave in different ways, and that each has a role in driving adoption.

Researchers have studied past innovations and determined the extent to which innovators (p coefficient) and imitators (q coefficient) played a role in their adoption. Mathematically, we can extract p and q from adoption data by studying the growth rate of the adoption curve. As a result, marketers can obtain p and q values for many past innovations by referring to innovation diffusion marketing research papers, or simply conducting an Internet search for the term, "bass coefficients."

For example, we performed an Internet search for the term, "Bass coefficients" and found several tables of p and q coefficients for various innovations over the years. In virtually every case, the q coefficient was significantly larger than the p coefficient. Although innovators "get the ball rolling" in new product/service adoption, it is imitators who represent the "engine" of adoption for many innovations. [6-13, 6-14]

Market Situations and Bass Coefficients: Existing coefficient tables tend to group items by physical category, such as "home appliances," "business products," and "consumer products." We do not find this grouping useful, because it makes finding analogous market situations difficult. We introduce an alternative model here, where we group product/service p and q coefficients by market situation. Figure 6.29 shows an overview of these categories based on the market situation.

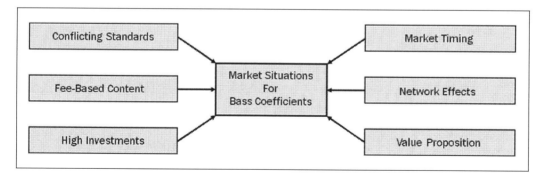

Figure 6.29: Diffusion Models: Market Situations for Bass Coefficients

We list several example products and services for each market situation category, so marketers can apply them in the "forecasting by analogy" approach we review later.

- **Conflicting Standards**: Many technical products and services rely on standardized interfaces to communicate with existing devices. The electronics industry refers to these communications interfaces as "standards" or "formats." Sometimes, several competitors introduce the same or similar products at the same time, each with its own standard. In industry parlance, this is called a "standards war" (also sometimes called a "format war").

  In standards wars, different companies advocate different technical standards, each benefiting their own company. Consumers are reluctant to purchase any device until the standards get settled (nobody wants to purchase a device that will soon be in the "wrong" standard), so adoption of all devices stalls. Adoption cannot start in earnest until the parties (or the market) can agree on the standard.

  This situation existed in the 1980s with the VHS vs. Betamax standards dispute in video cassette recorders (VCRs). It also occurred in the 1950s and 1960s with different formats for color television (NTSC vs. PAL vs. SECAM). More recently, Blu-Ray fought against the HD-DVD high definition digital versatile disc (DVD) format in the early 2000s, and won. Here are some example relevant p and q values for the Conflicting Standards market situation:

  - Color television (1954 – 1969): p = 0.00005; q = 0.6480
  - VCRs (1980 – 1987); p = 0.00637; q = 0.7501

- **Fee-based Content:** Many content providers, such as newspapers, entertainment studios, and publishers sell syndicated content to consumers for a fee. To predict adoption of innovations involving fee-based distribution of content in a network, we examine the adoption of consumer subscription to fee-based cable television programming.

  We can identify two phases in the delivery of content. The first phase is introduction. In the introductory stage of fee-based content, the content consumers are introduced to the concept of having to pay for something that was formerly free. When cable television producers introduced cable TV in the 1980s, consumers adopted slowly, and producers had to overcome significant resistance.

  The second phase is segmentation, which happens after consumers have accepted the notion of fee-based content. In the second phase, consumers have accepted the notion of paying for content. Now, they are more concerned with finding content matching their unique interests.

  For the second phase, we make the analogy of satellite television subscription in the 1990s. Producers had much greater market understanding than in the 1980s, thanks to their experience with cable TV. Producers were able to offer unique programming to match unique needs. Because of the added understanding, p-coefficient values are higher for the segmentation stage than they are in the introduction stage.

For example, satellite television provider DISH (dish.com) offers over 30 sports channels, a variety of movie channels, and more than 200 international channels, in 28 languages. [6-15]

Here are some example relevant p and q values for the Fee-based Content market situation:

- Cable television subscription (1953 – 1971); p = 0.00001; q = 0.5013
- Satellite television subscription (1994 – 1998); p = .04693; q = 0.3346

- **High Investments**: Some products and services demand significant infrastructure investment by businesses to encourage adoption. For example, the introduction of the compact disc (CD) player and its corresponding new digital music format in the 1980s required significant investments by multiple stakeholders. Music studios had to invest in digital recording equipment, music publishers had to invest in disc manufacturing equipment, radio stations had to invest in digital playback equipment, and so forth.

Stakeholders are reluctant to invest such large amounts unless they are certain of the innovation's success. Similar to the situation of network effects, the value of the innovation increases as more people adopt.

Here is an example set of relevant p and q values for the High Investment market situation:

- Compact disc (CD) players (1983 – 1996): p = 0.0017; q = 0.3991

- **Market Timing**: Sometimes, the market is just not ready to accept an admittedly great new product or service. For example, banks introduced automated teller machines (ATMs) in the early 1970s, but they took almost a decade to catch on with the public. Older consumers did not associate technology with banking, and resisted the change. Eventually, though, people came to realize the convenience and speed of ATMs (and other innovations, such as online banking) and the product eventually succeeded.

Similarly, consumers thought of blenders as commercial machines, not as household appliances, so initial adoption was slow. Products with poor market timing generally have low values for p (if they succeed at all) because many people are just not ready for them yet.

Here are some example relevant p and q values for the Market Timing market situation:

- ATM Machines (1971 – 1985): 0.00053; q = 0.4957
- Household blenders ((1955 – 1970): p = 0.00027; q = 0.4724

- **Network Effects**: As we mentioned earlier, some products and services deliver most of their value through networking across multiple individuals. The usefulness of such innovations increases as more people adopt them, encouraging ever-increasing adoption.

For example, the value of cell phones increased with the number of subscribers. Similarly, transmitting fax machines rely on receiving fax machines on the other end of the line. The value of fax machines therefore increases the more widely they are adopted. Consequently, the q coefficient (representing imitators who adopt after others adopt) will greatly outweigh the p coefficient (representing innovators who adopt without regard to others).

Here are some example relevant p and q values for the Network Effects market situation:

- Cellular phone service (1984 – 1995): p = 0.00074; q = 0.4132
- Fax machines (1987 – 1998): p = 0.0122; q = 0.2535

- **Value Propositions:** Some products and services feature clear value propositions, where consumers instantly understand the offerings deliver, and the adoption is not encumbered by network effects or other issues.

  For example, consumers rapidly adopted clothes washers when manufacturers introduced them in the 1920s. Consumers found the value proposition compelling, and sales did not depend on other washers to be sold. Sales of washers and similar appliances such as ranges and freezers soared. In cases where consumers find the innovation's value proposition clear and compelling, p values tend to be relatively large, because innovators quickly flock to the useful new devices.

  By contrast, the introduction of super audio compact discs (SACDs) in the early 2000s performed poorly in the market, because many people did not find the value to justify their super-premium prices.

  Here are some example relevant p and q values for the Value Proposition market situation:

  - Clothes washers (1922 – 1930): p = 0.03623; q = 0.234
  - Electric ranges (1925 – 1931); p = 0.04543; q = 0.4554
  - Freezers (1946 – 1954); p = 0.02359; q = 0.3578

Figure 6.30 summarizes the different market situations.

Situation	Description	Example
Conflicting Standards	Clashing technical standards/ formats for new innovations	VCRs
Fee-Based Content	Distribution of fee-based content through networks	Cable TV Satellite TV
High Investments	Financial commitment required to adopt new innovation	CD players
Market Timing	Ability of market to accept new innovation	ATM machines
Network Effects	Value increases as more people adopt	Cellular phone service Fax machines
Value Proposition	Products and services with clear, compelling value propositions	Clothes washers Electric ranges

Figure 6.30: Diffusion Models: Market Situations Summary

In the next section, we show how to apply p and q coefficients to typical marketing forecasting problems.

Process: Figure 6.31 outlines the steps to apply the model. Some refer to the application of the Bass model as **forecasting by analogy**. We explain the process below. [6-16]

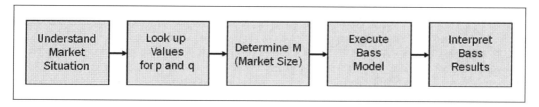

Figure 6.31: Diffusion Models: Bass Forecasting Process

- **Understand Market Situation**: Marketers must seek first to understand the characteristics of the product or service under study, and the situation in which the organization will launch them.

  For example, Acme Electronics (fictitious name) decides to introduce a new computer monitor. The new monitor delivers dazzling colors and outstanding resolution, partly because it uses a new method (called a standard or format) to communicate with the computer. The new standard clashes with existing standards. Therefore, we categorize the situation as one of "conflicting standards."

- **Look up the values of p and q**: Tables of Bass parameters (p, q, and M) of past innovations are available on the Internet. The marketer looks up the Bass parameters of the past innovation whose characteristics and situation are most analogous to the product or service being forecasted. We can access tables for p and q values for past innovations in marketing research books or simply conduct an Internet search for "Bass coefficients."

  In our Acme Electronics example, we would search for p and q coefficients for innovations embroiled in standards wars during their introduction. We decide that the bitter standards war faced by VCRs is analogous to our situation, so we apply those values to our case.

- **Determine M, the size of the potential market:** We can apply the techniques discussed in Chapter 2 to size the potential market for the new innovation. In our Acme Electronics example, we can calculate market size using a top down or a bottom up approach.

  In a top down approach, we would multiply the target "universe" population by a factor representing the portion relating to our product or service. For the target "universe", we find that Acme plans to target the United States market, which contains a population of about 300 million people. For the multiplying factor, we consider the analogous market of high-definition televisions (HDTV) to establish the percentage of people who appreciate high resolution and color quality. According to the Consumer Electronics Association (ce.org), approximately 36% of US households have HDTV sets in their homes. Multiplying the two factors, we arrive at a top-down market size of 108 million. [6-17]

  In a bottom up approach, we would identify market segments which appreciate high resolution and high quality color in monitors, and then calculate the size and purchase rate of those groups. In our example, we would identify segments which depend on high quality image reproduction such as photographers, graphic artists, web developers, video editors, filmmakers, map makers, and visual artists. We would calculate the size and purchase rate of each, and then sum up the totals to determine the bottom-up market size.

- **Execute Bass model:** Many commercial statistics packages include Bass diffusion models. For those without such packages, a quick Internet search will identify several Excel-based Bass models, many available for free download. Users simply enter the values of p, q, and M, and the program displays the adoption plot. We recommend running "best case" and "worst case" scenarios, with values of p and q increased and decreased by 20%, respectively, to gain further insight.

  In our Acme Electronics example, we conduct an Internet search for "Bass algorithm Excel." We find a Microsoft Excel spreadsheet already containing the Bass equation in it. We enter the values for p, q, and M, and the spreadsheet displays the "baseline" adoption curve, given nominal values for p and q (rounded to p = 0.0064; q = 0.75).

  We repeat the process to obtain the "best case" and "worst case" adoption curves. To obtain the "best case" curve, we increase our p and q values by 20% (to p = 0.0077 and 0.90) to reflect conditions favoring faster adoption. For example, we could face a situation where we quickly won the format wars, our product performed flawlessly, and consumers showed strong demand for the product.

  To obtain the "worst case" curve, we decrease our p and q values by 20% (to p = 0.0051 and q = 0.60) to reflect conditions threatening slow adoption. For example, we could face protracted standards war debates (as the VCR market faced in the 1980s), "bugs" in the product, and lackluster consumer demand.

  Figure 6.32 shows the adoption curves for the baseline case, the "best case," and the "worst case." We have maintained the same scales on the x and y axes for easier comparison.

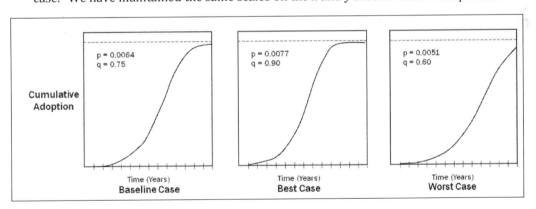

Figure 6.32: Diffusion Models: Acme Electronics Adoption Curves

- **Interpret results:** After running the model, some marketers are surprised by the length of time required for markets to adopt new innovations. Marketers can use a process called **back-casting** to identify opportunities for faster adoption. In back-casting, we "propel ourselves into the future" by examining the predicted adoption in the coming years. We then "look back to the present" to see what actions we can take right now to increase adoption rates.

In our Acme Electronics example, we interpret the results by studying the adoption graphs. The "worst case" scenario concerns us. After 13 years, the new innovation has still not reached 100% cumulative adoption. We cannot wait that long.

Using back-casting, we understand that we must take action now to prevent the "worst case" scenario from occurring in the future. Therefore, we resolve ourselves to quickly winning the standards war, building high quality into the product, and advertising heavily to boost consumer demand.

MARKETING MADE MEASURABLE

Tellabs: Forecasting Mobile Broadband: Telecom network equipment manufacturer Tellabs (tellabs.com) published a white paper forecasting the adoption of mobile broadband services. In the white paper, Tellabs investigates several different approaches to forecasting demand for such services.

Approaches include extrapolation (i.e, extending existing broadband trends), scenario planning (such as "low-cost data pipes," where unlimited cheap data plans proliferate), qualitative diffusion models (such as Geoffrey Moore's thoughts on how innovations can "cross the chasm" from early adopters to mainstream users), and quantitative diffusion models (such as the Bass diffusion model).

The paper does not offer a quantitative forecast on mobile broadband usage. Instead, it ends by quoting the late French mathematician Henri Poincare, who said, "It is far better to foresee without certainty than not to foresee at all." [6-18]

Triangulation of Forecast Results

We recommend applying multiple forecasting models to avoid dependency on any one model (and its inherent weaknesses). Triangulate the results of the models to arrive at a final number. To triangulate, calculate a weighted average of the results from the different models. For example, if we had results from three different forecasting approaches, we would calculate the final forecast using the equation below:

$$\text{Forecast} = (W1 * \text{Forecast 1}) + (W2 * \text{Forecast 2}) + (W3 * \text{Forecast 3})$$

In the equation, W1, W2, and W3 represent the weighting factors for the three different forecast results. We adjust the weights to reflect the importance of the results. For example, if we based our Forecast 1 on sound, verifiable data, but Forecast 2 incorporated many unsubstantiated estimates, we can weight Forecast 1 higher than Forecast 2.

We recommend comparing the triangulation result with the sales force estimate and a simple extrapolation of sales history (if available) to arrive at an informed estimate. Figure 6.33 shows the process.

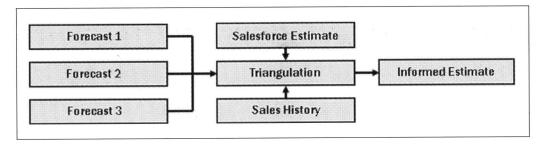

Figure 6.33: Triangulating Multiple Forecasts to Arrive at Informed Estimate

Gathering sales force estimates applies to both business to business markets (B2B) and business to consumer markets (B2C). For B2B markets, we can survey our sales force to gather their estimate for future sales. For B2C markets, we can reach out to distribution channel members, such as retail store managers, to gather their estimate on sales for the coming period.

For our sales history comparison, we simply extrapolate existing sales. We study extrapolated sales histories as a "sanity check" to ensure the forecast does not differ radically from sales predicted by existing trends. We differentiate simple extrapolations from time series analysis, which is more robust.

Comparing sales force estimates and simple extrapolations of sales histories gives assurance to our estimates. The comparison allows us to avoid careless mistakes, because we do not expect forecasts to change significantly from sales force estimates or sales history trends, unless market conditions change drastically.

Marketers may or may not wish to factor in the sales force estimate into their final triangulated figure, depending on the confidence they have in the data. The advantages to this approach are the knowledge of the market that sales representatives bring and the ease of gathering the information. On the other hand, salespeople often deliver a low forecast value (sometimes called "lowballing"), realizing the estimate they give could form the basis of their sales quotas.

PREDICTIVE ANALYTICS

In this section, we extend our treatment of model-based predictions from sales forecasting to the wider field of predictive analytics. Predictive analytics extract information from existing data to predict future trends and behavior. Similar to causal regression, it captures the relationships between explanatory variables and predicted variables.

For example, we might wish to know the relationship between the number of complaint calls from customers (explanatory variable) and the customers' likelihood to switch to another brand (predicted variable).

Predictive analytics applications frequently produce a single score representing the expected conditions or behavior. Perhaps the most famous example is the score representing credit worthiness developed by the Fair Isaac Corporation (FICO), which we study in the brief case study below.

MARKETING MADE MEASURABLE

FICO: Credit-Worthiness in a Single Score: Financial predictive analytics company Fair Isaac Corporation, known as FICO (fico.com) introduced the FICO scoring system in 1989.

The scoring system analyzes customer payment history, outstanding loan balances, and other information. Based on the information, it assigns a single value representing the likelihood of that person making payments on time. Banks, credit unions, and other lenders consider the score when deciding on loan availability and rates.

In 2009, FICO introduced its latest US version, called FICO 8, which the company claims increases predictive accuracy by up to 15%. [6-19]

Predictive Analytics Trends

Several trends have contributed to the growth of predictive analytics, as summarized in Figure 6.34. We discuss each trend below. [6-20]

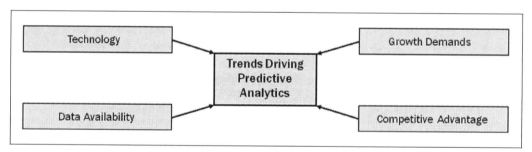

Figure 6.34: Trends Driving the Growth of Predictive Analytics

Technology: Predictive analytics processes can require thousands (or millions) of complex calculations. The increasing availability of sophisticated software and hardware technologies at a reasonable cost has made predictive analytics more accessible than in the past. The rich data and high computing requirements are a good match for **cloud computing**, which can leverage the computational power of advanced data centers against complex problems.

Data Availability: Organizations track substantial amounts of data, and have made much of it available online. The availability of detailed data from multiple sources permits researchers to conduct rich analyses into predicting outcomes.

Growth Demands: Many companies find themselves in markets with slow growth. Marketers can apply predictive analytics techniques to target competitors' customers in stagnant markets.

For example, most people interested in cellular telephones have already purchased one. Therefore, the overall growth rate of new subscribers for cell phone users is very low. The slow growth rate forces cell phone carriers such as AT&T and Verizon to grow their own market share by taking customers away from competitors.

Competitive Advantage: Predictive analytics techniques give new capabilities to organizations. Organizations can apply the techniques for competitive advantage in areas such as market definition, pricing, and operations. For market definition, organizations can target subsets of markets that they predict will be more profitable than the market as a whole. For pricing, companies can now accurately price products and services based on individuals' profiles. For operations, organizations can focus on fulfilling the special needs of the subset on which they are focusing their efforts.

Predictive Analytics Applications

The versatility of predictive analytics lends itself to many applications. Figure 6.35 provides an overview of the applications. We discuss each below. [6-21]

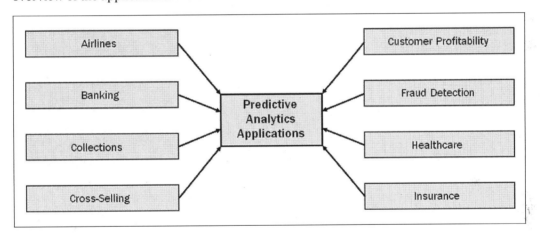

Figure 6.35: Predictive Analytics Applications

Airlines: Airlines can use predictive analytics to prevent equipment failures. By tracking aircraft maintenance logs, airlines can predict needed maintenance before failures cause service interruptions. Because air carriers can lose $10,000 per hour when planes sit idle, analytics can result in significant cost savings.

Banking: Predictive analytics methods study payment histories of customers to predict maximum loan amounts and interest rates. Banks offer lower maximum loan amounts and higher interest rates (or reject the loan application completely) to customers with low FICO scores.

Collections: Similar to the situation in banking, predictive analytics methods study payment histories and other behaviors to predict which customers will fail to make their loan payments, forcing collections agencies to initiate proceedings against the customer.

Cross-Selling: We can study sales histories to predict which products or services customers will find relevant for sales associated with other purchases (i.e., so-called "cross-selling"). For example, online ecommerce giant Amazon (amazon.com) displays related products to buyers, indicating "Customers who bought X (the current product) also bought Y (a related product)."

Customer Profitability: Predictive analytics examines the profitability of specific customer groups to decide which ones to grow and which to screen out. For example, Southwest Airlines (southwest.com) realizes that frequent fliers represent significant profits to the airline, so it provides them with perks to grow their loyalty.

Fraud Detection: We can study patterns of claims to predict which will be fraudulent. We examine characteristics of valid and fraudulent claims and look for telltale signs.

Healthcare: Predictive analytics methods examine patient histories to predict patients at risk for developing chronic conditions such as asthma, diabetes, and heart disease.

Insurance: Many leading insurance companies apply predictive analytics techniques. We already covered fraud detection, often used by insurance companies. In addition, insurance companies examine customer histories to assign prices to insurance policies. For example, health insurance companies consider customer health history when pricing health insurance policies, and auto insurance companies look at driving records to price auto insurance policies.

To execute predictive analytics, we collect all relevant data and use it to assess relationships between explanatory variables and predicted variables.

For example, insurance provider esurance (esurance.com) requests the following data to generate an automobile insurance quote: ZIP code, automobile information, annual mileage, gender, marital status, date of birth, current insurance status (insured or not insured), and driving history.

The company assesses prices for policies based on its history with drivers in similar groups. Drivers with spotty driving records or those driving high-performance cars receive higher insurance premiums, because the insurance company has found that these types of drivers result in higher claims payouts.

Many database and business intelligence vendors offer tools for predictive analytics. For large, cross-enterprise projects, consider large business intelligence vendors, such as IBM (powered by Cognos and SPSS), Oracle (powered by Hyperion), SAP (powered by Business Objects), and SAS.

For medium-sized projects, consider standard business intelligence vendors, such as Actuate (actuate.com) and MicroStrategy (microstrategy.com). Due to the inherent complexity of dealing with the large amounts of data predictive analytics entails, we do not recommend common spreadsheet tools such as Microsoft Excel for the task. [6-22]

MARKETING MADE MEASURABLE

Elie Tahari: Applying Predictive Analytics to Fashion: Upscale women's fashion brand and retail chain Elie Tahari (elietahari.com) applies the power of predictive analytics to forecast shipments to its retailers, such as Nordstrom.

The detailed forecast includes the styles, colors, and sizes to ship to each of its retail outlets. Nihad Aytaman, director of business operations at Elie Tahari, acknowledges the benefit of the predictive analytics forecast, stating, "That protects the customer, ensuring that any style or color they order is in stock, but also protects us so we don't overproduce."

Fashion executives hope to apply predictive analytics someday to forecast which new styles will be winners in the market. So far, this ability eludes computer-based systems, because predictive analytics relies on historical data to forecast future conditions. "We can't accumulate enough history to really do something like this," states Aytaman.

To address this shortcoming, fashion companies are investigating the combination of traditional analytics tools and collective intelligence. Collective intelligence applies social media techniques to predict future trends based on consumers' intentions to buy and actual purchasing behavior.

Many retailers remain skeptical of the notion that predictive analytics and fashion can mix. But Greg Petro, CEO of retail analytics firm First Insight (firstinsight.com), believes that will change as merchants begin to see the results and understand the tools. [6-23]

DATA MINING

In data mining, we extract patterns from data, with the goal of providing actionable information. Data mining is sometimes used as shorthand for the entire process of preparing and interpreting data to gain insight. [6-24]

The same trends that are driving predictive analytics are also propelling the popularity of data mining. Advances in data storage (with lower pricing per Terabyte) are encouraging companies to amass more data. Social media usage and other online trends are producing volumes of available data to study. Demands for growth in competitive markets mean that marketers need to find new tools to compete, and data mining has been found to be very effective. New insight into customer behavior can fuel new strategic initiatives, leading to significant profitability.

Figure 6.36 shows an overview of the overall data mining process. As the figure shows, the actual data mining portion is but one step in the overall process of gaining insight from data.

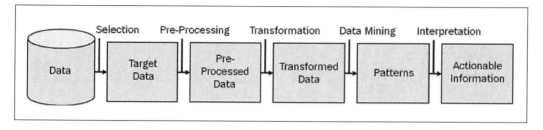

Figure 6.36: Data Mining: Data Extraction, Transformation, Mining, and Interpretation

Each step in the process plays an important role in developing actionable insight from the vast quantities of data that companies have at their disposal. We discuss each step in turn.

Selection: We start with the overall database of the company, which includes sales of all products for all markets. This data source is sometimes called a **data mart** or a **data warehouse**. Through the selection process, we filter out all irrelevant data. The process of extracting the data from outside sources, such as large organizational databases, is sometimes known as **extraction**. The result of this stage is our target data.

Pre-Processing: In pre-processing, we perform remedial preparation functions such as **cleaning** the data. By cleaning the data, we remove duplicate records, information known to be inaccurate, and other errors. The result of this stage is pre-processed data.

Transformation: In transformation, we finalize the preparation of data for the data mining process. Sometimes, the data just require a simple cleaning. Other times, the data requires significant work, depending on the business and technical needs of the database to be mined.

Typical transformation tasks include sorting (ordering the data alphabetically or numerically), pivoting (turning multiple columns into multiple rows or vice-versa), aggregation (totaling multiple rows for total sales or other values), merging (adding data from another source), and other similar preparatory tasks. The result of this stage is transformed data.

Data Mining: Data mining seeks to find patterns in data. Analysts apply one of four different approaches, as shown in Figure 6.37. We discuss each approach below.

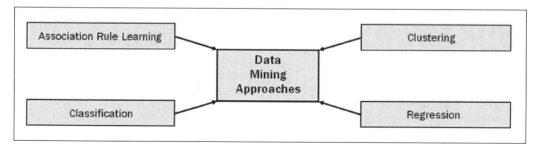

Figure 6.37: Data Mining: Approaches

- **Association Rule Learning**: Also called **market basket analysis**, this approach searches for associations in the data. With association rule learning, we search the database for products or services that are purchased together.

  The classic application is supermarket scan analysis, where we determine which products are purchased together. In this approach, we gain the insight of which products the customer finds to be related. For example, in the insurance industry, we could find that auto insurance buyers buy home insurance at the same time.

- **Classification**: Classification sorts data into different known categories by examining the structure (pattern) of the data.

  The classic application is spam filtering, where email algorithms classify incoming emails into either legitimate email or spam. For example, in the insurance industry we could assign higher premiums to teenage automobile insurance applications, due to their known pattern of having a higher incidence of claims.

- **Clustering**: Clustering identifies similarities in the structures (or patterns) of different data, with the goal of grouping the data using those patterns. Clustering is different from classification in that we do not know the structure (or patterns) ahead of time.

  The classic application for clustering is segmentation of data and markets. For example, in the insurance industry we could discover that teenagers and seniors tend to have higher accident rates than other market segments.

- **Regression**: Regression analysis seeks to find functions that describe the data with the minimum amount of error. The analysis finds relationships between variables, with the intent of predicting outcomes. Regression analysis can be used for many applications, such as predictive analytics.

  For example, in the insurance industry we could identify the age at which the high incidence of accidents for teenagers stops.

Interpretation: In interpretation, we form judgments based on the patterns we find in the data. We apply those judgments to gain insight and to develop strategic initiatives to act on the opportunities identified by the data.

Continuing our auto insurance example, if we found teenagers with high grade point averages suffered fewer accidents, we would offer lower rates to those individuals, thus stealing market share away from competitors charging higher rates and treating all teenagers the same.

Figure 6.38 summarizes the data mining process.

Step	Description	Example
Selection	Selecting relevant data to analyze	Filtering out irrelevant data
Pre-Processing	Removing obvious errors in data	Removing duplicate records in data
Transformation	Sorting, pivoting, merging, and otherwise preparing the data for mining	Merging sales records from two divisions into one large data set
Data Mining	Finding patterns in data	Correlating higher accident rates for teenage drivers using regression analysis
Interpretation	Forming judgments based on data patterns	Reducing insurance rates for teenage drivers with high grade point averages

Figure 6.38: Data Mining: Summary of Process

Tools required for data mining depend on the application. Simple data mining activities, such as sorting and informal analyses to find profitable areas with databases of limited size require little more than common spreadsheet tools, such as Microsoft Excel.

More advanced analysis requires dedicated tools such as those available from Statistical Analysis Software (SAS, available at sas.com) and Salford Systems (salford-systems.com). For large enterprise data mining initiatives, consider large, complex data mining solutions such as those offered by International Business Machines (IBM, available at ibm.com) and Oracle (oracle.com).

Example: Acme Cosmetics (fictitious company) sells its lines of cosmetics through different brand names to the following markets:

- Active Market: Mid-priced organic cosmetics sold to outdoor-loving women
- Luxury Market: High-priced cosmetics sold to fashion-conscious women
- Consumer Market: Low-priced cosmetics sold to price-sensitive women
- Professional Market: High-priced cosmetics sold through salons

Acme wishes to discover which markets within the United States generate the most profit for the company. Acme could execute a data mining initiative using the following steps:

- **Selection**: In the first step, we extract U.S. sales from our general sales database.

- **Pre-Processing**: In the second step, we clean up the records, eliminating faulty entries.

- **Transformation**: In the third step, we prepare the data for mining by calculating total revenue for each market, total costs for each market, and subtracting the two to calculate total profitability.

- **Data Mining**: In the fourth step, we seek to find patterns in the data. We discover through association rule learning that women at salons tend to purchase more items at the same time than those in other markets, resulting in greater profitability than the other markets.

- **Interpretation**: In the fifth step, we decide to launch a strategic initiative aimed at salons to drive sales of cosmetics to the professional market.

MARKETING MADE MEASURABLE

Big Data: Big Market for Data Mining: Industry analysts define Big data as collections of data sets so large and complex that traditional data mining methods are inadequate to analyze the data.

Large data sets can be found in Internet search indexes, call detail records in call centers, astronomy, genomics, medical records, photography archives, and other areas. Data sets can be on the order of a Petabyte (1 million Gigabytes) or an Exabyte (1 billion Gigabytes).

Analyzing such massive datasets will not work with standard relational databases and desktop workstations, instead requiring massively parallel software running on hundreds or even thousands of high-performance servers.

Industry analyst firm Gartner (gartner.com) predicts that companies will need to spend $232 billion in information technology (IT) by 2016 to build the infrastructure required to analyze big data. One major area driving the infrastructure spending is Social Media Revenue. In Social Media Revenue, companies analyze the vast amount of social media content to find patterns that can be leveraged into revenue. [6-25]

BALANCED SCORECARD

The **balanced scorecard** is a tool to track and manage financial and operational metrics, with the goal of transforming vague mission statements and general strategies into concrete actions. The scorecard gives management a quick overview of essential metrics that characterize the performance of the organization. Authors Robert Kaplan and David Norton popularized the tool in their 1996 book, "The Balanced Scorecard," in addition to their earlier Harvard Business Review paper. [6-26]

Kaplan and Norton felt that a strict focus on financial measures, such as return on investment (ROI) and earnings per share (EPS) could sacrifice long-term results for the sake of short-term financial gains. The authors also felt that initiatives concentrating exclusively on non-financial measures, such as development time and customer satisfaction, do not always lead to profitable operations. Therefore, the balanced scorecard includes both types of measures.

The tool is "balanced" in that it includes both financial and non-financial measures, as shown in Figure 6.39.

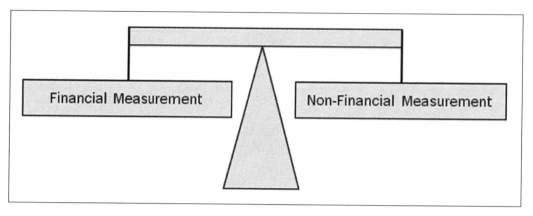

Figure 6.39: Balanced Scorecard: Balancing Financial and Non-Financial Measurements

The balanced scorecard considers business from four different areas: customers, financial, innovation and learning, and internal business processes. The scorecard examines multiple metrics in multiple areas because Kaplan and Norton believed that no single measure can capture the overall performance of the organization. We now examine the four areas.

Customers: According to Kaplan and Norton, customer concerns tend to fall into four categories: time, quality, performance and service, and cost.

- **Time**: In the balanced scorecard model, time refers to the lead time between the initial customer order and the time of delivery.

- **Quality**: Quality can be measured as manufacturing defects in the case of products, or service issues in the case of services.

- **Performance and Service:** Performance and service concern the degree of overall responsiveness a company has to their customer base.

- **Cost:** Cost refers to the total cost that customers experience, including the price of the product or service, along with associated costs, such as shipping, returns costs, and so forth.

Companies can benchmark their performance against that of competitors to determine how they compare. Companies must also survey customers to gain direct feedback.

For example, the Southwest airlines organization (southwest.com) prides itself on making its travel experience different from those of other airlines for the sake of their customers. The airline demonstrates its commitment to its customers with its consistently low fares, freedom to select any seat, and avoidance of baggage fees. [6-27]

Financial: Kaplan and Norton cite typical financial goals as profitability, growth, and shareholder value.

- **Profitability**: Organizations can measure profitability using a number of different measures, such as profitability by product (or by service, by geography, and so forth), using income statements, and other similar approaches.

- **Growth:** Growth can be measured using company-based metrics such as sales growth by quarter or by year, or market-based metrics such as market share.

- **Shareholder Value:** Shareholder value can be measured directly by examining the value of the organization's stock price over time, or by using shareholder value analysis. Shareholder value analysis (SVA) estimates current shareholder value based on future cash flows, discounted to account for the time value of money.

For example, the Financial Times commissioned a survey to find the companies creating the most value for their shareholders. Fund managers interviewed by analyst firm Price Waterhouse Coopers (pwc.com) for the Financial Times ranked L'Oreal fifth worldwide among companies creating the most value for shareholders. [6-28]

Innovation and Learning: Kaplan and Norton acknowledge that organizations must continue to innovate and learn to increase their chances for long-term success. They mention three critical areas: the ability to launch new products and services, the ability to create more value for customers, and the ability to improve operating efficiencies.

- **Ability to Launch**: The ability to launch new products and services allows companies to take advantage of new opportunities in the market. Failure to develop continuous streams of new innovations can make customers wonder about the company's relevance in the market (and its financial health).

- **Ability to Create Value**: Companies must also examine how to create additional value for customers. For example, online electronics retailer Crutchfield (crutchfield.com) added its "white glove" service to respond to customer queries on installation of big ticket items (such as large flat screen televisions) in their homes. [6-29]

- **Ability to Improve Operating Efficiencies**: Companies can improve operating efficiencies for both products and services. For product-oriented companies, operating efficiencies can come from specialized equipment, economies of scale, and experience curves. In **economies of scale**, unit costs are reduced through higher volume operations. In **experience curves**, unit costs are reduced through greater understanding of operations leading to new manufacturing processes. For service-oriented companies, specialized training and improved service processes can improve operating efficiencies.

For example, video card manufacturer Nvidia (nvidia.com) manufactures dozens of different products, including video cards, graphics processors, wireless communications processors, chipsets, and digital media player software. It has developed a keen ability to launch new products and show value to its customers. [6-30]

Internal Business Processes: Businesses must develop internal business processes to support their mission. The actual processes will vary from company to company, but all should result in added value to the customer to be successful. For example, companies in markets demanding constant innovation must develop the processes to succeed in those markets, such as idea generation, fast development times, and rapid market feedback mechanisms.

For example, social gaming company Zynga (zynga.com) developed a core competency around speed of development. With its core competency, it can address the dynamic demands of its market.

To execute the balanced scorecard approach, the company develops key criteria for each of the four areas that correspond to the over-arching mission of the organization. Next, the company assigns target values to the criteria. The company then measures its results and compares them to its targets.

For example, an organization with a mission statement of "delivering innovative products to our customers" could select the following criteria and metrics:

- **Customers**: The organization could translate its mission around innovation into a customer-oriented action, such as adopting customer-based design, where the organization gathers customer input in user groups before and during the design process. The organization could establish a target of ten such meetings for each new product, and track the actual performance over time.

- **Financial**: Here, the organization can translate its innovation focus to financial measures, such as the percentage of sales from new products over the past three years, as compared to overall sales. It could then benchmark its competitors to set a target value and track its actual performance over time against its target.

- **Innovation and Learning:** For this area, the organization can introduce value-added services that contribute to its perception as an innovative firm. For example, the organization can introduce training sessions for users to take advantage of the new innovations of the product. It could establish a target value of ten training sessions per quarter (by asking customers how frequently they want training), and monitor its performance over time.

- **Internal Business Processes**: The organization could develop its internal capabilities in idea generation through creativity training. It could establish a target of a minimum of ten new ideas for every new product idea generation meeting, and track its actual performance over time.

Figure 6.40 summarizes the balanced scorecard approach.

Perspective	Contributors	Example
Customers	Time Quality Performance and service Cost	**Southwest:** Prides itself on delivering customer value with low fares, no seat assignment, and no baggage fees
Financial	Profitability Growth Shareholder value	**L'Oreal:** 5th in the world for shareholder value creation
Innovation and Learning	Ability to launch Ability to create value Ability to improve operating efficiencies	**Nvidia:** Acquired ability to efficiently manage and launch dozens of different products
Internal Business Processes	Core competencies for market	**Zynga:** Core competency in development speed to respond to dynamic market

Figure 6.40: Balanced Scorecard: Summary

Like any other approach, the balanced scorecard method holds advantages and disadvantages.

Advantages: One of the principal advantages of the balanced scorecard is its ability to translate vague organizational mission statements into specific metrics that organizations must meet to realize that statement. For example, an organization could translate a murky mission statement of "We will be the best," into actionable metrics, such as customer satisfaction ratings, sales revenue growth, development speed, and service quality.

Disadvantages: The empirical nature of the approach can make the implementation of scorecards somewhat arbitrary, leading to low confidence in the approach.

For example, executive management translations of mission statements such as "We will deliver superior value to our customers" into scorecard metrics for sales revenue growth could leave some wondering about the relationship of the two. Observers might wonder if sales revenue growth indeed contributes to customer value, or if the quest for sales revenue growth served other purposes, such as executive bonuses.

We recommend against using balanced scorecard instruments from other organizations, even if they are successful with theirs. Organizations should develop their own scorecards, because much of the benefit derives from the design process of the scorecard itself.

The design of the scorecard forces organizations to clearly translate their mission statements into actionable metrics. The translation process reveals the true priorities of the organization, and gives management clear metrics to target.

CRITICAL SUCCESS FACTORS

Critical success factors (CSFs) are organizational attributes that contribute to meeting company objectives. Key performance indicators (KPIs) are metrics we can use to measure how well the organization is meeting its CSFs.

D. Ronald Daniel of consulting firm McKinsey pioneered the concepts of CSFs and KPIs in the 1960s, and MIT Sloan Professor Jack Rockart popularized them in the 1980s. Organizations can apply CSFs and KPIs to define and measure business objectives. [6-31]

For example, a cellular telephone carrier such as AT&T or Verizon could have an objective to increase customer retention through superior customer service. The carrier would consider its ability to provide outstanding customer service as a critical success factor. It could use its customer satisfaction rating as a key performance indicator.

Rockart defined four different types of critical success factors: industry, strategy, environmental, and temporal, as shown in Figure 6.41. We discuss each one in turn.

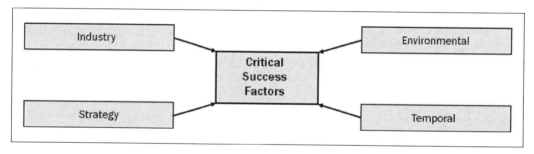

Figure 6.41: Critical Success Factors: Types

Industry: Industry-related critical success factors are areas of competency required for all organizations in their industry to remain competitive.

For example, organizations within the cell phone carrier industry, such as Verizon, require critical success factors in customer retention (to keep customers happy), network maintenance (to keep the network up), billing (to gain revenue), and other related areas.

Strategy: Strategy-related critical success factors are based on the strategies of individual organizations. Different organizations in the same industry could apply different CSFs, depending on their strategies. One organization might adopt a differentiation-based strategy, and would therefore require CSFs related to differentiation. It could maintain a CSF in product/service development and positioning to ensure its differentiation in the market. Another organization could adopt a low-cost strategy, and would therefore require CSFs related to low-cost development and production.

For example, cupcake manufacturer The Cupcakery (thecupcakery.com) maintains a focus strategy. It limits its offerings to cupcakes to maintain a profitable niche in the crowded bakery industry. As such, its critical success factors would differ from those of general bakeries.

Whereas general bakeries could measure pounds of product baked per day, The Cupcakery would find such a metric ill suited to its operations, which feature special creations such as "Peppermint Bliss" and "Gingerbread Chick" cupcakes. [6-32]

Environmental: Environmental-related critical success factors are factors needed to respond to changes in the environment. As we learned in Chapter 2, we can examine changes in the environment in terms of political changes (e.g., new government legislation affecting the products and services of the organization), economic changes (e.g., rising interest rates), social changes (e.g., increasing obesity rates), technological changes (e.g., availability of high speed, low power processors for mobile computing), and other types of changes.

For example, a solar panel manufacturer will need to develop critical success factors to respond to political changes (such as alternative energy subsidies), economic changes (the impact of rising interest rates on sales), social changes (societal beliefs surrounding solar power), and technological changes (availability of higher density solar panel technology).

Temporal: Temporal-related critical success factors result from the internal forces of organizations. Temporal CSFs become relevant during times of significant change for organizations. Temporal CSFs address different kinds of barriers and challenges the company is likely to experience during times of significant change. Organizations develop temporal CSFs before the change events occur as a kind of contingency planning.

For example, companies can decide to expand into new markets, develop significant new products or services, or launch major company re-organizations, all of which can stress unprepared organizations. Companies prepare for such stressful events by developing their temporal CSFs.

Figure 6.42 summarizes the four types of critical success factors.

Type	Description	Example
Industry	Competencies required to stay competitive in the company's industry	**Verizon**: Must maintain competencies in customer retention and other areas to remain competitive
Strategy	Critical success factors based on the strategy of individual organizations	**The Cupcakery**: Focuses efforts on cupcake niche in industry.
Environmental	Competencies to respond to changes in environment	**Solar Panel Manufacturing**: Must respond to political, economic, social, and technological changes
Temporal	Success factors to weather organizational changes	**Internal Organizations**: Prepare for stresses from market expansions, new product development, or major company re-organizations

Figure 6.42: Critical Success Factors: Summary

Execution of critical success factors and key performance indicators follows the steps shown in Figure 6.43. We discuss the steps.

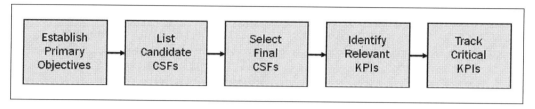

Figure 6.43: Critical Success Factors: Execution Steps

Establish Primary Objectives: Establish the organization's primary objectives and the strategies to achieve the objectives.

For example, we might decide on a strategy of market development to achieve an objective of growth. Recall that in the market development growth approach, we sell existing products and services to new markets.

List Candidate Critical Success Factors: We consider all of the different competencies that we could need to execute the chosen strategy and list them as candidate CSFs. When listing the candidate CSFs, use the four types of CSFs as a guide.

In our market development example, we could need the following CSFs: Ability to provide expected levels of customer service to the new market (industry CSF); ability to increase our competitiveness relative to companies currently serving our new market (strategy CSF); ability to respond to pending legislation affecting the new market (environmental CSF), and ability to secure additional financing in case the organization has insufficient funds to finance the venture with its existing assets (temporal CSF).

Select Final Critical Success Factors: From the list of candidate CSFs, we select only those absolutely essential to success of the strategy. Limit the number of CSFs to three (or five at the very most) to avoid dilution of effort.

In our market development example, we could decide that our principal CSFs are customer service, competitiveness, and legislative responsiveness.

Identify Relevant Key Performance Indicators: For each final CSF, identify one or more KPIs to monitor and measure the CSF. Some CSFs will require several KPIs to monitor.

In our market development example, we could measure customer service using customer satisfaction ratings, competitiveness using market share and relative brand preference (our brand compared to those of competitors), and legislative response using cost to implement new mandated changes.

Track Critical Performance Indicators: Track KPIs for each CSF during the execution of the strategy to ensure success of the CSF.

In our market development example, we would continue to track and monitor the KPIs identified in the previous step.

Figure 6.44 summarizes the process.

Step	Description	Example
Establish Primary Objectives	Establish primary objectives and strategy to achieve them	**Market Development**: Company decides on strategy of market development to achieve growth
List Candidate CSFs	Consider all possible required competencies to achieve objectives	**Market Development**: Create list of CSFs: industry, strategy, environmental, and temporal
Select Final CSFs	Identify top 3 – 5 CSFs	**Market Development**: Focus on customer service and other critical areas
Identify Relevant KPIs	Assign one or more KPIs for each CSF	**Market Development**: Measure customer service using satisfaction ratings
Track Critical KPIs	Monitor KPIs to evaluate execution of CSFs	**Market Development**: Track customer service over time to ensure quality

Figure 6.44: Critical Success Factors: Execution Summary

With the effective use of critical success factors and key performance indicators, organizations can identify which competencies are essential to its success, and measure their performance against those competencies using relevant metrics.

In the next chapter, we will begin our treatment of analytics for the marketing mix by examining models and metrics for products and services.

SUMMARY

Business operations support the implementation of strategy through the tactics of the marketing mix (product, price, place, and promotion). In this chapter, we covered the following business operations: forecasting, predictive analytics, data mining, balanced scorecard, and critical success factors.

Forecasting: Sales forecasts predict the volume of products and services expected to be sold by a given organization for a given time period, usually one year. We covered four different types of forecasts:

- **Time Series**: Time series forecasting leverages known sales history to extrapolate future sales. It works well for rapid predictions of sales in the immediate future. It is not recommended in cases where high accuracies are required, due to the inherent limitations of extrapolation.

- **Causal Analysis:** Causal analysis examines underlying causes to predict future conditions. It is best used for in-depth analyses of sales data, where time and cost are not issues. The technique requires large volumes of data, because multiple factors might be relevant.

- **Trial Rate:** Trial rate forecasting uses market surveys of initial trials (as well as actual short-term trials) to predict future market share. It is for use during the introduction phase of new products and services. Trial rate forecasting can be expensive due to the market testing involved.

- **Diffusion Models:** Diffusion models use analogous situations to predict adoption rates of new products and services. Like trial rate forecasting, it is for use during the introduction phase of new products and services, where no sales data are available yet.

Predictive Analytics: Predictive analytics extracts information from existing data to predict future trends and behavior. Perhaps the best known example of predictive analytics at the consumer level is the FICO score, which captures an individual's credit-worthiness in a single number, based on analyzing significant amounts of data. Trends such as technology improvements, data availability, and growth demands are driving higher adoption of predictive analytics techniques. The techniques are used for many applications, from determining interest rates for loans through banks, to assigning risk ratings for insurance policies.

Data Mining: In data mining, we extract patterns from data, with the goal of providing actionable information. In data mining, we select our target data, pre-process it to remove obvious errors, transform it to make it ready for mining, search it for patterns in the data, and then form judgments based on the patterns we observe.

Balanced Scorecard: The balanced scorecard balances financial and non-financial measures. It delivers a comprehensive view of the performance of the organization by studying multiple areas. It considers areas related to customers, financial performance, innovation and learning, and internal business processes. Businesses can use the balanced scorecard approach to translate general mission statements and strategies into concrete actions.

Critical Success Factors: Critical success factors (CSFs) are organizational factors that contribute to meeting objectives. We covered four types of CSFs: industry CSFs (what we need to remain competitive in our industry), strategy CSFs (factors related to our company's strategy), environmental CSFs (how we respond to changes in our environment), and temporal CSFs (how we prepare for times of organizational stress). Key performance indicators (KPIs) are metrics we can use to measure how well the organization is meeting its CSFs.

Terminology
Balanced Scorecard: Tool to track and manage financial and operational metrics, with the goal of transforming vague mission statements and general strategies into concrete actions
Bass Diffusion Model: Diffusion-based forecasting model developed by Professor Frank Bass
Causal Analysis Forecasting Method: Forecasting method seeking underlying causes to predict future behaviors

Critical Success Factors: Organizational attributes contributing to meeting company objectives

Data Mining: Extracting patterns from data, with the goal of providing actionable information

Diffusion Models: Forecasting method seeking to predict the time of adoption of new products and services

Exponential Average: Technique to filter noise out of data using exponential techniques. Weighs more recent data more heavily than past data.

Imitators: Imitators adopt new innovations primarily through the influence of other individuals. They wait for others to try the innovation first.

Innovators: Innovators seek new ideas and technologies, motivated by personal interest, with little concern if others have adopted the new innovation

Key Performance Indicators: Metrics to measure how well the organization is meeting its critical success factors

Moving Average: Technique to filter noise out of data using simple arithmetic averaging

Network Effects: Market situations where consumers find innovations increasingly useful as more people adopt them, such as telephone networks and the Internet

P (Coefficient of Innovation): Coefficient used in the Bass diffusion model to represent the degree to which innovators influence adoption rate

Penetration: The total number of people who have purchased the product or service

Predictive Analytics: Predictive analytics extracts information from existing data to predict future trends and behavior

Q (Coefficient of Imitation): Coefficient used in the Bass diffusion model to represent the degree to which imitators influence adoption rate

Repeat Rate: Percentage of people re-purchasing or re-using a new product or service, compared to the number of people who purchased or used the new product or service at least once

Time Series Forecasting Method: Forecasting method that identifies underlying trends and predicts future conditions based on those trends

Trial Rate: Percentage of people buying a new product or service for the first time, in a given population, and in a given time period

Trial Rate Forecasting Method: Uses market survey results, as well as short-term market trials, to estimate future sales of new products and services

Trial Volume: The total number of units we can expect to sell to the population over a given time period.

Triangulation: Aggregating multiple results into one final result, as in combining multiple forecast results

Class Discussion

1. What methods does your organization currently use to forecast sales?
2. For the causal analysis forecasting method, which variables would you identify as being relevant to your organization's sales?
3. How does your organization structure its surveys to its target market?
4. Of the market situations identified in the Bass Diffusion section, which one most accurately describes the situation facing your organization?
5. How many applications for predictive analytics can you identify for your organization?
6. What are your organization's critical success factors?

Practice Problems

1. Forecast sales for the coming year for your organization using the Time Series Forecasting Method.

2. Obtain sales data for your organization and plot the sales history. Filter out the noise using the moving averages and exponential smoothing techniques. Plot the smoothed history and note the difference.

3. Identify at least two likely variables influencing sales at your organization. Using the Causal Analysis Forecasting Method, determine the quantitative contribution of each variable toward your organization's sales.

4. Determine Bass diffusion model p and q coefficients for a new product or service about to be developed by your organization, using the market situations described in this chapter.

5. Using the Bass diffusion model p and q coefficients you found in the previous question, execute the Bass algorithm for nominal, best, and worst case scenarios.

6. Apply the back-casting technique described in the Bass diffusion model section to identify actions to take in the present which would improve adoption performance of the worst case scenario you identified in the previous exercise.

7. Prepare a draft balanced scorecard for your organization, showing how your organization's mission statement and strategies can be realized through customer, financial, innovation and learning, and internal business processes.

8. Identify critical success factors needed by your organization, including industry, strategy, environmental, and temporal factors.

Chapter 7.

PRODUCT AND SERVICE ANALYTICS

Chapter Outline

We cover the following marketing analytics topics in this chapter:

- ☑ **Conjoint Analysis**: Identifying important features
- ☑ **Decision Tree Model**: Deciding among different development options
- ☑ **Portfolio Resource Allocation**: Allocating investments among different projects
- ☑ **Product and Service Metrics**: Monitoring sales performance
- ☑ **Attribute Preference Testing**: Using the Internet to assess product preferences

"The more alike two products are, the more important their differences become."
- Regis McKenna

Silicon Valley marketing and public relations expert Regis McKenna (regis.com) definitely understands the power of differentiation. One of his most famous accomplishments was his work with Apple (then Apple Computer) in the 1970s to market the Apple II. Apple designed the Apple II as consumer-friendly.

By comparison, other computer manufacturers at the time aimed their machines more at hobbyists, such as the MITS Altair 8800, which required soldering and assembly after purchase. Mr. McKenna worked with Apple to leverage its consumer-friendly design by positioning it as the world's first "personal computer" to differentiate the Apple II from other machines. [7-1]

This chapter includes models to guide decision-making in product and service development. Organizations differ with respect to the decision-making authority for product and service development efforts. Although some companies insist that the engineering or product development group make all the product/service decisions, most successful organizations emphasize collaboration between development and marketing for market success. To that end, this chapter discusses tools marketers can apply to product and service decision making.

Many organizations seek to find the product or service features that customers desire most, and we address this need with the conjoint analysis model. Businesses also face difficult decisions in choosing among different new products or services to develop. We describe the decision tree model to cover the situation. Organizations must also decide how to allocate their limited resources toward products and services in their portfolio. We discuss portfolio resource allocation models.

This chapter also covers different methods to track relevant metrics, such as sales-based metrics. Using sales-based metrics, managers can gain insight into different adoption rates across markets and geographies. We also cover the use of web-based tools, such as pay per click search engine marketing, to quickly identify market demand for different features.

We use the term "products and services" in this book instead of just "products" to emphasize the relevance to both products and services. For example, hotel chain Marriott (marriott.com) applied conjoint analysis techniques to identify the most important features to include in its hotel services.

MARKETING MADE MEASURABLE

Courtyard by Marriott: Courting the Business Customer: Hotel chain Marriott (marriott.com) applied conjoint analysis to design a new hotel chain catering to business travelers. It started the conjoint process by identifying seven sets of attributes (characteristics) governing hotel design. Marriott called these sets "facets." The facets included "External Factors" (such as the type of pool the property should include), "Rooms" (such as the size of the guest rooms), "Food" (such as the availability of room service), "Lounge" (such as the availability of bars at the hotel properties), and so forth.

Overall, the study considered 50 attributes, each ranging from two to eight levels. For example, the "Room" facet included the attribute "Size of Room." The attribute "Size of Room" incorporated five levels: small (standard), slightly larger, much larger, small suite, and large suite.

Marriott's researchers developed forms to collect data from respondents. The forms asked respondents to select which level of attribute they preferred for each facet. The researchers associated costs for each attribute so respondents could trade off personal preferences for extra room cost.

For example, under the attribute "Entertainment," respondents could select either "Color TV" (no extra charge) or "Color TV with free in-room movies" ($2.50 per night extra charge). Marriott gathered the data by asking frequent hotel travelers (their target market) to complete the forms.

Using the data collected from respondents, Marriott developed its Courtyard by Marriott hotel chain. The chain proved a hit with its target market. The new chain generated more than $200 million with its first 90 hotels in 1987. Revenues grew to over $1 billion by 1994 as the chain grew to 300 hotels. [7-2]

CONJOINT ANALYSIS

Conjoint analysis is a statistical market research technique to examine the trade-offs consumers make between two or more attributes (features or benefits in a product or service). By examining the trade-offs consumers make, we can infer the value they place on individual attributes. Marketers can use the technique to decide which bundle of features to include in new products and services. [7-3]

For example, when shopping for tablet devices, consumers must decide between the ample screen size provided by larger tablets, such as the original Apple iPad series, and the portability (but smaller screens) of smaller tablets, such as the seven inch Samsung Galaxy Tab.

Terminology

Conjoint analysis uses the terms listed below, applicable for both products and services. Figure 7.1 shows the concepts.

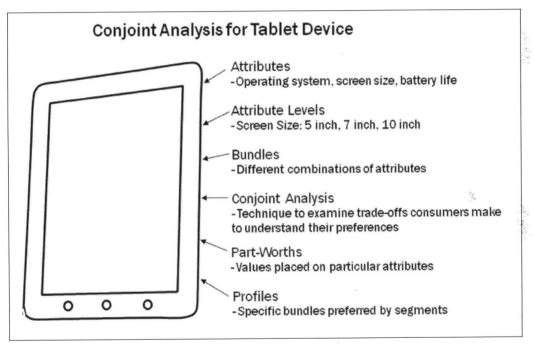

Figure 7.1: Conjoint Analysis: Terminology Demonstration for Tablet Device

Attributes: **Attributes** are characteristics consumers consider when evaluating products and services.

As a product-based example, consumers could consider operating systems, screen size, and battery life when evaluating tablet devices. As a service-based example, we can include location, cleanliness, price, and amenities when evaluating hotels for vacations.

Attribute Levels: Attributes can be present in various degrees, called **levels**.

In our tablet example, consumers could consider the attribute of screen size in different levels. Example of "levels" of screen size include 5 inch screens, such as the HTC One X and Samsung Galaxy Note, 7 inch screens, such as the Amazon Kindle Fire and the Apple iPad mini (the iPad mini has a 7.9 inch screen), and 10 inch screens, such as the original Apple iPad and the Samsung Galaxy Tab 10.1. In our hotel example, the location of one hotel could be 10 miles away from the beach, while another boasts a beach-front location.

Bundles: In conjoint analysis, we consider products and services as **bundles** of attributes.

For our tablet example, we could study consumer preferences for different bundles of attributes, such as a tablet with an Android operating system, a 7 inch screen, and a 16 hour battery life, compared to a tablet with an Apple iOS operating system, a 10 inch screen, and an 8 hour battery life. We can consider hotel rooms as bundles of location, cleanliness, price, amenities, and other attributes. When we evaluate products and services, we consider all the attributes bundled together.

Conjoint: Conjoint analysis is a technique to examine the trade-offs consumers make to determine marketable combinations (bundles) of attributes at different levels.

Coming back to our tablet example, Apple marketed its original iPad to consumers who preferred the usability of its reasonably large 10 inch screen size over the portability of a smaller-screened device. For services, we discussed how the Marriott hotel organization applied conjoint analysis to meet the needs of business travelers in its new Courtyard chain of hotels.

Part-Worths: Conjoint analysis decomposes overall preferences into values that designate the utility, or usefulness, of particular features. The conjoint analysis approach calls these utility values "**part-worths**."

With our tablet example, some consumers place a high value on high resolution screens, such as the Retina display Apple designed into the Apple iPad 3. For services, the Marriott study found that guests were willing to pay extra for restaurants located on the hotel property, so they were included in the design.

Profiles: **Profiles** are specific bundles preferred by customer segments.

In our tablet example, the Samsung Galaxy Tab 10.1 represents a number of different attributes at certain levels (Android operating system, 10 inch screen, 9 hours+ battery life) to make a marketable tablet device. For services, the Courtyard Marriott is a specific offering by the Marriott organization to fulfill the specific needs (represented by part-worths) of business travelers.

Application

Conjoint analysis is appropriate for situations where we need to quantify customer preferences for attributes. As a result, organizations often use conjoint analysis in product and service development. As we have seen in chapter 3, organizations also apply conjoint analysis for market segmentation.

Advantages

The market-based approach of conjoint analysis provides it with many advantages. Its versatile nature makes the technique relevant for many situations. Conjoint analysis is well known, with a deep body of research behind it, giving it credibility. The results are directly applicable to consumer behavior. Because the process uses actual product/service choices instead of surveys, the results can uncover hidden drivers not revealed during discussions with consumers.

Disadvantages

Conjoint analysis also suffers from disadvantages. The approach requires market research into consumer preferences for different variations of products and services. The research can be complex, time-consuming and expensive. Poorly conducted research could result in faulty data. Also, because conjoint analysis does not incorporate the quantity of goods purchased, the technique is limited in predicting resulting market share.

Technique

Figure 7.2 provides an overview of the conjoint analysis technique.

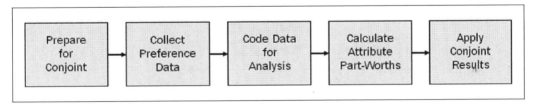

Figure 7.2: Conjoint Analysis: Technique Overview

Prepare for Conjoint: We prepare for the conjoint analysis study by identifying the evaluation attributes, assigning different levels to those attributes, and forming bundles using combinations of the different attributes at the various levels.

Collect Preference Data: Next, we ask consumers to state their preference for each bundle.

Code Data for Analysis: We prepare the data for analysis by coding it in a special form.

Calculate Attribute Part-Worths: We then calculate the preference consumers have for each attribute (called a part-worth).

Apply Conjoint Results: We interpret the results of the conjoint analysis and apply them for marketing purposes. For example, we might use the results to investigate possible market segmentation or to estimate market size using market simulation.

Example

We now demonstrate a method to conduct conjoint analysis using simple spreadsheet tools such as Microsoft Excel. We intend for the example to provide insight into the conjoint process. We do not intend for the simplified method described here to act as a replacement for commercial software packages.

The approach uses multiple regression analysis to determine the coefficients of an equation describing the respondent's preference for a product or service concept. The equation's coefficients express the degree to which each variable (representing an attribute) contributes to the preference. In this way, one can think of the coefficients as part-worths.

We can express a consumer's preference for a product or service, based on a certain set of attributes, using the following equation:

$$\text{Preference} = (\text{Constant}) + A1 * (\text{Attribute 1}) + A2 * (\text{Attribute 2}) + A3 * (\text{Attribute 3})$$

In the equation, A1, A2, and A3 are coefficients expressing the contribution for Attributes 1, 2, and 3, respectively. The illustrative example that follows describes how to find the part-worths.

For example, suppose we want to conduct a conjoint analysis on behalf of Acme Espresso Machines, a fictitious manufacturer of premium coffee makers. Acme competes in the small appliance industry, with major manufacturers such as Braun (braun.com), and specialty manufacturers, such as DeLonghi (delonghi.com), Gaggia (gaggia.com), and Rancilio (rancilio.com). Figure 7.3 displays one of Acme's espresso machines.

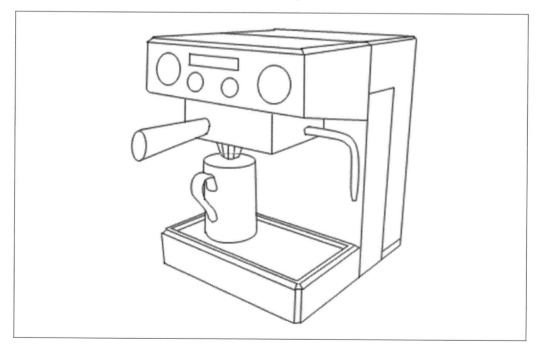

Figure 7.3: Conjoint Analysis: Acme Espresso Machine

With an overall goal of increasing sales of our espresso machines, we plan to analyze the market with three objectives in mind. First, we seek to understand how we can segment the overall market based on the types of features. For example, we might find that casual coffee drinkers prefer machines emphasizing convenience, whereas coffee aficionados prefer machines giving users complete control over every function. Second, we want to identify specific features desired by the different segments. For example, we might wish to know if convenience-oriented people prefer machines that grind coffee beans automatically. And third, we desire to select marketing messages that resonate with the target segments. For example, if we choose to target casual coffee drinkers, we will need to select messages emphasizing convenience.

We plan to conduct conjoint analysis to accomplish the objectives, using a step by step process. We will follow the steps shown in the Technique section, beginning with preparation.

Prepare for Conjoint: In the preparation step, we identify the evaluation attributes, select the different levels required for each attribute, and then form bundles (candidate "products" for evaluation) by combining different levels of attributes. Figure 7.4 shows an overview.

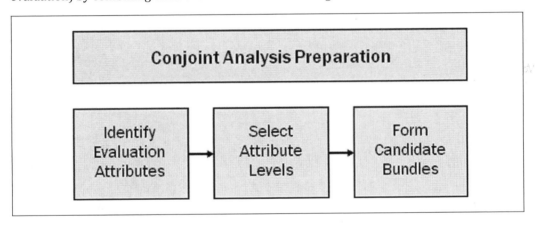

Figure 7.4: Conjoint Analysis: Preparation Step

We start by identifying the evaluation attributes. We recommend starting the process by reviewing available consumer evaluation sources. We can examine general sources, specialty sources, and trade information:

- **General Sources:** General sources include published consumer product/service evaluations, such as those found in Consumer Reports magazine, Epinions.com, and Amazon.com.

- **Specialty Sources**: Specialty sources focus on particular topics. In our case, we would examine sources such as Coffee Geek (coffeegeek.com), which includes consumer reviews of espresso machines and Home Barista (home-barista.com), with professional reviews of several machines.

- **Trade Information**: Trade information includes industry trade journals such as Barista Magazine (baristamagazine.com) and Coffee Talk (coffeetalk.com).

As we review the various sources, we should get a sense of the attributes consumers consider when deciding on a new espresso machine to purchase. If we need further data, we can administer a survey such as that shown in Figure 7.5. The survey asks respondents, "When purchasing an espresso machine, how important are the following attributes?" The figure shows a typical sample completed survey with entries for each of the four evaluation attributes included in the survey.

Evaluation Attributes	Not Important	Somewhat Important	Neutral	Important	Very Important
Speed					X
Capacity				X	
Price				X	
Cord length	X				

Figure 7.5: Conjoint Analysis: Survey to Identify Important Evaluation Attributes

The survey examines the importance of four attributes. The first attribute is the speed of the machine, as measured by the number of minutes the machine takes to make its drinks. The second attribute is the capacity, as measured by the quantity of liquid (in cups, ounces, or liters) the machine produces in each cycle. The third attribute is price, as measured by the manufacturer's suggested retail price (MSRP) for the machine. The fourth attribute is the length of the power cord, as measured in inches, feet, or meters.

We conduct the survey to a random sampling of espresso-drinking individuals. We ask them to rate the importance of each of the four criteria, using the scale shown in the figure. The scale extends from not important to very important, with five possible choices in the scale.

We analyze the results of the survey, and find out that speed, capacity, and price consistently rate as important or very important, but that respondents do not find cord length important. Therefore, we proceed with the conjoint analysis using three primary attributes: speed, capacity, and price.

Having determined the primary evaluation attributes, we need to select the levels for each. Here, we can apply our knowledge of espresso machines gained from our study in consumer evaluation sources to develop the levels shown in Figure 7.6. In the figure, we assign two levels to each attribute. For example, we assign two levels to speed, with level 1 indicating one minute or less, and level 2 indicating times greater than one minute.

Attribute	Level 1	Level 2
Speed	Speed1 (S1): Fast 1 minute or less	Speed2 (S2): Slow Greater than 1 minute
Capacity	Capacity1 (C1): Small 1 cup or less	Capacity2 (C2): Large Greater than 1 cup
Price	Price1 (P1): Budget $300 or less	Price2 (P2): Premium Greater than $300

Figure 7.6: Conjoint Analysis: Attribute Levels

In addition to the numerically-based attributes described in our example, we can also include non-numeric values. For example, if respondents indicated color as an important attribute, we would include it in our analysis. To include non-numeric values, we will need to assign codes to each level of attribute for computational purposes. For example, we can code the non-numeric attribute of color as shown in Figure 7.7. In the figure, we assign a number (1, 2, or 3) to each of the possible colors. We discuss the special coding required for this approach in Figure 7.17.

Attribute	Level 1	Level 2	Level 3
Color	1: Red	2: Blue	3. Green

Figure 7.7: Conjoint Analysis: Attribute Levels for Non-Numeric Values

We now form bundles, which represent candidate "products" for us to test. We form the bundles using the three attributes we selected, varying the levels of the attributes. Marketing researchers often refer to the bundles as "cards" because researchers in the past would use 3 inch by 5 inch index cards to represent individual bundles. Researchers would then give the cards to respondents for them to rate their preference for each one.

Our example includes three attributes of two levels each, so we will need 2^3 cards, or 8 cards. The carat (^) operator indicates an exponential, and is pronounced "to the power of." Thus, "2^3" is evaluated as "2 to the power of 3", which is 2 * 2 * 2 = 8. Figure 7.8 lists the eight cards. We sometimes refer to this type of complete listing as a "full-factorial" version.

Card	Speed	Capacity	Price
1	1	1	1
2	1	1	2
3	1	2	1
4	1	2	2
5	2	1	1
6	2	1	2
7	2	2	1
8	2	2	2

Figure 7.8: Conjoint Analysis: Candidate Bundles, or Cards

Each of the cards signifies potential products. For example, Card 1 designates the following espresso machine:

- Speed = 1: Designates small amount of time to deliver drinks (and therefore fast)
- Capacity = 1: Indicates small capacity (one cup or less)
- Price = 1: Declared as "small" (low) price (costing $300 or less)

Note that the values of the cards "count up" from right to left, similar to the counter of an automobile odometer. The last attribute (in this case, price) counts up quickly, then the second-to-last (capacity), followed by the first attribute (speed). Similarly, an automobile odometer counts up tenths of miles/kilometers first, then miles/kilometers, and so on, from right to left.

As we can see from the above example, the exponential nature of the conjoint card approach results in many cards. A typical analysis with many attributes and many levels could result in hundreds (or even thousands) of cards.

We can reduce the number of cards by applying fractional factorial techniques, such as the application of orthogonal arrays. Genichi Taguchi developed orthogonal arrays to improve the quality of manufactured goods. With orthogonal arrays, we could reduce our card count from eight to four. More dramatically, we could reduce a data set involving four factors at three levels each from 81 cards (3^4 cards) to only 9 cards. However, we lose some information during the reduction process. Our eight-card data set is manageable, so we will continue the rest of our discussion using the original eight cards. [7-4]

Collect Preference Data: In this step, we collect preference data for different candidate bundles from respondents. We begin by selecting the type of technique we will use to collect the data. We review three commonly-used techniques in this section. Figure 7.9 shows the three techniques.

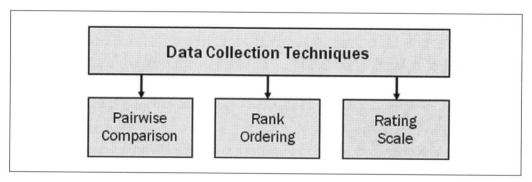

Figure 7.9: Conjoint Analysis: Data Collection Techniques

The first data collection technique we discuss in this section is called **pairwise comparison**. In the pairwise comparison technique, respondents compare pairs of options. In conjoint analysis, respondents compare two different cards and tell us which one they prefer.

Pairwise comparison has advantages and disadvantages relative to other approaches. As an advantage, some respondents find pairwise comparison easier than ranking. In ranking, researchers ask respondents to sort their choices in order of preference. Many respondents find pairwise comparison easier because they only deal with two choices at a time, rather than the many simultaneous choices required for ranking. As a disadvantage, pairwise comparison requires many comparisons to determine the relative preferences for multiple items.

Figure 7.10 presents a simplified example. The figure shows a typical pairwise comparison survey question. Respondents indicate their preference for the left card, the right card, or their indifference to either card by marking the relevant selection of the form.

The left card, Card #1, represents a candidate espresso machine with fast speed (S1), small capacity (C1), and small price (P1). In shorthand, we would refer to Card #1 as Card #1 (S1—C1—P1). Similarly, we can express the right card as Card #7 (S2—C2—P1).

In the card shown in the figure, the respondent preferred Card #1, so she marked her preference on the left hand side of the form.

Prefer Left Card	Indifferent	Prefer Right Card
Preference: __X__ . Card #1 (S1 – C1 – P1) Speed: 1 minute Capacity: 1 cup Price: Under $300	Preference: _____.	Preference: _____. Card # 7 (S2 – C2 – P1) Speed: 2 minutes Capacity: 2 cups Price: Under $300

Figure 7.10: Conjoint Analysis: Data Collection Using Pairwise Comparison

We can study the results of several pairwise comparisons to gain an understanding of the overall rankings of the various candidate choices. For example, Figure 7.11 shows a typical progression of pairwise comparisons and how we can interpret the ultimate ranking of choices by the respondent. At each step, we can see how the respondent makes their choice clear, leading to a final ranking. In our example, the series of choices made during pairwise comparison results in a rank order of Card 2 as #1, Card 3 as #2, and Card 1 as #3.

Pairwise Comparison	Result	Interpretation
Card 1 vs. Card 2	Card 2	Card 2 preferred over Card 1
Card 2 vs. Card 3	Card 2	Card 2 preferred over Card 3.
Card 1 vs. Card 3	Card 3	Among the remaining cards (Card 1 & Card 3), Card 3 is preferred, so Card 3 is the #2 choice and Card 1 is #3; Resulting Ranking: Card 2, 3, 1

Figure 7.11: Conjoint Analysis: Respondent Ranking through Pairwise Comparison

The second data collection technique is called **rank ordering**. In this technique, we provide all cards at once to the respondent, and ask the respondent to rank them in order of preference, from first choice to last choice. In the example above, we could have provided all three cards to the respondent and have the respondent rank them instead of having the respondent engage in pairwise comparison.

The advantage of rank ordering is speed. In the example above, we could have simply asked the respondent to provide their first, second, and third choices of the three cards. The approach would take less time than three separate pairwise comparisons.

The disadvantage of rank ordering is the complexity respondents face. For example, if we had asked the respondent to rank 128 different combinations, they might find the task daunting. In general, many respondents quickly establish their most preferred choices and least preferred choices, but find it difficult to rank the choices in the middle.

The third data collection technique is the **rating scale**. In the rating scale technique, we ask respondents to rate each choice on an absolute scale. In our example above, we could ask our respondent to independently rate each choice on a scale from 1 to 100, where 1 indicated a very low preference and 100 indicated a very high preference.

The rating scale technique enjoys several advantages. First, respondents can find it easier to rate each alternative independently than comparing all possible choices and being asked to rank them. Second, the technique simplifies computation using common spreadsheet tools such as Microsoft Excel.

The disadvantage of the rating scale approach is that some respondents might find difficulty in assigning ratings for fine rating scales. In the example above, if we had asked respondents to rate each choice on a 1 – 100 scale, some might find it hard to discern between the qualities that make a choice deserve a rating of 63, instead of a rating of 67.

To counter the disadvantage, and to improve the consistency of results, we recommend providing guidance to respondents on how they should assign ratings to choices. Figure 7.12 shows a sample rating scale guidance tool for a scale of one to five, five being best.

Rating	Assessment	Characteristics
1	Poor	Unacceptable in multiple areas, such as quality, design, and function. Definitely would not make it on consideration list.
2	Fair	Flawed in one or more important areas. Highly unlikely to make it on a final consideration list.
3	Neutral	Unit is neither particularly good nor bad. Only somewhat likely to make it on a final consideration list.
4	Good	Represents a good quality unit. Would be one of several units to be considered for purchase.
5	Outstanding	Represents the best available. Definitely would consider buying.

Figure 7.12: Conjoint Analysis: Sample Rating Scale Guidance for Scale of One to Five

The next step is to ask respondents to state their preferences for each bundle and record the data, using one of the data collection techniques from the previous section. In our ongoing example, we will use the rating scale technique due to its suitability for spreadsheet-based applications.

 In our example, we ask respondents to rate each card on a scale from one to five stars, using the rating scale guidance supplied in the previous figure. To assist in segmenting the market into accessible groups, we also ask respondents to provide market segment identification data. The identification data will take different forms for different types of markets. (This approach assumes "a priori" segmentation techniques; we could also apply post hoc techniques, as explained in Chapter 3).

For example, for our espresso machine example, we could ask about demographic data (such as age and income), geographic data (such as ZIP code), behavioral data (such as their intended usage for use the product), and psychographic data (such as favorite interests or activities).

Figure 7.13 and Figure 7.14 show the result of our data collection efforts for one individual. The first figure shows preference data for each card, along with the descriptions for each card (speed, capacity, and price levels). The second figure shows sample identifying information we can use for future demographic, geographic, behavioral, and psychographic segmentation.

Card	Speed	Capacity	Price	Preference
1	1	1	1	4
2	1	1	2	3
3	1	2	1	5
4	1	2	2	4
5	2	1	1	3
6	2	1	2	1
7	2	2	1	3
8	2	2	2	2

Figure 7.13: Conjoint Analysis: Sample Respondent Preference Results

Segmentation Type	Question	Response
Demographic	Gender	Female
Geographic	ZIP Code	94111
Behavioral	Anticipated usage	For use at work
Psychographic	Favorite sport	Snowboarding

Figure 7.14: Conjoint Analysis: Sample Respondent Segmentation Identification Results

Code Data for Analysis: To make our analysis run smoothly in computer-based tools such as Microsoft Excel, we need to prepare the data for analysis by coding it into a special form. The coding includes two steps--converting the data into binary form, and removing redundant data. Figure 7.15 provides an overview.

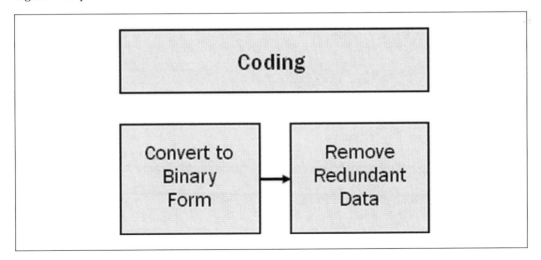

Figure 7.15: Conjoint Analysis: Coding Process

We start by coding the data into binary form. Binary form allows only zeros (0) and ones (1). We use two columns to represent attributes with two levels. We assign two levels to the attribute Speed. We will designate Speed 1 as the first level and Speed 2 as the second level. We assign a "1" to each "True" entry, and a "0" to each "False" entry. We repeat the process with capacity and price.

Figure 7.16 shows the data converted into binary form.

Card	Speed 1	Speed 2	Cap. 1	Cap. 2	Price 1	Price 2	Preference
1	1	0	1	0	1	0	4
2	1	0	1	0	0	1	3
3	1	0	0	1	1	0	5
4	1	0	0	1	0	1	4
5	0	1	1	0	1	0	3
6	0	1	1	0	0	1	1
7	0	1	0	1	1	0	3
8	0	1	0	1	0	1	2

Figure 7.16: Conjoint Analysis: Sample Respondent Results, using Binary Coding

For example, an espresso machine which completes the preparation of its drinks in under 60 seconds would be coded as Speed 1 = 1 and Speed 2 = 0. We code it as Speed 1 = 1 because we have defined Speed 1 to indicate fast speeds. If Speed1 = 1, then Speed 2 must equal 0, because our espresso machine cannot be both slow and fast at the same time.

Similarly, the figure shows coded values for capacity (Cap. 1 and Cap. 2) and price (Price 1 and Price 2). We do not code preference because it represents a ratio (in this case, a rating based on a scale of 1 to 5).

We can extend the process from two levels (as in our example) to as many levels as we wish. For example, Figure 7.17 shows a sample coding for three possibilities for color—red, blue, and green. We can code the three levels with three columns. In our example, Card A represents the product in a red color, Card B in blue, and Card C in green.

Card	Red	Blue	Green
Card A	1	0	0
Card B	0	1	0
Card C	0	0	1

Figure 7.17: Conjoint Analysis: Binary Coding with Three Levels

In our espresso machine example, the observant reader might wonder, "The data appears redundant. If Speed 1 = 1, then Speed 2 must equal zero. Will this redundancy cause a problem during computation, such as when using Microsoft Excel?" Indeed, the reader is correct. We refer to this problem as **linear dependency**. In regression analysis, we cannot allow one independent variable to be perfectly predictable on the state of other predictable variables.

To resolve the linear dependency problem, we omit one of the columns for each attribute. We only need (n – 1) columns to express all the possible levels of the attribute, where n is the number of levels. Because the redundant column for each attribute is completely dependent on the remaining columns, we do not lose any information when we remove one column.

Figure 7.18 shows the revised binary coding for our example. In the figure, we have removed one column for each attribute.

Card	Speed 1	Cap. 1	Price 1	Preference
1	1	1	1	4
2	1	1	0	3
3	1	0	1	5
4	1	0	0	4
5	0	1	1	3
6	0	1	0	1
7	0	0	1	3
8	0	0	0	2

Figure 7.18: Conjoint Analysis: Sample Respondent Results, with Redundancies Removed

Calculate Attribute Part-Worths: We now calculate the preference consumers have for each attribute (called a part-worth) using multiple regression analysis. The multiple regression process fits a function that approximates the data for multiple variables (in our case, speed, capacity, and price). The process fits a function by minimizing the sum of the squares of the errors. The errors are the discrepancies between the fitted curve and the given data.

Our example uses speed, capacity, and price as the evaluation attributes. Therefore, we use the following mathematical equation to predict preference levels:

Preference = (Constant) + A1 * (Speed 1) + A2 * (Capacity 1) + A3 * (Price 1)

In the equation, A1, A2, and A3 are coefficients expressing the contribution for the three attributes Speed 1, Capacity 1, and Price 1. Because part-worths express the importance of each attribute toward preference, we estimate the part-worths by calculating the coefficients for each variable in the describing equation. During the process, we also solve for the Constant, which represents the y-intercept of the equation.

Just as we did in Chapter 3, we can execute regression analysis using the regression function provided in Microsoft Excel's set of data analysis functions.

The description of the process we provide here provides general guidelines. The exact procedure and layout will depend on the version of Excel used.

As shown in Figure 7.19, we start the regression analysis process by selecting the Data menu tab, and then selecting Data Analysis in the area below the tab.

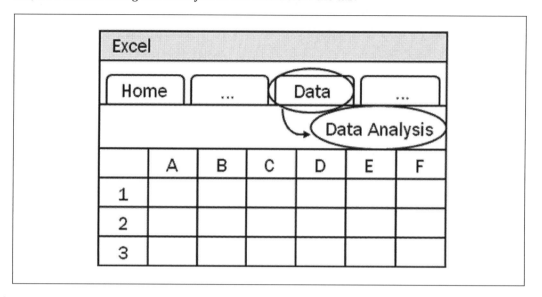

Figure 7.19: Conjoint Analysis: Launching Data Analysis in Microsoft Excel

Select "Regression" in the Data Analysis dialog box that follows, and click OK. Doing so will reveal the Regression dialog box, as shown in Figure 7.20. Select the preference data for Input Y Range, because it represents our dependent variable. For Input X, select three columns of data—speed, capacity, and price, because they represent independent variables. Keep the "Constant is Zero" box unchecked, because we will need to evaluate our constant for the Y-intercept. Click "OK" once the data is entered.

Figure 7.20: Conjoint Analysis: Entering Data into the Regression Dialog Box

Microsoft Excel will output a summary output table, a portion of which is shown in Figure 7.21. The regression analysis indicates that our constant is 2.0 and our attribute coefficients for A1, A2, and A3 are 1.75, -0.75, and 1.25, respectively.

Parameter	Coefficient
Intercept	2
Speed1	1.75
Capacity1	- 0.75
Price1	1.25

Figure 7.21: Conjoint Analysis: Microsoft Excel Regression Results

We plug in the values for the constant and the A1, A2, and A3 coefficients to arrive at the following preference equation:

$$Preference = Constant + A1 * Speed\ 1 + A2 * Capacity\ 1 + A3 * Price\ 1$$

$$Preference = 2.0 + 1.75 * Speed\ 1 - 0.75 * Capacity\ 1 + 1.25 * Price\ 1$$

The coefficients represent the utility the respondent places on the attributes. Because A1, the coefficient for Speed 1, is relatively large, we assert that the respondent places a high value on speed when selecting an espresso machine. The positive sign (+1.75) indicates that the respondent prefers Speed 1 (the fast machine) over the alternative speed, Speed 2.

The negative sign in front of the coefficient for Capacity 1, A2, shows that the respondent holds a preference against the smaller machine (Capacity 1), preferring the larger machine instead (Capacity 2). The positive coefficient for A3 indicates a respondent preference for the lower priced machine (Price 1) over the higher price unit (Price 2).

Apply Conjoint Results: In the final step, we interpret the results of the conjoint analysis, applying it for marketing purposes. For example, we might use the results to investigate possible market segmentation or to estimate market share using market simulation. Figure 7.22 provides an overview.

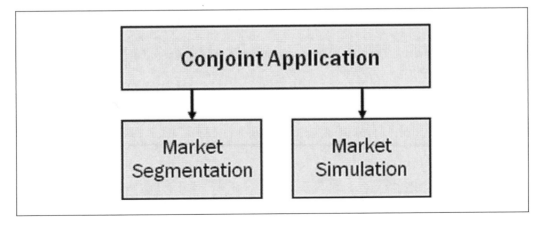

Figure 7.22: Conjoint Analysis: Application

Generally, we solve separate regression equations for each respondent, which is why we recommend commercial tools to avoid the tedium of manually calculating coefficients for each respondent. We can correlate the data against the respondents' segmentation data (demographic, geographic, behavioral, or psychographic). The correlation will guide us in segmenting the market, first in terms of identifying segments, and second in terms of determining the messages for each segment.

For example, suppose we ask each respondent to identify the purpose for which they intend to use the espresso machine (i.e., applying behavioral segmentation) during our data gathering process. We might discover that the segment that indicates that "the machine will be used at work" will have a high part worth utility for speed. Therefore, in our marketing communications to the "work" segment, we will emphasize the machine's speed. If sufficient demand exists, we might develop special high speed machines dedicated to that segment.

We can also apply conjoint analysis to estimate market share for new products and services. To do this, we build market simulators. We can think of market simulators as the collective voice of hundreds (perhaps thousands) of respondents with their preferences stored in the conjoint analysis database.

For example, if we planned to come out with a new model of espresso machine with a particular combination of speed, capacity, and price, we could predict how many people would prefer such a machine, using our respondent preference database.

Market simulators use choice rules to estimate market share, based on the calculated part-worths of respondents. The most straightforward choice rule is the first choice rule (also called the maximum utility rule). Other, more advanced, approaches include logit and Bradley-Terry-Luce models.

The first choice rule assumes that respondents can choose or vote for only one product, and that one alternative captures 100% of the share for each respondent. The first choice rule is well suited for high-involvement purchases. For example, consumers considering the purchase of a new home would select the home that maximizes their criteria (i.e. provides the highest utility).

Using the first choice rule, we can compute the market share for a proposed new product or service by determining the number of customers for whom it would offer the greatest utility (by considering their part-worths), divided by the total number of customers in the study. The first choice rule assumes that the respondents surveyed during the conjoint analysis accurately represent a cross-section of the market.

In our espresso machine example, we might want to estimate the market share for a proposed new "extra-fast" espresso machine with a certain capacity and price. To calculate the share, we would determine the percentage of respondents in our database for whom the machine would offer the greatest utility.

Examining the database, we find out that 30% of our respondents would make such a machine their first choice. Using the first choice rule (assuming that buyers only purchase one machine), we would predict that the new machine has the potential to capture 30% of the overall market for espresso machines.

Execution

To execute conjoint analysis, we recommend the use of commercial software packages, such as those by Qualtrics (qualtrics.com), SAS, (sas.com), and Sawtooth Software (sawtoothsoftware.com). Conjoint analysis can be complex to execute, especially for larger problems, and the results can be flawed if the supporting research is not conducted properly. [7-5]

MARKETING MADE MEASURABLE

Conjoint: Dare to be Bad? Frances Frei and Anne Morris, authors of the book "Uncommon Service: How to Win by Putting Customers at the Core of Your Business," suggest that companies must emphasize the product or service attributes that customers care about, even if it means other attributes suffer.

The book discusses the process the authors call "modified conjoint analysis" where companies work with customers to understand the preferences about which customers care deeply. The authors cite several successful companies making such trade-offs, or as they put it, "daring to be bad" at some things so they can be outstanding in others. Some examples:

- **Apple**: The Apple MacBook Air meets consumers' needs for an ultra-lightweight laptop, but "dares to be bad" with fewer ports and the lack of a user-replaceable battery. Customers give up these features for light weight.
- **Mayo Clinic**: The clinic offers patients same-day appointments, but "dares to be bad" by making patients give up control over which provider they see. Patients give up choice for speed.
- **Southwest Airlines**: The airline provides low prices and frequent departures, but "dares to be bad" with fewer on-board amenities, such as lack of a Business Class option. Travelers give up perks for price.
- **Zappos**: The online retailer offers its customers a dazzling inventory of shoes and other products, but "dares to be bad" by selling them at higher prices than discount websites. Shoppers give up price for selection.

The authors contend that companies must understand the attributes that customers most want, and build systems to deliver on those attributes—even if it means "disappointing" them in areas that they do not care much about. [7-6]

DECISION TREE MODELS

We can apply decision tree models to situations where we must decide among multiple product or service development projects or other decision alternatives. Decision trees take the form of hierarchical tree diagrams, where two or more branches (representing different scenarios) connect to nodes (connection points where the branches meet). The nodes represent decision points where we must decide on one branch or the other. [7-7]

Application

Product and service development organizations frequently apply decision tree models to decide among potential new product or service development projects. Many product and service development projects have certain probabilities of succeeding or failing. Decision tree models incorporate those probabilities, making the models relevant to product and service development decisions.

We are not just limited to product and service development, though—we can extend the application of decision trees to any situation where we must decide on one of multiple scenarios, each with its own predicted outcome and probability of occurrence.

Advantages

Because of the structured, hierarchical nature of decision tree models, they can bring order and structure into the decision-making process. Sometimes, the discipline required to obtain the probabilities and potential revenues (or other outcomes) of each potential choice is the principal benefit with the approach. Structured tools such as decision tree models guard against decisions strictly based on emotions or organizational politics.

Disadvantages

Like any model, decision tree models are only as good as the data on which they are founded. Incorrect or unsubstantiated data will result in erroneous conclusions, no matter how well the model is executed. Also, decision tree models with many scenarios can become complex and marketers can lose track of the various nodes. In these cases, we recommend preparing visual diagrams to show each branch of the tree, along with the corresponding data.

Technique

Figure 7.23 shows an overview of the technique for decision tree models. We follow our brief description of the technique with an example demonstrating its use.

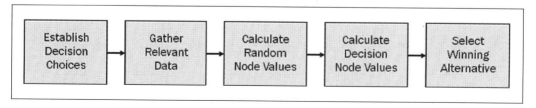

Figure 7.23: Decision Tree Model: Technique

Establish Decision Choices: We start by establishing the decision choices available to the marketer. For example, we can decide between two alternative products—one that delivers high revenue, but involves substantial market risk, or one delivering lower revenue at low risk.

Gather Relevant Data: We must gather the data for the alternatives, such as the amount of revenue we can expect given strong, average, and poor scenarios of market acceptance. When the market eagerly accepts our new product or service, we can generate significant profits. But in poor scenarios, we make meager profits or could even lose money.

Typical data to collect includes the potential revenue available with each scenario, the probability of that scenario occurring, and the cost associated with the scenario. Organizations typically apply historical data and industry information for the probability and potential revenue data. Costs will depend on the scope of the project.

Calculate Random Node Values: Random nodes in decision trees represent random selections among multiple scenarios. The marketer has no direct control over which scenario will occur. For example, if we launch a new product, it has a certain chance of winning and a chance of failing. To calculate the random node values, we calculate the expected value for each scenario reporting to that node. We calculate the expected value by multiplying the predicted outcome of the scenario by its probability of occurring.

Calculate Decision Node Values: Decision nodes in decision trees represent situations where marketers must decide on two or more alternatives, based on the data available. Unlike random nodes, marketers have full control over decision nodes.

Select Winning Alternative: We select the alternative with the highest net expected value (i.e., the total expected value, less development costs) as the winning alternative.

Example

Figure 7.24 shows a typical example. An organization must decide whether to develop a new product, or to enhance an existing product. If the organization develops a new product, it must decide whether to apply its standard development budget toward it, or to use a reduced budget in an effort to cut costs. If it decides to enhance an existing product instead, it will add features.

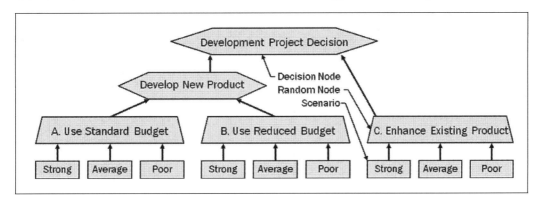

Figure 7.24: Decision Tree: Typical Development Project Selection Scenario

The figure shows two types of nodes connecting the branches together:

- **Random Nodes**: Four-sided trapezoids represent random nodes (sometimes also called chance nodes or uncertain nodes). Random nodes reflect the random nature of the branches reporting to the node. In our case, Random node A, "Use Standard Budget," incorporates a random selection among three scenarios: strong market reaction (labeled as "Strong"), average market reaction ("Average"), and poor market reaction ("Poor"). The scenarios are random in that the marketer does not have control over which will occur.

- **Decision Nodes**: Six-sided hexagons represent decision nodes. Decision nodes reflect situations where marketers must decide on two or more alternatives, based on the data available. In our case, Decision node "Develop New Product" asks the marketer to decide between two alternatives: "Use Standard Budget" and "Use Reduced Budget." Unlike random nodes, marketers have direct control over decision nodes.

In the figure, we represent possible scenarios as rectangles. In our case, the "Use Standard Budget" path could result in Strong, Average, or Poor scenarios.

Establish Decision Choices: We begin by establishing the decision choices. We face a choice of three alternatives, as summarized in Figure 7.25.

Alternative	Description
A. New Product, Standard Budget	Develop new product using standard development budget
B. New Product, Reduced Budget	Develop new product using reduced budget to cut costs
C. Existing Product, New Features	Enhance existing product with new features

Figure 7.25: Decision Tree: Example Decision Choices

Gather Relevant Data: We gather the data for the three alternatives and their scenarios.

Figure 7.26 shows data for three different scenarios for new product development with the standard budget.

Scenario	Probability	Potential Revenue
Strong market adoption	0.3	$800,000
Average market adoption	0.4	$200,000
Poor market adoption	0.3	$20,000
(Total probability for all scenarios)	*1.0*	*N/A*

Figure 7.26: Decision Tree: Data: New Product Development with Standard Budget

In the first scenario, customers react strongly to the new product, quickly adopting it. The result is substantial potential revenues. In the second scenario, the market reacts in a more typical way, with an adoption rate that is average for most product launches for the company. In the third scenario, customers react negatively, with low adoption rates and low resulting revenue. The probabilities for the different scenarios must sum to 1.0 (100%).

Figure 7.27 shows the potential revenue for three different scenarios of new product development with reduced development funding. The data acknowledge the effect of the reduced budget by assigning a lower probability to the more successful outcomes. For this example, the potential revenues remain unchanged.

Scenario	Probability	Potential Revenue
Strong market adoption	0.1	$800,000
Average market adoption	0.3	$200,000
Poor market adoption	0.6	$20,000

Figure 7.27: Decision Tree: Data: New Product Development with Reduced Budget

Figure 7.28 shows the predicted resulting revenue for developing an enhanced version of an existing product. The potential revenues have reduced substantially from the revenues generated by new products. The revenues are lower due to the existing level of penetration within the market for the current product. Enhanced versions of existing products do not generate the same kind of excitement (and potential revenues) as new products.

Scenario	Probability	Potential Revenue
Strong market adoption	0.2	$200,000
Average market adoption	0.5	$40,000
Poor market adoption	0.3	$10,000

Figure 7.28: Decision Tree: Data: Likely Outcomes for Existing Product Development

Figure 7.29 shows the expected development budget planned for the projects. The standard budget shown in the table reflects the typical amount spent during previous development projects of similar scope. The reduced budget represents efforts to reduce costs in the development organization. The budget to enhance the existing budget is significantly less than that for a new product. The lower budget acknowledges the decreased amount of work (and risk) required to enhance an existing product.

Development Project Type	Costs
New product, standard budget	$200,000
New product, reduced budget	$100,000
Enhanced existing product	$40,000

Figure 7.29: Decision Tree: Data: Development Costs for Different Projects

Calculate Random Node Values: Now that we have the data we need, we can calculate the values for each random node. We determine the random node values by calculating the expected value for each scenario reporting to that node. We then add up the expected values to arrive at the random node value total.

Figure 7.30 demonstrates the process for new product development projects with standard budgets. We calculate the expected value for each scenario by multiplying the potential revenue by the probability of the scenario occurring. We repeat the process for each scenario, and then total the expected values.

Scenario	Probability	Potential Revenue	Expected Value
Strong market adoption	0.3	$800,000	0.3 x 800,000 = $240,000
Average market adoption	0.4	$200,000	0.4 x $200,000 = $80,000
Poor market adoption	0.3	$20,000	0.3 x $20,000 = $6,000
Total			$326,000

Figure 7.30: Decision Tree: Calculating Random Node Values: New Products, Standard Budget

In Figure 7.31, we repeat the process to determine the sum of expected values for product development using reduced budgets. The calculations reveal that the sum of expected values is lower for projects using reduced budgets.

Scenario	Probability	Potential Revenue	Expected Value
Strong market adoption	0.1	$800,000	0.1 x $800,000 = $80,000
Average market adoption	0.3	$200,000	0.3 x $200,000 = $60,000
Poor market adoption	0.6	$20,000	0.6 x $20,000 = $12,000
Total			$152,000

Figure 7.31: Decision Tree: Calculating Random Node Values: New Products, Reduced Budget

In Figure 7.32, we complete the sum of expected values process by calculating the decision tree values for enhancing existing products. We find that the sum of expected values for enhancing existing products is less than either of the new product development projects.

Scenario	Probability	Potential Revenue	Expected Value
Strong market adoption	0.2	$200,000	0.2 * $200,000 = $40,000
Average market adoption	0.5	$40,000	0.5 * $40,000 = $20,000
Poor market adoption	0.3	$10,000	0.3 * $10,000 = $3,000
Total			$63,000

Figure 7.32: Decision Tree: Calculating Random Node Values: Enhanced Existing Products

Calculate Decision Node Values: Next, we calculate the value for each decision node. We designate the value of the decision node as the highest net expected value (Net EV) of the alternatives reporting to it. We calculate the net expected value by subtracting development costs from each alternative.

For example, for the alternative "Use Standard Budget," we had calculated the expected value as $326,000. We know from our data-gathering that the development organization expects to spend $200,000 for this alternative. Therefore, the net expected value is $326,000 - $200,000 = $126,000. We repeat the process for the other alternatives.

Figure 7.33 shows the result.

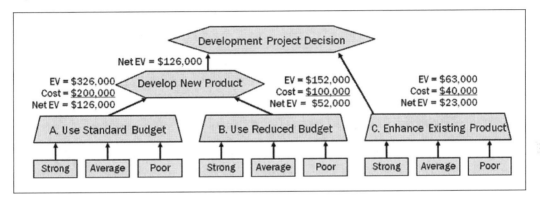

Figure 7.33: Decision Tree: Calculating Decision Node Values

The figure shows the net expected value for the three alternatives. We determine the value for the decision node "Develop New Product" by observing that the "Use Standard Budget" alternative represents the highest net expected value. Therefore, we assign the net expected value for "Use Standard Budget" ($126,000) to the "Develop New Product" decision node.

We now must decide between "Develop New Product" and "Enhance Existing Product." We make the decision by selecting the highest net expected value. Because "Develop New Product" represents a greater net expected value ($126,000) than "Enhance Existing Product" ($23,000), we select "Develop New Product."

In our illustrative example, we only considered two levels of decision nodes. We can easily accommodate additional levels by extending the process. We recommend preparing a hierarchical tree diagram, like that shown earlier, to keep track of the net expected values at each decision node.

Execution

Marketers can execute simple decision tree models with common spreadsheet tools such as Microsoft Excel using the tabular format demonstrated in the example. For more advanced decisions, such as those with many decision points, we recommend the use of commercial decision tree software. Examples include software from Palisade (palisade.com), SmartDraw (smartdraw.com), Treeage (treeage.com), and TreePlan (treeplan.com, an Add-In for Excel).

MARKETING MADE MEASURABLE

GeekWire: Decision Tree for Entrepreneurs: Seattle-based technology news site GeekWire (geekwire.com) postulated a unique type of decision tree for entrepreneurs. Entrepreneurs, GeekWire says, think about opportunities differently from others. [7-8]

GeekWire presents an example. A non-entrepreneurial couple wakes up one morning and decides to go camping. They learn that their favorite camping spot attracts many campers and that it offers only two tent sites, both available on a first-come, first-served basis. The couple builds a decision tree to guide their decision. The tree has two branches—Not Going Camping and Going Camping. Because of the proximity of the campground to their home, they do not associate a cost with traveling to the camp. We study each:

- **Not Going Camping:** Value of 0, because they have not lost anything by not going.
- **Going Camping:** We can split the "going camping" branch into two sub-branches: "Getting a Camping Spot" and "Not Getting a Camping Spot." In the case of "Getting a Camping Spot," the couple definitely wants to find a camping spot, so they assign a (+10) value to the scenario. They do not expect to get it, so they assign a probability of only 5%. In the case of "Not Getting a Camping Spot," the couple assigns a negative value (-2) to the unfortunate situation of not finding a camping spot, with a probability of 95%, because of the many other people competing for the same spot.

Figure 7.34 shows the resulting table for non-entrepreneurs. Because the value of not going camping (value of 0) exceeds the value of going camping (expected value of – 1.4), they decide not to go camping.

But entrepreneurs think differently. We re-calculate the decision tree:

- **Not Going Camping:** Here, we assign a value of (- 1), not of 0, because entrepreneurs believe in factoring in the cost of regret. Not going camping represents a missed opportunity and should therefore be assigned a negative value. Amazon.com founder Jeff Bezos actually came up with a model he called the "Regret Minimization Framework" to rationalize his decision to leave his well-paying job for the risky move of starting Amazon.com.
- **Going Camping:** Again, we split the "going camping" branch into same two sub-branches as before. In "Getting a Camping Spot," entrepreneurs believe in not over-estimating the competition. Many people may have had the idea to go camping, but not everyone will execute on it. Therefore, the probability of getting a camping spot rises from 5% to 10%. In " Not Getting a Camping Spot," entrepreneurs understand that failure can happen even with the best plans, so they discount the cost of failure. Therefore, we reduce the value of not getting a spot from (- 2) to (- 1).

Figure 7.35 shows the resulting table for entrepreneurs. Because the value of going camping (expected value of 0.1) exceeds the value of not going camping (value of – 1), the entrepreneurial couple decides to go camping. Moreover, they decide to purchase their camping food only if they get the campsite, thereby minimizing their monetary risk.

Scenario	Probability	Potential "Revenue"	Expected Value
Get a camping spot	0.05	+ 10	0.05 * 10 = 0.5
Not getting a spot	0.95	- 2	0.95 * (-2) = (- 1.9)
Total			(- 1.4)

Figure 7.34: Decision Tree: Camping Decision: Non-Entrepreneur

Scenario	Probability	Potential "Revenue"	Expected Value
Get a camping spot	0.10	+ 10	0.10 * 10 = 1
Not getting a spot	0.90	- 1	0.90 * (- 1) = (- 0.9)
Total			+ 0.1

Figure 7.35: Decision Tree: Camping Decision: Entrepreneur

PORTFOLIO RESOURCE ALLOCATION

Most organizations market several different types of products and services. We must decide how to allocate investments (resources) among the company's portfolio of products and services. Investing the same amount for each would not make sense, because we would ignore the higher potential profitability of winning products over losing ones.

Consulting organization Boston Consulting Group (bcg.com) introduced its product portfolio model for resource allocation model in 1968. Despite developing many models over its lifetime, most people know the Boston Consulting Group for its resource allocation model. In fact, many refer to Boston Consulting Group's product portfolio resource allocation model simply as the "BCG model." [7-9]

The objective of the framework is to promote investment into products and services that command high market growth rates along with high relative market share. BCG defines relative market share as the market share of a company relative to that of its principal competitors. The framework categorizes products into four quadrants—stars, dogs, cash cows, and question marks--according to the dimensions of their corresponding market growth rate and relative market share.

Stars: The BCG model refers to products with high market growth and high relative market share as "**Stars**." BCG founder Bruce Henderson denoted such products "stars" because of their attractive combination of market growth and market share. Mr. Henderson would tell clients, "The payoff for leadership [in market share] is very high indeed, if it is achieved early and maintained until growth slows."

As such, BCG recommended investing cash into stars because of the profitability such an approach would give. As Mr. Henderson said, "Increases in share increase the profit margin...the return on investment is enormous." For example, the Apple iPhone became a star product for Apple, with rapid growth rates and a high relative market share despite its premium price. [7-10]

Dogs: At the opposite end of desirability, the BCG model refers to products with low market growth and low relative market share as "**Dogs**." BCG refers to them as dogs because of their tendency to "dog," or slow, market growth. Investment in such areas should be eliminated, the model asserts, and the products should be divested.

For example, analysts considered the Microsoft Millennium Edition operating system (referred to as Microsoft ME) in the early 2000s a "dog" product. The system's error messages, incompatibility problems, failed or stalled shutdowns and BSODs (blue screens of death) caused low adoption rates. Accordingly, Microsoft ended the product after only one year, replacing it with Windows XP, which was greeted with wide acclaim. [7-11]

Cash Cows: The BCG model designates products with a relatively low market growth rate and high relative market share as "**Cash Cows**." Such products generate more cash than they need to maintain market share, because required investment in the product is relatively low. According to the BCG model, organizations should invest the cash generated by their cash cows into their star products or services.

For example, the Apple iPod digital music player became a cash cow once Apple introduced the iPhone in 2007. The iPod does not command the high growth rate it once did, but in 2004 it maintained an 87% market share for hard drive-based digital music players. [7-12]

Question Marks: The BCG model refers to products with high market growth rate but relatively low market share as "**Question Marks**" (sometimes also referred to as "problem children"). The actions to take with a question mark are uncertain. While the low market share makes market dominance unlikely, the high growth rate makes such investments attractive.

Application
Because of its focus on resource allocation, the model works well for apportioning monetary and personnel resources among multiple product and service development projects.

Advantages
The Boston Consulting Group product portfolio model provides a fairly simple, rational method of shifting investment from low-performing assets to high-performing ones.

Disadvantages
Some have criticized the BCG product portfolio model as overly simplistic. The model relies heavily on increasing market share, which can be expensive to achieve. In addition, the model considers market size a given. In practice, the company might grow the overall market size. For example, analysts estimate that the Apple iPhone grew the overall size of the smartphone market.

In response to the limitations of the BCG model, some analysts point to the **GE/McKinsey matrix** as an alternative. The GE/McKinsey matrix is similar to the BCG model in that its goal is to allocate scarce resources by evaluating market conditions.

The GE/McKinsey matrix is different in that it uses "Industry Attractiveness" and "Business Unit Strength" as its axes instead of market growth rate and relative market share. Industry attractiveness is a weighted combination of market growth rate, industry rivalry, and other measures. Business unit strength is a weighted combination of distribution channel access, production capacity, and other measures. A disadvantage of the GE/McKinsey matrix is its relative complexity and somewhat subjective weighting. [7-13]

Technique

Many marketing books advocate the construction of the classic BCG graph with its four quadrants. While we acknowledge the importance the classic graph format has made, we have found problems with the approach. For example, the classic graph inverts the market share axis, making the graph misleading without explanation. Therefore, we introduce a simplified approach.

Figure 7.36 introduces a simplified approach to product portfolio allocation using the BCG methodology. Figure 7.37 shows a sample table using the approach.

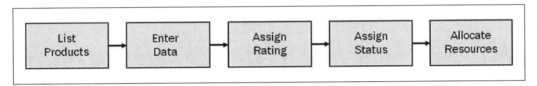

Figure 7.36: BCG Portfolio Resource Allocation: Technique

Product	Market Growth Rate	Relative Market Share	Status → Allocation
Product A	High	High	Star → Invest
Product B	Low	Low	Dog → Divest
Product C	Low	High	Cash Cow → Harvest
Product D	High	Low	Question Mark → Evaluate

Figure 7.37: BCG Portfolio Resource Allocation: Sample Table

We follow the steps below:

- **List products**: List the organization's products and services in the table, one product or service per row. Here, the word "product" can designate an individual product (for small firms), a service for service-oriented firms, or a product line for large firms.

- **Enter Data**: Enter the corresponding market growth rates and relative market shares for each product.

- **Assign Rating**: Assign a rating, "high" or "low" according to the situation. Indicate a market growth rate cut-off point, beyond which are "high" ratings and below which are "low" ratings. The cut-off point will vary by industry and situation. For relative market share, assign "high" relative market share for products with market shares greater than the company's most important competitor.

- **Assign Status**: Assign a status—Star, Dog, Cash Cow, or Question Mark—according to the combination of market growth rate and relative market share.

- **Allocate Resources**: Allocate resources to each product, based on its status. For example, Stars will warrant resource investment, while Dogs should be eliminated.

Example

Figure 7.38 shows a typical portfolio of products. The company has assigned a market growth rate cutoff of 6%. The figure shows the growth rate for each product's market, along with each product's relative share of that market.

Product	Market Growth Rate	Relative Market Share	Status → Allocation
Product A	12%	2.0	Star → Invest
Product B	1%	0.2	Dog → Divest
Product C	5%	2.0	Cash Cow → Harvest
Product D	10%	0.2	Question Mark → Evaluate

Figure 7.38: BCG Portfolio Resource Allocation: Example

From the figure, we see that product A commands a relative market share of 2.0, meaning that it holds twice the share of its principal competitor. Product A also benefits from participating in a market with a swift growth rate of 12%. Because both the market growth rate and relative market share are strong, we identify product A as a star, and seek to invest resources into it.

Product B, on the other hand, has captured a relative market share of only 20% (0.2) of its principal competitor, placing it in a weak position. In addition, the market is relatively flat, growing at only 1%. Therefore, we identify product B as a dog, and recommend divesting it.

The figure shows product C with a strong 2.0 relative market share in a market with a moderate growth rate of 5%. This situation of market leadership and steady market conditions works well for producing respectable cash flows from product C. Indeed, the BCG technique would label product C as a cash cow, and would recommend harvesting the cash to invest in product A.

Product D presents a problem. On the one hand, it is in a quickly growing market, with a robust 10% growth rate, making its prospects bright. On the other hand, it holds a relative market share of only 0.2, placing it in a weak position in the market. The BCG technique would identify product D as a question mark. In the cases of question marks, we need to further evaluate the situation surrounding the product to decide on its allocation of resources.

For example, if product D represents a strategic move into a new market of great importance to the organization, we might seek to increase investment in it to improve its market position. However, if product D represented a "me-too" product, perhaps obtained through an acquisition of another company, we would consider divesting it.

Execution

Marketers can create the traditional BCG graph using market growth rate and relative market share axes. The graph can be crafted using graphing tools such as Microsoft Excel. The graph can also be generated using tools from online analytics vendors such as Marketing Objects (marketingobjects.com) and SmartDraw (smartdraw.com). Alternatively, marketers can use the tabular approach discussed in this section. [7-14, 7-15]

MARKETING MADE MEASURABLE

Yahoo!: Searching for a Credible Service Portfolio: Yahoo! (yahoo.com) enjoyed a golden age during the 1990s and early 2000s. Consumers flocked to its search engine and relished the rich media content the company offered.

Fast-forward to the 2010s, and we find a company badly in need of a service portfolio strategy. Its former star, its search engine, has since been replaced by Microsoft's Bing after Yahoo! conceded defeat to search giant Google.

One could argue that its display advertising plays the role of cash cow, keeping the company afloat during stormy seas. Another source of cash came from the proceeds of the sale of its stake in Chinese company Alibaba, amounting to $7.1 billion. Yahoo! indicated it planned to keep part of that cash (originally earmarked for shareholders) to turn around the company and rebuild its service portfolio. Without a credible service portfolio, no company will survive long. [7-16]

PRODUCT AND SERVICE METRICS

In this section, we review some basic but useful metrics for tracking sales, profitability, and other results of products and services. We recommend applying the metrics to track how well (or poorly) the organization's products and services fare in the market.

Input Data

To calculate the metrics we cover in this section, we will need to gather the data shown in Figures 7.39 and 7.40. In addition, we will also need to obtain the costs to manufacture our products or deliver our services so that we can calculate gross margins.

Figure 7.39 shows total revenue by month for different products and services. Using the data, we can determine how the sales of product A vary by month.

Product/ Service	Jan	Feb	Mar	Apr	May	Jun	Jul	Aug	Sep	Oct	Nov	Dec
Product/Service A												
Product/Service B												
Product/Service C												

Figure 7.39: Product/ Service Sales Input Table: Total Revenue by Month, Products A, B, and C

Figure 7.40 displays the revenue in different markets for different products or services. The different markets (Market 1, Market 2, and Market 3) represent different groups of people purchasing the same products or services.

Product A: Market	Jan	Feb	Mar	Apr	May	Jun	Jul	Aug	Sep	Oct	Nov	Dec
Market 1												
Market 2												
Market 3												

Figure 7.40: Product/ Service Sales Input Table: Revenue in Different Markets by Month, Product A

Revenue Trends and Contribution Metrics

Having collected the required data, we can now apply it to assess key characteristics of the organization's sales of its products and services.

Figure 7.41 shows a plot of revenue trends. We plot out sales data over time to determine if we can assess certain trends. The figure shows three typical trends.

- **Steady Rise:** The sales data for product A show the first trend, a steady rise over time. We will want to identify possible drivers to the increasing sales.

- **Declining Sales:** Product B sales data demonstrate the second trend, where sales decline over time. We need to find out why.

- **Seasonal Patterns:** The sales data for product C show a third pattern, that of seasonality. The data show that sales are strong in the winter, and decrease in the summer. Such seasonal patterns would be indicative of winter-oriented products and services, such as snow chains and ski rental services.

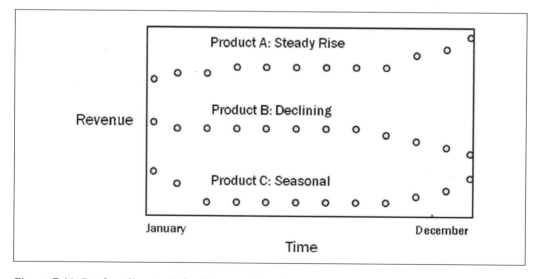

Figure 7.41: Product/Service Sales: Revenue Trends

Market Adoption Metrics

Figure 7.42 shows a plot of market adoption. We plot out sales data across markets to determine adoption rates of different products/services in different markets. In the figure, we see that product A performs significantly better than products B and C in markets one and two, but performs poorly in market three. Conversely, we see that product C out-performs product A in market three.

We can conduct market surveys or even conjoint analysis to identify the attributes that make product A such a hit in markets one and two, but less popular in market three. We could then apply what we learned to new product development for markets one and two.

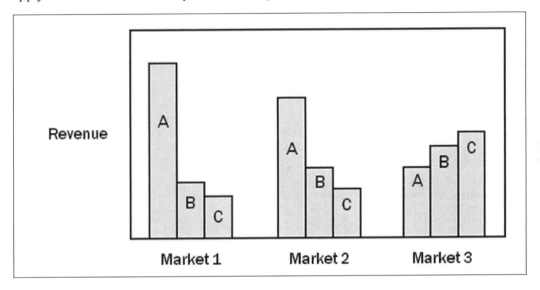

Figure 7.42: Product/Service Sales: Market Adoption

Product/Service Profitability Metrics

Figure 7.43 shows a Product Success Quadrant tool to analyze product/service profitability, in graphical format. Using the tool, we can assess how each product contributes to organizational profitability. In the figure, the gross margin (GM) threshold of 50% represents a particular organization's goals for gross margin. Different markets and organizations will have different goals for gross margin. [7-17]

The four quadrant nature of the tool makes it appear similar to the format of the Boston Consulting Group (BCG) portfolio allocation model. Organizations may find the Product Success Quadrant tool more useful than the BCG model in situations where market share data for competitors is not available.

For example, companies in niche markets often compete against small private firms. The SEC does not require such firms to disclose their revenues or gross margins. The Product Success Quadrant model gives companies the ability to calculate product/service success as measured by internal standards, even if it cannot obtain competitor data to assess its performance relative to that of its competitors.

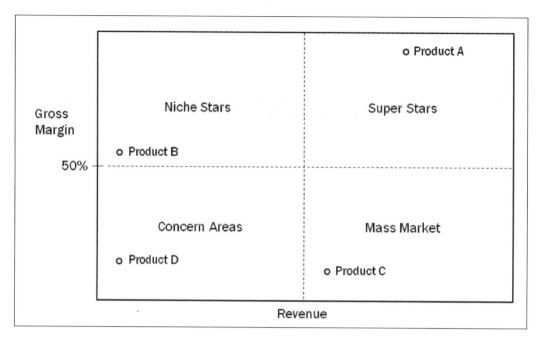

Figure 7.43: Product/Service Profitability: Product Success Quadrant Tool: Graphical Format
Adapted from product profitability analysis tool by Demand Metric (demandmetric.com)
Used with permission

To use the tool, we must first calculate the gross margin for each product or service. Product/service gross margin is defined as the financial contribution provided to the organization by the sales of the product or service. Gross margin is typically expressed as a percentage, and is calculated using the formula below.

$$\text{Gross Margin (Percentage)} = (\text{Revenue} - \text{COGS}) / \text{Revenue} * 100\%$$

In the formula, COGS stands for the **cost of goods sold**. The cost of goods sold is the cost incurred in manufacturing the product or delivering the service. It includes the cost of labor and materials to make the product, as well as other directly related costs, such as shipping. [7-18]

Figure 7.44 shows a convenient tabular format to execute the product/service profitability tool. The figure includes entries for average revenue (i.e., revenue averaged over one year or one quarter), cost of goods sold, and gross margin.

Product/ Service	Average Revenue	Cost of Goods Sold	Gross Margin	Quadrant
Product/ Service A	High	Low	High	Super Stars
Product/ Service B	Low	Low	High	Niche Stars
Product/ Service C	High	High	Low	Mass Market
Product/ Service D	Low	High	Low	Concern Areas

Figure 7.44: Product/Service Profitability: Product Success Quadrant Tool: Tabular Format

Using the data in the table, we can plot the revenue and gross margin for each product or service on the graphical format. The tool superimposes four quadrants over the data, signifying the profitability potential for various types of products and services.

- **Super Stars Quadrant**: This quadrant designates high levels of profitability. The products or services in the quadrant are "superstars" in that they generate significant revenue at high gross margin, resulting in robust profits for the organization.

- **Niche Stars Quadrant**: This quadrant designates products or services with good profitability but relatively low revenue. They are "niche stars" because they are profitable, but do not generate high revenues because they are purchased by a limited audience.

- **Mass Market**: This quadrant designates products or services with high revenues and relatively low profitability, targeted to a mass audience. The products or services in the quadrant are "mass market" in that they generate high revenues (due to high unit sales), but at low gross margins.

- **Concern Areas**: This quadrant designates products or services with low revenues and low gross margins. We must determine why the products or services in the quadrant are performing so poorly. If we cannot improve the product or service's revenue or gross margin, we should discontinue it.

MARKETING MADE MEASURABLE

Apple: Superstar in Revenue and Gross Margin: Apple (apple.com) reported a gross margin (GM) result of 44.7% in the first quarter of 2012. According to chief financial officer (CFO) Peter Oppenheimer, the gross margin was "higher than we've seen since I've been with Apple in 15 years." Apple's gross margin has steadily increased from approximately 30% in 2007, to 35% in 2008 and 2009, to 40% in 2010, and finally to its all-time high of 44.7% in 2012. Chief executive officer (CEO) Tim Cook stated that favorable component prices in its supply chain aided the high gross margin metrics. [7-19]

According to Price Waterhouse Coopers' (PWC, at pwc.com) Global Technology Scorecard for consumer electronics, Apple's performance deserves "Super Star" status on our Product Success Quadrant approach. PWC found the following metrics for the top performing consumer electronics companies in the first quarter of 2012 (PWC estimates): [7-20]

- **Apple:** Revenue of $39.2 billion; Gross margin of 47%
- **Canon:** Revenue of $10.1 billion ; Gross margin of 47%
- **Philips:** Revenue of $7.3 billion; Gross margin of 38%
- **Sony:** Revenue of $19.5 billion; Gross margin of 31%
- **Toshiba:** Revenue of $21.3 billion; Gross margin of 26%

Apple thus led the pack in terms of total revenue and tied for highest gross margin.

ATTRIBUTE PREFERENCE TESTING

Earlier in the chapter, we discussed the ability of conjoint analysis to determine the attributes that certain market segments prefer in our products and services. This section discusses an alternative approach. The alternative approach applies paid search engine marketing (SEM) tools, such as Google's AdWords service, to gauge respondent preference of different attributes.

Figure 7.45 shows the layout of a typical Google search engine results page (SERP). At the top of the page is the familiar search box where users enter search queries. Navigation within search products offered by Google, such as images, maps, videos, and so forth, is shown on the left hand side of the page, designated in the figure as "Left Nav."

Google places featured AdWords ads at the top center of the page for ads that it finds particularly relevant to the user's search. Google places other more general AdWords ads at the right hand side of the page. Google presents organic (non-paid) search results below the featured AdWords ads.

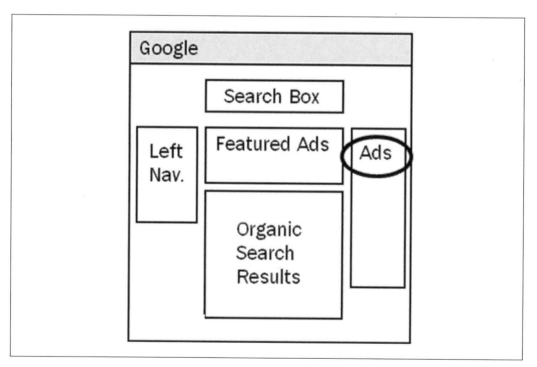

Figure 7.45: Attribute Preference Testing: Google Search Engine Results Page Layout

Google developed its AdWords paid search engine marketing tool to deliver advertisements relevant to the user's search terms. We can extend the application of AdWords to determine the interest level in various product or service attributes.

Figure 7.46 demonstrates the approach. We can test three different AdWords ads to gauge respondent preferences for three different product attributes. For example, we can test interest in three different attributes for vacuum cleaners made by fictitious company Acme Vacuum. We can run the three ads in Google AdWords for a period of time, and then measure the response for each ad:

- **Advertisement A: "Vacuum Carpets Fast."** This ad tests respondent preference for the attribute of speed, citing the vacuum's "Turbo-Vortex" design. The results of the test show the popularity of the speed attribute, with 240 "clicks" and 12 "purchases." "Clicks" represent situations where users demonstrated their interest in the speed attribute by clicking on the ad to learn more. "Purchases" designate scenarios where users found the speed attribute so compelling that they placed an order on the spot. Based on the results, we conclude that speed is an important (and revenue-generating!) attribute.

- **Advertisement B: "Hey Allergy Sufferers!"** This ad tests respondent preference for the attribute of particulate filtration, citing the vacuum's "Hyper-HEPA filter" to remove small particles, such as allergens. The results of the test show an unusual situation. Many respondents appeared interested in such an attribute, with 200 clicks, but only two respondents actually purchased the vacuum. Such a result could indicate a potential conflict between the ad's claims and actual product information revealed on the company's website. We tentatively conclude that attribute filtration is an important attribute, but that we must investigate the poor conversion rate between clicks and buys.

- **Advertisement C: "Vacuum Drapes Easily."** This ad tests respondent preference for the attribute of accessories provided with the vacuum cleaner, citing the "EZ-DRAPE" drape cleaning attachment. The test fared poorly, with only four clicks, none of which resulted in a sale. Based on the results, we conclude that the respondents have a lower preference for the accessories attribute than they do for speed or particulate filtration.

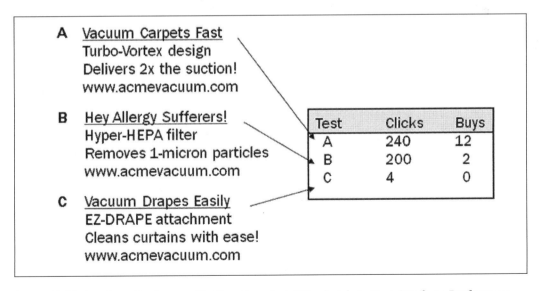

Figure 7.46: Attribute Preference Testing: Google AdWords Ads to Test Attribute Preferences

For situations where speed is required but high accuracy is not, we have found that the AdWords-based attribute preference testing technique provide a fast and cost-effective alternative to conjoint analysis techniques.

SUMMARY

We can apply analytics tools and techniques to support the development and marketing of products and services. In this chapter, we covered the following product and service models and metrics: conjoint analysis, decision tree models, portfolio resource allocation, product and service metrics, and attribute preference testing.

Conjoint Analysis: Conjoint analysis is a statistical market research technique where consumers make trade-offs between two or more features or benefits of a product or service. By examining the trade-offs consumers make, we can determine which features to include in new products and services. To execute conjoint analysis, we proceed with the following steps:

- **Prepare for Conjoint:** We identify key attributes (characteristics) of the product or service and assign levels to each attribute. We then form candidate bundles, each representing a combination of the attributes at different levels.

- **Collect Preference Data**: We ask consumers to evaluate their preference for each bundle.

- **Code Data for Analysis**: We prepare the data for conjoint analysis by coding it in a form that avoids computational problems during the analysis.

- **Calculate Attribute Part-Worths**: We calculate the preference for each attribute (called the part-worth) using regression analysis or other technique.

- **Apply Conjoint Results**: We can investigate possible market segmentation using the part worths we have calculated.

Decision Tree Model: Decision tree models are hierarchical tree diagrams to assist in the decision among multiple product or service development projects. The models identify outcomes (such as revenue) for alternative scenarios for each project, and assign probabilities to each. We multiply the different outcomes by their probabilities to come up with their expected values. We sum up the expected values for each of the scenarios for the different projects. We select the project with the largest sum of expected values.

Portfolio Resource Allocation: We can use portfolio resource allocation models to decide how much money to invest in the organization's different products and services. The Boston Consulting Group developed its product portfolio model informally known as the BCG model. The BCG model identifies products and services as stars, dogs, cash cows, or question marks, depending on their market growth rate and relative market share. Companies can then invest cash from the cash cows into the rising stars, and divest themselves of poorly performing dogs.

Product and Service Metrics: We can monitor products and services by examining product and service metrics. For example, we can create plots of the revenue from products and services and identify trends over time. We can also study the adoption of different products and services in various markets to determine their suitability for each market. By calculating the gross margins of our various products and services, we can assess the profitability for each and determine if they are "superstars" or "concern areas."

Attribute Preference Testing: We can take advantage of the immediate feedback available from the Internet with attribute preference testing. In the testing, we use search engine marketing (SEM) tools, such as Google's AdWords service, to gauge respondent preference of different attributes. We run several different SEM ads, each emphasizing different attributes of the product. We can then use the analytics function built in to SEM tools to calculate the number of clicks and conversions for each SEM advertisement.

Terminology

Attribute: In conjoint analysis, the characteristics consumers consider when evaluating products and services, such as battery life for cell phones

Attribute Levels: In conjoint analysis, the degree of each attribute, such as levels of four hours, eight hours, and twelve hours for the attribute of battery life for cell phones.

BCG Model (aka Boston Consulting Group product portfolio resource allocation model): Resource allocation model providing a graphical mechanism to guide investment into different products in a company's portfolio

Bundles (of Attributes): In conjoint analysis, the combination of attributes defining potentially marketable products and services

Cash Cow: In the Boston Consulting Group product portfolio resource allocation model, products with low market growth and high relative market share

Coding: In conjoint analysis, transforming raw conjoint data into a format useful for computer processing

Conjoint Analysis: Statistical market research technique to examine the trade-offs consumers make to determine marketable combinations (bundles) of attributes at different levels

Decision Nodes: In decision tree models, decision nodes represent situations where marketers must decide on two or more alternatives, based on the data available

Decision Tree Model: Decision analysis tool using hierarchical tree diagrams to show potential scenarios and their probabilities of occurrence

Dogs: In the Boston Consulting Group product portfolio resource allocation model, products with low market growth and low relative market share

GE/McKinsey Matrix (aka GE/McKinsey product portfolio resource allocation model): Resource allocation model guiding product investment using industry attractiveness and business unit strength measures

Linear Dependency: Situation where two or more independent variables are related

Part-Worths: In conjoint analysis, the utility presented by particular attributes

Profiles: In conjoint analysis, profiles are specific bundles preferred by customer segments

Question Marks (aka Problem Children): In the Boston Consulting Group product portfolio resource allocation model, products with high market growth and low relative market share

Random Nodes: In decision tree models, random nodes represent random selections among multiple scenarios.

SERP (Search Engine Results Page): Web page delivering Internet search results

Stars: In the Boston Consulting Group product portfolio resource allocation model, products with high market growth and high relative market share

Class Discussion

1. What principal attributes do consumers evaluate during the purchase decision of your organization's products and services?

2. What products or services in your organization do you believe could benefit from a conjoint analysis study?

3. Regarding decision tree models, why do outcomes (such as revenue) vary so greatly with different scenarios?

4. Regarding portfolio resource allocation, which products and services in your organization would you classify as "cash cows"? Which are "stars" and "dogs"?

5. What type of product and service metrics does your organization monitor on a routine basis?

Practice Problems

1. To support a conjoint analysis project, identify the principal attributes and their levels for a product or service of your choice.

2. Using the attributes and levels identified in Exercise 1, form candidate bundles ("cards").

3. Using the cards identified in Exercise 2, ask your class teammates or co-workers to rate their preferences for the different cards.

4. Using the data you gathered in Exercise 3, code the data and determine the part-worths for each attribute.

5. Using the part-worths you calculated in Exercise 4, identify market segments to target and corresponding messaging.

6. Develop a decision tree model to select between two alternatives. The first alternative is to develop a standard product for $200,000. The standard product has 3 possible scenarios: Strong adoption (probability = 0.1, Revenue = $400,000), average adoption (0.8, $100,000), or poor adoption (0.1, $10,000). The second alternative is to develop a deluxe product for $400,000. The deluxe product has 3 possible scenarios: Strong adoption (probability = 0.2, Revenue = $500,000), average adoption (0.5, $200,000), or poor adoption (0.3, $20,000).

7. Identify the stars, dogs, cash cows, and question marks in a portfolio consisting of four services. Service 1 maintains a market growth rate (MGR) of 1% and a relative market share (RMS) of 10%. The remaining services have the following data: Service 2 (MGR = 6%, RMS = 1%), Service 3 (MGR = 10%, RMS = 10%), and Service 4 (MGR = 1%, RMS = 1%).

8. Develop a market adoption plot for four products: A, B, C, and D. Product A commands a 10% market share in market 1, a 5% share in market 2, and a 1% share in market 3. Product B holds market shares of 2%, 5%, and 1% in markets 1, 2, and 3, respectively. Product C holds market shares of 11%, 1%, and 2% in markets 1, 2, and 3, respectively. Product D holds market shares of 1%, 2%, and 3% in markets 1, 2, and 3, respectively.

Chapter 8.
PRICE ANALYTICS

Chapter Outline

We cover the following marketing analytics topics in this chapter:

- ☑ **Pricing Techniques**: Reviewing different techniques and when to apply them
- ☑ **Pricing Assessment**: Checking profit results from pricing techniques
- ☑ **Profitable Pricing**: Incorporating consumer demand into pricing
- ☑ **Pricing for Business Markets**: Establish pricing for B2B markets
- ☑ **Price Discrimination**: Increasing profit using different prices for different segments

---

"The bitterness of poor quality is remembered long after the sweetness of low price has faded from memory."
– Aldo Gucci

Aldo Gucci, son of Guccio Gucci, the founder of luxury retailer Gucci (gucci.com), drove premium prices for the brand during his lifetime. He is credited with masterminding Gucci's successful move into the American luxury market.

Aldo's eldest son Giorgio said, "He was the first to see the huge opportunities in the U.S...It's thanks to our store on Fifth Avenue that our name became well known among Americans."

Aldo positioned the company as one of the premier providers of fashion merchandise to the world's elite, commanding luxury prices for luxury goods. President Kennedy once told Aldo Gucci, "You are the first Italian ambassador of fashion." [8-1]

This chapter covers a variety of analytical pricing approaches. We start by covering different pricing techniques to address different situations, products/services, and markets. Next, we describe how pricing and consumer demand can affect profitability. We then show several approaches especially suited for sales to businesses, also known as B2B sales. We close the chapter by discussing price discrimination.

PRICING TECHNIQUES

In this section, we cover pricing techniques to equip marketers for pricing under virtually any scenario. With each technique, we include a brief description, indicate the application or scenario for which the technique is suited, discuss its advantages and disadvantages, and demonstrate examples of the techniques. [8-2]

We will use a running example of the fictitious Acme Light Bulb Company, makers of electric light bulbs (lamps). Acme manufactures three lines of light bulbs. It manufactures its premium Acme LUX high efficiency light bulbs using light emitting diode (LED) technology, its midline halogen light bulbs, and its economy compact fluorescent lamps (CFLs).

Figure 8.1 shows the three different types of light bulbs manufactured by Acme.

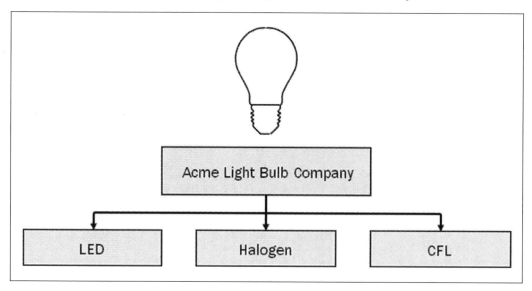

Figure 8.1: Acme Light Bulb Company: Example to Demonstrate Pricing Techniques

Creaming Pricing

Description: In **creaming pricing** (also known as **skimming**), we set prices high during the introduction of a new product or service. The technique gets its name from the analogy of "skimming" the "cream" off the market by targeting the top 1 – 5% of the market. The "cream" of the market represents individuals who value the product or service highly and show low sensitivity to price.

Figure 8.2 shows the concept behind creaming pricing, where companies "skim the cream off the top of the market."

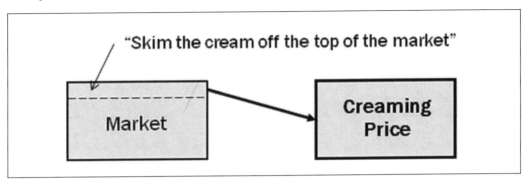

Figure 8.2: Pricing Techniques: Creaming Pricing

Application: Creaming pricing works well for unique, glamorous products and services that face few (if any) substitutes. For example, Panasonic charged very high prices for its new three dimensional (3-D) television sets when the company first introduced them to the consumer market. Once competitors offered similar products, Panasonic had to lower the price. Creaming pricing will not work once competitors offer similar products, because consumers can purchase the product or service more cheaply from the competition.

Advantages: The high prices used in creaming pricing results in higher initial revenue during the launch of the new product or service. Companies use the revenue to offset the significant cost required to develop new products and services.

Disadvantages: Creaming pricing only works if consumers cannot purchase the same product or service from another company for less. If competitors sell similar products and services, consumers will purchase the lower-price versions instead, and the creaming pricing technique will fail.

Example: After significant research and development, Acme has introduced its new Acme LUX LED-based replacement light bulbs (lamps). The Acme LUX light bulb replaces regular incandescent light bulbs, using standard medium base light bulb sockets, similar to products offered by competitors. Unlike competitors' products, the Acme LUX light bulb offers high illumination levels and natural spectrum lighting. By comparison, competitors' models look dim and throw off a blue tint, characteristic of many LED light bulbs.

Using creaming pricing, we could decide to charge $30 for the light bulb during the introductory period, even though incandescent light bulbs are available for under $1, and competitors offer models for $10.

Even at this high price, some consumers will choose to purchase the Acme LUX model because the value they place on the higher light output and natural spectrum light is greater than the value of the price charged. The increased revenue from the high prices accelerates payback of research and investment costs.

Demand-Based Pricing

Description: In demand-based pricing, we set prices to maximize profit, based on consumer demand for the product or service. Economics tells us that for most goods, quantity demanded increases as we decrease price, and vice versa. Economists call this relationship the demand function, plotted out as the demand curve.

If we adopt very low prices, we sell high quantities, but our profits will suffer because our prices are so low. If we set very high prices, we will sell far fewer units, so our profits will again be low. Demand-based pricing sets the pricing between these two extremes to maximize profitability.

Figure 8.3 shows the concept behind demand-based pricing, where the technique applies the demand curve to pricing decisions.

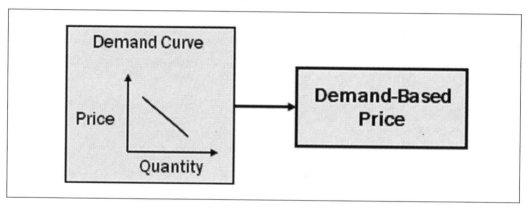

Figure 8.3: Pricing Techniques: Demand Based Pricing

Applications: Demand-based pricing works well for situations where companies have the freedom to adjust prices to market demand. Demand-based pricing works especially well when companies can change prices quickly based on market demand. For example, online retailer Amazon.com adjusts prices over time to maximize profitability.

Advantages: Demand-based pricing represents an effective method to maximize long-term profit. Also, many organizations use demand-based pricing, resulting in vast bodies of knowledge about the subject. Furthermore, the technique is rooted in sound economic theory, lending confidence in the approach.

Disadvantages: We must know the demand curve for the product or service to apply demand-based pricing. To construct the demand curve, we find out the quantity sold at different price points. Obtaining the data for the demand curve could prove time-consuming and expensive.

Example: Acme carefully monitors the quantity of its premium Acme LUX light bulbs it sells at different prices. Over time, the company has developed a demand curve for the quantity of light bulbs it can expect to sell at different prices. Acme uses the demand curve as part of its strategy to maximize profits on its Acme LUX light bulb.

MARKETING MADE MEASURABLE

Demand-Based Pricing for Parking in Demand: Parking space unavailability accounts for as much as 33% of auto traffic in some areas of San Francisco, due to drivers circling areas as they hunt for spaces. To cut down on the resulting congestion, the city has initiated a new parking program using demand-based pricing. The program raises the price of parking when empty lots are scarce, and lowers the price when lots open up.

Sensors embedded in the street detect when lots become available. Connections from the sensors feed availability data to new computerized parking meters, which adjust prices according to parking lot availability.

For example, parking on Drumm Street near popular coastside Ferry Building restaurants formerly cost $3.50 per hour. At that price, drivers often filled every available parking space. With the new program, prices are up to $4.50 per hour, but at least restaurant patrons can find parking. [8-3]

Everyday Low Pricing

Description: Everyday low pricing (EDLP) sets prices consistently low to attract price-sensitive customers and increase sales quantities. The technique avoids deep discounts and sales promotions. Retail giant Walmart (walmart.com) and home improvement store Lowes (lowes.com) use everyday low pricing to position their brands as providing good value for money. Both avoid deep discount sales in favor of consistently low pricing.

Figure 8.4 shows the concept of everyday low pricing, where the technique discourages deep discounting, opting instead to maintain steady prices.

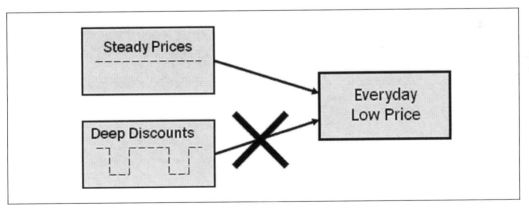

Figure 8.4: Pricing Techniques: Everyday Low Pricing

To execute an everyday low pricing approach, companies must wield a competitive advantage in low cost operations. For example, Walmart boasts sophisticated supply chain technology to keep costs low and profits high. Walmart leverages its low cost advantage to expand operations internationally, and is growing its presence in Argentina, Brazil, Canada, China, Japan, Mexico, South America, and other markets. [8-4]

Applications: Everyday low pricing works well for consumer packaged goods with well-known brands. For example, Walmart sells Hoover vacuum cleaners, LEGO toys, and Tide laundry detergent at consistently low prices.

Advantages: Everyday low pricing tends to smooth out the demand for products. Without everyday low pricing, companies face peaks of demand during sales promotions. The peaks of demand strain the supply chain to keep up, forcing manufacturing factories to work overtime. Once the promotion ends, demand wanes. The manufacturing inefficiencies from the rapidly varying demand can cause costs to increase.

Disadvantages: Everyday low pricing avoids deep discounts and sales promotions to keep manufacturing costs down, contributing to lower prices. But many companies rely on sales promotions to temporarily boost revenues in certain situations, such as slow sales cycles. The companies might also find themselves responding to consumer expectations for sales promotions at certain times, such as the end of year holiday season.

Example: Acme sells its midline halogen light bulbs to kitchen and bath supply stores. Acme designs the light bulbs to replace existing halogen light bulbs in kitchen and bath light fixtures. The light bulbs are specially designed for certain fixtures, and few substitute products exist.

Acme charges an everyday low price for the light bulbs, giving the company two benefits. In the first benefit, Acme avoids attracting new competitors into the replacement light bulb industry, which could happen if Acme set very high prices for its bulbs. In the second benefit, Acme reduces spikes in demand for light bulbs (and the high manufacturing costs that would result), which could occur if Acme ran frequent price promotions.

MARKETING MADE MEASURABLE

J.C. Penney: Fair and Square Every Day Pricing: Department store chain J.C. Penney (jcp.com) launched a new everyday low pricing policy in 2012 as part of its plan to transform the 110 year old chain into a 21st century retail powerhouse. Called "Fair and Square Every Day," the policy divorces the chain from its dependency on deep discounts to drive sales.

Instead of deep discount sales and promotions, the chain offers only three types of prices: "Every Day," which reflects typical pricing, "Month Long Value," which represents seasonal events such as back to school sales, and "Best Prices," to move clearance items. Also, prices will now end in "0" instead of "99" to emphasize the "fair and square" notion.

While analysts commend J.C. Penney on breaking its alliance on deep discount sales, they do not believe the approach will result in increased sales. Fixed-price sales (no discounting permitted) works best only for highly differentiated items, such as those from Bose and Cartier, the analysts state. The analysts find that neither the merchandise (which consists largely of undifferentiated, mass market goods) nor the store (which does not enjoy the same cachet as differentiated stores such as the Apple Store) has the differentiation needed to pull off this type of pricing approach. [8-5]

Going Rate Pricing

Description: In going rate pricing, companies align their prices with those of competitors and adopt a so-called market price. Companies thus charge identical (or nearly so) prices for similar goods. For example, adjacent gas stations of different brands often post very similar prices, often within a few pennies of each other.

Figure 8.5 shows the concept behind going rate pricing, where companies set prices using the "going rate" for goods, as established by its competitors.

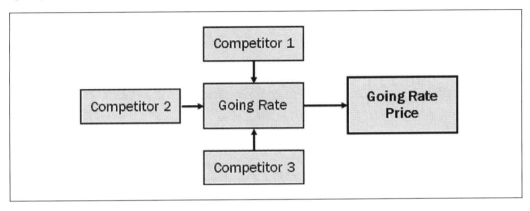

Figure 8.5: Pricing Techniques: Going Rate Pricing

Applications: Companies use the technique of going rate pricing for products that vary little from supplier to supplier, such as gasoline, steel, and meat. Going rate pricing is also common in concentrated industries, where a few companies dominate the market. Smaller companies believe that they must align their prices with the leaders to survive.

Advantages: Proponents of going rate pricing state that the technique "reflects the collective wisdom of the industry" in that each company applies uniform pricing throughout the industry. Smaller companies benefit from the approach by avoiding potential price wars that could occur if they set significantly different prices than those of the larger firms.

Disadvantages: Problems arise in the theory behind the approach as well as the execution. The theory of the "collective wisdom of the industry" is flawed, because the industry could be wrong. For example, some critics blame the housing industry on inflating home prices in the late 1990s and early 2000s, resulting in painful losses for many individuals when house prices returned to sustainable levels.

Going rate pricing also threatens to violate antitrust laws. Specifically, the Sherman Antitrust Act of 1890 prohibits business activities that reduce competition, including colluding to fix prices. For example, the Sherman Act strictly forbids two gas station owners from meeting to set a price that both will charge.

Example: Acme sells compact fluorescent lamps (CFLs) to home improvement retailers, for sale to consumers. Retailers face many alternative suppliers for such a common product. The retailers will choose to purchase the CFLs for a certain price.

Suppliers setting their price significantly above this "going rate" are not likely to sell their CFLs. Suppliers setting their price significantly below this "going rate" might trigger a price war with the other suppliers, which could undercut profits for the entire industry.

Markup/ Cost Plus Pricing

Description: **In markup/ cost plus pricing**, we simply add an arbitrary percentage, such as 20%, to the unit cost to arrive at the final price. Figure 8.6 shows the concept. The term **markup** is used when applying the technique to products, such as retail sales to consumers. The term **cost plus** is used when applying the technique to services. We cover a related technique, called target-return pricing, later in this chapter.

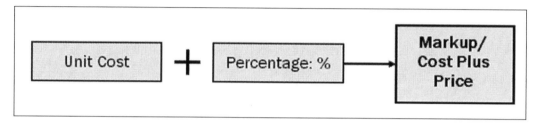

Figure 8.6: Pricing Techniques: Markup/ Cost Plus

Applications: The markup/ cost plus pricing technique is widely used for both products and services. Typical products include consumer packaged goods, such as frozen pizza and casual apparel. The technique is popular for these near-commodity products because higher profit margins could attract additional competitors. Typical services include building contractors and attorneys, who add a percentage to their costs to arrive at their billing fees.

Advantages: The markup/ cost plus pricing technique is fast and easy to calculate, as we demonstrate with the example below.

Disadvantages: The technique fails to incorporate customer demand in the price. Perhaps customers are willing to pay much more for the product or service than the company is charging using markup/ cost plus. Therefore, the technique is not likely to result in the highest profit. In addition, the actual markup percentage is arbitrary, and might not reflect the cost of capital or project risk.

Example: To calculate the markup price, we first calculate the unit cost, and then use the unit cost to determine the markup price. The following formula calculates the unit cost:

$$\text{Unit Cost} = (\text{Variable Cost}) + (\text{Fixed Cost}) / (\text{Unit Sales})$$

The unit cost is the cost to manufacture each unit, and consists of the variable cost and the fixed cost allocated over each unit. Variable costs are defined as the labor and materials to manufacture each unit. Fixed costs are defined as costs that remain fixed as we increase the number of units manufactured, such as rent and insurance. Unit sales are defined as the number of units that we sell.

In Acme's case, if the Acme LUX light bulb has a variable cost of $10 per light bulb, fixed costs of $400,000, and a unit sales estimate of 40,000, we would calculate unit cost as follows:

Unit Cost = (Variable Cost) + (Fixed Cost) / (Unit Sales)
Unit Cost = ($10) + ($400,000) / (40,000) = $10 + $10 = $20 per light bulb

We then calculate the markup price using the formula below, where Markup Percentage refers to the company's desired return on sales. If Acme plans to mark up their light bulbs by 20%, we would arrive at the following markup price:

Markup Price = (Unit Cost) / (1 – Markup Percentage)
Markup Price = ($20) / (1 – 0.20) = $25 per light bulb

Penetration Pricing

Description: In **penetration pricing**, we set prices very low to attract new customers and expand market share. For example, Japan priced its computer semiconductor chips at "bargain-basement" prices in the 1980s to stimulate demand and capture market share from United States chip manufacturers. The approach did stimulate demand, but the U.S. government declared the practice unfair to U.S. chip companies and invoked $84 million in sanctions.

Figure 8.7 shows the concept behind penetration pricing, where companies set prices lower than many of its competitors to increase market share.

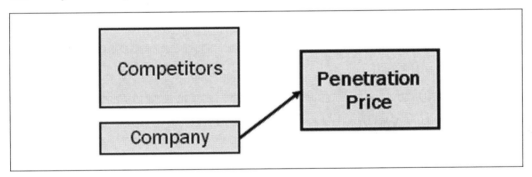

Figure 8.7: Pricing Techniques: Penetration Pricing

Applications: Companies apply penetration pricing when they plan to capture market share as quickly as possible with new products (some people refer to this type of situation as a "land grab"). The company with the largest market share will become the leader. Market leaders can wield a great deal of power in the market, and can have greater profitability than smaller players. Penetration pricing works best when companies can take advantage of economies of scale to reduce manufacturing costs as volumes increase.

For example, consumer packaged goods vendors such as Procter and Gamble and Unilever apply penetration pricing when penetrating into new and unknown international markets. The companies hope the market will become hooked on the offering and continue to purchase it after the companies increase the price. Hewlett-Packard sells its printers at low prices to enter the market, and then makes money by selling ink cartridges at very high prices.

Many Internet-based companies apply penetration price to garner market share. For example, social networking site LinkedIn (linkedin.com) allows users to sign up for free. They monetize their venture by selling ads, as well as Pro memberships with additional features.

Advantages: Penetration pricing can increase sales volume and market share quickly. Once customers purchase from the company offering the lowest price, they can be reluctant to switch to a competitor's version, even if prices begin to rise. Switching costs, such as those to switch suppliers for computer software or industrial goods, make it very expensive to switch. Many computer software programs and industrial goods include proprietary elements which cannot be transferred to competitor's versions, making switching very costly.

Disadvantages: Penetration pricing will not yield maximum profitability in the short term, due to the low prices involved. The technique might also result in a price war, where competitors undercut the company's low price with an even lower one. Price wars can devastate industries. For example, the airline industry suffered in the "air fare wars" of the 1990s, where airlines felt they had to reduce their prices to match competitors' discounted fares. [8-7]

Example: Acme might choose to engage in penetration pricing with its economical compact fluorescent lamps (CFLs). Consumers perceive CFLs as commodities, with few differentiating physical characteristics and no clear brand name leader. And yet, Acme chooses to participate in the CFL market because of the huge market size.

The U.S. Department of Energy estimated that businesses and consumers spent $252 million on CFLs in 2010 alone. Acme could cut its price to penetration levels to increase its market share, but it might exercise caution to avoid triggering a price war. It must also calculate if the resulting price still meets company-mandated rates of return (see the capital budgeting section later in this chapter). [8-8]

Prestige Pricing

Description: **Prestige pricing** sets prices high to signal high quality or status. Prestige pricing is sometimes also known as **image pricing**, **perceived value pricing**, or **premium pricing**. Figure 8.8 shows the concept behind prestige brands, where prestige brands (shown wearing a crown, to denote prestige status) can leverage their great brand equity to command high prices. For example, luxury watchmaker Rolex (rolex.com) sets prices very high to signal that the product is of high quality.

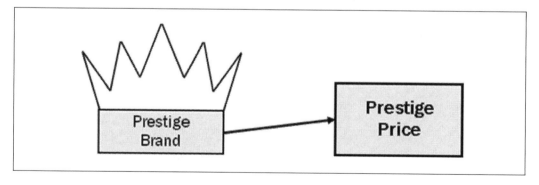

Figure 8.8: Pricing Techniques: Prestige Pricing

Applications: Image-oriented products, such as high-end perfumes, luxury watches, exotic automobiles, and haute couture clothing, use prestige pricing to convey an aura of high quality. Beyond traditional image-oriented products, companies can apply prestige pricing to virtually any highly differentiated product or service. For example, Apple uses premium pricing with its line of notebook computers.

Advantages: Prestige pricing's high prices can result in high revenue for the organization. For example, by growing the allure of its brand, Apple improved its profit margin from 13.3% in 2007 to 28.2% in 2011. [8-9]

Disadvantages: Prestige pricing demands strong brand equity and highly differentiated products and services. Unknown or poorly regarded brands cannot command the high pricing premiums used with prestige pricing. Companies can spend a great deal to obtain high brand equity. For example, Apple spent $691 million in advertising in 2010 (according to its Securities and Exchange Commission 10-K form), the year in which Apple launched the first iPad and the new iPhone 4. [8-10]

Example: Acme could choose to apply prestige pricing to its premium Acme LUX LED light bulbs. The Acme LUX differentiates itself from competitors' models by producing high illumination levels and natural spectrum lighting. By comparison, competitors' models look dim and throw off a blue tint, characteristic of many LED light bulbs.

In addition to high product performance, we will need to position the brand as a premium provider for discriminating users. To that end, Acme could run image-based advertisements showing how celebrities who demand high-quality light sources (such as famous artists and architects) prefer the Acme LUX light bulb.

Target-Return Pricing

Description: Target-return pricing calculates price to achieve a company-defined return on investment (ROI). The technique is similar to the markup/ cost plus technique described earlier, but substitutes the target return (the ROI required by the company) in place of an arbitrary percentage, such as 20%.

Figure 8.9 shows the concept behind target-return pricing, where companies set prices based on achieving a target rate of return.

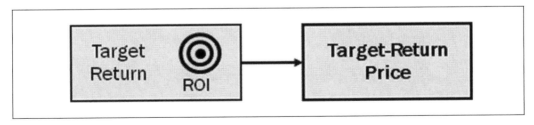

Figure 8.9: Pricing Techniques: Target-Return Pricing

Applications: Companies selling industrial products to businesses often set prices according to the target-return technique. Typical categories include tools, safety equipment, fasteners, maintenance supplies, industrial supplies, and other related areas. Regulated public utilities also use this method to ensure a fair return on investment.

Advantages: Similar to markup/ cost plus techniques, target-return pricing is quick and easy to calculate, and has been used for many years.

Disadvantages: Similar to markup/ cost plus techniques, target-return pricing rarely results in the highest possible profit, because it fails to incorporate market demand. Companies with unique products or services will likely generate higher profits by applying demand-based methods. In addition, target-return pricing calculations are dependent on the assumptions we make for our sales forecast (see the Example below).

Example: From the markup/ cost plus example, we recall that the Acme LUX light bulb has a variable cost of $10 per light bulb, fixed costs of $400,000, and a unit sales estimate of 40,000, for a resulting unit cost of $20 per light bulb.

Acme demands that its products achieve a 20% return on investment (ROI). The company has invested $800,000 in research and development for the new Acme LUX light bulb.

We can price our Acme LUX light bulbs for that level of ROI by applying the following target-return pricing equation:

Target-Return Price = (Unit Cost) + (Target ROI) * (Investment) / (Unit Sales)
Target-Return Price = ($20) + (20%) * ($800,000) / (40,000) = $24

Note that the target return price at a 20% ROI differs from the markup price we calculated earlier, despite also using a 20% rate. The difference is the result of different equations used to calculate the price.

Note also that the target return price is dependent on the accuracy of our estimation of unit sales. If we fail to sell the quantity we estimated, we will not deliver the ROI promised. To demonstrate the relationship, we re-write the target-return price equation to solve for ROI. For example, we can determine our ROI if our unit sales come in at 20,000, instead of 40,000:

ROI   = (Unit Sales) * (Target-Return Price – Unit Cost) / (Investment)
          = (20,000) * ($24 – $20) / ($800,000) = 10%

As part of the investment discussions, we want to know when our products will begin to generate profit for the firm. This point is known as the break-even point. The break-even point is defined as the point at which the total revenue from the product (calculated as units multiplied by price) equal total cost (calculated as the sum of fixed cost and variable cost). We discuss break-even further later in this chapter.

Using the break-even equation below, we can calculate the break-even point for the Acme LUX:

Break-even Quantity   = (Fixed Cost) / (Price – Variable Cost)
                         = ($400,000) / ($24 - $10) = 28,570 units

From the equation, we can see that fixed cost, price, and variable cost will all affect the point at which the product begins to turn a profit for the organization.

Tiered Pricing

Description: **Tiered pricing**, also known as **good-better-best pricing** or **price lining**, sets different price points for different levels of features or quality for the same type of product or service. Customers can self-select the level most suited to them from the three levels offered.

Figure 8.10 shows the concept behind tiered pricing, where companies can charge tiered pricing for different levels of features or quality.

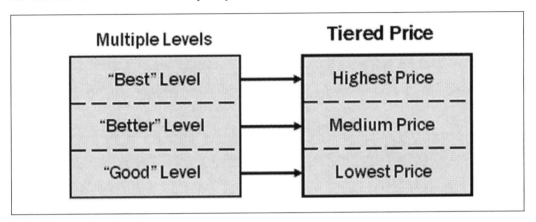

Figure 8.10: Pricing Techniques: Tiered Pricing

For example, automotive tire company Big O Tires (bigotires.com) offers three levels of automotive service. The first level is its Good Service package for $24.95, which includes basic engine oil and oil filter replacement. The second level is its Better Service for $34.95, which includes all of the services in the Good Service package, and also includes an engine flush. The third level is its Best Service package for $44.95, which includes all of the services in the Better Service package, along with the use of premium synthetic oil. [8-11]

Applications: Companies can use tiered pricing when they offer products or services at varying levels of features or quality to serve different needs within the same market. We can designate the different levels literally as "good, better, and best" or we can give names to our products and services that suggest the levels.

Advantages: Tiered pricing makes it easier for customers to select the particular product or service that suits their needs. Many will gravitate toward certain tiers. Tiered pricing also makes it easier for retailers to explain the inherent value of the different tier options. By making the options clear, customers face lower uncertainty in what they can expect.

Disadvantages: Tiered pricing for complex products and services can require skilled retail salespeople to explain the value of the different levels. Using the Big O Tires example discussed earlier, the retail salesperson would need to be able to explain to customers the benefits of synthetic engine oil over traditional petroleum-based oil when selling the Best Service package.

Example: Acme could offer its Acme LUX LED-based light bulbs in three tiers: Good, Better, and Best. The Good LUX tier would consist of light bulbs with a limited light output of 150 Lumens, about equivalent to the amount of light produced from a standard 25 Watt incandescent light bulb. We could price the Good tier at $10. The Better LUX tier would be priced at $20, and would produce a medium-level output of 800 Lumens, equivalent to that from a 60 Watt incandescent light bulb. The Best LUX tier would be priced at $30, and would develop 1700 Lumens of light, equivalent to that from a 100 Watt incandescent light bulb. [8-12]

Value-in-Use Pricing

Description: Value-in-use pricing, sometimes also called value-based pricing, sets prices based on the product or service's value to the customer, as opposed to the manufacturer's cost of production. We price the products or services to make customers indifferent as to whether to use their existing products or services, or switch to a new offering.

Figure 8.11 shows the concept behind value-in-use pricing, where companies set prices so that customers perceive the value of proposed alternative products or services to balance that of their existing products or services.

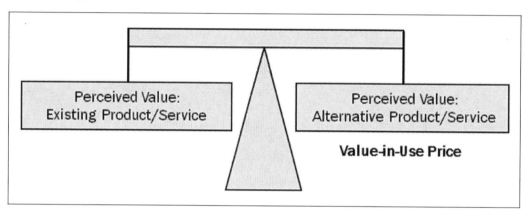

Figure 8.11: Pricing Techniques: Value-in-Use Pricing

For example, ceramic coating manufacturer Rhino Shield (rhinoshield.net) sells its product as an alternative to house paint, guaranteeing that its product will last 25 years, compared to only 3 – 5 years for traditional house paint. [8-13]

Similarly, synthetic automotive engine oils, such as Mobil 1, are priced significantly higher than petroleum-based engine oils, such as Pennzoil. But if the total cost per year for each type of oil is the same because synthetic oils permit longer intervals between oil changes, then customers are indifferent as to which to use.

Applications: Value-in-use pricing works well for differentiated products and services that hold identifiable value for certain groups of customers. The technique is frequently used for business-to-business sales, where companies can show that higher priced products can reduce total costs in the long run.

Advantages: Value-in-use pricing captures the value customers place on products and services. The technique separates the notion of price (what companies charge for products and services) and cost (the amount of money companies spend to manufacture products or provide services). The separation allows companies to gain profitability from products and services that provide real value to customers. By comparison, cost-based pricing schemes such as markup/ cost plus focus on costs instead of perceived value.

Disadvantages: In order to execute value-in-use pricing, companies must understand the benefits that customers realize from the product or service. In addition, companies must be able to reduce this benefit to monetary terms. Thus, companies must research the market and the usage scenarios that customers have for the product or service.

Example: Acme conducts market research on art galleries, and learns that they spend significant sums of money on changing light bulbs due to the many light bulbs in the gallery and the many lighting adjustments required to highlight new works. Galleries also demand a high quality of light, making the unique full-spectrum light of the Acme LUX LED light bulbs a good choice. Figure 8.12 summarizes the data.

Variable	Data	Description
Existing light bulbs: Price	$5	Price of existing halogen light bulbs
Existing light bulbs: Life	6 months	Life expectancy in demanding conditions
Existing light bulbs: Labor	$20/ unit	Labor cost to replace light bulbs
Existing light bulbs: Quantity	100	Quantity of light bulbs to be replaced
Acme LUX light bulbs: Price	VIU	Value in use (VIU) price we wish to calculate
Acme LUX light bulbs: Life	24 months	Life expectancy in demanding conditions
Acme LUX light bulbs: Labor	$20/ unit	Labor cost to replace light bulbs

Figure 8.12: Value-In-Use Pricing: Data Table

From the data, we can see that art galleries currently use halogen light bulbs to showcase their art. Acme has found that art galleries employ an average of 100 light bulbs per location. The light bulbs last 6 months, and cost $5 for the light bulb and $20 for the labor to replace each bulb. We can calculate the annual cost for light bulbs for the galleries by summing up the cost for the light bulbs themselves and the labor cost to replace them:

$$
\begin{aligned}
\text{Annual Light Bulb Cost} \quad &= \text{Cost for Parts (Light Bulbs)} \\
&+ \text{Cost of Labor (to Replace Light Bulbs)} \\
&= 100 \text{ light bulbs} * \$5/ \text{ each} * 2 \text{ changes}/ \text{ year} \\
&+ 100 \text{ light bulbs} * \$20/\text{each} * 2 \text{ changes}/ \text{ year} \\
&= \$1,000/ \text{ year} + \$4,000/ \text{ year} = \$5,000/ \text{ year}
\end{aligned}
$$

We see that the labor cost to replace the light bulbs is significantly more than the cost for the light bulbs themselves. In this example, we did not include any cost for lost productivity while changing the light bulbs, which would have driven the annual cost even higher.

We now calculate the value in use (VIU) price, maintaining the gallery's annual light bulb cost of $5,000 per year. We write out the same equation and solve for VIU. The equation is the same as the previous one, except that the Acme LUX light bulbs last 24 months, not six, so only require changing every 0.5 years.

$5,000   = 100 light bulbs * $VIU/ each * 0.5 changes/ year
           + 100 light bulbs * $20/ each * 0.5 changes/ year

→   VIU = $80 each for the Acme LUX LED light bulb

Therefore, a buyer could spend $80 for each Acme LUX LED light bulb and face the same annual light bulb cost. Note that this price is significantly above the markup price of $25 we calculated earlier, not to mention our unit cost of $20 per light bulb. We could price the light bulb between our unit cost and the VIU cost, provide lower annual light bulb costs to our gallery buyers, and still generate a handsome profit. Of course, Acme would need to adjust the price if competitors introduced similar light bulbs.

Variant Pricing

Description: The variant pricing technique sets different prices for different versions (variants) of products and services. The variants cater to specific market segments. Variant pricing works because different market segments have different priorities and evaluation criteria.

Variant pricing is different from price discrimination. We cover price discrimination later in this chapter. Variant pricing offers different variants of different products and services at a range of prices, whereas price discrimination offers the same products and services at a range of prices.

Figure 8.13 shows the concept behind variant pricing, where companies set different prices for different variants to cater to different segments.

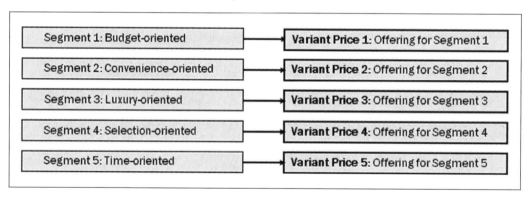

Figure 8.13: Pricing Techniques: Variant Pricing

For example, the automobile maker Volkswagen AG (volkswagenag.com) sells different cars (variants) to different market segments. Volkswagen AG sells its traditional Volkswagen automobiles, such as the Golf and Jetta models, to economy-minded customers. It sells its Bentley automobiles, such as the Continental Flying Spur, to luxury-minded customers. Volkswagen AG sells its Lamborghini automobiles, such as the Gallardo, to sport-minded customers. [8-14]

Applications: Organizations can develop different variants at different price points to satisfy the various needs of market segments. Consider a sampling of the different types of variants available in the market today:

- **Budget-oriented segment**: Hotel chain Motel 6 (motel6.com) advertises its prices as the "lowest price of any national chain." In addition to its standard hotel properties, it operates its extended-stay hotels, Studio 6, also offered at budget-friendly prices. [8-15]

- **Convenience-oriented segment:** Supermarket chain Safeway (safeway.com) offers home delivery (at an additional fee) to target convenience-oriented shoppers.

- **Customization segment:** Toyota's Scion line of automobiles (scion.com) offer wide customization options. Customization-oriented customers can select from hundreds of possible choices for exterior colors and trim, interior colors and trim, sound systems, and performance parts.

- **Luxury-oriented segment**: Airline Emirates Airways (emirates.com) offers posh accommodations for luxury-oriented customers willing to pay for first class service. Its first class cabin seats fully recline, allowing weary travelers to relax on their journey.

- **Risk-oriented segment**: Electronics retailer Best Buy (bestbuy.com) offers its Buy Back program for risk-oriented customers. Customers can pay a fee to sell back their electronic devices when new models come out. The Best Buy website even includes a "BuyBaculator" for consumers to calculate how much money Best Buy will give them for their devices. [8-16]

- **Selection-oriented segment**: Online retailer Amazon.com (amazon.com) claims it has the "Earth's Biggest Selection." Indeed, the retailer offers dozens of different categories, from audio-books to riding lawn mowers.

- **Time-oriented segment**: Shipping service United Parcel Service (ups.com) offers various shipping options (and corresponding prices) to cater to various segments. For the same shipment of a three pound package from Chicago to New York, prices range from $11 for UPS Ground service (for patient customers) to $24 for UPS 2nd Day Air (for moderate time-oriented customers) to $100 for UPS Next Day Air Early AM (for customers who value time greater than money). [8-17]

Advantages: Variant pricing allows us to capture the value different market segments place on their particular needs. As we saw above, some customers will pay ten times the amount to ship a package from one location to another, just to get it there earlier. The special variants often face little competition, allowing great freedom in pricing.

Disadvantages: Variant pricing requires companies to understand their market and the segments within it. Companies must conduct market research to determine the segments interested in their products and services, and the amounts the segments are willing to spend for the different variants. Companies must also stock additional products and services to accommodate the needs of those segments.

Example: Through market research, Acme discovers that some of its customers value durability. The customers operate in physically demanding environments, such as industrial plants, and have requested extra-durable light bulbs. The inherent ruggedness and long life of Acme's Acme LUX LED light bulb makes it a good basis for a special variant for the durability-oriented segment.

Acme can choose to offer extra-durable variants of its Acme LUX light bulb to the durability-oriented segment. It will need to determine which special attributes the customers expect in the new light bulbs, such as vibration resistance, crush-resistance, etc. Acme also needs to assess the value the segment places on the light bulb, which will contribute in determining the price point for the variant. With this information, Acme can decide if expected profits of the variant warrant the development of the new light bulb.

Figure 8.14 summarizes the pricing techniques we discussed.

Technique	Description	Example
Creaming Pricing	Set prices high during new product/ service introduction	Panasonic set high prices for its new 3D TVs
Demand-Based Pricing	Set prices to maximize profit, based on consumer demand	Amazon.com adjusts prices over time to maximize profitability
Everyday Low Pricing	Set prices consistently low to attract price-sensitive customers	Walmart uses everyday low pricing to emphasize good value
Going Rate Pricing	Set prices to align with those of competitors	Gasoline stations in same area often sell gas at similar prices
Markup/ Cost Plus Pricing	Set prices by adding percentage to unit cost	Consumer packaged goods often use markup pricing
Penetration Pricing	Set prices low to attract new customers and expand share	P & G and Unilever use penetration pricing at times
Prestige Pricing	Set prices high to signal high quality or status	Rolex sets prices very high to align with its luxury brand
Target-Return Pricing	Set prices to achieve company-defined return on investment	Industrial supply companies often use target-return pricing
Tiered Pricing	Set prices at different price points for different levels of features	Big O Tires offers Good, Better, and Best oil change packages
Value-in-Use Pricing	Set prices based on product or service's value to the customer	Rhino Shield ceramic coating lasts 25 years
Variant Pricing	Set different prices for different variants, for different segments	Volkswagen sells different cars to different market segments

Figure 8.14: Pricing Techniques: Summary

PRICING ASSESSMENT

In the previous section, we selected a pricing technique based on our situation and application. Before moving forward with the technique, we must assess how the technique (and the resulting price) will affect the organization's financial goals. [8-20]

In this section, we review three popular models to assess the impact of pricing on organizational goals. First, we cover break-even analysis, which estimates the quantity of units we must sell before we turn a profit. Second, we address net present value capital budgeting, which assesses if new proposed projects will meet organizational goals for return on investment based on the projects' expected revenue stream. Third, we review internal rate of return capital budgeting, which determines the rate of return expected on new projects.

Break-even Analysis

Description: Organizations use break-even analysis to predict the quantity we must sell before a new product or service becomes profitable. The break-even point is defined as the point at which revenue from a proposed new product or service equals its costs.

We use break-even to calculate if the proposed price will meet organizational revenue goals in certain time periods. If the price is too low, the break even time will be too long, and organizations will not move forward with the project. Many organizations state an objective for break-even time of one year.

Applications: The break-even financial decision model is widely used as a "go/no-go" decision tool for new product or service development. Projects not meeting the organization's break-even threshold do not move forward.

The break-even model can also be used for sensitivity analysis, to predict how the break-even point will change with respect to changes in prices. We can also predict the impact of cost-related changes.

Advantages: The break-even model is simple to compute and is widely used. The model can quickly indicate if a proposed price will meet a one-year break-even objective.

Disadvantages: The break-even model makes some strong assumptions and ignores several important factors. It assumes that sales prices are constant at all levels of output. It also assumes that all products produced are immediately sold. In addition, the model can only apply to a single product or single mix of products. Projects involving radically new processes or technologies often take longer than the common one year threshold. Therefore, dogmatic use of the break-even model can yield an excessive short-term focus.

Technique: Figure 8.15 shows an overview of the break-even analysis technique.

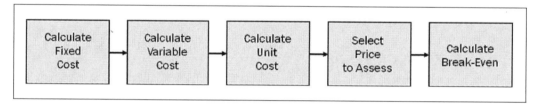

Figure 8.15: Pricing Assessment: Break-Even Analysis Technique

- **Calculate fixed cost**: Fixed cost for a project is defined as all costs assigned to a project that stay constant as volume (production quantity) increases. Typical examples include insurance, property taxes, and depreciation. We make the assumption here that the production increases do not require significant additional resources such as new machinery

- **Calculate variable cost (raw)**: Variable cost is defined as costs which vary according to volume, such as parts and materials per unit, as well as direct labor expended per unit.

- **Calculate variable unit cost (allocated)**: As we covered earlier, variable unit cost is the cost to produce each unit. For companies which allocate the fixed cost of certain tooling that wears out (such as dies) over the units manufactured, we use the equation below. Otherwise, we set unit cost equal to the variable cost.
    Variable Unit Cost = (Variable Cost) + (Fixed Cost / Unit Sales).

- **Select price to assess**: Select the price we wish to test. We could need to test several prices before we find one that meets the organization's break-even criteria.

- **Calculate break-even:** Calculate the break-even volume using the following formula:
    Break-even = (Fixed Cost) / (Price – Variable Unit Cost)

In some cases, we will need to cycle through the process multiple times, each time testing new prices, until we find a price that provides us with in an acceptable break-even.

Example: Acme wants to know if the new proposed Acme LUX light bulb will meet the organizational objective for break-even in the first year. Acme expects to sell 20,000 units in year one.

- **Calculate fixed cost**: Acme has a fixed cost of $200,000 for the project.

- **Calculate variable cost (raw):** Acme spends $10 per unit on (raw) variable cost.

- **Calculate variable unit cost (allocated):** Var. Unit Cost = $10 + ($200,000 / 20,000) = $20

- **Select price to assess:** Based on pricing of similar units, we expect to charge $40 per unit.

- **Calculate break-even:** We calculate the break-even point using the following formula:

  Break-even   = (Fixed Cost) / (Price – Variable Unit Cost)
                  = ($200,000) / ($40 - $20) = 10,000 units

According to the formula, we reach the break-even point well before the one year mark, so the price is acceptable from the standpoint of the break-even criterion. From the formula, we can see that any price lower than $40 will result in longer break-even quantities, given current fixed and unit costs.

Execution: The equations to calculate break-even are easily implemented in common spreadsheet programs such as Microsoft Excel. The advantage to implementing them in a spreadsheet program is the ability to conduct sensitivity analyses. For example, we could determine how changes in price and cost would affect break-even quantities.

Net Present Value Capital Budgeting Model

Capital budgeting models assess the likely profitability of proposed new products or services (or enhancements to existing ones).

Description: In this section, we address **net present value (NPV) capital budgeting**, which assesses if proposed projects will meet organizational goals for return on investment (ROI), based on the projects' expected revenue stream. Because the expected revenue stream is dependent on price, the net present value capital budgeting model can be viewed as a tool to validate price selection.

Capital budgeting analysis is a category of techniques that assess if proposed projects represent sound investments for organizations. Proposed projects, such as new products/services, expansions into new markets, and other ventures, require money and can be considered investments in the future of the organization.

Different projects will have different cash flows. Cash flows are the revenues that projects make over time, with a certain amount being made in the first year, another amount in the second year, and so forth. We calculate revenue by multiplying price by quantity, so price is an important component of cash flow. Capital budgeting analysis techniques determine if the cash flows associated with a project warrant investment in it.

Applications: Companies can apply net present value capital budgeting analysis to assess if proposed new products and services meet ROI goals, based on assumed prices and resulting cash flows. Because of its versatility, net present value capital budgeting analysis can be used to virtually any new product or service. We can also apply the technique for proposed enhancements to existing products and services.

Advantages: The net present value capital budgeting technique is straightforward to execute, as we shall see by example. The technique is popular.

Disadvantages: The simplistic approaches of capital budgeting techniques ignore possible threats and make significant assumptions. For example, the approaches do not take into account future competitive environments. The approaches are also highly dependent on the accuracy of cash flow calculations.

Technique: The **net present value** technique assesses whether a project is worthy of investment by calculating the sum of its cash flows discounted to reflect the **time value of money**. The time of value of money is the value of money acknowledging the effects of compounding interest over a period of time. The interest rate used is designated as the **discount rate**. The discount rate is typically the rate of return the organization could make with an investment of equivalent risk.

Net present values greater than zero indicate that the investment generates a greater rate of return than the discount rate, and should therefore be pursued. NPVs less than zero should be avoided, because the rate of return is less than the discount rate.

Figure 8.16 shows an overview of the process.

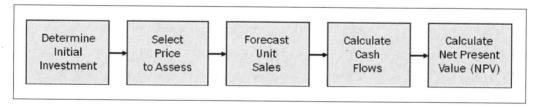

Figure 8.16: Pricing Assessment: Net Present Value Capital Budgeting Model

- **Determine initial investment:** We identify the required initial investment.

- **Select price to assess**: Next, we select the price we wish to test. As with the break-even technique, we might test several prices before we find one that meets our goals.

- **Forecast unit sales**: Based on historical company sales, or of sales of similar units from other companies, we forecast the number of units we expect to sell each year throughout the unit's lifetime.

- **Calculate cash flows**: We multiply the price by the units we expect to sell each year to arrive at the expected cash flow for each year. For example, if the unit price is $10, and we expect to sell 100 units, then the annual cash flow would be $10 * 100 = $1,000.

- **Calculate net present value:** We calculate the net present value using the formula:

NPV   =[(Cash flow from year 0) / (1 + discount rate) $^{t=0}$]
        +[(Cash flow from year 1) / (1 + discount rate) $^{t=1}$]
        +[(Cash flow from year 2) / (1 + discount rate) $^{t=2}$]
        +[remaining discounted cash flows]

Example: Acme wants to know if its proposed Acme LUX LED light bulbs will meet its organizational objective of generating 10% ROI.

- **Determine initial investment**: Acme expects an initial investment of $250,000, which equates to a negative (- $250,000) cash flow in year zero.

- **Select price to assess:** Acme plans to sell the units for $40 each.

- **Forecast unit sales**: Based on sales of similar units, Acme forecasts sales of 2,000 units in year one, 2500 in year two, and 3,250 in year three.

- **Calculate cash flows**: With the price and unit quantities established, we can calculate the cash flow from the units in year one as $40 * 2,000 = $80,000, in year two as $40 * 2,500 = $100,000, and year three as $40 * 3,250 = $130,000.

- **Calculate net present value**: We enter our information into the NPV equation:

NPV   =[(-$250,000) / (1 + 0.10)^{0}] + [($80,000) / (1 + 0.10)^{1}]
           +[($100,000) / (1 + 0.10)^{2}]+ [($130,000) / (1 + 0.10)^{3}] = $3,043; NPV > 0

The resulting NPV is greater than zero; therefore the cash flows more than cover the initial investment and it makes financial sense to invest in the project. The price thus passes the net present value capital budgeting test.

Internal Rate of Return Capital Budgeting Model

The internal rate of return model is an alternative capital budgeting model that companies can administer to directly determine the expected rate of return for a proposed product or service.

Description: The **internal rate of return** (IRR) model is similar to the NPV method. The IRR also uses a sum of discounted cash flows to decide whether to invest in a project. Again, the cash flows are dependent on the selected price. In fact, the IRR method uses the same equation as that for NPV. But instead of determining if NPV is greater than zero, we set NPV to zero and solve for the interest rate.

The resulting interest rate is called the internal rate of return. The internal rate of return is compared to the company's cost of capital, sometimes called the **hurdle rate**. The hurdle rate is defined by the company, and is often the interest rate it is required to pay on its loans.

If the internal rate of return is greater than the hurdle rate, the project is financially justified. If not, then the company should not move forward with the project.

Applications: Like with the NPV capital budgeting method, companies can apply the IRR approach to test the financial feasibility of new product and services, or enhancements to existing ones, based on our price we wish to test.

Advantages: The principal advantage of the IRR method over the NPV approach is the calculation of the actual rate of return in the IRR method. By comparison, the NPV approach only returns a go/no-go decision.

Disadvantages: In addition to the disadvantages of the NPV model, the IRR approach is a bit more difficult to calculate. Spreadsheet tools can make the process easier, as we will see in the example below.

Technique: To calculate the internal rate of return, we use the same formula as that for NPV. We set NPV equal to zero, and solve for interest rate, designated by IRR in the formula.

Figure 8.17 shows an overview of the process. It is similar to the process of the net present value capital budgeting model.

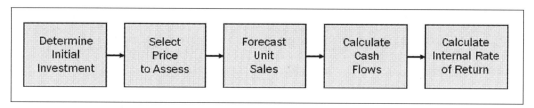

Figure 8.17: Pricing Assessment: Internal Rate of Return Capital Budgeting Model

- **Determine initial investment:** We start by estimating the initial investment required to launch the project, just as we did with the net present value capital budgeting process.

- **Select price to assess**: Next, we select a price we wish to test.

- **Forecast unit sales**: We examine the sales history for previous similar products, as well as that of relevant competitive products in the marketplace, to forecast the quantity of units we expect to sell each year.

- **Calculate cash flows**: Just as with the net present value capital budgeting technique, we multiply the price we wish to assess by the quantity of units we expect to sell to obtain the expected cash flow for each year.

- **Calculate internal rate of return:** To calculate the internal rate of return (IRR), we apply the net present value (NPV) equation. We set NPV to zero and solve for IRR.

$$\text{NPV} = [(\text{Cash flow from year } 0)/(1 + \text{IRR})^{t=0}]$$
$$+ [(\text{Cash flow from year } 1)/(1 + \text{IRR})^{t=1}]$$
$$+ [(\text{Cash flow from year } 2) / (1 + \text{IRR})^{t=2}]$$
$$+ [\text{remaining discounted cash flows}] = 0 \rightarrow \text{Solve for IRR}$$

Example: We repeat the example we used in the net present value capital budgeting model to highlight the similarities and differences between the IRR and the NPV models.

Acme wants to know the internal rate of return (IRR) for the proposed Acme LUX LED light bulbs, and if the IRR will meet the minimum internal return of 10%.

- **Determine initial investment**: Just as in the example for the net present value model, Acme expects an initial investment of $250,000, which equates to a (- $250,000) cash flow in year zero.

- **Select price to assess:** Acme plans to sell the units for $40 each.

- **Forecast unit sales**: Based on sales of similar units, Acme forecasts sales of 2,000 units in year one, 2,500 in year two, and 3,250 in year three.

- **Calculate cash flows**: Just as with the net present value model, we calculate the cash flow as $40 * 2,000 = $80,000 in year one, $40 * 2,500 = $100,000 in year two, and $40 * 3,250 = $130,000 in year three.

- **Calculate internal rate of return**: We enter our information into the NPV equation, set NPV = 0, and solve for IRR.

$$\text{NPV} = [(-\$250,000) / (1 + \text{IRR})^0] + [(\$80,000) / (1 + \text{IRR})^1]$$
$$+ [(\$100,000) / (1 + \text{IRR})^2] + [(\$130,000) / (1 + \text{IRR})^3] = 0 \rightarrow \text{IRR} = 10.6\%$$

Therefore, the proposed project meets the organizational requirement, and the selected price passes the internal rate of return capital budgeting assessment.

We can apply spreadsheet tools such as Microsoft Excel to determine IRR. For example, we can enter the formula into the spreadsheet with a test cell for IRR. Then, we test different values for IRR until the entire expression equals zero. With practice, users will find they can quickly converge to the final answer. Alternatively, one can use the NPV and IRR functions built into Microsoft Excel.

MARKETING MADE MEASURABLE

Disney: Capital Budgeting and the Disney Vacation Club: Entertainment and media enterprise Disney (disney.com) offers guests its Disney Vacation Club. In the Disney Vacation club, guests pay a one-time payment for 50 years of holidays. Alternatively, guests can "mortgage" their initial payment over 10 years. Guests may select from 200 possible locations at any time of the year they want. Club members earn points, so they may take a longer vacation next year if they miss a vacation this year.

Guests accrue several benefits from the Disney Vacation Club. Frequent vacationers (especially those with children) can save up to 70% on accommodations over the life of the club membership. A Forbes editor calculated that membership in the Club paid for itself in about 8 visits. Restrictions apply, and club members must seek permission from Disney if they want to sell their points to others.

Disney benefits from the Disney Vacation Club as well, because it allows Disney to forecast demand for an important segment of their guests at their resorts. In order to justify building new resorts, Disney management must predict expected cash flows from future resort revenues for capital budgeting. The Disney Vacation Club allows them to forecast part of the demand, as well as generate revenue in the near term (from the one-time payment) to fund future resort development. [8-21]

PROFITABLE PRICING

We can incorporate consumer demand into our pricing approach to increase product and service profitability. Economics tells us that consumers generally purchase less of a product or service when we charge more for it. Exceptions exist. Some products, such as luxury electronics, jewelry, and perfumes, can show the opposite behavior.

Demand Curves

The field of economics labels the relationship between sales quantity and price as the **demand curve**. The demand curve indicates the quantities of goods and services consumers purchase at given prices. [8-22]

Economics designates the **price elasticity** of a product or service as the rate at which the percentage of the change in quantity demanded varies with respect to the percentage change in price. The equation below expresses price elasticity:

Elasticity = (Percentage change in quantity demanded) / (Percentage change in price)

Because consumers generally purchase fewer goods and services as prices increase, elasticity is often a negative number. Nevertheless, we customarily express elasticity as a positive amount for convenience (i.e., we express it as the absolute value of the negative amount).

We refer to **elastic demand** as situations where the elasticity is greater than 1. In elastic demand, the quantity demanded depends a great deal on the price in the short term.

For example, consumers tend to purchase more non-perishable consumer packaged goods, such as frozen vegetables at lower prices than they do at higher prices. They feel they can "stock up" at the lower prices in the short term. In the long term, they do not continue to buy; there is a limit to the amount of frozen vegetables they want to own, even at very low prices.

Figure 8.18 shows a demand curve demonstrating elastic demand.

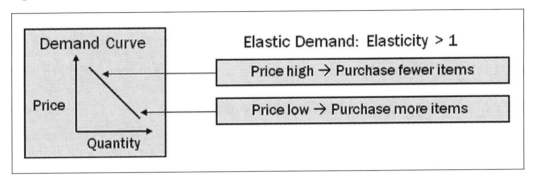

Figure 8.18: Demand Curves: Elastic Demand

We refer to **inelastic demand** as situations where the elasticity is less than 1. In inelastic demand, the quantity demanded depends little on the price in the short term.

For example, consumers tend to purchase about the same quantity of gasoline regardless of price in the short term. Consumers feel they have little choice because they need the gasoline to commute to work or perform other required tasks. We include the caveat "in the short term" to recognize long-term changes in behavior. For example, consumers can purchase fuel-efficient cars or start commuting to work on gas-sipping motorcycles in the long term.

Figure 8.19 shows a demand curve demonstrating inelastic demand.

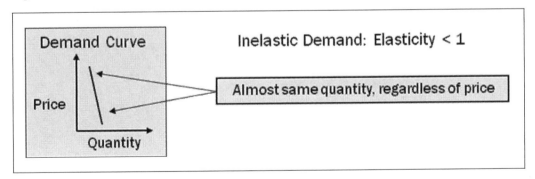

Figure 8.19: Demand Curves: Inelastic Demand

We can generate demand curves by determining the quantities that customers purchase at different prices. We can gather the demand data using three different approaches.

Surveys: We can conduct market surveys, asking customers how many units they would purchase at certain prices. We will need to specify the buying motivation (for a gift, for oneself, etc.) to ensure we gather relevant data.

Analysis: We can statistically analyze past sales data to determine how demand changed as we changed prices. For example, a company can examine how the quantity demanded changes during sales promotions launched in the past.

Experiments: We can conduct market experiments. In the experiments, we nudge prices up and down and observe the results. For example, we can track how sales vary in relation to discounts and price hikes.

Figure 8.20 shows a sample demand curve data set, in this case for the Acme LUX LED light bulb. Acme conducted experiments in the market to gather the data. The demand curve data shows that the average consumer will purchase only one light bulb when priced at $50. When the price is lowered to $40, the consumer will purchase two light bulbs. The pattern continues, with additional price decreases resulting in customers purchasing additional light bulbs. We can detect a linear relationship, based on the pattern of the values.

Price	Quantity
$10	5
$20	4
$30	3
$40	2
$50	1

Figure 8.20: Demand Curves: Sample Demand Curve Data for Acme LUX LED Light Bulb

We can calculate the elasticity for the Acme LUX LED light bulb using the elasticity equation. We use the two end points of the figure: (P1, Q1) = ($10, 5) and (P2, Q2) = ($50, 1).

Elasticity = (Percentage change in quantity demanded) / (Percentage change in price)
= [(Q2 – Q1) / Q1] / [(P2 – P1) / P1]
= [(1 – 5) / 5] / [($50 - $10) / $10] = -0.80 / 4 = -0.20

In this case, we see that the elasticity is negative (consistent with virtually every non-luxury product and service), with the absolute value much less than one, indicating that demand is relatively inelastic.

Optimal Pricing

We define the optimal price as the price yielding maximum profit. Once we know a product or service's demand curve, we can find its optimal price. We discuss optimal pricing by examining the impact the demand curve has on the optimal price. We demonstrate the process through a numerical example, and then discuss pricing optimization software that automates the process.

For each point on the demand curve, we can calculate the resulting revenue and cost. Once we know revenue and cost, we can calculate profits (Profit = Revenue – Cost).

For example, consider optimal pricing for Acme LUX LED light bulbs. Figure 8.21 repeats the demand curve (price and quantity demanded) in the first two columns. The next two columns show revenue and cost. We calculate revenue for each quantity by multiplying price by quantity (Revenue = Price * Quantity). We calculate cost for each quantity by multiplying cost per unit by quantity (Cost = Cost/Unit * Quantity). To get profit, we subtract total cost from total revenue.

From the figure, we observe that the maximum profit occurs at quantity of two (designated in the figure with an asterisk *). Pricing optimization software automates this tedious process.

Price	Quantity	Revenue	Cost	Profit
$10	5	$10 * 5 = $50	$20 * 5 = $100	$50-$100= ($50)
$20	4	$20 * 4 = $80	$20 * 4 = $80	$80 - $80 = $0
$30	3	$30 * 3 = $90	$20 * 3 = $60	$90 - $60 = $30
$40	2	$40 * 2 = $80	$20 * 2 = $40	$80 -$40 =$40 *
$50	1	$50 * 1 = $50	$20 * 1 = $20	$50 - $20 = $30

Figure 8.21: Optimal Pricing: Optimal Pricing Table for Acme LUX LED Light Bulbs.

MARKETING MADE MEASURABLE

Vendavo, Zilliant, and Others: Price Optimization: Demands for improved profitability in increasingly competitive and dynamic markets have driven interest in price optimization software. Price optimization software carefully examines costs and customer demand, and uses the data to calculate prices to boost profitability.

Marketing consulting firm Accenture (accenture.com) estimates that improving pricing by 1 percent can result in as much as 10 percent increased profits, so correct pricing is essential to long-term profitability.

Industrial coatings company PPG (ppg.com) manufactures house paint (sold under the Olympic brand at Lowe's), automotive paint for auto makers and refinishers, glass for houses and commercial buildings, and other industrial products. PPG turned to price optimization computer software vendor Zilliant (zilliant.com) to boost its revenues. Some of PPG's coatings include petroleum ingredients, which have increased in price. Zilliant software automates the process of incorporating cost increases into the price, to ensure that PPG maintains its profit margins despite dynamic petroleum costs.

Price optimization software companies specialize in different markets. For general business to business sales, example price optimization companies include PROS (prospricing.com), Vendavo (vendavo.com), and Zilliant (zilliant.com). For specialty industries, example companies include DemandTec (demandtec.com) and Revionics (revionics.com) for retail and Veritec Solutions (veritecsolutions.com) for transportation and hotel sales. [8-23]

PRICING FOR BUSINESS MARKETS

In this section, we expand our coverage of pricing to include several techniques specifically suited to business to business (B2B) situations. While some of the pricing models discussed in this section can also be used for business to consumer (B2C) markets, such as auction-based pricing, most are best suited for B2B.

Business Market Pricing Techniques

B2B organizations often apply three different approaches to pricing in business markets: cost-plus, channel-driven, and value-based. Figure 8.22 shows an overview of the approaches. [8-24]

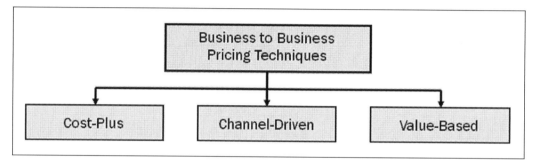

Figure 8.22: Business Market Pricing: Overview of Pricing Techniques

Cost-Plus: We can apply the cost-plus technique we covered earlier in the chapter to business to business sales. Just as we did for business to consumer sales, we add an arbitrary percentage, such as 20%, to the organization's cost to produce the good or service.

Similar to cost-plus for consumer markets, the approach has the advantage of quick and easy calculation, and the disadvantage of not incorporating demand.

Businesses use cost-plus pricing techniques for commodity products and services, such as industrial supplies.

Channel-Driven: Many smaller businesses distribute their products and services through distribution channels that sell to businesses. Some of the companies comprising the channel are quite large, and as such wield power over the sales environment, essentially dictating the prices they are willing to accept from suppliers. [8-25]

This situation is similar to the going rate pricing technique we covered earlier. As with going rate pricing, businesses face a "going rate" that the channel is willing to pay. Businesses that exceed that going rate price will find themselves shunned by channel members. The channel members will look for other suppliers willing to accept lower prices.

As with going rate pricing, channel-driven pricing holds few advantages and several disadvantages. The only true advantage is the survival of smaller suppliers willing to accept the terms of large channel members. The disadvantages include the lack of a "common wisdom of the industry" and potential allegations of unfairly manipulating prices.

Value-Based: The value-based pricing technique for businesses is similar to prestige pricing for consumer markets. The customer (in this case, a business) perceives high value from the product or service being sold, and is willing to pay premium prices to get it.

To execute this technique, companies must develop differentiated products and services and support them with brands of exceedingly high reputation.

Typical examples of this approach include top brands such as Cisco systems (cisco.com) for network hardware, Salesforce.com (salesforce.com) for software, and McKinsey consulting (mckinsey.com) for strategic consulting services.

Pricing Models

In general, we seek to set prices on business-oriented goods and services by placing a value on the "scalable enjoyment of customer success." The phrase means that customers (in this case, businesses) should pay more for products and services from which they derive great value.

For example, large companies using employee payroll services from Automated Data Processing (adp.com) should pay more than smaller companies, because larger companies have many more employees, and thus enjoy more "success" (in this case, payroll services for more employees).

Scaling by number of employees is one of many ways to show "scalable enjoyment." Businesses can apply any of several mechanisms to show "scalable enjoyment" depending on the situation. Many companies find software pricing models particularly vexing, so this section focuses primarily on software. Figure 8.23 shows an overview of the different pricing models. [8-26]

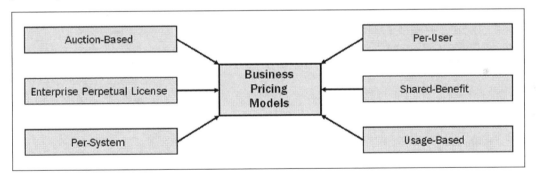

Figure 8.23: Business Market Pricing: Overview of Pricing Models

Auction-Based Pricing: This pricing model uses eBay style auctions to discover the market price by having potential buyers bid on items for sale.

- **Application:** Companies can use the technique to sell used equipment and other items where the exact value is not clear.

Enterprise Perpetual License Pricing: Also called "**all you can eat**" licensing, this pricing model allows customers to use the product or service freely, with no restrictions. The term comes from enterprise software, which is software sold to large organizations.

- **Application**: The technique can be used for products and services whose cost does not increase with usage. For example, software costs the same to make whether 10 people use it or 1,000 people use it. In fact, many software companies applied this technique during the late 1990s and early 2000s for enterprise software sales. Software marketers now frown on this technique, preferring instead to apply per-user or per-seat pricing to more accurately capture scale.

Per-system Pricing: This pricing model charges by the number of instances of the product installed, or alternatively by the number of computer servers running the product.

- **Application:** Companies use this technique to charge for large-scale implementations of products and services. For example, enterprise software companies apply the technique to capture the added value obtained by customers who execute the software on many systems.

Per-User Pricing: This pricing model charges customers for each person using the product or service. The intent of the technique is to capture the added value enjoyed by the customer as more people use the product or service.

- **Application**: Companies often use this technique to charge for services. Traditionally, companies have used it for training and other services involving personnel. More recently, computer software companies charge per user for **Software as a Service (SaaS)** offerings, which deliver functionality over the Internet rather than through a desktop application.

Shared-Benefit Pricing: This pricing model charges on a percentage of the benefit that the customer enjoys when using the product or service.

- **Application:** Companies apply this technique when customers do not fully understand or believe the benefits of a product or service. For example, companies offering employee training could charge customers a fee amounting to 5% of the added productivity of employees who receive the training. This technique can be difficult to apply, because proving the monetary benefit can be an arduous task.

Usage-Based Pricing: We can charge usage rates, such as hourly rates for usage instead of full purchase price.

- **Application**: Companies use this technique when customers express interest in lowering initial investments, and are more interested in the service a product provides than owning the product itself. For example, Rolls-Royce's aviation division sells its F405 jet engines to the Navy to power their T-45 training aircraft. Instead of charging a fixed price for the engines, Rolls-Royce charges by usage, in their "Power by the Hour" pricing model. [8-27]

PRICE DISCRIMINATION

We sometimes face situations where different types of people place different values on our products and services. We can apply price discrimination to capture the extra value some segments find in our offerings. [8-29]

Description: Organizations apply price discrimination to charge different prices for identical products and services. Price discrimination acknowledges that different market segments value the same product or service differently. Unlike the variant pricing technique we discussed earlier, which charges different prices for different variants tailored to each segment, price discrimination charges different prices for identical items.

Application: Figure 8.24 shows a sampling of price discrimination applications.

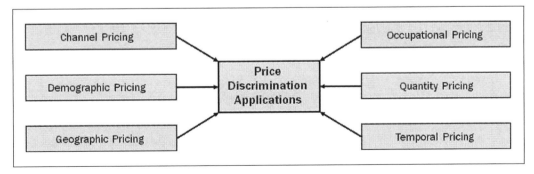

Figure 8.24: Price Discrimination: Sample Applications

- **Channel Pricing**: Companies can vary prices by distribution channel. For example, we can charge $2 for a bag of Fritos corn chips at a Safeway supermarket, and charge $4 for the same bag at an AM/PM convenience store. In channel pricing, we target the value some customers place on convenience.

- **Demographic Pricing**: Organizations can vary prices by demographic attributes of individuals. For example, ski resorts offer lower prices to senior citizens to encourage that demographic group to enjoy their facilities. Nightclubs offer lower prices to women on "ladies nights" to encourage that demographic group to attend.

- **Geographic Pricing**: Companies can vary prices by location or geography. For example, baseball stadiums charge increased prices for seats near home plate. Automobile manufacturers offer the same vehicles at different net prices, based on the state where customers purchase the vehicle, due to different state tax rates (although this practice is changing; see below).

- **Occupational Pricing**: Organizations can vary prices according to customer occupations. For example, clothing retailers offer employee discounts as a benefit to employees (and also to encourage employees wearing the company's garments). Theme parks offer reduced prices for active military members.

- **Quantity Pricing and Two-Part Pricing**: Companies can vary prices according to the quantity customers purchase. For example, fast food restaurant McDonalds applies quantity pricing, encouraging customers to "supersize" their orders, for a lower price per amount of food. Cellular phone provider Verizon (verizon.com) employs two-part pricing, charging a fixed rate per month for basic service, and then a per-minute rate for extra usage.

- **Temporal Pricing**: Companies offer different prices depending the time the product or service is offered. For example, movie theaters offer reduced prices for afternoon matinee show times. Some museums offer free admission once per month, such as the first Tuesday. Companies manufacturing seasonal items, such as snow-blowers, reduce prices during the off-season to stimulate sales.

Advantages: Price discrimination matches the prices of products and services with the perceived value of customers, which is the intent of efficient pricing methods. In economic terms, we would describe this situation as "extracting the full buyer surplus." Price discrimination benefits customers, in that they receive the value they sought. Price discrimination benefits companies in that it increases profits (see our example below).

Disadvantages: Price discrimination faces several disadvantages:

- **Reservation Prices**: Organizations can find difficulty in discovering buyers' reservation prices. The reservation price is the maximum price customers will pay. Without knowing how different people value the product or service, we cannot assign the appropriate price.

- **Arbitrage:** When companies sell the same product at different prices, some enterprising individuals will seek to profit by buying the product at the lowest price and re-selling it at a higher price (known as arbitrage). For example, some California citizens purchased automobiles in nearby Nevada to avoid paying California sales tax. Individuals could re-sell these "used cars" at a profit by avoiding the tax. The problem became so great that California had to enact complex legislation to combat the practice.

- **Legalities:** The Robinson-Patman Act of 1936, the Clayton Act, and the Sherman Antitrust Act prohibit charging different prices to different customers with the intent to harm competitors. For example, a company cannot charge different prices to two or more purchasers within a reasonably close time period where the practice could harm competitors. [8-30]

- **Unfair:** Legalities aside, some individuals consider the practice of price discrimination unfair, because it treats different people differently. Customers may complain about paying the full rate when certain classes of individuals enjoy a lower rate.

Example: Acme investigates the application of price discrimination in its pricing of its Acme LUX LED light bulbs. To do so, the company compares the profitability between charging a standard rate of $40 to all customers, or charging different rates for different groups. The light bulbs cost $20 to manufacture.

Acme has identified three different groups with different reservation prices. Market research has discovered relevant attributes about the three markets to which it sells. Figure 8.25 shows an overview of the three markets. We discuss each market.

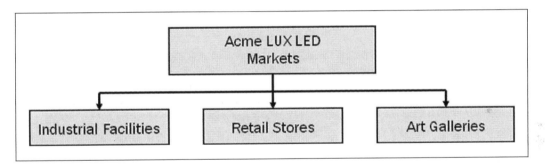

Figure 8.25: Price Discrimination: Example: Acme LUX LED Light Bulb Markets

- **Industrial Facilities**: Warehouses, factories, and other industrial facilities have limited needs for small-wattage light bulbs, such as those Acme supplies. Industrial facilities get most of their light from high-output fixtures, such as high-pressure sodium lighting. Industrial supply houses such as Grainger (grainger.com) supply these types of fixtures. Some lighting opportunities are available in break rooms and other areas. Industrial facilities are very price sensitive because they face many lighting substitutes. They do not place a very high value on the full-spectrum light the Acme LUX light bulb provides.

  The U.S. Census Bureau cites about 300,000 manufacturing facilities in the United States (NAICS 31 - 33). Acme estimates that 1% of the market would be interested in purchasing the Acme LUX at $40, and 2% at $30. [8-31]

- **Retail Stores**: Clothing stores, department stores, and other retail outlets place a high value on the full spectrum light the Acme LUX light bulb provides. They will need limited consulting assistance in the application of the light bulbs.

  The U.S. Census Bureau cites about 46,000 retail stores in the United States (NAICS code 452). Acme estimates that 20% of the market would be interested in purchasing the Acme LUX at $40, and 15% at $50. [8-32]

- **Art Galleries**: Art galleries need full spectrum light to properly showcase their artwork. Galleries currently use halogen lighting to obtain the quality of light needed. Halogen lighting provides high-quality light, but the low efficiency of the light bulbs results in high energy costs and excessive heat, requiring air conditioning to cool the interior space to comfortable temperatures. The Acme LUX offers an ideal alternative, with full spectrum light and cool temperature operation. The galleries will need extensive consulting services to make the most of the Acme LUX light bulbs.

  The U.S. Census Bureau cites 6,700 art dealers in the United States (NAICS code 453920). Acme estimates that 80% of the market would be interested in purchasing the Acme LUX at $40, and 60% at $80. [8-33]

Figures 8.26 and 8.27 show the calculations. The first figure shows the profit calculations for a fixed price of $40 for all segments. The second figure shows the profit calculations for varying prices for the three different markets, addressing the different values the three markets place on the Acme LUX light bulb.

According to the calculations, Acme earns 45% more profit through price discrimination than with fixed prices. This significant profit increase demonstrates why price discrimination remains such a popular technique.

Segment	Reservation Price	Profit per Segment
A: Industrial Plants	$40	1% * 300,000 * ($40 - $20) = $60,000
B: Retail Stores	$40	20% * 46,000 * ($40 - $20) = $184,000
C: Art Galleries	$40	80% * 6,700 * ($40 - $20) = $107,200
Total		$60,000 + $184,000 + $107,200 = $351,200

Figure 8.26: Price Discrimination: Example: Profit Calculations for Fixed Price

Segment	Reservation Price	Profit per Segment
A: Industrial Plants	$30	2% * 300,000 * ($30 - $20) = $60,000
B: Retail Stores	$50	15% * 46,000 * ($50 - $20) = $207,000
C: Art Galleries	$80	60% * 6,700 * ($80 - $20) = $241,200
Total		$60,000 + $207,000 + $241,200 = $508,200

Figure 8.27: Price Discrimination: Example: Profit Calculations for Varying Price

MARKETING MADE MEASURABLE

Couponing as Price Discrimination: Money magazine (money.cnn.com) reported on a new trend taking hold in America—extreme couponing. With the lingering poor economy, many Americans have adopted the role of "coupon enthusiast." Coupon enthusiasts can spend hours clipping coupons, but enjoy lower shopping bills. In some cases, shoppers can save half of their weekly grocery bills through their efforts.

Couponing represents a form of price discrimination. Manufacturers charge the "coupon segment" less in exchange for the inconvenience of clipping coupons. The policy is similar to that used by airlines, which charge less for tickets in exchange for the inconvenience of non-refundable fares.

Coupon website Coupons.com estimates that shoppers can save $1,400 per year on groceries by spending 40 minutes per week on coupons. Coupon enthusiasts report a certain sense of accomplishment—of not being "suckers"—through their couponing activities.

Indeed, Matt Sharp, executive producer of Extreme Couponing (extremecouponing.com) states that couponing has extended to an emerging subculture, saying "Yes, it's about saving money, but not in the regular way of being on a budget, giving up your Starbucks, and neglecting yourself...For couponers savings is fun, almost a sport." [8-34]

SUMMARY

We can use analytics tools and techniques to determine pricing for different situations, products/services, and markets. In this chapter, we described how pricing and consumer demand can affect profitability. We also showed several approaches especially suited for business to business sales. We closed the chapter by discussing price discrimination.

Pricing Techniques: We cover a variety of pricing techniques, to equip marketers with pricing approaches for virtually any scenario.

- **Creaming Pricing**: Also known as skimming pricing, creaming pricing sets prices high during the introduction of a new product or service. It is best used for unique, glamorous products and services that face few, if any, substitutes.

- **Demand-Based Pricing**: Demand-based pricing sets prices to maximize profit, based on consumer demand for the product or service. It is best used for situations where companies can adapt prices quickly based on market demand.

- **Everyday Low Pricing**: Everyday low pricing, also known as EDLP, sets prices consistently low to attract price-sensitive customers. It is best used for consumer goods with well-known brands.

- **Going Rate Pricing**: Going rate pricing aligns prices with those of competitors, adopting a so-called market price. It is best used for commodity-like products that vary little from supplier to supplier.

- **Markup/Cost Plus Pricing**: Markup/Cost Plus Pricing adds an arbitrary percentage to the unit cost of products and services to arrive at the final price. It is best used for near-commodity goods, where higher prices would encourage new market entrants.

- **Penetration Pricing**: Penetration pricing sets prices very low to attract new customers and build market share. It is best used for situations where companies wish to capture market share as quickly as possible.

- **Prestige Pricing**: Prestige pricing sets prices high to signal high quality or status. It is best used for image-oriented products.

- **Target Return Pricing**: Target return pricing sets prices to achieve a company-defined return on investment (ROI). It is best used for situations where ROI is closely monitored, such as public utilities.

- **Tiered Pricing**: Tiered pricing sets different price points for different levels of features, quality, or service. It is best used for companies who need to serve different needs for quality within the same market.

- **Value in Use Pricing**: Value in use pricing sets prices based on the product or service's value to the customer, as opposed to the manufacturer's cost of production. It is best used for differentiated products and services that can save money for customers.

- **Variant Pricing:** Variant pricing sets different prices for different versions (variants) of products and services. It is best used for companies which cater to different market segments.

Pricing Assessment: Pricing assessment determines the impact of pricing on organizational goals. We covered three popular techniques.

- **Break-even Analysis**: We conduct break-even analyses to determine the quantity of units we must sell before a new product becomes profitable. Many organizations check if proposed prices for new products and services will meet the objectives for break-even within one year.

- **Net Present Value Capital Budgeting Model:** We study if the net present value (future cash flows discounted by the organization's cost of capital) of proposed new projects meets organizational goals for return on investment.

- **Internal Rate of Return Capital Budgeting Model**: Similar to the net present value capital budgeting model, the internal rate of return model checks if the expected rate of return for a proposed new project meets or exceeds the company's rate of return goal, often called the hurdle rate.

Profitable Pricing: We can incorporate consumer demand into our pricing approach to increase product and service profitability. We capture the effect of consumer demand and price using demand curves. Demand curves show the relationship between sales quantity and price.

Demand curves vary between elastic demand (where consumers are highly influenced by price) and inelastic demand (where consumers purchase goods and services regardless of price). Knowing a product or service's demand curve allows us to calculate its optimal price, which is the price yielding maximum profit.

Pricing for Business Markets: Business markets often use cost-plus pricing techniques (where business add arbitrary percentages to unit cost), channel-driven pricing techniques (where companies adapt their prices to meet the "going rate" that powerful distribution channels are willing to pay), and value-based pricing techniques (where businesses set premium prices for highly differentiated goods and services). Businesses can apply several different types of pricing models, all of which are designed to place a value on the "scalable enjoyment of customer success."

Price Discrimination: Price discrimination sets different prices for groups of people who value the same products and services differently. We can apply price discrimination in many ways:

- **Channel Pricing**: Charging different prices for the same product, depending on where consumers purchase it

- **Demographic Pricing**: Charging different prices to different age, income, or gender groups

- **Geographic Pricing**: Charging different prices based on location

- **Occupational Pricing**: Charging different prices based on consumers' occupations

- **Quantity Pricing**: Charging different prices per unit depending on how many units consumers purchase

- **Temporal Pricing**: Charging different prices depending on the time the product or service is offered

Terminology

Break-Even Analysis: Pricing assessment technique to determine if proposed pricing will result in break even within a certain period of time, often one year

Creaming Pricing: Pricing technique that sets prices high during the introduction of a new product or service

Demand-Based Pricing: Pricing technique that sets prices to maximize profit, based on consumer demand

Demand Curve: Relationship between sales quantity and price

Elasticity: Percentage change in quantity demanded, divided by the percentage change in price

Everyday Low Prices: Pricing technique that sets prices low to attract price-sensitive customers

Going Rate Pricing: Pricing technique that aligns company prices with those of competitors, adopting a so-called market price

Internal Rate of Return Capital Budgeting: Pricing assessment technique to check if the expected rate of return from a proposed new project meets or exceeds the company's rate of return goal, often called the hurdle rate.

Markup/ Cost Plus Pricing: Pricing technique that adds an arbitrary percentage to the unit cost of products and services to arrive at the final price.

Net Present Value Capital Budgeting: Pricing assessment technique to determine if the net present value of expected cash flows from new projects meets organizational goals for return on investment.

Optimal Price: Price yielding maximum profit

Penetration Pricing: Pricing technique that sets prices very low to attract new customers and build market share

Prestige Pricing: Pricing technique that sets prices high to signal high quality or status

Price Discrimination: Setting different prices on the same goods and services to capture individual perceived value

Target Return Pricing: Pricing technique that sets prices to achieve company-defined return on investment

Tiered Pricing: Pricing technique that sets different price points for different levels of features, quality, or service.

Value in Use Pricing: Pricing technique that sets prices based on the product or service's value to the customer, as opposed to the manufacturer's cost of production

Variant Pricing: Pricing technique that sets different prices for different versions (variants) of products and services

Class Discussion

1. What type of pricing technique does your organization use? How well do you believe the technique suits your organization's products, services, and markets? What technique would suit the organization better?

2. How would you apply variant pricing in your organization to cater to multiple markets?

3. ECommerce applications can provide near real-time data on online sales. What impact can such immediate data make?

4. What type of pricing assessment technique does your organization use to evaluate pricing for proposed new products and services?

5. Some people believe price discrimination is unfair; others think it "levels the playing field" by adjusting price to people's ability to pay. Split your team into two groups and have the two groups argue different sides of the case.

Practice Problems

1. Calculate the markup price for the Acme LUX II light bulb, with a variable cost of $20, fixed costs of $500,000, unit sales of 25,000, and a markup rate of 25%.

2. Determine the target-return price for the Acme LUX II light bulb, with a variable cost of $20, fixed cost of $500,000, unit sales of 25,000, and a target return on investment of 25%.

3. Calculate the value in use price for the Acme LUX II light bulb to replace existing compact fluorescent lamps (CFLs). We have 100 CFLs, with a price of $3, a life of 2 years, and which cost $10 each to replace. The Acme LUX II light bulb has a life of 5 years and costs $10 to install.

4. Determine the break-even point in units for the Acme LUX II light bulb, with a fixed cost of $500,000, price of $50, and unit cost of $30.

5. Calculate the net present value of the Acme LUX II light bulb. Acme expects to charge $50 for the light bulb, seeks a 10% return, and forecasts sales of 3,000 units for the first year, 4,000 in the second year, and 3,000 in the third year. The Acme LUX II light bulb development project requires an initial investment of $300,000.

6. Determine the price elasticity for the Acme LUX II light bulb using the elasticity equation. (P1, Q1) = ($20, 10) and (P2, Q2) = ($40, 5).

Chapter 9.

DISTRIBUTION ANALYTICS

Chapter Outline

We cover the following marketing analytics topics in this chapter:

☑ **Distribution Channel Characteristics**: Reviewing channel attributes and roles
☑ **Retail Location Selection**: Determining locations for new retail stores
☑ **Channel Evaluation and Selection**: Assessing channel performance
☑ **Multi-Channel Distribution**: Analyzing multi-channel distribution scenarios
☑ **Distribution Channel Metrics**: Monitoring distribution channel performance

"Many entrepreneurs who build great products simply don't have a good distribution strategy. Even worse is when they insist that they don't need one, or call no distribution strategy a 'viral marketing strategy.'"
– Marc Andreessen

As the developer of early Internet browser Mosaic and co-founder of Netscape, Marc Andreessen certainly qualifies as an entrepreneur who built great products. Unlike others, though, Andreessen did have a good distribution strategy. In the 1990s, Andreessen's team gave away Mosaic for free to attract users. Thanks to the compelling distribution model, soon two million people were using the new browser.

Since then, Andreessen has been involved in many Internet start-up ventures such as Loudcloud, ColabNet, and others. Andreessen also spoke at Stanford University's CS 183 Course, "Startup," where he was heard saying the quote above. [9-1]

Companies use distribution channels to deliver products and services to their target market. Distribution channels consist of organizations that channel goods from manufacturers to end users. Example channel members include wholesalers and retailers. In a typical consumer model, goods can move through multiple channel members, as the Kraft example demonstrates.

MARKETING MADE MEASURABLE

Kraft Distribution Channels: Kraft Foods (kraftfoodscompany.com) manufactures, distributes, and sells a variety of food merchandise. Fox example, it markets Lunchables lunch snacks, Jell-O gelatin and Grey Poupon mustard. Kraft manufactures its products in facilities all over the United States, such as its Lunchables plant in Fullerton, California.

Kraft maintains a hub and spoke style distribution system to distribute its products from the manufacturing plants to retailers. From the manufacturing plants, the products move to regional distribution centers. Kraft strategically locates its regional distribution centers near major metro areas, such as the following:

- Aurora, Illinois: Services the greater Chicago area
- Bethlehem, Pennsylvania: Services the New England area
- Fort Worth, Texas: Services the Texas area
- Ontario, California: Services the Southern California area
- Stockton, California: Services the Northern California area

The regional distribution centers supply about 4,900 customer distribution centers across America. Products move from the customer distribution centers directly to large retailers (such as supermarkets), and through wholesale distributors to smaller retailers (such as convenience stores). [9-2]

DISTRIBUTION CHANNEL CHARACTERISTICS

This section provides an overview of distribution channel characteristics to provide the background necessary to apply the metrics and models presented in this chapter.

We start by describing the different roles distribution channel members play. We continue the discussion with covering the services members provide, and how different companies structure their distribution channels. We then cover distribution intensity. We complete the section by discussing the effects distribution channels can have on pricing and profitability. [9-3]

Distribution Channel Members

Companies employ the services of different types of distribution channel members to address the varying needs of their markets. Marketers sometimes refer to distribution channel members as intermediaries. Intermediaries represent any organization involved in distribution between producers and consumers. Each channel member plays a vital role and performs essential services in the movement of goods and services to end users.

In this section, we discuss the following types of distribution channel members:

- Non-Internet retailers, such as convenience stores and mass merchandisers
- Internet-based retailers, such as corporate websites and aggregator websites
- Non-retailer intermediaries, such as distributors and wholesalers
- Services-based channel members, such as dealerships and Internet-based services

Figure 9.1 shows different examples of **non-Internet retailers**. Each type plays a specific role and performs important services for the company and the consumer.

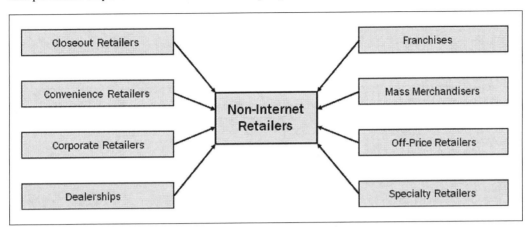

Figure 9.1: Distribution Channel Members: Non-Internet Retailers

Closeout Retailers: Closeout retailers liquidate unpopular merchandise that did not sell at full retail prices in traditional mass merchandise stores, such as department stores. For example, closeout retailer Big Lots (biglots.com) features a changing mix of discounted merchandise.

Convenience Retailers: Convenience retailers offer fast service (compared to supermarkets and mass merchandise retailers) for convenience goods, such as snack foods. For example, convenience store 7-Eleven (7-eleven.com) sells Big Gulp soft drinks, Slurpee drinks, and other fast food items.

Corporate Retailers: Some corporations choose to manage locations owned by the corporation itself, in addition to franchisee-owned stores and other locations. For example, sports retailer Nike (nike.com) operates Niketown retail stores in several States. [9-4]

Dealerships: Dealerships specialize in motor vehicles, such as automobiles, motorcycles, and powersports vehicles (snowmobiles, all-terrain vehicles, etc.). In addition to sales to end users, it performs several other roles, such as carrying inventory, negotiating for final price, delivering service, and collecting market feedback. For example, Ford supplies vehicles to about 3,100 dealers in the United States. [9-5]

Franchises for Products: Companies grant licenses to operate stores carrying the company's brand and operating principles to franchisees. Generally, franchisees own and operate the stores, although many franchises include a mix of privately-owned and company-owned units. For example, fast food franchise Taco Bell operates a mix of restaurants, with 80% privately-owned, and 20% company-owned. [9-6]

Mass Merchandisers: Mass merchandise retailers, such as department stores, sell a wide variety of goods to end users. For example, department store Sears (sears.com) carries appliances, automotive products, clothing, electronics, jewelry, lawn mowers, office supplies, sporting goods, tools, and many other categories.

Off-Price Retailers: Off-price retailers sell name-brand merchandise for reduced prices. For example, off-price retailer Marshalls (marshallsonline.com) became successful by buying manufacturers' discontinued, over-run, and closeout stock at a discount. It then sells the stock at prices 20 - 60 % less than those of department stores. [9-7]

Specialty Retailers: Specialty retailers sell narrow assortments of goods to buyers looking for specific needs or usages. Often, specialty retailers provide consulting and advice on applications for the niche they serve. Specialty retailers will stock merchandise general stores do not carry, in order to accommodate unique customer needs. For example, specialty retailer Sunglass Hut (sunglasshut.com) focuses exclusively on sunglasses and their accessories.

Figure 9.2 summarizes our sampling of non-Internet retailers.

Retailer Type	Description	Example
Closeout	Liquidates unpopular merchandise	Big Lots
Convenience	Fast service for snack foods	7-11
Corporate	Owned by company	NikeTown
Dealership	Carries inventory for sale to consumers	Ford auto dealer
Franchise	License to run store, granted by company	Taco Bell
Mass Merchandise	Sell wide variety of goods	Sears
Off-Price	Sell discontinued items	Marshalls
Specialty	Focus on narrow product line	Sunglass Hut

Figure 9.2: Distribution Channel Members: Sample Retailers, Non-Internet

Figure 9.3 shows examples of several types of **Internet-based retailers**. Similar to non-Internet retailers, different types of Internet-based retailers play a variety of roles.

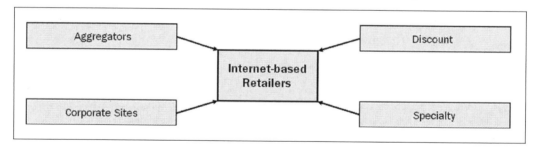

Figure 9.3: Distribution Channel Members: Internet-based Retailers

Aggregators: Aggregator Internet retail distribution channels sell multiple brands of goods. Some sell a wide variety of goods. For example, Internet retailer Amazon.com offers 34 categories of goods on its website, such as Amazon Kindle e-books, cell phones, consumer electronics, music, office products, software, tools, and many others. As a testament to its selection, it offers 76 different models of riding lawn mowers. [9-8]

Corporate Sites: Most consumer-oriented companies maintain a corporate website to sell directly to consumers. Companies sometimes offer unique models on their website not available at retail stores. For example, computer maker Dell (dell.com) offers its computers at Best Buy retail stores, at aggregator websites such as Amazon.com, as well as on its corporate website, Dell.com. Ordering through Dell.com allows consumers to configure the machine to their specifications and not be limited to the merchandise stocked at retail stores.

Discount: Discount Internet retailers sell discontinued merchandise at discount prices. For example, discount Internet retailer Overstock.com sells housewares and other items at deeply reduced prices. The retailer also features its online clearance center, "The Clearance Bin," where shoppers can find additional discounts. [9-9]

Specialty: Specialty retailers focus on niche markets and categories. The retailers carry multiple brands of products and services which they believe will benefit the niche market. For example, Tiger Direct (tigerdirect.com) specializes in online sales of high technology consumer products, especially personal computers.

Figure 9.4 summarizes examples of Internet-based retailers.

Retailer Type	Description	Example
Aggregator	Sell multiple brands of goods	Amazon.com
Corporate Site	Owned by company	Dell.com
Discount	Sell discontinued items	Overstock.com
Specialty	Focus on market niche or category	TigerDirect.com

Figure 9.4: Distribution Channel Members: Sample Retailers, Internet-based

Figure 9.5 shows examples of **non-retailer intermediaries**. Intermediaries generally either assist retailers in consumer sales or sell directly to businesses. Only in rare cases do non-retailer intermediaries sell directly to consumers.

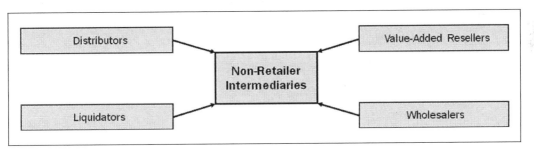

Figure 9.5: Distribution Channel Members: Non-Retailer Intermediaries

Intermediaries represent any organization involved in distribution between producers and consumers. They execute an assortment of necessary functions to get products to final users. In addition to retailers (covered earlier), intermediaries include organizations such as distributors and wholesalers. Here, we cover several common intermediary types.

Distributors: Distributors purchase products from companies and then resell them to businesses. Some distributors sell directly to consumers, but most do not. The products remain in their stock form, without modifications (unlike value-added resellers, which we cover later).

For example, distributor Arrow Electronics (arrow.com) sells to 120,000 businesses through a global network of more than 390 locations in 53 countries. [9-10]

Liquidators: Liquidators purchase all or most of the closeout stock of another company and sells it to other businesses. For example, product lifecycle logistics company GENCO (genco.com) purchases surplus inventories of companies and liquidates them through its subsidiary, GENCO Marketplace. [9-11]

Value-added Resellers: Value-added resellers (VARs) purchase products from others, add features or services to them, and then resell the products to other businesses. Some VARs also sell to consumers. VARs modify the products to make them more suitable for specific applications. For example, distributor and value-added reseller Tech Data (techdata.com) launched its StreamOne Solutions Store to customize options for clients. [9-12]

Wholesalers: Wholesalers purchase products from suppliers, and then resell them (generally in large quantities) to retailers. For example, wholesaler Jacobs Trading Company (jacobstrading.com) sells by the truckload to discount stores and other retailers.

Figure 9.6 summarizes examples of non-retailer intermediaries.

Intermediary Type	Description	Example
Distributors	Sells standard stock to businesses	Arrow
Liquidators	Sells discontinued items to businesses	GENCO
Value-added Resellers	Sells modified stock to B2B; some B2C	Tech Data
Wholesalers	Sells standard stock to retailers	Jacobs Trading

Figure 9.6: Distribution Channel Members: Examples of Non-Retailer Intermediaries

Figure 9.7 shows examples of several types of distribution channel members specializing in delivering services. **Services-based channel members** differ from product-oriented members in that they manage the infrastructure to deliver services to customers. For example, coffeehouses must maintain coffee-making machinery and tables for patrons. Here, we cover several common services-oriented channel members.

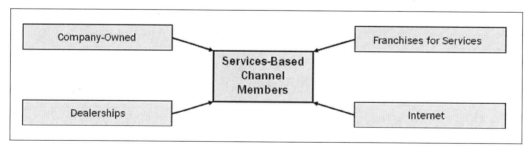

Figure 9.7: Distribution Channel Members: Services-Based Channel Members

Company-Owned: Some businesses prefer to own their branches, instead of permitting independent ownership by franchisees. Company ownership ensures tight control over the brand, but can limit expansion rate.

For example, coffee retailer Starbucks (starbucks.com) operates virtually all its stores as company-owned entities. Doing so permits Starbucks to offer consistent levels of service to their customers. Instead of expanding using the independent franchise model, Starbucks resells its products through "licensed stores." Licensed stores sell Starbucks products through large organizations such as airlines (Alaska Airlines serves Starbucks coffee on its flights) and supermarkets (Safeway supermarkets sell bags of Starbucks coffee). [9-13]

Dealerships: Dealerships, such as automotive, motorcycle, and snowmobile dealerships, specialize in service at the point of sale. Services can include repair by factory-certified technicians, as well as installation of accessories, such as customization kits from the factory. Dealers can generate revenue from service operations, especially in recessionary times where new car purchases slow down.

For example, recreational vehicle (RV) dealer Shabbona Creek RV (shabbonacreekrv.com) in Atkinson, Illinois, operates a complete service center, as well as sales of new and used recreational vehicles. [9-14]

Franchises for Services: Franchises fulfill two important roles. First, they permit individuals to engage in business opportunities with existing brands and operations guidelines. Second, they permit businesses to expand their geographic reach without tying up corporate capital. Franchises generally operate a mix of locally owned franchise locations (owned by franchisees) and company-owned franchise locations.

For example, plumbing repair franchise Roto-Rooter (rotorooter.com) structures its operations into two separate divisions. Roto-Rooter Services Company owns and manages company-owned Roto-Rooter service locations. Roto-Rooter Corporation manufactures Roto-Rooter machinery and oversees agreements with independent Roto-Rooter franchises. [9-15]

Internet: Organizations can deliver services over the Internet where operations do not require face-to-face relations. Many organizations maintain websites that fulfill elements of its product and service mix, such as software drivers, user manuals, software downloads, and customer support services. Some companies conduct all of their business over the Internet.

For example, Internet domain registrar Go Daddy (godaddy.com) provides domain registration services and web hosting services over the Internet. [9-16]

Figure 9.8 summarizes our sampling of services-based distribution channel members.

Service Provider Type	Description	Example
Company-owned	Company owns and manages locations	Starbucks
Dealership	Service at point of sale	Shabbona Creek RV
Franchise	Locally owned by franchisee	Roto-Rooter
Internet	Delivery of services over Internet	Go Daddy hosting

Figure 9.8: Distribution Channel Members: Services-Based Channel Members

Distribution Intensity

Companies can operate different types and quantities of distribution channel members depending on their goals. We identify three levels of intensity: intensive, selective, and exclusive. Figure 9.9 shows an overview of distribution intensity and its levels.

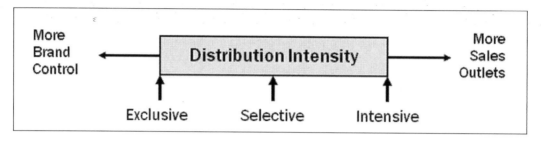

Figure 9.9: Distribution Channel Members: Distribution Intensity Overview

Intensive Distribution: Companies select intensive level distribution intensity when they plan to saturate markets with their products or services. Mass-market products and services, such as beer and snack foods, benefit from this level of intensity because their sales depend on the number of outlets offering the product or service. Such mass-market products and services often face many similar offerings from competitors. Offering products and services in many locations avoids customers selecting competitor brands because the customer could not find the company brand at their present location.

For example, cellular phone service provider Verizon (verizonwireless.com) offers its cellular phones and plans in a wide variety of locations. According to verizonwireless.com's store finder, Verizon offers its services in 74 locations within the Chicago, Illinois area. The locations consist of company-owned stores, Apple retail stores, Best Buy retail stores, Costco warehouse stores, Radio Shack retail stores, Walmart warehouse stores, and independent cell phone retailers. [9-17]

Exclusive Distribution: In exclusive distribution, companies limit themselves to only one type of retail outlet. The company often owns and/or controls the retail outlet. Companies who rely heavily on their brand's equity tend to select exclusive distribution. Companies operating company-owned stores can showcase their brand in a tightly controlled setting. Exclusive distribution limits potential sales because so few locations offer the products or services.

For example, tool maker Snap-on (snapon.com) manufactures and sells its line of professional-grade tools exclusively through its Snap-on franchise. Snap-on franchisees drive to mechanics' shops within their territories in Snap-on branded vans and sell tools directly from them. Snap-on thus focuses exclusively on sales to professionals. Snap-on's e-commerce website requires shoppers to enter the name of the local franchisee to avoid channel conflict. [9-18]

Selective Distribution: Companies choose selective distribution as a middle ground between intensive and exclusive distribution intensities. Selective distribution offers some of the brand control of exclusive distribution, while offering the product or service in more locations, as with the intensive distribution approach. With selective distribution, companies can focus their retail support efforts, such as training, toward a handful of different outlets. The approach works best when consumers hold brand preferences and are willing to search out outlets to find them.

For example, fashion manufacturer Coach (coach.com) offers its line of leather handbags, accessories, and other goods through only a handful of stores. According to coach.com's store locator, Coach offers its goods to 17 stores in the Chicago, Illinois area. The locations consist of five company-owned stores, as well as high-end department stores such as Bloomingdales, Macy's, and Nordstrom. [9-19]

Distribution Costs

Companies can incur different types of distribution costs, depending on the nature of their distribution channels and structure. Companies must consider the costs when evaluating and selecting their distribution channel partners.

Figure 9.10 shows an overview several typical types of costs incurred by the manufacturer when selling goods through distribution channels. [9-20]

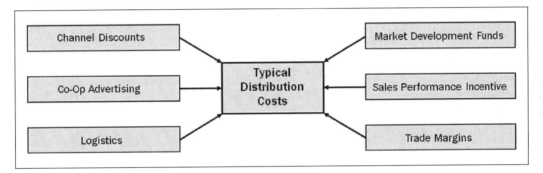

Figure 9.10: Distribution Channel Characteristics: Typical Distribution Channel Costs, Overview

Channel Discount Costs: Many retailers set their own prices for goods and services, generally within guidelines set by the manufacturer. Discounts on merchandise, such as those for consumer sales promotions, are "costs" in that they result in lower net sales amounts.

Co-op (Cooperation) Advertising Costs: Companies can choose to co-market their products and services in advertising with distribution channel members. For example, electronics retailer Radio Shack (radioshack.com) runs weekly advertisements in major metropolitan newspapers, such as the New York Times. Cell phone service provider Verizon Wireless could choose to pay Radio Shack for a portion of the advertisement cost in exchange for Radio Shack featuring Verizon products in the advertisement.

Logistics Costs: Distributors expect manufacturers to pay for any logistics-related costs to transport and manage product inventory.

Such costs can include inventory holding costs (such as warehouse rental costs), order management (the cost of computer systems to manage orders), returns costs (costs for shipping goods back to manufacturers), general shipping costs (costs for shipping from manufacturer to retailer, and through distributor if applicable), after-sales service, and others.

Market Development Funds (MDF) Costs: Some manufacturers choose to work with channel partners to promote certain products and services, such as newly introduced offerings.

Manufacturers will prepare agreements stating the type of promotional activities channel partners will provide. In exchange for the promotional activities, manufacturers pay market development funds (MDF).

Companies make MDF payments to the channel member's department of marketing or business development, depending on the channel member organizational structure.

Sales Performance Incentive Fund (SPIF) Costs: Similar to MDF payments, SPIF payments are incentives paid by a company to a distribution channel member to promote certain products and services. Unlike MDF payments (which get paid to the channel member's marketing or business development function), SPIF payments get paid directly to salespeople.

Business to business and technology companies frequently use SPIF payments to boost sales of lagging products and services. Companies should use SPIFs with caution. By paying salespeople directly, SPIF arrangements might conflict with general agreements between companies and channel members. [9-21]

Trade Margins Costs: Distribution channel members expect payments from companies to carry the company's products and services. Typically, companies pay a percentage of the product or service's retail price. We refer to this percentage as a trade margin, sometimes also called a mark-up or commission. Powerful channel members can charge substantial amounts, often over 40% of the retail price.

Figure 9.11 summarizes typical distribution costs.

Distribution Cost Type	Description
Channel Discounts	Cost incurred when retailers sells products or services at a discount from retail price.
Co-op Advertising	Cost to co-market company products and services by sharing costs to feature brands in advertisements.
Logistics	Cost for distribution logistics, such as inventory, returns, shipping, order management, service, and others.
Market Development Funds	Cost for co-marketing products and services with distribution channel member, often part of a specific plan.
Sales Performance Incentive Funds	Cost for incentive to channel member sales team to promote specific products and services.
Trade Margins	Cost for participating in distribution channel. Typically a percentage of the retail price. Also called mark-up or commission.

Figure 9.11: Distribution Channel Members: Typical Distribution Costs

RETAIL LOCATION SELECTION

In the next section, we discuss evaluation criteria for assessing and selecting distribution channel members. Because retail location selection forms such an important part of the assessment process, we devote a special section to it here. [9-22]

Several factors contribute to the crucial nature of retail location selection. First, location can have a direct effect on customer acquisition. Second, location decisions have large cost implications. New retail stores can require millions of dollars of investment. Third, location decisions can have long-lasting impact. Unlike pricing decisions, which companies can quickly change if they do not produce the desired effect, contracts governing retail locations (such as leasing contracts) can often cover several years. Thus, a bad retail location decision can haunt a company for years.

Successful companies follow a three step process for selecting a new retail store location, as shown in Figure 9.12.

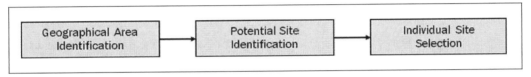

Figure 9.12: Retail Location Selection: Overview

- **Geographic Area Identification**: The first step is to identify the general geographic areas (such as cities or towns) that contain the types of people we want to target. Marketers refer to these areas as "attractive markets."

- **Potential Site Identification**: The second step is to identify the set of retail locations that will best meet the company's retail goals.

- **Individual Site Selection**: The third step is to narrow down the set of retail locations to only one location (or more, if the company plans to open several stores).

The three step process thus starts at a general level and converges to a specific location. As Figure 9.13 indicates, we can apply different decision models toward each step in the process.

Retail Location Selection Process	Description	Example Model
Geographic Area Identification	Identify geographic areas where individuals of target market reside	GIS; Market Sizing
Potential Site Identification	Identify set of retail locations meeting company's retail goals.	GIS; Gravity Model
Individual Site Selection	Select one location from set of retail locations identified earlier	Company-specific decision criteria

Figure 9.13: Retail Location Selection: Example Models

Geographic Area Identification

As we covered earlier, the first step in retail store location selection is to identify the general geographic areas, such as cities and towns, which contain the types of people we want to target (our target markets).

We can identify geographic areas rich in target market individuals by estimating area market sizes of various locations, and then selecting the greatest ones. We covered how to estimate market sizes in chapter two of this book. Estimating market demand of multiple geographic areas can be tedious, so we will consider an alternative: Geographic Information Systems (GIS).

Geographic information systems combine physical geographic features (such as terrain) with cultural geography (such as areas of high personal income) to provide guidance in retail location selection.

GIS systems examine nearby trading areas when considering retail store locations. Trading areas are geographic areas from which a retailer, or group of retailers, draws its customers. GIS systems check distances and physical impediments (rivers, highway access, etc.) between proposed retail store locations and nearby trading areas to assess their desirability.

GIS systems display cultural characteristics of physical spaces using thematic maps. Thematic maps use visual techniques such as colors, shading, and boundary lines. The techniques highlight areas of special interest for the retailer. Effective retail locations match the characteristics of the trading area with those of the company. For example, the area might represent populations particularly interested in outdoor activities, or fine arts, or with high personal income.

Marketers can apply geographic information systems for other uses as well. GIS systems can prevent new store cannibalization by checking potential overlap areas between proposed new stores and existing stores. Geographic information systems can assist with advertising management by indicating the demographic and other characteristics of the nearby market that advertisers should emphasize during local promotion campaigns. Retailers can also apply GIS systems for merchandise management, by checking the mix of product and service offerings with the anticipated needs of the trading area.

Figure 9.14 shows a map of the San Francisco Bay Area, showing shaded areas to designate geographic zones rich in relevant customers, such as those seen in GIS output maps. For demonstration purposes, we have overlaid several of Apple's retail stores on the map, shown as dots (GIS maps do not ordinarily show actual store locations). We see on the map that many of Apple's stores lie in or near the highlighted areas. [9-23]

Several specialty vendors supply GIS systems. For example, Environmental Systems Research Institute (ESRI, at esri.com) develops geographic information systems for many uses, including retail location. ESRI supplements its mapping functionality with different types of data. Available data types include U.S. Census demographics, estimated consumer spending and purchase potential data, and business data, such as traffic counts. [9-24]

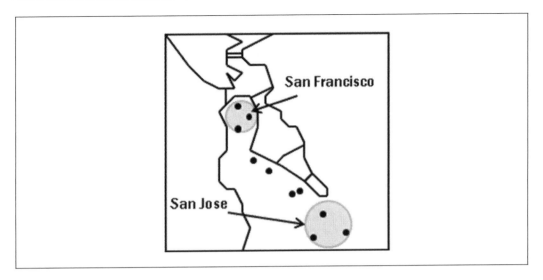

Figure 9.14: San Francisco Bay Area Map with Population Centers Shaded

Potential Site Identification

In the second step, we identify potential retail location sites within the geographic areas we determined in the first step. For example, our analysis in the first step might have resulted in the identification of two promising geographic retail areas for a new store. In the second step, we will select one of the two areas. In the third step (discussed in the next section), we drill into the specific location within the geographic area we selected in step two.

We can apply the power of geographic information systems to the second step. Indeed, many companies employ this approach. To consider an alternative approach, we will cover the retail gravity model for the second step, which was popular before the advent of GIS systems.

The **gravity model** asserts that shoppers are attracted to retail stores located with convenient access, and maintaining a good "image." We use the word "attracted" because the model assumes that stores pull in shoppers with a force similar to that of gravity. [9-25]

In the model, the term "convenient access" is generally interpreted as the distance from the store to the center of a geographic area rich in potential customers. We can modify direct distance measurements to reflect impediments to travel, such as areas of slow traffic.

The term "image" in the model is interpreted as the size of the retail store. The model assumes that larger stores translate to greater image for shoppers, due to the greater variety and lower prices larger stores offer.

The gravity model states that the probability of a store pulling in a customer is calculated by dividing the size of a store by its distance from shoppers, and then dividing the resulting expression by the sum of similar expressions for alternative store locations. We can modify the equation using alpha and beta adjustment parameters. See the discussion below.

The gravity model applies the following formula:

$$\text{Probability} = [\,(\text{Size})^{\alpha} / (\text{Distance})^{\beta}\,] / \Sigma\,[\,(\text{Size})^{\alpha} / (\text{Distance})^{\beta}\,]$$

- **Size**: Size refers to the size of the store in square feet or square meters. The units of size do not matter, as long as they are used consistently. The entire expression is dimensionless (no units) because the same terms are used in both the numerator and denominator, and are thus canceled out.

- **Distance**: Distance refers to the length in kilometers or miles from the store to the center of the target market. Again, the units do not matter as long as they are used consistently.

- **α (Alpha):** Alpha is a parameter to adjust the degree of importance the target market has for the size of stores. The default value is 1.0. If we found our customers held a strong preference for large stores, we could increase alpha to emphasize its importance.

- **β (Beta):** Similar to alpha, Beta is an adjustment parameter to reflect the degree of importance customers hold for the distance of stores.

- **Σ (sigma):** Sigma is an operator that sums expressions. Here, it sums size divided by distance (modified by the parameters Alpha and Beta) for all stores in consideration.

We now demonstrate the use of the approach using a retail store location example.

Example: Discount mass merchandise retailer Acme Mart (fictitious) plans to open a new store. Acme Mart sells to its target market in nearby city Small City. Figure 9.15 shows three possible locations for Acme Mart's new retail store.

- **Store location A** has a size of 5,000 square feet and is four miles away from the target market area, the center of Small City.
- **Store location B** has a size of 10,000 square feet and is five miles away.
- **Store location C** has a size of 15,000 square feet and is eight miles away.

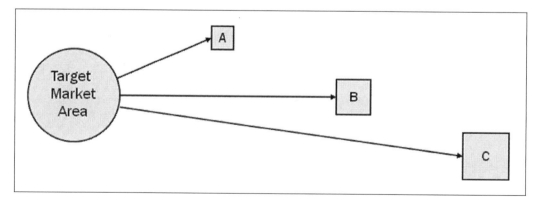

Figure 9.15: Gravity Model Retail Store Location Example

We start by assuming that customers value size and distance equally. Therefore, we set our Alpha and Beta parameters to one. We use the gravity model equations to calculate the probability of attraction for each store.

- **Step One**: Calculate the expression $[(Size)^\alpha / (Distance)^\beta]$ for each store location.

  Store A: $[(Size)^\alpha / (Distance)^\beta]$: $[(5)^1 / (4)^1] = 1.25$
  Store B: $[(Size)^\alpha / (Distance)^\beta]$: $[(10)^1 / (5)^1] = 2.00$
  Store C: $[(Size)^\alpha / (Distance)^\beta]$: $[(15)^1 / (8)^1] = 1.88$

- **Step Two**: Sum the expression $[(Size)^\alpha / (Distance)^\beta]$ for each store location.

  $\Sigma [(Size)^\alpha / (Distance)^\beta]$ $= 1.25 + 2.0 + 1.88 = 5.13$

- **Step Three**: Evaluate the expression $[(Size)^\alpha / (Distance)^\beta] / \Sigma [(Size)^\alpha / (Distance)^\beta]$ for each store location.

  Store A: $[(Size)^\alpha / (Distance)^\beta] / \Sigma [(Size)^\alpha / (Distance)^\beta]$: $1.25 / 5.13 = 0.24$
  Store B: $[(Size)^\alpha / (Distance)^\beta] / \Sigma [(Size)^\alpha / (Distance)^\beta]$: $2.00 / 5.13 = 0.39$ ←
  Store C: $[(Size)^\alpha / (Distance)^\beta] / \Sigma [(Size)^\alpha / (Distance)^\beta]$: $1.88 / 5.13 = 0.37$

From the results, we see that Store B has the greatest probability of customer visits, based on the gravity model. We can repeat the process, this time assuming that customers value distance more important than size. To test how the shopper assessment will change, we set Alpha = 1.0 and Beta = 2.0, and calculate the probabilities for each store location:

- **Step One**: Calculate the expression $[(Size)^\alpha / (Distance)^\beta]$ for each store location. This time, we set Alpha = 1.0 (customer preference for store size) and Beta = 2.0 (customer preference for store distance).

  Store A: $[(Size)^\alpha / (Distance)^\beta]$: $[(5)^1 / (4)^2] = 0.31$
  Store B: $[(Size)^\alpha / (Distance)^\beta]$: $[(10)^1 / (5)^2] = 0.40$
  Store C: $[(Size)^\alpha / (Distance)^\beta]$: $[(15)^1 / (8)^2] = 0.23$

- **Step Two**: Sum the expression $[(Size)^\alpha / (Distance)^\beta]$ for each store location.

  $\Sigma [(Size)^\alpha / (Distance)^\beta]$ $= 0.31 + 0.40 + 0.23 = 0.94$

- **Step Three**: Evaluate the expression $[(Size)^\alpha / (Distance)^\beta] / \Sigma [(Size)^\alpha / (Distance)^\beta]$ for each store location.

  Store A: $[(Size)^\alpha / (Distance)^\beta] / \Sigma [(Size)^\alpha / (Distance)^\beta]$: $0.31/ 0.94 = 0.33$
  Store B: $[(Size)^\alpha / (Distance)^\beta] / \Sigma [(Size)^\alpha / (Distance)^\beta]$: $0.40/ 0.94 = 0.43$ ←
  Store C: $[(Size)^\alpha / (Distance)^\beta] / \Sigma [(Size)^\alpha / (Distance)^\beta]$: $0.23/ 0.94 = 0.24$

Therefore, customers have a greater likelihood of visiting Store B if we increase the value they place on short distances to the stores they visit.

The gravity model suffers from several disadvantages. First, customers do not always value short distances to stores. Customers will visit distant stores if they feel the stores offer the exact merchandise they seek, or provide some other attribute, such as lower prices. For example, many cities offer outlet stores of major brand names on the outskirts of town. Many customers visit the outlet stores despite the many closer stores available, in the hope of finding a bargain.

In the second disadvantage, not all customers want the largest possible store. Some customers prefer shopping at boutiques for their specialized selection, informed salespeople, and more intimate environment.

In the third disadvantage, the standard form of the gravity model does not reflect the implications of different modes of access, such as travel by personal vehicle or public transport (although the Beta parameter could be increased to reflect greater effective distance).

The gravity model has enjoyed good success, but many companies now find GIS systems to be a more attractive alternative for today's retail store location selection. But both approaches only find the general location. Companies still need to select the individual site location. We discuss individual site selection in the next section.

Individual Site Selection

In this section, we cover guidelines on specific store locations, depending on the company's retailing objectives. Each company will likely have different retailing objectives, making a universal site selection model infeasible.

For example, a list of location objectives for an automotive maintenance retail store, such as Jiffy Lube (jiffylube.com) would be quite different from one for a designer clothing store, such as Kate Spade (katepade.com).

The selection of the type of location must be consistent with the customer shopping situation. We separate customer shopping situations into three types: convenience shopping, comparison shopping, and specialty shopping.

Convenience Shopping: Convenience shopping retailers cater to people's need for convenience. Example retailers include 7-Eleven and AM/PM convenience stores. Convenience-oriented retail stores must be located near their customers, so companies tend to locate them in highly populated areas. See our discussion on central business districts below.

Comparison Shopping: Comparison shopping retailers cater to people's needs for comparing choices when shopping for high-consideration, expensive items. Example retailers include those for furniture, automobiles, apparel, and consumer electronics. Competing brands in the same category often locate next to each other to drive comparison shoppers to their stores. See our discussion on agglomerated retail areas later in this section.

Specialty Shopping: Specialty shopping retailers cater to people's occasional needs for specialty products and services. At the time when consumers need these types of specialty offerings, they are more interested in selection (to be sure they find what they need) than distance from their home or work (because they rarely shop for specialty goods). Therefore, we can place such stores in freestanding buildings. See our discussion on freestanding retailers later in this section.

We continue this section by discussing common locations for store-based retailers, stating the advantages and disadvantages of each. We offer insight into the selection process by providing guidelines on the types of usage scenarios (convenience-oriented, comparison-related, etc.) that generally work well in each type of location.

Figure 9.16 provides an overview of common types of retail locations.

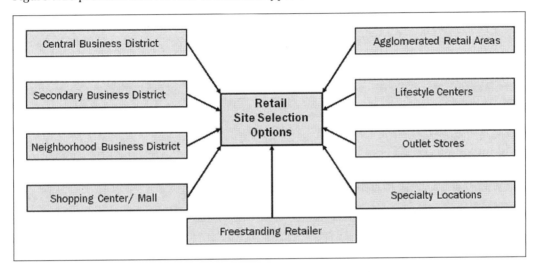

Figure 9.16: Retail Location Selection: Overview of Common Retail Locations

Central Business District: Central business district (CBD) locations are unplanned shopping areas near city centers. Central business districts have strong advantages. Public transportation services often converge on city centers, making access convenient. The location also ensures a steady stream of urban foot traffic and vehicle traffic. Central business districts also have disadvantages. Landlords can charge high rents. Cities can charge high taxes. Shoppers that drive their cars to stores often suffer scarce and expensive parking. Shoppers must also endure traffic congestion. Many older cities are plagued by high crime rates and decaying conditions.

Central business district store locations work well for brands associated with urban lifestyles. Such brands include so-called urban brands and luxury brands. Urban brands include brands popular with youth in cities, such as Diesel brand jeans in the 2000s. Luxury brands include brands such as Hermes, located in posh retail stores in Manhattan. Of course, basic necessities (food, clothing, etc.) will also work in cities.

Retail chain stores, such as Walmart and Home Depot, do not work as well in central business districts. The crowded nature of central business districts often do not allow sufficient space for large stores of this type. Also, some cities pass ordinances to avoid proliferation of so-called big box stores in their areas.

Secondary Business District: Secondary business district (SBD) locations are similar to central business districts, but smaller. They revolve around at least one major store, such as a department store, at a large street intersection.

Secondary business districts work well for department stores and specialty stores. For example, fashion apparel stores offering unique clothing not ordinarily found in department stores fare well in secondary business districts.

Neighborhood Business District: Neighborhood business district (NBD) locations are shopping areas designed to satisfy the convenience needs of a local neighborhood. Neighborhood shopping areas consist of several small stores, often accompanied by a major retailer, such as a supermarket. Neighborhood business districts are generally located on major streets in residential areas. Many people refer to such shopping areas as "strip malls." [9-26]

Neighborhood business districts work well for convenience-oriented retail stores, such as dry cleaning establishments.

Shopping Centers and Malls: Shopping centers and malls are centrally owned or managed shopping districts. They are planned, with each store complementing the others in merchandise offerings (called balanced tenancy). Shopping centers differ from malls in that shopping centers are located outdoors, while malls are enclosed.

Convenient parking facilities surround shopping centers and malls. Shopping centers and malls benefit from heavy foot traffic, low crime rate, and sharing of common costs. Disadvantages include high rents, inflexible hours and policies, and competition from nearby stores.

Shopping centers and malls work well for chain stores of major brands, such as clothing and footwear sales. Most shopping centers and malls feature at least one anchor store, such as a major department store. Anchor stores draw customers to shopping centers, helping to generate foot traffic for surrounding smaller stores.

Freestanding Retailer: Freestanding retailers are stand-alone buildings, with no adjacent retailers to share traffic. Companies should place freestanding retail stores along prominent highways to boost incoming traffic.

Advantages can include absence of nearby competition, differentiation from similar offerings, lower rents, freedom in policies, and inexpensive parking. Disadvantages can include lack of drawing power for complementary stores, difficulties in attracting initial customers, and high initial costs (if buildings must be erected).

Freestanding retailers work well for retail environments that buyers perceive as destinations, such as specialty retailers. For example, customers could justify special trips to popular restaurants such as Olive Garden (olivegarden.com), automotive maintenance facilities such as Jiffy Lube (jiffylube.com), and specialty stores such as golf retailer Golfsmith (golfsmith.com).

Agglomerated Retail Areas: Agglomerated retail areas are shopping districts which combine competing brands of one category. They are the opposite of freestanding retailers. Many customers prefer to shop in agglomerated retail areas because they offer one-stop shopping for purchases. The customer convenience of the approach can drive incoming traffic to the stores.

Agglomerated retail areas work well for situations where customers appreciate the convenience of conducting comparison shopping for multiple brands in one area. Examples include so-called "auto malls" (with multiple auto dealerships), "restaurant rows" (with competing restaurants), and "hotel rows" (with several different hotel chains).

Lifestyle Centers: So-called lifestyle centers feature trendy brands associated with certain types of lifestyles, especially relatively affluent ones.

Lifestyle centers work well for specialty retail brands, especially those that satisfy needs and wants associated with fairly affluent lifestyles. Examples include centers populated with retail stores such as cookware and tableware specialist Williams-Sonoma (williams-sonoma.com), furniture and accessory retailer Restoration Hardware (restorationhardware.com), and home décor specialist Pottery Barn (potterybarn.com).

Outlet Centers: Outlet centers offer a method for manufacturers and retailers to dispose of excess inventory without the steep discounting of liquidation stores. In the past, merchandise consisted of previous year models discounted to stimulate sales. More recently, manufacturers often develop special models for outlet store sales. [9-27]

Outlet centers work well for major consumer brands, especially those selling fashion and home goods merchandise.

Specialty Locations: In addition to the standard retail locations listed above, many other options exist. Stand-alone kiosks can be made available and are popular in urban areas.

Specialty locations work well for products and services related to their particular location. For example, airports often sell books and magazines for long flights, hotels often sell sundries that forgetful travelers left at home, beachside resorts sell suntan lotion, and hospitals sell flowers and other gifts to give to patients.

Figure 9.17 summarizes several specific location options and recommended uses for each option.

Retail Store Location	Description	Recommended Uses
Central Business District (CBD)	Business district near center of city with an unplanned shopping area.	Urban brands; Luxury brands; Specialty
Secondary Business District (SBD)	Business district smaller than central business district, anchored by at least one major store at a major street intersection.	Department stores; Specialty stores; Comparison shopping
Neighborhood Business District (NBD)	Business district satisfying convenience needs of neighborhood.	Grocery stores; Convenience stores
Shopping Center/ Mall	Centrally owned or managed, with balanced tenancy.	Chain stores of major brands
Freestanding Retailer	Stand-alone facilities, with no adjacent retailers to share traffic.	Destination stores; Specialty shopping
Agglomerated Retail Areas	Collections of competing brands in one category	Comparison shopping: Auto malls
Lifestyle Centers	Upscale retail locations catering to high income lifestyles	Specialty retail brands; Specialty
Outlet Stores	Clearance stores for major brands. Often located on outskirts of major metro areas.	Major consumer brands, esp. fashion
Specialty Locations	Locations other than the common types of locations mentioned above.	Kiosks; Airports; Hotels; Resorts

Figure 9.17: Retail Site Selection: Individual Site Selection Options

MARKETING MADE MEASURABLE

Walmart as Magnet: Using Location to Pull in Customers: Businesses must consider how the type of location they select for retail stores will affect sales.

For example, if foot traffic is vital to the success of the business, companies must avoid independent locations in small strip centers and opt instead for centers anchored by large traffic generators, such as Walmart. According to retail consultant Bob Kramer, "Walmart is not likely to carry the top brands, but they will draw customers towards you."

Specialty products, as opposed to mass market products, will warrant different locations. According to Devon Wolfe, a managing director at Pitney Bowes MapInfo, a location consultancy, "The more mainstream your appeal, the broader your array of competition, which will mean that...you need to co-locate with your competitors to be a contender."

For specialty products, Wolfe says, "If you're going the specialty route, your store will be more of a destination, which means that you can locate closer to your target customer and worry less about competitive positioning." [9-28]

CHANNEL EVALUATION AND SELECTION

In this section, we cover a simple technique to assess the performance of existing distribution channel members, as well as select new members. This book introduces a new channel evaluation and selection model that incorporates the guidelines for retail location selection we just discussed, along with profitability and other objectives.

Evaluation Criteria Overview

We base the new channel evaluation and selection model on four categories of evaluation criteria. By "channel," we primarily refer to retail channel members. The evaluation categories include profitability and customer evaluation criteria.

To recognize the importance of customers in distribution channel evaluation, we include three different customer-oriented aspects. The aspects recognize the life cycle of customers—from acquiring them, to keeping them, to gaining additional revenue from them.

Customers follow a certain relationship with company distribution channels. Customers value different criteria as the relationship matures. For example, we find that customers value location and brand alignment strongest at the beginning of the relationship (the acquisition phase). With the relationship established, customers value strong customer support for them to continue the relationship (the retention phase). As customers gain trust in the company, they become open to recommendations for relevant new products and services (the customer revenue growth phase).

Figure 9.18 shows an overview of the four evaluation criteria categories to guide us in our evaluation and selection of the most effective channel. We cover the four criteria in general here, and expand upon them in the next section.

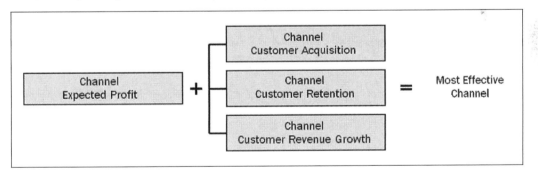

Figure 9.18: Channel Evaluation and Selection: Overview of Model

Channel Expected Profit: We define profitability through the channel as the estimated revenue expected from the channel, less the total costs. We can calculate revenue by multiplying the number of units sold by the retail price per unit. We can calculate costs using the cost components given in the earlier section (trade margins, logistics, discounts, etc.). For example, Internet-based distribution channels can yield high profits due to their relatively low costs.

Channel Customer Acquisition: This category recognizes the role distribution channels play in bringing in new customers, such as when entering new markets. For example, many marketers emphasize the importance of location when selecting retail stores to attract new customers.

Channel Customer Retention: This category captures the role distribution channels play in keeping existing customers, ensuring they do not defect to competitors. For example, many customers change companies when customer service does not meet their expectations.

Channel Customer Revenue Growth: This category acknowledges the role distribution channels play in developing new revenue streams from customers. Marketers also call this revenue growth technique as growing "share of wallet." Some companies offer value-added services to complement their products. For example, electronics retailer Best Buy (bestbuy.com) acquired electronics services firm Geek Squad (geeksquad.com) to repair and maintain computers, home theater components, and other electronic equipment.

Figure 9.19 summarizes the categories of evaluation criteria used in the model.

Channel Evaluation Criteria Category	Description
Channel Expected Profit	Total expected revenue (quantity multiplied by price) less total expected costs (trade margins, logistics costs, discounts, etc.)
Channel Customer Acquisition	Effectiveness in attracting new customers
Channel Customer Retention	Effectiveness in keeping existing customers
Channel Customer Revenue Growth	Effectiveness in developing additional revenue streams from existing customers

Figure 9.19: Channel Evaluation and Selection: Criteria Categories

Because distribution channel members routinely report revenue and cost figures, the information is readily available, and so we will not discuss those areas further. Instead, we focus on developing measurement criteria for the customer-focused areas.

Customer Acquisition Criteria

Our model incorporates four criteria to assess the distribution channel member's efforts to acquire customers. Figure 9.20 shows an overview.

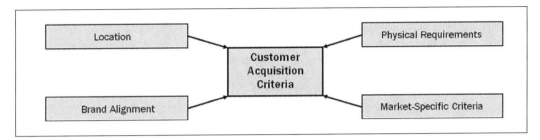

Figure 9.20: Channel Evaluation and Selection: Customer Acquisition Criteria, Overview

Location: As we covered earlier in the chapter, location plays a vital role in the selection of new distribution channel members. In the model, we define the location criterion as the effectiveness of the location in attracting new customers.

For example, we might choose to place an AM/PM convenience store (ampm.com) at the intersection of major streets to boost traffic to the store.

Brand Alignment: Companies selling products or services through non-exclusive retail stores must ensure that the brand associations of the retail store, as perceived by the target market, match the brand associations of the company.

For example, luxury product manufacturer Hermes (hermes.com) sells fashion accessories, leather goods, jewelry, fragrances, and other goods to affluent buyers. Hermes sells its goods through Nordstrom high-end department stores (nordstrom.com), because the Nordstrom's brand associations of luxury and affluence align with those of Hermes. By contrast, Hermes would not sell its wares through convenience store 7-Eleven, because the brand associations do not match. [9-29]

Physical Requirements: Companies must check that the distribution channel member meets its physical requirements. We will separate this topic into two areas: mandatory requirements and physical criteria.

Mandatory requirements deal with legal ordinances that must be met to open new retail stores. Legal requirements include zoning laws (store owners must follow city regulations on the use of buildings for commercial purposes), building and safety codes (store owners must follow building codes, such as plumbing and electrical construction adequacy), as well as other federal, state, and local ordinances. We will assume that the ordinances have been met, or that the store owner has a plan to meet them.

Physical criteria deal with physical attributes desirable for retail operations. Physical attributes include characteristics such as available retail floor size (measured in square feet or square meters), parking availability (parking lot quantity and parking distance to the store), driving access (the ease of driving to the store), loading access (the ease of access for supply trucks to pick up and deliver merchandise), store visibility (the ease of seeing the store), and so forth.

Market-Specific Criteria: Companies in certain markets require evaluation criteria in addition to those outlined in this section. The markets require retailers to provide value-added services as part of the store experience. Services include customization, training, installation, and others. Companies in those markets will need to evaluate the retail channel to determine if those services are available through the channel.

For example, fine men's clothing retailer Men's Wearhouse (menswearhouse.com) offers customization services (tailoring) to their customers. Apple provides training for its Macintosh computers and other products through its One to One training program. Consumer electronics store Best Buy (bestbuy.com) offers installation of complex items such as large-format televisions, computer hardware and software, and home theater components through its Geek Squad (geeksquad.com) services division. Each company needs to ensure that personnel and other resources are available to deliver these services.

Figure 9.21 summarizes the customer acquisition criteria used in the model.

Evaluation Criteria	Description	Example
Location	Effectiveness of location in attracting new customers	AM/PM at major intersection
Brand Alignment	Degree of fit between product brand and channel brand	Bloomingdale's vs. 7-Eleven
Physical Requirements	Degree to which channel meets physical needs, e.g., size, garage access, zoning	Square footage
Market-Specific Criteria	Degree to which channel fulfills market-specific criteria	Customization; Training; Installation

Figure 9.21: Channel Evaluation and Selection: Customer Acquisition Criteria, Summary

MARKETING MADE MEASURABLE

Foursquare: Social Media Location Apps and Customer Acquisition: According to a study by online analytics company comScore (comscore.com), 20% of those using smartphones use location-based "check-in" services on their phones.

Retailers can take advantage of the popularity of these social media location apps, such as Facebook Places (facebook.com/about/location) and Foursquare (foursquare.com). According to the study, 60% of check-in service users were between the ages of 18 and 34, a prime demographic for many retailers.

Businesses can leverage this trend by offering specials and deals to attract new customers to local retail outlets. [9-30]

Customer Retention Criteria

Having acquired our customers, we must now retain them. Many experts agree about the importance of customer retention to the ongoing success of the business. Not only does increased customer retention fuel ongoing revenue, it can reduce costs in several areas:

- **Marketing Costs**: Increased customer retention reduces marketing costs because it costs more to acquire new customers than to retain existing ones.

- **Operations Costs**: Increased retention reduces operations costs, such as the cost to decommission customer accounts.

- **Transaction Costs**: Increased customer retention reduces transaction costs, such as up-front contract negotiation and order processing costs.

Our model incorporates three criteria to assess the distribution channel member's efforts to retain customers. The three criteria are customer support, feedback, and programs. Figure 9.22 shows an overview.

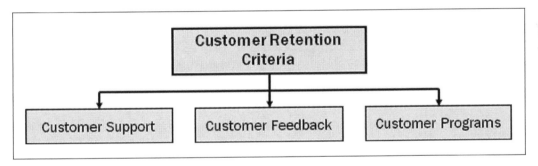

Figure 9.22: Channel Evaluation and Selection: Customer Retention Criteria, Overview

Customer Support: We refer to the term "customer support" instead of "customer service" to distinguish ongoing support from value-added services such as consulting, training, and so forth. Some of the factors affecting customer support include the following:

- **Interpersonal skills**: Companies rated high in customer support often employ agents skilled in interpersonal communications. The agents empathize with discontented customers. Some agents manage customers so well that customer satisfaction actually increases after the handling of a customer complaint. For example, online and catalog outdoor gear retailer L. L. Bean (llbean.com) earned a reputation for customer support excellence, in part due to their highly skilled team of customer support agents.

- **Technology skills**: Companies with high-technology products and services need skillful technology support. For example, Apple staffs its Genius Bar (apple.com/retail/geniusbar) in its retail stores with highly informed technicians who can quickly diagnose and resolve technical issues.

- **Administration skills**: Large companies and those with wide product lines need administration skills, such as the ability to quickly process orders and returns. For example, online retailer Amazon.com (amazon.com) has developed a reputation for quickly processing customer orders and returns.

Customer Feedback: Companies rely on distribution channel members, such as retailers, as part of their customer feedback mechanism. Retailers spend a great deal of time with customers and can sense potential opportunities and threats based on daily interactions. Timely feedback of this information from retailers to companies can ensure that the company develops products and services relevant to the wants and needs of the target market. See the Container Store brief case study below.

Customer Programs: Structured loyalty programs can keep profitable customers from defecting to competitors. Effective loyalty programs offer attractive incentives to their customers to stay loyal, with the incentives increasing as customers stay with the company. For example, luxury retailer Neiman Marcus (neimanmarcus.com) offers its InCircle Rewards customer loyalty program. Neiman Marcus supports the program with retailer employee training, consistent communications, and incentives their customers appreciate. [9-31]

Figure 9.23 summarizes the customer retention criteria used in the model.

Evaluation Criteria	Description	Example
Customer Support	Effectiveness of resolving customer issues	Amazon.com
Customer Feedback	Degree of customer feedback from channel partner to company	The Container Store
Customer Programs	Effectiveness of customer loyalty programs for customer retention	Neiman Marcus

Figure 9.23: Channel Evaluation and Selection: Customer Retention Criteria, Summary

MARKETING MADE MEASURABLE

The Container Store: Feedback Tools and Customer Retention: Storage and organization products retailer The Container Store (containerstore.com) gathers and applies feedback from customers to boost customer retention. The Container Store used OpinionLab's (opinionlab.com) feedback and survey service to collect comments from customers' use of the Container Store's Design Center tool. The tool leads online shoppers through the process of designing custom closet and organizational systems. The feedback they received helped the Container Store improve their conversion rate metrics.

The OpinionLab also measured feedback from the Container Store's mobile website. Feedback showed that consumers wanted to see more of the desktop site's functionality replicated on the mobile website. In particular, consumers desired the ability to access the gift registry and organizational tips, neither of which the mobile site offered. According to Catherine Davis, direct marketing director of the Container Store, "The feedback really helps us prioritize what we should do first." [9-32]

Customer Revenue Growth Criteria

Many companies face pressure to grow revenue. In addition to growing revenue from acquiring new customers, companies can increase revenue by growing the amount of money earned from each customer. Companies can sell complementary goods and services to existing customers to increase customer revenue growth. Sometimes this concept is referred to as growing "share of wallet," in that the company captures more total income from customers.

The model considers three criteria to evaluate the customer revenue growth capability of the distribution channel member. The three criteria are consulting and guidance, customer-centered metrics, and channel growth. Figure 9.24 shows an overview.

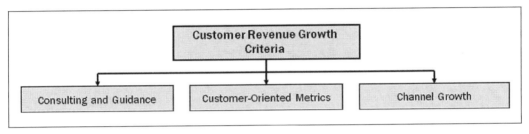

Figure 9.24: Channel Evaluation and Selection: Customer Revenue Growth Criteria, Overview

Consulting and Guidance: Companies have long relied on consulting and guidance to drive customer revenue growth. Many customers consider retailers to be trusted advisors, guiding them in their purchase decisions. Retailers knowledgeable about their products and services can grow revenue for the firm by suggesting complementary offerings to customer purchases.

For example, sports retailer Fleet Feet Sports (fleetfeetsports.com) specializes in providing expert guidance to runners, from running equipment selection to training techniques. Fleet Feet Sports employees receive training to provide customers with the best possible equipment. Fleet Feet Sports started out specializing strictly in running shoes. The company now offers shorts, shirts, sports bras, jackets, and other technical running apparel. What might start out as a simple shoe purchase could turn into fitting a customer with an entire running ensemble. [9-33]

Customer-Centered Metrics: Companies must implement and maintain systems to track sales by customers if they plan to increase revenue per customer. In the Wild West, the corner general store clerk remembered the few patrons of the store. In today's fast-paced society, companies cannot rely strictly on memory, so they turn to **customer relationship management (CRM) systems**. CRM systems integrate customer data from various sources (such as customer orders and support) to gain insight into customer wants and needs.

For example, luxury hotel services provider Ritz Carlton (ritzcarlton.com) implemented its Customer Loyalty Anticipation and Satisfaction System (CLASS) to provide top quality service to its guests. The CLASS system uses a simple CRM system to keep track of customer preferences, such as bed type, their favorite table at the restaurant, and their preferred room. [9-34]

Channel Growth: To maximize customer revenue growth, companies must consider the overall growth rate of the distribution channel itself. Customer revenue growth relies on the strength of the distribution channel. Recent shopping trends by consumers show a shift in the types of distribution channels they prefer, moving away from the mass merchandisers popular in the past, to the growth of specialty and online retailer channel members today.

For example, companies formerly sold through mass merchants such as Montgomery Ward to maximize sales of its merchandise. But the mass merchant distribution channel has been shrinking due to competition from Internet retail sales and other factors. In fact, Montgomery Ward stopped its retail operations because it could not thrive in the crowded retail field. [9-35] Figure 9.25 summarizes the customer revenue growth criteria used in the model.

Evaluation Criteria	Description	Example
Consulting & Guidance	Effectiveness of consulting to increase revenue per customer	Fleet Feet Sports
Customer-Centered Metrics	Ability to track revenue at customer level	Ritz Carlton
Channel Growth	Degree to which channel will grow over time	Internet growth

Figure 9.25: Channel Evaluation and Selection: Customer Revenue Growth Criteria, Summary

MARKETING MADE MEASURABLE

Walmart: Retailers Battling for Share of Wallet: Traditional supermarkets, dollar-discount stores, drug store chains, big-box department stores, and wholesale clubs all seek to generate more revenue per customer.

To build "share of wallet," many non-supermarket retailers are now adding groceries to their mix of merchandise. Retailers believe that shoppers coming into discount or other non-grocery stores will want to take advantage of the convenience of picking up grocery store items while at the store.

Some companies are already noticing the shift toward grocery shopping at non-supermarket retailers. Walmart, the nation's biggest retailer, reported that U.S. comparable-store sales grew only 1.5% in 2011, below analysts' estimates of 1.8%, in part due to shoppers choosing other stores to purchase groceries. As a result, Walmart indicated it planned to spend $1 billion in 2012 to cut prices on grocery goods to bring shoppers back.

According to Standard & Poor's Capital IQ analyst Joseph Agnese, "The struggle today is to maximize share of wallet by trying to fulfill as many of the consumers' needs as possible and to do it well." [9-36]

Evaluation and Selection Model

With our evaluation criteria established, we now describe the distribution channel member evaluation and selection model. We describe the model as follows:

- **Goal of Model**: The goal of the model is to act as a structured decision making tool for the evaluation and selection of new distribution channel members, such as retail stores.

- **Inputs to Model**: The inputs to the model include revenue and cost data, as well as the assessments of individual evaluation criteria described earlier.

- **Outputs from Model**: The outputs from the model include expected profit from each channel member under consideration, as well as aggregate scores for the customer acquisition, retention, and revenue growth abilities of each member.

Figure 9.26 shows an overview of the inputs and outputs of the model.

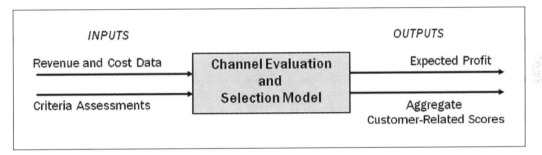

Figure 9.26: Channel Evaluation and Selection Model: Inputs and Outputs

We do not assert that the model replaces the role of skill and judgment. Rather, we developed the model as a decision aid, to frame the decision and provide structure around it. In fact, much of the model's value comes from the discipline required to collect and assess the various evaluation criteria data.

We built the model to fulfill the following criteria:

- **Expected Profit**: The model acknowledges the importance of revenue and cost, and calculates expected profit for each candidate channel member.

- **Additional Evaluation Criteria**: Users can easily include additional evaluation criteria as needed for the model, due to its simple structure. We recognize special circumstances can exist in some situations, and the model accommodates them.

- **Evaluation Criteria Weighting**: Different market situations demand more emphasis on some evaluation criteria than others. For example, newly launched brands often must emphasize customer acquisition over retention, at least until the brand establishes itself. Therefore, we have incorporated weighting of evaluation criteria to adjust the model to those situations.

- **General Relevance:** The flexibility of the model, because of its ability to incorporate additional evaluation criteria and weighting, makes it relevant to a wide range of channel member decisions.

In the calculations that follow, we express all values in profitability entries in monetary terms, such as U.S. Dollars or Euros. For the customer acquisition, retention, and revenue growth figures, we would prefer to continue working directly in monetary terms for consistency with the profitability calculations. However, it can be difficult to determine exact monetary values for all evaluation criteria. Therefore, we will work using non-monetary evaluation ratings.

We suggest the rating systems shown in Figure 9.27. For quick evaluations, we recommend the 5-Star system shown in the figure, similar to that used on Amazon.com. For more thorough evaluations requiring finer accuracy, we recommend the 0 – 100 percentage system.

Rating: Stars	Rating: Percentages	Description
5 Stars	100%	Perfect performance. This level will rarely, if ever, be achieved. Values of 5 in key areas, such as location, are very important.
4 Stars	80%	Excellent performance. This level will be reached by a handful of top-caliber channel members.
3 Stars	60%	Good performance. This level represents the minimum standard for passing.
2 Stars	40%	Fair performance. This level is unlikely to be accepted unless the channel member is outstanding in other areas.
1 Stars	20%	Poor performance. One evaluation at this level in an important area will likely remove the channel member from all consideration.

Figure 9.27: Distribution Channel Member Selection: Percentage Assignment Guidelines

The model applies weights to criteria in each evaluation group to emphasize or de-emphasize their importance. For example, in the Customer Acquisition evaluation group, we can assign a higher weight to location than the other criteria if we believe it to be significant.

Weights will vary with the retailing situation. For example, locations with great foot traffic are more important with convenience stores than with destination stores, so we would assign a higher weight to location for convenience stores. The weights are expressed in percentages. The sum of the weights for each group must equal 100%.

The model also applies weights to each evaluation group to emphasize one group over the other. For example, a newly established brand will want to place a higher weight on customer acquisition, to emphasize the store's ability to attract customers to try the new brand. By comparison, a well-known brand can place more emphasis on customer revenue growth. Again, the sum of the weights should equal 100%. Because each retailing situation will differ, we cannot offer universal guidance for weighting.

To summarize, the model uses three types of data:

- **Financial Data**: Financial data consists of amounts in monetary terms, such as dollars or Euros. We can obtain the data by estimating the market size for the relevant geographic area, by considering sales of similar stores in the same area, or by asking the channel member for the amounts they expect to generate based on the proposed product or service to be sold.

- **Evaluation Criteria**: The model incorporates evaluation criteria for the channel member's ability to acquire, retain, and grow revenue from customers. For example, a retail store dealing in luxury goods located near a high income area could score well (4 – 5 stars) in its "location" evaluation criterion. It scores well because its proximity to its target market aids it to acquire relevant customers. The score should agree fairly well no matter who performs the assessment; i.e. most people would agree that a store like that should score well in its "location" criterion.

- **Model Weights:** The model allows users to vary the importance of different criteria. For example, we can emphasize profitability over customer retention. Unlike the assessment of the evaluation criteria (which generally should not vary), the weights will vary depending on the situation facing the company. One company, with a long history and sufficient customers, could wish to weight profitability higher than customer acquisition. Another company, just starting out with a new product, will likely want to weight customer acquisition higher than customer revenue growth, at least in the short term.

Execution of the model follows a three-step approach, as shown in Figure 9.28.

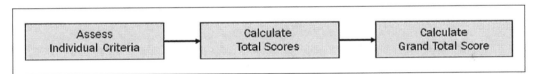

Figure 9.28: Distribution Channel Member Selection Model: Three-Step Approach

- **Assess Individual Criteria**: First, we calculate the scores for the individual decision criteria (location, brand alignment, etc.) for each evaluation criteria group (customer acquisition, retention, and revenue growth).

- **Calculate Total Scores:** Second, we calculate the total scores for each criteria group.

- **Calculate Grand Total Score**: Third, we calculate the grand total score for each distribution channel member alternative.

Assess Individual Criteria: In the first step, we calculate the scores for the decision criteria for each evaluation group. We start with the decision criteria for the profitability evaluation group, and then move on to customer acquisition, retention, and revenue growth.

- **Profitability**: We must estimate the expected revenues and costs for each candidate distribution channel member. We enter the values in a spreadsheet modeled after Figure 9.29. The figure shows expected revenue for different products or services as designated by Revenue (1) for product/service #1 and Revenue (2) for product/service #2. We can expand the figure to include more products or services.

Alternative	Revenue (1)	Revenue (2)	Cost	Total (Monetary)	Total (Normalized)
Member A				$10	16.6%
Member B				$20	33.3%
Member C				$30	50.0%
Total				$60	100.0%

Figure 9.29: Distribution Channel Member Selection: Profitability Calculations

Similarly, we estimate total costs for each alternative. See the Distribution Costs section earlier in this chapter for a discussion of typical costs to expect.

We complete the spreadsheet by subtracting costs from revenue to arrive at a total for each channel member. In the Total (Monetary) column, we calculate the expected profit for each channel member in monetary terms, such as U.S. Dollars or Euros. In the Total (Normalized) column, we calculate the expected profit for each channel in normalized terms.

To calculate the **normalized** amounts, we find the sum of the expected profits for all channel members, and then divide each channel member expected profit by the sum. For example, if channel members A, B, and C generated expected profits of $10, $20, and $30, respectively, we add up the profits to arrive at $10 + $20 + $30 = $60. Next, divide each profit by the sum to find normalized values of $10/$60 = 16.6%, $20/$60 = 33.3%, and $30/$60 = 50.0% for channel members A, B, and C respectively.

- **Customer Acquisition**: Figure 9.30 shows a recommended spreadsheet format for customer acquisition calculations. We must estimate the degree to which each alternative channel member satisfies customer acquisition-related criteria. For each channel member, assign a rating (1 – 5 stars or equivalent) assessing how well the member achieves each criterion. For example, we rate a store located in a highly trafficked area as a "5" in location, whereas a store in a near-abandoned mall with poor traffic we rate as a "1."

In addition, we assign a weight for each criterion in the group. The weights are designated with capital letters representing their function. For example, Weight (L) represents the weight for Location and Weight (BA) represents the weight for Brand Alignment. Weights must total 100%. For example, we could assign a weight of 50% for location, 20% for brand alignment, 20% for physical requirements, and 10% for market-specific criteria for a new brand with few market-specific needs, for a total of 100%.

Evaluation Criteria	Description	Weight
Location	Effectiveness of location in attracting new customers	Weight (L)
Brand Alignment	Degree of fit between product brand and channel brand	Weight (BA)
Physical Requirements	Degree to which channel meets physical needs, such as size, garage access, etc.	Weight (PR)
Market-Specific Criteria	Degree to which channel fulfills market-specific criteria	Weight (MC)

Figure 9.30: Distribution Channel Member Selection: Customer Acquisition Calculations

- **Customer Retention**: Figure 9.31 shows the evaluation criteria for customer retention. We repeat the same process we used for customer acquisition. Here, we enter expected effectiveness values for customer support, customer feedback, and customer programs for each candidate channel member. We also enter corresponding weights for each criterion.

Evaluation Criteria	Description	Weight
Customer Support	Effectiveness of resolving customer issues	Weight (CS)
Customer Feedback	Degree of customer feedback from channel partner to company	Weight (CF)
Customer Programs	Effectiveness of customer loyalty programs for customer retention	Weight (CP)

Figure 9.31: Distribution Channel Member Selection: Customer Retention Calculations

- **Customer Revenue Growth**: We execute the same process as in the previous sections, this time for customer revenue growth. Figure 9.32 shows the evaluation criteria for customer revenue growth. Consulting and guidance should receive a higher weight for specialty stores than for stores selling general merchandise. Customer-centered metrics will be more important for companies with complex customer needs.

Evaluation Criteria	Description	Weight
Consulting and Guidance	Effectiveness of consulting to increase revenue per customer	Weight (CAG)
Customer-Centered Metrics	Ability to track revenue at customer level	Weight (CM)
Channel Growth	Degree to which channel will grow over time	Weight (CG)

Figure 9.32: Distribution Channel Member Selection: Customer Revenue Growth Calculations

Calculate Total Scores: Having calculated the assessments for individual criteria, we now calculate the total for each group.

Use the spreadsheet structure shown in Figure 9.33 to enter evaluation values for each group of evaluation criteria. The figure shows a typical spreadsheet layout, using the evaluation criteria for customer acquisition as an example. The left column lists the various alternative channel members. The columns in the middle of the spreadsheet show evaluations for each criterion and their corresponding weights.

Alternative	Weight (L)	L	Weight (BA)	BA	Weight (PR)	PR	Weight (MSC)	MSC	Total
Member A									
Member B									
Member C									
Total	100%		100%		100%		100%		

Figure 9.33: Distribution Channel Member Selection: Spreadsheet Entries for Evaluation Groups

The spreadsheet abbreviates the titles to save space. For example, L designates location; Weight (L) designates the weight for location, and so forth. BA indicates brand alignment, PR stands for physical requirements, and MSC represents market-specific criteria. The right column shows the total.

We compute the total by summing the weighted values for each criterion. For example, we would compute the total score for customer acquisition for each channel member using the following formula:

Total (Customer Acquisition, Channel Member A)
= Weight (L) * L + Weight (BA) * BA + Weight (PR) * PR + Weight (MSC) * MSC

Repeat the process for the customer retention and customer revenue growth evaluation groups.

Calculate Grand Total Score: The third step is to calculate the grand total for each channel member. We calculate the grand total by summing the weighted scores for each evaluation group. Figure 9.34 shows the spreadsheet layout for the grand total calculation. Similar to the spreadsheet layout for evaluation groups, the left column lists the alternatives, the middle columns show the values for each evaluation criteria group and their corresponding weights, and the right column shows the grand total.

Alternative	Weight (EP)	EP	Weight (CA)	CA	Weight (CR)	CR	Weight (RG)	RG	Total
Member A									
Member B									
Member C									
Total	100%		100%		100%		100%		

Figure 9.34: Distribution Channel Member Selection: Grand Total

As before, the spreadsheet abbreviates titles to save space. EP designates expected profit. CA stands for customer acquisition. CR represents customer retention. RG indicates customer revenue growth. Weights for each use the same nomenclature. For example, Weight (EP) designates the weight for expected profit.

We enter weights for each category. The weights will emphasize or de-emphasize different evaluation groups. The process of assigning the weights can be valuable, because it forces the organization to make important trade-offs. The values of the weights will depend on the situation of the company. As before, the sum of all weights must equal 100%.

- **Expected Profit**: Companies in financial peril with a short term focus on survival can choose to assign a high weight to expected profitability and much lower weights for the other evaluation criteria groups. Financially healthy companies should not take this extreme approach.

- **Customer Acquisition**: Businesses wishing to grow their customer base would assign higher weights to the customer acquisition area.

- **Customer Retention**: Companies indicating a desire to keep their existing customers would place a high weight for customer retention.

- **Customer Revenue Growth**: Established companies with wide product lines wishing to grow the "share of wallet" per customer would enter a high weight for customer revenue growth.

Check the values in the totals column. The highest value will represent the preferred channel member, based on the criteria given.

Example: Acme Cosmetics (a fictitious company) manufactures and sells two brands of premium anti-wrinkle face cream derived from a rare form of green tea. The first brand is their super-premium brand. The second brand is their standard brand. Some say that the green tea gives the creams their unique rejuvenating powers. Whatever the reason, sales are increasing. Therefore, the company plans to expand sales to additional retail stores.

Acme Cosmetics completed an evaluation of available retail store locations in its target area. The company has narrowed down its choices to three alternatives—Store X, Store Y, and Store Z. To make an informed choice on the alternatives, Acme Cosmetics researched each alternative.

Figure 9.35 presents the results of their research, presenting the attributes for the three candidates. The data in the figure represents the "inputs" into the assessment model. Acme has assigned weights for profitability, customer acquisition, customer retention, and customer revenue growth at 40%, 20%, 20%, and 20%, respectively. We now review the attributes for the three alternatives.

Attribute	Weight	Store X	Store Y	Store Z
Profitability: 40%				
Revenue (1)		$120	$100	$110
Revenue (2)		$60	$80	$50
Cost		$90	$72	$32
Customer Acquisition: 20%				
Location	50%	80%	60%	20%
Brand Alignment	20%	80%	60%	40%
Physical Requirements	20%	60%	80%	100%
Market-Specific	10%	60%	60%	100%
Customer Retention: 20%				
Customer Support	50%	80%	40%	40%
Customer Feedback	30%	60%	40%	40%
Customer Programs	20%	60%	20%	20%
Customer Revenue Growth: 20%				
Consulting / Guidance	50%	100%	60%	20%
Customer Metrics	30%	80%	40%	60%
Channel Growth	20%	20%	20%	100%

Figure 9.35: Distribution Channel Member Selection: Acme Cosmetics Example: Store Attributes

Store X is a premium retail store located in an upscale mall situated in a prime location in the city. We evaluate the revenue and cost attributes as follows:

- **Revenue**: Acme expects Store X to generate generates $120,000 in revenue (abbreviated in the Figure as $120 for brevity) for brand #1 of our anti-wrinkle cream. Therefore, Revenue (1) is $120. Revenue (2), for brand #2 of our cream, is $60.

- **Cost**: The store charges a rate of 50% of total sales in costs. Therefore, we calculate the costs associated with Store X as 50% * ($120 + $60) = $90.

We now evaluate the customer acquisition attributes, along with their corresponding weights:

- **Location**: Acme Cosmetics rated Store X 80% (excellent) in location due to its upscale mall presence, giving it great exposure to its target audience. Acme believes the location of the store is critical, so it assigns a 50% weight to the location.

- **Brand Alignment**: The upscale mall presence of Store X aligns well with its premium brand, so Acme rated brand alignment at 80% (excellent). Acme desires to keep the brand aligned, so it assigns a moderate weight of 20% to brand alignment.

- **Physical Requirements**. Because Store X is in a premium mall, all of the legal requirements (zoning, etc.) have been met. Acme found limited available floor space in Store X, so it scored only 60% (good) on the physical requirements attribute. Acme needs adequate floor space to properly showcase its products, so it assigns a moderate weight of 20%.

- **Market-Specific Criteria**: Store X appears willing to provide adequate, but not industry-leading, training services to its staff to properly describe the benefits of the Acme Cosmetics line, so we rate it 60% (good). Acme requires only minor training assistance for store sales staff, so it assigns a relatively low 10% weight to market-specific criteria.

Next, we evaluate criteria and weights for customer retention:

- **Customer Support**: Store X's helpful and efficient staff make customer support a breeze. Acme rates it 80%. Acme places a lot of value in support, and so assigns it a relatively high weight of 50%.

- **Customer Feedback**: Store X encourages (but does not require) its sales staff to provide feedback to manufacturers, so Acme Cosmetics rates it 60%. Acme believes customer support to be moderately important, and so assigns it a moderate weight of 30%.

- **Customer Programs**: Store X maintains a customer loyalty program, but does not emphasize it to customers, so Acme Cosmetics rates it 60%. Acme finds customer programs to be moderately important (but not as important as customer feedback), and so assigns it a moderate weight of 20%.

We complete our evaluation process for Store X by considering customer revenue growth:

- **Consulting and Guidance**: Store X employs sales staff with outstanding knowledge in cosmetics. Customers value their expertise. Acme rates it 100%. Consulting and guidance are of high importance to Acme, so Acme assigns a high weight of 50% to the criterion.

- **Customer Metrics**: Store X maintains a customer relationship management database. Salespeople rely on its information to acknowledge customer preferences during the shopping experience. Acme rates it 80%. Acme finds such systems important, and so rates the criterion a moderate weight of 30%.

- **Channel Growth**: Store X has a proud history of serving the community well, with premium brands in a convenient location. Alas, shoppers increasingly choose to shop elsewhere, looking for bargains on the Internet. Because the channel has few growth prospects, Acme assigns it a very low score of 20%. Channel growth is of moderate importance to Acme, which it rates at 20%.

Store Y is a retail outlet store located in an outlet mall on the outskirts of the city. Acme applies the same approach to scoring Store Y as it did Store X. Acme keeps the same weighting. We briefly review Store Y's evaluation:

- **Revenue**: Store Y is expected to generate $100 for Revenue (1) and $80 for Revenue (2).

- **Cost**: Store Y has less overhead than Store X, and so charges less than store X for merchandising manufacturer's products. Store Y charges 40% of total sales, for a cost of 40% * ($100 + $80) = $72.

- **Location**: Store Y's location only generates moderate traffic, so Acme rates it 60%.

- **Brand Alignment**: Store Y's emphasis on outlet merchandising (less posh than true premium malls) makes it a less-than-ideal choice for brand alignment. Acme rates it 60%.

- **Physical Requirements**: Store Y offers abundant floor space. Acme rates it 80%.

- **Market-Specific Criteria**: Store Y agrees to provide training to sales staff. Acme rates it 60%.

- **Customer Support**: Store Y's customer support staff is efficient but not as customer-friendly as those in Store X. Acme rates it 40%.

- **Customer Feedback**: Store Y allows sales staff to provide feedback to manufacturers, but provides no active encouragement to do so. Acme rates it 40%.

- **Customer Programs**: Store Y maintains a store loyalty program, but few customers appear to use it. Acme rates it a low 20%.

- **Consulting and Guidance**: Store Y sales staff know a bit about cosmetics, but are not experts. Acme rates it 60%.
- **Customer Metrics**: Store Y maintains a CRM system, but salespeople rarely use it. Acme rates it 40%.

- **Channel Growth**: Store Y's popularity is decreasing as shoppers look for bargains elsewhere. Acme rates it 20%.

Store Z is an Internet-based retail store with several product lines. Store Z maintains a moderately well known brand, but is not a superstar such as Amazon.com. Acme repeats the same evaluation process as with Stores X and Y. We review the results:

- **Revenue**: Store Z is expected to generate $110 for Revenue (1) and $50 for Revenue (2).

- **Cost**: Store Z enjoys a much lower cost structure because of its Internet basis. Store Z charges only 20% of total sales, for a cost of 20% * ($110 + $50) = $32.

- **Location**: Store Z has only a moderately well known brand name, giving it a lackluster "location" on the web, unlike major etailers such as Amazon.com. Acme rates it at 20%.

- **Brand Alignment**: Store Z features many brands, not all of which are premium, reducing the overall brand appeal. Acme rates it at 40%.

- **Physical Requirements**: Store Z offers unlimited floor space. Store Z can simply add new web pages to accommodate more products. Acme rates it 100%.

- **Market-Specific Criteria**: Store Z has many applications (apps) available to perform a variety of different tasks. Acme rates it at 100%.

- **Customer Support**: Store Z customer service is Internet-based. Without telephone support, some customers might feel slighted. Acme rates it 40%.

- **Customer Feedback**: Store Z includes some limited algorithms to collect aggregate customer feedback and return it to the manufacturers. Acme rates it 40%.

- **Customer Programs**: Store Z offers occasional coupons sent via email, but few customers opt in to such communications from Store Z. Acme rates it 20%.

- **Consulting and Guidance**: Store Z consulting and guidance is limited to usage charts and recommendations on the website. Acme rates it 20%.

- **Customer Metrics**: Store Z maintains an order management system, carefully tracking customer orders and returns, but not tracking customer preferences. Acme rates it 60%.

- **Channel Growth**: Store Z's popularity is booming as shoppers flock to the Internet in search of bargains. Acme rates it 100%.

With our attributes evaluated, we begin the calculation process. We begin with revenues and cost. Figure 9.36 shows profitability calculations for the three stores. The figure shows the totals in monetary and normalized formats.

Alternative	Revenue (1)	Revenue (2)	Cost	Total (Monetary)	Total (Normalized)
Store X	$120	$60	$90	$90	28%
Store Y	$100	$80	$72	$108	33%
Store Z	$110	$50	$32	$128	39%

Figure 9.36: Distribution Channel Member Selection: Acme Profitability Calculations

We now calculate our evaluation scores for customer acquisition. Figure 9.37 shows how to format computer spreadsheets to enter and calculate such scores.

Alternative	Weight (L)	L	Weight (BA)	BA	Weight (PR)	PR	Weight (MSC)	MSC	Total
Store X	.50	.80	.20	.80	.20	.60	.10	.60	.74
Store Y	.50	.60	.20	.60	.20	.80	.10	.60	.64
Store Z	.50	.20	.20	.40	.20	1.00	.10	1.00	.48

Figure 9.37: Distribution Channel Member Selection: Acme Customer Acquisition Calculations

We move to calculations for customer retention attribute evaluation. Figure 9.38 shows how the values are entered into the spreadsheet.

Alternative	Weight (CS)	CS	Weight (CF)	CF	Weight (CP)	CP	Total
Store X	.50	.80	.30	.60	.20	.60	.70
Store Y	.50	.40	.30	.40	.20	.20	.36
Store Z	.50	.40	.30	.40	.20	.20	.36

Figure 9.38: Distribution Channel Member Selection: Acme Customer Retention Calculations

We proceed to the final set of evaluations, those for customer revenue growth attributes. Figure 9.39 shows the format.

Alternative	Weight (CAG)	CAG	Weight (CM)	CM	Weight (CG)	CG	Total
Store X	.50	1.00	.30	.80	.20	.20	.78
Store Y	.50	.60	.30	.40	.20	.20	.46
Store Z	.50	.20	.30	.60	.20	1.00	.48

Figure 9.39: Distribution Channel Member Selection: Acme Customer Revenue Growth Calculations

We finish the process by calculating the grand total. Figure 9.40 shows the recommended spreadsheet format for the grand total calculations.

Alternative	Weight (EP)	EP	Weight (CA)	CA	Weight (CR)	CR	Weight (RG)	RG	Total
Store X	0.40	.28	0.20	.74	0.20	.70	0.20	.78	.55
Store Y	0.40	.33	0.20	.64	0.20	.36	0.20	.46	.42
Store Z	0.40	.39	0.20	.48	0.20	.36	0.20	.48	.42

Figure 9.40: Distribution Channel Member Selection: Acme Grand Total Calculations

From the figure, we can see that Store X scored the highest, and therefore performed the best in the evaluation, given the selected weightings. Had Acme chosen a more well known Internet-based retailer, we might have seen Store Z's score top that of Store X. Had Acme applied different weights, the model would have likely selected a different winner.

Acme Cosmetics might consider selling its super-premium brand in the premium mall stores, and sell its standard brand through Internet-based retailers, thus adopting a multi-channel distribution approach. We discuss multi-channel distribution in the next section.

MULTI-CHANNEL DISTRIBUTION

In this section, we consider multi-channel distribution, where companies employ multiple distribution channels to reach customers.

Companies with multi-channel distribution enjoy several advantages. First, multiple channels can increase sales by offering the company's products and services to more potential customers within existing geographic areas. Second, multiple channels can aid company efforts to expand into new geographic areas. Third, savvy companies can use the characteristics of different channels to align their efforts to idiosyncrasies of different markets. Fourth, companies can reduce the overall cost of sales by serving some markets with lower cost distribution channels, such as Internet-based channels.

Channel Performance Charts

We can track sales of company products and services through different channels to compare the performance of each. Marketers can use sales comparison charts to determine the effectiveness of different types of sales channels.

Figure 9.41 shows a sample sales comparison chart for different channels. The chart shows how sales vary by channel. Channel A represents the company's retail store channel. The chart shows that the retail store channel contributes the majority of sales for the organization. Channel B characterizes the company's Internet-based sales channel. Channel C is the company's specialty store sales channel.

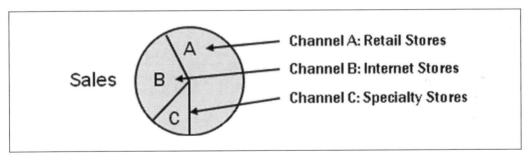

Figure 9.41: Channel Sales Comparison Chart

Figure 9.42 shows an alternative approach to presenting the same data. The comparison chart discussed above highlighted how each distribution channel contributed to total sales. The incremental sales chart shown in the figure below highlights how each additional distribution channel adds to incremental revenue. Marketers can use incremental sales charts to show the role each channel plays in adding to company revenue.

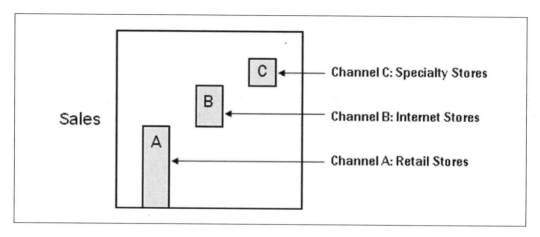

Figure 9.42: Incremental Channel Sales Chart

Multi-Channel Market Tables

Companies selling into multiple markets (such as business and consumer markets) apply different distribution channels to reach the different markets. Each type of distribution channel has a set of characteristics that make it well-suited for a certain type of market. Distribution channels selling to businesses, such as value-added resellers, must have the capability to modify products and services to meet unique business demands. Distribution channels selling to consumers, such as retail stores, must have the capability to provide easy ordering, returns, and customer support.

We illustrate the concept with an example. Computer networking company Cisco (cisco.com) manufactures connectivity hardware and software for multiple markets. It applies savvy multi-channel strategy to target its different markets with different distribution channels.

Figure 9.43 shows Cisco's strategy for multi-channel sales to consumers. Cisco services two types of consumer markets. The first type is basic consumers with modest networking needs, such as setting up home networks. For basic consumers, Cisco sells its wireless routers and other products through its corporate consumer web store at home.cisco.com. It also sells the same products through online etailers such as Amazon.com and retail stores such as Best Buy.

Market	Corporate Consumer Web Store: home.cisco.com	Etail Web: Amazon.com	Retail Stores: Best Buy
Basic Consumers	✓	✓	✓
Mobile Consumers	✓		

Figure 9.43: Multi-Channel Market Table: Cisco Consumer Markets

Cisco also sells products and services to the mobile consumer market. For mobile consumers, Cisco sells its Cisco Connect Cloud set of products (such as its Smart Wi-Fi Routers) and software applications, available for leading smartphones. Cisco sells its Cisco Connect Cloud offerings exclusively through Cisco-branded websites. [9-37]

Figure 9.44 shows Cisco's strategy for multi-channel sales to businesses. Cisco generates the majority of its revenue through sales to businesses. Therefore, the company applies a robust set of distribution channels to the different business markets it serves.

Market	Corporate Business Website: cisco.com	Distributor (CDW, etc.)	Value-added Reseller (Nexus IS, etc.)
Small Business	✓	✓	
Enterprise		✓	✓
Service Provider			✓
Industry Specialist			✓

Figure 9.44: Multi-Channel Market Table: Cisco Business Markets

Cisco serves small businesses through its corporate business-oriented web store at cisco.com. For small businesses with more advanced needs, such as basic consulting, it also sells its products through distributors such as CDW (cdw.com). [9-38]

Cisco also sells its business-oriented products and services to large business enterprises, such as Fortune 500 companies. Because of the additional demands these companies have, Cisco services their needs through distributors (for relatively basic needs) and value-added resellers (VARs) such as Nexus IS (nexusis.com). [9-39]

In addition to small businesses and enterprises, Cisco also supplies service providers (such as Internet service providers, which need powerful networking gear) and specific industries (such as healthcare, which has special needs for networking equipment in hospitals and other areas). Because of the extensive services needed by service providers and specific industries, Cisco emphasizes sales through its VAR network to those markets.

MARKETING MADE MEASURABLE

Improvements: Multi-Channel Retailing through Internet and Printed Catalogs:
Home solutions company Improvements (improvementscatalog.com) applies a multi-channel retailing model, collecting orders through Internet-based sales and printed catalogs. Companies mailed 12.7 billion catalogs in 2010—a large investment.

It turns out that printed catalogs represent a viable distribution channel for retailing, even in the age of online shopping. First, many people find the tactile nature of printed material more inviting and less passive than sitting in front of a computer. Second, companies find a spike in website activity when print catalogs arrive in customers' mailboxes. And third, companies can emphasize their broad selection using multiple niche catalogs.

For example, apparel retailer L.L. Bean (llbean.com) offers no fewer than nine different catalogs, for general markets, fashion-oriented markets (in its "Signature" catalogs), and outdoors-oriented markets (in its hunting and fishing catalogs). [9-40]

DISTRIBUTION CHANNEL METRICS

In this section, we cover metrics useful for tracking distribution channel effectiveness. The metrics measure the availability of a company's products and services in retail outlets. We discuss all commodity volume, product category volume, and category performance ratios. Each measures specific aspects of a company's distribution effectiveness.

All Commodity Volume

The **all commodity volume** (ACV) metric measures the total sales of company products and services in retail stores that stock the company's brand, relative to total sales of all stores. ACV is often used over a specific area, addressing stores in a specific neighborhood, city, or state. [9-41]

Two formulas express ACV. The first declares ACV as a percentage. The second formula abbreviates the expression to include only total sales of all stores carrying the company's brands. The two formulas are distinguished by their units. The first uses percentages. The second uses monetary terms, such as dollars or Euros.

> ACV in Percentage Units:
> $$ACV = \frac{[\text{Total Sales of Stores Carrying Brand (\$)}]}{[\text{Total Sales of All Stores (\$)}]}$$
>
> ACV in Monetary Units:
> $$ACV = [\text{Total Sales of Stores Carrying Brand (\$)}]$$

Example: Acme Cosmetics sells its products through a distribution network consisting of two stores, Store D and Store E. The other store in the area, Store F, does not stock Acme. Total sales of Stores D, E, and F, are $30,000, $20,000, and $10,000, respectively. We calculate the all commodity volume as follows:

> ACV   = [Total Sales of Stores Carrying Brand] / [Total Sales of All Stores]
>   = [$30,000 + $20,000] / [$30,000 + $20,000 + $10,000] = 83.3%

The advantage of the all commodity volume metric is that it provides a measure of the customer traffic through the stores stocking the brand. It tells us if we are in the most popular stores (i.e., those with the highest sales). The disadvantage of the metric is that it tells us nothing about sales in our category. We discuss a metric that addresses this disadvantage in the next section, product category volume.

Product Category Volume

Product category volume (PCV) refines the all commodity volume (ACV) metric by emphasizing sales within the product or service category. Using the metric, marketers can understand the effectiveness of different distribution channels in category sales. [9-42]

Product category volume is defined as the total category sales by stores that carry the company's brand, divided by the total category sales of all stores. Here is the formula:

PCV   = [Total Category Sales by Stores Carrying Company Brand]
                [Total Category Sales of All Stores]

Example: As we saw earlier, Acme Cosmetics sells its products through two stores, Store D and Store E. Stores D and E sell $1,000 and $800 of Acme products, respectively. The other store in the area, Store F, does not sell Acme products. Stores D, E, and F sell $1,000, $800, and $600 in the cosmetics category, respectively. We calculate the product category volume metric:

PCV   = [Total Category Sales by Stores Carrying Company Brand]
                [Total Category Sales of All Stores]

PCV   = [$1,000 + $800+ $0]   = 75.0%
                [$1,000 + $800 + $600]

The advantage of the product category volume metric is that it can provide an indication of the effectiveness its channel partners have in sales within the category. The disadvantage is that sometimes the data on category sales for the different stores can be difficult to collect. In that case, we recommend physically visiting the stores and measuring the areas devoted to the relevant category. Multiply the areas by the expected sales per area (such as sales per square foot) for the store to arrive at the category sales for the store.

For example, department store JC Penney (jcpenney.com) generates about $200 per square foot in its retail stores. If JC Penney allocated 100 square feet to cosmetics, then we would expect JC Penney to earn $200 * 100 = $20,000 in total sales for cosmetics. [9-43]

Category Performance Ratio

The category performance ratio is defined as the ratio of product category volume over all commodity volume. In formula form, we state the following: [9-44]

Category Performance Ratio =   [Product Category Volume]
                                                     [All Commodity Volume]

Example: Acme Cosmetics wishes to determine how the product category volume (sales in the category) for the relevant distribution channels compare to the market as a whole. We can use the category performance ratio to compute this.

Category Performance Ratio = [Product Category Volume] / [All Commodity Volume]

= [75.0%] / [83.3%] = 90.0%

The metric gives us insight into the effectiveness of the company's distribution efforts, relative to the average effectiveness of all categories. Category performance ratios greater than one indicate that the retail stores in the company's distribution network perform more effectively in the category than the market as a whole.

In our example, because 90% is under 100%, we can assert that the stores carrying Acme Cosmetics demonstrate a reduced emphasis on cosmetic sales than the overall collection of stores in the market as a whole.

MARKETING MADE MEASURABLE

Stage Stores vs. Wet Seal: Winner & Loser in Distribution Channel Sales Metrics: Apparel retailers measure sales revenue in stores open at least one year. By focusing on sales from stores open one year or more, the metric focuses on long-term success in its chosen market, and excludes results from stores recently opened or closed. Analysts closely watch the metric, due to its strong predictor of a retailer's health.

Using that measure, we can find winners and losers in the apparel market. Family apparel and accessories retailer Stage Stores (stagestores.com) revenue at stores open at least a year rose 5.3% in 2012. The company cited particularly strong sales in accessories, cosmetics, misses' sportswear, and young men's. [9-45]

By comparison, we find struggling teen clothing seller The Wet Seal (wetseal.com) not faring as well. Revenue at Wet Seal stores open at least one year fell 15.9% in 2012. As a result, the company fired its CEO and planned to reduce the number of new Wet Seal stores it will open in an effort to control costs as sales deteriorate. [9-46]

SUMMARY

We can use analytics models and metrics to guide our decisions for product distribution. Companies use distribution channels to deliver products and services to their target market. Distribution channels are organizations that supply goods to end users. Example channels include wholesalers and retailers.

In this chapter, we covered distribution channel characteristics, retail location selection, distribution channel evaluation and selection, multi-channel distribution, and distribution metrics.

Distribution Channel Characteristics: In order to apply the models and metrics in this chapter, marketers must have an understanding of distribution channel characteristics.

- **Distribution Channel Members**: In this chapter, we reviewed different examples of distribution channel members. Retailers include non-Internet retailers, such as convenience stores, and Internet-based retailers, such as corporate websites. Non-retailers include distributors, liquidators, value-added resellers, and wholesalers.

- **Distribution Intensity:** Companies can select from intensive distribution, where products are stocked in many locations to maximize sales, to exclusive distribution, where products are stocked in only a few carefully controlled outlets, to maximize brand equity.

- **Distribution Costs**: Companies can incur different types of costs for distributing products, such as co-op (cooperation) advertising costs, discounts costs, logistics costs, market development funds costs, and sales performance incentive fund costs.

Retail Location Selection: Successful companies follow a three-step process for selecting a new retail store location:

- **Geographic Area Identification**: First, companies must identify the general geographic areas (such as cities or towns, or portions thereof) that contain the types of people we wish to target. We can use geographic information systems (GIS) and market sizing models to accomplish this step.

- **Potential Site Identification**: The second step is to identify the set of retail locations that will best meet the company's retail goals. We can use GIS systems and the gravity retail location model to accomplish this step.

- **Individual Site Selection:** The third step is to narrow down the set of retail locations to only one location. Companies use their own specific decision criteria (such as the exact goals for the store) for this step.

Channel Evaluation and Selection: Companies can evaluate existing distribution channels and select new ones using the channel evaluation and selection model described in the chapter. The model uses four sets of criteria, listed below. Within each set of criteria, we evaluate several areas contributing to the channel's performance in one of the four sets of criteria.

- **Channel Expected Profit:** We define expected profitability through the channel as the estimated revenue expected from the channel, less the total costs.

- **Channel Customer Acquisition:** Distribution channels play a vital role in gathering new customers, so one of our primary criteria is the channel's ability to acquire customers.

- **Channel Customer Retention:** Channels also play a role in keeping existing customers, ensuring they do not defect to competitors.

- **Channel Customer Revenue Growth:** In an effort to grow revenue, many companies offer value-added services and other initiatives to develop new revenue streams from customers.

Multi-Channel Distribution: Many companies, especially those that service several markets, employ multiple distribution channels to reach customers. We discussed two tools to track multi-channel performance—channel performance charts and multi-channel market tables. Channel performance charts track sales of company products and services through different channels to compare the performance of each. Multi-channel market tables show how the various channels map to different markets the company wishes to target.

Distribution Channel Metrics: We discussed several distribution channel metrics:

- **All Commodity Volume (ACV):** The ACV metric indicates the total sales of company products and services in retail stores that stock their brand, relative to total sales of all stores. It is useful for gauging customer traffic through stores carrying the brand.

- **Product Category Volume (PCV):** The PCV metric refines the ACV metric by emphasizing sales within the product or service category. It is useful for gauging the effectiveness of channel partners in sales within the category.

- **Category Performance Ratio:** The category performance ratio is defined as the ratio of product category volume (PCV) over all commodity volume (ACV). Category performance ratios greater than one tell us that the retail stores in the company's distribution network perform more effectively in the category than the market as a whole.

Terminology

Agglomerated Retail Areas: Shopping districts which combine competing brands of one category, such as "auto malls" or "restaurant rows"

All Commodity Volume (ACV): Distribution channel metric which measures the total sales of company products and services in retail stores stocking the brand, relative to total sales of all stores

Category Performance Ratio: Distribution channel metric that divides Product Commodity Volume by All Commodity Volume, i.e., PCV / ACV, to provide insight into the effectiveness of the company's distribution efforts, relative to the average effectiveness of all categories

Central Business District: Unplanned shopping areas near city centers

Co-op Advertising: Arrangement between company and distribution channel member to split advertising costs

Distribution Intensity: Selecting the number of distribution channels for a company's products and services, based on the sales and brand goals of that company

Distributor: Distribution channel member that purchases products from companies and then resells them to businesses

Exclusive Distribution: Distribution intensity level where companies limit themselves to only one type of retail outlet to defend brand equity

Geographic Information Systems (GIS): As used in retail store location, systems which combine physical geography features with cultural geography

Gravity Model: Retail site identification decision model which considers store size and distance from the target market

Intensive Distribution: Distribution intensity level where companies saturate markets with their products and services using many distribution channels

Liquidator: Distribution channel member which purchases all or most of the closeout stock of another company and sells it to other businesses

Market Development Funds (MDF): Arrangement between company and distribution channel member to have channel promote certain products and services, in exchange for MDF payments to channel

Neighborhood Business District: Shopping areas designed to satisfy convenience needs of local neighborhoods

Product Commodity Volume (PCV): Distribution channel metric which measures total category sales by stores that carry the company's brand, divided by the total category sales of all stores

Sales Performance Incentive Fund (SPIF): Arrangement between company and distribution channel member to have channel salespeople promote certain products and services, in exchange for SPIF payments to salespeople

Secondary Business District: Shopping areas similar to central business districts, but smaller

Selective Distribution: Distribution intensity level where companies select a middle ground between the fury of intensive distribution and the control of exclusive distribution

Trade Margin: Mark-up or commission paid by company to distribution channel member for carrying company's products and services in its channel

Value-added Reseller: Distribution channel member which purchases products from others, adds features or services to them, and then resells the products to other businesses

Wholesaler: Distribution channel member that purchases products from suppliers, and then resells them (generally in large quantities) to retailers

Class Discussion

1. How is the Internet changing the distribution of products?
2. Why do luxury goods makers shy away from intensive distribution?
3. What are some limitations of the gravity model, as it pertains to retail store location?
4. What trends are occurring in many cities that affect city shopping areas?
5. What other evaluation criteria would you add to the channel evaluation and selection model, as explained in this chapter?
6. How effective are loyalty programs in generating customer retention?

Practice Problems

1. Determine the store most likely to attract customers, as predicted by the gravity model. Store A has a size factor of 10 and a distance factor of 5. Store B has a size factor of 15 and a distance factor of 8. Store C has a size factor of 20 and a distance factor of 10.

2. In the channel evaluation and selection model described in the chapter, select a store you know and assess it using the criteria shown in the model. Substitute the data for Store X in the example shown in the chapter. Identify which store generates the highest score.

3. Company A sells its products in two stores, Store 1 and Store 2. The area's other store, Store 3, does not stock company A's products. Calculate the all commodity volume for Company A if total sales in Store 1, Store 2, and Store 3 are $20,000, $50,000, and $30,000, respectively.

4. Company A sells its products in two stores, Store 1 and Store 2. The other store in the area, Store 3, does not stock company A's products. Calculate the product category volume for Company A if category sales in Store 1, Store 2, and Store 3 are $1,000, $2,000, and $3,000, respectively.

5. Calculate the category performance ratio for Company A, using the all commodity volume and product category volume determined in the previous questions.

Chapter 10.

PROMOTION ANALYTICS

Chapter Outline

We cover the following marketing analytics topics in this chapter:

- ☑ **Promotion Budget Estimation**: Establishing an overall promotion budget
- ☑ **Promotion Budget Allocation**: Deciding on most effective way to spend budget
- ☑ **Promotion Metrics for Traditional Media**: Covering metrics for traditional vehicles
- ☑ **Promotion Metrics for Social Media**: Addressing metrics for social campaigns

---

"Half the money I spend on advertising is wasted, and the problem is I don't know which half."
– John Wanamaker

Historians credit the concept of the department store to John Wanamaker. In 1876, he converted an abandoned Pennsylvania Railroad depot into Wanamaker's, a clothing and specialty store. He continued to improve the store, adding an in-store restaurant, electric lights, and elevators.

Historians also credit him for printing the world's first copyrighted advertisement. He adhered to the promises made in the ad, earning him the public's trust and boosting sales.

His third big contribution was the invention of the price tag. Before the price tag, buyers and sellers haggled over items to determine the final price. His invention was moved by faith. He believed that if everyone was equal before God, then everyone should pay the same price. [10-1]

In this chapter, we cover tools and techniques to analyze promotion. We define the term promotion broadly in this chapter, to mean any method we can use to promote our products and services to our target market(s).

Figure 10.1 shows an overview of several popular promotion methods. Of course, many other means exist, such as outdoor advertising on billboards and transit stations, product placement in movies and video games, point of purchase displays in retail stores, mobile advertising delivered to cell phones, and so forth. [10-2]

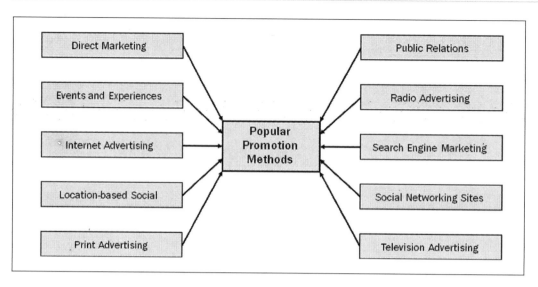

Figure 10.1: Popular Promotion Methods, Overview

Direct Marketing: In direct marketing, we target individuals directly through email, postal mail, and other means. For example, Apple applies direct marketing to send ads through email, advertising its new products and services.

Events and Experiences: Companies hold and sponsor events to promote its brands in relevant settings. For example, the off-road automaker Jeep (jeep.com) sponsored the 2012 Winter X Games to promote its rugged vehicles.

Internet Advertising: We can advertise over the Internet to promote our products and services, using banner ads, pop-up ads, and other techniques. For example, Radio Shack (radioshack.com) promotes ads on Yahoo! web pages for its cellular phones.

Location-based Social Networking: To promote businesses near smartphone users, companies can apply location-based social networking to run ads for local businesses. For example, companies can run promotions using location-based social networking company Foursquare (foursquare.com) to promote "check-ins" to local businesses.

Print Advertising: Businesses can run print advertisements in magazines, newspapers, and other printed media. For example, cosmetics maker Maybelline (maybelline.com) inserts ads for their cosmetics products in fashion magazines such as Vogue.

Public Relations: Companies execute public relations (PR) activities to build and maintain their reputation with stakeholders, such as its customers.

For example, the BBC News reported that Britain's Royal Mail painted 110 of its postboxes gold to honor the British gold medal winners in the London 2012 Olympics. The boxes have since become "cherished local landmarks." In November 2012, the Royal Mail announced the boxes were to remain gold, and that each would be fitted with a plaque commemorating the winning athlete's name. Many news outlets picked up the story, making it a successful PR effort. [10-3]

Radio Advertising: Many companies use radio advertising to promote services. Radio is popular for automobile-related advertising, since much radio listening takes place in automobiles. For example, budget hotel chain Motel 6 (motel6.com) promotes its hospitality services through radio commercials.

Search Engine Marketing: Also called pay per click (PPC), search engine marketing techniques place relevant ads near non-paid search results on search engine results pages. For example, search engine marketing ads for home improvement store Lowes (lowes.com) appear in search engine results when users search for the term "washing machines."

Social Networking Sites: Many businesses place advertisements on popular social networking sites. For example, Facebook, LinkedIn, and Twitter all offer paid advertising opportunities to reach vast audiences.

Television Advertising: Many companies use television advertising to broadcast their messages to mass market audiences. For example, the Government Employee Insurance Company (GEICO, at geico.com) promotes its insurance services in television commercials featuring its GEICO gecko.

Figure 10.2 summarizes several different popular promotion methods.

Promotion Type	Description	Example
Direct Marketing	Targeting individuals directly through email and other channels	**Apple:** Ads sent via email, promoting new products
Events and Experiences	Holding or sponsoring events to promote brand in relevant settings	**Jeep:** Sponsored 2012 Winter X Games to promote its vehicles
Internet Advertising	Banner ads or pop-up ads in web sites with high traffic	**RadioShack:** Ads for cell phones on Yahoo! web pages
Location-based Social Networking	Advertising emphasizing relevant businesses in area near user	**Foursquare:** Tool to promote local restaurants and other businesses
Print Advertising	Print ads, often found in magazines, newspapers, etc.	**Maybelline:** Ads for cosmetics in fashion magazines such as Vogue
Public Relations	Activities to build and maintain reputation with stakeholders	**Royal Mail:** Painted British postboxes gold to commemorate 2012 Olympic athletes
Radio Advertising	Commercials, often 60 seconds long	**Motel 6:** Commercials for budget hotels targeting travelers in cars
Search Engine Marketing	Also called pay per click (PPC), ads show up in search engine page results	**Lowes:** Ad for Lowes shows up in search engine results for "washing machines"
Social Networking Sites	Paid advertisements on popular social networking sites	**Facebook, LinkedIn, Twitter:** Each offers paid advertising
Television Advertising	Commercials, often 30 seconds long	**GEICO:** Commercials featuring the GEICO gecko to sell insurance

Figure 10.2: Popular Promotion Methods, Summary

We start the chapter by discussing methods to establish organizational promotion budget levels. We then show how to allocate the budget over multiple promotion vehicles to maximize marketing effectiveness. We review popular metrics for traditional promotion techniques, such as TV and print advertisements. We close the chapter with a section on social media metrics.

MARKETING MADE MEASURABLE

Advertising Age: 37% of All Advertising Is Wasted: Advertising online journal Advertising Age (adage.com) reviewed the book "What Sticks: Why Most Advertising Fails and How to Guarantee Yours Succeeds." The book is the result of five years of research on campaigns from 36 of the nation's top advertisers. Rex Briggs, a veteran market researcher, authored the book. Briggs studied marketing giants such as Procter & Gamble (P&G), Unilever, Johnson & Johnson (J&J), Kraft Foods, and McDonald's.

In general, the book disparages many of the techniques used by the largest advertising agencies. The book shows that a considerable amount of the agencies' efforts are wasted. One reason for the high waste is that many ad agencies are unable to define success. The book states that only two of the 36 marketers the author researched had a clear definition of success for each marketing effort at the beginning of the campaign.

In the book, the author notes the difference in advertising approaches by the companies, from the highly analytical techniques of Procter & Gamble and Johnson & Johnson, to the instinct-driven Target. In fact, Target was so instinct-driven that Chairman-CEO Robert J. Ulrich would make snap decisions on creative executions displayed in the corporate lobby. Such an approach would never work at P&G or J&J. [10-4]

PROMOTION BUDGET ESTIMATION

In this section, we discuss methods to estimate the total budget required for promotion. In many organizations, promotion accounts for the majority of marketing budgets. In fact, we can use the first three promotion budget estimation approaches (percentage of sales, affordable, and competitive parity) to establishing marketing budgets as well. [10-5]

Figure 10.3 shows an overview of several popular promotion budget estimation methods.

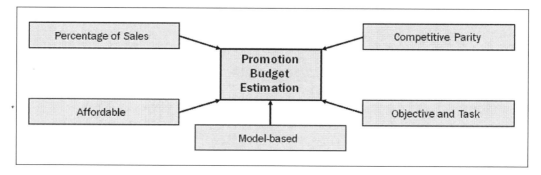

Figure 10.3: Promotion Budget Estimation: Overview

Percentage of Sales Method

Many organizations set their total promotion budget as a percentage of annual sales revenue. Companies that sell to other businesses (B2B) often employ this approach. To execute the approach, one first obtains the total sales generated by the company in the previous year. We then multiply that number by a percentage to calculate the promotion budget for the next year.

Figure 10.4 shows the approach, where companies set aside a percentage of their annual revenues for promotional efforts.

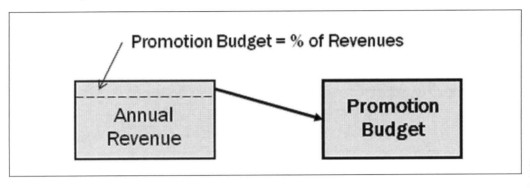

Figure 10.4: Promotion Budget Estimation: Percentage of Sales Method

Different businesses and market conditions warrant different percentage levels. Legal services firm LegalZoom (legalzoom.com) reports that many businesses allocate between 9 – 12% of annual sales for their annual marketing budget. Small businesses with less promotion needs, such as those selling a well-known product or service, may go as low as 2%. [10-6]

The calculation follows the formula below:

(Budget for Next Year) = (Sales Revenue from Previous Year) * (Percentage)

For example, if our company generated $100,000 in revenue last year, and we applied a 10% promotion spending level, we would establish $100,000 * 10% = $10,000 for the budget.

The method benefits from several advantages. First, it has intuitive appeal for managers, who can understand that marketing contributes to sales. Second, it promotes stability among competitors (avoiding one overly dominant competitor) because they spend an industry average percentage. Third, it ensures a minimum level of promotion spend (unlike the "affordable" method we discuss below). Fourth, the method establishes a ceiling on marketing spending, ensuring that marketing spending will not exceed sales revenue.

The method suffers from several disadvantages. First, it employs cyclical reasoning. We spend money on promotion to drive sales revenue, not the other way around. Second, it can block companies from accelerating ahead of their competition, because we are locked into a certain spending level. And third, we might wish to grow our business during recessionary times. Recessions often bring periods of low sales revenues. Tying the marketing spending to sales during recessionary sales years will hamper promotion spending, which can inhibit growth.

Affordable Method

Some organizations set their promotion budgets to what they believe they can afford. In such scenarios, promotion efforts get whatever funds the company does not spend on other uses. For example, if a company budgets $20,000 for all expenses, and spends $18,000 on non-marketing expenses, such as information technology, etc., that leaves $2,000 for promotional expenses.

Figure 10.5 shows the approach, where leftover company funds go for promotion.

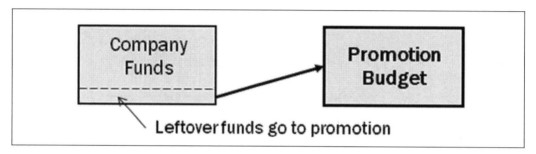

Figure 10.5: Promotion Budget Estimation: Affordable Method

For example, some companies in the prolonged recession of the late 2000s cut marketing budgets to extremely low levels just to keep companies solvent.

We do not recommend the method due to its many disadvantages. The method fails to acknowledge promotion spending as an investment toward future sales. The method can cripple the company if it needs to react quickly to a competitive threat, because it will not have the resources to compete. Lastly, the affordable method makes long-range planning uncertain, because marketers cannot predict the available promotion budget for future time periods.

Competitive Parity Method

Some companies set their promotion budget to approximate the spending level of similar organizations in the same industry. Figure 10.6 shows the approach, where companies set their promotion budget to equal that of its competitors.

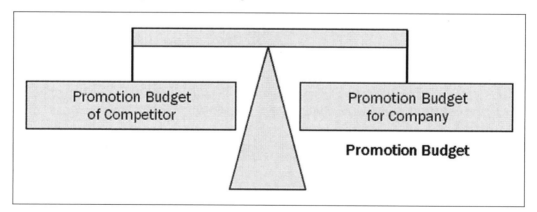

Figure 10.6: Promotion Budget Estimation: Competitive Parity Method

In the book, "What Sticks: Why Most Advertising Fails and How to Guarantee Yours Succeeds," author Rex Briggs alleges that two of the Big Three automakers (Ford, GM, Chrysler) based their annual media budgets based on one another's media spending from the prior year. [10-7]

To execute this pricing technique, marketers observe the promotion vehicles (print advertisements, radio commercials, television commercials, etc.) initiated by competitors and calculate the funds required to replicate their promotion efforts.

For example, a marketer in Company A notes that her competitor, Company B, promotes its offerings using 30 print magazine advertisements per year in Magazine X, 20 radio commercials per year on Radio Station Y, and 10 television commercials per year on TV Channel Z. The marketer contacts the advertising salesperson at Magazine X and learns that ads similar to those of Company B cost $1,000 each. The marketer then calls the advertising salespeople at Radio Station Y and TV Channel Z and learns that radio and TV ads similar to those of Company B cost $5,000 and $10,000 each, respectively.

Figure 10.7 outlines the approach to determining the total spending of Company B, given the information gathered by the marketer.

Promotion Vehicle	Cost per Ad	Quantity of Ads	Subtotal
Print Magazine Ads	$1,000	30	$1,000 * 30 = $30,000
Radio Commercials	$5,000	20	$5,000 * 20 = $100,000
TV Commercials	$10,000	10	$10,000 * 10 = $100,000
Total Spending			$230,000

Figure 10.7: Calculating Competitor Promotion Spending

Proponents of the competitive parity method state that the method holds the advantage of reflecting the "collective wisdom" of the industry. However, companies' objectives, brands, and offerings differ so widely (even in the same industry) to render such an assertion suspect. What works well at one company may not work well at another. One aspect is certain—companies spending the same as their competitors are unlikely to beat them.

Objective and Task Method

Some companies estimate promotion budgets using the objective and task method. They develop promotion budgets in three general steps. In the first step, they declare certain objectives. In the second step, they determine the tasks to accomplish those objectives. In the third step, they estimate the costs to complete the tasks.

Advertisers often employ the objective and task method, especially those in large consumer packaged goods (CPG) firms. The objective and task method benefits from a direct relationship between promotion objectives and promotion budget. The objective and task method fails to allow the user to prioritize and select specific objectives from lists of objectives. It also does not permit the user to decide whether the outcome of the objective (increased sales, etc.) warrants the promotion budget allocated to it.

To demonstrate the technique, we show a typical use case of the objective and task method. Acme Cosmetics plans to introduce a new travel-friendly version of its popular face cream, fortified with green tea extract. Acme plans to target the new cream to corporate professionals who travel often and who wish to counter the drying effect of airplane interiors. Acme estimates a total market size of 40 million potential users. [10-8]

Figure 10.8 shows the specific sequence of tasks Acme must perform to determine the advertising budget to meet its new product introduction goals.

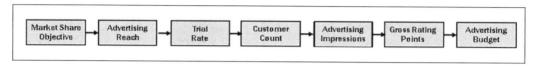

Figure 10.8: Advertising Budget Objective and Task Method: Example Tasks

Acme next establishes the tasks required to reach its declared objective:

Market Share Objective: Acme declares that it plans to achieve a market share objective of 10% in the category within the total market of 40 million potential users. We can calculate that we need 10% * 40 million = 4 million users to accomplish the objective.

Advertising Reach: Acme plans to reach 80% of its potential users with its advertisements. 80% of 40 million people equates to 32 million people. Many advertising agencies target 80% reach levels in their campaigns.

Trial Rate: Acme would like to have 25% of informed prospects (people reached by the advertising message) try the product to determine if they like it. 25% of 32 million people equates to 8 million people.

Customer Count: Based on previous product introductions, Acme has found that about 50% of prospects who try new Acme products like them and become customers. Acme will thus target 50% of 8 million people, for a total of 4 million users, which is our market share objective.

Advertising Impressions: Advertisers define exposures to advertisements as impressions. For example, we count every time a prospect views a magazine ad, or sees an Internet ad, or views a television commercial as an impression. Based on previous campaigns, Acme has found that it takes 30 impressions during a four week advertising campaign to achieve a 25% trial rate for each 1% of the population.

Gross Rating Points: Advertisers define gross rating points (GRP) as one exposure to 1% of the target population. Acme plans to achieve 30 impressions (exposures) to 80% of the population. Gross rating points are calculated as reach multiplied by frequency. In our case, we have a reach of 80% and a frequency of 30, so Acme needs 30 * 80 = 2,400 gross rating points.

Advertising Budget: Acme needs to determine the budget required to achieve 2,400 gross rating points. Advertisers sometimes refer to the cost per gross rating point as CPP (cost per point). The cost of gross rating points varies by designated market area (geographic location) and over time.

For example, the National Journal reported the cost for its America Leads On Trade national advertising campaign in 1997 as $14.68 per GRP in Wichita, $61.55 in Grand Rapids, $77.63 in Las Vegas, $105.83 in Cleveland, $121.56 in Denver, $134.80 in Dallas, $142.93 in Seattle, $172.78 in Phoenix, $180.30 in Washington, D.C., and $550.93 in Los Angeles. By the 2000s, the CPP for the Los Angeles market had increased to $2,300. [10-9, 10-10]

In our case, Acme determines the average CPP for its target areas to be $1,800. To achieve its target of 2,400 gross rating points, it must allocate 2,400 * $1,800 = $4,320,000 toward its advertising budget.

Model-Based Method

In response to demands for accurate methods for promotion budget determination, marketing researchers have developed various types of promotion budget decision models.

The ADBUDG model represents a typical example of the promotion budget decision model. John Little introduced the model in 1970. He based the model on four assumptions: [10-11]

- **Zero Level Advertising**: If the company stops all advertising, over one time period (typically one quarter), market share will drop to a lower level (labeled as "minimum share"), but will not drop to zero.

- **Maintenance Level Advertising**: If the company advertises at a certain level called the "maintenance level," market share will neither increase nor decrease.

- **50% Boost Advertising**: Advertising increased by 50% will grow market share to a point between the share at maintenance level and the share at saturation level.

- **Saturation Level Advertising**: If a company substantially increases its advertising to the point where it is saturating the market, the market share will grow to a point labeled as "maximum share" in Little's model.

Therefore, to run the model, we must know (or be able to estimate) the resulting market share for a given company for each of the four conditions. Ideally, we would establish this data by examining sales history to find times in the company's past when it advertised at these levels. In practice, companies simply estimate the resulting market share for each of the four conditions.

Marketers then input the four market share estimates into the model, along with other data for calibration purposes. Using the data, the model builds a response curve with advertising levels as the input and expected market share at the end of the period as output. The model also provides a "contribution" output, which it defines as the value of expected sales less the advertising budget to achieve those sales.

Interested readers can find various examples of spreadsheets demonstrating the ADBUDG model by simply searching for "ADBUDG Model filetype:xls" on the Internet. In search engines such as Google, the "filetype" operator searches for files of a particular type, such as Microsoft Excel's xls format.

The ADBUDG model has several advantages and disadvantages. Its principal advantages are simplicity (the model is based on four simple assumptions) and availability (simple searches can locate sample spreadsheets).

One of its disadvantages is the subjective nature of the input data, because they are often based on management estimates of market share at varying advertising levels. Second, the ADBUDG fails to include competition, so we cannot predict how our sales might react if our competitors choose to match our changes in advertising levels. Third, the ADBUDG model considers market share changes over one time period only. Thus, it cannot predict how market share will change over long-term conditions.

Because of its limitations, we believe the model is best suited for long-standing firms in mature, stable industries. Such firms are more likely to be able to accurately predict resulting market share from different promotion spending levels. By comparison, startup firms in dynamic markets would find it difficult to predict future market share using the model.

Figure 10.9 summarizes the different promotion budget estimation methods.

Estimation Method	Description	Example
Percentage of Sales	Set promotion budget as a percentage of company annual revenue	**Legal Zoom:** Many companies spend between 9 – 12% of sales on marketing
Affordable	Set promotion budget to whatever the organization can afford	**Recession Spending:** Marketing budgets slashed during recession
Competitive Parity	Set promotion budget to match that of competitors	**GM, Ford, Chrysler:** Big three auto makers matched promotion spending
Objective and Task	Set promotion budget to achieve specific promotion objectives	**Consumer Packaged Goods:** Create objectives-based campaigns
Model-based	Set promotion budgets using predictive models	**Long-standing Firms, Mature Industries:** Best for stable situations

Figure 10.9: Promotion Budget Estimation: Summary

MARKETING MADE MEASURABLE

CMO Survey: Marketing Budget Trends: Business magazine Forbes (forbes.com) reported on the results from a study by the CMO Survey organization (cmosurvey.org). The CMO Survey found that marketing spending is increasing, but at a rate lower than initially forecast.

The CMO Survey tracks total marketing budgets as a percent of company revenues (the Percentage of Sales method). The organization found the percentage rising steadily over the 2011 to late 2012 time period: [10-12]

- February 2011: 8.1%
- August 2011: 10.0%
- February 2012: 10.4%
- August 2012: 11.4%

The CMO Survey also surveyed companies of different sizes to determine their spending on marketing analytics, as a percentage of their overall marketing spending. The results included spending in 2012 (the year of the survey) and 2015 (forecasting three years out). Here, we show the results for small companies (less than $25 million in annual revenues), medium-sized companies (between $100 million and $499 million in annual revenues), and large companies (more than $10 billion in revenues): [10-13]

- Small companies: 4.8% in 2012; 7.3% in 2015
- Medium companies: 5.5% in 2012; 7.6% in 2015
- Large companies: 7.3% in 2012; 10.8% in 2015

From the data, we can see a strong trend toward increasing spending at marketing analytics in every size of company.

PROMOTION BUDGET ALLOCATION

In the previous section, we examined how to determine the promotion budget for all promotional efforts. In this section, we will discuss how to allocate that promotion budget over different vehicles to maximize the number of impressions (exposures) for a given budget. Vehicles include traditional methods, such as television and radio, as well as newer methods, such as social media.

In promotion budget allocation, we aim to maximize the effectiveness of our promotional efforts (our objective) for a given budget (our constraint).

In the world of mathematics, we refer to situations of this type as linear optimization problems. Mathematicians sometimes refer to the category as linear programming. Linear optimization seeks to find maximum and minimum values for an expression called the objective function, subject to a set of constraints. For example, we could wish to maximize revenue or minimize cost, given constraints of marketing budgets and other considerations.

Figure 10.10 shows an overview of the linear optimization model. The inputs to the model are objective functions and constraints. The output of the model is the maximized or minimized objective, depending on the goal of the model.

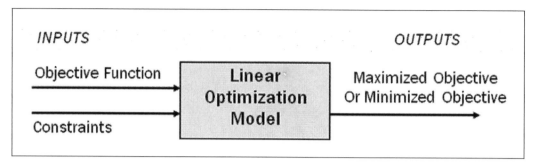

Figure 10.10: Promotion Budget Allocation: Linear Optimization Model Overview

We apply linear optimization to promotion budget allocation to decide on the best mix of inputs for the best output. In our case, our inputs are promotion vehicles and the output is the number of resulting impressions, which we wish to maximize. [10-14]

Allocation Model Inputs

In order to run the model, we need to know information about the objective, the contribution from each vehicle, and the constraints.

Objective: The objective is what we want to achieve. Our objective with promotion campaigns is to maximize the number of impressions (exposures) delivered to our target audience.

Contribution: We define contribution here as the amount each promotion vehicle provides toward the objective. We can measure the contribution by determining the number of viewers (also called the audience) exposed to each type of promotion vehicle.

Constraints: Constraints are conditions that limit the number of possible solutions to problems. Figure 10.11 offers an overview of four typical types of constraints facing many organizations when executing promotion campaigns.

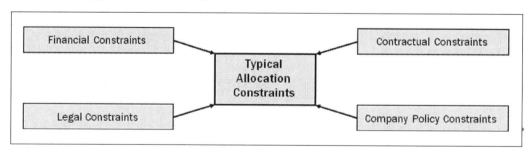

Figure 10.11: Promotion Budget Allocation: Typical Types of Constraints

- **Financial Constraints:** Organizations are increasingly asking marketers to do more with less, so financial constraints are common. Examples include constraints such as, "stay within a maximum budget of $2,000 per month" and "maintain a minimum spending of $1,000 to continue marketing momentum."

- **Legal Constraints**: Companies must follow legal regulations. Examples include constraints such as, "marketers must comply with CAN-SPAM regulations in the United States."

- **Contractual Constraints**: Organizations must observe contractual obligations as the result of performance contracts with outside suppliers such as advertising agencies. Examples include constraints such as, "Our contract with our advertising agency states that they are not required to create more than 100 promotion campaigns per month."

- **Company Policy Constraints**: Companies must follow internal regulations. Examples include constraints such as, "Executive management must review all marketing campaigns before executing them."

Figure 10.12 shows the process for executing promotion budget allocation using linear optimization. We start by establishing the goal of the campaign. We then determine the contribution from each type of promotion vehicle, based on our historical data. We express our objective function, as a basis of the promotion vehicle contribution. We define our constraints. We apply the contribution, objective, and constraint data to run the model. The model reveals our optimal budget allocation. We will demonstrate the technique through an example.

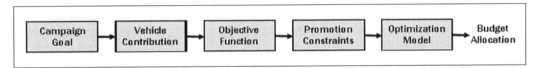

Figure 10.12: Linear Optimization Process for Budget Allocation

Example

Acme Cosmetics plans to promote its new green tea-based anti-wrinkle cream to generate brand awareness. Acme promotes its products using three promotion vehicles: direct marketing, pay per click, and social media.

Figure 10.13 shows the number of impressions each vehicle generates per ad, along with the cost per advertisement. The figure also shows the maximum quantity of campaigns permitted each month under its contract with its advertising agency. Acme Cosmetics does not want to exceed $2,000 per month in its total promotion budget.

Promotion Vehicle	Audience/ Ad	Cost/ Ad	Maximum Quantity
D: Direct Marketing	30 Viewers/ Ad	$30/ Ad	30
P: Pay Per Click	30 Viewers/ Ad	$40/ Ad	20
S: Social Media	40 Viewers/ Ad	$60/ Ad	10

Figure 10.13: Promotion Budget Allocation: Acme Promotion Data

Acme wishes to determine the optimum number of direct marketing campaigns, pay per click campaigns, and social media campaigns to maximize the number of total impressions for its given budget.

We demonstrate the process of executing the linear optimization approach, step by step.

Campaign Goal: In our case, our goal is to maximize the number of total impressions, given the constraints of budget and limits on the quantities of different kinds of vehicles.

Vehicle Contribution: We calculate the contribution of each type of vehicle:

- **Direct Marketing**: The first vehicle to consider is direct marketing campaigns. The campaigns consist of emails sent directly to individuals within its target market. The emails describe the new product and its benefits. The emails also inform the reader of retailers near them, where they can go to obtain a free sample of the product. Upon reviewing its historical data, Acme finds that 30 people are exposed to each direct marketing ad, and that each ad costs $30. Therefore, the audience/ ad = 30 and the cost/ ad = $30.

- **Pay per Click**: The second vehicle is pay per click (PPC) marketing campaigns. Pay per click campaigns display ads relevant to user searches, generally on the top or sides of the search engine results page (SERP). For example, Microsoft's Bing Search Advertising (advertising.microsoft.com) and Google's AdWords (adwords.google.com) services offer pay per click online advertising. Companies pay the search engine provider each time a user clicks on an ad, which is why the vehicle is known as pay per click. For pay per click, audience/ ad = 30 and cost/ ad = $40.

- **Social Media**: The third vehicle is social media campaigns, which consist of paid advertisements and other vehicles on popular social platforms. For example, Facebook (facebook.com/advertising), LinkedIn (linkedin.com/advertising), and Twitter (advertising.twitter.com) offer paid advertising opportunities. For social media, audience/ ad = 40 and cost/ ad = $60.

For brevity, we will denote the three vehicles as D for direct marketing, P for pay per click, and S for social media.

Objective Function: Our next step is to develop our promotion objective function, given our contribution data. We know that our objective is to maximize impressions (exposures) to our target audience with our promotion campaigns. We can state the objective in equation form:

$$Z = 30 * D + 30 * P + 40 * S$$

The equation applies the following variables:

Z = Our objective, in this case the total number of impressions from all promotion vehicles.

D = Quantity of direct marketing campaigns to run, given that each direct marketing campaign results in 30 viewers per advertisement.

P = Quantity of pay per click campaigns to run, with 30 viewers per campaign.

S = Quantity of social media campaigns to run, with 40 viewers per campaign.

Promotion Constraints: We then express our constraints in equation form. We start with an equation for the budgetary constraint of $2,000 for all programs:

$$B = 30 * D + 40 * P + 60 * S \le \$2,000$$

The equation applies the following variables:

B = Our monthly budget

D = Quantity of direct marketing campaigns, which cost $30 each to run.

P = Quantity of pay per click campaigns, which cost $40 each to run.

S = Quantity of social media campaigns, which cost $60 each to run.

$\le$ = Inequality sign, indicating that we may not exceed our maximum budget.

In our example, Acme also faces additional constraints in the form of contractual obligations. Acme's contract with its advertising agency stipulates that it cannot exceed a certain number of campaigns per month for each type of promotion vehicle. We express the contractual obligation constraints using the equations below:

D $\le$ 30 $\rightarrow$ Cannot exceed 30 direct marketing campaigns per month

P $\le$ 20 $\rightarrow$ Cannot exceed 20 pay per click campaigns per month

S $\le$ 10 $\rightarrow$ Cannot exceed 10 social media campaigns per month

Figure 10.14 summarizes the governing equations for our example.

Linear Optimization Element	Equation
Objective Function	Z = 30 * D + 30 * P + 40 * S
Constraint #1: Budget	B = 30 * D + 40 * P + 60 * S $\le$ $2,000
Constraint #2: Maximum campaigns/ month: D	D $\le$ 30
Constraint #3: Maximum campaigns/ month: P	P $\le$ 20
Constraint #4: Maximum campaigns/ month: S	S $\le$ 10

Figure 10.14: Promotion Budget Allocation: Acme Governing Equations

Optimization Model: We now introduce the linear optimization model. To implement the model, we will use the Solver tool available within Microsoft Excel. Solver works well for optimization problems involving maximums and minimums. Solver defines optimization models using three parts: the target cell, the changing cells, and the constraints: [10-15]

- **Target Cell**: Solver refers to the objective as the target cell. Solver requires the user to allocate a spreadsheet cell as a target cell. Any cell will do. Solver places the answer for the objective in the target cell. Solver uses multiple target cells for optimization problems involving multiple objectives. For example, Acme might have a secondary goal to maximize market share.

- **Changing Cells**: Solver refers to the contribution variables as changing cells. In our case, we would need three changing cells for the quantities of direct marketing, pay per click, and social media programs.

- **Constraints**: Solver manages a variety of constraints, such as maximums (e.g., "budget cannot exceed $2,000"), minimums (e.g., "we must run at least three programs per month), and equals (e.g., "we must run exactly four social media campaigns per month"). Unless otherwise specified, Solver assumes nonnegative constraints (i.e., we cannot run a negative number of campaigns).

Figure 10.15 shows the process to apply the linear optimization tool for promotion budget allocation. We start by setting up the model. We then execute the model, and interpret the results. We will review each step, starting with setup.

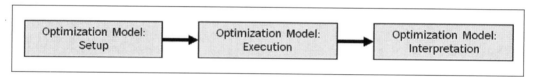

Figure 10.15: Promotion Budget Allocation: Optimization Model Process

Optimization Model: Setup: Our first step in developing the model is to set up a spreadsheet in the form expected by Solver.

Figure 10.16 shows our suggested format for setting up the spreadsheet. We divide the workspace into three sections: changing cells, target cell, and constraints.

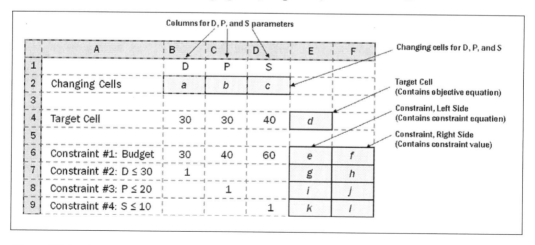

Figure 10.16: Promotion Budget Allocation: Spreadsheet Format

- **Changing Cells**: The upper section of the spreadsheet shows the changing cells, shown in the figure as *a*, *b*, and *c* (spreadsheet addresses \$B\$2, \$C\$2, and \$D\$2). Excel will place the answers for the decision variables in these cells. Leave them blank. We recommend adding labels above the changing cells for reference. In the figure, we added the labels for D, P, and S above the corresponding changing cells *a*, *b*, and *c*. We recommend organizing the parameters (the coefficients in front of the variables) for D, P, and S in all equations under the D, P, and S labels. The format allows us to easily change the parameters later.

- **Target Cell**: The middle section of the spreadsheet shows the target cell, shown in the figure as *d* (address \$E\$4 in the spreadsheet). Excel expects to find the equation for the objective function in the target cell. Therefore, we enter the objective function into the cell, "= 30 * D + 30 * P + 40 * S".

- **Constraints**: The bottom section of the spreadsheet shows the constraint cells, shown in the figure as *e*, *f*, *g*, *h*, *i*, *j*, *k*, and *l*. The spreadsheet shows two sides to each constraint—the left side and the right side. The left side contains the constraint equations. The right side contains the constraint values.

  For complex constraints, such as our constraint for the budget, we enter the equation on the left side and the value on the right. In our case, we enter the constraint equation for budget (= 30 * D + 40 * P + 60 * S) in the left side for constraint #1 (cell *e* in the figure). For the right side of constraint #1 (cell *f* in the figure), we enter the constraint value for budget (2000). To make it easier to change the parameters of the budget equation later, we enter the parameters in separate cells. This permits more flexibility than "hard-coding" the parameters into the Excel formula itself.

  For simple constraints, such as our constraint for the limit of 30 direct marketing campaigns (D) per month, we enter the address of the corresponding changing cell into the left constraint cell. We enter the constraint value in the right constraint cell. In our case, we would enter the address for changing cell for D (shown as *a* in the figure) into the left side constraint for D (shown as *g* in the figure). For the right side, enter the constraint value (30). Just as we did with the complex constraint, we show the parameters in separate cells. In this particular example, all the parameters are "1".

Optimization Model: Execution: Having set up the model, we now execute it using the Solver Add-in in Microsoft Excel.

To launch Solver, select the Data top menu tab and click "Solver" in the Analysis section, as shown in Figure 10.17. If the Data menu does not display the Solver option, then the Solver Add-In has not been enabled for Excel. Follow the instructions at the Microsoft support page (support.microsoft.com) to enable the Solver Add-In for Excel.

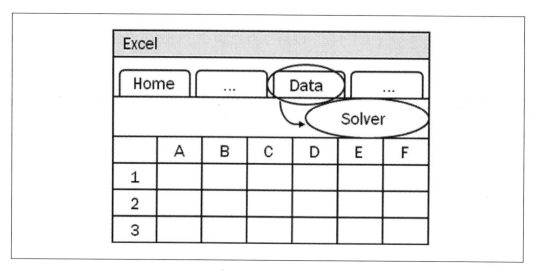

Figure 10.17: Promotion Budget Allocation: Launching Solver Add-In

Clicking on "Solver" will bring up the Solver Parameters dialog box, as shown in Figure 10.18.

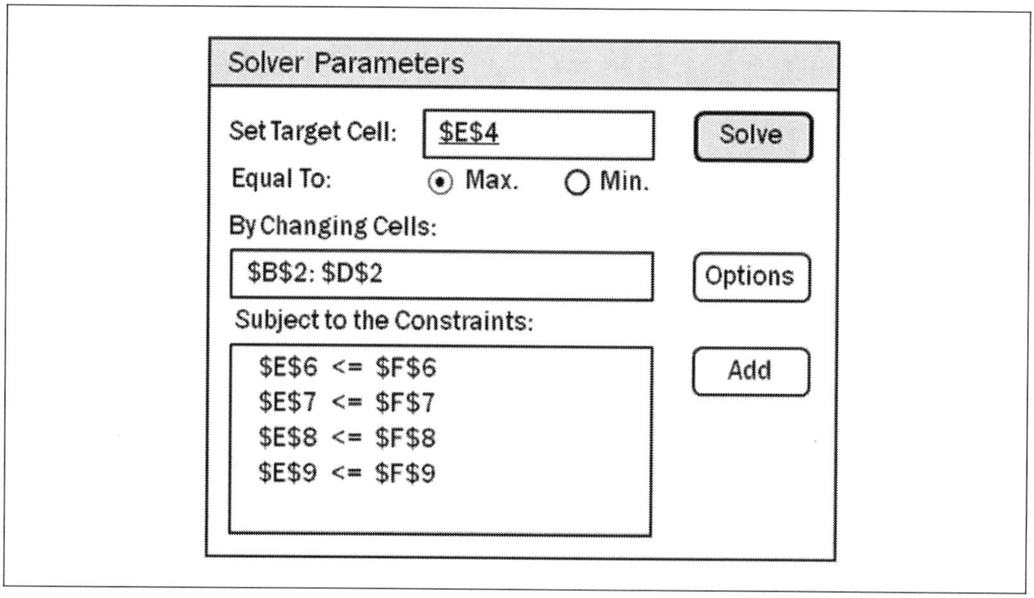

Figure 10.18: Promotion Budget Allocation: Solver Parameters Dialog Box

Under "Set Target Cell", we enter the location of the target cell. In our case, we enter "$E$4" (also denoted as *d* in our spreadsheet).

Under "Equal To", we want to maximize our solution, so we select the "Max." radio button.

Under "By Changing Cells", we enter the location of the changing cells. In our case, we enter "$B$2:$D$2" (also denoted as *a*, *b*, and *c* in our spreadsheet).

Under "Subject to the Constraints", we enter our constraints. To add constraints, click the "Add" button. Doing so will reveal the "Add Constraint" dialog box in Figure 10.19.

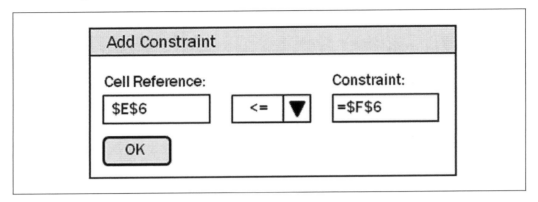

Figure 10.19: Promotion Budget Allocation: Add Constraint Dialog Box

To add a constraint, enter the address of the constraint equation in the box marked "Cell Reference". In our case, the equation for the first constraint (budget) is located in cell *e*, with a location of $E$6. Next, we select the inequality from the pull-down menu in the middle of the dialog box. We can choose from <= (less than or equal to), = (equal to), or >= (greater than or equal to). In our case, we must keep budget less than or equal to a certain amount, so we select the <= inequality sign.

We click OK to return to the Solver Parameters dialog box, and repeat the process for the remaining constraints. Once we have completed entering our information, we click the Solve button in the Solver Parameters dialog box.

Solver returns the results by automatically entering the optimal values into the changing cells, target cell, and constraint cells on the spreadsheet. Figure 10.20 shows the spreadsheet after Solver has entered the solution results.

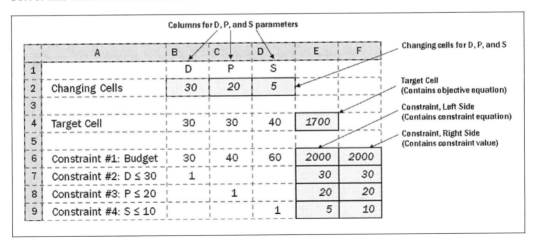

Figure 10.20: Promotion Budget Allocation: Solver Results in Spreadsheet

Figure 10.21 summarizes the results. Totaling the budget for all three types of promotion vehicles, we arrive at $900 + $800 + $300 = $2,000. Therefore, we have not exceeded our maximum budget of $2,000. Solver also tells us that we can expect a total of 1,700 impressions from our combination of promotion vehicles.

Promotion Vehicle	Solver Result	Cost/ Ad	Total Cost/ Vehicle
D: Direct Marketing	30 (30 maximum)	$30/ Ad	$900
P: Pay Per Click	20 (20 maximum)	$40/ Ad	$800
S: Social Media	5 (10 maximum)	$60/ Ad	$300
Total			$2,000

Figure 10.21: Promotion Budget Allocation: Solver Results Summary

Optimization Model: Interpretation: In addition to providing the optimal values, Solver also presents a Solver Results dialog box. In the dialog box, we can elect to view an Answer Report to interpret information about the constraints in our solution. If we select Answer Report and click OK, we get a new tab in Excel. Figure 10.22 shows the information from the Answer Report.

Promotion Vehicle	Solver Result	Maximum Allowable	Status
D: Direct Marketing	30	30	Binding
P: Pay Per Click	20	20	Binding
S: Social Media	5	10	Not Binding
Budget	$2,000	$2,000	Binding

Figure 10.22: Promotion Budget Allocation: Solver Constraint Results

Solver refers to a value limited by the given constraint as "binding" and one not limited by the constraint as "not binding." We can see that the direct marketing and pay per click promotion vehicles hit their constraint limit, and therefore they are binding. The social media vehicle did not, and is therefore not binding. The model thus indicates that we have more capacity to deliver social media campaigns than we need.

MARKETING MADE MEASURABLE

Inc. Magazine: Allocating Marketing Dollars: Small business magazine Inc. (inc.com) gave the following tips for allocating marketing budgets:

- **Audience:** Define the target market clearly and precisely to avoid wasting money on irrelevant prospects.
- **Media:** Select media that the target market views and respects.
- **Tracking:** Track effectiveness of different vehicles, such as print, radio, and direct mail to forecast success of future promotional campaigns.

Marketers should not be afraid to change programs to make them work even better. According to Peter Geisheker, chief executive of marketing consultancy The Geisheker Group (geisheker.com), "There's a reason why the best race car drivers have the best mechanics...They're always tweaking and adjusting the car's performance." [10-16]

PROMOTION METRICS: TRADITIONAL MEDIA

In this section, we cover metrics for traditional promotion media, such as television, radio, and print advertising. Later, we cover metrics for the web and social media vehicles.

We hinted at several types of metrics earlier in this chapter in the Objective and Task Method for promotion budget estimation. We now go into the metrics in more detail. The metrics will prove useful in discussions with media planners, as they often use the metrics described here.

Media planners are individuals within an advertising agency responsible for selecting different media (such as television commercials and print ads) for placement in different vehicles on behalf of their clients.

Figure 10.23 shows an overview of several popular metrics to measure traditional media.

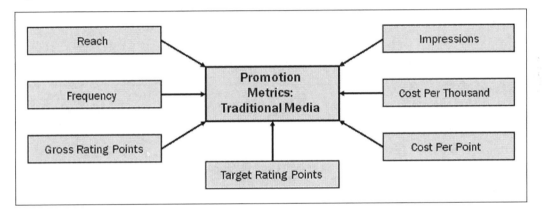

Figure 10.23: Promotion Metrics for Traditional Media: Popular Metrics

Reach

Reach measures the size of the intended audience targeted by the promotion. Figure 10.24 shows the concept. [10-17]

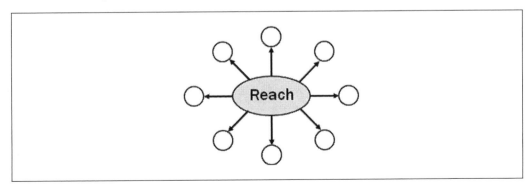

Figure 10.24: Promotion Metrics for Traditional Media: Reach

For example, Conde Nast, publisher of fashion magazine Vogue (vogue.com), features a Media Kit section on its website, as do many companies offering advertising opportunities. The Media Kit cites the magazine's circulation as 1.25 million. One could interpret the circulation as the magazine's reach. The Media Kit also includes other pertinent advertising information, such as advertising rates for ads in its print magazine, website, and tablet publications. [10-18]

In lieu of a Media Kit, some companies offering advertising opportunities refer to a rate card, which shows advertising pricing, specifications (size of ads, etc.) and other relevant information. Some advertising salespeople quote a pass-along rate representing the number of people to which the original reader passes along the magazine. The salespeople will multiply the basic circulation by the pass-along rate to arrive at a total effective circulation. In the Vogue example above, if the magazine has a pass-along rate of four, the total effective circulation would be 4 * 1.25 million, or 5.0 million.

In addition to website Media Kits and rate cards, marketers can obtain third party information to calculate reach. For example, media data firm Standard Rate and Data Service (SRDS, at next.srds.com) offers a host of data for different media, such as print, radio, television, and cable. For web-based versions of publications (such as Vogue.com), marketers can use website research tools such as Alexa. Alexa (alexa.com) provides web analytics for websites, such as number of visitors, which could be considered the website's reach.

The popularity of the reach metric makes it an indispensable tool for media planning. However, the reach metric provides little insight or analysis. For example, the metric does not tell us about the relevance of our messaging to our target audience. Nor does it tell us about the publication's credibility with its intended audience. Therefore, do not make the assumption that bigger (e.g., higher circulation rates) is always better (i.e., more effective at promoting our goods and services).

Frequency

Frequency measures the average number of exposures of an advertisement to an individual within the target market over a specified time period. Media planners balance frequency with reach as they work within the allocated budget to achieve stated promotion goals.

For example, a marketer in Company A works with advertising agency X to produce and air television commercials. Due to repetition, over a four week time period the television commercials reached a total of 15 million households in a geographical region with 5 million households. We calculate the frequency as 15 million / 5 million = 3.

Herb Krugman, a marketing researcher at General Electric, is credited for suggesting that a frequency of three works well for consumer advertising. Thus, a consumer must be exposed to the same advertisement three times in order for it to be effective. The repeated exposure aids the consumer's thought process. Each exposure plays a specific role in the decision making process to purchase (or not purchase) the offering. [10-19]

Figure 10.25 shows the concept.

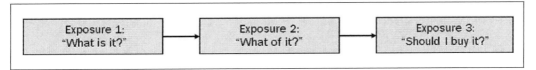

Figure 10.25: Promotion Metrics for Traditional Media: Frequency

- **Exposure #1**: He suggested that the first exposure evokes a "What is it?" response from average consumers. Exposure #1 thus represents the "curiosity" step, where consumers strive to understand the offering.

- **Exposure #2**: Consumers use the second exposure to determine the personal relevance of the product or service to their lives. Exposure #2 thus represents the "What of it?" response.

- **Exposure #3**: Krugman suggests that not until the third exposure does the consumer seriously contemplate purchasing the new offering. Exposure #3 thus represents the decision step.

- **Exposure #4 and Beyond**: Exposures beyond the first three do little to sway the consumer. Krugman states that "there is no such thing as a fourth exposure psychologically: rather fours, fives, etc., are repeats of the third exposure effect."

Krugman's work notwithstanding, other marketing researchers offer different theories. In his book, "When Ads Work," Professor John Philip Jones states that just one exposure (a frequency of one) should suffice to sway consumers. While Jones acknowledges that the "rule of three" was used as a rule of thumb, he states that the frequency can depend on a number of factors, such as purchase motivation (ads for products or services requiring consumers to change their habits will take more than one exposure to work), purchase price (ads for expensive products and services require more than one exposure), message complexity (complex ads for products and services with subtle value propositions require multiple exposures), and other elements. [10-20]

Just as with reach, the widespread popularity of the frequency metric has made it an important element of media planning. We recommend working with a skilled media planner to determine the optimal frequency. As Professor Jones states, a frequency of three can work as a good rule of thumb, but the final frequency decision will depend on a variety of factors.

Gross Rating Points (GRPs)

Gross rating points measure the level of intensity of a media plan, such as a plan to advertise a new product through a television commercial campaign. One gross rating point (GRP) represents one exposure to 1% of the target population. The total gross rating points of an advertising campaign measure the total of all rating points achieved during the campaign. The total number of GRPs can be calculated by multiplying reach by frequency. [10-21]

Figure 10.26 shows the concept.

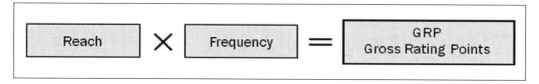

Figure 10.26: Promotion Metrics for Traditional Media: Gross Rating Points

For example, television advertising research company Nielsen (nielsen.com) conducts its TV Rating research through electronic metering technology to determine how many viewers tuned to specific channels at certain times. To assess the effectiveness of a particular television advertising campaign, we could measure that 20% of all targeted viewers were tuned into the channel with our television commercial when it aired. [10-22]

Advertisers refer to gross rating points as "gross" because they count every single exposure, with no efforts to calculate a "net" amount. For example, if we measured our television viewing audience the next time our commercial aired, and determined that 30% of the audience tuned in, our gross rating points would increase to 20 + 30 = 50 points. The gross rating points calculation thus double-counts audiences, giving us the potential of realizing percentages greater than 100%.

Gross rating points work on media other than television. In fact, gross rating points are widely used for radio, print, and other media. Media planners routinely calculate total reach, average frequency, and gross rating points in advertising campaigns. Media planners focus on delivering the maximum number of gross rating points for the lowest possible cost.

The gross rating points metric shares the same advantages and disadvantages as the reach and frequency metrics. The primary advantage of the GRP metric is its widespread use and understanding of what is measured.

The disadvantage of GRP is that it measures actions (what was done), not results (how sales increased as a result of the commercial). We can determine that the message was delivered (such as through the Nielsen method), but we cannot assume that the individual actually paid attention to the commercial. They might have left the room, ignored the commercial, or passed over the commercial because they were watching the program on a digital video recorder (DVR), such as those made by Tivo (tivo.com).

Target Rating Points (TRPs)

Target rating points represent the exposure level of an advertisement to a specific target market. One target rating point is defined as reaching one percent of the particular target market we want to reach. We calculate TRPs by multiplying gross rating points by the ratio of the size of the specific target market over that of the total audience. [10-23]

Figure 10.27 shows the concept.

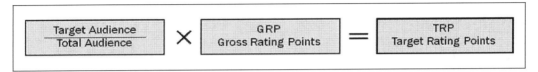

Figure 10.27: Promotion Metrics for Traditional Media: Target Rating Points

We can determine the ratio of our target market to the total audience by researching the company's publication demographic information. For example, suppose we want to target college-educated working women through the Vogue print magazine. Conde Nast, the publisher of Vogue, provides us with audience information on its website (condenast.com).

Figure 10.28 shows audience facts for Vogue magazine, as well as its competitor, Elle magazine, published by the Hearst Publishing Group. [10-24, 10-25]

Audience Data	Vogue	Elle
Total Audience	11,398,000	6,302,000
Circulation	1,250,000	1,145,000
Gender: Female %	89%	87%
Education: Any College	64%	70%
Employed	64%	67%

Figure 10.28: Audience Information for Vogue and Elle Print Magazines

From the data, we can calculate the ratio of our target market (college-educated working women) to the overall audience for Vogue magazine as follows:

Vogue: %College * %Employed * %Female = 64% * 64% * 89% = 36.5%
Elle: %College * %Employed * %Female = 70% * 67% * 87% = 40.8%

We can also examine other data sources for the information. For example, we can access web metrics company Alexa (alexa.com) for information on the audience visiting Vogue's website, vogue.com. Entering "vogue.com" in Alexa's search box and clicking on the "Audience" tab reveals that vogue.com website visitors are primarily female (about 60% female to 40% male), childless (about 70% with no children), and college-educated (about 50% have attended some college). [10-26]

In a previous example, we had calculated a total of 50 gross rating points for a television commercial advertising campaign.

We can calculate the target rating points for an advertising campaign in Vogue magazine:

Target Rating Points = (Target Audience) / (Total Audience) * Gross Rating Points

= 36.5% * 50 = 18.25 Target Rating Points

The target rating points metric represents a coarse measurement of how effectively the advertising budget was spent to reach a specific target audience. Looking at the example above, one could assert that we "wasted" 63.5% (100% - 36.5%) of our money on the "wrong" audience when advertising in Vogue magazine. By comparison, we only "waste" 59.2% (100% - 40.8%) when advertising in Elle.

Impressions

Impressions are simply the total number of exposures to the target audience during the campaign. Like gross rating points, impressions are "gross" in that we count multiple exposures to the same individual.

For example, if we ran an advertisement campaign in Vogue magazine (with a circulation of 1.25 million) consisting of six ads over a six month period, we would calculate the total impressions:

Impressions   = (Advertisement Placements) * (Reach)
                  = (6) * (1.25 million) = 7.5 million

Cost Per Thousand (CPM)

Cost per thousand measures the cost to deliver an advertisement to 1,000 individuals in the audience, through a given advertising medium, such as television or print. In the CPM abbreviation, the letter M signifies the Roman numeral for 1,000. [10-27]

Figure 10.29 shows the concept.

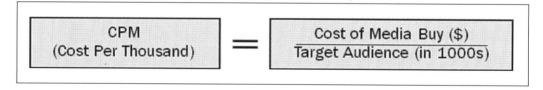

Figure 10.29: Promotion Concepts for Traditional Media: Cost Per Thousand

In our previous Vogue magazine example, we accessed the Media Kit for the print version of Vogue by navigating through the website of its publisher, Conde Nast. In the Media Kit, we learned that Vogue reaches 1.25 million people. The Vogue print magazine Media Kit also includes its advertising rates. From the Media Kit, we learn that a four-color full page advertisement in the magazine runs $165,000. We can calculate the cost per thousand: [10-28]

CPM   = (Cost of Media Buy) / (Target Audience / 1,000)
              = ($165,000) / (1.25 million / 1,000) = $132

CPM varies by media type. According to a 2010 Morgan Stanley study, the average cost per thousand for different media types in the United States ran $5 for outdoor advertising, $10 for radio, $17 for magazines and newspapers, and $28 for television. Outdoor advertisements, sometimes referred to as out-of-home (OOH), enjoy low CPMs due to the many people exposed to an outdoor ad, such as that on a billboard. Television takes its place as the king of traditional media, commanding the highest CPM. [10-29]

Marketers can use CPM metrics to compare the relative cost efficiency of different media types. For example, some advertising campaigns use multiple media types, and we can compare the CPM for each. In order to ensure accuracy, we should only compare media types that reach the same audience.

Cost Per Point (CPP)

Cost per point measures the cost to deliver an advertisement to one percent of the individuals in the audience. We sometimes refer to one percent of the target population as one rating point. Therefore, we can define the cost per point as the cost of buying one rating point. In this way, cost per point is sometimes called cost per rating point. [10-30]

Ratings measure the percentage of the target market exposed to an advertisement. For example, we can examine the number of individuals exposed to a commercial on television or an advertisement in a print magazine. The cost per point measures the relative efficiency of media vehicles relative to a company's target market.

We calculate cost per point by dividing the cost of the media buy by the vehicle rating, as shown in Figure 10.30.

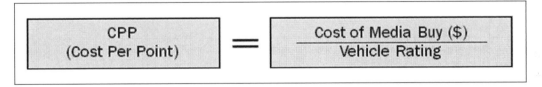

Figure 10.30: Promotion Budget for Traditional Media: Cost per Point

In our earlier Vogue magazine example, we learned that a full-page advertisement cost $165,000 and reached 1.25 million viewers, resulting in a cost per thousand of $132. Referring to the Elle Media Kit, we find out that a similar four-color full-page ad runs $148,000 in Elle, reaching 1.14 million viewers, resulting in a cost per thousand of $129.

Figure 10.31 summarizes the data in a table.

Magazine	Cost/ Ad	Circulation	CPM	Rating	CPP
Vogue	$165,000	1,250,000	$132	36.5	$4,520
Elle	$148,000	1,145,000	$129	40.8	$3,627

Figure 10.31: Cost per Point Calculations for Vogue and Elle Print Magazines

Referring to our earlier Vogue example, we wanted to target a specific subset of the readers, specifically college educated working women. We saw that such women comprised 36.5% of Vogue readership and 40.8% for that of Elle. We enter the values in the table's Rating column. The ratings show how well each magazine rates in terms of its effectiveness of reaching the target market. It is customary to drop the percentage symbol (%) in tables of this type. We then divide the cost of the media buy (the cost of the ad) by the rating to obtain the cost per point.

From the data, we see that the advertisement in Elle is the better buy, because its CPP is significantly cheaper than that for Vogue. At this point, the reader might wonder, why not just consolidate all advertising in the magazine with the lowest CPP? Advertisers use multiple vehicles because one vehicle cannot reach the entire target market. It takes multiple vehicles to reach the target market, especially for large markets, such as the fashion clothing market addressed by Vogue and Elle magazines.

MARKETING MADE MEASURABLE

Forbes: Measuring Print Advertising by Tracking Online Behavior: For many markets, such as business to business sales of complex computer software and equipment, print advertising remains an effective medium, even in today's digital world. With print, discerning buyers can easily review the details of complex products to see if the products will work for their situation. Many buyers can find it difficult to skim computer screens for such information.

At the same time, print advertising can pose challenges to measure. Many marketers find it difficult to confirm that print advertisements generate revenue because print does not enjoy the online measurement techniques of Internet-based advertising.

To combine the advantages of print advertising with online measurement, Forbes Media, comScore, and Starcom MediaVest teamed up. The result was a new methodology for measuring the effectiveness of print advertising by tracking changes in online behavior by readers.

The process compares two groups. Both groups receive an invitation to a survey. The survey asks them if they read the issue in which an ad appeared. If they say yes, they get included in the test group. If not, they go to the control group. The process tracks respondents using cookies. With the cookies, the process watches their online behavior to determine if people reading the ad are more likely to perform certain behaviors, such as go online to read more about the product they saw in the print advertisement. [10-31]

PROMOTION METRICS FOR SOCIAL MEDIA

In the previous section, we covered metrics for traditional promotion media, such as television and print advertising. In this section, we extend the discussion to include social media vehicles. Examples include social networking metrics (such as measuring fans on Facebook) and other metrics from other social media efforts (such as tracking the number of followers on Twitter).

Marketers must begin any analytics project, including ones involving social media, with a clear objective in mind. In social media interactions, our objective is typically to increase conversions. Here, we use the term "conversions" to signify anything that would qualify as a successful interaction that aligns with the company's objectives.

Figure 10.32 shows a list of several different types of conversion sources, as well as specific events triggering the conversion. Selection on the type of conversion to use will depend on the goals of the company.

Source	Event
Blog Subscription	Prospect signs up to be notified of new blog posts
Call Back Requests	Prospect requests callback
Contact forms	Prospect enters information and clicks Submit
Content Downloads	Prospect requests download of datasheet or other content from website
Contest Entry	Prospect enrolls in contest by filling out form
Demo Signup	Prospect signs up for live demo or other interactive event
Live Chat	Prospect engages in live chat with company representative
Purchase	Prospect places online order for product or service
Subscriptions	Prospect requests subscriptions to newsletters or similar content
User Registration	Prospect registers to receive ongoing access
Video Viewing	Prospect watches featured video on website
Webinar Signup	Prospect signs up for webinar

Figure 10.32: Promotion Metrics for Social Media: Conversion Sources and Events

To gather the data we need to evaluate our progress toward our objective, we need to employ a measurement tool. In the next section, we cover several popular types of social media measurement tools.

Social Media Measurement Tools

In this section, we discuss several types of tools to measure social media activities and their contributions to organizational goals.

In Figure 10.33, we introduce a categorization of social media measurement tools. The categories include built-in tools, aggregators, and professional tools.

Built-in tools are those native to the social media channel, such as the metrics provided within Twitter. Aggregators are measurement tools that gather metrics from multiple social media channels. Professional tools are those designed for dedicated social media professionals. The figure shows a small sampling of the wealth of social media tools available. The developers of the tools target the tools for different purposes, and for different types of users.

Category	Description	Target User	Example
Built-in Tools	Metrics capabilities included with social media application itself	Small businesses or Personal use	Facebook metrics LinkedIn metrics Twitter metrics YouTube metrics
Aggregators	Combines metrics from multiple sources	Small businesses or Serious amateurs	Hootsuite Klout Samepoint SocialMention TweetDeck
Professional	Provides deep dive into significant amounts of data	Dedicated social media professional	Cision Cymfony (Visible Technologies) Radian6 (Salesforce.com) Scout Labs (Lithium) Techrigy (Alterian)

Figure 10.33: Social Media Measurement Tool Categories

We now present a brief overview of the categories of tools, citing examples of each and the types of users targeted by the tools:

Built-in Tools: Many social media vehicles include basic measurement tools. The tools have the advantages that they are free and are easy to access within the application. The primary disadvantages with the tools are their limited capabilities and the requirement for users to check multiple tools to get an overview of their social footprint. The time required to check each social media channel (Facebook, LinkedIn, Twitter, and so forth) can be daunting for companies communicating through multiple channels.

Popular social media sites all include basic metrics, with some (such as LinkedIn) offering extra metrics at additional cost:

- **Facebook**: Built-in measurement functionality includes metrics around fans (total fans, new fans, and removed fans), subscribers (total subscribers, un-subscribers, and re-subscribers), demographics (age, gender) and other attributes.

- **LinkedIn**: For standard personal accounts, LinkedIn limits metrics to profile views and inclusions in search results. Users can upgrade (at extra monthly fees) to gain metrics around traffic sources for "My Profile" views. LinkedIn Groups offer additional metrics around members, discussions, and updates.

- **Twitter**: Built-in metrics include number of followers, number of followings, and number of Tweets to date. Twitter also offers Twitter Grader, to measure users' power and reach on Twitter, and Twitter Search, which allows users to search topics for relevant Tweets.

- **YouTube**: YouTube offers a fair amount of functionality built into the product, such as views (total views and unique viewers), popularity (relative popularity and top videos), and discovery (breakdown of sources of views for each video). YouTube also provides its Hot Spots analytics tool, which compares viewership of users' videos with those of other videos of the same length.

Figure 10.34 presents a summary of some of the built-in measurement capabilities for several popular social media vehicles.

Vehicle	Sample Measurement Capabilities
Facebook	Fans: Total fans; New fans; Removed fans Subscribers: Un-subscribers; Re-subscribers Demographics: Age; Gender Media: Photo; Video; Audio Interactions: Total number of comments; Wall posts
LinkedIn	Personal account, standard: Profile views; Inclusions in search results Personal account, Business Plus: Traffic sources for "My Profile" views LinkedIn Groups: Total members; Total discussions; New postings
Twitter	Twitter Account: Number of followers and followings; Number of tweets Twitter Grader: Measure power and reach on Twitter Twitter Search: Search Twitter postings for all relevant tweets
YouTube	Views: Total views; Unique viewers Popularity: Relative popularity; Top videos Demographics: Age; Gender Discovery: Breakdown of sources of views for each video Hot Spots: Viewership compared to other same-length videos

Figure 10.34: Social Media Measurement Tools: Built-in Tools

Aggregators: Aggregator social media measurement tools collect data from multiple social media vehicles and present the aggregated data in one place. Professional tools, discussed later, can also aggregate data, but professional tools target a different type of user and can cost several hundred dollars per month to use. By comparison, the aggregator tools mentioned below cost very little, and many are free.

The advantage of this category of tools is the convenience of having all the data at one's fingertips. The disadvantage is the slow speed of most aggregators—it takes time to scour the web for all social media mentions of a particular brand or topic. People interested in the convenience provided by aggregators can turn to several different aggregator tools. [10-32]

- **Hootsuite**: Hootsuite (hootsuite.com) provides a social media dashboard to manage and measure social networks. The tool works with Facebook, Foursquare, LinkedIn, and Twitter. Hootsuite allows users to track brand mentions and analyze social media traffic.

- **Klout**: Klout (klout.com) estimates the level of influence for a brand, based on more than 35 variables on Facebook and Twitter. The tool displays a list of the most influential followers and their topics of expertise.

- **Samepoint**: Samepoint (samepoint.com) assigns real-time engagement points, based on the number of comments on a topic and the number of sources discussing the topic. Samepoint allows the user to view the data in different ways, such as Real-time (focusing on Twitter tweets and other up-to-the-minute social discussions) and Groups (focusing on discussions related to the brand in group forums, such as those on LinkedIn Groups and Meetup).

- **Socialmention**: Socialmention (socialmention.com) gathers data from Facebook, Twitter, YouTube, and other sources to present a comprehensive view of the social media attributes for a topic or brand. The tool adds insight through four key measures. The first measure is strength, which Socialmention defines as the ratio of the number of mentions in the past 24 hours compared to all possible mentions. The second measure is sentiment, which is the number of positive mentions compared to negative mentions. The third measure is passion, which is the number of authors repeatedly discussing the brand. The fourth measure is reach, which Socialmention defines as the number of unique authors mentioning the brand compared to the total number of mentions.

- **TweetDeck:** TweetDeck (tweetdeck.com) condenses social media profiles and data streams into one customizable application. TweetDeck incorporates feeds from Twitter, Facebook, LinkedIn, and MySpace.

Figure 10.35 summarizes the capabilities of some popular aggregator tools.

Tool	Sample Measurement Capabilities
Hootsuite	Social media dashboard to manage and measure social networks Tracks brand mentions and analyzes social media traffic
Klout	Estimates level of influence based on data from Facebook and Twitter Displays list of most influential followers
Samepoint	Engagement points, based on number of comments and sources Different views, such as Real-time and Groups
Socialmention	User-selected sources: Facebook, Twitter, YouTube, etc. Social media insight: strength, sentiment, passion, and reach
TweetDeck	Combines social media profiles and data streams Incorporates feeds from Twitter, Facebook, LinkedIn, and MySpace

Figure 10.35: Social Media Measurement Tools: Aggregators

Professional: Professional social media measurement tool providers target organizations employing teams of dedicated social media professionals. Professional tools allow managers to assign different social media tasks (such as following up on a customer request) to social media team members.

The advantage of such tools is that they provide deep analytics capabilities, essential for dedicated social media operations. The disadvantages of the tools are that they can be complex to learn and operate, and can be expensive to purchase. For example, Salesforce.com charges about $600 per month per topic for its powerful Radian6 (radian6.com) professional social media analytics dashboard and engagement console.

- **Cision**: Cision (us.cision.com) develops social media software tailored to public relations, marketing, and media relations. The tool includes media monitoring, media list building, press release distribution, and media analysis.

- **Cymfony**: Cymfony (cymfony.com) provides social media monitoring and analytics. Visible Technologies (visibletechnologies.com) acquired Cymfony in 2012. [10-33]

- **Radian6**: Radian6 (radian6.com) provides a social media dashboard with real-time monitoring of social media. The tool integrates with Salesforce.com and Webtrends.com. Radian6 is one of the industry leaders. Salesforce.com acquired Radian6 in 2011.

- **Scout Labs** : Scout Labs (scoutlabs.com) scans blogs, forums, open social networks, Twitter, and other sources, analyzes the data, and identifies trends and customer sentiment. Lithium acquired Scout Labs in 2010.

- **Techrigy**: Techrigy (alterian.com/socialmedia) offers a robust social media monitoring tool with analytics. The tool searches the Web for relevant trends, much like Google Alerts. In fact, TechCrunch refers to Techrigy as "Google Alerts on Steroids." Alterian acquired Techrigy in 2009. [10-34]

Figure 10.36 summarizes the capabilities of several professional-grade social media tools.

Tool	Sample Measurement Capabilities
Cision	Tailored to public relations, marketing, and media relations Includes media monitoring, media list building, and other PR tasks
Cymfony	Social media monitoring and analytics Acquired by Visible Technologies in 2012
Radian6	Social media dashboard and console Acquired by Salesforce.com in 2011
Scout Labs	Scans Web, analyzes data, identifies trends and customer sentiment Acquired by Lithium in 2010.
Techrigy	Searches web and analyzes data for relevant trends Acquired by Alterian in 2009

Figure 10.36: Social Media Measurement Tools: Professional-Level Tools

In the following section, we introduce a hierarchical structure to measure social media data, in relation to its worth to achieving organizational objectives.

Social Media Pyramid of Persuasion

Different types of social media interactions will have different levels of marketing effectiveness in satisfying marketing objectives. For example, a user signing up for an email newsletter (which can designate strong interest in the company's offerings) can contribute more to meeting an objective of boosting online sales than a user simply viewing one of the company's web pages.

In this section, we introduce the social media pyramid of persuasion. The pyramid groups different types of social media interactions into different levels of contribution toward reaching organizational objectives. The pyramid employs a hierarchical approach to capture the varying levels of importance for different types of social engagement regarding the company's brand. Here, the company's brand represents the company's products, services, reputation, category, or other relevant attribute.

As shown in Figure 10.37, the social media pyramid of persuasion contains four tiers:

- **Viewer Level**: The first and lowest level, where users simply view content without actively engaging with it

- **Engagement Level**: The second level, where users perform actions to engage with the brand

- **Dialog Level**: The third level, where users actively communicate with the brand

- **Referral Level**: The fourth and highest level, where users refer the company's brand to other users

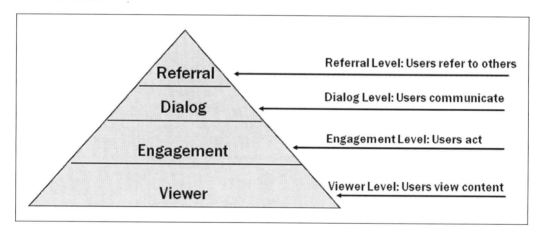

Figure 10.37: Social Media Metrics Pyramid of Persuasion

We now discuss the different levels and sample metrics for each.

Viewer Level: The lowest level, the Viewer Level, represents passive activities by users toward the brand. This level contains the most users, and represents the "universe" of potential users. At this level, viewers come to sites to view web pages, watch videos, or other similar activities, but choose not to extend the relationship at this time. Because the user has not provided any means of contacting them, we can only engage in one way communications with them. They can get content from us, but we do not know their reaction to it.

We can measure viewer level activity using metrics appropriate to the channel, as shown in Figure 10.38. For example, on websites, we can measure user visits on the different pages. On photograph and video sharing sites such as Tumblr and YouTube, we can measure pictures and videos viewed.

Measurement	Equations and Examples
Activity	Corporate websites: Views by page Social networking sites: Total views Photo and video sharing sites: Number of pictures and videos viewed

Figure 10.38: Viewer Level Sample Metrics: Examples

Engagement Level: In the next level, the Engagement Level, users choose to engage with the brand beyond passively viewing content. We can measure users on the engagement level with different metrics suited to different channels. For email, we can measure the number of people who have "opted in" to email communications. For micro-blogs such as Twitter, we can measure the number of followers. For social networking sites such as Facebook, we can measure the number of fans. For websites requiring registration (sign-ups) for participation, such as local area-focused social networking site Foursquare, we can measure number of registrations.

Figure 10.39 shows a table of sample metrics of interest when examining social media effectiveness at the engagement level (multiply ratios by 100 to obtain percentages):

- **User Count**: This metric expresses the quantity of users choosing to engage with the brand, such as the number of Twitter followers.

- **User Growth**: In this metric, we calculate the percentage of users we have gained over a certain period (usually over 30 days)

- **User Relevance**: This metric shows the percentage of users that represent our target

- **User Influence Level**: Here, we examine the percentage of users with above-average influence so we can estimate our potential reach

Measurement	Equations and Examples
User Count	Email: Number of opt-ins over time Twitter: Number of followers Facebook: Number of fans Websites: Number of registrations
User Growth	$\dfrac{\text{(End Number of Users)} - \text{(Beginning Number of Users)}}{\text{(Beginning Number of Users)}}$
User Relevance	$\dfrac{\text{Number of Target Market Users}}{\text{Number of All Users in Community}}$
User Influence Level	$\dfrac{\text{Users with Above-Average Influence}}{\text{Quantity of All users in Community}}$

Figure 10.39: Engagement Level Sample Metrics: Equations and Examples

Dialog Level: At the Dialog level, users participate in two way communications with the brand. This level goes beyond the passive activities of the first level, and the "sign-ups" of the second level. Here, users choose to make the brand a part of their lives.

Figure 10.40 shows metrics of interest when evaluating social media performance at the dialog level:

- **Activity**: This metric represents dialog activities performed by the user, such as comments on blogs, content created by users on sites promoting user-generated content (UGC), discussion themes (such as those designated by hashtags on Twitter), and mobile usage, such as Foursquare check-ins or scanning of quick response (QR) codes to learn more about an offering.

- **Brand Discussion:** Here, we measure the number of mentions of the company's brand as a percentage of all brand discussions (the company and its competitors) in a given community. For example, we might wish to know how often users mention "iPad Mini" in Apple forums.

- **Dialog Level**: This metric measures the level of dialog, such as postings and comments, as a percentage of all activities, such as web page views. For example, a low dialog level could represent a relatively low level of interest toward a particular brand or topic.

- **Dialog Sentiment**: Here, we measure the degree of positive, neutral, and negative mentions of a particular brand as a percentage of all brand mentions. For example, a high percentage of negative brand mentions could indicate growing dissatisfaction with a brand.

- **Topic Intensity**: This metric measures the number of mentions of a company's brand as percentage of all the messages in a given online community. For example, we might notice that mentions of the brand "iPad Mini" account for fewer than 5% of all messages in an online Apple forum.

Measurement	Equations and Examples
Activity	Blogs: Number and depth of blog comments UGC Sites: Amount and relevance of content Themes: Number of brand discussions using Twitter hashtags Mobile: Number of local spot check-ins in Foursquare or QR code scans
Brand Discussion	Mentions of Company Brand in Past 30 Days All Brand Mentions (Company & Competing Brands)
Dialog Level	Dialog Level (Postings, Comments, etc.) Total Quantity of User Views
Dialog Sentiment	Positive/ Neutral / Negative Mentions All Company Brand Mentions
Topic Intensity	Number of Mentions of Company Brand Quantity of All Messages in Community

Figure 10.40: Dialog Level Sample Metrics: Equations and Examples

Referral Level: At the highest level, the Referral Level, users refer brands, events, and other areas of interest to other users. Communications of this type go beyond dialog to provide word of mouth recommendations (or criticisms) to other users. Figure 10.41 shows metrics of interest when evaluating social media performance at the referral level:

- **Referral Level**: This metric measures the level of intensity of referral activity. For example, we could measure the number of Twitter re-tweets and Facebook shares over the past 30 days, and compare that number with the quantity of all messages sent during that period.

- **Referral Influence**: Here, we measure the influence level of users performing referrals, as compared to the average influence level of the community. For example, we might notice that users re-tweeting #iPadMini tweets have a high influence level.

- **Referral Depth**: In this metric, we estimate the level of depth (the specificity of content) by counting the number of words in referral messages, and comparing that quantity with the average message length. For example, we might observe that referrals involving "iPad Mini" contain 30% more words than average messages.

Measurement	Equations and Examples
Referral Level	Re-Tweets + Facebook Shares in Past 30 Days Quantity of All Messages
Referral Influence	Influence Level of Referrers Average Influence Level
Referral Depth	Quantity of Words in Referral Messages Average Message Length

Figure 10.41: Referral Level Sample Metrics: Equations and Examples

MARKETING MADE MEASURABLE

Google Panda and Penguin: SEO beyond the Website: Search engine giant Google (google.com) wants its search engine optimization (SEO) algorithms to reflect users' true engagement with brands, instead of being tricked by gimmicks to artificially boost search engine rankings. To that end, it launched a new type of SEO algorithm, code-named Panda, in February of 2011. Panda used artificial intelligence to enforce Google's best practice guidelines. Google has long advocated best practices to gain SEO status, such as quality content, originality, and good overall user experience.

Google then took the process a step further with the next algorithm, code-named Penguin, in April of 2012. Penguin looks beyond the website to assess brand presence. Much of the brand conversation now occurs outside the website, on social media channels. Penguin considers social media conversations when determining website ranking.

As a result, a well-optimized website is no longer sufficient for a strong Google ranking. Companies must now encourage conversation on social media channels to enhance their reputation and earn a high Google Page Rank. [10-35]

SUMMARY

Marketers can draw from a number of techniques to promote their products and services. They can choose traditional promotion vehicles such as print advertising and television, and/or newer methods, such as Internet advertising and location-based social networking.

In this chapter, we covered analytics models and metrics for promotion, including promotion budget estimation, promotion budget allocation, promotion metrics for traditional media, and promotion metrics for social media.

Promotion Budget Estimation: Promotion accounts for the majority of marketing budgets, so we must estimate the amount needed accurately. We can turn to several techniques to estimate promotion budgets:

- **Percentage of Sales Method**: In the first method, we can set our total promotion budget as a percentage of annual sales revenue. While the method is fast and simple, the approach makes it difficult to leapfrog competitors.

- **Affordable Method**: Here, we can set promotion budget to what companies believe they can afford. This method can cripple companies which need to react quickly to competitive threats.

- **Competitive Parity Method**: In this method, companies set promotion budgets to approximate what competitors spend on promotion. Proponents of the method state that the resulting budget reflects the "collective wisdom of the industry."

- **Objective and Task Method:** Some companies develop promotion budgets by declaring certain objectives, determining the tasks to accomplish those objectives, and then estimating the costs to complete the tasks.

- **Model-Based Method**: We can also turn to promotion budget estimation models, such as the ADBUDG model. With the ADBUDG model, we can estimate future market share as a function of promotion spending.

Promotion Budget Allocation: Once we establish the overall promotion budget, we allocate it among marketing programs. To do so, we can apply linear optimization models. Linear optimization models include objective functions, which specify intended outcomes. The models also include constraints, such as budget and legal constraints. The model then maximizes the outcome (as defined by the objective function), subject to the constraints specified.

Promotion Metrics for Traditional Media: Many companies use traditional media, such as print advertisements, radio, and television. We can measure such media using metrics such as reach, frequency, and gross rating points. Reach measures the size of the intended audience to whom we will be targeting the promotion. Frequency measures the average number of exposures of an advertisement to an individual within the target market over a specified time period, such as one month. Gross rating points (GRPs) measure the level of intensity of media plans, and are calculated by multiplying reach by frequency.

Promotion Metrics for Social Media: Companies are adopting social media campaigns, often to supplement campaigns using traditional media. To measure social media campaigns, we can use different types of tools. Tool categories include built-in tools, such as those native to social media applications, aggregators, which combine metrics from multiple sources, and professional tools, designed for dedicated social media professionals.

Terminology

Affordable Method: Promotion budget estimation method that sets budgets to whatever a company can afford.

Competitive Parity Method: Promotion budget estimation method that sets budgets to approximate those of competitors.

Constraint Function: Equation (or set of equations) used in linear optimization that expresses financial, legal, or other limitations that must be met for a valid solution.

Cost per Thousand: In promotion metrics for traditional media, cost per thousand measures the cost to deliver an advertisement to 1,000 individuals in the audience through a given advertising medium.

Cost per Point: In promotion metrics for traditional media, cost per point measures the cost to deliver an advertisement to one percent of the individuals in the audience.

Frequency: In promotion metrics for traditional media, frequency measures the average number of exposures of an advertisement to an individual within the target market over a specified time period.

Gross Rating Points: In promotion metrics for traditional media, gross rating points measure the level of intensity of a media plan. Gross rating points are calculated by multiplying reach by frequency.

Linear Optimization: Technique used to maximize or minimize a value (expressed as an objective function) subject to limitations (expressed as constraint functions).

Model-Based Method: Promotion budget estimation method that sets the budget in accordance to a decision model, such as the ADBUDG model.

Objective and Task Method: Promotion budget estimation method that sets a budget to achieve specific promotion objectives.

Objective Function: Equation used in linear optimization (such as that for promotion budget allocation) to specify intended outcome to maximize or minimize.

Percentage of Sales Method: Promotion budget estimation method that sets budgets as a percentage of annual sales revenue.

Reach: In promotion metrics for traditional media, reach measures the size of the intended audience to whom we will be targeting promotions.

Solver: Add-in in Microsoft Excel enabling users to solve simultaneous equations to seek a solution. Used in linear optimization.

Target Rating Points: In promotion metrics for traditional media, target rating points represent the exposure level of an advertisement to a specific target market.

Class Discussion

1. What types of promotion vehicles (direct marketing, events, radio, television, etc.) do you find effective in persuading you to purchase something, or take some other action?
2. What method does your organization use to set promotion budgets?
3. What method does your organization use to allocate the promotion budget across marketing vehicles?
4. How would the concept of "reach" apply to Internet audiences?
5. How would you measure "success" for a social media measurement tool?
6. What forces cause consumers to advance in the pyramid of persuasion, such as moving from the dialog level to the referral level?

Practice Problems

1. Calculate the promotion budget for next year for a company using the "percentage of sales" method of promotion budget estimation. The company annual revenue is $500,000, and they typically spend 10% of revenue on promotion.
2. Determine the promotion budget for next year for a company using the "comparative parity" method of promotion budget estimation. The company's competitor purchases 10 print ads at $1,000 each, 20 radio ads at $5,000 each, and 30 television ads at $10,000 each.
3. Indicate how to allocate a company's budget across its three promotion vehicles to maximize the number of exposures given the available budget. The company uses direct marketing, Internet advertising, and Google AdWords pay per click search engine marketing. The direct marketing ads result in 30 views per ad, and cost $20 each. We are limited to 100 direct marketing ads per month. The Internet ads result in 40 views per ad, and cost $30 each. We are limited to 50 Internet ads per month. The AdWords ads result in 50 views per ad, and cost $60 each. We are limited to 60 ads per month. The company has a $20,000 monthly marketing budget.
4. Calculate the GRP (gross rating points) for an advertising campaign with a reach of 500,000 and a frequency of 3.
5. Calculate the CPM (cost per thousand) for an advertising campaign costing $10,000 sent to 2,000 individuals.
6. Determine the user growth in a Twitter account starting the month with 300 users and ending it with 400 users.

Chapter 11.
SALES ANALYTICS

Chapter Outline

We cover the following marketing analytics topics in this chapter:

- ☑ **Consumer Sales Process**: Analyzing the consumer sales process for insight
- ☑ **ECommerce Sales Model**: Calculating online sales campaign effectiveness
- ☑ **Sales Metrics**: Evaluating sales performance in multiple areas
- ☑ **Profitability Metrics**: Assessing gross margin using profitability metrics
- ☑ **Support Metrics**: Measuring support performance

"Good marketers measure."
– Seth Godin

Marketing guru Seth Godin (sethgodin.com) urges marketers to measure the results of their efforts. Godin believes effective measurement quickly shows which efforts work and which do not.

Before the Internet made it easy to look up phone numbers, the telephone company made a lot of money through its Yellow Pages advertising business. According to Godin, one of the secrets of their success was that the phone company would give companies a second phone line when they purchased big ads. The phone on that line would ring every time someone called about the ad.

When it came time for renewal, the salesperson would look at the phone, imagining it would never ring again. The salesperson knew they must renew the ad. And the phone company knew it could charge high prices for its ads because businesses could not bear to imagine their phones silent.

The ringing of the phone provided a clear measurement of the effectiveness of the ads. Businesses will continue to invest in techniques they know will provide results. [11-1]

This chapter covers models and metrics for sales processes. We begin by analyzing the sales process for sales of goods and services to consumers, examining how we can measure our effectiveness at each step in the process. We then introduce an eCommerce sales model to calculate the performance of online sales campaigns. We close the chapter by covering metrics for sales, profitability and support.

CONSUMER SALES PROCESS

In this section, we analyze the process for sales of products and services to consumers. We break the process down into steps to study how we can measure our sales effectiveness at each step, and identify actions to improve our effectiveness. Of course, consumers do not always follow every step, especially for routine purchases, such as household staples. Nevertheless, we can learn much about the sales process by examining each step.

The general consumer sales process follows five distinct steps, as summarized in Figure 11.1. We will go through each of the steps, using a running example of a female consumer considering the purchase of a new motorcycle. [11-2]

Sales Step	Description	Survey Metric	Marketing Actions
Problem Description	Consumer recognizes problem and wants to solve it	Identified applications for product or service	Consumer advertising to show how product solves problem
Information Search	Consumer gathers information to make decision	Sources of information	Distribution of relevant information to multiple venues
Evaluation of Alternatives	Consumer judges different alternatives	Beliefs, attitudes, and decision criteria	Framing of problem to benefit company
Purchase Decision	Consumer decides on specifics of the purchase	Brand, dealer, quantity, timing, and payment method	Purchase attributes and purchase experience
Post-purchase Behavior	Consumer wonders if they made the right choice	Satisfaction and likelihood to recommend to others	Follow-up actions to assure consumer

Figure 11.1: Consumer Sales Process: Summary

Problem Description

In the problem description stage, the consumer recognizes a problem she has and decides she wants to solve it. The trigger for the problem can stem from an internal stimulus (such as a feeling of boredom, and wanting a change) or an external stimulus (such as rising fuel costs).

In the case of our female consumer, she wants to save money on gasoline for commuting to work (a reaction to an external stimulus), and she also desires something sporty (internal stimulus). She evaluates fuel-efficient automobiles, but finds them too slow for her sporty nature. She turns her attention to sporty cars, only to find them fuel guzzlers. A friend suggests a motorcycle—thrifty on fuel, and still quite sporty. She decides to consider a new motorcycle.

Even in this early stage, we can measure our success in engaging consumers in the sales cycle. We can survey people in our target market and calculate how many associate our product or service with their intended applications.

For example, market research firm J.D. Power and Associates (jdpower.com) sends out multi-part surveys to people purchasing new motor vehicles. As part of its efforts, J.D. Power sends out its New Motorcycle Buyer Survey to purchasers of new motorcycles. In the survey, J.D. Power asks the question, "What type of riding do you do with your new motorcycle?" and asks the respondent to check all the riding types that apply. Riding types include Commuting, Riding Around Town, Short/Day Trips, Fast Paced Trips, Extended/Overnight Travel, and others. [11-3]

Figure 11.2 shows a typical multi-part survey.

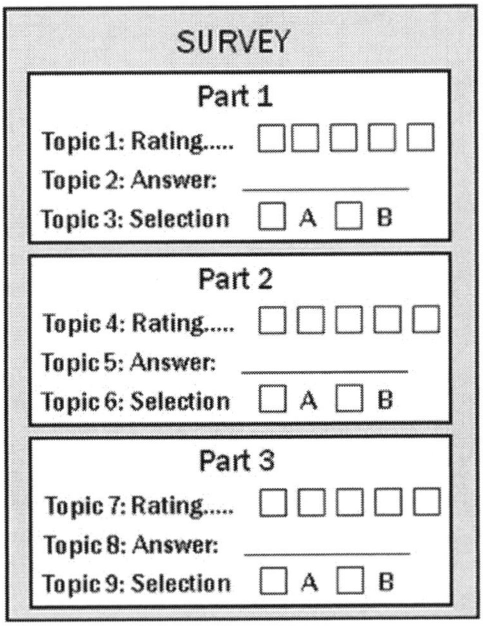

Figure 11.2: Consumer Sales Process: Typical Multi-Part Survey

J.D. Power offers the data from the survey to motorcycle manufacturers so they will know the perceived relevance of their motorcycles for different applications. In the case of our female consumer, she might state that she intends to use a new motorcycle for both Commuting and Fast Paced Trips.

We can take steps to increase the conversion rate for consumers to proceed from the first step (problem description) to the second step (information search). We can advertise how our products and services relate to the target market. In the case of our female consumer, the motorcycle manufacturer can run advertisements in motorcycle magazines, websites, and other locations showing people commuting on their bikes.

Information Search

In the information search stage, consumers gather information to make their decision. Consumers search for information in four sources: personal, commercial, public, and experiential. [11-4]

Personal sources include individuals known by the consumer, such as friends, colleagues, and acquaintances. Commercial sources include information provided by companies, such as websites and advertising. Public sources include material from mass media (such as magazines and television) and consumer rating organizations (such as J.D. Power and Associates). Experiential sources include feedback from trial of the product or service.

In the case of our female consumer, she can ask her friends about the type of motorcycle to purchase (Personal), look at advertisements from motorcycle manufacturers (Commercial), read motorcycle-related magazines (Public), and take a test ride at a local dealer (Experiential).

As we did in the first step, we can measure our progress in the sales cycle through a survey. In this case, we can ask the consumer about the sources of information they consult when making new purchases.

For example, J.D. Power includes the following question in its New Motorcycle Buyer Survey: "Which of the following sources did you use for gathering information about your new motorcycle?" J.D. Power provides a list of various sources and asks the respondent to select all that apply. The survey shows answer choices such as Magazine Articles, Dealer Displays, Product Brochures, Friends/Relatives, Dealer Personnel, Motorcycle Websites, and others. [11-5]

We can use the feedback from surveys such as this to increase the effectiveness of information distribution. For example, J.D. Power sends the results of the surveys to motorcycle manufacturers so they know which sources consumers use. If manufacturers find high scores for magazine articles, they will want to consider increasing exposure of their bikes in magazines.

Evaluation of Alternatives

In the third stage, Evaluation of Alternatives, consumers apply the information they gathered in the previous step to evaluate the various alternatives that face them. Consumers use a combination of beliefs (opinions held by consumers), attitudes (evaluations and feelings toward an object, such as a product, service, person, or idea), and decision criteria (specific desires to be evaluated during the decision making process). [11-6]

In the case of our female consumer, she will judge different alternatives by examining motorcycle models from a variety of manufacturers. Based on her research and life experiences to date, she has formed beliefs, such as: "Honda makes reliable products." She has developed attitudes, such as: "I like the styling of cruiser-style motorcycles." She has also created decision criteria, such as: "I want to maximize fuel economy and sportiness while not exceeding a budget of $5000."

We can measure our sales effectiveness in this step through a survey. In this case, we inquire about the consumer's attitudes, beliefs, and decision criteria.

For example, J.D. Power includes specific questions in its New Motorcycle Buyer Survey to cover these areas. [11-7]

- **Beliefs**: The survey gathers data from the consumer about the beliefs she holds by asking her to rate the degree (from "strongly disagree" to "strongly agree") that she agrees in statements such as "My motorcycle must be made in the USA."

- **Attitudes**: The survey asks for her attitudes to specific styling features, such as those of the exhaust, wheels, fenders, engine, and fuel tank.

- **Decision Criteria**: J.D. Power also inquires into decision criteria with questions such as, "Why did you select this motorcycle model?" and provides answer choices such as Quality, Performance, Comfort, Size, Availability, Price, and so forth.

We can improve our marketing effectiveness during this stage by framing the evaluation criteria to benefit the company. Depending on the situation facing the manufacturer, we can use different approaches—real repositioning, psychological re-positioning, competitive de-positioning, altering the importance weights, focusing on neglected attributes, or changing the consumers' ideals. [11-8]

Figure 11.3 shows an overview.

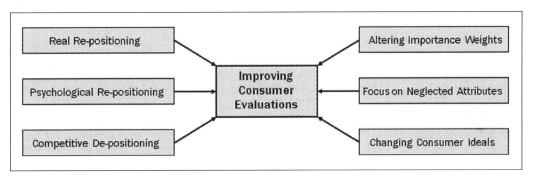

Figure 11.3: Consumer Sales Process: Improving Consumer Evaluations: Overview

- **Real Re-positioning**: We can redesign our products and services if consumers find them inadequate. For example, if our female consumer purchased a motorcycle but later found it to have excessive service costs, we could consider changes to the design for cheaper servicing.

- **Psychological Re-positioning**: We can alter beliefs about the product, service, or brand. For example, if the J.D. Power survey results showed that female consumers found the brand to overly emphasize male riders, we could implement an advertising campaign advocating female ridership.

- **Competitive De-positioning**: We can change beliefs about competitors' brands if we believe they incorrectly portray their products or services. For example, if the J.D. Power survey results found that Kawasaki brand motorcycles came in as a close second choice to

Hondas due to lower maintenance costs, we could run a comparison chart on our website showing the actual maintenance costs between Honda and Kawasaki motorcycles, showing virtually the same costs for each.

- **Altering Importance Weights**: We can focus attention to areas in which the product, service, or brand excels, demonstrating superiority in that area. For example, we can advertise that the Honda Rebel motorcycle achieves 84 miles per gallon, one of the highest ratings for motorcycles in its class. [11-9]

- **Focusing on Neglected Attributes**: We can direct attention to areas seldom discussed, but potentially relevant to the buying decision. For example, we can advertise that the Honda Rebel features a seat height less than 27 inches, a specification not always mentioned in ads, unlike fuel economy, which is almost always mentioned. The low seat height can benefit riders with short inseams.

- **Changing Consumer Ideals:** We can show the importance of a specific attribute with the intention of changing the ideal level for a particular attribute. For example, the curb weight of the Honda Rebel motorcycle is only 331 pounds, which is 48% lighter than the average for all cruiser motorcycles. Heavy motorcycles can intimidate some beginners. Because the Honda aims its Rebel at beginners, Honda could consider defining the weight of 331 pounds as the "standard" that all beginning riders should prefer when considering a new motorcycle. [11-10]

Figure 11.4 summarizes methods to improve consumer evaluations.

Method	Description	Example
Real Re-Positioning	Redesign existing products and services to make them better suited to consumers	Physical changes in design of motorcycle
Psychological Re-Positioning	Alter beliefs about the product, service, or brand	Advertising campaign advocating female ridership
Competitive De-positioning	Change beliefs about competitors' brands	Comparison charts contrasting performance of different brands
Altering Importance Weights	Focus attention to areas where brand excels	Emphasis on superior fuel economy
Focusing on Neglected Attributes	Direct attention to important areas not often considered	Benefits of low seat height
Changing Consumer Ideals	Change ideal level for certain attributes	Define new "standard" for ideal weight for entry-level motorcycles

Figure 11.4: Consumer Sales Process: Improving Consumer Evaluations: Summary

Purchase Decision

In the previous step, the consumer formed brand preferences (and perhaps preferences around specific models), based on an evaluation of the alternatives. The purchase decision step takes the process to the next stage, where the consumer decides on specific areas of the purchase.

Consumers can make up to five sub-decisions to make the final purchase decision: brand, dealer, quantity, timing, and payment method. Consumers consider the attitudes of others (such as what their friends say) and unanticipated situational factors (such as a potential loss in employment) during the final purchase decision process. [11-11]

Figure 11.5 shows an overview of these five sub-decisions. We discuss the relevancy of each for our female consumer contemplating a new motorcycle.

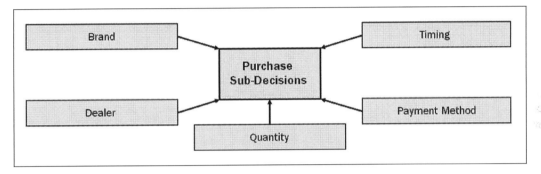

Figure 11.5: Consumer Sales Process: Purchase Sub-Decisions: Overview

- **Brand**: Our consumer will select the final brand choice, based on the information gathered to date and any new information. In addition to her earlier research, she will listen intently to the attitudes of others as she becomes more serious in her decision-making process. She might visit online forums to gather more information. For example, she might visit a Honda Rebel forum, such as hondarebelforum.com, to learn more about her intended purchase from current owners.

- **Dealer**: In addition to the brand, our consumer will need to decide where to purchase the new motorcycle. Again, she could consult forums for advice. She can also consider postings of dealers on service provider evaluation websites, such as Yelp (yelp.com).

- **Quantity**: In this case, our consumer will likely only purchase one motorcycle. However, she must also decide if she wants to increase her initial purchase through extended warranties, accessories, and other optional extras. Many dealers discount such items at the point of initial sale to encourage higher initial purchases.

- **Timing**: Our consumer might decide to modify, postpone, or avoid a purchase decision based on the risk she perceives. Perceived risk includes several types of risk: **Functional risk**: "Will the product live up to my expectations?", **Physical risk**: Will I be involved in an accident?", **Financial risk**: Can I afford a new motorcycle now?", **Social risk**: Will my friends tease me about riding a motorcycle?", **Psychological risk**: "Will the bike fail to fulfill my need for sportiness?", and **Time risk**: "Should I hold off buying the bike until the end-of-year sales, or will my model be gone by then?"

- **Payment method**: When making the actual purchase, our consumer must decide on the method of payment. Payment terms and financing could influence the final sale.

We can measure our sales effectiveness in this step by direct feedback from the consumer in the form of a general survey, such as that by J.D. Power, or through a focused survey, such as that from the motorcycle dealer.

For example, the J.D. Power New Motorcycle Buyer Survey includes the following questions to measure the effectiveness of the purchase decision step: [11-12]

- **Brand:** "What other motorcycles (brand and model) did you seriously consider while shopping for your new motorcycle?" Respondents write in the make and model of the competing brands.

- **Dealer**: "What are the main reasons for buying your new motorcycle at this dealership?" Answer choices include items such as price, location, financing, and so forth.

- **Quantity**: "Did you receive any of the following at no additional cost when purchasing this motorcycle?" Answer choices include items such as extended service plans, maintenance programs, accessories, and so forth.

- **Timing**: The survey assesses the consumer's familiarity and risk comfort level with motorcycles by asking the following question: "What type of rider do you consider yourself?" Answer choices include beginner, intermediate, advanced, and expert.

- **Payment Method**: "How did you pay for your new motorcycle?" Answer choices include items such as dealer financing, credit line, credit card, and so forth.

Figure 11.6 summarizes the different purchase sub-decisions.

Sub-Decision	Description	Example
Brand	Narrowing down list of top brands to consider	Deciding on Honda brand due to strong brand reputation
Dealer	Selecting channel from which to purchase item	Purchasing new motorcycle from nearby dealer for easy servicing
Quantity	Determining quantity to purchase, along with accessories	Selecting extended warranty for peace of mind with new machine
Timing	Evaluating functional risk, financial risk, social risk, and psychological risk in consideration of postponing decision	Postponing purchase of new motorcycle until after completion of Motorcycle Safety Foundation (MSF) Basic Rider Course
Payment Method	Selecting method of payment	Paying with dealer financing

Figure 11.6: Consumer Sales Process: Purchase Sub-Decisions: Summary

We can improve our marketing efforts at this stage through consumer communications on brand (through brand-oriented advertisements), dealer (through high dealer ratings on evaluation websites such as Yelp), quantity (through offers on packages available at time of purchase), timing (by understanding the class of buyer attracted to different models, such as beginning riders attracted to some motorcycles, advanced riders attracted to other bikes, and so forth), and payment method (by offering flexible payment plans).

In addition, we also want to understand the consumer's perception of the entire purchase experience. In fact, the J.D. Power New Motorcycle Buyer Survey devotes an entire section to the buying experience, including questions on model availability, courtesy, knowledge, and so forth.

Post-Purchase Behavior

Consumers continue to evaluate their decision even after they have completed the purchase. They wonder if they made the right choice. They notice disadvantages with the product or service they failed to see during the evaluation process. Consumers hear favorable news about competing makes and models (or the announcement of a 50% off sale!). They might feel pressure to return the product or discontinue the service within the first 30 days (or similar), before it is too late to get their money back. Therefore, marketers must evaluate this portion of the sales cycle even though it occurs after the sale.

In the case of our female consumer, she purchases her new Honda motorcycle. She enjoys riding it, but finds a few areas she dislikes. For example, she almost burns her leg on the hot exhaust pipe because of the pipe's exposed location. She might decide to keep her new Honda anyway, but will consider other brands when purchasing her next motorcycle.

Marketing researchers sometimes refer to this conflict between initial assessment and post-purchase perceptions as post-purchase dissonance (PPD), and it represents a major challenge in consumer marketing.

We can evaluate the sales effectiveness at this step by surveying our new customer to understand her satisfaction level with key attributes of the product or service, and any related services, such as dealer performance.

For example, the J.D. Power New Motorcycle Buyer Survey dedicates a significant part of the survey to understanding the buyer's satisfaction with their new motorcycle, and their likelihood to recommend the motorcycle and the dealer to others. The survey includes several sections to assess satisfaction: [11-13]

- **Attribute Ratings**: The survey includes many questions covering multiple attributes of the motorcycle, such as comfort, controls, styling, engine performance, and ride.

- **Quality Ratings**: The survey asks the respondent about any quality issues, such as poor paint, engine noises, transmission problems, electrical concerns, and other areas.

- **Buying Experience Ratings**: The survey assesses the consumer's satisfaction with the dealer and the overall purchase experience.

- **Service Experience Ratings**: The survey asks detailed questions about the quality of the service experience.

- **Overall Ownership Experience Ratings**: The survey inquires about the overall ownership experience and asks how likely the consumer would be to recommend the motorcycle brand and dealer to others.

We can improve our marketing efforts at this stage by addressing any pressing issues identified by the survey. In addition, we can avoid many instances of post-purchase dissonance by following up with the consumer after the sale. Such follow-up demonstrates the manufacturer's commitment to quality and service, and can change consumers' perceptions of the brand.

In our motorcycle example, the Honda dealer could call the new owner and ask her how she likes her new bike. She would proceed to tell the dealer about the poor placement of the hot exhaust pipe, and how she almost burned her leg on it. The dealer could ask her to bring the bike in to the service shop for fitment of a protective heat shield around the pipe. This action would address the complaint she had with the motorcycle. In addition, it would leave a lasting impression on the commitment the dealer (and the brand) had for her satisfaction with her new Honda motorcycle.

MARKETING MADE MEASURABLE

Intuit: Decision Simplicity: Advisory company Corporate Executive Board (CEB, at executiveboard.com) surveyed more than 7,000 customers and interviewed 200 marketing executives to find out the best way to influence consumers' purchase decisions. The #1 answer: decision simplicity. Consumers want companies to simplify the decision making process. [11-14]

Instead, many companies try too hard to engage with consumers through social media and other channels. Companies push out too much information, causing consumers to over-think purchase decisions. As a result, consumers become less confident in their purchase choices and less likely to remain loyal to the brand.

Accounting software maker Intuit (intuit.com) simplifies the decision making process with three steps:

- **Trust:** Intuit offers more than 160,000 unfiltered reviews and ratings, so prospects can make up their own minds.
- **Learn:** Intuit provides its TurboTax Live Community forum to learn about the product from other customers.
- **Consider Options:** Intuit shows comparisons of its products on its home page to help consumers easily decide which is right for them.

ECOMMERCE SALES MODEL

The potential profitability of eCommerce sales has attracted many merchants to sell online. ECommerce merchants have found that different types of goods and services require different sales techniques.

In the case of inexpensive goods and services, many merchants find it sufficient to post detailed descriptions of their offerings on their websites. They then rely on search engine optimization (SEO) techniques to pull potential customers (prospects) to their site when the prospects search for relevant items using Internet search engines. [11-15]

But eCommerce merchants of expensive goods and services often find that SEO techniques alone do not result in adequate sales. Such situations require more active sales efforts. For example, many merchants selling expensive home theater electronics find it necessary to execute outbound marketing campaigns in order to engage prospects.

Sample outbound campaigns include emails sent to prospects to promote new products and services, pay per click (PPC) search engine marketing advertisements, and social media campaigns.

Prospects often deliberate over purchase decisions for expensive goods and services, and require multiple campaigns from the merchant before they make their decision. Merchants execute the campaigns to generate responses from prospects that propel them forward in the decision-making process. Because not all prospects will buy from the company, and because each prospect will likely need multiple communications from us before they are ready to buy, we need to generate many responses for each sale.

Responses can include opening an email (we can track the number of opened emails), clicking on a search engine advertisement (we can track the number of PPC clicks), or replying to a social media campaign (we can track social media responses). Over time, we count the number of responses required to generate a sale, which merchants refer to as the conversion rate.

ECommerce marketing and sales campaigns require budget to execute and we desire to maximize our sales efforts based on the budget.

To gain maximum effectiveness from our eCommerce sales efforts, we must predict the outcomes of the campaigns, compare them to the actual results, and make adjustments as necessary. To that end, we introduce an eCommerce sales model to predict eCommerce marketing and sales results.

The structure of the model, with its well-defined inputs, outputs, and straightforward governing equations, lends itself well to implementation using popular spreadsheet programs, such as Microsoft Excel.

Business to business (B2B) marketers can also apply the model to their sales activities. In the explanation above, replace the word "responses" with "leads" to signify that each lead represents an expression of interest from a prospect. Companies will have their sales force personnel follow up after leads to close the sale. In the model, we also replace the word "orders" with "customers" to indicate that relationships with business customers often last longer than those with consumers. [11-16]

Figure 11.7 shows an overview of the inputs and outputs of the model.

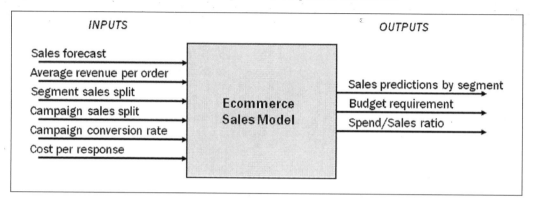

Figure 11.7: ECommerce Sales Model: Overview

Model Inputs

We start our treatment by discussing the inputs to the model. Figure 11.8 summarizes the inputs to the model.

Input	Description	Example
Sales Forecast	Amount of sales revenue expected to be made in next year	"We expect to generate $40,000 in sales next year"
Average Revenue/ Order	Average revenue generated per order; also called Order Size	"The average customer spends $1,000 per order"
Segment Sales Split	Percentage of sales per market segment	"Segment A accounts for 30% of overall sales"
Campaign Sales Split	Percentage of sales per marketing campaign	"Social media campaigns account for 25% of overall sales"
Campaign Conversion Rate	Ratio of sales to campaigns for different marketing campaigns	"PPC campaigns result in one sale for every 100 clicks, a 1% conversion rate."
Cost per Response	Average marketing spend per prospect response	"Our social networking program costs us about $2.00 to get a response from a prospect"

Figure 11.8: ECommerce Sales Model: Inputs

Sales Forecast: The sales forecast is the amount of sales revenue that the organization expects to generate in the coming year. For example, the company might plan to generate $40,000 in sales in the coming year.

Average Revenue per Order: To obtain the average revenue per order, we sum the revenue from all orders in the previous year and divide by the total number of orders. For an online retailer selling expensive goods, we might find that the average customer spends $1,000 per order.

Segment Sales Split: Different market segments will generate different levels of revenue. The segment sales split variable is the percentage of sales for each market segment, based on historical data. For example, we might examine our previous year's sales and determine that a certain segment accounts for 30% of overall sales.

Campaign Sales Split: Different types of marketing campaigns (email newsletters, social media campaigns, etc.) will generate different levels of revenue. The campaign sales split variable is the percentage of sales for each type of campaign. We might find that social media campaigns account for 25% of overall sales.

Campaign Conversion Rate: Campaign conversion rate is the percentage of successful sales efforts relative to the overall campaign effort. For example, we might find that pay per click (PPC) campaigns result in one sale for every 100 clicks on an online advertisement, which equates to a one percent campaign conversion rate.

For expensive goods and services, we might target different goals for conversion. For example, a realtor would not expect a buyer to purchase a home directly from an Internet ad. She might consider a "conversion" as a contact from an interested buyer. Chapter 10 discusses various conversion goals.

Cost per Response: We can observe the cost we incur to generate responses from prospects. In the case of email and social media campaigns, we calculate the total cost required to execute the campaigns, and divide by the number of prospect responses (which we can track) to obtain the cost per response. In the case of PPC campaigns, search engine organizations such as Google provide cost per click (response) data in their PPC campaign dashboards.

Model Outputs
We turn our attention now to the outputs of the model. Figure 11.9 summarizes the outputs from the model.

Output	Description	Example
Sales Predictions by Segment	Amount of sales revenue predicted for each market segment	"We predict we will generate $100,000 in Segment #1"
Budget Requirement	Amount of marketing budget required to execute campaigns	"Our campaigns will require a total campaign budget of $20,000"
Spend/ Sales	Marketing budget spent, as a percentage of sales generated	"We spent about 10% of sales on marketing campaigns"

Figure 11.9: ECommerce Sales Model: Outputs

Sales Predictions by Segment: The model predicts the amount of sales revenue we can expect to generate for each market segment. For example, the model could predict we will generate $100,000 in segment #1 as a result of our eCommerce efforts.

Budget Requirement: The model calculates the amount of budget required to execute the campaigns. For example, the model could indicate that the campaigns will require a campaign budget of $20,000.

Budget/ Sales: The model calculates the ratio of the campaign budget relative to the revenue those campaigns generate. The inverse of this ratio (Sales/ Budget) represents the return on investment (ROI) for the campaigns. For example, the model could state that we can expect to spend about 10% of our sales amount on marketing campaigns.

Governing Equations

We complete our introduction of the model by reviewing the governing equations. Figure 11.10 summarizes the equations governing the model.

Variable	Equation
Orders	Orders = (Sales Forecast) / (Revenue / Order)
Orders by Segment	Orders by Segment = (Total Orders) * (Segment Sales Split)
Responses	Responses = (Orders) / (Conversion Rate)
Budget	Budget = (Responses) * (Cost per Response)
Sales by Segment	Sales = (Sales Forecast) * (Segment Sales Split)
Budget/ Sales	Budget/ Sales = (Budget) / (Sales)

Figure 11.10: ECommerce Sales Model: Governing Equations

Orders: The model calculates the total number of orders required to generate the sales forecast by dividing the sales forecast (in currency units, such as dollars or Euros) by the revenue generated per order (also in currency units).

Orders by Segment: We multiply the total orders by the segment sales split (the percentage of sales predicted for each market segment) to obtain the predicted orders by segment.

Responses: The model calculates the number of responses we predict we will need from prospects to generate our estimated number of orders. To calculate the anticipated number of responses we will need, we divide the number of orders by the conversion rate.

Budget: We calculate the budget required to execute our marketing campaigns by multiplying the number of responses by the cost per response. The cost per response can vary by the type of campaign, so the model calculates budgets for each type of campaign separately, and then sums them together to obtain the total budget.

Sales by Segment: We determine the sales by segment by multiplying the sales forecast (which includes sales for all segments) by the segment sales split.

Budget/ Sales: The model calculates the ratio of required budget (i.e., the marketing spending) to sales revenue by dividing the budget required to execute our marketing campaigns by the sales we anticipate generating through our campaigns. The budget/sales ratio represents our marketing effectiveness. A small budget/ sales ratio indicates high effectiveness, with a small amount of money spent to generate sales revenue.

Example

We will show the structure of the model and demonstrate its use through an example.

Luxury electronic sales eCommerce merchant Acme.com (fictitious company) specializes in high-end home theater and electronics equipment for discriminating home owners. Acme.com estimates it will generate $200,000 in sales over the next year, spread evenly throughout the year. Because Acme.com specializes in high-end merchandise, it generates an average of $1,000 in revenue per order.

Acme.com sells to three segments:

- **Segment 1: Early Adopters**: The first segment, high-income early adopters, constitutes fifty percent of the total sales of Acme.com. The segment demands the latest advances in high technology that money can buy.

- **Segment 2: Mid-Income Pragmatists:** The second segment, mid-income pragmatists, generates thirty percent of total sales. The segment also appreciates high technology, but also requires reliability and ease of use.

- **Segment 3: Value-Conscious Shoppers:** The third segment, value-conscious shoppers, makes up twenty percent of Acme.com sales. The segment cares more about price than about the latest features.

Figure 11.11 summarizes the sales input data for the eCommerce model. The figure shows the annual sales forecast spread out evenly over the four quarters of the year, and then totaled for the fiscal year of the organization. The figure also shows the average revenue per order and segment sales splits remaining constant throughout the year. If we wish, we can change this situation to show the average revenue per order or segment sales splits changing over time. For example, we might realize greater order sizes near the holiday season at the end of the year.

Input: Sales	Quarter 1	Quarter 2	Quarter 3	Quarter 4	Fiscal Year
Sales Forecast	$50,000	$50,000	$50,000	$50,000	$200,000
Average Revenue/Order	$1,000	$1,000	$1,000	$1,000	$1,000
Segment Sales Split: Segment 1	50%	50%	50%	50%	50%
Segment Sales Split: Segment 2	30%	30%	30%	30%	30%
Segment Sales Split: Segment 3	20%	20%	20%	20%	20%

Figure 11.11: ECommerce Sales Model, Acme.com Example: Sales Input Data

Acme.com drives eCommerce sales using three types of campaigns:

- **Campaign A: Email Newsletter**: About forty percent of its sales derive through its email newsletter campaign. The newsletter discusses new products and promotions, results in two sales for every 100 responses (a 2.0% conversion rate), and costs an average of $2.20 per response to create and distribute.

- **Campaign B: PPC:** Thirty-five percent of its sales come from pay per click (PPC) advertisements using Google AdWords. Acme.com has found the PPC campaign to generate a 1.0% conversion rate and costs $1.00 per response.

- **Campaign C: Social Media:** The third type of campaign, social media, accounts for 25% of its sales, achieves a 1.5% conversion rate and costs an average of $1.40 per response to execute.

Figure 11.12 summarizes the campaign input data.

Input: Campaigns	Campaign Sales Split	Conversion Rate	Cost per Response
A: Email Newsletter	40%	2.0%	$2.20
B: PPC	35%	1.0%	$1.00
C: Social Networking	25%	1.5%	$1.40

Figure 11.12: ECommerce Sales Model, Acme.com Example: Campaign Input Data

We start the model by calculating the results for each market segment. Figure 11.13 shows the results table for Segment 1. Results tables for segments two and three would be similar.

Campaign	Orders	Responses	Budget	Sales	Budget/Sales
Campaign A (Email)	40	2,000	$4,400	$40,000	11.0%
Campaign B (PPC)	35	3,500	$3,500	$35,000	10.0%
Campaign C (Social)	25	1,667	$2,333	$25,000	9.3%
Total	*100*	*7,167*	*$10,233*	*$100,000*	*10.2% (Ave.)*

Figure 11.13: ECommerce Sales Model, Acme.com Example: Results for Segment 1

We now discuss how to calculate the entries in the figure, starting with the Orders column on the left and working our way across to the Budget/Sales column on the right.

We begin by calculating the number of orders Acme.com needs to achieve to generate its sales forecast of $200,000.

We calculate the total number of orders using the following equation:

Orders   = (Sales Forecast) / (Revenue / Order)
              = ($200,000) / ($1,000) = 200

We now calculate the number of orders for segment 1 using the following equation and the segment sales split for Segment 1 of 50%:

Orders by Segment   = (Total Orders) * (Segment Sales Split)
                      = (200) * (50%) = 100

We multiply the total number of orders for Segment 1 by the campaign sales split for the three different types of campaigns to arrive at the order quantity for the three campaigns:

Orders for Campaign A   = (Orders for Segment 1) * (Campaign Sales Split, Campaign A)
                         = (100) * (40%) = 40

Orders for Campaign B   = (Orders for Segment 1) * (Campaign Sales Split, Campaign B)
                         = (100) * (35%) = 35

Orders for Campaign C   = (Orders for Segment 1) * (Campaign Sales Split, Campaign C)
                         = (100) * (25%) = 25

We now calculate the number of responses we must generate to achieve the quantity of orders we need. We apply the equation to calculate responses, inserting the order quantities and conversion rates for the three different types of campaigns:

Responses   = (Orders) / (Conversion Rate)

Responses, Campaign A = (40) / (2.0%) = 2,000

Responses, Campaign B = (35) / (1.0%) = 3,500

Responses, Campaign C = (25) / (1.5%) = 1,667

We calculate the budget to generate the responses. We apply the equation to calculate the required budget, substituting the total responses and cost per response for the three campaign types:

Budget   = (Responses) * (Cost per Response)

Budget, Campaign A   = (2,000) * ($2.20) = $4,400

Budget, Campaign B   = (3,500) * ($1.00) = $3,500

Budget, Campaign C   = (1,667) * ($1.40) = $2,333

Next, we calculate the sales for Segment 1, as well as the sales for each campaign contributing to the sales for Segment 1. We use the equation to calculate sales by segment, and then insert the campaign sales split percentages to obtain the sales by campaign for that segment:

Sales, Segment 1 (All Campaigns) = (Sales Forecast) * (Segment Sales Split)
= ($200,000) * (50%) = $100,000

Sales, Segment 1, Campaign A = (Sales, Segment 1) * (Campaign Sales Split, Campaign A)
= ($100,000) * (40%) = $40,000

Sales, Segment 1, Campaign B = (Sales, Segment 1) * (Campaign Sales Split, Campaign B)
= ($100,000) * (35%) = $35,000

Sales, Segment 1, Campaign C = (Sales, Segment 1) * (Campaign Sales Split, Campaign C)
= ($100,000) * (25%) = $25,000

We finish the calculations for the results of Segment 1 by determining the budget/ sales ratio for each of the three campaigns. We substitute the values for budget and sales for each of the three campaign types in Segment 1:

Budget/ Sales   = (Budget) / (Sales)

Budget/ Sales, Campaign A   = ($4,400) / ($40,000) = 11.0%

Budget/ Sales, Campaign B   = ($3,500) / ($35,000) = 10.0%

Budget/ Sales, Campaign C   = ($2,333) / ($25,000) = 9.3%

We have now completed the calculations for the results table for Segment 1. We repeat the process to generate the values for the results tables of Segments 2 and 3.

Figure 11.14 summarizes the total results for the three segments (includes results from all three campaigns).

Segment	Orders	Responses	Budget	Sales	Budget/Sales
Segment 1	100	7,167	$10,233	$100,000	10.2%
Segment 2	60	4,300	$6,140	$60,000	10.2%
Segment 3	40	2,867	$4,093	$40,000	10.2%
Total	200	14,333	$20,467	$200,000	10.2% (Ave.)

Figure 11.14: ECommerce Sales Model, Acme.com Example: Summary Results for All Segments

This model has several advantages. First, marketers can quickly and easily use the model to predict the orders, responses, budget, and sales for different market segments. Second, one can compare the predicted results of the model with actual results and make corrective actions if necessary. Third, marketers can change parameters, such as segment sales splits, campaign sales splits, and conversion ratios to calibrate the model to actual behavior to maintain accuracy over time.

The model also has several disadvantages. First, it does not take competition into account. Second, the buying habits of market segments might change over the period of study. Indeed, such factors can definitely occur over the long period (one year) covered by this model. Marketers should keep these issues in mind when applying the model.

MARKETING MADE MEASURABLE

Nordstrom: Evolving to ECommerce: In a trend called "showrooming," consumers go to retail stores to check out products, but then go online to buy them for less. In protest, major retailers such as Best Buy, Target, and Walmart stopped selling Amazon.com Kindle tablets. They figure they do not want to enable showroomers. [11-17]

But analysts do not perceive this protest as a viable long term strategy. They cite that the number of active mobile devices will soon exceed the world's population. Therefore, slowing the sales of Kindle devices will have little impact.

Nordstrom provides an example of successful retailing in the eCommerce world. Instead of fighting the trend, they embrace it. They meet the challenge head on with three steps:

- **Selection:** Online shoppers can access any item in any retail location.
- **Simplicity:** Nordstrom sets up its website so users can quickly find what they seek.
- **Service:** Online shoppers enjoy the same great service Nordstrom retail shoppers have come to enjoy, including liberal return policies.

SALES METRICS

In this section, we examine sales metrics to understand the effectiveness of marketing and sales efforts. Many companies consider sales revenue the most important outcome of marketing efforts, so marketers take sales metrics seriously.

We study sales results in different ways. We analyze overall sales in our chosen market to get a high-level view of our efforts. We also review sales metrics at other levels (at the market segment level, at the product/service level, etc.) to understand our effectiveness in a more detailed fashion. [11-18]

To comprehend sales effectiveness at different levels, we introduce a hierarchy of sales metrics, starting at a high level with sales to entire markets, down to sales to individual customers. Figure 11.15 shows an overview of the different levels.

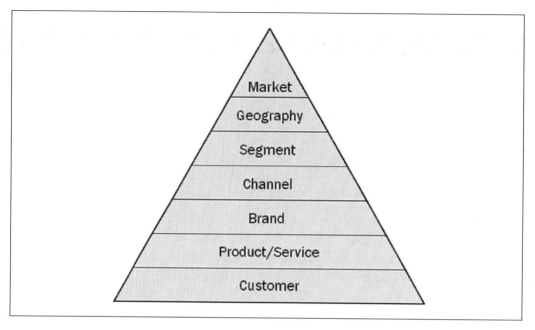

Figure 11.15: Sales Metrics: Hierarchy Overview

We now discuss the different types of metrics for each level in the hierarchy. Each level provides us with different insights into our sales effectiveness. We illustrate the concepts using running examples of Apple products and services.

Sales at Market Level

Market-level sales metrics measure overall sales in a market, such as market share. By examining market-level sales metrics, we can assess our degree of competitiveness.

We can apply several metrics to assess sales at the market level:

Market Share: To determine market share, we divide the sales revenue of the company in a market by the total revenue from that market. Many organizations monitor this popular metric. Experts recommend defining the market very carefully to avoid confusion. For example, marketers can define the applicable market in terms of a list of specific competitors, products/services, geographic areas, or market segments. We calculate market share using the equation below:

$$\text{Market Share} = \frac{\text{(Company Sales Revenue)}}{\text{(Total Market Sales Revenue)}}$$

Relative Market Share: Relative market share emphasizes our degree of competitiveness in a chosen market. It acknowledges that a specific market share level, such as twenty percent, might represent leadership in one market and a weak position in another. We calculate the relative market share using the equation below:

$$\text{Relative Market Share} = \frac{\text{(Company Market Share)}}{\text{(Largest Competitor's Market Share)}}$$

Figure 11.16 shows sample charts for sales metrics to monitor and evaluate sales at the market level. The pie chart on the left illustrates Company A's percentage of the total market. The vertical bar chart on the right displays the market share values for Company A and Company B. Such a bar chart vividly shows how the market shares for the two companies compare.

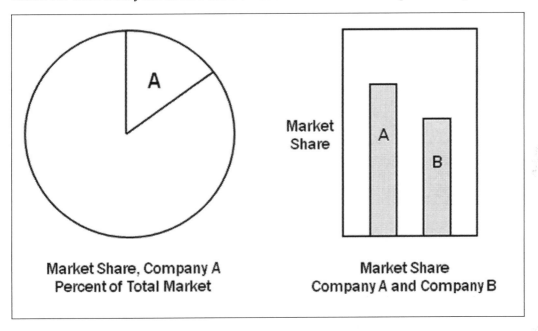

Figure 11.16: Sales Metrics: Sales at Market Level

MARKETING MADE MEASURABLE

Apple: Tablet Market Share Leader: According to Forbes, Apple's 9.7 inch iPad enjoyed a 63% market share for all original equipment manufacturer (OEM) tablet shipments in 2011. By comparison, its competitor Android grew to only 31% by the end of 2011. [11-19]

Forbes noted the highly connected nature of tablets, citing market share-like statistics:

- 100% of tablets have Wi-Fi
- 81% of tablets have Bluetooth
- 27% have mobile broadband (3G/4G)

Sales at Geography Level

Companies doing business internationally track sales into different geographical areas. Many large organizations sell into domestic and international geographies to reduce exposure to risk in any one area. Such a strategy demands strong international operations performance. By examining geography-level sales metrics, we can determine our ability to maintain and grow sales into different geographies.

We can apply several metrics to assess sales at the geography level.

Sales by Geography: We can measure the percentage of sales from each major geographical area served by the organization. This metric provides us with a snapshot of our geographical performance. We calculate sales by geography using the equation below:

$$\text{Sales by Geography} = \frac{(\text{Sales into Geography 1, Geography 2, etc.})}{(\text{Overall Sales})}$$

Growth Rate, Sales by Geography: We can measure our growth rate of sales into different geographical areas. The metric gives us insight into our success in growing operations into our chosen geographical areas. We generally assess the growth rate on an annual basis, also called a Year over Year (YOY) basis.

Growth Rate, Sales by Geography

$$= \frac{[(\text{Sales into Geography at End of Year}) - (\text{Sales into Geography at Beginning of Year})]}{(\text{Sales into Geography at Beginning of Year})}$$

MARKETING MADE MEASURABLE

Apple: Sales by Geography: Apple enjoys significant international sales. It tracks sales by geography to assess its international sales performance. According to Apple's 2011 Form 10-K Annual Report, Apple's sales by geography are as follows: [11-20]

- Americas: 35% of net sales
- Europe: 25% of net sales
- Japan: 5% of net sales
- Asia-Pacific: 20% of net sales

Sales at Segment Level

Earlier in this book, we covered the importance of market segmentation. We can track sales metrics at the segment level to understand how different segments respond to our offerings.

Similar to our study of sales to different geographies, we can examine internally-oriented metrics, such as sales percentages into particular segments, as well as growth rates. Additionally, we can determine externally-oriented metrics, such as comparing company sales in the segment to all sales to the segment (similar to the market share calculation above).

Sales by Segment: We can measure our sales for each of our targeted market segments. The metric provides us with insight into the assessment of our offerings by the different segments. For example, we might find that our services sell much stronger into some segments.

$$\text{Sales by Segment} = \frac{\text{(Sales into Segment 1, Segment 2, etc.)}}{\text{(Overall Sales)}}$$

Growth Rate, Sales by Segment: In addition to total sales into segments, we can examine our growth rate into different segments. The metric offers us insight into the change in demand of different market segments over time.

Growth Rate, Sales by Segment

$$= \frac{[\text{(Sales into Segment at End of Year)} - \text{(Sales into Segment at Beginning of Year)}]}{\text{(Sales into Segment at Beginning of Year)}}$$

MARKETING MADE MEASURABLE

Apple: Sales by Segment: In 2012 Apple offered its new iPad 3 with Retina display to the early adopter market segment, while simultaneously selling its previous model, the iPad 2, for the price-sensitive market segment for $100 less than the previous list price. [11-21]

Sales at Channel Level

Tracking sales of products and services through different distribution channels allows us to compare the effectiveness of each. Distribution channels can include organizations such as company-retail stores, general retail stores, eCommerce sites, and direct sales forces. We track metrics for direct sales forces for business to business sales and high-priced consumer goods, such as real estate. We wish to determine the percentage of sales contributed by each channel. Similar to sales by geography and by segment, we can calculate sales by channel.

Sales by Channel: We measure our sales by different channels, with the goal of determining how each contributes to overall sales.

$$\text{Sales by Channel} = \frac{\text{(Sales by Distribution Channel 1, Channel 2, etc.)}}{\text{(Overall Sales)}}$$

Growth Rate, Sales by Channel: We measure the rate of the different channels to determine our channel sales trends.

Growth Rate, Sales by Channel

$$= \frac{[\text{(Sales by Channel at End of Year)} - \text{(Sales by Channel at Beginning of Year)}]}{\text{(Sales by Channel at Beginning of Year)}}$$

MARKETING MADE MEASURABLE

Apple: Sales by Channel: Apple sells through multiple distribution channels. [11-22]

- **Apple-branded Retail Stores**: Physical Apple Stores
- **Apple-branded Online Stores**: Apple.com, iTunes.com, etc.
- **Apple Catalog & Internet Resellers**: Amazon.com, Frys.com, J&R Computerworld
- **Apple Industry Stores**: Apple Store for Education, Apple Government Stores, etc.
- **Cellular Telephone Service Providers**: AT&T, Verizon, etc.
- **Others:** Apple Corporate Resellers, Apple Value Added Resellers, etc.

According to Apple's Form 10-K Annual Report, filed October 2011, sales through its Apple retail stores accounted for 13.0% of overall sales. [11-23]

Sales at Brand Level

Companies invest considerable time and money developing their brands. The resulting brand equity contributes significantly to company sales. Consumers grow to trust and prefer brands with high brand equity, such as Apple, McDonald's, UPS, and BMW.

We can calculate both internally-focused (sales by brand) and externally-focused (brand penetration) brand metrics.

Sales by Brand: Many organizations own multiple brands. In addition to the over-arching corporate brand, companies maintain brands for individual products and services. We can measure the sales for each brand owned by the company, as they compare to total sales. This metric provides us with an internally-focused metric on the popularity of different brands the company offers.

$$\text{Sales by Brand} = \frac{\text{(Sales by Brand 1, Brand 2, etc.)}}{\text{(Overall Sales)}}$$

Brand Penetration: We can also calculate the degree to which the company's brand has penetrated the market population. In this case, we divide the number of customers who have purchased the company's brand with the number of people in the target market. [11-24]

$$\text{Brand Penetration} = \frac{\text{(Customer Purchasing Brand 1, Brand 2, etc.)}}{\text{(People in Target Market)}}$$

MARKETING MADE MEASURABLE

Apple: Sales by Brand: Forbes magazine reported that the brand equity of Apple climbed to the top position of the brands studied in 2012, to almost $183 billion. In addition to the over-arching Apple brand, we can study brands representing specific product and service lines. For example, we can consider "iPod", "iPhone" and "iPad" as brands representing product lines. [11-25]

We can examine sales by brand to gain a sense of the power of the Apple product line brands. According to Apple's Form 10-K Annual Report, filed in October 2011, Apple cites the following sales by brand: [11-26]

- **iPhone:** Total sales for all models: $47.0 billion
- **iPad:** Total sales for all models: $20.4 billion
- **iPod:** Total sales for all models: $7.5 billion

Sales at Product/Service Level

Organizations commonly report sales at the product or service level for several reasons. First, we need to know how the sales of different products and services compare so we can decide how much money to invest in their development. Second, manufacturers of products need to track product-level sales for production planning. If sales metrics show increasing volumes, manufacturers will need to adjust their production plans to build more units. Similarly, service providers need to track demand for services to determine if they need to build up services capability, such as training additional service personnel. Third, many companies hold their product managers accountable for sales of their products, so we need product/service-level sales to judge their performance.

We can calculate sales at the product/service level by revenue and by units. We examine unit sales because some decisions depend on knowing the number of units. For example, many companies monitor the cost of sales at the unit level.

Sales Revenue by Product/Service: We can calculate the percentage of sales revenue each product or service contributes to overall sales. To do so, we divide the sales revenue of the product or service by total sales.

Sales Revenue by Product/Service

$$= \frac{\text{(Sales Revenue of Product 1, Product 2, etc.)}}{\text{(Overall Sales Revenue)}}$$

Unit Sales by Product/Service: We calculate the percentage of unit sales each product or service contributes to the overall sales by dividing the product/service units over total units.

Unit Sales by Product/Service

$$= \frac{\text{(Unit Sales of Product 1, Product 2, etc.)}}{\text{(Overall Units Sold)}}$$

Figure 11.17 shows sample charts for sales metrics to monitor and evaluate product/service sales performance. The pie chart on the left illustrates the percentage of total sales contributed by each of the company's five products, A, B, C, D, and E. The vertical bar chart on the right displays the individual sales levels for the five products.

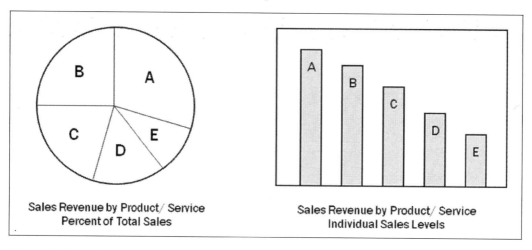

Figure 11.17: Sales Metrics: Sales by Product/Service

MARKETING MADE MEASURABLE

Apple: Sales by Product: In late 2011, Apple sold three products in its iPhone product line. Each product required the consumer to sign up for a new two-year service agreement with a cellular service carrier to obtain the advertised price. The products apply unique feature sets and prices to target different market segments. [11-27]

- **Apple iPhone 4S:** Apple sold its iPhone 4S with Siri voice-recognition for $399 (for its 64GB version) through AT&T, Sprint, and Verizon. The iPhone 4S targeted the early adopter market segment with its advanced features.
- **Apple iPhone 4:** Apple also sold its iPhone 4 for $99 (limited to 8GB of storage) through AT&T, Sprint, and Verizon. The iPhone 4 targeted the mainstream market segment with its balance of strong features and low price.
- **Apple iPhone 3GS:** Apple offered its Apple iPhone 3GS for "free" (again, with a two-year contract) to target price-sensitive late adopters. Unlike the other products, consumers could only obtain the iPhone 3GS through AT&T.

Sales at Customer Level

Some companies benefiting from long-term relationships from customers monitor sales at the customer level. The companies acknowledge dealings with customers as more than transactions. Instead, they seek to assess the value over the lifetime of the customer. We can use a metric called the customer lifetime value to express the total sales revenue expected by particular customers through the lifetime of their relationship with the company. [11-28]

Customer Lifetime Value: This metric captures the dollar value of a customer relationship, projected into the present using the concept of net present value. Net present value uses the time value of money to convert a future series of sales into an equivalent value today. The time value of money acknowledges money values change over time due to the power of compounding interest.

Figure 11.18 shows how we can represent future cash flows from a customer into an equivalent value today.

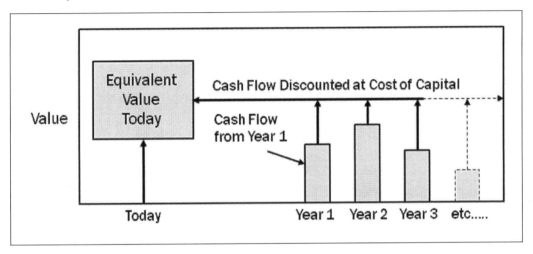

Figure 11.18: Sales Metrics: Net Present Value, Used for Customer Lifetime Value

Use the following equation to calculate customer lifetime value (CLV):

Customer Lifetime Value (CLV) $= \dfrac{\text{Margin} * [(\text{Retention Rate})]}{[1 + (\text{ Discount Rate }) - (\text{ Retention Rate })]}$

The equation uses the following terms:

Margin: Margin represents the amount of money contributed to the organization with each sale. It is calculated by subtracting the cost of sales (such as advertising) from sales revenue.

Retention Rate: Retention rate expresses the degree to which the organization can keep its customers for an extended period. It is calculated by determining the percentage of customers continuing to do business with the company over the time period of the calculation.

Discount Rate: Discount rate states the cost of capital companies use to discount future cash flows. For some companies, the discount rate can be the interest rate they pay on their loans. For other companies, the discount rate can be an internal interest rate they must achieve on their investments. Some companies refer to this rate as a hurdle rate.

MARKETING MADE MEASURABLE

Apple: Customer Loyalty for High Lifetime Value: Apple promotes long-term customer loyalty by producing a stream of innovative products and services. It also offers its One to One personalized training program. The One to One program gives consumers one year of personalized, face-to-face classes at their local Apple retail store. The One to One program offers several advantages to Apple: [11-29]

- First, by providing the training through its retail stores, Apple continues to expose consumers to the Apple brand experience.
- Second, Apple trainers show how multiple Apple products and services work together, thus encouraging additional purchases of new products and services by the consumer.
- Third, Apple trainers continually encourage and motivate consumers during the training sessions, and reinforce the merits of the Apple brand.

Figure 11.19 summarizes sales metrics at each level.

Category	Description	Metrics
By Market	Determining the big picture by measuring sales performance at the market level	Market Share Relative Market Share
By Geography	Measuring sales volumes into different geographical areas	Sales by Geography Growth Rate, Sales by Geography
By Market Segment	Estimating the sales engagement level of different market segments	Sales by Market Segment Growth Rate, Sales by Market Segment
By Channel	Evaluating the go to market sales performance of distribution channels	Sales by Channel Growth Rate, Sales by Channel
By Brand	Assessing popularity of company brands in target markets	Sales by Brand Brand Penetration
By Product/ Service	Measuring sales levels of individual products and services	Sales Revenue by Product/ Service Unit Sales by Product/ Service
By Customer	Assessing potential revenue (and profit) at the customer level	Customer Lifetime Value

Figure 11.19: Sales Metrics: Hierarchy Summary

PROFITABILITY METRICS

In this section, we examine metrics to monitor and evaluate profitability. As we did in the Sales Metrics section, we break profitability metrics into a hierarchy. In the case of profitability, though, we use fewer levels. We use fewer levels because we need both revenue and cost data to calculate profit, and most companies maintain cost information only at certain levels.

For example, virtually every organization collects cost information for the following levels:

- **Company:** Organizations require company-level cost information for financial reports.
- **Channel:** Distribution channel members often track costs of distribution.
- **Products and Service:** Companies require cost at the product/service level for operations.
- **Customer:** Organizations maintain customer data in their customer relationship management systems.

Few companies, however, keep detailed financial cost data at the other levels. Therefore, we focus on the profitability of the company, channel, product/service, and customer levels in this section.

Figure 11.20 shows an overview of the different levels for profitability metrics.

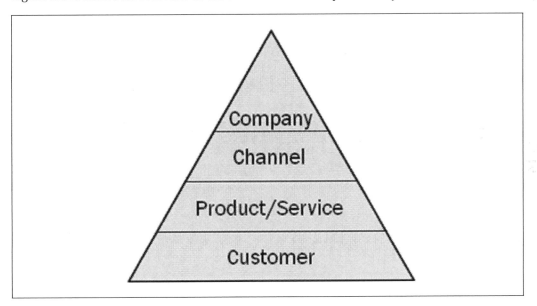

Figure 11.20: Profitability Metrics: Hierarchy Overview

We now discuss the different types of profitability metrics at each level in the hierarchy. Each level provides us with different insights into marketing effectiveness. We discuss popular profitability metrics for each level and illustrate examples using Apple products and services.

Profitability at Company Level

Companies closely monitor profitability at the overall company level. Private companies (companies not traded on public stock exchanges) must track revenue, cost, and profitability data to monitor financial health and complete income tax returns. Public companies must report financial data to the United States Securities and Exchange Commission (SEC).

Marketers are most often interested in gross margin (the amount of money contributed by products and services once the cost of sales has been subtracted) as opposed to total company profitability (which subtracts operating expenses and other expenses from gross margin). Companies leave calculations of total company profitability to finance departments because the calculations of operating expenses and cost allocations are complex and unique to specific company situations. Therefore, we concentrate on gross margin metrics in this section.

Company Gross Margin Amount: Companies often report gross margin both as an amount, expressed in monetary terms, and as a percentage. To calculate the company gross margin amount, subtract the total cost of sales from total sales revenue. We calculate the total cost of sales by summing the total amount of direct material, direct labor, and company overhead incurred in producing company products and services. We can show the calculations in equation form: [11-30]

$$\text{Company Gross Margin Amount} = (\text{Total Sales}) - (\text{Total Cost of Sales})$$

Company Gross Margin Percentage: To calculate the gross margin percentage, we divide the gross margin amount by total sales.

$$\text{Company Gross Margin Percentage} = \frac{(\text{Company Gross Margin Amount})}{(\text{Total Sales})}$$

MARKETING MADE MEASURABLE

Apple: Company Gross Margin: According to the Apple Form 10-K Annual Report filed on October 2011, Apple enjoyed a company-wide gross margin percentage of 40.5%.

Apple calculated its gross margin percentage by subtracting its cost of sales of $64.4 billion from its net sales of $108 to arrive at a gross margin amount of $43.8 billion, and then divided the gross margin amount by the net sales.

Apple incurred about $10.0 billion in operating expenses (including research and development and selling, general and administrative costs), as well as about $8.3 billion in income taxes, to arrive at a net income (profitability) of $25.9 billion for 2011. [11-31]

Profitability at Channel Level

Companies with networks of distribution channels (such as manufacturers of consumer goods) monitor and evaluate profitability at the channel level.

Channel Margins: As we saw in the Distribution Analytics chapter, the sale of goods to consumers involves multiple channel members, such as distributors, wholesalers, and retailers. Each member charges for their value-added services by marking up the product with a margin.

Each member considers the next member in the distribution chain as their "customer." Thus, wholesalers consider retailers as their customers. Conversely, retailers consider wholesalers as their "suppliers." Therefore, we use the terms "customer" and "supplier" when calculating channel margin metrics.

We can calculate the price at each point in the chain using the following formulas: [11-32]

$$\text{Customer Selling Price} = \frac{(\text{Supplier Selling Price})}{[1 - (\text{Customer Margin Percentage})]}$$

$$\text{Customer Selling Price} = (\text{Supplier Selling Price}) + (\text{Customer Margin Amount})$$

$$\text{Supplier Selling Price} = (\text{Customer Selling Price}) - (\text{Customer Margin Amount})$$

The equations use the following variables:

- **Customer Selling Price**: The price for which the distribution channel member sells its products to the next member in the distribution chain (its customer).

- **Supplier Selling Price**: The price the distribution channel member pays to acquire the product.

- **Customer Margin Amount**: The monetary amount (such as dollars or Euros) the channel member charges to move the product through their channel.

- **Customer Margin Percentage**: The percentage markup the channel member charges to move the product through their channel.

Example: Acme Cosmetics manufactures and sells its green tea-enriched wrinkle cream through a distribution channel consisting of a distributor, a wholesaler, and a retailer. The retail price of the cream is $10.00. Each channel member expects to make money from the product because of the value they add. The money comes from the margin each member takes from the retail sales of the product. We can show how the "chain of margins" affects the cost for which the manufacturer must make the product.

- **Retailer**: The retailer sells the Acme wrinkle cream to consumers for $10.00. It adds the value of stocking, displaying, and selling the merchandise. In return, it expects to generate a margin of 40% of the cost to its customer (the consumer).
    - **Supplier Selling Price:**
      In our case, we assume that the consumer does not resell the wrinkle cream to others, so the notion of "supplier selling price" here is not applicable.
    - **Margin:** The margin amount is thus $4.00 (40% * $10.00 = $4.00).

- **Wholesaler**: The wholesaler supplies the cream to its customer, the retailer. In this case, the wholesaler acts as the supplier, and the retailer acts as the customer. We can calculate the supplier selling price (the amount the wholesaler charges the retailer for the product) using the following equation:
    - **Supplier Selling Price:**
      Supplier Selling Price = (Customer Selling Price) – (Customer Margin Amount)
      In our case:
      Wholesaler Selling Price = (Retailer Selling Price) – (Retailer Margin Amount)
      Therefore:
      Supplier Selling Price = ($10.00) – ($4.00) = $6.00
      Thus, the wholesaler (the supplier, in this instance) sells the cream to its customer (the retailer) for $6.00.
    - **Margin:** The wholesaler adds value by purchasing large quantities of goods from various producers, warehousing them, and reselling them to retailers. For its services, it expects to generate a margin of 25% of the cost to its customer (the retailer). The margin amount is thus $1.50 (25% * $6.00 = $1.50).

- **Distributor:** The distributor supplies the cream to its customer, the wholesaler. Here, the distributor acts as the supplier, and the wholesaler acts as the customer. We can calculate the supplier selling price using the equation:
    - **Supplier Selling Price:**
      Supplier Selling Price = (Customer Selling Price) – (Customer Margin Amount)
      In our case:
      Supplier Selling Price = ($6.00) – ($1.50) = $4.50
    - **Margin:** The distributor adds value by distributing goods for manufacturers. Distributors differ from wholesalers in that distributors carry many different items, whereas wholesalers carry large quantities of fewer items. For its services, the distributor expects to generate a margin of 20% of the cost to its customer (the wholesaler). The margin amount is $0.90 (20% * $4.50 = $0.90)

- **Manufacturer**: The manufacturer supplies the cream to its customer, the distributor. We can calculate the supplier selling price using the equation:
    - **Supplier Selling Price:**
      Supplier Selling Price = (Customer Selling Price) – (Customer Margin Amount)
      In our case:
      Supplier Selling Price = ($4.50) – ($0.90) = $3.60
    - **Margin:** The manufacturer adds value by making the product. For its services, the manufacturer expects to generate a margin of 50% of the cost to its customer (the distributor). The margin amount is $1.65 (50% * $3.60 = $1.80).

Therefore, if the manufacturer expects to make a 50% margin, it must not exceed a manufacturing cost of $1.80, which appears quite low for a $10.00 jar of wrinkle cream. This steep reduction is common for consumer goods, which pass through multiple channel members before they reach the hands of consumers. Because of high channel costs, many manufacturers prefer to sell with direct channels (such as company-owned Internet sites) which sell directly to consumers.

Profitability at Product/Service Level

Companies routinely monitor and analyze profitability of their products and services. Marketers measure the contribution each unit of product or service makes to profit. The contribution is the sales revenue from the unit less the cost incurred to make it. We call this contribution the unit margin. Just as with gross margin at the company level, we can express unit margins as amounts (in monetary terms, such as dollars or Euros) or percentages. [11-33]

Unit Margin Amount: To get the unit margin, we subtract the cost per unit from the selling price of the unit. We calculate the unit margin amount using the equation below.

$$\text{Unit Margin Amount} = (\text{Selling Price per Unit}) - (\text{Cost per Unit})$$

Unit Margin Percentage: To calculate the unit margin percentage, we divide the unit margin amount by the selling price per unit.

$$\text{Unit Margin Percentage} = \frac{(\text{Unit Margin Amount})}{(\text{Selling Price per Unit})}$$

MARKETING MADE MEASURABLE

Apple: Unit Margin: Apple does not publicly reveal unit margins for each of its products and services. In its Form 10-K Annual Report filed in October 2011, Apple states that its overall gross margin percentage is 40.5%.

The report mentions that its iPad product line suffered from lower gross margins than the average because it had higher cost structures. The report also explains that the iPhone product line enjoyed higher gross margins than the company average. [11-34]

According to CNET (cnet.com), Apple generated gross margins of 49% to 58% on United States iPhone sales between April 2010 and March 2012. The Apple iPad generated lower margins, estimated at 23% to 32% between October 2010 and March 2012. [11-35]

Profitability at Customer Level

Companies seeking to benefit from long-term relationships with customers calculate and monitor profitability at the customer level. The customer profit metric indicates which customers profit the organization and which do not. Gathering data at the customer level is not trivial. Companies will benefit from customer relationship management (CRM) systems to collect revenues and costs for each customer. [11-36]

Customer Profit: To calculate customer profit, subtract the total cost to serve each customer from the revenue generated from the customer. We express the concept in the equation below:

$$Customer\ Profit = (Customer\ Revenue) - (Customer\ Cost)$$

Once we calculate profit at the customer level, we quickly find that some customers profit organizations more than others. Some customers generate significant amounts of profit, while others actually cost the company money in the long run. We therefore waste money if we treat each customer the same. We want to encourage our profitable customers to stay with us, and discourage the unprofitable ones from doing so. With customer profit data, we can structure the customer base into three levels:

- **High Profitability Customers**: The most profitable customers represent a valuable asset to the organization. Losing high profitability customers to competitors can substantially reduce profitability. Therefore, companies should reward their continued loyalty. For example, airlines reward top level frequent flyers with free upgrades and other incentives.

- **Medium Profitability Customers**: Companies should encourage customers with middle-level profitability to ascend up to the top level. For example, airlines frequently remind travelers about the perks of their top tier elite frequent flyer programs, so that travelers will aspire to grow to that level.

- **Low Profitability Customers**: Companies lose money on low profitability customers. They can cost more to serve than the customers generate in revenue. Companies can take two actions with this tier of customers. First, it can reduce the cost of service by servicing them through low-cost channels such as the Internet, or by charging extra for some services. For example, some airlines charge bottom level customers extra to access the airplane's wireless Internet service, while top level customers enjoy free usage. Second, companies should identify common characteristics of bottom level customers and avoid acquiring such customers in the future.

Figure 11.21 shows the concept of the hierarchical approach to customer profitability.

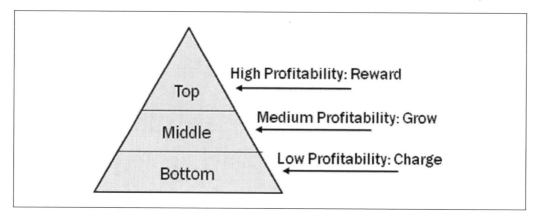

Figure 11.21: Customer Profit: Hierarchical Approach to Customer Care

MARKETING MADE MEASURABLE

Apple: Customer Profit: As part of its decision to carry the Apple iPhone, cell phone service carrier Sprint (sprint.com) considered potential customer profitability. [11-37]

Sprint CEO Dan Hesse found that users of the iPhone yielded a higher potential profit than users of competing Android-based smartphones. Mr. Hesse cited two reasons for higher potential profitability.

- First, iPhone customers exhibited lower churn rates (i.e., they tended to stay with the carrier longer), resulting in higher revenues over the customer's expected lifetime.
- Second, iPhone customers use less data on average than other smartphone customers using premium 4G Android-based devices.

Figure 11.22 summarizes profitability metrics at each level.

Category	Description	Metrics
By Company	Determining the big picture by measuring profitability at the company level	Company Gross Margin Amount Company Gross Margin %
By Channel	Evaluating the go to market profit performance of distribution channels	Channel Margins
By Product/ Service	Measuring the profitability of individual products and services	Unit Margin Amount Unit Margin Percentage
By Customer	Assessing the potential profit at the customer level	Customer Profit

Figure 11.22: Profitability Metrics: Hierarchy Summary

SUPPORT METRICS

Companies rarely hold marketing departments accountable for customer support. Nevertheless, marketers can benefit by monitoring support metrics that can affect sales. Rather than cover every possible support metric, we focus our efforts on two selected metrics—customer satisfaction and the Net Promoter Score. We discuss the metrics and provide illustrative examples using Apple products and services.

Customer Satisfaction

Companies seeking to maintain long-term relationships with customers know that customer satisfaction represents an important driver for future sales. To that end, many companies measure customer satisfaction to assess how well they have fulfilled customers' expectations. In addition, companies have found that customers' likelihood to recommend the brand to their friends provides another good indicator into customer satisfaction level. [11-38]

Customer Satisfaction: Companies measure customer satisfaction as the percentage of customers whose survey ratings of experiences with the brand exceed specified satisfaction goals. Many surveys use a standard five point scale:

- **Very Satisfied**: Also called the top box, this maximum score represents the peak of customer satisfaction.
- **Somewhat Satisfied**: Marketers often report this score, as well as the Very Satisfied responses, as the top two boxes.
- **Neither Satisfied nor Dissatisfied**: This box represents a neutral rating.
- **Somewhat Dissatisfied**: This box indicates a fair amount of dissonance between the customers' expectations and the company's ability to deliver.
- **Very Dissatisfied**: This box signals major problems in the company's ability to meet customers' expectations for the brand.

Willingness to Recommend: Some companies also measure the percentage of surveyed customers who indicate that they would recommend the company to their friends. Such surveys often apply the same five-point scale used for customer satisfaction measurements.

Companies find several difficulties in measuring customer satisfaction and applying it to predict future customer behavior. First, many surveys suffer from response bias. In response bias, survey scores do not represent the total population because only very irate (or very pleased) customers feel motivated to respond to a survey. Second, satisfaction scores could increase because dissatisfied customers are leaving the brand. Third, customer expectations could rise over time, leading to a gradual erosion of scores.

MARKETING MADE MEASURABLE

Apple: Customer Satisfaction: The American Customer Satisfaction Index (ACSI) tracks consumer feelings toward consumer electronics and appliances.

In 2011, Apple's Macintosh computer product line earned a score of 87 out of a possible 100, the top score for all personal computer (PC) manufacturers. With the 2011 high score, Apple remained in the first rank of all PC makers for the eighth year in a row.

In addition, Apple took the top spot in a J.D. Power study on customer satisfaction with smartphone makers. [11-39]

Net Promoter Score

Frederick R. Reichheld developed the Net Promoter Score (NPS) to capture the relatively complex notion of customer satisfaction in a single number. Mr. Reichheld, together with Bain & Company and Satmetrix, holds a registered trademark for the term. [11-40]

Net Promoter Score: To calculate the net promoter score, companies issue surveys to their customers. The surveys ask customers how likely they are to recommend the company or brand to a friend or colleague. The company collects the responses and divides them into three tiers:

- **Promoters**: The Net Promoter Score defines promoters as customers who provide a score of 9 or 10 (highly likely to recommend).

- **Detractors:** The NPS defines detractors as customers giving a score of 6 or less (not likely to highly unlikely to recommend).

- **Passives**: Passives represent the remaining customers, somewhat satisfied but unenthusiastic over the brand, with scores of 7 or 8.

Figure 11.23 illustrates the concept.

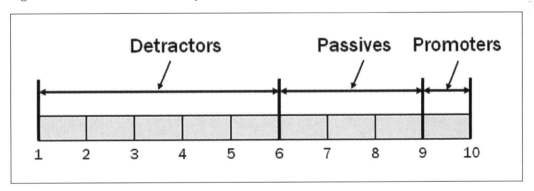

Figure 11.23: Support Metrics: Net Promoter Score

The Net Promoter Score applies the following formula:

Net Promoter Score = (Percentage of Promoters) – (Percentage of Detractors)

High Net Promoter Score values suggest high degrees of customer satisfaction. Conversely, low NPS scores signal trouble. Companies should monitor their NPS values over time to detect any trends in customer satisfaction.

The advantage of the Net Promoter Score is that it summarizes the complex concept of customer satisfaction in a single metric. The disadvantage of the score is that it suffers from the same problems as traditional customer satisfaction surveys, namely, response bias, population changes due to defecting customers, and increasing customer expectations.

MARKETING MADE MEASURABLE

Apple: Net Promoter Score: PC Magazine (pcmag.com) holds its annual Readers' Choice Awards to understand which brands its readers like best. In 2010, it asked readers if they would recommend certain brands to friends and colleagues. They applied the findings to create Net Promoter Scores for popular brands.

Apple earned the highest Net Promoter Score in several categories:

- Notebook computers: Best score, at 81%
- Desktop computers: Best score, at 79%
- Cell phone operating systems: Best score, at 66%
- Network routers: Best score, at 73%
- Media players (such as iPod): Best score, at 58%

Some other brands scored well, but none scored so well in so many categories. Some brands even showed negative Net Promoter Score results, meaning that they had many more unhappy customers than happy ones. [11-41]

Figure 11.24 summarizes our selected customer support metrics.

Category	Description	Metrics
Customer Satisfaction	Determining the percentage of customers whose customer satisfaction ratings exceed specified goals	Customer Satisfaction Likelihood to Recommend
Net Promoter Score	Predicting future customer satisfaction and loyalty	Net Promoter Score

Figure 11.24: Selected Support Metrics: Summary

SUMMARY

By analyzing each step of the sales process, we can gain understanding of sales opportunities. Many companies evaluate marketing performance by measuring sales growth, so the ability to analyze sales is an important area for marketing analysts to master.

In this chapter, we covered analytic models and metrics for sales, including an analysis of the consumer sales process, an eCommerce sales model, and metrics for sales, profitability, and support.

Consumer Sales Process: We can break down the consumer sales process into steps. At each step, we study how we can measure our sales effectiveness and identify actions to improve it. We identify five steps in the process:

- **Problem Description**: In the problem description stage, the consumer recognizes a problem and decides they want to solve it. We can improve sales effectiveness at this step by surveying people in our target market and determine how many associate our product or service as solutions to problems such as theirs.

- **Information Search**: In the information search stage, consumers gather information to make their decision. We can improve sales effectiveness at this step by ensuring that consumers can readily access information about our products and services.

- **Evaluation of Alternatives**: In the third stage, consumers apply the information they gathered in the previous step to evaluate the alternatives that face them. We can improve sales effectiveness at this step by framing the evaluation criteria to benefit the company.

- **Purchase Decision**: Here, the consumer decides on specific areas of the purchase, such as brand, retail store, quantity, timing, and payment method. We can improve sales effectiveness at this step by surveying our target market and asking them to evaluate those specific areas.

- **Post-Purchase Behavior**: After the sale, consumers might feel dissatisfied. They wonder if they made the right choice. We can reduce the feeling of dissatisfaction by following up with the customer and settling any issues they might have with the product or service.

ECommerce Sales Model: We developed an eCommerce model to predict our sales by segment, our required marketing budget, and our resulting spend/sales ratio. As inputs to the model, we need the sales forecast (the amount of revenue we expect to make in the next year), the average revenue per order (also known as order size), the percentage of total sales per market segment, the percentage of sales per marketing campaign, the campaign conversion rate, and the cost per response. We can execute the model using standard spreadsheet programs.

Sales Metrics: We examine sales metrics to understand the effectiveness of marketing and sales efforts. We recommend examining the following hierarchy of sales metrics:

- Sales at market level, such as market share
- Sales at geography level, such as sales by region
- Sales at segment level, such as sales by segment
- Sales at channel level, such as sales by channel
- Sales at brand level, such as brand penetration
- Sales at product/service level, such as unit sales
- Sales at customer level, such as customer lifetime value

Profitability Metrics: We examine profitability metrics to assess the contribution our products and services are making to the financial success of the organization. As with sales metrics, we recommend considering a hierarchy of profitability metrics:

- Profitability at company level, such as company gross margin
- Profitability at channel level, such as channel margins
- Profitability at product/service level, such as unit margins
- Profitability at customer level, such as customer profit

Support Metrics: Although companies rarely hold marketing functions accountable for customer support, we still recommend tracking support metrics. Quality of support can greatly affect sales. We recommend tracking the following groups of metrics:

- Customer satisfaction, such as surveys of customers using the brand
- Net Promoter Score, which uses a proprietary method to assess satisfaction

Terminology

Brand Penetration: Sales metric assessing the degree to which the company's brand has penetrated (sold into) the market population.

Competitive De-Positioning: Technique used for framing consumer evaluation criteria to benefit the company. Competitive de-positioning refers to altering beliefs about competitors' brands.

Cost of Sales: Direct material and labor costs for producing goods or delivering services. Does not include indirect costs such as sales force costs.

Customer Profit: Contribution provided by each customer, calculated by subtracting the total cost to service each customer from the total revenue they earn for the organization.

Discount Rate: The cost of capital companies use to discount future cash flows.

Gross Margin Amount: Monetary contribution of products and services per unit sold.

Gross Margin Percentage: Gross margin amount divided by total sales.

Net Promoter Score: Proprietary method to capture customer satisfaction as a single number; asks customers about their likelihood to recommend the company or brand to a friend or colleague.

Post-Purchase Dissonance (PPD): Perceived dissatisfaction after purchasing a new product or service.

Psychological Repositioning: Technique used for framing consumer evaluation criteria to benefit the company. Psychological re-repositioning refers to altering beliefs about the product, service, or brand.

Real Repositioning: Technique used for framing consumer evaluation criteria to benefit the company. Real repositioning refers to redesigning product or service to make it suit customer needs.

Retention Rate: The degree to which an organization can keep its customers for an extended period, such as one year.

Class Discussion
1. What decision process steps do you take when you shop for a new product or service?
2. How has the Internet changed the consumer sales process?
3. What post-purchases dissonance scenarios have you experienced?
4. On the eCommerce sales model, why do we split out sales by different segments?
5. How should the measurement period change as we go down the sales metric hierarchy? In other words, should we be assessing sales at market level with the same frequency as sales at the product/service level?
6. What are some actions we can take to increase customer lifetime value?
7. How are customer lifetime value and customer profit related?
8. What are some actions we can take to improve our Net Promoter Score?

Practice Problems
1. Develop a spreadsheet-based eCommerce sales model, using the textbook as a guide. Calculate the expected quarterly sales for the following scenario (each value constant over four quarters): Sales forecast: $100,000; Average revenue per order: $1,500; Segment sales split, segment 1: 40%; Segment sales split, segment 2: 35%; Segment sales split, segment 3: 25%. The campaign input data includes the following information: Direct marketing: 40% sales split, with a 2% conversion rate, and a $3.00 cost per response; Pay per click marketing: 30% sales split, with a 1% conversion rate, and a $4.00 cost per response; Social networking marketing: 30% sales split, with a 1.5% conversion rate, and a $2.50 cost per response.
2. Calculate Company A's relative market share if its sales are $1,000,000, its largest competitor's sales are $800,000, and the market size is $10,000,000.
3. Determine the customer lifetime value for a margin of $100, a retention rate of 99%, and a discount rate of 10%.
4. Company A sold 1,000 units of Service A. Company A surveyed its customers asking them if they would recommend Service A to their friends. The survey showed that 20% of respondents scored 9 – 10 (on a 10 point scale), 50% scored between 7 and 8, and 30% scored 6 or lower. How would you interpret the result?

Chapter 12.

ANALYTICS IN ACTION

Chapter Outline

We cover the following marketing analytics topics in this chapter:

- ☑ **Rapid Decision Models**: Easing the way into an analytics mindset
- ☑ **Metrics in Marketing Campaigns**: Citing metrics in marketing campaigns
- ☑ **Excel Excellence**: Converting data into drama
- ☑ **Data-Driven Presentations**: Influencing decision-makers

"Knowledge is of no value unless you put it into practice."
– Anton Chekhov

Literary critics acknowledge Russian physician and writer Anton Chekhov as one of Russia's greatest writers. They say he single-handedly revolutionized both the drama and the short story. His plays "Uncle Vanya" and "The Cherry Orchard" garnered acclaim.

Chekhov abandoned the traditional story structure. Instead, he told stories through an early use of the stream of consciousness technique. James Joyce and other modernists would later adopt this technique.

Chekhov exhibited a deep insight into human emotion, and "put his knowledge into practice" with such subtlety that readers often find it difficult to decide whether a particular work is a comedy or a tragedy. In fact, by the time of his death, the Russian public regarded him second in literary celebrity only to Leo Tolstoy. [12-1]

This chapter discusses how to set analytics in action. It shows marketers how they can incorporate models and metrics into their daily routine. Marketers do not need to limit their use of models and metrics to major strategic situations. Instead, they can take advantage of the power of marketing analytics in their everyday professional lives.

To that end, this chapter reviews several sections. The first section covers developing fast, easy decision models to quickly demonstrate the power of analytics in their organization. The second shows how to form campaigns applying metrics in the ad. The third section discusses modeling and graphic tips using Microsoft Excel. The fourth section covers how to craft data-driven presentations to influence decision-makers.

RAPID DECISION MODELS

The models shown thus far in the book serve marketers well for strategic marketing decisions. But some might find few occasions to use strategic models, and desire models for more everyday uses. In addition, some marketers may long for a fast, easy to build models to introduce their organization to marketing analytics. To that end, we present three such models in this section.

The first model uses Pareto prioritization analysis to identify important market segments on which to focus our efforts. The second model boosts sales of related goods and services (called "cross-selling") by studying patterns of sales to date. The third model provides a framework with which to select a new business partner or supplier, such as a public relations agency.

Pareto Prioritization Analysis Model

In this section, we show to use the Pareto prioritization analysis model to identify important market segments.

The analysis technique is named after Vilfredo Pareto, an Italian engineer, sociologist, economist, political scientist and philosopher. Pareto observed that 80% of the land in Italy was owned by 20% of the population. Therefore, we sometimes refer to the Pareto approach as the 80 – 20 Rule, to indicate that a majority percentage of results (80%) are often caused by a minority percentage of drivers (20%). [12-2]

In marketing, we often find that 80% of company sales result from just 20% of market segments. The 20% can come from different types of market segments: [12-3]

- **Demographic Segments**: Demographic segments can have different ages, incomes, or industries. For example, younger age groups account for most download-based music sales.

- **Geographic Segments**: Geographic segments involve different physical locations, such as specific cities or towns. For example, people in coastal areas purchase more surfboards and wetsuits than those living inland.

- **Behavioral Segments**: Behavioral segments include groups of people who vary in their consumption behavior. For example, 20% of the population (heavy beer drinkers) account for the majority of beer sales (close to 80%).

- **Psychographic Segments:** Psychographic segments include groups of people with different attitudes, opinions, and beliefs. For example, people with beliefs about healthy lifestyles are more likely to purchase organic produce.

We now demonstrate the process using an example. Figure 12.1 shows a typical customer data set. The data set includes the customer's name, the amount of sales they have done with the organization, their age, their geography, and available psychographic information. In our example, Alex Alpha has generated $1,100 for the organization, is 25 years in age, hails from Atlanta, and when asked about his favorite animal, answered "aardvarks."

Name	Sales	Demographics	Geography	Psychographics
Alex Alpha	$1,100	Age 25	Atlanta	Aardvark lover
Betty Beta	$100	Age 44	Boston	Bat lover
Debbie Delta	$300	Age 35	Denver	Dog lover
Edie Epsilon	$200	Age 38	El Paso	Egret lover
Gary Gamma	$1,300	Age 24	Galveston	Goose lover

Figure 12.1: Pareto Prioritization Analysis: Original Customer Data

We want to determine which segmentation variable (demographic, geographic, or psychographic) accounts for the most change in sales. We sort the data using the sales variable, from high sales to low sales. We sort by sales because it acts as the dependent variable. Figure 12.2 shows the resulting table.

Name	Sales	Demographics	Geography	Psychographics
Gary Gamma	$1,300	Age 24	Galveston	Goose lover
Alex Alpha	$1,100	Age 25	Atlanta	Aardvark lover
Debbie Delta	$300	Age 35	Denver	Dog lover
Edie Epsilon	$200	Age 38	El Paso	Egret lover
Betty Beta	$100	Age 44	Boston	Bat lover
Total Sales	$3,000			

Figure 12.2: Pareto Prioritization Analysis: Sorted Customer Data

As the figure shows, sales for all customers totaled $3,000. Sales for the top two customers (Gary and Alex) totaled $2,400. This value accounts for 80% of all sales ($2,400 / $3,000 = 80%). We can study how different demographic, geographic, and psychographic characteristics affect sales. Geography does not appear to change sales results, because our top two customers live quite far from each other. Psychographics does not play much of a role, either, because they prefer quite different animals.

But we do see a correlation with demographics, in this case age. We see that our top two customers represent the 20 – 25 year old age group, whereas the other customers do not. Therefore, based on the data shown, we should concentrate our marketing efforts on the 20 – 25 year old market segment.

Cross-Sales Model

Many organizations sell related products and services. These organizations have the opportunity of increasing total sales by cross-sales of certain products and services.

Figure 12.3 shows a typical scenario. It shows a customer (represented by a shopping cart) purchasing Product A and considering the purchases of related products and services Product B and Service C. For example, the customer could purchase a smartphone (Product A), along with a smartphone case (related Product B) and an accidental breakage warranty service (Service C).

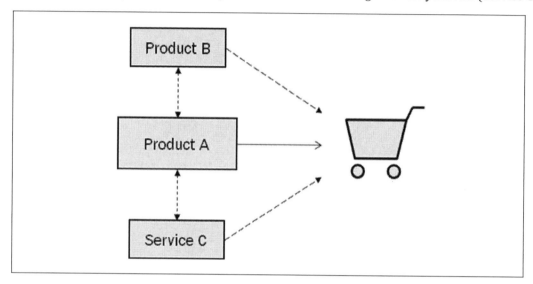

Figure 12.3: Cross-Sales Model: Typical Cross-Sell Scenario

For example, eCommerce retailer Amazon.com increases total sales by suggesting products related to the principal product for which the shopper is shopping. Amazon.com indicates the relation by stating, "Those that purchased [principal product] also purchased [suggested related products]."

Figure 12.4 re-examines the sales data we analyzed earlier. We see total sales for each shopper in the left column. The total sales represents the sum of sales for Product A, Product B, and Service C, shown in the right columns. Product A represents the company's principal offering. The company also sells related offerings Product B and Service C.

Name	Sales, Total	Sales, Product A	Sales, Product B	Sales, Service C
Alex Alpha	$1,100	$600	$300	$200
Betty Beta	$100	$0	$100	$0
Gary Gamma	$1,300	$800	$300	$200
Debbie Delta	$300	$0	$300	$0
Edie Epsilon	$200	$0	$200	$0

Figure 12.4: Cross-Sales Analysis: Related Product and Service Sales Data

As we saw in the Pareto prioritization analysis example earlier, we can more easily discern patterns by first sorting by the variable of interest. In this case, we sort by total sales to identify what the top customers purchase. Figure 12.5 shows the result. Alternatively, if the organization desires to stimulate sales for a certain product, such as Product B, we could sort by sales of that product instead to determine which products cross-sold with it.

Name	Sales, Total	Sales, Product A	Sales, Product B	Sales, Service C
Gary Gamma	$1,300	$800	$300	$200
Alex Alpha	$1,100	$600	$300	$200
Debbie Delta	$300	$0	$300	$0
Betty Beta	$100	$0	$100	$0
Edie Epsilon	$200	$0	$200	$0

Figure 12.5: Cross-Sales Analysis: Data Sorted by Total Sales

The figure presents some clear cross-sales patterns:

- 50% ($600/$1200) of Product B sales comes from cross-sales with Product A. Therefore, cross-sales represent a significant source of sales revenue for the organization.

- Service C only sells when customers purchase Product A and Product B. Therefore, we should not market Service C alone, but rather in conjunction with Product A and Product B.

- Our top customers (identified earlier as age 20 – 25) regard Product B and Service C as essential related products. Therefore, cite Products A, B, and C in our messaging to 20-25.

The analyses are quick to execute and can result in significant potential incremental revenue.

Supplier Selection Framework

In this section, we present a framework to select marketing-related suppliers (sometimes called vendors). We have found the framework presented here to be fair, fast, and effective.

Figure 12.6 shows a typical scenario. An organization decides to outsource the public relations (PR) function. The organization invites three agencies (PR Agency 1, PR Agency 2, and PR Agency 3) to present their capabilities to the marketing managers.

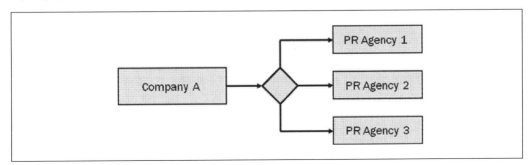

Figure 12.6: Supplier Selection Framework: Typical Scenario

In such a situation, we recommend the usage of a supplier selection framework as shown in Figure 12.7. The figure shows a list of selection criteria in the first column, with ratings for each of the three suppliers in the remaining columns. The marketer must determine the selection criteria before evaluating the suppliers. Indeed, this step represents the most difficult aspect. We recommend carefully evaluating how "success" is defined for this function to help guide the selection of the criteria. Criteria will vary with the situation.

Once the marketer has established the selection criteria, she applies them to each supplier. For example, we can rate each criterion on a 1 to 10 scale, where 1 represents completely unacceptable performance and 10 signifies perfect performance. In the figure, we designate the ratings, along with comments in parentheses noting the reasoning behind the score. In a spreadsheet implementation, we recommend dedicating a separate column for the rating values for ease in summing the total scores.

Once we have established the rating for each supplier, we tally the scores to find a winner. We face different ways to sum the scores:

- **Straight Sum**: We can simply add the scores to find the total, and declare the supplier with the most points as the winner. For example, we show the total scores in the figure using straight sums.

- **Modified Sum**: We can sum the scores, as in the first approach. But we can automatically disqualify a supplier if they fail in any one important category. For example, PR Agency 1 scored a 1 (unacceptable performance) in Cost Structure, which could disqualify it from contention even if its total score turns out high otherwise.

- **Weighted Sum**: In this approach, we weight each selection criterion to adjust its significance in the final decision. We select individual weights so that the total does not exceed 100% for the entire set of criteria. For example, we could assign 25% for Industry Contacts and 25% for Cost Structure to acknowledge their high importance, 20% for Social Media Expertise to signify a medium-level importance, and 10% each for the remaining three, for a total of 100%.

Selection Criteria	PR Agency 1: Large PR Agency	PR Agency 2: Midsize PR Agency	PR Agency 3: Small PR Agency
Industry Contacts	8 (Many new contacts)	6 (Out of date)	8 (Many new contacts)
Social Media Expertise	8 (Strong focus)	5 (Not a focus)	5 (Some experience)
Article Opportunities	5 (Not a focus)	5 (Not a focus)	8 (Strong experience)
Award Opportunities	5 (Not a focus)	8 (Strong experience)	5 (Some experience)
Crisis Management	8 (Many resources)	3 (No focus)	5 (Some focus)
Cost Structure	1 (Very expensive)	3 (Expensive)	7 (Reasonable)
Total Scores	*35*	*30*	*38*

Figure 12.7: Supplier/ Partner Selection Framework

MARKETING MADE MEASURABLE

Entrepreneur Magazine: Supplier Selection Criteria Recommendations: Startup company resource Entrepreneur magazine (entrepreneur.com) recognizes that suppliers can turn into valued partners. Effective suppliers can help companies cut costs, improve on product designs, and contribute to the company's marketing efforts. Therefore, companies should take care in how they select the suppliers with which they work. [12-4]

Entrepreneur recommends the following supplier selection criteria:

- **Price:** Company budgets often specify acceptable prices for supplier services. Suppliers must fall within the acceptable price range for companies to select them.
- **Reliability:** Companies often value reliability in their suppliers. An inexpensive but unreliable supplier is no bargain. Some companies prefer larger suppliers due to the reliability-enhancing backup systems bigger suppliers can offer.
- **Stability:** Look for a long track record of success and well-tenured senior executives to ensure high stability, Entrepreneur states. Also look for telltale signs of poor stability, such as supplier deliverables arriving ahead of schedule. Such early shipments suggest the company is in trouble, and needs to accelerate its cash inflows.
- **Location:** Companies find it easier to work with nearby suppliers. Not only can nearby suppliers offer faster service, they might be able to deliver free shipping as well.
- **Competency:** Finally, look for signs that point to high competency. Signs include advanced products and services, well-trained employees, and flexibility in operations, such as providing different finance options.

METRICS IN MARKETING CAMPAIGNS

So far, this book has covered how to apply metrics to monitor and diagnose marketing efforts. In this section, we extend the discussion to show how marketers can cite metrics in the headline or body copy of an email or other marketing communications vehicle to gain attention.

Numbers stand out like a red rowboat in a blue sea of text. Some people believe that numbers can add credibility to an argument. Most importantly, numbers can motivate people to act, which is our goal as marketers. In fact, entrepreneur resource Inc. magazine found that metrics can be more motivating than bonuses. [12-5]

The first step in the approach is to find a bold metric that supports the goals of the campaign. The metric should cause the target audience to gasp in amazement. Brief scans of current events on the Internet will give one ample metrics for the approach. [12-6]

Figure 12.8 lists several sample bold metrics and some possible campaign applications. Of course, we can add many other potential applications to the list. [12-7, 12-8, 12-9, 12-10, 12-11, 12-12, 12-13, 12-14, 12-15, 12-16]

Sample Bold Metrics	Potential Campaigns
70% of people 12 and older who abuse prescription drugs say they get them from a friend or relative	Campaigns with anti-drug message
49%: The rise in dog-napping from 2010 to 2011	Campaigns for dog security
33 Million: The number of Americans living alone	Campaigns for single-serving meals
53%: The percentage of dogs who are overweight	Campaigns for diet dog food
13.9 Hours/Week: The amount of time spent per week on tablets	Campaigns for tablet devices and their apps
80%: Increase in emails opened in smartphones and tablets in first 6 months of 2012	Campaigns using mobile advertising techniques
61%: Non-essential email delivered to professional accounts	Campaigns for spam filters
64% of smartphone owners use their devices to shop online	Campaigns for mobile device eCommerce apps
73% of smartphone owners access social media apps at least once per day	Campaigns for mobile device social media apps
3 Billion: Hours of video watched per month watched by YouTube users	Campaigns to promote the use of online video

Figure 12.8: Sample Bold Metrics and Potential Campaigns for Their Use

The next step in the approach is to craft a campaign that applies the bold metric. Here, we look for a product or service attribute to associate with the metric. We might also look for a trend supported by the metric and capitalize on that aspect for our campaign. Of course, we can also reverse the procedure, first identifying the product or service to promote, and next correlating a bold metric to it.

In addition to applying bold metrics as the stars of campaigns, we can invert and juxtapose the metrics for added impact.

In inversion, we take the opposite of a number to emphasize its importance. For example, we might wish to run a marketing campaign motivating citizens to vote in elections. In the marketing campaign, the statement "40% of registered voters voted" might not appear particularly compelling, because it implies that a large percentage of citizens actually did vote. Through inversion, we can change our statement to, "60% of registered voters failed to vote."

In juxtaposition, we place two related metrics in context with each other for added impact. For example, we might wish to run a marketing campaign motivating unhappy workers to change their unwanted careers to ones they desire. The statement, "80% of people over 45 consider changing careers" might fail to motivate people. It might imply that the simple act of considering a new career is sufficient.

To add impact, we juxtapose the 80% metric with another metric: "Only 6% of those considering a change in career actually make the change." The juxtaposition of the two metrics (one large, the other small) adds excitement and can motivate the reader to action. Figure 12.9 shows a sample ad inspired by the juxtaposition. [12-17]

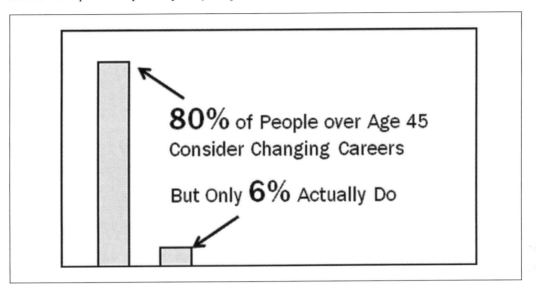

Figure 12.9: Metrics in Marketing Campaigns: Juxtaposition

MARKETING MADE MEASURABLE

Sharpie: Metrics to Measure What Matters: Writing instrument maker Sharpie (sharpie.com) turned to agency DraftFCB (draftFCB.com) to create a campaign for its popular markers. DraftFCB found out that handwriting constitutes only 13% of all communication. The agency applied the bold metric to create a theme around the use of Sharpie markers to break through the clutter of regular writing. [12-18]

The ad read, "In a world where only 13% of communications is handwritten, we need all the help we can get to break through the technological clutter." The ad paired the bold metric and the emphasis on "breaking through" with a photo. The photo showed a writer in the act of using the Sharpie pen to write a deeply personal note, writing, "I Love...." [12-19]

EXCEL EXCELLENCE

In this section, we show special techniques to leverage the versatility and impact of Microsoft Excel spreadsheets and charts. We start by reviewing pivot tables, which highlight and summarize specific aspects of data. We then discuss chart selection to emphasize different attributes of marketing results. We end by showing chart enhancements to increase the effectiveness of plots and graphs on the target audience.

Pivot Tables

Many organizations collect vast amounts of data. Typical databases can include hundreds (or even thousands) or rows, with information such as revenues, products, services, locations, salespersons, distribution channels involved, and so forth. Organizations with customer relationship management (CRM) systems can also capture customer-related data, such as age, income, purchase history, shopping preferences, and others.

Working with such large databases can prove cumbersome because of their size. It can also prove unnecessary, because we often need only a small subset of the data for our analysis.

To make it easier to make sense out of data, Microsoft Excel enables PivotTable reports. The reports allow users to quickly analyze data and gain insight. In this section, we will cover the basic approach to generating pivot tables. [12-20]

We will apply a running example to explain the creation of pivot tables. Acme Industries (a fictitious company) sells two products, Product A and Product B. It sells its products through two distribution channels--a corporate-owned Internet site and a retail store. Acme wants to compare the sales revenue of its different products, and how those sales vary over time. It also wishes to determine the performance of its different channels.

Figure 12.10 shows the relevant Acme sales data, including total sales by customer for the period, the date of the sale (by month), the product each customer purchased, and the distribution channel through which they purchased it.

Customer	Sales	Date of Sale	Product	Channel
Alex Alpha	$1,100	January	Product A	Store
Betty Beta	$100	February	Product B	Internet
Debbie Delta	$300	February	Product B	Store
Edie Epsilon	$200	January	Product B	Internet
Gary Gamma	$1,300	January	Product A	Store

Figure 12.10: Pivot Tables: Original Data Set

We could accomplish the analysis Acme requests through traditional sorting techniques. For example, to get sales by product, we could sort by Product, and then total up the sales for each product. But we can achieve the goals Acme desires quicker and more elegantly using pivot tables. We will go through the process of creating them, step by step.

Launch Pivot Table: First, we select the data we wish to analyze. When selecting the data, include the top row (the column labels). Next, select the Insert tab in the Excel menu, and then click on Pivot Table, as shown in Figure 12.11.

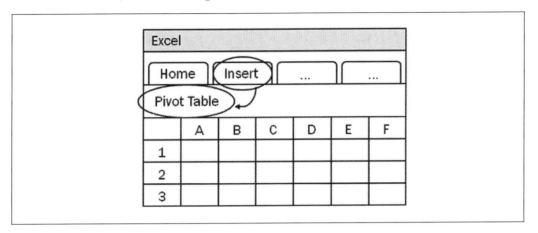

Figure 12.11: Pivot Tables: Launch Pivot Table

Clicking on Pivot Table will launch the Create Pivot Table dialog box. Figure 12.12 shows a simplified version of the box. The box includes a top section and a bottom section. The top section asks the user to tell Excel where to find the data source. Because we already selected the data in the first step, we click on the "Select a table or range" radio button. The Table Range input box should already be filled in. If not, select the radio button and enter the data range.

On the bottom section, we recommend clicking on the "New Worksheet" radio button to present the pivot table on a new worksheet. Doing so will provide the marketing analyst with additional room with which to work.

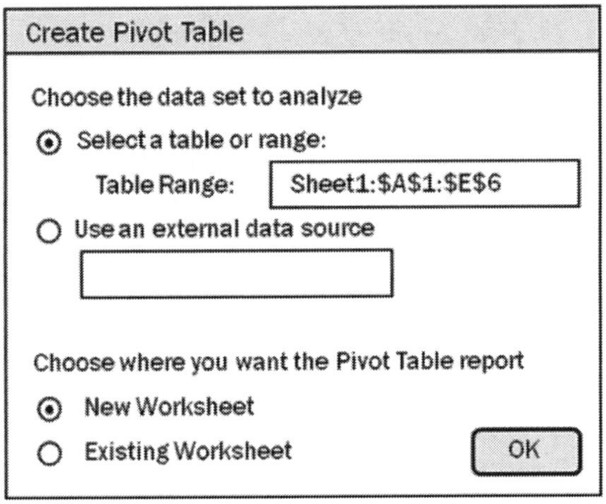

Figure 12.12: Pivot Tables: "Create Pivot Table" Dialog Box

PivotTable Field List: Clicking OK in the Create PivotTable dialog box brings up the PivotTable Field List shown in Figure 12.13. Excel refers to the column headings in our original data as fields. In our case, the fields consist of Customer, Sales, Date, Product, and Channel.

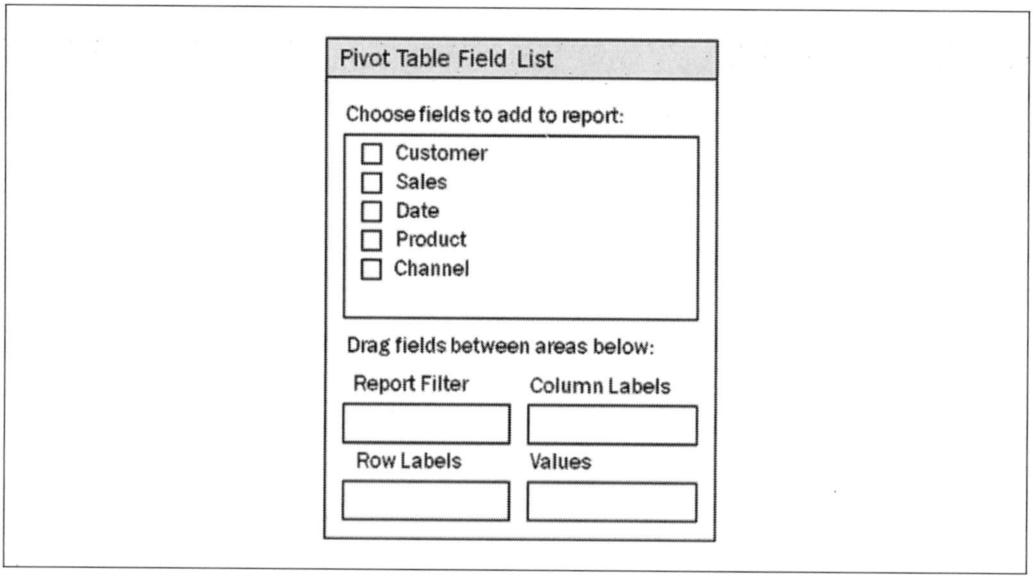

Figure 12.13: Pivot Tables: PivotTable Field List

Basic Report: Acme wishes to know the total sales revenue of its different products, so we will start by building a pivot table showing that data. To do this, select the Product and Sales boxes in the PivotTable Field List. Selecting the two boxes Product and Sales brings up the basic report shown in Figure 12.14. We can now see sales by product, and note that Product A easily outsells Product B.

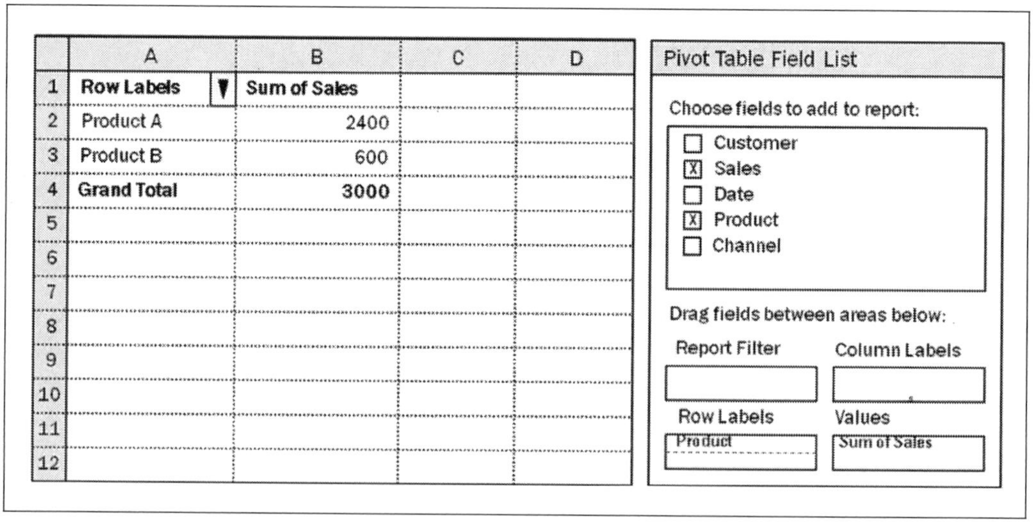

Figure 12.14: Pivot Tables: Basic Report: Sales by Product

Adding Fields to Report: Acme indicated it wanted to see a report showing product sales over time. Therefore, we select the Date box in the Pivot Table Field List to add the time dimension. The pivot table now shows sales by product, broken out by time (sales in January vs. sales in February), as shown in Figure 12.15.

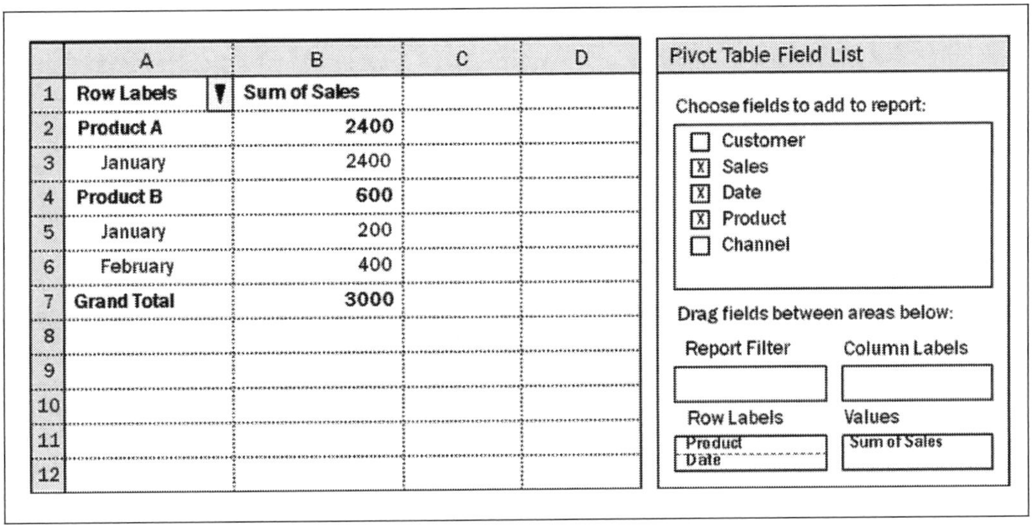

	A	B	C	D
1	Row Labels ▼	Sum of Sales		
2	Product A	2400		
3	January	2400		
4	Product B	600		
5	January	200		
6	February	400		
7	Grand Total	3000		
8				
9				
10				
11				
12				

Pivot Table Field List

Choose fields to add to report:
- [ ] Customer
- [X] Sales
- [X] Date
- [X] Product
- [ ] Channel

Drag fields between areas below:

Report Filter | Column Labels

Row Labels | Values
Product / Date | Sum of Sales

Figure 12.15: Pivot Tables: Adding Fields to Report

Adding Fields to Report, Continued: Acme indicated it wanted to see a report showing the relative performance of its distribution channels (the amount of sales for each channel). We can accomplish this by adding the Channel field to the report. The resulting report will show a table of product sales over time and distribution channel. Figure 12.16 shows the result.

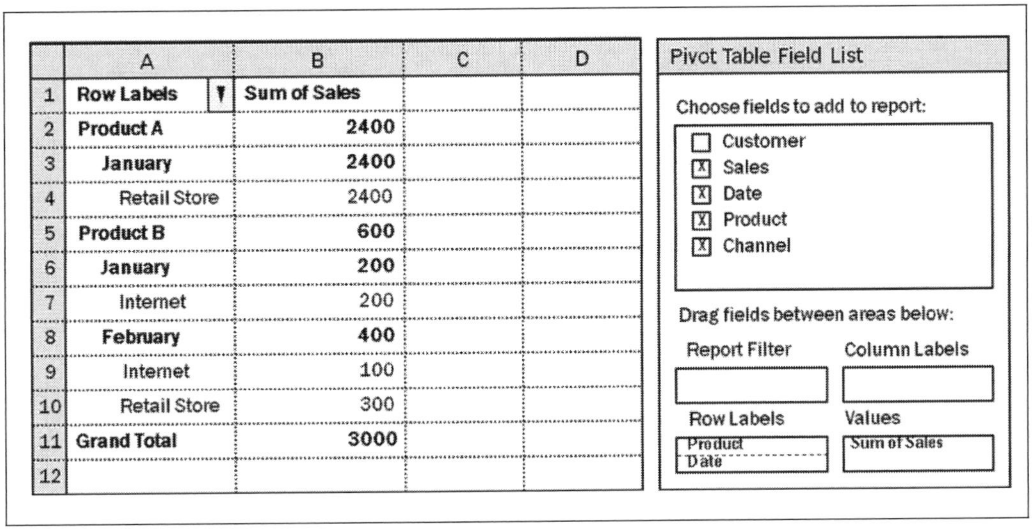

	A	B	C	D
1	Row Labels ▼	Sum of Sales		
2	Product A	2400		
3	January	2400		
4	Retail Store	2400		
5	Product B	600		
6	January	200		
7	Internet	200		
8	February	400		
9	Internet	100		
10	Retail Store	300		
11	Grand Total	3000		
12				

Pivot Table Field List

Choose fields to add to report:
- [ ] Customer
- [X] Sales
- [X] Date
- [X] Product
- [X] Channel

Drag fields between areas below:

Report Filter | Column Labels

Row Labels | Values
Product / Date | Sum of Sales

Figure 12.16: Pivot Tables: Adding Fields to Report: Adding Date, and then Channel

Note that the structure of the table depends on the order in which the user selects the fields. Figure 12.17 shows what happens if we chose Demand first, and then Date.

	A	B	C	D
1	Row Labels ▼	Sum of Sales		
2	Product A	2400		
3	Retail Store	2400		
4	January	2400		
5	Product B	600		
6	Internet	300		
7	January	200		
8	February	100		
9	Retail Store	300		
10	February	300		
11	Grand Total	3000		
12				

Pivot Table Field List

Choose fields to add to report:

☐ Customer
☒ Sales
☒ Date
☒ Product
☒ Channel

Drag fields between areas below:

Report Filter   Column Labels

Row Labels   Values
Product   Sum of Sales
Date

Figure 12.17: Pivot Tables: Adding Fields to Report: Adding Channel, and then Date

Adding Fields to Report Filter: As an alternative to adding the Channel field to get sales by distribution channel, we can achieve the same result through Excel's Report Filter function. To use Report Filter, right-click on the Channel field in the PivotTable Field List, and select Add to Report Filter. Figure 12.18 shows the "Add to Report Filter" option that pops up when Channel is right-clicked.

	A	B	C	D
1	Row Labels ▼	Sum of Sales		
2	Product A	2400		
3	January	2400		
4	Product B	600		
5	January	200		
6	February	400		
7	Grand Total	3000		
8				
9				
10				
11				
12				

Pivot Table Field List

Choose fields to add to report:

☐ Customer
☒ Sales
☒ Date
☒ Product
☐ Channel

▽ Add to Report Filter

Drag fields between areas below:

Report Filter   Column Labels

Row Labels   Values
Product   Sum of Sales
Date

Figure 12.18: Pivot Tables: Adding Fields to Report Filter

Selecting Reports Using Report Filter: The Report Filter creates one table for each of the values of the field added to the Report Filter. In our case, the field Channels has two values— Internet and Retail Store, so Report Filter will present us with two reports.

We can select which report we wish to see by selecting the Channel selector at the top of the spreadsheet, as shown in Figure 12.19. Selecting Internet from the list will provide us with a report showing products sold through the Internet distribution channel. Similarly, selecting Retail Store shows store-only sales. Selecting the All option shows sales through all channels.

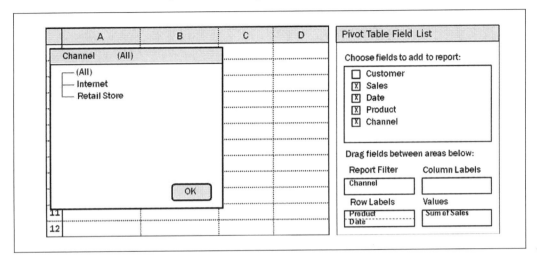

Figure 12.19: Pivot Tables: Selecting Reports using Report Filter

Pivoting PivotTables: At this point, we have presented the sales data by product, date, and channels that Acme requested. But the two column layout makes the content difficult to read. To address this, Excel can pivot the table, which transposes sections of the table by converting fields from rows to columns.

For example, we can convert the field Channel from row to column to give that field its own set of columns to display the data. To pivot the table, right-click on the field of interest (in this case, Channel), and select Add to Column Labels. Figure 12.20 shows the result.

	A	B	C	D
1	**Sum of Sales**	Column Labels ▼		
2	**Row Labels** ▼	Internet	Retail Store	Grand Total
3	**Product A**		2400	2400
4	January		2400	2400
5	**Product B**	300	300	600
6	January	200		200
7	February	100	300	400
8	**Grand Total**	300	2700	3000
9				
10				
11				
12				

Pivot Table Field List

Choose fields to add to report:

- ☐ Customer
- ☒ Sales
- ☒ Date
- ☒ Product
- ☒ Channel

Drag fields between areas below:

Report Filter	Column Labels
	Channel

Row Labels	Values
Product / Date	Sum of Sales

Figure 12.20: Pivot Tables: Pivoting Pivot Tables

We encourage readers to test the different features of Excel's pivot table functionality to gain a true understanding of its power. A few minutes spent with pivot tables will quickly expand one's expertise with the subject.

Chart Selection

This section discusses how to select the appropriate type of chart (also called graph) for different situations. We emphasize the unique attributes of different types of charts by comparing them in pairs. For example, we discuss the unique attributes of pie charts and vertical bar charts individually, and then showcase their differences by comparing the two with each other. In this way, marketers will have a greater understanding of when to use each type of chart. [12-21]

For each type of chart, we begin with an overview of the basic characteristics of the chart. We then discuss "triggers." Triggers are keywords and key-phrases indicating that certain types of charts should be used. For example, the words "constituents" and "breakdown" should trigger displaying the data in a pie chart, because pie charts suit themselves well for showing parts of a whole.

We follow up with typical uses for the charts in marketing situations. We end by providing presentation tips, discussing guidelines on using the charts to their best advantage during presentations.

Pie Charts: We use pie charts to show how each element relates to a whole. Figure 12.21 shows a typical pie chart, in this case showing sales revenue by product. Products A, B, C, D, and E each contribute to the overall revenue of the organization. The pie chart format quickly shows the relative amount each product contributes.

- **Triggers**: We know we should use pie charts when we hear words such as "constituents" (which indicate parts of a whole), "total" (which indicate that the total will include several components), and "breakdown" (which indicates how the total breaks down into individual pieces). For example, we could receive a request to "show the breakdown of total revenue by product," which would indicate that we should apply a pie chart.

- **Typical Uses**: Although pie charts have many uses, marketers most often use them for three situations.

    o **Market Share:** The first use is to display market share, where each pie slice represents a different company, and the size of the slice indicates the relative market share.

    o **Revenue Breakdown:** The second use is for revenue breakdown. We can break down revenue by product/service, by location (city or state), and so forth.

    o **Marketing Budgets:** The third common usage is for marketing budgets, where each slice represents an expense category, such as social media spending.

- **Presentation Tips**: When including pie charts in presentations, indicate areas of interest (such as a featured product or service) through cross-hatching, shading, or color to make it stand out from the rest. Otherwise, the pie slices will appear fairly similar. The figure deliberately does not include cross-hatching or shading. Note the similarity between the pie slices of Product A and Product B due to lack of shading.

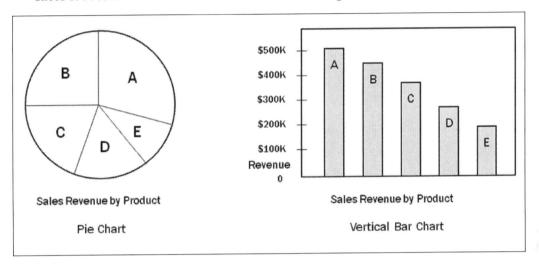

Figure 12.21: Comparison of Pie Chart (left) and Vertical Bar Chart (right)

Vertical Bar Charts: We use vertical bar charts to show how each element differs from other elements. Figure 12.21 shows a typical vertical bar chart, in this case displaying the revenue for Products A, B, C, D, and E. The vertical bar chart format quickly shows the difference in sales among the different products. Microsoft Excel refers to vertical bar charts as column charts.

- **Triggers**: We should use vertical bar charts when we hear the phrases "comparison" and "differences." For example, we could receive a request to "compare the sales of Product A and Product B," indicating we should use a vertical bar chart.

- **Typical Uses**: Marketers can use vertical bar charts any time they want to emphasize differences or comparisons of data. Marketers often use them for three situations.

  o **Sales Revenue Comparisons:** The first is sales revenue comparisons. For example, the figure compares sales revenue for different products. We could also compare sales revenue by market segment, geographic location, distribution channel, and so on.

  o **Before-After Comparisons:** We can also apply vertical bar charts for before-after comparisons. For example, we might wish to show brand awareness ratings before and after an advertising campaign to demonstrate the difference.

  o **Competitive Comparisons:** Marketers also use vertical bar charts for competitive comparisons. For example, we can show how fuel economy metrics of the vehicles we manufacture compare to those of our competitors.

- **Presentation Tips**: Microsoft Excel offers vertical bar chart variations beyond the single column format. Microsoft refers to these variations as clustered column, stacked column, and 100% stacked column charts.

  Figure 12.22 shows an example of each. Clustered column charts place two columns side by side and are useful for comparing pairs of data points. Stacked column charts stack one data point on top of another, and are useful for showing the contribution of each toward the total. 100% Stacked column charts also show the contribution of each data point toward the total, but expresses the data in percentages.

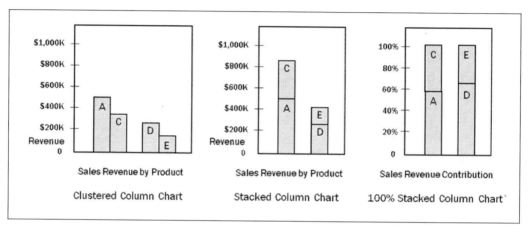

Figure 12.22: Vertical Bar Chart Variations: Clustered, Stacked, and 100% Stacked (right)

Horizontal Bar Charts: As with vertical bar charts, we use horizontal bar charts to show how each element differs from the others. Figure 12.23 shows a typical horizontal bar chart displaying the same data shown in the earlier figure, namely, the revenue for products A, B, C, D, and E. Microsoft Excel refers to horizontal bar charts simply as bar charts.

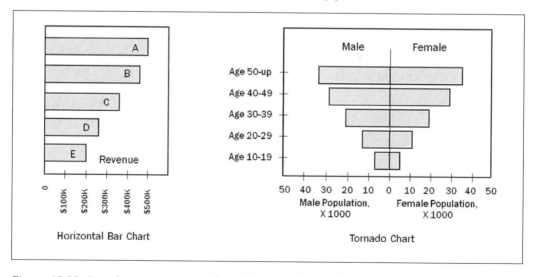

Figure 12.23: Sample Horizontal Bar Chart (Left) and Tornado Chart (Right)

- **Triggers**: Similar to vertical bar charts, we can use horizontal bar charts when we hear the phrases "comparison" and "differences." We can also use horizontal bar charts when we hear the phrase "population comparisons" (see Typical Uses below).

- **Typical Uses**: Both horizontal and vertical bar charts display differences well. Many marketers prefer to use vertical bar charts (aka column charts) instead of horizontal bar charts, because readers easily associate "higher" with "better." The choice is largely a matter of personal preference, with two exceptions.

  o **Long Category Names**: The first exception is the plotting of charts with long category names. Such charts should be plotted as horizontal bar charts to avoid truncating the category names on the x-axis (or positioning the text vertically, making it difficult to read). In the figure, we have deliberately oriented the x-axis text vertically, to demonstrate the problem.

  o **Tornado Charts:** The second exception is the plotting of so-called tornado charts. The term "tornado" is used because some believe the shape of such charts resemble a tornado funnel cloud. Such charts compare characteristics of two populations. Marketers and statisticians use tornado charts to display population comparisons between male and female, Republicans and Democrats, etc. Figure 12.23 shows a typical tornado chart.

- **Presentation Tips**: Microsoft Excel offers horizontal bar charts in various formats, including clustered bar charts, stacked bar charts, and 100% stacked bar charts, just as it does with column (vertical) charts. Excel does not provide a tornado chart format.

  To create a tornado chart in Excel with two series of data (such as male and female), enter the data in two columns, one for each series of data. Next, reverse the sign of all of the values in one column, such as the population values of all the males. Now plot the data in Microsoft Excel using the Stacked Bar function. The data will present itself in tornado chart form, due to the changes in the sign. Figure 12.24 shows a sample data chart modified to reverse the signs of the population values for the males.

Age Group	Males	Females
Ages 10 - 19	- 8,000	5,000
Ages 20 - 29	- 12,000	11,000
Ages 30 – 39	- 22,000	20,000
Ages 40 – 49	- 30,000	30,000
Ages 50 – up	- 34,000	34,000

Figure 12.24: Data Set Preparation for Tornado Chart

Line Charts: We use line charts to display data over time. Line charts highlight the pattern of change over time, aiding us in identifying trends. Figure 12.25 shows a comparison of the same data plotted as a clustered vertical bar chart and a line chart to highlight the differences.

- **Triggers**: We know we should use line charts when we hear words such as "trends" (changes over time), "long term" (emphasis on multiple weeks, months, or quarters), and "overtaking" (the situation that occurs one data series grows larger than another, as we discuss in the example below).

- **Typical Uses**: Marketers use line charts whenever they want to emphasize long term trends. Two common uses of line charts include:

    o **Trends Comparing Internal Data with Other Internal Data**: An example of comparing internal data with other internal data would be showing long term sales of one product with that of another (as shown in the figure).

    o **Trends Comparing Internal Data with External Data**: An example of comparing internal data with external data would be showing overall sales over time for one company with those of its competitor.

- **Presentation Tips**: Marketers should label the trend implied with the line chart to ensure that audience members identify it. For example, in the line chart shown in the figure, we add the headline, "Sales of Product B Overtaking Product A."

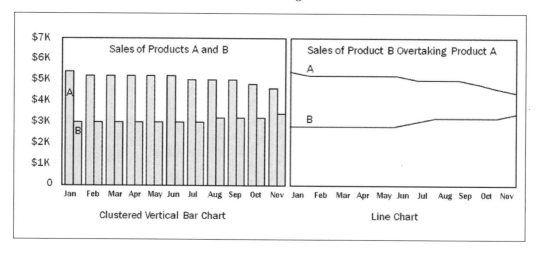

Figure 12.25: Comparison of Clustered Vertical Bar Chart (left) and Line Chart (right) using Same Data for each Chart

Other Types of Charts: Beyond the charts listed above, we might occasionally make use of other charts. We caution the reader to use such other charts sparingly when presenting to general audiences. Their unusual nature can make interpretation of the data difficult. Figure 12.26 summarizes a sampling of these types of charts. We discuss them briefly here.

- **Scatter Charts**: Scatter charts, also known as scatter diagrams, display raw data as points. Marketers use scatter charts to deduce possible relationships between the two variables. In the example shown in the figure, the chart suggests a positive slope relationship between the horizontal axis variable and the vertical axis variable.

- **Doughnut Charts**: Doughnut charts display constituents of a whole, similar to the role of pie charts. Unlike pie charts, doughnut charts can display multiple data series. In the example shown in the figure, outer doughnut A1-B1-C1 denotes one data series, and inner doughnut A2-B2-C2 denotes the other data series. For example, we could designate A1-B1-C1 as sales of products A, B, and C in market segment 1, and A2-B2-C2 as sales of the products in market segment 2.

- **Radar Charts**: Radar charts enable marketers to plot multiple dimensions of several data series. We occasionally refer to radar charts as **spider charts** because they can appear similar to a spider's web. In the example shown in the figure, we display data along five axes.

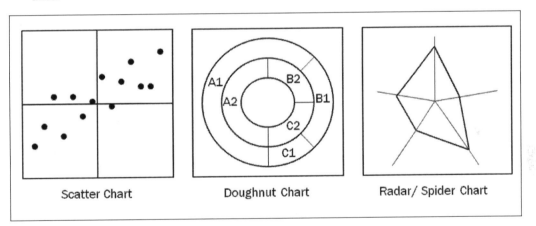

Figure 12.26: Other Types of Charts

Chart Enhancements

In this section, we discuss how to enhance charts so they can tell their story clearly and succinctly. We show the process of building enhanced charts, from initial chart creation, to adding explanatory comments, to adding insight to charts by using breakdowns and comparisons. [12-22]

Initial Chart Creation: Our first step is to create the initial chart. Figure 12.27 provides an overview of the process, showing three steps:

- **Words and Numbers**: As the figure demonstrates, our presentations often start with simple words and numbers. While words and numbers are a good place to start, they do not offer sufficient insight into marketing behavior. We therefore move on to the next step.

- **Data Table**: As we collect more detailed data, we make it easier to analyze the data by displaying it in tabular format.

- **Basic Chart**: Next, we create the basic chart from the data table. We select the relevant chart type based on the guidelines we just covered.

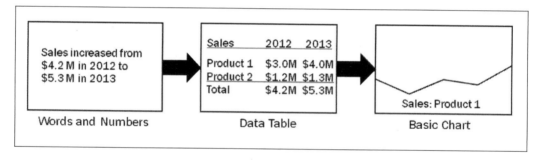

Figure 12.27: Chart Enhancements: Initial Chart Creation

Comment Additions: Our second step is to add explanatory comments to aid the chart in telling its story. Explanatory comments will vary depending on the intended role for the chart. Simple charts might get by with just a headline. More advanced charts might require headlines, trend arrows, thresholds and other enhancements. Figure 12.28 shows an overview of the process, with three steps:

- **Chart with Headline**: As the first diagram in the figure demonstrates, we can add clarity to a chart by simply adding a headline to it. The headline can quickly clarify the intended message of the chart by focusing the viewer's attention on the key aspect of the chart. Without the headline, the viewer will be forced to find meaning in the chart, and could come to the "wrong" conclusion (i.e. not what the marketer intended).

- **Chart with Trend Arrow**: Many marketing-related charts include time as the horizontal axis. For those time-oriented charts, marketers can add a trend arrow to emphasize the change of data over time. Because the human eye naturally follows geometric shapes such as arrows, the addition of trend arrows adds impact to time-related charts.

- **Chart with Threshold**: Many organizations implement strategic initiatives. Often, those initiatives involve achieving important goals, such as reaching specific sales revenue targets. In these types of situations, our charts will benefit with the addition of threshold lines representing those goals. For example, our organization might target exceeding $3.0 million in sales for a specific product. By adding the $3.0 million threshold to the chart, we can quickly communicate our actual sales relative to the sales target.

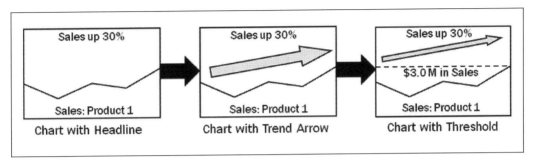

Figure 12.28: Chart Enhancements: Comment Additions

Breakdowns and Comparisons: In some cases, we require added insight into the data. In those cases, we can prepare breakdown and comparison charts, as shown in Figure 12.29 and Figure 12.30.

- **Breakdown Charts**: As shown in the Breakdown Charts figure, we can break the data down into constituent elements to show how each element contributes to the total. For example, organizations often break down sales data by products/services (to determine their relative sales) and by distribution channels (to determine the contributions of each to overall sales).

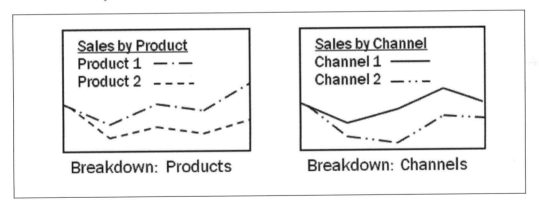

Figure 12.29: Chart Enhancements: Breakdown Charts

- **Comparison Charts**: We can add insight to the data by comparing it to important benchmarks. For example, organizations might wish to track how actual sales compare to those forecasted, or how they compare to sales by competitors, as shown in the figure.

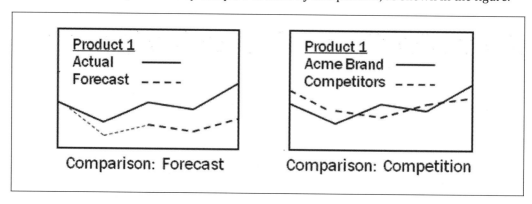

Figure 12.30: Chart Enhancements: Comparison Charts

Figure 12.31 shows how an example chart to illustrate the techniques discussed in this section. The figure displays a typical sales chart, plotting sales revenue over a one year period. The chart includes several enhancements, including a threshold to highlight the crossing over the five million dollar sales target, a trend arrow to emphasize increasing sales, and a headline summarizing the intended message of the chart.

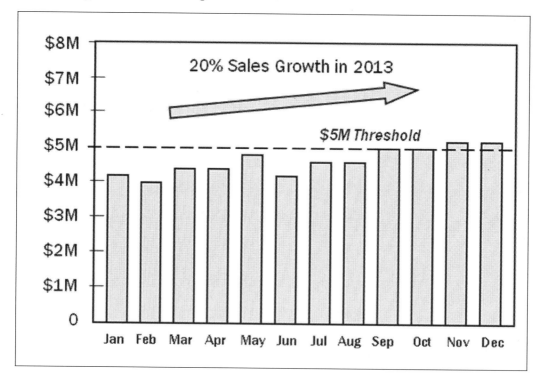

Figure 12.31: Chart Enhancements: Example Showing Several Enhancements

Charting Ethics

With the great power of marketing analytics comes great responsibility. Marketing analytics tools and techniques offer great persuasive ability. The ability derives from the sound marketing theories supporting the field. But deceptive people can abuse the power and distort the truth by manipulating the presentation of the data. We urge our marketing colleagues not to engage in this practice.

Figure 12.32 shows a typical example. The example summarizes the results of a customer survey. The survey asks Acme customers to answer the following question: "Would you recommend Acme to others?" The answer choices are "Yes" (I would recommend) and "No" (I would not recommend).

The chart on the left depicts what we call "truncating trickery," making it appear that the "Yes" results easily outnumber the "No" responses. The truncation of the axis distorts the truth. The right side of the figure portrays the data ethically, showing in fact that the "Yes" and "No" responses are almost equal in number.

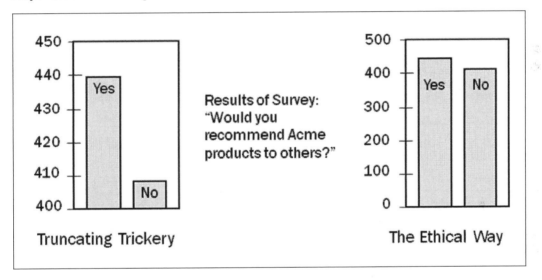

Figure 12.32: Charting Ethics: Avoiding Truncating Trickery

MARKETING MADE MEASURABLE

Pat Hanrahan: From Academy Award to Data Visualization: Graphics expert Pat Hanrahan is certainly one of the few data scientists ever to win an Academy Award, let alone two. And yet, Hanrahan won the Academy Award for technical achievement in 1993 for his graphics work at Pixar Animation Studios. He won his second Academy Award in 2004 for new artistic rendering techniques for skin and other materials.

Hanrahan found that adding drama to animation was not enough. He wanted to add drama to data. So he co-founded data visualization company Tableau Software (tableausoftware.com) in 2003. Tableau integrates with company databases and spreadsheets to transform uninspiring columns of data into interactive maps and graphs. The tool aids people's ability to interpret the data, making it come "alive."

Hanrahan claims the tool encourages user interactivity for rapid understanding of the data, saying that "We let any user ask questions of their data by a simple drag and drop interface."

According to Ted Corbett at Tableau customer Seattle Children's Hospital, "I've never seen people get this excited about data." The hospital expects revenue to double, thanks to the opportunities identified by Tableau. [12-23]

DATA-DRIVEN PRESENTATIONS

Most corporate executives are "outcome-driven." That is, they are driven by results. Therefore, presenting information with data quantifying the anticipated results of a particular plan or proposal can be a powerful way to influence executives.

Many executives respect decisions based on quantifiable metrics and sound models. As such, the marketing analytics models and metrics presented in this book can be a valuable ally when presenting important findings and ideas to executive audiences. In this section, we cover how to develop data-driven presentations with the goal of persuading executive-level audiences. [12-24]

Metrics Alignment

When developing data-driven presentations, marketers must ensure that the metrics used in the presentation match those the executive tracks. Marketers sometimes present on intermediate variables, such as brand awareness or Facebook Likes, only to find that executives are more concerned with financial metrics, such as sales and profits. The discord caused by the mismatch of metrics can cause presentations to fail.

Therefore, we recommend that marketers find out first which metrics the executives in their organization respect. To find out, attend some executive-level briefings to determine which metrics the executives track. Alternatively, ask the chief financial officer (CFO) about the type of metrics the CEO requests in financial status reports.

The example below demonstrates the missed opportunity when marketers fail to keep executive audiences in mind when selecting metrics to report.

MARKETING MADE MEASURABLE

McDonald's: Marketing Analytics Execution: On April 2010, fast food restaurant chain McDonald's (mcdonalds.com) executed a promotion campaign using location-based social media tool Foursquare (foursquare.com). In the campaign, customers could come into McDonald's to check-in for a chance to win $5 and $10 gift cards.

McDonald's head of social media reported that the campaign was a success, with a 33% increase in check-ins. The social meda head indicated he considered check-ins to be equivalent to foot traffic. Critics retorted that Foursquare check-ins should not be counted as physical foot traffic.

The ISM Travels blog (ismtravels.com) indicated both the check-ins metric and the foot traffic metric missed the point. ISM contends McDonald's should have measured incremental revenue from the campaign, because that is the principal metric that executives find credible in evaluating such a promotion. [12-25, 12-26, 12-27]

Executive Presentations

Executives face many promising projects with which to move forward. Therefore, persuading them to approve proposed projects or ideas could present challenges..

In this section, we present a systematic approach to thwart common attacks others make to kill proposed projects. The approach suggests analytics-based countermeasures to address common ways that ideas fail to gain organizational buy-in. We demonstrate the approach using a real-world example. [12-28]

Harvard professor John P. Kotter and University of British Columbia educator Lorne A. Whitehead identify four types of attacks on new ideas in their book, "Buy-In: Saving Your Idea from Getting Shot Down." Each type of attack can threaten a valid proposed project. By examining each type of attack, we can prepare for them. We will discuss the four types: [12-29]

- **Death by Delay**: In the first type of attack, people attempt to kill the idea by introducing delays to its discussion. The attackers might feel threatened by the idea, and believe that delaying its discussion will cause the marketer to forget the idea or give up. To combat this type of attack using marketing analytics, introduce the importance of time in the discussion. Show the data on a timeline, indicating the future benefit that the organization will lose if the idea is allowed to sit idle.

- **Confusion**: In the second type of attack, people present contrary data to confuse the audience. Here, the best defense is a good offense. Mount a pre-emptive strike against the attackers by presenting the idea using metrics and arguments the decision makers find relevant. For example, show the incremental revenue the company will generate as a result of the proposed project.

- **Fear-Mongering**: In this attack, people invoke fear in the audience, such as the fear of change. We can defend against this type of attack by discussing the consequences which will occur if the idea is not executed. For example, we can discuss a likely upcoming event that will spell disaster if the organization fails to implement the marketer's idea.

- **Character Assassination**: In the fourth type of attack, people go after the marketer's personal reputation and credibility. To fight this type of attack, emphasize the importance of the data over any personal feelings or beliefs. Many decision makers find data more reliable and credible than personal opinions.

Figure 12.33 summarizes the four types of attacks and the defensive strategies for each.

Attack Type	Description	Defensive Strategy
Death by Delay	Deferring discussion of the idea to the future, hoping marketer will give up	Present data using time orientation, indicating consequences in the future if the idea is not implemented
Confusion	Presenting contrary data to confuse the audience	Concentrate on metrics and other attributes vitally important to the principal decision makers
Fear Mongering	Invoking fear in the audience, such as the fear of change	Present data showing that the consequences of not executing the idea will far outweigh any possible negative outcomes
Character Assassination	Targeting the marketer's personal reputation or credibility	Shift discussion away from personal beliefs to data

Figure 12.33: Executive Presentations: Attacks and Defensive Strategies

To demonstrate the approach, we cite a real-world example, modified to protect the identities of the company and people involved. The example involves a leading enterprise software company. The company sells its software packages to large businesses, and tailors each package to the requirements of the customer firm through its professional services function. The professional services function customizes and implements the software package for the customer firm, and earns revenue from the customer for its services.

The division of the enterprise software company responsible for much of the company revenues held a quarterly operations review meeting. In the meeting, each department head (engineering, marketing, professional services, and so forth) presented the status of their departments to the chief executive of the division.

At the meeting, the department head of engineering presented the slide shown in Figure 12.34. He stated that the perceived lack of personnel hampered morale and productivity. He requested that the chief executive provide him with more personnel for his department to address the problems. The executive refused to grant him additional personnel, largely because he failed to portray an argument the executive found convincing.

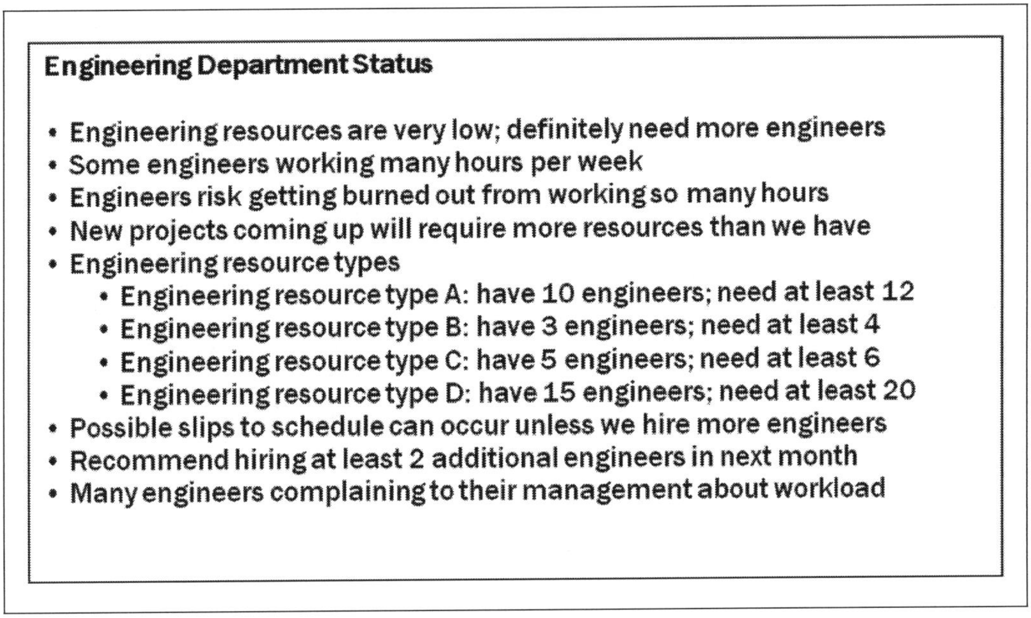

Engineering Department Status

- **Engineering resources are very low; definitely need more engineers**
- **Some engineers working many hours per week**
- **Engineers risk getting burned out from working so many hours**
- **New projects coming up will require more resources than we have**
- **Engineering resource types**
    - **Engineering resource type A: have 10 engineers; need at least 12**
    - **Engineering resource type B: have 3 engineers; need at least 4**
    - **Engineering resource type C: have 5 engineers; need at least 6**
    - **Engineering resource type D: have 15 engineers; need at least 20**
- **Possible slips to schedule can occur unless we hire more engineers**
- **Recommend hiring at least 2 additional engineers in next month**
- **Many engineers complaining to their management about workload**

Figure 12.34: Executive Presentations: Example of the Wrong Way to Gain Buy-In

In denying the engineering department head's request, the executive mentioned the following points:

- "We will keep an eye on the problem to see if the situation worsens." This phrase demonstrates an example of the **death by delay** attack.
- "It was my understanding that the department was already fully staffed." Here, we see an example of a **confusion** attack.
- "Adding new staff now could result in increased training and office costs." This statement shows a **fear mongering** attack.
- "Your incessant complaints about workload make me wonder about your commitment to the division." This phrase demonstrates an attack based on **character assassination**.

In addition to the problems mentioned above, the engineering department head failed to discuss the principal concern of the chief executive: increasing organizational revenue.

Next on the operations review meeting agenda was the head of the professional services organization. As with the head of engineering, the head of professional services also wanted to increase staff in her department. But unlike the head of engineering, she developed her presentation using the principles of this section.

Long before the meeting started, she had identified the principal metric that mattered to the chief executive--revenue. She therefore crafted her presentation around revenue. In her presentation, she showed how her department contributed to revenue. Furthermore, she showed how her desire for additional personnel aided the GM's quest for additional revenue.

Figure 12.35 shows the presentation slide she used. The figure shows the relationship between department resources (personnel) and projected revenue. The figure adds a trend arrow to make that relationship clear. It also indicates that as sales increase, the department will need additional personnel to service those sales. The figure communicates that a lack of resources in the future will halt incremental revenue—a situation the chief executive will not tolerate.

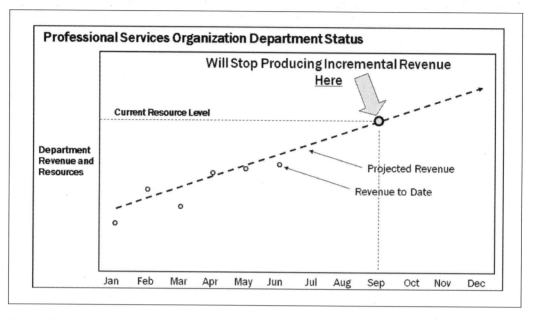

Figure 12.35: Executive Presentations: Example of the Right Way to Gain Buy-In

Her approach effectively eliminates the four types of attacks:

- **Death by delay** attacks will not work, because the timeline indicates that delaying the introduction of additional personnel will compromise incremental revenue, a matter of intense urgency for the chief executive.

- **Confusion** attacks will not likely prove effective either, because the chart is based on actual revenue performance data (marked by points on the chart), which hold great credibility to the executive.

- **Fear mongering** attacks will not stop our department head, because the consequences of not adopting the plan (the certain elimination of incremental revenue) far outweigh possible negative outcomes (such as the fear of not being able to find sufficient office space for the new hires).

- **Character assassination** attacks have themselves been assassinated here, by simply shifting the conversation away from discussions about subjective topics such as personnel morale (as the head of engineering did), instead focusing on the data.

We therefore advise marketers to pay heed to the marketing analytics approach to presentations, or risk failing in executive presentations.

MARKETING MADE MEASURABLE

Peter Drucker: Influencing Decision-Makers: According to management guru Peter Drucker (druckerinstitute.com), "The great majority of people tend to focus downward. They are occupied with efforts rather than results...As a result they render themselves ineffectual." [12-30]

Management expert Marshall Goldsmith agrees. Goldsmith extended Drucker's comments and cited guidelines for knowledge workers to follow in order to influence decision makers with proposed new ventures. Goldsmith refers to knowledge workers as "people who know more about what they are doing than their managers do." Some of the guidelines include the following:

- **Decisions are made by the person with the power to make the decisions**. Decisions are not made by the "right" person or the "smartest" person. Knowledge workers can sometimes feel that this situation is "not fair." Once knowledge workers learn to accept the situation, they become more effective in influencing others and making a positive difference.

- **It is your responsibility to sell, not their responsibility to buy.** Knowledge workers can mistakenly believe that decision makers must "buy" their arguments. This assumption will lead to failure. Instead, knowledge workers must understand that a large part of their role is the ability to educate decision makers, and present their arguments in ways they can respect. For example, "sell" the arguments using results-oriented language, stating the outcome that is likely to occur if the organization embarks upon the proposed plan.

- **Focus on the contribution to the greater good.** Too many knowledge workers focus on how proposed ventures will benefit themselves or their own departments. They place little thought into the benefits for the organization as a whole. Decision-makers often control a greater sphere of influence than that of knowledge workers. Just as an effective salesperson focuses on the needs of the buyer, knowledge workers must learn to focus on the needs of the decision maker.

In summary, one can think of decision-makers as outcome-driven. They are driven by results, by the outcomes of processes. Most knowledge workers, on the other hand, are driven by the process itself.

The situation is a bit like author John Gray's book, "Men Are from Mars, Women Are from Venus." Knowledge workers must learn to frame their conversations to decision-makers in terms of outcomes, not of processes.

SUMMARY

This chapter described several approaches to set analytics into action. It discussed how marketers can incorporate models and metrics into their daily routine. They can take advantage of the power of marketing analytics in their everyday professional lives.

In this chapter, we covered developing rapid decision models to quickly demonstrate the power of analytics in their organization, creating marketing campaigns based on citing metrics, transforming data into drama with different spreadsheet techniques, and influencing decision makers with data-driven presentations.

Rapid Decision Models: Decision models need not be complex. We can quickly demonstrate the power of analytics using rapid, simple decision models:

- **Pareto Prioritization Analysis Model**: We can apply the Pareto model to determine areas on which to focus the majority of our efforts. Sometimes called the 80 – 20 rule, the Pareto approach identifies the 20% of the market delivering 80% of the results.

- **Cross-Sales Model:** We can increase revenue in organizations by cross-selling related products and services. The cross-sales model shows how to quickly correlate products and services to identify cross-sell candidates customers find most relevant.

- **Supplier Selection Framework:** We can develop spreadsheets using specific selection criteria to select suppliers that will most benefit our organization.

Metrics in Marketing Campaigns: Metrics can not only measure the results of marketing campaigns. They can act as the "star" in campaigns. We can cite bold metrics that demonstrate the value of our products and services. We can invert and juxtapose the metrics for added impact.

Excel Excellence: We can apply spreadsheet-based software, such as Microsoft Excel, to visualize data. We discussed different means of converting data into drama:

- **Pivot Tables**: In pivot tables, we sort and transpose existing data for a unique view that displays our intended message.

- **Chart Selection**: We covered guidelines to select the most relevant chart type, depending on the objectives of the data presentations. We discussed pie charts, vertical bar charts, horizontal bar charts, line charts, and other special types of charts.

- **Chart Enhancements**: No matter which type of chart we select, we can enhance it to improve its storytelling ability. Enhancements include items such as headlines, trend lines, thresholds, and so forth.

- **Charting Ethics**: With the great power of marketing analytics comes great responsibility. Marketers must avoid distorting the truth.

Data-Driven Presentations: We can apply the power of marketing analytics to create presentations based on our data and findings. Such presentations can be powerful tools to influence decision makers. We offered some guidelines to aid in this application of analytics:

- **Avoiding a Mismatch of Metrics:** Ensure that the metrics used in the presentation are those the decision-maker respects. Find out which metrics they track, and focus the presentation on those metrics.

- **Executive Presentations**: Executives face many promising projects with which to move forward, so persuading them to approve a marketer's proposed project, idea, or request presents challenges. We presented a systematic method to thwart common attacks used by others to kill proposed projects.

When presenting to decision makers, marketers must frame their arguments in the "outcome-focused" world of the decision maker, rather than the "process-focused" world to which many marketers are accustomed.

Terminology

Clustered Column Chart: Type of vertical bar chart that places two columns side by side for ease in comparing pairs of data points.

Cross-Selling: Selling related products and services to customers, with the intention of increasing revenue.

Doughnut Charts: Type of chart displaying constituents of a whole using portions of rings. Rings are often placed concentrically.

Pareto Prioritization Analysis Model: Also known as the 80 – 20 rule, this model identifies areas on which to focus efforts.

Pivot Table: Computer spreadsheet functionality that sorts, organizes, and transposes data to aid in interpreting it.

Radar Chart: Also called a Spider Chart. Type of chart displaying multiple dimensions of several data series.

Stacked Column Chart: Type of vertical bar chart that displays data of different elements by stacking one bar on top of another.

Scatter Charts: Type of chart displaying raw data as points.

Tornado Charts: Type of chart, often displayed as a horizontal bar chart, comparing characteristics of two populations, such as male and female.

Class Discussion

1. What types of analyses would be relevant for the Pareto prioritization analysis model?
2. What criteria do consumers use to determine that some products and services are relevant to others?
3. What is the best way of determining selection criteria when using the supplier selection framework described in the chapter?
4. How can we locate bold metrics for use in campaigns citing metrics?
5. Study the types of charts your organization normally uses. Are they more likely to be pie charts, bar charts, line charts, or some other types of charts?

6. Think of a time when you had to present a proposed project to a decision maker. How would you have applied data-driven presentations in that case?

Practice Problems

1. Obtain a subset of sales data from your organization, such as that for a one year period. Using the Pareto prioritization analysis model, identify customer attributes that correlate with higher than average sales levels.

2. Gather product/service sales data from your organization. Using the cross-sales analysis model described in this chapter, identify relevant cross-selling opportunities for your organization's principal products or services.

3. Prepare a supplier selection framework model, as described in the chapter. If your organization is not planning to hire a new supplier, look for potential examples in your personal life. Personal suppliers could include hair stylists, doctors, dentists, etc.

4. Obtain sales data from your organization and experiment with different ways to analyze and display the data using pivot tables. Experiment by creating pivot tables evaluating sales by product/service, by geography, and by market. Build pivot tables combining two or more sales variables.

5. Create a tornado chart showing a comparison between two populations. If the relevant data is available, compare sales to male and female customers. Otherwise, select two other related variables, such as domestic and international sales, etc.

6. Prepare two slides for use in presenting a proposed project to a decision maker. In the first slide, adopt the "wrong way" approach, focusing on efforts taken instead of results achieved. In the second slide, apply the "right way" approach, emphasizing the outcome likely to occur because of your proposed project.

REFERENCES

Chapter 1

1-1. "William Thomson, 1st Baron Kelvin of Largs." Biography.com

1-2. Mangel, M and F.J. Samaniego, F.J., "Abraham Wald's Work on Aircraft Survivability." Journal of the American Statistical Association. June 1984.

1-3. McNary, Tim. "Chief Marketing Officer Tenure Now at 43 Months." Spencer Stuart press release. July 5, 2012.

1-4. Rodgers, Ceci. "Data Analysts: The New Masters of the Universe." CBSnews.com. April 16, 2010.

1-5. Sorger, Stephan. *Marketing Planning: Where Strategy Meets Action*. New Jersey: Pearson, 2012.

Chapter 2

2-1. "The Forbes 400." Forbes.com, Listing 188, Mortimer Zuckerman. September 20, 2007.

2-2. Sorger, Stephan. *Marketing Planning: Where Strategy Meets Action*. New Jersey: Pearson, 2012. Page 25.

2-3. Crothers, Brooke. "iPad, MacBook Torpedoing Ultrabook Sales, Says Analyst." CNET.com. August 6, 2012.

2-4. Sorger, Stephan. *Marketing Planning: Where Strategy Meets Action*. New Jersey: Pearson, 2012. Page 25.

2-5. United States Census Bureau, census.gov

2-6. United States Bureau of Labor Statistics, bls.gov

2-7. United States Bureau of Economic Analysis, bea.gov

2-8. Metro Atlanta Chamber (chamber of commerce for metropolitan Atlanta, Georgia area), metroatlantachamber.com

2-9. United States Census Bureau, North American Industry Classification System (NAICS), census.gov/naics

2-10. United States Census Bureau, NAICS 52421, Insurance Agencies and Brokerages, Industry Snapshot.

2-11. Sorger, Stephan. *Marketing Planning: Where Strategy Meets Action*. New Jersey: Pearson, 2012. Pages 27 – 28.

2-12. "Insurance Brokers & Agencies in the US: Market Research Report." IBISWorld.com. July 2012.

2-13. Nielsen Website, nielsen.com

2-14. Kolakowki, Nicholas. "Apple iPad Will Lead Tablet PC Market." Eweek.com. July 8, 2010.

2-15. Adweek website, Adweek.com

2-16. Kotler, Philip and Keller, Kevin Lane. *Marketing Management*. 13th edition. New Jersey: Pearson Prentice-Hall, 2009. Pages 108 – 109.

2-17. Vernon, Patrick. "Venture Capital Tutorial for Entrepreneurs Considering Presenting at VCIC." vcic.unc.edu.

2-18. Kotler, Philip and Keller, Kevin Lane. *Marketing Management*. 13th edition. New Jersey: Pearson Prentice-Hall, 2009. Pages 108 – 109.

2-19. Pettey, Chrisy. "Gartner Says PC Shipments to Slow to 3.8 Percent Growth in 2011; Units to Increase 10.9 Percent in 2012." Gartner Press Release. September 8, 2011.

2-20. Kotler, Philip and Keller, Kevin Lane. *Marketing Management*. 13th edition. New Jersey: Pearson Prentice-Hall, 2009. Pages 113-116.

2-21. U.S. Census Bureau. "U.S. Census Bureau Announces 2010 Population Counts—Apportionment Counts Delivered to President." December 21, 2010.

2-22. "NHE Fact Sheet." Center for Medicare and Medicaid Services. Accessed via cms.gov.

2-23. U.S. Bureau of Transportation Statistics, Research and Innovative Technology Administration, Table 1-11: Number of U.S. Aircraft, Vehicles, Vessels, and other Conveyances. Accessed via bts.gov.

2-24. U.S. Census Bureau. "U.S. Census Bureau Announces 2010 Population Counts—Apportionment Counts Delivered to President." December 21, 2010.

2-25. American Dental Association statistic. Accessed via dentistry website wowdentistry.net.

2-26. Walgreens. Walgreen's price for Glide-branded floss. Accessed via Walgreens.com.

2-27. Bonini, Sheila and Oppenheim, Jeremy. "Helping Green Products Grow." McKinsey Quarterly, October 2008.

2-28. Swicofil Dental Floss web page. Accessed via swicofil.com.

2-29. Kotler, Philip and Keller, Kevin Lane. *Marketing Management*. 13th edition. New Jersey: Pearson Prentice-Hall, 2009. Pages 113-114.

2-30. "State and County QuickFacts, Ohio." U.S. Census Bureau.

2-31. "State and County QuickFacts, Ohio." U.S. Census Bureau.

2-32. The Robbins Company website. Accessed via robbistbm.com

2-33. "American Hospital Association Benchmarking Network 2002 Survey". Reported by the Journal of the Medical Library Association. Accessed via ncbi.nlm.nih.gov.

2-34. "Fast Facts on US Hospitals."American Hospital Association. Accessed via aha.org.

2-35. "NAICS 541213, Tax Preparation Services, 2007. Geographic Distribution." U.S. Census Bureau.

2-36. "Summary Statistics by NAICS, Arizona." U.S. Census Bureau.

2-37. Ferrari dealer locator. Accessed via Ferrari.com website.

2-38. "Light Vehicle Sales per Dealership." Department of Energy, Energy Efficiency and Renewable Energy, Vehicle Technologies Program. February 23, 2009.

2-39. Kotler, Philip and Keller, Kevin Lane. *Marketing Management*. 13th edition. New Jersey: Pearson Prentice-Hall, 2009. Pages 79 – 86.

2-40. "India Slashes Import Duty on IT Equipment." Inquirer.net. January 9, 2004.

2-41. "Forrester: Global IT Purchases Will Decline in 2009." Forrester Research press release. January 13, 2009.

2-42. "Taking the Lug Out of Luggage." Financial Times. Accessed via ft.com.July 22, 2010.

2-43. Golman, David. "Ultrabooks Could Save the PC." Accessed via money.cnn.com. November 28, 2011.

2-44. Noyes, Katherine. "Patent Trolls Cost Businesses $80 Billion Per Year, Study Finds." PC World magazine: pcworld.com. November 15, 2011.

2-45. Mayfield, Kendra. "E-Waste: Dark Side of Digital Age." Wired Magazine: wired.com. January 10, 2003.

2-46. Porter, Michael. *Competitive Strategy*. New York: The Free Press, 1980. Pages 3-28.

2-47. Keller, Kevin Lane. *Strategic Brand Management: Building, Measuring, and Managing Brand Equity*. 2nd edition. New Jersey, Prentice Hall, 2003. Page 501.

2-48. McGlaun, Shane. "Luna Personal Robot Can Walk the Dog." Technabob.com. May 11, 2011.

2-49. Kain, Erik. "Amazon Price Check May Be Evil But It's the Future." Forbes: forbes.com. December 14, 2011.

2-50. Gongloff, Mark. "Groupon? More Like Group-Off!" Wall Street Journal: MarketBeat Blog. November 23, 2011.

Chapter 3

3-1. BiographyBase.com, "Aesop Biography."

3-2. Procter and Gamble Tide website: tide.com

3-3. P&G Products web page, Egypt: "Caring About Your Home." Accessed via pg.com.

3-4. Dyer, David; Dalzell, Frederick; Olegario, Rowena. "How Tide Cleaned Up the Competition." Harvard Business School. July 12, 2004.

3-5. Professor E. Jerome McCarthy is credited for developing the Marketing Mix concept (product, price, place, and promotion) in 1960.

3-6. "Post Reseearch – Segmentation – Response Variables." AngelSEO.co.uk. August 28, 2010.

3-7. "World's Most On-Time Airlines." Forbes.com. February 23, 2010.

3-8. Mutzabaugh, Ben."J.D. Power: JetBlue, Alaska Air are Highest-Rated Airlines." USA Today. June 14, 2012.

3-9. "Customer Ratings Rise for Low-Cost Airlines." Wall Street Journal. June 13, 2012.

3-10. Reed, Dan. "Thanksgiving Airline Traffic Forecast to Drop 4%." USA Today. November 10, 2009.

3-11. Higgins, Michelle. "How to Fly V.I.P., Perk by Perk." New York Times. June 8, 2012.

3-12. Mitchell, Jacqueline. "What Your Car Says About You." Forbes.com. November 21, 2008.

3-13. Sorger, Stephan. *Marketing Planning: Where Strategy Meets Action*. New Jersey: Pearson, 2012. Pages 44 – 47.

3-14. Sorger, Stephan. *Marketing Planning: Where Strategy Meets Action*. New Jersey: Pearson, 2012. Pages 56 – 60.

3-15. Myers, James. *Segmentation and Positioning for Strategic Marketing Decisions*. Chicago: American Marketing Association, 1996. Page 31.

3-16. Myers, James. *Segmentation and Positioning for Strategic Marketing Decisions*. Chicago: American Marketing Association, 1996. Page 17.

3-17. Myers, James. *Segmentation and Positioning for Strategic Marketing Decisions*. Chicago: American Marketing Association, 1996. Page 17 – 23.

3-18. Green, Joshua. "The Luxurious Lives of Preferred Travelers." Business Week. March 8, 2012

3-19. Moskowitz, Clara. "SpaceX's Dragon Capsule on Way to Space Station." MSNBC.com. May 22, 2012.

3-20. Coppock, David. "Market Segmentation and Best Customers." Information-Management.com. August 22, 2002.

3-21. Burns, Alvin and Bush, Ronald. *Basic Marketing Research*. 3rd Edition. New Jersey: Pearson Prentice Hall, 2012. Pages 317 – 320.

3-22. Burns, Alvin and Bush, Ronald. *Basic Marketing Research*. 3rd Edition. New Jersey: Pearson Prentice Hall, 2012. Pages 330 – 335.

3-23. "About Statistical Analysis Tools." Microsoft office website: Office.Microsoft.com.

3-24. Evans, James. *Statistics, Data Analysis, and Decision Modeling*. New Jersey: Pearson Prentice Hall, 2010. Page 198.

3-25. Evans, James. *Statistics, Data Analysis, and Decision Modeling*. New Jersey: Pearson Prentice Hall, 2010. Page 209.

3-26. Myers, James. *Segmentation and Positioning for Strategic Marketing Decisions*. Chicago: American Marketing Association, 1996. Pages 68 – 75 and 126 – 127.

3-27. Myers, James. *Segmentation and Positioning for Strategic Marketing Decisions*. Chicago: American Marketing Association, 1996. Pages 55 – 56.

3-28. Myers, James. *Segmentation and Positioning for Strategic Marketing Decisions*. Chicago: American Marketing Association, 1996. Pages 146 – 154 and 164 – 165.

3-29. Sorger, Stephan. *Marketing Planning: Where Strategy Meets Action*. New Jersey: Pearson, 2012. Pages 65 – 68.

3-30. Pomerantz, Dorothy. "Rise in Digital Film Sales Doesn't Help Home Video Market." Forbes. January 10, 2012.

3-31. "VCRs Face Digital Recording Future." Consumer Electronics Association, at ce.org. 2005.

3-32. Paul, Ian. "Best Buy May Slash HP TouchPad Prices." PC World. August 17, 2011.

3-33. "Brands." Brands overview page. L'Oreal website, at loreal.com.

3-34. Kotler, Philip and Keller, Kevin Lane. *Marketing Management*. 13th edition. New Jersey: Pearson Prentice-Hall, 2009. Pages 228 – 229.

3-35. Bare Escentuals investment page. WikiInvest, at wikinvest.com.

3-36. Selectica website, selectica.com

3-37. Starwood Hotels and Resorts website, starwoodhotels.com

3-38. American Hospital Supply website, americanhospitalsupply.com

3-39. Oracle website, oracle.com

3-40. Chanel website, chanel.com

3-41. Hardy, Quentin. "The Big Business of Big Data." New York Times Bits Blog. October 24, 2011.

3-42. Cisco website, cisco.com

3-43. Dell website, dell.com

3-44. Home Depot website, homedepot.com

3-45. Ries, Al and Trout, Jack. *Positioning: The Battle for Your Mind*. Warner Books. 1993.

3-46. Sorger, Stephan. *Marketing Planning: Where Strategy Meets Action*. New Jersey: Pearson, 2012. Pages 69 -70.

3-47. Projects section, Staples page.Prophet website, prophet.com.

3-48. Myers, James. *Segmentation and Positioning for Strategic Marketing Decisions*. Chicago: American Marketing Association, 1996. Pages 68 – 75 and 182 – 188.

3-49. Lilien, Gary L. and Rangaswamy, Arvind. *Marketing Engineering*. Revised Second Edition. Victoria, British Columbia: Trafford Publishing, 2004. Pages 122 – 127.

3-50. KYST Multidimensional Scaling Program, online user guide. Accessed via netlib.org.

3-51. MDSCAL Multidimensional Scaling Program, online user guide. Accessed via netlib.org.

3-52. Lilien, Gary L. and Rangaswamy, Arvind. *Marketing Engineering*. Revised Second Edition. Victoria, British Columbia: Trafford Publishing, 2004. Pages 128 – 136.

Chapter 4

4-1. Wikipedia, Aristophenes biography.

4-2. McGregor, Jena. "Reading Your Rival's Mind." Business Week. July 10, 2006.

4-3. Feder, Barnaby. "Resignation at Quaker Oats Over Snapple's Poor Sales." New York Times. July 20, 1996.

4-4. Sorger, Stephan. *Marketing Planning: Where Strategy Meets Action*. New Jersey: Pearson, 2012. Pages 90 – 96.

4-5. AIG website,.aig.com

4-6. Hoovers website, hoovers.com

4-7. InsideView website, insideview.com

4-8. Jigsaw website, jigsaw.com

4-9. Manta website, manta.com

4-10. Alexa.com website

4-11. Compete.com website

4-12. TweetDeck website, tweetdeck.com

4-13. Samepoint website, samepoint.com

4-14. Socialmention website, socialmention.com

4-15. Radian 6 website, radian6.com

4-16. Sorger, Stephan. *Marketing Planning: Where Strategy Meets Action*. New Jersey: Pearson, 2012. Pages 81 – 84.

4-17. Siegler, MG. "Google Rents Goats to Replace Lawnmowers." TechCrunch. May 1, 2009.

4-18. Sorger, Stephan. *Marketing Planning: Where Strategy Meets Action*. New Jersey: Pearson, 2012. Pages 81 – 84.

4-19. Lawnbotts robotic lawn mower website,.lawnbotts.com

4-20. The Toro Company, Company History website page. Accessed at thetorocompany.com.

4-21. Addante, Frank. "Focus on the Right Competitors." Founderblog.com. March 29, 2011.

4-22. Halpern, Steven. "Blenders and Juicers Boost Deer Consumer Products (DEER)." Blogginstocks.com. March 17, 2010.

4-23. Mufson, Steven. "China Asks WTO to Block U.S. Tariffs." Washington Post. May 25, 2012.

4-24. Chengalpattu. "Seducing Shoppers in Sticksville." Economist. July 14, 2012.

4-25. BlendTec.com website

4-26. Cuisinart.com website

4-27. Kansasstatutes.lesterama.org website

4-28. "Wastes – Resource Conservation – Common Wastes & Materials – eCycling." EPA.gov website.

4-29. Alibaba.com website, search on Blender Products by Country.

4-30. "Beehive Blender: Oster vs. Waring – Help a Girl Decide, Please!" Chowhound.chow.com.

4-31. "Pureeing Soups with An Immersion Blender." Williams-Sonoma.com website.

4-32. Somheil, Tim. "No Going Back to Pre-Recession Spending." ApplianceMagazine.com. July 24, 2009.

4-33. MacMillan, Douglas. "Living Social Aims to Be Different from Groupon." BusinessWeek. September 22, 2011.

4-34. Kotler, Philip and Keller, Kevin Lane. *Marketing Management*. 13th edition. New Jersey: Pearson Prentice-Hall, 2009. Pages 49 – 52.

4-35. Jarden.com website

4-36. "James E. Lillie Appointed Chief Executive Officer of Jarden Corporation; Martin E. Franklin to Serve as Executive Chairman." Jarden press release. June 13, 2011.

4-37. Jarden, 2011 Annual Report. June 15, 2012.

4-38. Russo, Nick. "Jarden has the Highest Debt to EBITDA Ratio in the Housewares & Specialties Industry)." MySmartTrend.com. August 30, 2012.

4-39. "Jarden Reaffirms Confidence in Growth Strategy and 2009 Outlook at Analyst and Investor Day." Jarden press release. March 3, 2009.

4-40.Jarden, 2011 Annual Report. June 15, 2012.

4-41. "In the Kitchen: Jarden VillaWare." FrogDesign.com website.

4-42. Jarden, 2011 Annual Report. June 15, 2012.

4-43. Jarden, 2011 Annual Report. June 15, 2012.

4-44. "Average User Rating, Oster Blenders."Consumer Reports website, consumerreports.org.

4-45. "Average User Rating, Waring Blenders." Consumer Reports website, consumerreports.org.

4-46. Coursey, David. "Apple Premium Pricing Buys More Than a Logo." PCWorld.com. March 22, 2009.

4-47. "Price & Shop: Buy a Blender."Consumer Reports website, consumerreports.org.

4-48. Jarden, 2011 Annual Report. June 15, 2012.

4-49. "Customer Reviews: Oster BLSTET-C Blender, Brushed Nickel."Amazon.com.

4-50. "Waring Pro MBB Series Professional Food and Beverage Blender Review." BestBlenderReviews.com.

4-51. Jarden Corporation, Annual Report 2011. Page 3.

4-52. MacMillan, Douglas. "In Some Virtual Worlds, the Thrill is Gone." BusinessWeek. November 23, 2011.

4-53. Kotler, Philip and Keller, Kevin Lane. *Marketing Management.* 13th edition. New Jersey: Pearson Prentice-Hall, 2009. Page 306.

4-54. Kahney, Leaner. "Apple: It's All about the Brand", Wired. December 4, 2002.

4-55. "Starbucks Caffeinates its China Growth Plan." BusinessWeek. October 25, 2006.

4-56. Casey, Kevin P. "Nintendo Hopes Wii Spells Wiiner." USA Today. August 15, 2006.

4-57. Chu, Kathy. "Bank of America Raises ATM Surcharge." USA Today. September 12, 2007.

4-58. Hoover, J. Nicholas. "Cisco Preps Server-Switch As HP Prepares Flank Attack." InformationWeek. December 19, 2008.

4-59. "FedEx Ground Completes National Expansion of FedEx Home Delivery." Business Wire. September 17, 2002.

4-60. Yue, Lorene. "U of I Part of %500M Energy Research Program." Chicago Business. February 1, 2007.

4-61. Sasseen, Jane. "How Sara Lee Left Hanes in its Skivvies." BusinessWeek. September 18, 2006.

4-62. McNichol, Tom. "Can Microsoft's Bing Take a Bite Out of Google?" Time. July 31, 2009.

4-63. Trefis Team, "Bing's Market Share Squeaks Higher, Google Still Gorilla of Search." Forbes. January 17, 2012.

4-64. Sorger, Stephan. *Marketing Planning: Where Strategy Meets Action.* New Jersey: Pearson, 2012. Pages 106 – 109.

4-65. Janicek, Karel. "AP Interview: Czechs Turn to New Markets." BusinessWeek. August 17, 2011.

4-66. Lenovo website, lenovo.com

4-67. Westin Hotels and Resorts website, starwoodhotels.com/westin/difference

Chapter 5

5-1. Silverstein, Joshua. "Grand Strategies of the Great Powers: Churchill in World War I." Accessed at WinstonChurchill.org. July 14, 2009.

5-2. Satow, Julie. "Homework Trumps Gut Instinct in Retail Brokering." New York Times." March 13, 2012.

5-3. Tirrell, Meg. "Varian Medical jumps as Siemens Exits Radiation Therapy Market." Business Week. November 16, 2011.

5-4. Narayan, Adi. "Pfizer Teams with India Brewmaster in Return to $14 billion Insulin Market." Bloomberg.com. February 24, 2011.

5-5. Porter, Michael. *Competitive Advantage: Creating and Sustaining Superior Performance.* Boston: Free Press. 1985.

5-6. Glaberson, William. "Where You Are What You Wear; At the Sunglass Hut, Selling Image and Status by the Pair." New York Times. April 9, 1992.

5-7. Ansoff, H. Igor. "Strategies for Diversification." Harvard Business Review. 1957.

5-8. Trefis Team. "Dunkin' Donuts Hits 10,000 Stores on China Push, Stock Going to $29." Forbes. January 4, 2012.

5-9. "Decision Making Techniques." Mindtools.com website.

5-10. "Quantitative Strategic Planning Matrix." Zideate.com.

5-11. "Monte Carlo Analysis: Bringing Uncertainty and Risk into Forecasting." MindTools.com.

5-12. Saaty, Thomas. *The Analytic Hierarchy Process: Planning, Priority Setting, Resource Allocation.* New York: McGraw Hill, 1980.

5-13. "The Analytic Hierarchy Process: Choosing by Weighing Up Many Subjective Factors." MindTools.com.

5-14. Wauters, Robin. "Global Smartphone App Download Market Could Reach $15 Billion by 2013: Report." TechCrunch.com. March 5, 2010.

5-15. Jones, Healy. "Market Size and Venture Capital." Startable.com. February 17, 2009.

5-16. Bryant, Adam. "Wang Files for Bankruptcy; 5,000 Jobs to Be Cut." New York Times. August 19, 1992.

5-17. "Revenue Cycle Explorer" product page. Marketo.com website,

5-18. Farris, Paul W., Bendle, Neil T., Pfeifer, Phillip E., Reibstein, David J. *Marketing Metrics: The Definitive Guide to Measuring Performance.* Second Edition. New Jersey: Pearson, 2010. Page 101.

5-19. Farris, Paul W., Bendle, Neil T., Pfeifer, Phillip E., Reibstein, David J. *Marketing Metrics: The Definitive Guide to Measuring Performance.* Second Edition. New Jersey: Pearson, 2010. Pages 350 – 351.

5-20. Farris, Paul W., Bendle, Neil T., Pfeifer, Phillip E., Reibstein, David J. *Marketing Metrics: The Definitive Guide to Measuring Performance.* Second Edition. New Jersey: Pearson, 2010. Pages 125 – 127.

5-21. Apple Form 10-K Annual Report, filed October 26, 2011.

5-22. Farris, Paul W., Bendle, Neil T., Pfeifer, Phillip E., Reibstein, David J. *Marketing Metrics: The Definitive Guide to Measuring Performance.* Second Edition. New Jersey: Pearson, 2010. Page 129.

5-23. Keller, Kevin Lane. *Strategic Brand Management: Building, Measuring, and Managing Brand Equity.* 2nd edition. New Jersey, Prentice Hall, 2003. Pages 76 – 77.

5-24. Farris, Paul W., Bendle, Neil T., Pfeifer, Phillip E., Reibstein, David J. *Marketing Metrics: The Definitive Guide to Measuring Performance.* Second Edition. New Jersey: Pearson, 2010. Pages 138 – 139.

5-25. Farris, Paul W., Bendle, Neil T., Pfeifer, Phillip E., Reibstein, David J. *Marketing Metrics: The Definitive Guide to Measuring Performance.* Second Edition. New Jersey: Pearson, 2010. Pages 167 – 171.

5-26. Farris, Paul W., Bendle, Neil T., Pfeifer, Phillip E., Reibstein, David J. *Marketing Metrics: The Definitive Guide to Measuring Performance.* Second Edition. New Jersey: Pearson, 2010. Pages 161 – 165.

5-27. Aktiv project page. Ideabox.us website, ideabox.us/models/aktiv

5-28. "Custom Shop Guitar Features."Carvin Guitars website, carvinguitars.com.

5-29. Cook, Kathleen. "TacAir Team Now Gets Components Just In Time." Boeing.com press release. September 2004.

5-30. Sopranos, Katherine. "Lean On Me." Boeing.com press release. November 2004.

5-31. Cooke, James. "Metamorphosis of a Supply Chain." SupplyChainQuarterly.com. 2007.

5-32. "About Steinway." Steinway.com website.

5-33. "Surgical Care" webpage. OneidaHealthcare.org,

5-34. "Experienced Leadership Programs" page. GE.com website.

5-35. Moore, Malcolm. "Royal Wedding: Chinese Tailors Rush to Copy Kate Middleton's Dress." Telegraph.co.uk. April 30, 2011.

5-36. "Sommelier Training" web page. French Culinary Institute website, frenchculinary.com.

5-37. Mullaney, Tim. "Social Media is Reinventing How Business is Done." USA Today, May 16, 2012.

5-38. Kay, Roger. "How Apple Keeps Innovation Coming and Customers Buying." Forbes.com. October 3, 2011.

Chapter 6

6-1. "Yogi Berra Biography." Biography.com.

6-2. Christie, Les. "Real Recovery in Home Prices Not Expected Until Spring." CNNMoney.com. August 8, 2012.

6-3. Fuhrmann, Ryan. "Is Warren Buffett Really a Value Investor?" Forbes.com. May 16, 2011.

6-4. "Stock Chart for AAPL." Apple Inc. Bloomberg.com.

6-5. Newman, Jared. "Best Buy Kills Return Fees Amid Poor Sales." PCWorld.com. December 20, 2010.

6-6. Farris, Paul W., Bendle, Neil T., Pfeifer, Phillip E., Reibstein, David J. *Marketing Metrics: The Definitive Guide to Measuring Performance.* Second Edition. New Jersey: Pearson, 2010. Pages 112 – 121.

6-7. Farris, Paul W., Bendle, Neil T., Pfeifer, Phillip E., Reibstein, David J. *Marketing Metrics: The Definitive Guide to Measuring Performance.* Second Edition. New Jersey: Pearson, 2010. Pages 114.

6-8. Farris, Paul W., Bendle, Neil T., Pfeifer, Phillip E., Reibstein, David J. *Marketing Metrics: The Definitive Guide to Measuring Performance.* Second Edition. New Jersey: Pearson, 2010. Pages 117 – 119.

6-9. Rogers, Everett M. "Diffusion of Innovations." New York: Free Press. 1983.

6-10. "Forecasting the Take-Up of Mobile Broadband Services." Tellabs white paper. 2010.

6-11. Sundqvist, S and Frank, L and Puumalainen, K. "The Effects of Country Characteristics, Cultural Similarity, and Adoption Timing on the Diffusion of Wireless Communications." Journal of Business Research, Volume 58, Issue 1, January 2005, Pages 107 – 110.

6-12. Bass, Frank. "A New Product Growth for Model Consumer Durables." Management Science. Volume 15, 1969. Pages 215 – 217.

6-13. Robert-Ribes, Jordi. "Predicting the Speed of Technology Introduction: The Bass Model of Technology Diffusion." jordi.pro/bass.

6-14. Jiang, Zhengrui and Bass, Frank and Bass, Portia. "Virtual Bass Model and the Left-Hand Data-Truncation Bias in Diffusion of Innovation Studies." International Journal of Research in Marketing. 2006. Issue 23, Pages 93 – 106.

6-15. "DISH Entertainment: Find Your Package." Dish.com/entertainment.

6-16. "Forecasting the Take-Up of Mobile Broadband Services." Tellabs white paper. 2010.

6-17. "Guide to HDTV Formats – Part 1: 720p, 1080i, and 1080p HDTV." Practical Home Theater Guide. November 29, 2012.

6-18. "Forecasting the Take-Up of Mobile Broadband Services." Tellabs white paper. 2010.

6-19. "FICO Score." Fair Isaac Corporation web page, fico.com,

6-20. McKendrick, Joe. "Predictive Analytics: The Perfect Use Case for Cloud Computing." Forbes. June 18, 2012.

6-21. Koch, Christopher. "A Real Need for Big Data: Preventing Airline Equipment Failures." Forbes. June 27, 2012.

6-22. "Vendor Landscape of BI and Analytics." PracticalAnalytics.wordpress.com. May 1, 2011.

6-23. Mitchell, Robert L. "How BI is Helping to Predict Fashion Trends." Computerworld. September 12, 2011.

6-24. Kotler, Philip and Keller, Kevin Lane. *Marketing Management.* 13th edition. New Jersey: Pearson Prentice-Hall, 2009. Pages 143 – 145.

6-25. Columbus, Louis. "Using Search Analytics to See into Gartner's $232B Big Data Forecast." Forbes.com. October 15, 2012.

6-26. Kaplan, Robert and Norton, David. *The Balanced Scorecard: Translating Strategy into Action.* Boston, Massachusetts: Boston: Harvard Business School Press, 1996.

6-27. "The Southwest Experience." Southwest.com website.

6-28. "L'Oreal, World Number 5 for Value Creation According to Fund Managers Financial Times." L'Oreal website, finance page: loreal-finance.com, 2001.

6-29. Crutchfield website, crutchfield.com

6-30. Nvidia website, nvidia.com

6-31. Daniel, D. Ronald. "Management Information Crisis." Harvard Business Review. September – October 1961. Pages 111 – 116.

6-32. The Cupcakery website, thecupcakery.com

Chapter 7

7-1. Regis McKenna website, "About Regis McKenna." www.regis.com/about

7-2. Green, Paul; Scarbough, Marsha; Shifflet, Douglas; Wind, Jerry. "Courtyard by Marriott: Designing a Hotel Facility with Consumer-Based Marketing." Published by the Institute of Management Sciences, Interfaces 19: January – February 1989. Pages 25 – 47.

7-3. Orme, Bryan. *Getting Started with Conjoint Analysis: Strategies for Product Design and Pricing Research.* 2009. Research Publishers.

7-4. Ulrich, Karl and Eppinger, Steven. *Product Design and Development.* 5th Edition. New York, McGraw Hill, 2012. Pages 317 – 319.

7-5. "Statistical Analysis" web page. SAS.com website.

7-6. Denning, Steve., "Dare to Be Bad? Really? The Authors Reply." Forbes. March 15, 2012.

7-7. "How to Decision Trees Work." Ehow.com.

7-8. Pour-Moezzi, Pejman. "Think Different: How an Entrepreneur Makes Decisions to Go Camping." GeekWire. May 10, 2012.

7-9. Stern, Carl. *Perspectives on Strategy from the Boston Consulting Group.* New Jersey: Wiley, February 1998.

7-10. Boston Consulting Group website, bcg.com. About_BCG page.

7-11. "Five Product and Marketing Disasters." OddCulture.com.

7-12. Betteridge, Ian. "iPod Market Share Falls—to 87%." PC Magazine. November 4, 2004.

7-13. Collis, David and Campbell, Andrew and Goold, Michael. *Harvard Business Review on Corporate Strategy.* Harvard Business Press. August 1999.

7-14. "BCG Product Portfolio" web page. Marketing Objects website, marketingobjects.com.

7-15. "Easy Growth-Share Matrix Software" web page. SmartDraw website, smartdraw.com.

7-16. Pepitone, Julianne. "Marissa Mayer's Yahoo Turnaround Starts to Take Shape." Money.CNN.com. September 26, 2012.

7-17. Adapted from a product profitability analysis tool by Demand Metric (demandmetric.com), provider of sales and marketing analytics tools and templates.

7-18. Sorger, Stephan. *Marketing Planning: Where Strategy Meets Action.* New Jersey: Pearson, 2012. Page 249.

7-19. Hughes, Neil. "Apple's 44.7% Gross Margins are Highest in at Least 15 Years." Appleinsider.com. January 25, 2012.

7-20. Price Waterhouse Coopers, "Global Technology Scorecard: Consumer Electronics Market Analysis." July 2012.

Chapter 8

8-1. "Aldo Gucci, 84; Expanded Fashion House in U.S." New York Times. January 21, 1990.

8-2. Sorger, Stephan. *Marketing Planning: Where Strategy Meets Action*. New Jersey: Pearson, 2012. Pages 169 – 175.

8-3. Cooper, Michael and McGinty, Jo Craven. "A Meter So Expensive, It Creates Parking Spots." New York Times. March 15, 2012.

8.4. Welch, David. "Wal-Mart to Push Low Prices for Growth in China, Brazil." Bloomberg.com. April 12, 2012.

8-5. Mohammed, Rafi. "J.C. Penney's Risky New Pricing Strategy." Business Week. January 31, 2012.

8-6. "Reagan to Ease Japan Sanctions: Computer Chip Dumping Has Stopped, U.S. Says." Los Angeles Times. November 3, 1987.

8-7. Surowiecki, James. "Priced to Go." New Yorker Magazine. November 9, 2009.

8-8. "Energy Star CFL Market Profile: Data Trends and Market Insights." U.S. Department of Energy. September 2010.

8-9. Apple (AAPL) Financial Data, including profit margin. YCharts.com.

8-10. Dilger, Daniel Eran. "Apple's 2010 Ad Budget Increases by $190 Million, But Still Outpaced by New Sales Growth." Apple Insider. October 27, 2010.

8-11. Teneriello, Steven. "Price Positioning Strategies for Your Service Company, Part 2." TheServiceCoach.com. April 2, 2010.
http://blog.theservicecoach.com/blog-0/bid/20696/Price-Positioning-Strategies-for-your-Service-Company-Part-2

8-12. LaMonica, Martin. "Sylvania Takes on 60-Watt Bulb with LED Light." CNET.com. May 13, 2010.

8-13. "Rhino Shield vs. Paint." Rhino Shield web site, rhinoshield.net.

8-14. Volkswagen AG website, volkswagenag.com

8-15. Motel 6 website, motel6.com.

8-16. "Buy Back Program" web page. Best Buy website, bestbuy.com.

8-17. United Parcel Service website, ups.com

8-18. Apple.com

8-19. Musil, Steven. "iPad Mini Configuration and Prices Reportedly Revealed." CNET.com. October 14, 2012.

8-20. Sorger, Stephan. *Marketing Planning: Where Strategy Meets Action*. New Jersey: Pearson, 2012. Pages 245 – 253.

8-21. Gans, Joshua. "Why Disney Would Like You to Subscribe to Vacations." Forbes. March 25, 2012.

8-22. Kotler, Philip and Keller, Kevin Lane. *Marketing Management*. 13th edition. New Jersey: Pearson Prentice-Hall, 2009. Pages 385 – 388.

8-23. Lager, Marshall. "The Price is Right...You Hope." DestinationCRM.com. October 2008.

8-24. Taber, David. The Taber Report, "Pricing and Licensing." Taberconsulting.com.

8-25. Taber, David. The Taber Report, "Pricing and Licensing." Taberconsulting.com.

8-26. Taber, David. The Taber Report, "Pricing and Licensing." Taberconsulting.com.

8-27. "U.S. Navy renews Rolls-Royce Power by the Hour ® T-45 Trainer Engine Support with $66 million Contract." Rolls-Royce website, rolls-royce.com. October 2, 2007.

8-28. "Power by the Hour: Can Paying Only for Performance Redefine How Products are Sold and Serviced?" Wharton Business School, as reported on Knowledge at Wharton website, knowledge.wharton.upenn.edu, February 21, 2007.

8-29. Kotler, Philip and Keller, Kevin Lane. *Marketing Management*. 13th edition. New Jersey: Pearson Prentice-Hall, 2009. Pages 400 – 402.

8-30. "Antitrust Price Discrimination." United States Federal Trade Commission website, ftc.gov.

8-31. "NAICS 31-33 Manufacturing, Industry Sampler." United States Census Bureau.

8-32. "NAICS 4521 Department Stores, Industry Sampler." United States Census Bureau.

8-33. "NAICS 453920 Art Dealers, Industry Sampler." United States Census Bureau.

8-34. Keegan, Paul. "Extreme Couponing: Stockpiling Toothpaste, Meat." CNN Money. July 20, 2011.

Chapter 9

9-1. Constable, Giff. "Highlights from Andreessen's Stanford CS183 Talk." Giffconstable.com. May 13, 2012.

9-2. "Direct Store Delivery (DSD) vs. Central Distribution." MWPVL.com website.

9-3. Kotler, Philip and Keller, Kevin Lane. *Marketing Management*. 13th edition. New Jersey: Pearson Prentice-Hall, 2009. Pages 414 – 427 and 458 – 459.

9-4. Nike store locator, store.nike.com

9-5. "For First Time, Ford Tops Chevy in Number of U.S. Dealers." Autotrader.com. February 24, 2011.

9-6. "Taco Bell Franchise Review." About Franchises website, franchises.about.com.

9-7. "Marshalls." Wikipedia.

9-8. "Patio Lawn and Garden" (category of goods). Amazon.com.

9-9. Overstock.com Clearance Bin, overstock.com/clearance

9-10. Arrow Electronics, "Our Company" page. Arrow website, arrow.com.

9-11. GENCO Product Lifecycle Logistics, Product Liquidation page. GENCO website, genco.com.

9-12. Tech Data StreamOne Solutions Store web page, techdata.com/streamone.

9-13. Starbucks website, "Apply for a Licensed Store."

9-14. Shabbona Creek RV website, shabbonacreekrv.com.

9-15. Roto-Rooter Plumbing & Drain Service website, Corporate Office page. rotorooter.com.

9-16. Go Daddy website, godaddy.com

9-17. Verizon Wireless store finder, verizonwireless.com.

9-18. Snap-on e-commerce website, New User Registration: buy1.snapon.com.

9-19. Coach store finder, coach.com.

9-20. Sorger, Stephan. *Marketing Planning: Where Strategy Meets Action*. New Jersey: Pearson, 2012. Pages 175 – 176.

9-21. Rose, Wendy and Burek, Tanya. "What is a SPIF?" businessready.ca. March 4, 2008.

9-22. Kotler, Philip and Keller, Kevin Lane. *Marketing Management*. 13th edition. New Jersey: Pearson Prentice-Hall, 2009.. Page 455.

9-23. Apple Store Locator, apple.com/buy/locator.

9-24. "Geospatial Data" web page. Environmental Systems Research Institute (ESRI), esri.com.

9-25. Lilien, Gary L. and Rangaswamy, Arvind. *Marketing Engineering*. Revised Second Edition. Victoria, British Columbia: Trafford Publishing, 2004. Pages 379 – 384.

9-26. Offner, Jim. "Progress Edition: Neighborhood Districts Flourish." Cedar Valley Business. February 10, 2011.

9-27. Ross, Allison. "Outlet stores: Are you getting a good deal, or just a different kind of deal?" Palm Beach Post. February 1, 2011.

9-28. Klein, Karen. "How to Find the Best Retail Location." Business Week. September 16, 2008.

9-29. Hermes website, hermes.com

9-30. Belicove, Mikal. "Location-Based Check-Ins on the Rise with Consumers." Entrepreneur magazine. May 17, 2011.

9-31. Brooks, Roger. "Four Steps to Launching a Loyalty Program." Entrepreneur magazine. December 10, 2010.

9-32. Enright, Allison. "How Feedback Tools Help The Container Store Satisfy Customers." Internet Retailer. April 12, 2012.

9-33. Fleet Feet Sports, fleetfeetsports.com. About Us page.

9-34. Delio, Michelle. "For Ritz-Carlton, It All Begins with Customer Knowledge." Destination CRM magazine. April 17, 2000.

9-35. Webb, Steve. "Montgomery Ward Drops Out of Crowded Retail Field." National Real Estate Investor. January 1, 2001.

9-36. Byrt, Frank. "6 Companies Battling for Americans' Grocery Money." Forbes. April 10, 2012.

9-37. Cisco consumer website, home.cisco.com.

9-38. Cisco corporate website, How to Buy page: cisco.com/web.ordering.

9-39. Cisco corporate website, Partner Locator page: tools.cisco.com/WWChannels

9-40. Geller, Lois. "Why Are Printed Catalogs Still Around?". Forbes. October 16, 2012.

9-41. Farris, Paul W., Bendle, Neil T., Pfeifer, Phillip E., Reibstein, David J. *Marketing Metrics: The Definitive Guide to Measuring Performance*. Second Edition. New Jersey: Pearson, 2010. Pages 204 – 205.

9-42. Farris, Paul W., Bendle, Neil T., Pfeifer, Phillip E., Reibstein, David J. *Marketing Metrics: The Definitive Guide to Measuring Performance*. Second Edition. New Jersey: Pearson, 2010. Pages 206 – 207.

9-43. Poggi, Jeanine. "Retailers Look to the Department Store for Salvation." Advertising Age. March 19, 2012.

9-44. Farris, Paul W., Bendle, Neil T., Pfeifer, Phillip E., Reibstein, David J. *Marketing Metrics: The Definitive Guide to Measuring Performance*. Second Edition. New Jersey: Pearson, 2010. Pages 207.

9-45. "Stage Stores Key Revenue Metric Rises in July." Business Week. August 2, 2012.

9-46. "Wet Seal Posts 15.6% Drop in Key Sales Metric." Business Week. August 2, 2012.

Chapter 10

10-1. "John Wanamaker: Department Store." Who Made America? Biography series. PBS.org.

10-2. Sorger, Stephan. *Marketing Planning: Where Strategy Meets Action*. New Jersey: Pearson, 2012. Pages 208 – 212.

10-3. "Golden Postboxes to Keep Their Sheen to Honour British Athletes." BBC News UK. November 2, 2012.

10-4. Neff, Jack. "New Book Reports 37% of All Advertising is Wasted." Advertising Age. August 6, 2008.

10-5. Kotler, Philip and Keller, Kevin Lane. *Marketing Management*. 13th edition. New Jersey: Pearson Prentice-Hall, 2009. Pages 484 – 485.

10-6. "Cost of Marketing: What is the Average Budget?" LegalZoom website. Article Center. Legalzoom.com.

10-7. Neff, Jack. "New Book Reports 37% of All Advertising is Wasted." Advertising Age. August 6, 2008.

10-8. Kotler, Philip and Keller, Kevin Lane. *Marketing Management*. 13th edition. New Jersey: Pearson Prentice-Hall, 2009. Page 485.

10-9. "Spotlight Report: America Leads on Trade." National Journal. October 11, 1997.

10-10. Brill, Steven. "Mapping Out the Campaign Air War." Brill's Content. brillscontent.com.

10-11. Lilien, Gary L. and Rangaswamy, Arvind. *Marketing Engineering*. Revised Second Edition. Victoria, British Columbia: Trafford Publishing, 2004. Pages 315 – 318.

10-12. Moorman, Christine. "Marketing Spend on the Rise – Three Trends Worth Watching." CMOSurvey.org. October 19, 2012.

10-13. Moorman, Christine. "Spending on Marketing Analytics." CMOSurvey.org. March 28, 2012.

10-14. Harmon, Mark. "Using the Excel Solver to Optimize Your Marketing Budget." blog.excelmasterseries.com. January 14, 2011.

10-15. "Introduction to Optimization with the Excel Solver Tool." Microsoft Office website, Office.microsoft.com.

10-16. Johnson, Hilary. "How to Build Your Marketing Budget." Inc. magazine. September 27, 2010.

10-17. Clow, Kenneth and Baack, Donald. *Integrated Advertising, Promotion & Marketing Communications*. New Jersey: Prentice Hall, 2002. Page 261.

10-18. Media Kit for Vogue brand. Conde Nast publishing, condenast.com.

10-19. Ephron, Erwin. "A Frequency of Three: How a Marketing Researcher at General Electric Named Herb Krugman Gave the TV Networks Something Better than Money: The Gospel of Effective Frequency." Inside Media, January 2, 1992, as reported in eprononmedia.com.

10-20. Surmanek, Jim. "One Hit or Miss: Is a Frequency of One Frequently Wrong?" Advertising Age. November 27, 1995.

10-21. Clow, Kenneth and Baack, Donald. *Integrated Advertising, Promotion & Marketing Communications*. New Jersey: Prentice Hall, 2002. Page 261.

10-22. "Television Measurement" web page. Nielsen website, nielsen.com.

10-23. Farris, Paul W., Bendle, Neil T., Pfeifer, Phillip E., Reibstein, David J. *Marketing Metrics: The Definitive Guide to Measuring Performance*. Second Edition. New Jersey: Pearson, 2010. Pages 296 – 298.

10-24. Media Kit for Vogue brand. Conde Nast publishing, condenast.com.

10-25. Elle media kit, accessed on Elle.com website.

10-26. Alexa.com site information result page for vogue.com.

10-27. Clow, Kenneth and Baack, Donald. *Integrated Advertising, Promotion & Marketing Communications*. New Jersey: Prentice Hall, 2002. Page 261.

10-28. Rate card for advertisements, found in media kit for Vogue brand. condenast.com.

10-29. "Average Online CPMs Still Lagging Behind Other Media." ExchangeWire EMEA, exchangewire.com. June 15, 2010.

10-30. Clow, Kenneth and Baack, Donald. *Integrated Advertising, Promotion & Marketing Communications*. New Jersey: Prentice Hall, 2002. Pages 261 and 293.

10-31. Griffin, Marie. "Forbes to Measure Print Advertising by Online Behavior." B to B Media Business (btobonline.com). January 6, 2011.

10-32. Duffy, Jill. "21 Great Apps and Tools for Social Media." PC Magazine. March 13, 2012.

10-33. "Visible Technologies Acquires Cymfony to Expand Global Product Offering." Visibletechnologies.com press release. April 2012.

10-34. Wauters, Robin. "Alterian Acquires Techrigy, The 'Google Alerts on Steroids.'" TechCrunch.com. July 15, 2009.

10-35. Fielding, Veronica. "SEO Isn't What You Think It Is." Fast Company. August 10, 2012.

Chapter 11

11-1. Godin, Seth. "Measure THAT." Seth Godin blog, sethgodin.com. April 5, 2006.

11-2. Kotler, Philip and Keller, Kevin Lane. *Marketing Management.* 13th edition. New Jersey: Pearson Prentice-Hall, 2009. Pages 167 – 174.

11-3. "2010 New Motorcycle Buyer Survey." J.D. Power and Associates. Page 8, Question 56.

11-4. Kotler, Philip and Keller, Kevin Lane. *Marketing Management.* 13th edition. New Jersey: Pearson Prentice-Hall, 2009. Pages 167 – 174.

11-5. "2010 New Motorcycle Buyer Survey." J.D. Power and Associates. Page 2, Question 3.

11-6. Kotler, Philip and Keller, Kevin Lane. *Marketing Management.* 13th edition. New Jersey: Pearson Prentice-Hall, 2009. Pages 167 – 174.

11-7. "2010 New Motorcycle Buyer Survey." J.D. Power and Associates. Page 2, Question 5.

11-8. Kotler, Philip and Keller, Kevin Lane. *Marketing Management.* 13th edition. New Jersey: Pearson Prentice-Hall, 2009. Pages 167 – 174.

11-9. Honda website, powersports.honda.com

11-10. Honda Rebel motorcycle specifications. Access via motorcycles.findthebest.com website.

11-11. Kotler, Philip and Keller, Kevin Lane. *Marketing Management.* 13th edition. New Jersey: Pearson Prentice-Hall, 2009. Pages 167 – 174.

11-12. "2010 New Motorcycle Buyer Survey." J.D. Power and Associates. Page 2, Question 5.

11-13. "2010 New Motorcycle Buyer Survey." J.D. Power and Associates. Pages 2 – 8.

11-14. Spenner, Patrick. "Marketers Have It Wrong: Forget Engagement, Consumers Want Simplicity." Forbes. July 2, 2012.

11-15. Chaffey, Dave. "8 Online Revenue Model Options for Internet Businesses." Smart Insights. January 10, 2011.

11-16. Sorger, Stephan. *Marketing Planning: Where Strategy Meets Action.* New Jersey: Pearson, 2012. Pages 54 – 64.

11-17. Levick, Richard S. "How Nordstrom Evolved from Bricks to Clicks." Fast Company. October 3, 2012.

11-18. Farris, Paul W., Bendle, Neil T., Pfeifer, Phillip E., Reibstein, David J. *Marketing Metrics: The Definitive Guide to Measuring Performance.* Second Edition. New Jersey: Pearson, 2010. Pages 32 – 39.

11-19. Savitz, Eric. "Tablets by the Numbers: It's All About Apple and ARM." Forbes. July 10, 2012.

11-20. Apple Form 10-K Annual Report, filed October 26, 2011. Page 30.

11-21. "Apple Launches New iPad." Apple press release. March 7, 2012.

11-22. "Apple Catalog & Internet Resellers." Apple.com website, solutionprofessionals.apple.com

11-23. Apple Form 10-K Annual Report, filed October 26, 2011. Page 30.

11-24. Farris, Paul W., Bendle, Neil T., Pfeifer, Phillip E., Reibstein, David J. *Marketing Metrics: The Definitive Guide to Measuring Performance.* Second Edition. New Jersey: Pearson, 2010. Pages 42 – 45.

11-25. Savitz, Eric. "Apple Tops Ranking of World's Most Valuable Brands." Forbes.com. May 22, 2012.

11-26. Apple Form 10-K Annual Report, filed October 26, 2011. Page 30, Net Sales.

11-27. Friedman, Lex. "Buying Guide: Which iPhone Should You Get?" Macworld.com. November 24, 2011.

11-28. Farris, Paul W., Bendle, Neil T., Pfeifer, Phillip E., Reibstein, David J. *Marketing Metrics: The Definitive Guide to Measuring Performance.* Second Edition. New Jersey: Pearson, 2010. Pages 167 – 172.

11-29. Gallo, Carmine. "The Apple Store Improves its Secret Loyalty Weapon." Forbes.com. May 21, 2012.

11-30. Sorger, Stephan. *Marketing Planning: Where Strategy Meets Action.* New Jersey: Pearson, 2012.

11-31. Apple Form 10-K Annual Report, filed October 26, 2011. Page 30, Net Sales.

11-32. Farris, Paul W., Bendle, Neil T., Pfeifer, Phillip E., Reibstein, David J. *Marketing Metrics: The Definitive Guide to Measuring Performance.* Second Edition. New Jersey: Pearson, 2010. Pages 75 – 85.

11-33. Farris, Paul W., Bendle, Neil T., Pfeifer, Phillip E., Reibstein, David J. *Marketing Metrics: The Definitive Guide to Measuring Performance.* Second Edition. New Jersey: Pearson, 2010. Pages 69 – 75.

11-34. Apple Form 10-K Annual Report, filed October 26, 2011. Page 35, Gross Margin.

11-35. Reisinger, Don., "Apple's iPhone Margins Hit 58 Percent, Nearly Double iPad's." Cnet.com. July 27, 2012.

11-36. Farris, Paul W., Bendle, Neil T., Pfeifer, Phillip E., Reibstein, David J. *Marketing Metrics: The Definitive Guide to Measuring Performance.* Second Edition. New Jersey: Pearson, 2010.. Pages 161 – 166.

11-37. "Sprint Says iPhone Users 'More Profitable' Than Other Customers." Apple Insider. March 21, 2012.

11-38. Farris, Paul W., Bendle, Neil T., Pfeifer, Phillip E., Reibstein, David J. *Marketing Metrics: The Definitive Guide to Measuring Performance.* Second Edition. New Jersey: Pearson, 2010. Pages 56 – 59.

11-39. Reisinger, Don. "Apple Tops in Customer Satisfaction for 8th Year." Cnet.com. September 19, 2011.

11-40. Farris, Paul W., Bendle, Neil T., Pfeifer, Phillip E., Reibstein, David J. *Marketing Metrics: The Definitive Guide to Measuring Performance.* Second Edition. New Jersey: Pearson, 2010. Pages 60 – 62.

11-41. Gottesman, Ben. "Net Promoter Score: Which Companies Are Creating Good Customers?" PC Magazine. September 7, 2010.

Chapter 12

12-1. "Anton Chekhov."Encyclopedia Britannica.

12-2. "Vilfredo Pareto."Encyclopedia Brittanica.

12-3. "Pareto Analysis: Using the 80:20 Rule to Prioritize." Mind Tools, mindtools.com website.

12-4. "How to Find and Work with Suppliers." Entrepreneur. December 11, 2003.

12-5. Stillman, Jessica. "Metrics are More Motivating Than Bonuses." Inc.com. June 18, 2012.

12-6. Taylor, Bill. "What Surprising Number Will Change Your Business?" Harvard Business Review blog, blogs.hbr.org. May 21, 2010.

12-7. "National Survey on Drug Use and Health (NSDUH)." Substance Abuse and Mental Health Services Administration (SAMHSA), Office of Applied Studies. 2008.

12-8. Data compiled by the American Kennel Club, as reported by Southwest Airline's Spirit magazine, "The Numbers" section, December 2011.

12-9. Data compiled by U.S. Census bureau, as reported by Southwest Airline's Spirit magazine, "The Numbers" section, July 2012.

12-10. Data compiled by the Association for Pet Obesity Prevention, as reported by Southwest Airline's Spirit magazine, "The Numbers" section, September 2012.

International Facility Management Association, as reported by Southwest Airline's Spirit magazine, "The Numbers" section, November 2011.

12-11. Magid, Frank N. "A Portrait of Today's Tablet User Wave II." Online Publishers Association. June 2012.

12-12. Jordan, Justine. "Email Client Market Share: New Stats." Litmus.com blog. June 15, 2012.

12-13. "Only one in three emails received is essential for work." Mimecast.com. June 2012.

12-14. "mCommerce Quadruples in Just Two Years." Edigitalresearch.com.

12-15. "Apps: Fun or Functional?" LightspeedResearch.com. May 3, 2012.

12-16. "It's YouTube's 7th Birthday...And You've Outdone Yourselves, Again." YouTube blog website, youtube-global.blogspot.com. May 20, 2012.

12-17. "Changing Careers at 30." ChangingCareersAt30.net.

12-18. Silverthorne, Sean. "The Holy S***! Number." CBSNews.com. May 24, 2010.

12-19. DraftFCB.com agency website, Work detail for Sharpie account

12-20. "PivotTable I: Get Started with PivotTable Reports in Excel 2007."Microsoft Office website, Support section, office.microsoft.com.

12-21. "How to Choose the Right Chart Type in Excel 2010."Dummies.com.

12-22. "How to Add Titles to Excel 2010 Charts."Dummies.com.

12-23. Kharif, Olga. "Pat Hanrahan's Tableau Analytics Software." Business Week. December 8, 2011.

12-24. Peck, Wendi and Casey, William. "Some Simple Rules for Communicating with Executives." Denver Business Journal. June 29, 2003.

12-25. Van Grove, Jennifer. "McDonald's Foursquare Day Campaign Increased Checkins by 33%." Mashable.com. September 16, 2010.

12-26. "Make the Case for Social Media Campaigns with Metrics the C-Suite Respects." MarketingProfs website, marketingprofs.com. December 28, 2010.

12-27. Colman, Craig. "When Virtual Numbers Create Virtual Results." ISMTravels.com blog. October 10, 2010.

12-28. Sorger, Stephan. "The ABC Approach: Gaining Organizational Buy-In Through Analytics." Demand Metric blog, blog.demandmetric.com. December 2010. Based on content contributed by the author of this book to DemandMetric.com blog.

12-29. Kotter, John P. and Whitehead, Lorne A. *Buy-In: Saving Your Idea from Getting Shot Down.* Boston: Harvard Business Review Press. 2010.

12-30. Goldsmith, Marshall. "Effectively Influencing Decision Makers." Business Week. June 19, 2009.

INDEX

48689807R00272

Made in the USA
Columbia, SC
10 January 2019